ARTTALK

TEACHER'S WRAPAROUND EDITION

Rosalind Ragans, Ph. D.

Glencoe
McGraw-Hill

New York, New York   Columbus, Ohio   Woodland Hills, California   Peoria, Illinois

CONTRIBUTORS

Thomas Beacham
Art Teacher
Telfair County High School
McRae, GA

Claire B. Clements
Specialist, Meeting Special Needs
Associate Professor of
Education of Exceptional Children
The University of Georgia
Athens, GA

Robert D. Clements
Specialist, Meeting Special Needs
Professor of Art
The University of Georgia
Athens, GA

Faith Clover
Fine Arts Curriculum Specialist
Multnomah Education Service District
Portland, OR

Nelle Elam
Art Teacher
Starkville High School
Starkville, MS

Larry Hurt
Art Teacher
Ben Davis School
Indianapolis, IN

Audrey Komroy
Art Teacher
Akron High School
Akron, NY

Elaine McMichael
Supervisor of Art Education
Somerville High School
Somerville, MA

Bunyan Morris
Specialist, Studio Lessons
Marvin Pittman Laboratory School
Statesboro, GA

Jane Rhoades
Specialist, Cultural Perspectives
Teacher Educator
Georgia Southern University
Statesboro, GA

Faye Scannell
Specialist, Computer Options
Lead Art Technology Teacher
Bellevue, WA

Carlyne Seegraves
Elementary Art Teacher
East Grand Rapids Public Schools
Grand Rapids, MI

Becky Shopfner
Art Teacher
Chaffin Junior High School
Fort Smith, AR

Barbara Stodola
Executive Director
The John G. Blank Center for the Arts
Michigan City, IN

Jean Morman Unsworth
*Specialist, Art is Everywhere and
Sparking Creativity*
Art Consultant
Chicago, IL

Send all inquiries to:
Glencoe/McGraw-Hill
21600 Oxnard Street, Suite 500
Woodland Hills, CA 91367

ISBN: 0-02-640296-3 (Teacher's Wraparound Edition)
ISBN: 0-02-640295-5 (Student Text)

3 4 5 6 7 8 9   AGK   00 99 98 97

ONTENTS

TEACHING WITH *ARTTALK*   **TM 5**

USING THE STUDENT TEXT   **TM 6**
    Organization of the Text   TM 6
    Elements of Each Chapter   TM 6
    Other Text Features   TM 8

THE TEACHER'S WRAPAROUND EDITION   **TM 9**
    Organization of the Teacher's Wraparound Edition   TM 9
    Teacher's Manual   TM 9

OTHER PROGRAM COMPONENTS   **TM 10**
    Teacher's Classroom Resources   TM 10
        Application Activities
        Artist's Profiles
        Computers in the Art Classroom
        Cooperative Learning Activities
        Cultural Diversity in Art
        Enrichment Activities
        Reproducible Lesson Plans
        Reteaching Activities
        Studio Lessons
        Testing Program and Alternative Assessment
    Fine Art Color Transparencies   TM 10
    Fine Art Prints   TM 10

PROFESSIONAL ARTICLES   **TM 11**
    What is a Quality Art Program?   TM 11
        by Rosalind Ragans
    Recognizing the Importance of Cultural Diversity in an Art Program   TM 14
        by Jane Rhoades
    Meeting Special Needs in the Art Classroom   TM 16
        by Robert and Claire Clements
    Arts: The Vital Connection   TM 19
        by Jean Morman Unsworth

SAFETY IN THE ART CLASSROOM   **TM 21**

COURSE PLANNING   **TM 23**
    Pacing Chart   TM 23
    Scope and Sequence Chart   TM 29
    Art Supplies Grid   TM 31

TEACHING WITH ARTTALK

Welcome to ARTTALK—a lively, inviting, comprehensive art program written and designed for beginning and advanced level art classes. This popular program has been updated and expanded to include more interactive student activities, new multicultural studio lessons, integrated computer options, and over two hundred artworks representing a wide range of cultures, artistic styles, and art media.

This revised edition has been further enhanced with the addition of a Teacher's Wraparound Edition and the Teacher's Classroom Resources. These new correlated components not only provide additional teaching support, but enable you, the classroom teacher, to select those areas that are of greatest interest to your students and reflective of your curriculum emphasis and direction.

ArtTalk is based on several assumptions. These include:

- In order for students to comprehend art concepts, it is important to provide meaningful, hands-on learning experiences that allow for personal growth and creative expression.

- A comprehensive art program integrates the areas of aesthetics, art criticism, art history, and studio production.

- A quality art education program provides students with experiences that are sequentially planned, building on previous concepts, and providing learning opportunities that incorporate a variety of media, artistic styles, and historical periods.

- An up-to-date art program includes information about computer art and provides the opportunity for hands-on application.

To achieve these goals, *ArtTalk* provides a textbook program with fully integrated components for easy use. They include:

- **Student Text.** The 416-page text incorporates aesthetics, art criticism, art history, and studio production throughout the book, and presents detailed coverage of the elements and principles of art.

- **Teacher's Wraparound Edition.** This new component provides complete lesson plans, teaching suggestions, supplemental information, cross-references, and more—all conveniently "wrapped" around every page of the reduced student text.

- **Teacher's Classroom Resources.** The *ArtTalk* Teacher's Classroom Resources (TCR) contains reference material for your own use and reproducible activities for classroom use. Separate booklets enable you to select the most appropriate activities to meet your classroom needs. These booklets focus on application activities, enrichment activities, reteaching activities, and an alternative assessment and testing program. Other booklets cover specialized curriculum emphasis including cooperative learning activities, cultural diversity in art, and computers in the art classroom. Together these supplements provide a wide range of topics and curriculum emphasis.

- **Fine Art Color Transparencies.** Forty-eight ready-to-use, fine art transparencies provide effective ways to introduce topics, reinforce concepts, and provide comparisons between artworks and art styles.

- **Fine Art Prints.** Twenty-four poster-size masterpieces printed on self-supporting stock are available to supplement the artwork appearing in the student text.

Using the Student Text

ArtTalk is a visually oriented program incorporating reproductions of masters' works and student artworks. These examples enable students to expand their appreciation and understanding of various artists, works of art, and artistic styles. Each illustration is discussed within the narrative portion of the text. The teaching caption and credit line information reinforce chapter content and can be used as an effective learning tool in the classroom.

Artwork for this edition has been carefully selected from museums and private collections throughout the country. Each work of art has been reproduced in a size large enough to be visually "read" by the reader. The artists who have been selected are both males and females, and they represent a variety of times, places, and cultures.

The text is written in a friendly, informal style giving students practical information about art concepts without overloading them with theoretical concepts. This style gives students the confidence and skills they need to comfortably discuss works of art and critique their own works of art.

Organization of the Text

The organization of the text, its special features, and the visual presentation combine to make this book a positive learning experience for students. The text is divided into four units. Each unit brings together chapters which have a common theme. These include:

- **Unit 1: Appreciating the Visual Arts.** In Unit One, students explore the value of visual arts. They realize that the visual arts serve the same purpose today that they've served since the early history of humanity. For example, the visual arts satisfy human needs—both personal needs and group needs. They also satisfy our physical needs for useful objects and shelter, and fulfill our needs for personal expression and communication. In this unit, students learn about the language of visual arts and they begin to learn how to look at artworks in new ways. They examine the many different kinds of art created throughout history and explore the career opportunities available in art today. After completing Unit One, students will be ready to begin creating their own art.

- **Unit 2: The Elements of Art.** In Unit Two, students develop a greater understanding of each of the elements of art. Each chapter deals with an individual element. Within the chapter they learn to recognize, identify, and describe the element. They identify how the element appears within their environment and they study works of art from various periods of history to see how artists used the expressive qualities of the elements to enhance their works. In each chapter, students start by examining the elements as concrete, familiar things in their environment. Then they become acquainted with the more abstract, expressive qualities of the element. After finishing a chapter, students apply the concepts they have learned in that chapter to the intensive study of a work of art by a master artist using the art-criticism process. They also compare the masterpiece to a work of art by an old master, once more applying the concepts studied in the chapter.

- **Unit 3: The Principles of Design.** Unit Three explores the principles of design and helps students develop an understanding of how art objects are organized. Again, students begin by looking at their natural environment. Then they look at works of art to see how artists use a principle of art to express feelings and ideas. At the same time, students work at developing a skillful use of that principle in their own artworks. At the end of each chapter, students apply the concepts they have learned to study master artworks.

- **Unit 4: Technique Tips Handbook.** The Technique Tips Handbook gives students helpful hints for handling different media and tools. It contains step-by-step procedures or techniques that pertain to drawing, painting, printmaking, sculpting, and other art-production skills. Illustrations are included which help students visualize each technique.

Elements of Each Chapter

Each chapter of the text includes a number of carefully designed features to enhance student interest and learning. Within each chapter the following recurring learning aids and textbook features are presented:

Words to Know. Vocabulary development, which begins on the chapter opening pages with "Words to Know," is carried through the body of the chapter. When first used in the chapter, vocabulary terms appear in boldface type. A clear definition is given in italics as well as examples or further explanation when needed. (All vocabulary terms are included in the Glossary at the end of the book.) On the chapter review page there are review questions requiring students to identify the meaning of each term.

Chapter Opener. A full-page color reproduction of a work of art introduces each chapter, provides a visual clue to the contents of the chapter, and serves as motivation for the students. Included on the chapter spread is a list of objectives, which identify the learning outcomes of the chapter, introductory paragraphs, and a preview of key vocabulary terms. An independent section titled "First Impressions" encourages students to perceptively examine the chapter's opening artwork.

Activities. Application of content is essential if students are to grasp knowledge and comprehend material. In this edition, student activities provide immediate hands-on application of the key concepts within the chapter. The first activity "Applying Your Skills" is tailored for a beginning level art student. The second activity "Further Challenge" offers an alternative for those students who are more artistically inclined or for those who have had previous art experience. When appropriate, "Computer Option" gives students an opportunity to demonstrate their application of material by using the computer.

Looking Closely. This feature focuses students' attention on two or three artworks within each chapter. The expanded caption asks questions that encourage closer inspection of the work and requires students to use perceptive and interpretative skills.

Art Criticism in Action. This culminating feature appears at the end of each chapter, and challenges students to closely examine and apply the steps of art criticism to a work of art created by a contemporary artist. On the following page for comparison purposes, students are introduced to another work of art by an old master artist. In this way, students have the opportunity to use higher level thinking skills as they apply the steps of art criticism. In addition, they compare and contrast styles, techniques, and processes used by contemporary artists with those used by artists of the past. (To enhance students' understanding of how time and place affected the artists' styles, the contemporary artist is profiled within the student text. The old master is profiled in the TCR booklet *Artist's Profiles*.)

Meet the Artist. At the end of each chapter, a contemporary artist is profiled. This feature expands the multicultural coverage of contemporary artists and spotlights a wide range of media, techniques, and processes used by today's artists. The feature emphasizes how the artist's cultural heritage has influenced his or her choice of medium, artistic style, and use of indigenous materials.

Studio Lessons. Beginning in Chapter 5, studio lessons which are directly tied to the chapter contents are provided. Each studio has been field-tested by high school students and feature an exemplary work of art by a high school student. These studios require the use of two- and three-dimensional procedures and involve the students in a variety of media experiences including drawing, painting, ceramics, and printmaking.

These studio lessons in *ArtTalk* may require several class periods to complete. Because of the materials, some teachers may want all of the students to work on the same problem at the same time. Some teachers may wish to assign one studio lesson to one group of students, and another to another group. Some teachers may be able to let the students choose which lesson they prefer. This will depend upon the quality of the studio, the art materials available, and the maturity of the students. Some classes that do not run a full year may not have time to complete any studio lessons at all. However, during the field testing of this text, several teachers allowed gifted and talented students to move through the chapters at their own pace and complete more than one studio lesson on their own. Of course specific times for conferences were set up for these students. This gave the teacher more time to work with students who needed more instruction time.

More Portfolio Ideas. Throughout the course, students are encouraged to keep a sketchbook and develop a portfolio featuring their selected works of art. Naturally, many students will keep examples of the studio lessons in their portfolio. However, "More Portfolio Ideas" offers additional ideas and techniques for the portfolios. These projects are tied directly to the ideas, techniques, and style unique to the particular artist who is featured in "Meet the Artist."

Student Artwork. Exemplary student artwork by high school students is displayed within the studio lessons and provides motivation to aspiring student artists.

Chapter Review. A one-page cognitive review is provided for each chapter. It includes checking for comprehension of key terms, reviewing important concepts, using critical thinking skills, and implementing interdisciplinary activities.

Other Text Features

These additional features listed below appear in the student text and enable teachers and students to maximize the use and flexibility of the text.

Artists and Their Works. A comprehensive listing of all artists and the titles of their artworks and page references appears in this section. This handy reference for teachers and students enables readers to quickly identify the broad range of artists and artworks presented in the program.

Chronology of Artworks. All the artworks that appear in *ArtTalk* are arranged in a chronological listing so students can compare the artistic styles and techniques used by artists throughout history and throughout their career.

Glossary. Every vocabulary term (identified in boldface type) is listed and defined in the Glossary. Where needed, a pronunciation guide is also provided. Chapter references assist students in locating where the word is introduced and defined in context within the text.

Bibliography. A bibliography presents a range of supplementary reading material to expand students' knowledge about artists and art concepts.

Index. A comprehensive index is provided as a study aid to assist students in finding specific topics.

THE *TEACHER'S* *WRAPAROUND* EDITION

ArtTalk offers a Teacher's Wraparound Edition. The Teacher's Wraparound Edition (TWE) differs from the Student Text in the following ways: (1) material from the Student Text is reproduced in a slightly smaller size to allow more room for the teaching material, which fills the side and bottom columns; (2) a 32-page Teacher's Manual (the section you are reading now) is bound into the book.

Organization of the Teacher's Wraparound Edition

This unique component is labeled "wraparound" because its design offers the teacher consistent, specific suggestions in the left, right, and bottom margins that surround or "wrap around" each two-page spread of the Student Text. The Student Text, as it appears in the Teacher's Wraparound Edition, has been slightly reduced in size in order to provide more space for teacher notes and annotations. The TWE provides techniques for working with every aspect of the Student Text. It offers, in essence, a complete set of lesson plans, preview and extension activities, and alternative teaching strategies for adapting the program to your own teaching style and to the learning styles of your students. Its purpose is to save valuable teacher preparation time. A closer look at the various types of support that the notes provide may help you decide how you can most effectively use this Teacher's Wraparound Edition to its fullest advantage.

This teaching material follows a consistent, easy-to-use pattern. Note that the complete lesson cycle— FOCUS, TEACH, ASSESS, and CLOSE—is contained within each chapter. As you cover the pages of the Student Text in class, the teaching suggestions are right in the margins where you need them.

The Teacher's Wraparound Edition provides you with support material in three general categories:

- **Lesson Plans.** The "core" of the Teacher's Wraparound Edition, this material provides you with complete suggestions for introducing each unit and chapter, teaching the chapter content, and completing each segment of study. In addition, special self-contained lesson plans are provided for the text's feature titled "Art Criticism in Action," "Looking Closely," and "Activities."

- **Bottom Column Annotations.** Boxes at the bottom of the page give you additional information related to the content of the Student Text. This information

supplements the core lesson plan by focusing on various areas of interest. The categories are:
  - **Unit and Chapter Resources**
  - **Teacher Talk**
  - **More About . . .**
  - **Resources Beyond the Classroom**
  - **Cooperative Learning**
  - **Cultural Perspectives**
  - **Curriculum Connection**
  - **Meeting Special Needs**
  - **Art on a Shoestring**
  - **At the Museum**
  - **Technique Tips**
  - **Safety Tips**
  - **Developing a Portfolio**
  - **Alternative Assessment**

- **Teaching Aids.** A number of additional features save you time and help make the Teacher's Wraparound easy to use. These include unit and chapter overviews, resource lists, cross-references, and answers to review questions. The Teacher's Wraparound Edition provides a wealth of material. From this, choose what best fits your classroom situation, the needs of your students, and your individual teaching style.

Teacher's Manual

To assist in course planning and to increase teacher effectiveness, a Teacher's Manual is included in the Teacher's Wraparound Edition. This manual explains the program components and how to use them. Other parts of the Teacher's Manual include:

- **Professional Articles** to help you articulate the criteria of a quality art education program, explain how to teach students with varying ability levels, and suggest ways to create a positive classroom environment.

- **Safety in the Art Classroom** to help identify safety guidelines to follow when setting up an art classroom and cautioning students as they work with potentially hazardous materials and tools.

- **A Pacing Chart** to help you decide how much time to spend on each chapter.

- **A Scope and Sequence Chart** to help you identify where topics are introduced, emphasized, and reinforced.

OTHER PROGRAM COMPONENTS

The *ArtTalk* Teacher's Classroom Resource (TCR) is a resource of reference materials for your own use and reproducible activity sheets for classroom use. Its diversity enables you to select the most appropriate activities to meet the needs of your students and curriculum emphasis. The file includes the following supplemental booklets:

Application Activities. These activities are provided in each chapter and enable students to check their comprehension and ability to relate the key concepts within the chapter. Application activity sheets can be used to monitor students' comprehension of "Looking Closely" and "Art Criticism in Action."

Artist's Profiles. This booklet features biographical information of over forty master artists. Profiles 1 through 12 directly relate to the master artist who is featured in the "Art Criticism in Action" features. Profiles 13 through 44 provide background information about other artists whose works appears in *ArtTalk*. These profiles provide supplemental information and can be used to promote independent learning in the classroom.

Cultural Diversity in Art. Through the study of art, students have the unique opportunity to see how various cultures use art as a form of personal, social, and creative expression. These reproducible handouts give students greater exposure to the various ways that cultures throughout the world use art.

Computers in the Art Classroom. It is important to introduce students to the computer's use as an art tool in a manner which emphasizes its potential to aid an artist in creating imagery. Information in this booklet explains how to set up a computer station and lesson plan ideas which encourage students to either experiment and create imagery on the computer, or to find out and report on more information about the computer's potential as an art tool.

Cooperative Learning Activities. The art classroom is a natural setting for building teamwork and cooperation among students. Cooperative learning activities promote this goal and give students various opportunities to work in small groups to apply and extend the contents of the chapter. These activities use multiple teaching strategies, including role-playing, research projects, and debate activities.

Enrichment Activities. To provide further challenge for students, handout sheets give them additional background information and learning opportunities to extend their knowledge and application of content.

Reproducible Lesson Plans. Lesson plans (one for each chapter) are provided in an easy-to-follow, checklist format following a standard lesson cycle of FOCUS, TEACH, ASSESS, and CLOSE.

Reteaching Activities. To meet the various learning abilities of your students, reteaching activities are provided. The booklet includes both concept maps and study guides which enable students to visualize and identify key concepts of the chapter.

Studio Lessons. Studio production activities are the core of many art programs. In addition to the activities and studio lessons in the student text, the Studio Lessons booklet offers additional studio lessons correlated to the chapters. These studio lessons also include the "Critiquing" feature so that students can apply the steps of art criticism to their own works of art.

Testing Program and Alternative Assessment. A chapter and unit testing program along with alternative assessment ideas provide teachers with an objective evaluation tool for checking comprehension and giving students the opportunity to demonstrate their knowledge of the material in an exciting and creative fashion.

Fine Art Transparencies. The *ArtTalk* program includes a set of forty-eight ready-to-use, full-color, fine-art transparencies with an accompanying guide that provides teaching strategies and student activity pages. These transparencies can be used to introduce or extend the chapters and help students develop higher level thinking skills as students compare, analyze, and evaluate works of art. This program contains an Instructor's Guide with student activity sheets.

Fine Art Prints. Twenty-four poster-sized art masterpieces printed on self-supporting stock are available to supplement the artwork appearing in the student text. In addition, there is a large version of The Design Chart, providing the teacher with a display-size tool to aid students during the art-criticism activities. This package includes an Instructor's Guide with student activity sheets.

What Is a Quality Art Program?

Rosalind Ragans
Author
Associate Professor Emeritus
Georgia Southern University

A quality art program is for all students. It provides learning opportunities for the artistically-talented few as well as for the many students who may never produce art outside the art classroom.

A quality program in visual arts teaches students that they can communicate their ideas and emotions in many different ways. It teaches them that both verbal and nonverbal methods can be used to express abstract ideas and emotions. Students learn to trust their creative intelligence and learn that some problems have many different solutions. This gives students the confidence so they will not be afraid to make decisions in situations where there is more than one "right" answer. They learn concepts and techniques that give them expressive control over the visual images they produce.

In a quality art program students expand their perceptive, interpretive, and analytical abilities. They learn to find meaning in visual images, and learn to identify aesthetic qualities in a variety of works. By using the language of visual art, they have a precise vocabulary with which to express their ideas, and they develop the ability to make and defend aesthetic judgments.

In a quality program students become sensitive to and understand the broad cultural foundation upon which their own culture is based. The visual arts have always been an integral component in the history of humanity, and, through the study of art history, students develop a better understanding of beliefs and ideas that are different from their own.

The components of a quality art program fall under the following categories: aesthetics, art criticism, art history, and the production of art.

AESTHETICS IN ART EDUCATION

Aesthetics is the philosophy of art, the study of the nature of beauty and art. Aesthetics is concerned with the *Big Question:* "What is art?" In the past, aesthetics was defined as the study of beauty, because the creation of beauty was thought to be the purpose of art. Today, in our more complex society, the purpose of art has also become more complicated. Some artists still believe that the purpose of art is to create beauty, or beautifully organized arrangements of the elements of art. Some believe that art must imitate reality. Others think of art as a very strong means to communicate ideas and emotions.

As students begin a course in art, they have little experiential background upon which to draw when making judgmental statements about art. That is why *ArtTalk* introduces three aesthetic theories in Chapter 2 to help students make value judgments about works of art. Three were selected because no single theory of art was found to be satisfactory when applied to works of art representing different art styles. The introduction of more than one theory offers students several different aesthetic qualities from which to select when making and defending value judgments about specific works of art. The three theories are: Imitationalism, Formalism, and Emotionalism.

Imitationalism represents a point of view concerning art that is important to many secondary students. Generally, beginning students prefer art that shows subject matter they can recognize. They feel comfortable talking about the literal qualities in artworks they have seen. This theory offers students a comfortable starting place before they move on toward more unfamiliar styles and philosophies of art. Imitationalism is concerned with the first component of a work of art: the subject matter.

Formalism is the second theory offered to the students because it deals with the focus of *ArtTalk*: the language of art. This theory is concerned with the composition of a work of art: the arrangement of the elements of art using the principles of design. This theory is very important when students are producing and responding to works of art. In *ArtTalk*, students are taught how to control the elements and principles of art so that they can express their ideas, values, and emotions in visual form. They are also taught how to "read" the elements and principles in works of art so they can understand the ideas, values, and emotions being expressed in the works of other artists. They study how artists have used formal qualities, and this helps them solve production problems. Formalism is concerned with the second component of a work of art: composition.

Emotionalism is the third theory offered for the use of the students. This theory deals with the subjective aspects of a work of art. The expressive quality of a work of art is the focus of this theory. Emotionalism requires a strong communication of feelings, moods, or emotions from the work to the viewer. Emotionalism is concerned with the third component of a work of art: the content or meaning of the work.

ART CRITICISM IN ART EDUCATION

Art criticism is the sequential process used in this text to guide students through the procedures needed to learn from works of art. The four-step process will help students expand their perceptive, analytical, interpretive, and aesthetic judgment abilities. Art criticism will help them study a work of art noticing subject, composition, and meaning before making an aesthetic judgment. Too often beginners look at a work of art briefly and decide immediately upon a judgment. The sequential procedures in art criticism force students to postpone judgment while becoming immersed in the image. It forces them to have a fully founded visual experience before drawing conclusions about a work.

The four steps in the art-criticism process are *description, analysis, interpretation,* and *aesthetic judgment.* The first two steps, description and analysis, must be objective. Guessing must be saved for interpretation. During description the student makes a list of all the objects in the work. This helps to slow down the student's perceptive process. All of the objects listed must be objective. If the student sees a woman holding a child, that is what must be reported. To say, at this point, that a mother is holding her child tenderly would be subjective guessing. If the work is nonobjective and there are no objects to be listed, the elements of art become the subject matter. During the second step, analysis, the student describes the way the artist has used the elements and principles of art. During interpretation, the student tells what message he or she is receiving from the work. The interpretation must be based upon the facts collected during the first two steps, but the facts can be modified by each student's experiential background. In a class of thirty students there may be thirty different interpretations, and they can all be correct if they are based on the clues collected during the first two steps. During the last step, aesthetic judgment, the student is asked to make a value judgment about the work. The student is asked to decide if the work is successful or not, but the student is asked to use one or more of the aesthetic

theories explained above to back up the judgment.

Art criticism is important in helping students learn from works of art by other artists. It is also an important procedure to help students objectively study their own art products.

The sequential steps of art criticism are similar to those used in the scientific method. During the first two steps, description and analysis, students are asked to collect data objectively. During the third step, interpretation, students speculate about the meaning of the work based on the data collected; they make a hypothesis about the idea, emotion, or mood expressed by the artist. During the fourth step, aesthetic judgment, the students offer their conclusions about the work of art.

ART HISTORY IN ART EDUCATION

ArtTalk is not an art history book, yet there is no way a serious study of art can take place without learning something about the history of art and the broad cultural foundation upon which the students' cultures are based. Chapter 3 is an art history overview that helps students understand the chronology of art periods and cultures. Throughout the rest of the text, works of art from a variety of cultures and time periods are used to illustrate specific concepts. In addition, the credit lines and captions supply information that can help students place the works of art in time and place.

Biographical information about artists who are featured in the art-criticism activities and studio lessons also provide historical and cultural perspectives. Other material throughout the text and in the resource material will add to the students' knowledge about artists, cultures, and the time and place in which works of art were created.

ART PRODUCTION IN ART EDUCATION

ArtTalk offers a variety of production activities that help students practice, develop, and refine their production skills. In the beginning of the text, students are asked to keep a sketchbook in which all visual notes are kept. It is recommended that finished works be kept in a portfolio. The combination of sketchbook and portfolio gives the teacher and students a visual record of their progress through the course.

Short activities are presented within each chapter following a major concept. These student activities may be finished in one class period, although some may require more time. You may even want to use them as follow-up homework assignments. The activities are presented at two or three levels. The first level usually requires cutting, pasting, arranging, and simple drawing skills. The second level involves more advanced drawing skills. In most cases a "Computer Option" activity is also presented. Of course, the use of these will depend on the number of computers available to the art students. They are written with generic directions, however, and will apply to most of the drawing software programs.

At the end of each chapter in Units Two and Three, several studio lessons are presented. Each lesson is based upon a work of art and is directly related to the aesthetic concepts taught in the chapter. The student must recall the concepts and apply them to the creation of his or her art project. Then the student must consciously apply these concepts to the self-evaluation questions that pertain to the work. As the teacher, take time to evaluate each project according to its expressive qualities. If using a group critique, be sure it is based upon the objective criteria of the assignment. If you have a group of students who have difficulty in handling peer criticism, talk to each student privately, or write a note to the student regarding the work. Be sure to always include positive statements about the successful part of the studio lesson.

At the end of each "Meet the Artist" section, additional studio activities that relate to the work of the artist are presented. These activities are related to the art-criticism discussion. Teachers may wish to assign one of these problems to students, or they may be offered as optional projects for those who are interested in that particular artist.

ARTTALK — A BALANCED APPROACH

ArtTalk presents teachers with all the concepts needed to teach a quality art program. The program is designed to be used by both beginning and advanced level students, by students who will seek careers in art, and those who will become intelligent consumers of the arts. *ArtTalk* helps students expand their perceptive, interpretive, and analytical abilities by introducing them to art from different cultures and different times and providing them with the opportunity to express ideas and emotions in both visual and verbal means. *ArtTalk* accomplishes this by integrating the four components of a quality art program: aesthetics, art criticism, art history, and studio production.

Recognizing the Importance of Cultural Diversity in an Art Program

Dr. Jane Rhoades, Ph.D.
Teacher Educator
Georgia Southern University

*S*tudents learn about the art of their own culture and other cultures through their family and friends, through the mass media, and perhaps even by teaching themselves. Sometimes the information learned this way is valuable, but it should not be relied upon to always give adequate and correct information. Instead, schools are the most available and most effective place for giving students the opportunity to learn about the visual arts.

BENEFITS OF A QUALITY CULTURALLY DIVERSE ART PROGRAM

A quality art education program taught by a culturally sensitive and qualified art specialist benefits every student. When art educators teach in a systematic, meaningful way, students acquire knowledge about art and cultures that will benefit them throughout their lives. Such a program promotes growth in many areas. Some of these include:

Art Promotes Intracultural Understanding

Through a culturally sensitive art program, students begin to understand the role and function that art and artists play in a society. Through learning about the art of other cultures, they have the opportunity to identify similarities and differences between their culture and others. They learn that art reflects the religion, politics, economics, and other aspects of a culture.

Through a quality art program students can address issues of ethnocentrism, bias, stereotyping, prejudice, discrimination, and racism. Students can learn that no one racial, cultural, or national group is superior to another and that no one group's art is better than another.

Art Teaches Self-Esteem Through Diversity

Through a quality art program, students learn to recognize, acknowledge, and celebrate racial and cultural diversity through art within their own society. A good program helps promote the enhancement and affirmation of their self-esteem and encourages pride in one's own heritage. Personal expression is encouraged and the result is often a statement in visual form that is both inventive and filled with personal meaning.

Art Teaches Effective Communication

In order for students to become visually literate, they need to understand that the visual symbols created by artists transmit information that cannot be disclosed through other modes of communication. Art can symbolize concepts that are too complex or too threatening to internalize. Artists from all cultures develop visual symbols.

Students should be encouraged to learn visual literacy by looking, understanding, talking, writing, and making images, but also by learning that each society has its own way of communicating through images. Through a culturally sensitive art program, students will be able to discuss and compare art from other societies. Students learn to visually communicate by creating images that convey knowledge, create new knowledge, shape opinions, disclose the depths of human emotion, and impart the most profound value found universally throughout the world.

Art Teaches About Civilizations

Through a quality art program, students develop a sensitivity and understanding of the history of humankind. For many periods in history it is only through visual remains or material culture that societies' cultures can be pieced together. A study of art history reveals varied world views, concepts, symbols, styles, feelings, and perceptions. Experiences that students have with these art objects from the past teach them respect for others, challenge their minds, and stimulate not only the intellect but also the imagination.

Art Teaches Critical Thinking

A culturally sensitive art program encourages a variety of critical-thinking skills. When students are faced with looking at art from other cultures, they make critical judgments and develop their own opinions. Students are asked to identify and recall information; to organize selected facts and ideas; to use particular facts, rules, and principles; to be able to figure out component parts or to classify; and to combine ideas and form a new whole.

Art Teaches Perceptual Sensitivity and Aesthetic Awareness

As a result of a quality art program, students develop a keen sense of awareness and an appreciation for beauty. They learn that each culture has its own criteria for beauty. Art experiences help cultivate an aesthetic sensitivity and respect for the natural and humanmade environment around the globe. Art classes are the only place in the school curriculum where students learn about what constitutes quality visual design—about harmony, order, organization, and specific design qualities (such as balance, movement, and unity).

Art Teaches Creativity

When a culturally sensitive art program is implemented, creativity in all students is stimulated and nurtured. Students learn to solve problems creatively. They learn that every society has some form of creative expression. Students learn that artists in other cultures have expressed their creativity in a wide range of ways as a magician, mythmaker, teacher, propagandist, shaman, and catalyst of social change. In some societies there is not one special person called an artist—everyone in the culture makes beautiful objects.

UNDERSTANDING CULTURE

Which of the following are cultural experiences? (a) watching a friend quilt; (b) preparing dinner; (c) attending an art exhibition opening; (d) decorating a Christmas tree. (*Answer: They all are!*) All of the items are cultural experiences because they are based on knowledge learned as members of a society. Individuals do not learn about their culture by themselves. People acquire information about the world and how to deal with it as a member of a social group. This learned cultural knowledge varies greatly from one society to another.

In *Faces of Culture,* the author states that culture allows us to do more than survive. Our view of the nature of the world and our place in it is expressed and communicated culturally. All societies have religions, which are bodies of cultural knowledge and practices. We also elaborate our world through music, art, and dance. We decorate our world and our bodies either to please our gods or to please ourselves. We carve tree trunks into objects of art. We paint our faces and the walls of our houses. We make music with instruments and our voices. All this activity is shaped by our participation in a cultural tradition.

Culture is learned. Every society has institutions—family and school are the best examples in our society. As a teacher in the school, you are a cultural transmitter.

ARTWORKS IN CULTURAL CONTEXT

You can help students understand the cultural context of how and why artworks are created by asking a series of specific questions such as:

- What ideas, emotions, values, and/or qualities are being transmitted through the artwork? What does the work tell the viewer about the person who created it (that is, rank, status, or role in his or her culture)?
- What does this artwork tell the viewer about the culture it was created in? Does the artwork tell the viewer anything about the values of the culture?
- Is the art considered popular, traditional, or avant-garde?
- Was this work an innovation? If so, how and why did it come about?
- Why would one culture put more emphasis on the shape of a bowl, another on the pictorial decoration, another on size, another on texture, and so on?
  1) Does this difference indicate specific availability of materials, knowledge of tools, or specific needs of their personal, social, or religious life?
  2) Are these differences related to date, climate, or trade patterns?
  3) To what degree do differences depend on the skills and dedication of the individual artist?
- What evidence can be found that one culture has learned from (been acculturated with) another culture?
  1) Is there a similarity in utilitarian objects or pictorial subject matter?
  2) Is there a similarity in the treatment of materials?
  3) Is there a similarity in the depiction of the human figure or of other subject matter?

Throughout *ArtTalk* and its supplement *Cultural Diversity in Art,* teachers can extend and build upon the cultural aspects of the artworks presented in the Student Text. The bottom column information in the Teacher's Wraparound Edition titled "Cultural Perspectives" and the booklet in the Teacher's Classroom Resources help the teacher and students learn to appreciate cultural diversity through art.

At the beginning of your course, you may wish to take the "Cultural Sensitivity Self-Inventory" which appears in *Cultural Diversity in Art.* This checklist helps you assess the multicultural contents of your course. Following the inventory are suggestions which can help you become a more culturally sensitive art teacher.

ArtTalk and its related components can enable you to develop creative and empowering strategies for students who are living in a culturally diverse society.

Meeting Special Needs in the Art Classroom

Robert D. Clements
Professor of Art
The University of Georgia
Georgia University Affiliated Program Fellow

Claire B. Clements
Associate Professor of Education of Exceptional
Children
Director of Outreach Training and Technical Assistance
Georgia University Affiliated Program for Persons with
Developmental Disabilities

*M*eeting the needs of students with specific kinds of disabilities and adjusting the art classroom to accommodate their needs can be challenging for the art educator. However, the art classroom is an ideal setting to tailor instruction to help students with disabilities and to foster an environment that promotes self-esteem.

TEACHING ART TO STUDENTS WITH DIFFERENT ABILITIES

In 1975, federal legislation passed Public Law 94–142, the Education for All Handicapped Children Act. This required the inclusive education and integration of all students with and without developmental disabilities. This law mandates that testing, individualized educational plans, parental consent, confidentiality, least restrictive environment, and educational programming be given to all youths with developmental disabilities.

Developmental disability refers to any severe, chronic disability of a person which (a) is attributed to a mental or physical impairment or combination thereof; (b) is manifested before age 22; (c) is likely to continue indefinitely; (d) results in limitations in three or more areas of life activity: self-care, language, learning, mobility, self-direction, capacity for independent living, and economic self-sufficiency; and (e) reflects the need for a combination of long-duration, individually planned treatments.

The student with disabilities in your art class should be treated as much like the other students as possible. This is called the principle of *normalization*, the use of an environment to be as culturally normative as possible. As you work with students, also keep in mind the principle of *partial participation*. For example, can the individual participate in the lesson in some way? Perhaps a student who does not speak could hold the art reproduction while the class discusses it. Perhaps a student without sight could work with another student in cleaning the paintbrushes. Avoid giving students with disabilities unearned privileges or indulging them and making them dependent on you. Try to overcome your natural tendency to do for students with disabilities what they are capable of doing. It is very easy to "overdo" for these individuals and perpetuate their feelings of being unable to achieve. In order to empower the student for independent achievement, the less teacher assistance, the better.

Keep your choice of topics and media appropriate to the age. For example, instead of pudding paints for teenagers, use an adult material such as paper pulp. Even for students without disabilities, it is a good prevention strategy, when using art materials such as crayons (which make some students think of primary school), to emphasize how master artists, such as Picasso, have used this medium to create adult works of art.

While communicating with students, focus on the students' capability, such as, "George can vocalize about the patterns he draws." Use "people first" language. Negative language continues old attitudes of exclusion and promotes a "Them-Versus-Us" attitude. Positive language promotes positive attitudes and helps to promote independence, self-help, and community inclusion. While this article and the features in the Teacher's Wraparound Edition discuss each particular disability separately, in reality, disabling conditions share many common problems, such as discouragement, fear of failure, feelings of shyness, and feelings of being different. These common problems can be addressed by the regular art curriculum's components of discussion, perception, creation, and emotional expression.

Discussion activities clarify feelings and develop speaking abilities. Perceptual activities develop cognitive and observational skills. Artistic production activities develop the students' perceptual, cognitive, and psychomotor skills. Creating objects exerts a unifying, healing influence on its maker; even more so does creating an object when its maker strove toward expressions of beauty.

The following information discusses characteristics of specific learning disabilities and suggests ways that individuals with disabilities can successfully participate in an inclusive art classroom.

Students with Visual Impairments

Since most students with visual disability will have some vision (only one out of ten legally blind persons is totally blind), students must have learning experiences that provide for feeling and touching to supplement their seeing ability. Partially sighted individuals benefit from using media such as glue, grease pencils, crayons, or oil pastels that leave a slightly raised line. Media leaving a recessed line indentation is also recommended. These include using a stylus or dull pencil on foam meat trays, used X-ray film, or heavy aluminum foil inscribed on a padded surface. For those who do not require tactile assistance, bold marking instruments are suggested; wide-tip, felt marking pens give bold contrast lines. For students with total blindness, three-dimensional media and sensory stimulation materials are recommended. Fragrant, smell-coded colored marking pens are available.

In all cases, promote the students' pride in the activities they do well—folk dancing, marching, roller skating, swimming, dancing, and so forth. Pipe cleaner figures or wire figures that represent these activities can mentally reinforce and build self-esteem.

Art can be used to promote spatial understanding for students with visual disabilities. The students' spatial awareness of one's home, bedroom, or neighborhood can be depicted in relief maps made from cardboard, glue, felt, sandpaper, clay, yarn, foil, and so forth.

When talking with these students, use metaphoric language to create vivid mental images, for example "blue like the water in the swimming pool," or "a soft dim light like a summer evening."

Students with Hearing Impairments

Although all teens suffer from some insecurity and fear of being considered different from their peers, students with hearing disabilities are usually more self-conscious and shy. Help students gain security in the classroom by having an attitude that fosters acceptance of individual differences. You can promote peer relationships by having the student with the hearing disability team up with a friend and work cooperatively on a project.

When students with hearing disabilities fall behind academically, it is often in the areas of speech, language, and reading. You can use discussions of the art projects, as well as art criticism, art history, and aesthetic issues, as vehicles to develop these youths' desire to speak. However, since hearing aids readily pick up background noise and can prevent the student from hearing, hold art discussions in your classroom's quietest area, as far as possible from ventilation, fan, and air duct noise. Art-history reports on famous artists can develop ability in speaking and reading as well as acceptance of one's disability. Cite the great achievements of Beethoven and the great Spanish painter Francisco Goya who did their greatest masterpieces after becoming deaf. Having a hearing disability need not limit an individual's artistic expression.

Students with Orthopedic and Neurological Disorders

Individuals who are unable to use their arms can paint and draw with the brush held between their teeth. Cameras can be adapted to fit onto wheelchairs and the shutter can be released with a switch. Working with a peer, the student can point to illustrations in magazines and can help with tearing and gluing the illustrations in a sketchbook.

Students with Behavior Disorders

When students with behavior disorders look around the inclusive classroom, they may be overwhelmed by a sense of being less capable in art. You can encourage student satisfaction in their accomplishments by emphasizing how "we each make our artwork in our own way." Foster divergent work by using encouraging statements such as: "Sue has shown a completely different way of thinking about the problem. She uses blues and greens that feel to me like a picnic on a windy day in a field of blowing grass." If the teacher encourages and reminds the student of past successes while the student still feels good about the work, the student's inferior feelings can be lessened.

To minimize disturbances before they grow, establish a quiet corner in your classroom. Fill it with soothing features for the student's body, eyes, and hands; an aquarium, plants, posters with tranquil scenes and quiet colors on the walls, a small carpet, a beanbag chair, or a rocking chair or pillows on the floor can create a comfortable, sheltered reading place.

Students with Mild Mental Retardation

When working on group projects along with students without disabilities, students with mild levels of mental retardation may find pleasure in doing some of the project's more repetitive aspects. Often confronted by so much that is confusing, students with mild mental retardation seem to get satisfaction from doing over and over something in which they have achieved mastery. Art projects involving learning a sequence of steps can help these youths to be able to perform out-of-school jobs which often involve sequences of steps.

Make opportunities for cultural enrichment available to students with mental retardation. On class field trips to a museum, listen and take seriously their verbal responses to art. Teach the students how to act at an art reception. Without actively making cultural experiences available to the student, the student may develop feelings of fear and inadequacy about going to museums, concerts, art fairs, art receptions, and performances in your school. Help the student invite friends to a reception of his or her work. Because cultural events are a satisfying part of life, persons with developmental disabilities deserve to be equipped with the skills, etiquette, and experiences to enable them to participate.

Students with Moderate Retardation

Helping the student with moderate levels of mental retardation to be able to live independently in the community or in a group home is the major educational goal. Building functional clay objects, such as mugs, and construction activities with styrofoam, toothpicks, and blocks, develops fine motor skills. Help the student gain expressive language skills, not only during the motivation and working periods, but especially during a time of happy sharing and role-playing at the lesson's end. Acting in skits also allows students to practice public speaking skills. Promote students' managerial skills by enlisting their support in the collection and inventory of supplies.

Students Who Are Gifted

Generally, people tend to think of giftedness as more of a blessing than curse. Yet most teachers who have worked with gifted youths will probably agree that youths who are gifted have their special learning problems, such as lack of motivation and boredom. They may play a role as "the brains" behind the mischief. Though the playfulness of youths who are gifted can be nerve-racking, their imaginative play often precedes and serves as a catalyst for their cognitive development. Challenge them by brainstorming during all three parts of a lesson: the motivation period, the working period, and the evaluation period. Ask "What other ways can we use this media; how else can we show space?"; during the evaluation time, ask "How else have we shown perspective and space? Can anyone think of a way that no one used?"

Students need time to mull things over and the freedom to come up with an individual solution. Lead them to appreciate the rewards of losing themselves in their work. Encourage your students to use metaphors, which can let them put together thoughts and feelings about things that are taboo or frightening.

While your encouragement is essential, vague praise such as "That is good" is not usually helpful. Exhort your students who are gifted to put themselves into their work. "How can it be good if you dabble unconcernedly with it? I want to see love and caring and thought and involvement." Demand effort and feeling. Help the student to abstract, to boil down the size of the problem. Say to the student, "What is the big idea, the main idea, the essence, that you want to show?" By simplifying, the students can be helped to find a way through the vast maze of possibilities their fertile minds open up.

Some other ways that teachers keep students who are gifted motivated are with Advanced Placement (AP) art history and studio art courses for college credit. To help them link a rich imaginative life to the real world, help your gifted students to enter real-world competitions such as Scholastic Art Awards, county art fairs, state Governor's Honors Programs, state school art exhibitions, PTA art competitions, poster contests, art school portfolio review deadlines, and the National Arts Recognition Talent Search. Put the students into situations in which they can receive approbation, such as school and community exhibits, demonstrations, and competitions. Foster their growth through your phone calls and letters of recommendation to gain their admission into special enrichment programs.

ARTTALK—MEETING SPECIAL NEEDS

Practical suggestions are given in *ArtTalk's* Teacher's Wraparound Edition which explain ways in which visual arts programs and specific studio lessons and activities can be adapted so they contribute to the quality of life for students with disabilities and help them be a part of the inclusive art classroom. The inclusive art class presents students with disabilities with a wide range of peers so they can model appropriate responses. Inclusion also benefits the student with disabilities by providing creative and intellectual stimulation, progress in speech and social growth, and learning better ways of handling day-to-day life situations.

Arts: The Vital Connection

Jean Morman Unsworth
Author and Former Professor of Fine Arts
Loyola University of Chicago
Author of CONNECTING–Integrating Art Across the
Curriculum **and Teacher Resource Binders for** Exploring
Art, Understanding Art, **and** Art in Focus

Creativity—for some it is a remote power possessed only by "artists." For others it is a challenge to one's control. For the art teacher it is a gift in every child—a power that is waiting to be tapped and nurtured.

We are living in a time of information explosion. Aided by new technology, every field of knowledge is expanding with incredible speed. There is a great danger of schools becoming merely "fact-ories." More than ever before it is essential that we see education in its fullest sense—the "drawing out" or educating of the full potential of each student, not simply the "feeding in" of information.

The role of the arts in learning must be reassessed. Viktor Lowenfeld wrote, "Art is a fundamental human process...a dynamic and unifying activity, with great potential for the education of our children."

THE ARTS—A COMPLEMENTARY MODE OF LEARNING

Factual learning taps only the left brain powers of logic, objectivity, reason, judgment, knowledge, skill. The arts add and integrate the vital dimension of right-brain powers—intuition, imagination, and the rich resources of the senses. The whole child comes to school. We need to call forth all of his or her potential in the entire learning process, to encourage the dreamer to imagine how things might be. We need to reach individual children where their strengths lie.

I present the arts not as peripheral, not merely as a desirable cultural dimension, but as essential complementary modes of learning that should be integrated into the entire curriculum.

The skill of drawing is basic to this integration. Drawing is a most human way of seeing and expressing, more natural than writing. Everyone can draw. The problem is the dominance of left-brain thinking that convinces most people they can't draw. Teach a person to really look and to let the eyes draw and you have solved the problem. Drawing should be as personal as handwriting. We are all taught to make the same letter forms, yet our handwriting becomes a most essential identification. Drawing too is individual. It should not be subjected to a standardized form.

The self-confidence that comes with the skill of drawing allows the child to make learning personal, not simply the information needed for the test.

THE CREATIVE PROCESS CHALLENGES THINKING SKILLS AND RISK TAKING

Making connections, expressing ideas, transforming, symbolizing, experimenting, inventing, and the curiosity and self-discipline that comes from taking responsibility for one's decisions—all these and more thinking skills are involved in the process of creating. And the risk of trying one's own ideas and working through those that don't work is a vital experience not found in mastery of "right" answers. Often the brightest child is confident only with those right answers. Creative thinking, risking and making one's own art, music, dance, and poetry affirm the person in a way that no other learning can.

ALL THE ARTS INTERRELATE

All of the arts reach into the same reservoir of intuition, imagination, and sensory perception. All the arts are built on rhythm, proportion, and balance. All the arts transform ordinary knowledge into vision by emphasizing the color, texture, and form of nature, of human activity, and of human emotion. All the arts belong to every person. Their roots are in each of us.

To cultures we call primitive, this concept is normal and natural. Dance, song, visual image, ritual, and drama are interwoven in daily life. The sophistication of western civilization has separated us from the arts, has set them aside as specialties practiced by the few for the few. We need to reclaim them. We need to allow them to tap the spiritual in each of us—to reach the deeper levels of thought and perception of which we are all capable.

AWARENESS – THE SEEING THAT IS VISION

Plato said, "Wonder unsettles life, opens us to another dimension of the everyday world, namely, its being-full-of-wonder." It is this readiness to fall in love with a blade of grass or a glowworm, to be able to feast our eyes, to see the ordinary as if for the first time, that we need to nurture. The "Art is Everywhere" and "Sparking Creativity" features in the Teacher's Wraparound Edition of *ArtTalk* are aimed at this awareness. They reach into all of the senses, listening to both music and the sounds of our day, finding textures in touch as well as in sound, responding to the imagery of poets, and bringing an aesthetic sensibility to our environment. The examples below demonstrate that art is a life experience touching every aspect of our existence. It stretches us into new and exciting dimensions when we perceive and respond creatively. This habit of aesthetic awareness continues to enrich throughout one's life.

Art Is Everywhere

To foster students' awareness of line in everyday life, suggest this: Look for lines in your world–the meandering lines of a vine, the sway of telephone lines from pole to pole, the organic lines of wood grain, or the lines of sorrow, anger, laughter, and age in faces. Find dynamic diagonal lines, rigid verticals, quiet horizontals, and flowing curves. Follow the lines of the movement of birds, the converging lines of railroad tracks, or the squiggly lines of a plate of fettucini. Line is alive! Watch the lines of a dancer's movements or the swinging arms of a rollerblader.

Art Is Everywhere

To foster students' awareness of expressions of color in everyday life, suggest this: Poets use color in their poetry, sometimes to describe objects but also as metaphors of feelings, moods, or scenes. For example, Matthew Arnold wrote vivid descriptions of Dover Beach, England, at night. Look in Bartlett's Familiar Quotations for literary references to each color. You will find under red, for example, a reference to Percy Bysshe Shelley's "Ode to the West Wind." Find a copy of the poem and locate his description of autumn leaves. Write your own color metaphors.

Sparking Creativity

Want students to think creatively about aesthetics? Suggest this: We need a critical eye and aesthetic judgment in many aspects of our daily life. Skim through a catalog for furniture and housewares to see the many different tastes it shows. Test your own aesthetic sense. Cut out from catalogs the furnishings of what you consider a well-designed living room, bedroom, or den. Look for furniture, drapes, bedspreads, rugs, lamps, and decorative pieces. Cut out shapes for each room and arrange them on a sheet of paper. Then share your ideas with classmates. Plan rooms for children, teenagers, or adults.

SAFETY IN THE ART CLASSROOM

Art teachers and their students are often in contact with potentially harmful materials, although many may be totally unaware of the danger. Lead poisoning, cancer, nervous system disorders, anemia, silicosis, chemical pneumonia, asthma, and dermatitis are recognized as industrial diseases caused by hazardous chemicals. However, many fail to recognize that these same diseases are found among artists, craftspeople, teachers, and students using art and craft materials without adequate precautions.

Although studies have been conducted and the findings published, many teachers remain unaware that toxic substances may be in some of the art materials they use routinely in their teaching. Other teachers, aware of the problem, feel that they are exercising adequate precautions by referring to the labels on the art products they use.

Labeling of Art Materials

The labeling of art materials continues to be limited in many ways. Ingredients that caused laboratory animals to perish within two weeks after a single dose was administered were identified as "acutely toxic" and must bear a warning label. However, if fewer than half the animals die, the product may be labeled "nontoxic." In addition, when products are imported or repackaged, the hazards may not be listed or properly described on the label.

Teachers should be aware of the fact that the Federal Hazardous Substances Act, and other legislation introduced at the federal level, have not been entirely successful at rectifying problems of this kind. Moreover, some products known to cause long-term health problems have been excluded from regulation. For example, until recently, manufacturers could still use a "nontoxic" label on a product as dangerous as asbestos powder.

Industry Safety Standards

The art-materials industry has, for many years, supported the use of voluntary safety standards. These standards have been developed with the cooperation and input of various manufacturers. The Arts and Crafts Materials Institute (ACMI) has for some time adhered to a voluntary program designed to ensure the safety of younger students working with art materials. Most art teachers are familiar with the two ACMI safety labels—AP indicating Approved Product, and CP specifying Certified Product. These labels certify that the products on which they are placed have been found to contain no ingredients in sufficient quantities to be toxic or harmful to users. In addition, products bearing a CP seal abide by certain quality standards pertaining to workmanship, working qualities, and color. While the AP/CP seal applies to art products intended for use by younger students, a Certified Label (CL) is used to identify products considered to be more appropriate for older students and adults. The CL seal on a label indicates that the product's ingredients have been examined by toxicologists. The label lists any safety precautions required by law and by labeling standards developed by the American Society of Testing and Materials. Teachers are advised to read and adhere to these safety precautions.

Material Safety Data Sheets and Their Use

Teachers should realize that they may request a Material Safety Data Sheet (MSDS) from manufacturers pertaining to any art products they are unsure of. Among the items included on the MSDS are a listing of all the ingredients for which industrial standards exist, health-hazard information, fire-hazard data, and the chemicals with which the product might react dangerously.

In most school systems, central ordering procedures are— or should be—developed as a means of ensuring that all art materials entering the school are approved by appropriate authorities (for example, the Health Department or Board of Education). Requiring Material Safety Data Sheets from suppliers as a condition of purchase should effectively eliminate many of the toxic materials that might otherwise be brought into the classrooms by unsuspecting teachers.

Safety Precautions for Students

In order for a chemical in an art material to harm a student, it must first come into contact with or enter the body. Teachers should be aware of the following three ways in which this can occur.

Skin Contact. Some chemicals such as those used in etching, or solvents like lacquer and paint thinners, can irritate the skin on contact and result in a variety of skin problems. Other chemicals, known as sensitizers, can cause skin allergies. Examples of these sensitizers include formaldehyde found in some color photography solutions, turpentine, epoxy glues and resins, nickel and chromium compounds, and many tropical woods.

However, the danger with regard to skin contact does not end here. Many toxic chemicals do not just damage the skin itself. They can also be absorbed through the skin into the bloodstream where they can affect other organs. Examples include methyl alcohol found in some shellacs, toluene found in lacquer thinners and silk screen inks, and glycol ethers found in photoetching materials.

Inhalation. Dusts, powders, vapors, gases, aerosols, and other airborne substances may be readily inhaled and, therefore, represent a health hazard. Examples include solvent vapors from paints, inks, and thinners; spray mists from air brush or aerosol spray cans; gases from photographic baths; pottery kiln firing; metal fumes from soldering, welding, and metal casting; and dusts from dyes and pigments, pottery glazes, and woodworking. Some of the chemicals in these materials can result in lung damage from inhalation while others can be absorbed into the bloodstream, where they can lead to a variety of problems including lead poisoning, nerve damage, and kidney damage.

Ingestion. Ingestion is of particular concern with younger students who are inclined to experiment and put things in their mouths. However, ingestion of hazardous substances can occur in the case of older students as well. These students can be affected if they eat, drink, or apply make-up in a classroom where art materials can contaminate these items.

Precautions in Selecting and Using Art Materials

There are certain safety precautions that all teachers should take when selecting art materials for use in their classrooms. Included in these precautions are the following:

- Make certain that the materials obtained for younger students (age 12 or under) have an AP or CP seal of approval; materials secured for use by older students should have a CL seal.
- Incorporate into the art curriculum written information on the potential hazards of art materials and techniques; students should be tested on this information just as they are tested with regard to other aspects of curriculum content. Documentation of this type of instruction should be made and filed.
- Carefully supervise students in the classroom, making certain that safety rules are understood and observed. Teachers must also remember to obey these safety rules themselves in order to impress upon their students the seriousness of these regulations. Students should never be allowed to work in the classroom, during or after school hours, without direct teacher supervision.
- Avoid using solvents or products containing solvents in the art room. These include turpentine, lacquer, shellac, paint thinner, rubber cement, rubber cement thinner, permanent markers, and solvent-based inks such as silk-screen printing ink.
- Do not use acids, alkalies, or bleaches.
- Do not use aerosol spray cans in the classroom, since the inhalation of the spray mist can cause injury to lung tissue.
- Use dust-causing products with care in a well-ventilated area. This precaution applies to the use of pastels, chalks, plaster and clays in dry form, copper enamels, glazes, papier-mâché mixtures, and powdered tempera paints.
- Place kilns in a separate room, outdoors, or if this is not possible, in an out-of-the-way part of the room where students are not likely to come into contact with them when they are in operation. In addition, all kilns should have local exhaust ventilation.
- Remember that good ventilation is an absolute necessity whenever using any art or craft material. Solvents such as paint thinner or turpentine, if used at all, should be tightly sealed and stored away from work areas.
- Be prepared for emergencies by having written emergency procedures prepared, posted, and explained to students. This includes fire-drill procedures and the use of fire extinguishers.
- Report all accidents, even minor ones such as a small cut. Illnesses suspected of being related to art materials should be reported in writing to the school principal or other designated authority at once so that an investigation can be conducted and corrective action determined.

At the beginning of each school year or new term, teachers are urged to determine if any of their students are asthmatic, visually impaired or hearing impaired, or on prescribed medication. If asthmatic students are enrolled in the art class, they should not be exposed to dusts, fumes, or vapors. Visually impaired students understandably operate very close to their artwork and, as a consequence, are more likely to inhale harmful dusts, vapors, and fumes. Students with hearing impairments should not be exposed to activities requiring loud hammering or noisy machinery since this could aggravate their condition. If students are found to be on medication, the teacher should seek their physician's advice regarding the potentially harmful interaction between their prescribed medicine and the art materials they might use in class.

Similar precautions are recommended in situations involving students who are physically handicapped in other ways or who may be learning disabled or emotionally disturbed. These students are at an even greater risk from toxic materials and require special care and attention. In some instances, they might not be able to use the same materials and processes as other students. Careful evaluation is needed in each case to determine what special precautions might be necessary.

Clearly, the need to direct time and effort to safeguarding the health and safety of students in the art classroom is essential. Art teachers, aware of their responsibilities in this regard, recognize that assistance may be needed. Many have turned to the Center for Safety in the Arts (CSA) for this kind of assistance. CSA is a national clearinghouse for research and education on hazards in the visual arts, performing arts, education facilities, and museums. Teachers who wish to take advantage of the services and publications provided by this not-for-profit center can write to the following address for information:

The Center for Safety in the Arts
5 Beekman Street, Suite 1030
New York, New York 10038
(212) 227-6220

COURSE PLANNING

To implement a quality art education program, there is no standard formula or format that will work for every art class. The content of *ArtTalk* draws upon the fundamental disciplines that contribute to the understanding and making of art—art production or studio art, art criticism, aesthetics, and art history. Goals and objectives will be developed by the professional art teacher and will be dependent upon the interests, ability levels, learning styles, standards set by local or state educational requirements, and instructional time allotted for the individual program.

To assist with the planning and development of individual courses, a Pacing Chart and Scope and Sequence Chart are included in this section. These are only intended as suggested guidelines. Individual teachers will need to make necessary adjustments and modifications as required by their local, state, and national curriculum guidelines, as well as by the ability level and learning styles of their students.

Pacing Chart

On the following pages you will find suggested daily lesson plans for using *ArtTalk* as the main text in three of the most common time sequences allocated for art—9-weeks, 18-weeks, and 36-weeks.

Plan One was developed for the use of *ArtTalk* in a nine-week session. Plan Two was developed for a 18-week semester of art taught either in middle or junior high schools. Plan Three provides suggested lesson plans for using *ArtTalk* in a full year.

The following plans identify the number of days spent on chapter contents. It should be noted that during this time, students will have the opportunity for practical application of the material using media and techniques as they complete the Activities within the chapter. Larger blocks of time are allocated for the Studio Lessons because they are more complex than the Activities within the chapter. They also place greater emphasis on the chapter concepts, skill development, and aesthetic quality.

UNIT ONE — Appreciating the Visual Arts

	9 weeks 45 days	18 weeks 90 days	36 weeks 180 days
CHAPTER ONE			
The Language of Art	3	3	5
Art Criticism in Action: *Family Group* by Henry Moore and *The Tragedy* by Pablo Picasso	1	1	1
Meet the Artist: Henry Moore and **Chapter Review**	1	1	1
TOTAL	5	5	7

	9 weeks 45 days	18 weeks 90 days	36 weeks 180 days
CHAPTER TWO			
Art Criticism and Aesthetic Judgment	3	3	5
Art Criticism in Action: *Dawn* by Louise Nevelson and *Gates of Paradise* by Lorenzo Ghiberti	1	1	1
Meet the Artist: Louise Nevelson and Chapter Review	1	1	1
TOTAL	**5**	**5**	**7**
CHAPTER THREE			
Art History	4	5	10
Art Criticism in Action: *Lady with a Bowl of Violets* by Lilla Cabot Perry and *Ginevra de' Benci* by Leonardo da Vinci	1	1	1
Meet the Artist: Lilla Cabot Perry and Chapter Review	1	1	1
TOTAL	**6**	**7**	**12**
CHAPTER FOUR			
Careers in Art	2	2	5
Art Criticism in Action: *A Wrinkle in Time* by Leo and Diane Dillon and *The Third of May, 1808* by Francisco Goya	1	1	1
Meet the Artist: Leo and Diane Dillon and Chapter Review	1	1	1
TOTAL	**4**	**4**	**7**

	9 weeks 45 days	18 weeks 90 days	36 weeks 180 days
CHAPTER FIVE			
Line	4	4	5
Studio Lessons 1. Yarn Painting 2. Contour Wire Sculpture 3. Imagination Landscape 4. Drawing Expressing Movement		(3 days for studio, choose #3 or #4.)	(6 days for studio, choose #1 or #2 for 4 days. Choose #3 or #4 for 2 days.)
Art Criticism in Action: *Study for the Munich Olympic Games Poster* by Jacob Lawrence and *Death of Socrates* by Jacques Louis David	1	1	1
Meet the Artist: Jacob Lawrence and **Chapter Review**	1	1	1
TOTAL	**6**	**9**	**13**

	9 weeks 45 days	18 weeks 90 days	36 weeks 180 days
CHAPTER SIX			
Shape, Form, and Space	5	5	7
Studio Lessons 1. Drawing an Outdoor Scene 2. Clay Plaque with High Relief 3. Landscape Using Surreal Space		(2 days for studio, choose #1 or #3.)	(6 days for studio. #2 takes 4 days. Choose #1 or #3 for 2 days.)
Art Criticism in Action: *Spirits Soaring* by Michael Naranjo and *Nike of Samothrace*	1	1	1
Meet the Artist: Michael Naranjo and **Chapter Review**	1	1	1
TOTAL	**7**	**9**	**15**

	9 weeks 45 days	18 weeks 90 days	36 weeks 180 days
CHAPTER SEVEN			
Color	5	5	10
Studio Lessons 1. Photo Collage and Mixed Media 2. Photo Enlargement 3. Using Color to Create an Expressive Statement 4. Creating a Rainbow Creature		(2 days for studio. Choose #1 or #3.)	(7 days for studio. Choose #1 or #3 for 2 days. Choose #2 or #4 for 5 days.)
Art Criticism in Action: *Things to Come* by Elizabeth Murray and *The Annunciation* by Jan van Eyck	1	1	1
Meet the Artist: Elizabeth Murray and **Chapter Review**	1	1	1
TOTAL	**7**	**9**	**19**

	9 weeks 45 days	18 weeks 90 days	36 weeks 180 days
CHAPTER EIGHT			
Texture	3	3	7
Studio Lessons 1. Fantasy Landscape 2. Assemblage 3. Paper Sculpture Creature 4. Stitchery and Appliqué		2	1 2 2 4
Art Criticism in Action: *The Green House* by Sandy Skoglund and *Daniel in the Lions' Den* by Peter Paul Rubens	1	1	1
Meet the Artist: Sandy Skoglund and **Chapter Review**	1	1	1
TOTAL	**5**	**7**	**18**

	9 weeks 45 days	18 weeks 90 days	36 weeks 180 days
CHAPTER NINE			
Rhythm and Movement		4	7
Studio Lessons 1. Painting with a Rhythmic Activity 2. A Pattern Collage 3. Weaving with a Pattern 4. Coil Baskets		(2 days for studio. Choose #1 or #2.)	(9 days for studio. Choose #1 and #2 for 2 days. Choose #3 or #4 for 5 days.)
Art Criticism in Action: *Janet* by Chuck Close and *The Girl with the Red Hat* by Jan Vermeer		1	1
Meet the Artist: Chuck Close and **Chapter Review**		1	1
TOTAL		**8**	**18**
CHAPTER TEN			
Balance		3	7
Studio Lessons 1. Formal Portrait 2. Informal Group Picture 3. Linoleum Print Using Radial Balance 4. Clay Pot Decorated with Radial Designs		(2 days for studio. Choose #1 or #2.)	(10 days for studio. Choose #1 and #2 for 2 days. Choose #3 or #4 for 6 days.)
Art Criticism in Action: *Flower Day* by Diego Rivera and *David* by Gianlorenzo Bernini		1	1
Meet the Artist: Diego Rivera and **Chapter Review**		1	1
TOTAL		**7**	**19**

	9 weeks 45 days	18 weeks 90 days	36 weeks 180 days
CHAPTER ELEVEN			
Proportion		3	7
Studio Lessons 1. Storyteller Figure 2. Using Distortion for Expressive Effect 3. Papier-Mâché Mask 4. Soft Sculpture		(Choose #1 or #2 for 4 days.)	(Choose #1 or #2 for 6 days.) (Choose #3 or #4 for 5 days.)
Art Criticism in Action: *Waiting* by Isabel Bishop and *Pietà* by Michelangelo		1	1
Meet the Artist: Isabel Bishop and **Chapter Review**		1	1
TOTAL		9	20

	9 weeks 45 days	18 weeks 90 days	36 weeks 180 days
CHAPTER TWELVE			
Variety, Emphasis, Harmony, and Unity		3	7
Studio Lessons 1. Assemblage with Handmade Paper 2. Enlarge One Frame from a Comic Strip 3. Clay Sculpture Unifying Two Ideas 4. Designing a Mural		(6 days for studio. Choose #2 or #4 for 3 days; #3 for 3 days.)	4 3 3 6
Art Criticism in Action: *Apartment Hill* by Wayne Thiebaud and *The Mill* by Rembrandt		1	1
Meet the Artist: Wayne Thiebaud and **Chapter Review**		1	1
TOTAL		11	25

SCOPE AND SEQUENCE CHART

	Introduce ● Emphasize ■ Reinforce ▲	CHAPTER 1 The Language of Art	CHAPTER 2 Art Criticism and Aesthetic Judgment	CHAPTER 3 Art History	CHAPTER 4 Careers in Art	CHAPTER 5 Line	CHAPTER 6 Shape, Form, and Space
Aesthetics			■		▲	▲	▲
Art History				■	▲	▲	▲
Art Criticism			■	▲	▲	▲	▲
Elements of Art		●					
Line		●	▲	▲		■	
Shape, Form, and Space		●	▲	▲	▲	▲	■
Color		●		▲	▲		▲
Texture		●	▲		▲		
Principles of Art		●					
Rhythm and Movement		●	▲				
Balance		●	▲				
Proportion		●	▲				
Variety, Emphasis, Harmony, & Unity		●	▲				
Media, Tools, and Process		●					
Drawing		●			▲		▲
Painting		●		▲			▲
Printmaking		●		▲			
Sculpture		●	▲	▲		▲	▲
Architecture				▲	▲		▲
Other		●		▲	▲	▲	▲
Careers					■		

SCOPE AND SEQUENCE CHART

Legend:
- ● Introduce
- ■ Emphasize
- ▲ Reinforce

	CHAPTER 7 — Color	CHAPTER 8 — Texture	CHAPTER 9 — Rhythm and Movement	CHAPTER 10 — Balance	CHAPTER 11 — Proportion	CHAPTER 12 — Variety, Emphasis, Harmony, and Unity
Aesthetics	▲	▲	▲	▲	▲	▲
Art History	▲	▲	▲	▲	▲	▲
Art Criticism	▲	▲	▲	▲	▲	▲
Elements of Art						
Line			▲			▲
Shape, Form, and Space	▲	▲	▲	▲	▲	▲
Color	■		▲	▲		▲
Texture		■	▲	▲		▲
Principles of Art						
Rhythm and Movement	▲		■			▲
Balance				■		
Proportion					■	
Variety, Emphasis, Harmony, & Unity						■
Media, Tools, and Process						
Drawing					■	
Painting	■	▲	▲	▲	▲	▲
Printmaking		▲	▲	▲		
Sculpture		▲	▲	▲	▲	▲
Architecture		▲		▲	▲	▲
Other	▲	▲	▲	▲	▲	▲
Careers						

ART SUPPLIES GRID

	CHAPTER 1	CHAPTER 2	CHAPTER 3	CHAPTER 4	CHAPTER 5	CHAPTER 6
	The Language of Art	Art Criticism and Aesthetic Judgment	Art History	Careers in Art	Line	Shape, Form, and Space
Pencils	●	●	●	●	●	●
White Drawing Paper				●	●	●
Sketch Paper/Sketchbook	●	●	●		●	●
Brushes	●				●	
Tempera or Acrylic Paints	●		●		●	
Water Containers	●					
Mixing Trays	●					
Paint Cloths	●					
Found Objects	●	●				●
Newspapers, Magazines	●		●		●	●
Mat or Poster Board					●	●
Scissors			●		●	
White Glue					●	●
Felt-Tip Markers					●	
Colored Construction Paper						●
Rulers					●	●
Chalk (Pastels)						●
Oil Pastels					●	●
India Ink					●	
Pens & Penholders			●		●	
Clay	●					
Clay Modeling Tools	●					
Carving Tools	●					
Colored Pencils / Crayons					●	
Charcoal Pencils						
Charcoal						
Cardboard						●
Mixing Bowls						
Watercolor Paints	●				●	

ART SUPPLIES GRID

	CHAPTER 7	CHAPTER 8	CHAPTER 9	CHAPTER 10	CHAPTER 11	CHAPTER 12
	Color	Texture	Rhythm and Movement	Balance	Proportion	Variety, Emphasis, Harmony, and Unity
Pencils	●	●	●	●	●	●
White Drawing Paper	●	●	●	●	●	●
Sketch Paper/Sketchbook	●	●	●	●	●	●
Brushes	●	●	●	●	●	●
Tempera or Acrylic Paints	●	●	●	●	●	●
Water Containers	●	●	●		●	●
Mixing Trays	●	●	●		●	●
Paint Cloths	●	●				
Found Objects						
Newspapers, Magazines	●	●	●	●	●	●
Mat or Poster Board	●					
Scissors	●	●	●		●	●
White Glue	●	●			●	●
Felt-Tip Markers		●		●	●	●
Colored Construction Paper	●	●	●	●	●	
Rulers	●	●	●			
Chalk (Pastels)	●			●	●	
Oil Pastels	●					
India Ink						
Pens & Penholders						
Clay						
Clay Modeling Tools						
Carving Tools						
Colored Pencils / Crayons	●	●				
Charcoal Pencils					●	
Charcoal					●	
Cardboard		●				
Mixing Bowls						
Watercolor Paints	●					

ARTTALK

ARTTALK

SECOND
EDITION

Rosalind Ragans, Ph. D.
Associate Professor Emerita
Georgia Southern University

Glencoe
McGraw-Hill

New York, New York   Columbus, Ohio   Woodland Hills, California   Peoria, Illinois

CONTRIBUTORS AND REVIEWERS

Thomas Beacham
Art Teacher
Telfair County High School
McRae, GA

Leilani Calzada
Art Teacher
Burges High School
El Paso, TX

Sherry Christensen
Art Teacher
Lee High School
San Antonio, TX

Ron Durham
Art Coordinator
Arlington I.S.D.
Arlington, TX

Nell Elam
Art Teacher
Starkville High School
Starkville, MS

Joyce Hearne
English/Art Teacher
El Paso High School
El Paso, TX

Larry Hurt
Art Teacher
Ben Davis High School
Indianapolis, IN

Audrey Komroy
Art Teacher
Akron High School
Akron, NY

Ann Krone
Art Coordinator
Wichita USD 259
Wichita, KS

David McIntyre
Visual Arts Facilitator
El Paso Independent School District
El Paso, TX

Elaine McMichael
Supervisor of Art Education
Somerville High School
Somerville, MA

Sandra H. Moore
Art Specialist
John Sevier Middle School
Kingsport, TN

Virginia Neff
Art Teacher
Shawnee Mission
Shawnee Mission, KS

Christine Peña
Art Teacher
USC Magnet
Los Angeles, CA

Carlyne Seegraves
Elementary Art Teacher
Woodcliff Arts Center
East Grand Rapids
    Public Schools
Grand Rapids, MI

Becky Schopfner
Art Teacher
Chaffin Junior High School
Fort Smith, AR

Barbara Stodola
Executive Director
The John G. Blank Center
    for the Arts
Michigan City, IN

Send all inquiries to:
Glencoe/McGraw-Hill
21600 Oxnard Street, Suite 500
Woodland Hills, CA 91367

ISBN 0-02-640295-5 (Student Text)

Printed in the United States

    3 4 5 6 7 8 9   AGK   00 99 98 97

STUDIO LESSON CONSULTANTS

The author wishes to express her gratitude to the following art teachers who participated in field testing the Studio Lessons with their students:

Karen Anable-Nichols
Reseda High School
Reseda, CA

Thomas Beacham
Telfair County High School
Helena, GA

Pam Bergman
Hume-Fogg Academic High School
Nashville, TN

Wendy Bull
Colonial Junior High School
Memphis, TN

Craig Burkhalter
Southeast High School
Macon, GA

Barbara Cox
Glencliff High School
Nashville, TN

Maggie Davis
Northwestern Senior High School
Miami, FL

Marsha Hogue
Lake Highlands High School
Dallas, TX

Sandra H. Moore
John Sevier Middle School
Kingsport, TN

Bunyan Morris
Marvin Pittman Laboratory School
Statesboro, GA

PerriAnn C. Morris
Jenkins County High School
Millen, GA

Ted Oliver
Fannin County High School
Blue Ridge, GA

Kelly Pasman
Parkview Junior High School
New Castle, IN

David Sebring
Dobson High School
Mesa, AZ

Margaret M. Shearouse
Harlem High School
Harlem, GA

Rosanne Stutts
Davidson Fine Arts School
Augusta, GA

Nancy Walker
Colonial Junior High School
Memphis, TN

STUDENT CONTRIBUTORS

The following students contributed exemplary work for the Studio Lesson pages:

Dobson High School, Mesa, AZ: Joel Switzer 5.36A, Lyle Kinlicheenie 10.34A, Jacob Marx 11.32A; Reseda High School, Reseda, CA: Wesley Ashcraft 7.39A, Dago Chavarria 9.27A; Douglas Anderson High School, Jacksonville, FL: Jessica Erickson 9.8; Northwestern Senior High School, Miami FL: Manuel Cuellar 10.33A; Davidson Fine Arts School, Augusta, GA: Heather Story 7.40A, Therese Turman 9.28A; Fannin County High School, Blue Ridge, GA: Amy Jones 5.38A; Harlem High School, Harlem, GA: Josh Menefee 12.28A; Jenkins County High School, Millen, GA: Kristen Leonard 5.35A, Genie Wiggins 8.28A, Melissa Hurst 8.30A, Erin Reeves, Stephanie McMillan, Nimesh Solanki, Krystal Boyd 9.29A; Joy Crocket, Martha Pierce 9.30A; Marvin Pittman Laboratory School, Statesboro, GA: Sean Sanders 6.24, Eddie Dinello, 6.41, Dana Van Tassel 6.42, 6.43; Marian Puckett 7.9; Elisabeth Adams, Meg Chandler, Eric DeLoach, John Dewey, Nichalos Gordon, Christi Groover, Chrissy Joiner, Ashley MacCaughelty, Marco Marchionni, Katie J. Olliff, Shaana Perkins, Alison Powell, Elizabeth Price, Chad Prosser, Dawn Ross, Jenny Smith, Kelly Smith, Anna Woodyard, all 7.38A; Elizabeth Ariail 8.14; Dawn Ross 8.29A; Marissa MacCaughelty 9.21; Maggie Moore 9.22; Trip Healy 10.10; Maggie Horne 11.34A; Southeast High School, Macon, GA: Jennifer Maddox 12.27A; Telfair County High School, Helena, GA: Rebecca Renew 5.37A; Ware County High School, Waycross, GA: Dorothy Robbins 12.29A; Parkview Junior High School, New Castle, IN: Kevin Swiegart 7.37A; John Sevier Middle School, Kingsport, TN: Sarah Rains 8.8; Colonial Junior High School, Memphis, TN: Alexandria Hare 6.44A, Carey Arnett 6.46A; Glencliff High School, Nashville, TN: Jason Swafford 8.27A; Hume-Fogg Academic High School, Nashville, TN: Karianne Mattox 6.16; Dede Bacon 6.45A; Lake Highlands High School, Dallas, TX: Chip Cullum 10.31A; Ginna Ladd 10.32A; Rogher Jeri 11.33A.

Credits for the art details found throughout the Table of Contents are listed below. Following the credit information in parentheses are the figure number and the page on which the full work of art can be found.

CONTENTS

UNIT 1 *A*PPRECIATING THE VISUAL ARTS 2

CHAPTER 1 *The Language of Art* 4
The Elements and Principles 6
The Media and Process of Art 6
The Work of Art 17
The Credit Line 18
Art Criticism in Action 20
    Family Group by Henry Moore 20
    The Tragedy by Pablo Picasso 21
Meet the Artist: Henry Moore 22
Chapter Review 23

CHAPTER 2 *Art Criticism and Aesthetic Judgment* 24
Why Study Art Criticism? 26
How to Criticize a Work of Art 27
Aesthetic Theories and Qualities of Art 30
Art Criticism: Getting Started 32
Students Practice Art Criticism 34
Art Criticism in Action 36
    Dawn by Louise Nevelson 36
    Gates of Paradise by Lorenzo Ghiberti 37
Meet the Artist: Louise Nevelson 38
Chapter Review 39

C H A P T E R　3　　*Art History*　　　　　　　　　　40

Learning About Works of Art　　　　42

Art of Earliest Times　　　　43

Art of Asia　　　　47

Art of Greece and Rome　　　　48

Art of the Middle Ages in Europe　　　　50

Art of the Renaissance in Europe　　　　51

Art of Islam　　　　52

Art of the Native Americans　　　　53

Art of Europe in the Seventeenth　　　　53
　　　Through the Nineteenth Century

Art of Africa　　　　57

The Beginning of the Twentieth Century　　　　58

From the Fifties into the Future　　　　63

Art Criticism in Action　　　　66

　　Lady with a Bowl of Violets by　　　　66
　　　Lilla Cabot Perry

　　Ginevra de' Benci by Leonardo da Vinci　　　　67

Meet the Artist: Lilla Cabot Perry　　　　68

Chapter Review　　　　69

CHAPTER 4   *Careers in Art*   70

Art-Related Careers   72

Business and Industry   72

Environmental Planning and Development   76

Entertainment   78

Education and Cultural Enrichment   80

Thinking About an Art Career   81

Art Criticism in Action   82

   A Wrinkle in Time cover illustration   82
    by Leo and Diane Dillon

   The Third of May, 1808 by   83
    Francisco Goya

Meet the Artist: Leo and Diane Dillon   84

Chapter Review   85

UNIT 2

*T*HE ELEMENTS OF ART   86

CHAPTER 5   *Line*   88

What is Line?   91

Kinds of Lines   93

Line Variation   94

What Different Lines Express   97

Contour Drawing   100

Gesture Drawing   102

Calligraphic Drawing   103

Line and Value   105

Studio Lessons

   Yarn Painting   106

   Contour Wire Sculpture   108

   Imagination Landscape   110

   Drawing Expressing Movement   112

Art Criticism in Action   114

   Study for the Munich Olympic Games   114
    Poster by Jacob Lawrence

   Death of Socrates by Jacques Louis David   115

Meet the Artist: Jacob Lawrence   116

Chapter Review   117

CHAPTER 6   *Shape, Form, and Space*   118

Shapes   120

Forms   122

Space and Its Relationship to Shape and Form   124

How We Perceive Shape, Form, and Space   129

How Artists Create Shapes and Forms In Space   132

What Different Spaces, Shapes, and   139
    Forms Express

Studio Lessons

    Drawing an Outdoor Scene   144

    Clay Plaque with High Relief   146

    Landscape Using Surreal Space   148

Art Criticism in Action   150

    Spirits Soaring by Michael Naranjo   150

    Nike of Samothrace   151

Meet the Artist: Michael Naranjo   152

Chapter Review   153

CHAPTER 7   *Color*   154

How We See Color   156

Color Schemes   164

Color in Pigments   171

How Artists Use Color   174

Studio Lessons

     Photo Collage and Mixed Media   178

     Photo Enlargement   180

     Using Color to Create an Expressive Statement   182

     Creating a Rainbow Creature   184

Art Criticism in Action   186

     Things to Come by Elizabeth Murray   186

     The Annunciation by Jan van Eyck   187

Meet the Artist: Elizabeth Murray   188

Chapter Review   189

CHAPTER 8   *Texture*   190

How You Perceive Texture   193

Texture and Value   196

How Artists Use Texture   199

Studio Lessons

     Fantasy Landscape   206

     Assemblage   208

     Paper Sculpture Creature   210

     Stitchery and Appliqué   212

Art Criticism in Action   214

     The Green House by Sandy Skoglund   214

     Daniel in the Lions' Den by Peter Paul Rubens   215

Meet the Artist: Sandy Skoglund   216

Chapter Review   217

UNIT 3		
	𝒯HE PRINCIPLES OF DESIGN	218
CHAPTER 9	*Rhythm and Movement*	220
	How We Perceive Visual Rhythm	222
	Repetition	224
	Types of Rhythm	226
	How Artists Use Rhythm to Create Movement	235
	Studio Lessons	
	Painting with a Rhythmic Activity	238
	A Pattern Collage	240
	Weaving with a Pattern	242
	Coil Baskets	244
	Art Criticism in Action	246
	Janet by Chuck Close	246
	The Girl with the Red Hat by Jan Vermeer	247
	Meet the Artist: Chuck Close	248
	Chapter Review	249
CHAPTER 10	*Balance*	250
	Visual Balance	252
	The Expressive Qualities of Balance	263
	Studio Lessons	
	Formal Portrait	268
	Informal Group Picture	270
	Linoleum Print Using Radial Balance	272
	Clay Pot Decorated with Radial Designs	274
	Art Criticism in Action	276
	Flower Day by Diego Rivera	276
	David by Gianlorenzo Bernini	277
	Meet the Artist: Diego Rivera	278
	Chapter Review	279

CHAPTER 11   *Proportion*   280

The Golden Mean   282

Scale   285

Drawing Human Proportions   288

How Artists Use Proportion and Distortion   293

Studio Lessons

Storyteller Figure   300

Using Distortion for Expressive Effect   302

Papier-Mâché Mask   304

Soft Sculpture   306

Art Criticism in Action   308

Waiting by Isabel Bishop   308

Pietà by Michelangelo   309

Meet the Artist: Isabel Bishop   310

Chapter Review   311

CHAPTER 12   *Variety, Emphasis, Harmony, and Unity*   312

Variety   314

Emphasis   315

Harmony   322

Unity   324

Creating Visual Unity   324

How Artists Use Variety, Emphasis,   332

and Harmony to Enhance Unity

Studio Lessons

Assemblage with Handmade Paper   334

Enlarge One Frame from a Comic Strip   336

Clay Sculpture Unifying Two Ideas   338

Designing a Mural   340

Art Criticism in Action   342

Apartment Hill by Wayne Thiebaud   342

The Mill by Rembrandt   343

Meet the Artist: Wayne Thiebaud   344

Chapter Review   345

UNIT 4 — TECHNIQUE TIPS HANDBOOK — 346

Drawing Tips
1. Making Contour Drawings — 349
2. Making Gesture Drawings — 349
3. Drawing Calligraphic Lines with a Brush — 349
4. Using Shading Techniques — 350
5. Using Sighting Techniques — 350
6. Using a Viewing Frame — 351
7. Using a Ruler — 351
8. Making a Grid for Enlarging — 352
9. Measuring Rectangles — 352

Painting Tips
10. Mixing Paint to Change the Value of Color — 352
11. Making Natural Earth Pigment Paints — 353
12. Working with Watercolors — 353
13. Cleaning a Paint Brush — 353

Printmaking Tip
14. Making a Stamp Print — 354

Sculpting Tips
15. Working with Clay — 354
16. Joining Clay — 354
17. Making a Pinch Pot — 355
18. Using the Coil Technique — 355
19. Papier-Mâché — 355
20. Making a Paper Sculpture — 356

Other Tips
21. Making Paper — 356
22. Basic Embroidery Stitches — 357
23. Weaving Techniques — 358
24. Making a Coiled Basket — 360
25. Making a Tissue Paper Collage — 361

Display Tips
26. Making a Mat — 362
27. Mounting a Two-Dimensional Work — 363
28. Working with Glue — 363

Safety in the Art Room — 364

Artists and Their Works — 366
Chronology of Artworks — 371
Glossary — 376
Bibliography — 384
Index — 389

EATURES

Art Criticism in Action

Artist	Title of Artwork	
Henry Moore	*Family Group*	20
Pablo Picasso	*The Tragedy*	21
Louise Nevelson	*Dawn*	36
Lorenzo Ghiberti	*Gates of Paradise*	37
Lilla Cabot Perry	*Lady with a Bowl of Violets*	66
Leonardo da Vinci	*Ginevra de' Benci*	67
Leo and Diane Dillon	*A Wrinkle in Time*	82
Francisco Goya	*The Third of May, 1808*	83
Jacob Lawrence	*Study for the Munich Olympic Games Poster*	114
Jacques Louis David	*Death of Socrates*	115
Michael Naranjo	*Spirits Soaring*	150
	Nike of Samothrace	151
Elizabeth Murray	*Things to Come*	186
Jan Van Eyck	*The Annunciation*	187
Sandy Skoglund	*The Green House*	214
Peter Paul Rubens	*Daniel in the Lions' Den*	215
Chuck Close	*Janet*	246
Jan Vermeer	*The Girl with the Red Hat*	247
Diego Rivera	*Flower Day*	276
Gianlorenzo Bernini	*David*	277
Isabel Bishop	*Waiting*	308
Michelangelo	*Pietà*	309
Wayne Thiebaud	*Apartment Hill*	342
Rembrandt	*The Mill*	343

Meet the Artist

Henry Moore	22	Elizabeth Murray	188
Louise Nevelson	38	Sandy Skoglund	216
Lilla Cabot Perry	68	Chuck Close	248
Leo and Diane Dillon	84	Diego Rivera	278
Jacob Lawrence	116	Isabel Bishop	310
Michael Naranjo	152	Wayne Thiebaud	344

ACTIVITIES

Chapter 1

Testing Your Knowledge	10
Exploring Paints	11
Making a Printing Plate	14
Composing a Photograph	15
Using Credit Information	18

Chapter 2

Testing Personal Responses	27
Practicing Description	28
Interpreting a Work	29
Classifying Aesthetic Theories	32

Chapter 3

Analyzing Architecture	49
The Gothic Style	50
Analyzing a Work	54
Analyzing a Style	55
Analyzing a Style	63
Applying the Steps	65

Chapter 4

Analyzing Design	74
Using Design for Display	78
Critiquing Animation	79
Thinking About Careers	81

Chapter 5

Creating Lines	92
Identifying Lines	94
Creating Varied Lines	95
Using Lines Expressively	99
Using Contour Lines	100
Capturing Motion	102
Thick-to-Thin Lines	103
Using Line to Create Value	105

Chapter 6

Exploring Shapes	122
Creating Forms	123
Experimenting with Space	125
Using Three Dimensions	128

Shape and Point of View	131
Using Shading	133
Creating Depth	138
Active and Static Shapes	143

Chapter 7

Making a Color Wheel	159
Creating Values	162
Working with Intensity	163
Using Color Schemes	169
Mixing Colors	173
Using Color for Effect	176

Chapter 8

Creating Textures	194
Creating Contrasting Textures	197
Inventing Textures	204

Chapter 9

Using Visual Beats	223
Motifs and Patterns	226
Using Random Rhythm	226
Alternating Rhythm	230
Using Flowing Rhythm	233
Progressive Rhythm	235

Chapter 10

Using Symmetry	253
Creating Radial Balance	256
Using Informal Balance	261
Identifying Balance	267

Chapter 11

Experimenting with Scale	287
Human Proportions	290
Drawing the Head	292
Distorting Proportions	298

Chapter 12

Variety and Contrast	315
Using Emphasis	322
Creating Unity	331

LISTING OF STUDIO LESSONS BY MEDIA

Chalk

Landscape Using Surreal Space	148
Using Color to Create an Expressive Statement	182
Formal Portrait	268
Using Distortion for Expressive Effect	302

Clay

Clay Plaque with High Relief	146
Clay Pot Decorated with Radial Designs	274
Storyteller Figure	300
Clay Sculpture Unifying Two Ideas	338

Fibers

Yarn Painting	106
Stitchery and Appliqué	212
Weaving with a Pattern	242
Coil Baskets	244

Mixed Media

Photo Collage and Mixed Media	178
Creating a Rainbow Creature	184
Fantasy Landscape	206
Assemblage	208
A Pattern Collage	240
Papier-Mâché Mask	304

Other

Contour Wire Sculpture	108
Soft Sculpture	306
Assemblage with Handmade Paper	334

Paint

Imagination Landscape	110
Drawing Expressing Movement	112
Landscape Using Surreal Space	148
Photo Enlargement	180
Using Color to Create an Expressive Statement	182
Painting with a Rhythmic Activity	238
Formal Portrait	268
Informal Group Picture	270
Using Distortion for Expressive Effect	302
Enlarge One Frame from a Comic Strip	336
Designing A Mural	340

Paper

Paper Sculpture Creature	210
Papier-Mâché Mask	304

Pencil, Pen, Charcoal, and Markers

Drawing Expressing Movement	112
Drawing an Outdoor Scene	144
Formal Portrait	268
Using Distortion for Expressive Effect	302
Enlarge One Frame from a Comic Strip	336

Printmaking

Linoleum Print Using Radial Balance	272

APPRECIATING THE VISUAL ARTS

UNIT OVERVIEW

Learning about the language of visual art is a key to understanding, appreciating, and creating works of art. In Chapter 1, students are introduced to the elements and principles of art. (Each element and principle will be explained in much greater detail in Units 2 and 3.) Chapter 2 helps students analyze and evaluate artworks based on aesthetic qualities and the steps of art criticism—*describe*, *analyze*, *interpret*, and *judge*. In Chapter 3, students explore the many different types of art created throughout history, beginning with prehistoric art and progressing to contemporary times. In Chapter 4, students examine the career opportunities in art and art-related fields.

UNIT PLANNING GUIDE

The following chart shows the number of class periods suggested for each chapter.

	9 wks.	18 wks.	36 wks.
Ch. 1	5	5	7
Ch. 2	5	5	7
Ch. 3	6	7	12
Ch. 4	4	4	7

Jan Steen. *The Dancing Couple*. (Detail.) 1663. Oil on canvas. 102.5 × 142.5 cm (40⅜ × 56⅛″). National Gallery of Art, Washington, D.C. Widener collection.

2

RESOURCES FOR UNIT 1

Unit 1 Test
ArtTalk Fine Art Transparency
• Audrey Flack. *Marilyn*

ArtTalk Fine Art Print
• Faith Ringgold. *The Church Picnic Story Quilt*

APPRECIATING THE VISUAL ARTS

CHAPTER 1
The Language of Art

CHAPTER 2
*Art Criticism and
Aesthetic Judgment*

CHAPTER 3
Art History

CHAPTER 4
Careers in Art

In *ArtTalk* you will be learning about the visual arts. These are the arts that produce images and objects to look at. The visual arts include all objects created for visual appeal—including those that serve a useful purpose.

Why should you read about and learn how to make visual arts? Because they satisfy human needs for display, celebration, personal expression, and communication. We use the visual arts to enhance our visual environment, to express our innermost feelings, and to communicate ideas.

In the first unit of *ArtTalk* you will learn about the language of visual art. You will begin to learn how to look at art in new ways and to make judgments about its artistic merit. You will also learn about the many different kinds of art created throughout history and the career opportunities in art today. After completing Unit 1, you will be ready to begin creating your own art. You will also be on your way toward developing a fuller appreciation for the visual arts and for the natural art that surrounds you in the environment.

3

The Language of Art

INTRODUCE

CHAPTER OVERVIEW

Chapter 1 introduces students to the idea that there is a language of art. This language is a visual one, and communication is accomplished through the successful use of the elements and principles of art combined with the choice of media for a work of art. Unlike verbal and written languages, the language of art is common to the people of all countries.

CHAPTER SUPPLIES

For a list of the materials you will need for the Activities in this chapter, refer to the "Art Supplies Grid" in the Teacher's Manual. In addition, have on hand the following special items:

- automatic camera and film

FINE ART RESOURCES
Transparencies
- Käthe Kollwitz. *Seed for Sowing Shall Not Be Ground*
- Helen Lundeberg. *Double Portrait of the Artist in Time*
- Richard Diebenkorn. *Figure on a Porch*

Fine Art Print
- Dong Kingman. *Skaters in New York*

FIGURE 1.1 Grant Wood was an American artist who chose to paint the people and the landscapes of mid-twentieth-century Iowa in the realistic style he learned by studying the art of fifteenth-century German artists. His paintings are still popular today because they make people feel they are looking at America's "good old days."

Grant Wood. *Return from Bohemia*. 1935. Colored crayon, gouache, and pencil on brown paper. 59.7 x 51 cm (23½ x 20"). The Regis Collection, Minneapolis, Minnesota.

4

RESOURCES FOR CHAPTER 1

Application Activities 1, 2
Artist's Profiles 1, 21, 37
Cooperative Learning Activities 1, 2
Cultural Diversity in Art
Enrichment Activities 1, 2

Reteaching Activities
Study Guide 1
Concept Map 1
Chapter 1 Test

The Language of Art

When you talk to someone or write a letter, you *communicate*. You share your ideas and feelings with that person. You use words—either spoken or written—to communicate a message.

You can also communicate through the arts. They are languages for expressing ideas and feelings that everyday words cannot explain. The arts talk in ways that go beyond simply describing something or telling a story.

The arts can cross the language barriers of different countries. Someone who cannot speak English can understand what is happening in the painting by Grant Wood (Figure 1.1). Mikhail Baryshnikov may speak English with a Russian accent, but when he dances, the language of his movement is understood all around the world.

The arts may even help us communicate with beings from other worlds. In 1972 scientists of the National Aeronautics and Space Administration (NASA) attached a special plaque to *Pioneer 10*, the first exploratory vessel designed to leave our solar system. This spacecraft is out beyond our planets today, carrying this plaque, which has drawings of a human man and woman and a diagram of our solar system. The NASA scientists thought these visual symbols were the best way to try to communicate with any beings *Pioneer 10* might encounter.

FIRST IMPRESSIONS

In *Return from Bohemia* (Figure 1.1 on the opposite page) Grant Wood has shown himself at work on a painting. What is your first reaction to this work of art? What questions come to mind as you look at this group portrait? Does Wood use the concealed canvas and the title to help tell more than a simple story? How does he communicate to you?

Objectives

After completing this chapter, you will be able to:

■ Identify the elements of art and the principles of design.

■ Describe the media used in drawing and painting.

■ Explain how you can improve your perceptual skills.

■ List the processes used in printmaking and sculpture.

■ Name and identify the subject, composition, and content in a work of art.

Words to Know

composition
content
credit line
edition
elements of art
freestanding
medium
nonobjective art
perception
photography
principles of design
printmaking
relief
subject
symbol

5

FOCUS

INTRODUCING THE CHAPTER

Tell students that in this chapter they will learn that artists use a visual language to communicate their ideas, and that art viewers who understand this language are better prepared to make judgments about artworks.

MOTIVATOR

Display an assortment of media and artist's tools such as pencils, charcoal, crayons, clay, inks, and brushes. Ask students to experiment with the media and tell them that in this chapter they will learn more about the media and processes used by artists to create drawings, paintings, prints, sculptures, and crafts.

VOCABULARY PREVIEW

Have students preview the list of vocabulary words on this page. Also, acquaint them with these words that will appear in the chapter: pigment, solvent, printing plate, brayer, serigraph, fine art, and applied art.

USING FIRST IMPRESSIONS

Refer students to Figure 1.1 and remind them that Grant Wood is best known for his painting *American Gothic,* which captures the simple lifestyle and determination of rural Americans. Using the questions in the text, have students attempt to explain their reactions to *Return from Bohemia.*

TEACHER TALK

A Success Story When Larry Hurt of Ben Davis High School in Indianapolis, Indiana, teaches art, he encourages an open mind and an eagerness to examine critical issues of the day. One of his students followed through on his advice. After reading an article about the censorship of an art show at a local high school gallery, then writing an opinion paper on the topic, the student contacted all of the individuals involved, set up a forum on censorship, and served as moderator of the session. The forum was open to all Art Honor Society chapter members. The result was a lively discussion that promised more dialogue and more critical thinking at Ben Davis!

TEACH

(page 6)
- The Elements and Principles

GUIDED PRACTICE

Understanding Art History

To help students further appreciate the life and times of Grant Wood, whose work is shown in Figure 1.1, page 4, assign *Artist's Profile 37* in the TCR.

Developing Perceptual Skills

Ask students to write a description of the main entrance to the school. Challenge students to remember lines, shapes, forms, spaces, colors, and textures. Ask volunteers to read their descriptions aloud, then display a picture of the entrance, or, if possible, take the class to the entrance. Ask them to suggest ways that they can train themselves to observe more closely the elements of art found in their environment.

Developing Studio Skills

Instruct students to choose one element of art, such as line or color, and create an abstract composition emphasizing that element by limiting the others. For example, if they choose shape, they would vary the shape but keep the color uniform. Remind them to plan and organize their work so that it uses the principles of design.

INDEPENDENT PRACTICE

Keeping a Sketchbook

Using an ordinary pencil, have students make a value scale by starting with the lightest gray and progressing to the darkest gray.

THE ELEMENTS AND PRINCIPLES

You know that the people in our world speak many different languages. Spanish, Swahili, Japanese, Hindi, French, English, and Apache are only a few of the three thousand different languages that have been spoken on this planet Earth.

Each language has its own system of words and rules of grammar. To learn a new language you need to learn new words and a new set of rules for putting those words together.

The language of visual art also has its own system. All of the objects you look at in a work of art are made up of certain common elements. They are arranged according to basic principles. As you learn these basic elements and principles, you will learn the language of art.

Being able to use the language of visual art will help you in many ways. It will increase your ability to understand, appreciate, and enjoy art. It will increase your ability to express yourself clearly when discussing art. It will even help you improve your ability to produce artworks.

The Elements of Art

A **symbol** is *something that stands for, or represents, something else*. In a spoken language words are symbols. The word *chair* stands for a piece of furniture that has a seat, legs, a back, and sometimes arms. In the language of art we use visual symbols to communicate ideas.

The *basic visual symbols in the language of art* are known as the **elements of art**. Just as there are basic kinds of words—such as nouns, verbs, adjectives, and adverbs—there are basic kinds of art elements. These are *line, shape* and *form, space, color, value*, and *texture*. The elements are the visual building blocks that the artist puts together to create a work of art. No matter how a work is made, it will contain some or all of these elements.

When you are looking at a visual image, it is difficult to separate one element from another. For example, when you look at a painting, you may see a rough, red square outlined with a black line. However, rather than seeing the elements of texture (rough), color (red), shape (square), and line (black) separately, you see them all at once. You see

the object as a whole. You visually "read" the elements together.

Sometimes the differences between the elements are not clear-cut. A line may be so wide that it looks like a shape, or an artist may manipulate light and dark values to indicate different surface textures. Look at the variety of textures Janet Fish has created in *Fallen Vase* (Figure 1.2).

When you first learned to read, you did not begin with a full-length novel. You learned by reading one word at a time. That is how you will start to read the language of art: one element at a time.

The Principles of Design

After you have learned to recognize the elements of art, you will learn the ways in which the elements can be organized for different effects. When you learn a language, you learn the rules of grammar by which words are organized into sentences and paragraphs. Without these rules people would find it very difficult to communicate.

Visual images are also organized according to rules. The *rules that govern how artists organize the elements of art* are called the **principles of design**. They also help artists organize the elements for specific effects. The principles of design have a strong influence on the way art communicates, and they are the subject of the last four chapters in *ArtTalk*. The principles you will learn about are *rhythm, movement, balance, proportion, variety, emphasis, harmony*, and *unity*. In Figure 1.3 on page 8, the artist Julio Larraz has created a mysterious mood by the way he has used the principles of design to organize the elements in his painting *Papiamento*.

THE MEDIA AND PROCESSES OF ART

The *material used to make art* is called a **medium**. Tempera is an opaque medium used for painting. A medium can be something as ordinary as a crayon or as exotic as gold. You need to know that the word *medium* has an unusual plural form. It is **media**. Clay, wood, and marble are media used for sculpting.

CURRICULUM CONNECTION

Literature Writers use words like artists use the elements of art to communicate ideas. By explaining details about color and line, by describing the texture of objects, their shape and form, and how they take up space, a writer enriches a story and captures the interest of readers. Rather than simply naming an object or a scene, the writer may use descriptive phrases to vary his or her style and create a certain mood or impression. Writing is enhanced by effective use of description. Ask students to think of a book that uses vivid descriptions. Probably, the author used the elements of art to create the memorable images.

TEACH

(pages 7–17)
• The Media and Processes of Art

LOOKING
CLOSELY

FIGURE 1.2 Look closely at the different ways that Fish has used light values to indicate different surfaces. The transparent red glass bowl has different highlights than the slightly less shiny ceramic lamp base. Now notice the different way she uses light to show highlights on the soft, sheer curtains. How is the light different on the fruit than it is on the fallen vase? How has light been used to indicate that there is a lit lightbulb inside the translucent lamp shade? Look at the green leaves in the window and the leaves on the trees on the distant hill. What has the artist done with the edges of shapes to indicate distance?

Janet Fish. *Fallen Vase*. 1987. Oil on canvas. 178 × 101.6 cm (70 × 40″). Robert Miller Gallery, New York, New York.

GUIDED PRACTICE

Building Vocabulary

Have students define *medium* and *media*. Stress the uniqueness of the Latin plural form and ask for examples of similar words that form plurals by changing spellings, rather than adding *s/es*, (for example, foot/feet).

Developing Perceptual Skills

Have students browse through art books and identify at least one example of a drawing, a painting, a print, a photograph, a sculpture, and a craft. Instruct students to explain how they were able to determine the correct medium used.

LOOKING
CLOSELY

Have students study Figure 1.2 and answer the questions in the caption.
   Encourage them to see how the light reflected by the glass bowl is white, and it has a hard-edged outline. The lamp base has reflections that are a light value of dull-orange glaze, and the edges of the shapes do not have hard lines.
   In the center of the lamp shade there are white brushstrokes mixed with the yellow that indicate the shape of a bulb inside the yellow shade.
   The leaves in the vase have sharp, clearly defined edges. The leaves on the tree blend into bunches with soft edges while the leaves on the hill are a soft blend of green without any shapes or edges.

Just as the artist's choice of how to arrange the elements of art using the principles of design affects the look of the finished work, so do the medium and the process the artist chooses. A watercolor painting of an outdoor scene will look very different from an oil painting of the same scene. During your art class you will use many art media to make art. The following describes some of the most familiar media and processes that you will use and read about.

Drawing

Drawing is the process of moving a pointed instrument over a smooth surface to leave a mark. That mark is a line. Line is the most important element of art in drawing.

The most popular drawing media are graphite pencils, colored pencils, marking pens, charcoal, crayons, pastels, and colored chalk. Pen and ink, pen and brush, and brushes with watercolors are also used to make drawings.

CULTURAL PERSPECTIVES

Artists of every culture find ways to express their beliefs, rituals, and ideas. The materials they use for this expression can range from feathers, shells, and dye, to stitchery. Each material shows the ingenuity of the people who use it. Often, the chosen material can be found only in their particular locale and reveals the feeling for beauty that is a rich part of every culture. For example, feathers and shells are common to the art of the Native American, South Pacific, and African cultures. Silk thread is a feature of Asian, Chinese, Native American, and European stitchery. Have students bring in examples of art from various cultures and display them.

GUIDED PRACTICE
(continued)

Understanding Art History

Explain to students that when preliminary sketches are available, they prove to be vital to art historians. Art historians frequently use sketches to determine the authenticity of a discovered artwork that is thought to be the work of a major artist. The Maison de Renoir, for example, houses a collection of the materials left by Pierre Auguste Renoir. If someone "discovers" a painting by Renoir, these documents can be helpful in establishing the legitimacy of the work. Have students examine preliminary sketches done by artists.

Sparking Creativity

Want students to think creatively about media? Suggest this: Find a medium in the materials around you such as match sticks, pebbles, torn pieces of magazine, colorful scraps of fabric, buttons, and tiles. Then make a mosaic on a piece of firm cardboard or masonite. Try many arrangements of your pieces before gluing them down. Repeat and cluster colors. Carry movements through the design. Keep trying until your design begins to work. Look around you for ideas—tree lines, water going down a drain, crowds of people, or the cloverleaf of an expressway ramp. Pattern is everywhere.

FIGURE 1.3 Julio Larraz has camouflaged the figure of the woman in this painting by placing her against the textured trunk of the palm tree, using active lines for the palm fronds, and painting the water an intense blue. Why do you think the artist arranged the picture this way? What kind of mood did he create by using these techniques? Now that you have looked closely at the painting, what question do you think the artist wanted to raise in the viewer's mind?

Julio Larraz. *Papiamento.* 1987. Oil on canvas. 143.5 × 209.5 cm (56½ × 82½″). Nohra Haime Gallery, New York, New York.

There are many different purposes for drawing. Some of the most important are to develop perception, to record ideas, to help plan projects, and to make finished artworks. The drawing *Preacher* by Charles White is an example of a finished work of art drawn with pen and ink (Figure 1.4).

To an artist, looking and perceiving are not the same thing. Looking is simply noticing and labeling an object. **Perception** is *the act of looking at something carefully and thinking deeply about what is seen.* Developing perception requires that you really study the object being observed and that you notice every detail carefully. Through drawing, artists become better at perceiving.

Many artists use sketchbooks to record their surroundings and to study objects. Artists also record ideas and impressions in these sketchbooks that can be used later. The Renaissance artist Leonardo da Vinci (lay-oh-**nar**-doh da **vin**-chee) filled more than one hundred sketchbooks with his perceptions and ideas. He made visual drawings and added written notes. His sketchbooks included everything from perceptions of people to his notations on the movement of water (Figure 1.5) and his plans for flying machines.

Drawing is usually the first step in completing many paintings and other art projects. Rough sketches, or studies, are almost always done before creating a work in another medium such as paint or clay. Fashion designers draw their ideas for new styles long before any fabric is cut. Many creative people, such as stage designers, graphic designers,

CULTURAL PERSPECTIVES

Throughout this program you may wish to use activities from the supplement *Cultural Diversity in Art.* This booklet is designed to extend and build upon concepts learned in *ArtTalk* and to focus on helping the teacher and student learn to appreciate cultural diversity through art. Art educators need to address the changing complexion of the population of the United States which in turn manifests itself in the classroom. The guide will help you evaluate your current program, and offer suggestions to help you become a more culturally sensitive art educator. Reproducible student activity sheets are included and can be used with a variety of chapters in *ArtTalk.*

FIGURE 1.4 The artist has built up the dark areas in this drawing by carefully applying layers of lines that cross each other in different directions. It is easy to see the lines in the gray shadows, but some areas appear totally black.

Charles White. *Preacher*. 1952. Ink on cardboard. 54 × 75 cm (21⅜ × 29⅜"). Collection of Whitney Museum of American Art, New York, New York.

FIGURE 1.5 Da Vinci's observations of moving water could not be verified until this century, when we had cameras that could capture the movement of water in a photograph. Da Vinci filled his notebooks with sketches and notes that could be read only when held up to a mirror.

Leonardo da Vinci. Page from his sketchbook showing movement of water. Royal Library, Windsor Castle, London, England. The Royal Collection 1993, Her Majesty Queen Elizabeth II.

▨▨▨▨▨ COOPERATIVE LEARNING ▨▨▨▨▨

As an initial drawing experience, this exercise helps students become comfortable with collaborative efforts and peer review: Give each student a blank sheet of drawing paper. Instruct them to begin a drawing with one object or shape. Have them pass the drawing to the next person who adds something to the drawing. Continue the process until everyone has added something to every drawing. Hang the drawings and have everyone examine the final results. Ask: How did this approach affect the composition? How did it affect the subject? The content? Are any drawings stronger than others? Why?

Testing Your Knowledge

Throughout *ArtTalk,* activities have been interspersed to provide students with immediate hands-on application of key concepts. These activities are sequenced according to level of difficulty. Activity 1 is for beginning level students or students who feel unsure about their artistic ability. Activity 2 is a more challenging activity. When appropriate, computer options have also been added and may be optional or extension activities for those students who have access to a computer.

1. Applying Your Skills.
Assure students that these assignments will not be graded and are intended for diagnostic purposes only. You will use the information you collect to evaluate what they need to learn.

Set up a large still-life arrangement of odd objects, such as kitchen utensils, stuffed toys, an old type-writer, posters, big plants, and so on. Do not select a vase with pretty flowers as pretty objects often inhibit students.

2. Further Challenge.
Remember that the quality of a student's work should be a fair indicator of his or her drawing ability. Do not be impressed by quantity. Some talented students work slowly and meticulously. Look for quality of line, accuracy in proportions, relationship of one object to the next, use of negative space, overlapping, and detail.

3. Computer Option.
All of the elements and principles can be taught using the tools and menus on the computer. At the beginning level, students are more successful if they first use traditional drawing tools such as pencil and paper to complete the assignment before attempting the same activity on a computer.

and architects, must show presentation drawings for a client's approval. Figure 1.6 is an architect's loose perspective drawing that presents an exciting feeling about a new building. This kind of drawing is very different from the precise blueprints that an architect must prepare before the actual construction of a building can begin.

Throughout this book you will be asked to make several sketches and select the best one to carry out an assignment. You will also be asked to make perception drawings. You will be asked to keep all these sketches and drawings in a sketchbook. This sketchbook will be a record of your experiences in this class.

Testing Your Knowledge

1. Applying Your Skills.   Draw an arrangement of three everyday objects in your sketchbook. You will look back at this later to see how your work has improved.

FIGURE 1.6   Notice how the architect has indicated the features with a minimum of lines.

MEETING SPECIAL NEEDS

Visually Impaired   Students who are blind can think deeply about what they are perceiving. They can feel an object and describe what it seems like. They can model it in clay. If some students have limited vision, they can draw an object's shape into a styrofoam meat tray or onto a piece of heavy aluminum foil with a pad of paper beneath, making an embossed line which can be felt. Blind students can draw an object's outline shape into white sand on black paper. Students with partial vision can draw using a bold black marking pen. Students who are blind will enjoy the activity described in "More Portfolio Ideas" on page 22, creating an interesting form, solely from touch.

2. Further Challenge. Add two objects to the arrangement, placing one in the foreground and one in the background.

3. Computer Option. In the center of your screen, draw one rectangle and two circles of different sizes. You may use colors or patterns. The shapes in the center of your screen should not touch. Use Copy and Paste tools to create four different arrangements using all three shapes. The shapes in these arrangements may overlap. Save this file for future reference.

Painting

Painting is the process of applying color to a surface using tools such as a brush, a painting knife, a roller, or even fingers. Some paints can be diluted and blown as a fine mist onto a surface with an airbrush. The surface is the material to which the paint is applied. Canvas, paper, and wood are three examples of material. The look of a finished painting has much to do with the combination of media, tools, and the surface the artist chooses. In Figures 1.7 and 1.8 on page 12, you can see how Winslow Homer has created two images that are almost exactly alike. Figure 1.7 is made with thin, wet, flowing watercolor on white paper. The white in that painting is the white of the paper. Figure 1.8 is painted with thick, creamy oil paint on canvas, and the white in the oil painting is opaque white paint.

All paints have three basic ingredients: pigment, binder, and solvent. The *pigment* is a finely ground powder that gives every paint its color. Pigments are produced by chemical processes or by grinding up some kind of earth, stone, or mineral. The *binder*, sometimes called the vehicle, is a liquid that holds together the grains of pigment in a form that can be spread over a surface, where it is allowed to dry. The *solvent* is the material used to thin the binder.

The binder for oil paint is linseed oil, and the solvent is turpentine. The binder for watercolor is gum arabic, and the solvent is water. Acrylic paint, which first appeared in the 1950s, uses an acrylic polymer as a binder. When acrylic paint is wet, water is used as the solvent. Once acrylic is dry, it is waterproof.

ACTIVITY **Exploring Paints**

1. Applying Your Skills. Gather as many different kinds of paint of the same color as you can. For example, look for red watercolor, red tempera paint, and red acrylic. On a piece of paper, draw one shape for each kind of paint. Paint each shape with a different kind of paint. Display your results alongside those done by your classmates. Discuss the similarities and differences you observe.

2. Further Challenge. Follow the directions above but draw two shapes for each kind of paint. Paint one of each shape with thick paint; dilute the paint with the proper solvent to fill the second shape. Compare the results obtained with thick and thinned paint.

Printmaking

In printmaking the artist makes multiple original images. **Printmaking** is *a process in which an artist repeatedly transfers an original image from one prepared surface to another.* Paper is often the surface to which the printed image is transferred.

Notice that a print is not the same as a reproduction of an artwork such as those you see on the pages of this book. The making of a reproduction is a photographic process. Confusing original prints with reproductions is a mistake many people make because reproductions are often called prints. All prints made by the printmaking process are made using three basic steps:

- ▦ *Creating the printing plate.* A *printing plate* is a surface onto or into which the image is placed. In creating a plate, the artist makes a mirror image of the final print.
- ▦ *Inking the plate.* The artist applies ink to the plate. This is done with a *brayer,* a roller with a handle. For a multicolor print, one plate must be made for each color.
- ▦ *Transferring the image.* The paper or other material is pressed against the inked plate, and the ink is transferred to the new surface. Sometimes this is done by hand. At other times a printing press is used.

Understanding Art History

Tell students that Renaissance artists mixed pigments, which they had to grind up with a mortar and pestle, with linseed oil to make their paint. Turpentine had to be used as a solvent instead of water. An advantage was that the oil dried much slower than egg tempera or fresco, allowing the artist to work much longer. With the extended time available to work, artists could blend with a brush and add layers of transparent glazes, made by thinning the paint with turpentine.

Have students compare the works of Renaissance artists Leonardo da Vinci (Figure 3.36, page 67), Giotto (Figure 6.22, page 133), and Sandro Botticelli (Figure 6.25, page 135).

ACTIVITY **Exploring Paints**

1. Applying Your Skills. To make this activity as interesting as possible, collect as many different types of one hue of paint as you can find. Before class, set up trays that can be placed on each table. If you are going to include other painting materials such as artist's oil paint, house acrylic and enamel, gouache, and even make-up colors, place appropriate brushes in each tray. After students have finished drawing their shapes, have them use the paints on their table before moving to another station.

2. Further Challenge. If you are going to have students do the activity with solvents, place appropriate containers containing the solvent on each tray. Turpentine and artificial turpentine will melt plastic containers.

ART ON A SHOESTRING

To stretch your art budget, try these suggestions:

- A backing board with a lightweight acetate covering will take the place of mat board. If the drawing is on tracing paper or vellum, however, place a piece of inexpensive white poster or tagboard between the corrugated board and the drawing. The corrugated board will discolor any drawing in a few years. Thin paper shows the corrugation ridges from the backing.

- Check with art clubs, designers' associations, or a society of illustrators, to see if they have a fund for aid to education.

- Tracing vellum and some watercolor papers can be bought less expensively in rolls or by the foot.

GUIDED PRACTICE
(continued)

Cooperative Learning

Have students divide into groups of three or four to brainstorm examples of the types of media, tools, and surfaces that painters use or might use. To help get them started, encourage students to discuss what they have learned and read about so far. Also, ask them to think about paintings that they have seen in person or in books to get additional ideas.

Remind students that painters often experiment with different media, using different or unusual methods and tools. Too, painters consider the effect a particular surface will have on their work.

Interdisciplinary: Science

Point out to students that many improvements in paint technology have arisen out of advances made in the field of chemistry in the last fifty years. For example, since 1946, chemists have developed synthetic (human made) materials to use as binding vehicles. Some synthetic resins, like the acrylic polymer used in acrylic paint, are often stronger, more flexible, and more water resistant than some natural binders such as egg yolk (used in tempera paints) or gum arabic (used in watercolors). Ask students to examine the labels on the paints they use to find out the chemical make-up of each.

Understanding Art History

To help students further appreciate the life and times of Winslow Homer, whose work is shown in Figures 1.7 and 1.8, assign *Artist's Profile 21* in the TCR.

FIGURE 1.7   Winslow Homer. *Sketch for Hound and Hunter*. 1892. Watercolor. 35.4 x 50.3 cm (13⅞ × 19⅞"). National Gallery of Art, Washington, D.C. Gift of Ruth K. Henschel in memory of her husband, Charles R. Henschel.

FIGURES 1.7 AND 1.8   The images you see in these two works by Winslow Homer are almost exactly alike. The difference is that one is painted with thin, wet, flowing watercolor paint, while the other is painted with thick, creamy oil paint. Can you describe the different effects these two materials have on the same subject?

FIGURE 1.8   Winslow Homer. *Hound and Hunter*. 1892. Oil on canvas. 71.8 x 122.3 cm (28¼ × 48⅛"). National Gallery of Art, Washington, D.C. Gift of Stephen C. Clark.

COOPERATIVE LEARNING

As you incorporate cooperative learning into your classroom, keep in mind that some students may have little experience working cooperatively. Take time in the beginning to explain what will be expected of every group member—listening, participating, and respecting other opinions. Your role is one of coach. You introduce the project, set the parameters, create the teams, provide materials, offer support, monitor the progress of the students, and provide meaningful closure. Monitoring is an essential part of your relationship with learning groups. Otherwise, skepticism, distrust, or lack of self-discipline will be reinforced.

A series of identical prints made from the same plate is called an **edition.** The printmaker writes his or her name, the title of the work, and the number of each print, in pencil in the bottom margin. The number 10/20 indicates that you are looking at the tenth of twenty prints that were made from the same plate.

There are four main techniques artists use for making prints. They are relief, intaglio, lithography, and screen printing.

Relief printing. In this method the artist cuts away the sections of a surface not meant to hold ink. The image to be printed is, as a result, raised from the background. In Figure 1.9 Elizabeth Catlett has controlled the light and dark areas of her linoleum-cut relief print by the amount she has cut away. Notice that the white lines are wider in the very light area.

Intaglio. This name comes from the Italian word meaning "to cut into." Intaglio is a process in which ink is forced to fill lines that have been cut or etched into a metal surface, while the plate's surface is wiped clean. When the prints have been made, you can actually feel the lines of raised ink.

Lithography. This printmaking process is based on the principle that grease and water do not mix. In lithography the image to be printed is drawn on limestone, zinc, or aluminum with a special greasy crayon. When the drawing is completed, the surface is chemically treated with a nitric-acid solution to clean it, and it is rinsed with water. Then, when the surface is inked, the greasy area alone holds the ink.

Screen printing. This is the newest method for making prints. It was developed in the United States during this century. This technique makes

FIGURE 1.9 Catlett has devoted her artistic career to a socially conscious art that represents the struggles of African Americans.

Elizabeth Catlett. *Sharecropper.* 1970. Linoleum cut on paper. 45.2 × 43 cm (17¹³/₁₆ × 16¹⁵/₁₆"). National Museum of American Art, Washington, D.C.

GUIDED PRACTICE
(continued)

Using Art Criticism

Have the class choose two prints shown in other chapters of this book. Then help students compare those prints and the Catlett print in Figure 1.9. Ask: What printmaking method did each artist use to create the artwork? What effect was achieved with this type of medium? What mood do you think each artist was trying to create? How did the artist use the medium to create line, values, shape, and form? Which print do you consider to be the most successful? After the discussion, have each student write a short analysis of the print he or she likes best.

Understanding Art History

Ask a group of volunteers to find three or more reproductions of artworks that were created in different centuries. Have the volunteers share these reproductions—and a few facts about each artist and how the artwork was created—with the class. Then help students discuss these various artworks, noting differences in treatments using similar printmaking methods.

Developing Studio Skills

Explain to students that one relatively simple way to understand the printmaking process is to compare the printing plate to a low relief sculpture. Ask students to remember interesting relief designs on buildings, walkways, gates, fences, and other structures. Tell them to imagine rolling an inked brayer over the surface of these objects and then applying the paper and transferring the ink.

AT THE MUSEUM

The Heard Museum (Phoenix, Arizona) What does rain mean to you? Is it just water that falls from the sky, or is it a part of your livelihood, your religion, your music, or your art? At the Heard Museum, you can visit the "Rain" exhibit which focuses on native peoples of the American Southwest and Mexico whose cultures revolve around rain. The exhibit explores their expressions of rain through ceremony and dance, stories, and art. At several activity stations, visitors can make rain-like sounds with musical instruments, trace rain symbols of birds, rainbows, and water animals, or put up their own rain sayings, listen to authentic Native American rain songs, or look for rain symbols on the baskets, jewelry, pottery, and rugs.

ACTIVITY Making a Printing Plate

1. Applying Your Skills.
This activity helps students learn that printmaking requires thinking in reverse, and that the printing plate is always the reverse of the final print. When you choose newspaper for this activity, be sure the sheet that is under the students' design is full of print. The ink from the print will stick to the back of the paper, and when the student turns it over the letters will appear in reverse.

2. Further Challenge.
Suggested media with which to carry out the stamp print depends on what materials are readily available. Some examples include: erasers; vegetables such as potatoes, carrots, or turnips; yarn glued to a bottle cap or jar lid; found objects glued to a piece of cardboard; sponges; and inner tube material glued to heavy cardboard.

3. Computer Option.
After learning the Copy and Paste commands, students can easily create repeat patterns on the computer. When combined with their knowledge of symmetry, students have created designs using positive and negative space.

Exploring Aesthetics

Tell students that motion pictures, television shows, even popular music have aesthetic qualities that can be interpreted as a statement about a culture. For example, communities will sometimes preserve a time capsule that includes material specifically chosen because it would give clues about the culture to people who find it in the future. Ask students to discuss why people might disagree about what is appropriate material to include. In the same way, visual art can communicate the culture of our time period.

use of a stencil that is placed on a fabric screen stretched across a frame. The screen is placed flat on the printing surface, and a squeegee is used to press ink through the porous fabric areas not covered by the stencil. A screen print that has been handmade by an artist is called a *serigraph.* If more than one color is used, a separate screen is made for each color. How many screens do you think Miroslav Sutej used to create his serigraph in Figure 1.10?

ACTIVITY Making a Printing Plate

1. Applying Your Skills. A printmaker must think in reverse. The printing plate must be a mirror image of the final print. In your sketchbook make a small design using your initials. The design should be less than 1 inch (2.5 cm) square. Copy this design onto a sheet of thin paper. Place the thin paper over a thick pad of newsprint. Draw over the initials, pressing down hard. Turn the paper over and you will see your initials in reverse.

2. Further Challenge. Make a stamp print of your initials. See Technique Tip 14 on page 354 in the Handbook for directions.

3. Computer Option. Use the Text tool to type your name. Use the Select and Flip tools to produce a mirror image. You may also experiment with flipping a simple drawing to produce a mirror image.

Photography

Photography is *a technique of capturing optical images on light-sensitive surfaces.* Everyone can take a photograph. All you have to do is point a camera, trip the shutter, and you have a snapshot. To make a work of art using photography, however, one

FIGURE 1.10 This work has no recognizable objects as subject matter. The artist has created a work that is very interesting by emphasizing the elements of color and shape.

Miroslav Sutej. *Ultra AB.* 1966. Color silkscreen. 49.2 × 45 cm (19⅓ × 17¾"). Library of Congress, Washington, D. C. Pennell Fund, 1970.

FIGURE 1.11 Look closely at this work. What does it tell you about the financial condition of these people?

Dorothea Lange. *Migrant Mother.* 20.3 × 25.4 cm (8 × 10"). Courtesy of the Library of Congress, Washington, D.C.

must make decisions regarding the subject, composition, light conditions, lens opening, and shutter speed. Photography as an art also involves scientific control of what happens in the darkroom to control the look of the final image.

Dorothea Lange was a photojournalist who made the world aware of the problems of migrant workers during the Depression. She was a reporter who worked with a camera. Look closely at this work (Figure 1.11). What does it tell you about the financial status of these people? How many children are in the photo? Even though her face is creased with worry lines, the mother's posture tells you her relationship to the family.

Today, technology is changing the way photographs are made, but it still takes the artist's eye to *see* and the artist's technical skills to *make* a work of art.

 Composing a Photograph

1. Applying Your Skills.   With an automatic camera, you can make a photograph that looks more like art than a snapshot. Look carefully through the viewing lens. Try to frame your composition so that the object relates well to the background. If you take a picture of a person, come in close enough to catch the mood of the person. Bring your photos to class and compare your best shots with those of your classmates.

2. Further Challenge.   Take a carefully composed photograph of a building or a landscape scene. Include some nearby foliage on one side of your viewing lens but focus on the distant objects. Discover what happens visually when your film is developed.

MEETING SPECIAL NEEDS

Building Self-Esteem   Photography is particularly useful for persons with neurological and orthopedic disabilities. Persons who can move a finger can press a shutter release mechanism. Special tripod mounting systems and release switches are available for persons who use wheelchairs. Non-camera photographic techniques such as photograms and blueprint pictures do not use a lens, but instead rely upon specially coated paper and light. These techniques are also useful for students with disabilities, and the technique of making animated movies is appealing to students with behavior disabilities.

GUIDED PRACTICE
(continued)

Exploring Aesthetics

Divide the students into three groups. One group will represent the public, one the art community, and one the art critics. Have each group examine Nancy Grave's sculpture in Figure 1.13 and create a list of its strengths and weaknesses based on the criteria, interests, and agendas of the group they represent.

Developing Studio Skills

Collect some found materials such as twigs, pieces of broken toys, small empty boxes, discarded kitchenware, and anything else that is small and no longer useful. Working in small groups, sort through all the objects collected and choose several pieces to create an assembled sculpture. Use any joining materials such as glue, tape, string, and wire, as necessary.

Developing Studio Skills

Have students bring something to class that is a handmade, one-of-a-kind object. In small groups have them discuss the objects that have been brought. What is special about the objects? Are they rare? Do students like the objects? What criteria do they use to determine the value of each object? Ask each group to share their findings with the class.

INDEPENDENT PRACTICE

Keeping a Sketchbook

Ask each student to choose an artwork that they feel is successful. In their sketchbooks, have them write a description of the work and explain why they chose it. Have them show it to ten other people and ask them to also write a short paragraph or sentence about the work.

16

Sculpture

Sculpture takes up space. *Vaquero*, by Luis Jimenez (Figure 1.12), stands in front of the National Museum of American Art in Washington, D.C. As you walk toward the museum and then up the steps, you see the cowboy on his horse from changing points of view. This work is an example of sculpture in the round, or freestanding sculpture. **Freestanding** means *surrounded on all sides by space*. This kind of sculpture can be viewed from all sides.

FIGURE 1.12   Which elements has Jimenez used to make the sculpture so unusual?

Luis Jimenez. *Vaquero*. Modeled 1980, cast 1990. Fiberglass and epoxy. 5 m (16'6") high. National Museum of American Art, Washington, D.C.

Some sculpture is attached to a background, such as the wall of a building. That is called relief sculpture. **Relief** is *a type of sculpture in which forms project from a flat background*. Relief sculptures are designed to be viewed only from the front.

Artists use a variety of techniques and materials to create sculpture. The processes include modeling, carving, casting, and assembly.

Modeling. This is a process in which a soft, pliable material is built up and shaped. Materials such as clay, wax, and plaster are used in modeling. Because the sculptor gradually adds more and more material to build a form, modeling is referred to as an *additive* process.

Carving. Here the sculptor cuts or chips a form from a mass of material to create a sculpture. Carving is a *subtractive* process. Material is removed until the sculpture is completed. Wood and stone are materials that can be carved.

Casting. In this process melted metal or another liquid substance is poured into a mold to harden. This method allows the artist to duplicate something originally created in wax, clay, or plaster using a more permanent material. Just as with printmaking, an edition of sculptures can be made from the same mold. Once the edition is complete, the mold is destroyed.

Assembly. Assembly is a modern technique. In this process the artist gathers and joins together a variety of different materials to construct a sculpture. One assembly process involves welding together pieces of metal. Nancy Graves used a combination of casting and assembly to create *Zaga* (Figure 1.13).

Crafts

Before machines were invented, people made everything by hand. Fabric for clothing was woven by hand. Plates, bowls, and pots in which to cook were made by hand. Today, artists are still making one-of-a-kind items by hand. Some objects are created for practical use, and others are made purely for decorative purposes. Art made to be experienced visually is called *fine art*. Art made to be functional as well as visually pleasing is called *applied art*. Some crafts are considered fine art if they are made solely for decorative purposes.

Today, artists are creating both functional and decorative craft objects. Weavings are made from

FIGURE 1.13 Graves collects natural objects and casts them in bronze. Then she assembles the pieces of bronze to create new forms and paints them. Can you name some of the objects that were used to create this sculpture?

Nancy Graves. *Zaga.* 1983. Cast bronze with polychrome chemical patination. 182.9 × 124.5 × 81.4 cm (72 × 49 × 32″). Nelson-Atkins Museum of Art, Kansas City, Missouri. © Nancy Graves/VAGA, New York 1994.

natural wool, linen, silk, cotton, and manufactured fibers. Quilts are stitched from fine fabrics to be hung on the wall like paintings. Baskets are woven from reeds and wood slats as well as manufactured fibers. Pottery is made with clay from the earth. Handmade glass objects are formed by forcing air through a tube to shape globs of melted glass. Jewelry is crafted using expensive materials such as precious stones and gold, but it can also be made using paper. As wonderful as technology has become, we still appreciate having an object that is one-of-a-kind and made by hand.

THE WORK OF ART

Works of art may be defined by three basic properties, or features. These properties are *subject, composition,* and *content.*

The Subject

The **subject** is *the image viewers can easily identify in a work of art.* The subject may be one person or many people. It may be a thing, such as a boat. It may be an event, such as a dance. The subjects in John Trumbull's painting (Figure 1.14 on page 18) are easily recognized. The subjects are the soldiers, the white flag in the distance, and the sky.

In recent years some artists have chosen to create nonobjective artwork. **Nonobjective art** is *art that has no recognizable subject matter.* Figure 1.10 on page 14 is such a work.

The Composition

The second property of a work of art is the composition of the work. The **composition** is *the way the principles of design are used to organize the elements.* Notice how Trumbull has organized the lines, values, shapes, and color to lead your eyes to the center of interest: the two figures lying on the ground.

The Content

The third property of a work of art is the content. The **content** is *the message the work communicates.* The message may be an idea or a theme, such as patriotism or family togetherness. It may be an emotion, such as pride, love, or loneliness.

In the 1960s NASA recorded every step of the space program with photographs. However, NASA officials felt that they needed artists to communicate to the people of the future the wonder and excitement that everyone felt about leaving the bonds of earth and venturing into space. They asked the artists to come to Cape Canaveral in Florida, observe everything that was going on, and capture the emotions of the time. All the artists painted the same subject matter, but the

TEACH

(pages 17–19)
- The Work of Art
- The Credit Line

GUIDED PRACTICE

Promoting Discussion
  Remind students that although many artists may begin with the same subject, each will bring a different background and a different style to his or her interpretation. That interpretation becomes the content or meaning of the work. That meaning is like a metaphor; the work of art represents something more than just the subject of the work. The meaning of the work depends upon two key factors: the way the artist has manipulated the elements using the principles; and the emotions and knowledge the viewer brings to a study of the work. Choose an artwork from this chapter and ask students to explain what the work means to them.

Using Art Criticism
  Have students choose an artwork from the textbook and write a description of how the artist used the elements and principles of art. Ask them to decide which is most important in developing the work's composition and mood. Have them identify the focus of the artwork, if possible, and explain how the artist draws the viewer's attention to this focus.

MORE ABOUT . . . FINE ART AND APPLIED ART

The controversial distinction between fine art and applied art has been made only in modern times. In Europe, until the later part of the Middle Ages, painters, sculptors, and others we now consider artists were regarded as skilled craftspeople. During the Renaissance, these artists and their works gained new prestige and their art began to be distinguished from crafts, or applied arts. For example, some artists and critics regard certain paintings as merely decorative and therefore categorize these works as applied art. On the other hand, some artists and craftspeople insist that art is valid only if it can be used in daily life.

GUIDED PRACTICE
(continued)

Exploring Aesthetics

After reviewing the art-works in Figures 1.15, 1.16, and 1.17, ask students to list the similarities and differences they see. Ask them to create a new title for each work that invokes an emotional response to the subject.

Understanding Art History

Have students look through this chapter and identify the following: three works from the National Gallery of Art; three works that were created in different countries during the same century; three works that were created using media other than oil paint.

Developing Perceptual Skills

Have students work in small groups to practice visualizing metric measurements. First, have them estimate the metric measurements of these objects around them: a door frame, a textbook, a shoe, a desk, a pen or pencil, and a piece of notebook paper. Then, using a ruler or meter stick, have them measure the items and compare their estimate to the actual measurement.

 Using Credit Information

1. Applying Your Skills.
(Figure 1.9) Elizabeth Catlett; (Figure 1.1) *Return from Bohemia*; (Figure 1.2) *Fallen Vase*.

2. Further Challenge.
(Figures 1.7 and 1.8) *Sketch for Hound and Hunter* and *Hound and Hunter* by Winslow Homer; (Figure 1.12) *Vaquero* by Luis Jimenez; (Figure 1.5) Drawing by Leonardo da Vinci.

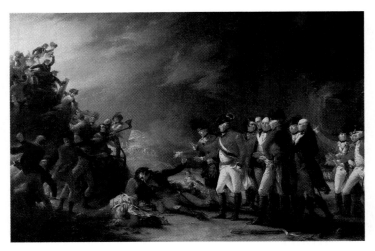

FIGURE 1.14 This large historical painting records one event in the siege of Gibraltar when the British defended the huge rock from the Spaniards in 1784. Everyone is carefully posed to create a scene of dignity.

John Trumbull. *The Sortie Made by the Garrison of Gibraltar*. 1789. Oil on canvas. 180.3 × 271.8 cm (71 × 107″). The Metropolitan Museum of Art, New York, New York. Purchase, Pauline V. Fullerton Bequest; Mr. and Mrs. James Walter Carter and Mr. and Mrs. Raymond J. Horowitz Gifts; Erving Wolf Foundation and Vain and Harry Fish Foundation, Inc. Gifts; Gift of Hanson K. Corning, by exchange; and Maria DeWitt Jesup and Morris K. Jesup Funds, 1976.

emotions the artists put into their individual works were different. The emotions the artists put into the paintings made up the content. Three of these paintings are shown in Figures 1.15, 1.16, and 1.17.

THE CREDIT LINE

Look at Figure 1.15. The credit line appears beneath the caption. A **credit line** is *a list of important facts about a work of art*. Every artwork in this book has a credit line.

Decoding a Credit Line

Most credit lines contain six or more facts. They are as follows:

- *Name* of the artist.
- *Title* of the work. This always appears in italics.
- *Year* the work was created. Sometimes, in the case of older works, "c." appears before the year. This is an abbreviation for *circa*, which means "around" or "about" in Latin.
- *Medium* used by the artist. If more than one medium is used, the credit line may read "mixed media."
- *Size* of the work. The first number is always the height, the second number is the width, and if the work is three-dimensional, the third number indicates the depth.
- *Location* of the work. Location names the gallery, museum, or collection in which the work is housed and the city, state, and country. The names of the donors may also be included.

 Using Credit Information

1. Applying Your Skills. Who is the artist of the work in Figure 1.9 on page 13? What is the title of the painting by Grant Wood (Figure 1.1, page 4)? Which work in this chapter was completed most recently?

2. Further Challenge. Which two works by the same artist have almost the same title and are created using two different media? Which is the largest work in this chapter? Which work in this chapter is not housed in the United States?

FIGURE 1.15 Kingman interpreted the subject in terms of his Oriental heritage. He transformed the rocket into a pagoda form. Why do you think he included the birds, a hot air balloon, helicopter, and single-engine plane? Notice the many areas of clear white paper.

Dong Kingman. *Higher, Faster, and Farther.* 1969. Watercolor on paper. 71.1 × 91.4 cm (28 × 36"). Courtesy of NASA.

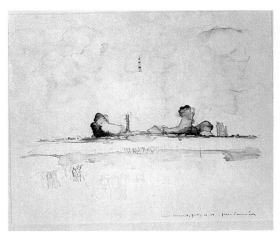

FIGURE 1.16 Fernandes saw the launch as a graceful leap from the earth's surface. He bathed his work in the glowing colors of the morning sun. If you look closely, you can see the audience along the bank of the Banana River, almost hidden in the brilliance of the light.

Julio Fernandes. *Apollo 11.* 1969. Watercolor on paper. 34.3 × 40.6 cm (13½ × 16"). Courtesy of NASA.

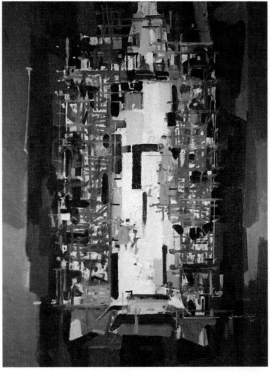

FIGURE 1.17 Dodd captures the glowing Saturn rocket encased in its web of red supports. He sees beyond the mechanical forms to portray for us the effect it has on his emotions.

Lamar Dodd. *Night Before Launch.* 1969. Oil on canvas. 127.5 × 91.4 cm (50 × 36"). Courtesy of NASA.

ART CRITICISM IN ACTION

INTRODUCTION

Because students have not yet been introduced to the steps of art criticism (these are presented in Chapter 2), this chapter directs students to analyze the subject, composition, and content of two works of art. Have students study and compare Moore's *Family Group* to Picasso's *The Tragedy*. Refer them to the questions in the student text and be sure they understand the following terms: *credit line, media, subject, composition,* and *content.*

CRITIQUING THE WORK

1. **Credit Line** The information requested is in the credit line. It is important to note that Moore's work is a freestanding sculpture. If students were standing in front of the sculpture, their heads would be about the same level as the adults' heads, even though the figures are seated.

2. **Subject** The subject of the sculpture is a group of people comprised of two adults (one male and one female) and a child.

3. **Composition** The forms in the sculpture are abstract and gently rounded. The two adults are seated on a bench with their bodies facing each other. Both adults hold the child who seems to be the link between them. Their backs are straight and all three forms hold their heads up to face whatever is coming. Their body language indicates that they are a united team.

4. **Content** Interpretations will vary.

FIGURE 1.18   Henry Moore. *Family Group.* 1948-49. Bronze (cast 1950). 150.5 × 118.1 cm (59¼ × 46½"). The Museum of Modern Art, New York, New York. A. Conger Goodyear Fund.

RESOURCES BEYOND THE CLASSROOM

Other Works By . . . Henry Moore
Large Interior Form
Reclining Figure
Large Torso: Arch

Other Works By . . . Picasso
Three Musicians

The Lovers
Glass of Absinthe
Glass, Guitar and Bottle
Guernica
The Blind Man's Meal
Les Demoiselles d'Avignon
Head of a Bull

CRITIQUING THE WORK

1. **Credit Line** Read the credit line for *Family Group* (Figure 1.18). List the following: the artist's name, the date the artwork was created, the medium used, the size, and the location of the work. If you were standing in front of *Family Group*, how would the level of your head relate to the heads of the people?
2. **Subject** What is the subject of *Family Group?* Can you easily identify the subject in this sculpture?
3. **Composition** Look at the shapes and forms of the people, including their posture and body language. How has Moore linked the figures? What has he done with the vertical and horizontal lines to provide a unified composition?
4. **Content** Looking at the composition of the sculpture, what message do you receive? How has Moore conveyed his message? Do you think he was successful in communicating his view? Why or why not?

COMPARING THE WORKS

Now look at *The Tragedy* by Pablo Picasso (Figure 1.19). Look at the credit line information. Note the date, medium used, the size of the work, and its location. If *The Tragedy* were hanging on the door to your classroom, how much of the door would it cover?

Compare the amount of realistic detail the artist uses in each work. Compare the space the artist has placed between the people. Compare the colors. Compare the surface textures of the people. Which work has real-looking texture, and which work shows the texture of the medium? How have the differences in composition affected the message of the artworks? Write a brief paragraph about the message each work communicates.

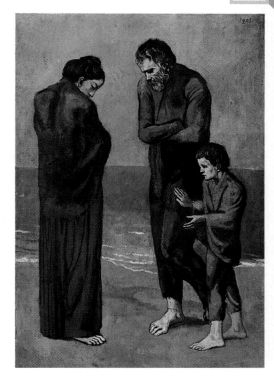

FIGURE 1.19 Pablo Picasso. *The Tragedy.* 1903. Oil paint on wood. 105.4 × 69 cm (41½ × 27⅛"). National Gallery of Art, Washington, D.C. Chester Dale Collection.

FYI Henry Moore was not easily discouraged. When he was asked to create a massive sculpture for the UNESCO (United Nations Educational, Scientific, and Cultural Organization) building, he searched the marble quarries in Italy until he found the perfect piece. There was only one problem—it weighed more than 60 tons (54 metric tons). Not to be defeated by the fact that he could not move the mountain of marble, Moore brought his tools to the quarry and carved for a year. When he had reduced the work to a movable size, it was transported to Paris so Moore could finish it in place. That work is the simplest and largest of Moore's reclining figures.

Have students measure the classroom door and compare the size of the door with the size of *The Tragedy*. (The painting will probably cover one half of the door.)

Moore has abstracted his people, eliminating almost all details. We can see a hint of nose and ears, folds in the woman's skirt, and marks on the feet to indicate toes. Picasso's painting exhibits realistic details such as hair, facial features, folds in the clothing, and clearly defined hands and feet.

Space is very important in both works. Figure 1.18 has some negative spaces, but they appear between the forms that are joined together. The figures seem to be tied together by the form of the child. In Figure 1.19, the large negative space between the adults separates them.

Moore's sculpture is the color of the aged metal. Picasso has limited the color scheme in *The Tragedy* to a variety of blues, indicating the difference between the face and clothing by changing values. The texture of the sculpture is the texture of smooth metal. The textures in the painting seem to imitate the textures of skin, hair, cloth, and so on. Picasso imitates textures while Moore shows the texture of his medium.

EXTENSION

- Have students read more about Henry Moore in the "Meet the Artist" feature on the following page.
- Assign *Artist's Profile 1* in the TCR.

21

MORE ABOUT . . . PICASSO

The Tragedy typifies Picasso's style during his Blue period. However, not all students know that in addition to painting, he was a gifted sculptor, collagist, ceramicist, and printmaker. Besides producing hundreds of lithographs, he created etchings. Around 1907, Picasso abandoned print-making when he began developing the Cubist style. Later, in 1944, he returned to his interest in lithography and created another series of prints. This series, in turn, renewed the public's interest in this art form.

- Have students complete "Building Vocabulary" and "Reviewing Art Facts" on page 23.
- Assign *Application 1* and 2 in the TCR.

ANSWERS TO BUILDING VOCABULARY

1. symbol
2. elements of art
3. principles of design
4. medium
5. perception
6. printmaking
7. edition
8. photography
9. freestanding
10. relief
11. subject
12. nonobjective

ANSWERS TO REVIEWING ART FACTS

1. Line, shape and form, space, value, color, and texture.
2. Rhythm, movement, balance, proportion, variety, emphasis, and unity.
3. Answers can include graphite pencils, colored pencils, markers, charcoal, crayons, pastels, and colored chalks.
4. Pigment, binder, and solvent.
5. Creating the printing plate, inking the plate, transferring the image.
6. Screen printing.
7. Carving.
8. Answers will vary.
9. Answers will vary.
10. Answers can include an increased understanding of architecture, clothing, hairstyles, color relationships, artworks of all kinds, and art media and processes.

MEET THE ARTIST

HENRY MOORE
English, 1898–1986

Henry Moore created sculptures that were completely unique. He made images in stone that retained the look of natural stone. When he worked with wood, it seemed as if the rain and wind had worn the wood down to the shape he gave it. When he worked with metals such as lead and bronze, his figures took on the shapes of the molten flow of the metal.

The year 1940 was a turning point for him. England was at war, and Moore became an official war artist. His sensitive, abstract drawings of Londoners huddled in subway tunnels to escape the Nazi bombing established him as a leading English artist.

Moore's work focused on three themes: the family, the reclining female figure, and the abstract form within a form. The motivation for *Family Group* (Figure 1.18) was the pending birth of his daughter. He was obsessed with the idea of family.

When Moore's sculptures came back from the foundry, they were shiny, like new pennies. He wanted them to be a dull green so that they would look older and softer. To do this he coated them with acids. Then he rubbed them down so that they looked like thousands of hands had been touching them for years.

Henry Moore is recognized as one of the greatest and most innovative sculptors of the twentieth century. His work can be seen in collections of modern art throughout the world.

MORE PORTFOLIO IDEAS

Hold a piece of clay behind your back and model and smooth it into a rounded but uneven form having at least one opening that goes completely through it. Keep turning the clay as you work so that every surface is affected. When you are finished, the form should look like a rock that has been worn down by the forces of nature.

Follow the above instructions. Then bring the work in front of you. Use clay modeling tools to refine the form. When the clay has become leather-hard (damp but unmovable), polish some of the surfaces with a smooth river rock or the back of a spoon to create a surface texture variation.

22

DEVELOPING A PORTFOLIO

Choosing a Project A portfolio should exhibit strong, confident examples of a student's work. Typically, evaluators would rather see fewer competent works than many that are mediocre and would call into question the student's overall ability. However, a diversity of artistic skill is also critical, so students must learn to balance both objectives. Encourage them to approach each assignment throughout the semester as a potential project for their portfolios, and as a method of isolating their strengths and weaknesses. Then students can concentrate on improvement in those areas that are weaker while continuing to develop the stronger ones.

CHAPTER 1 REVIEW

Building Vocabulary

On a separate sheet of paper, write the term that best matches each definition given below.

1. Something that stands for, or represents, something else.
2. The basic visual symbols in the language of art.
3. The rules that govern how artists organize the elements of art.
4. A material used to make art.
5. The act of looking at something carefully and thinking deeply about what is seen.
6. A process in which an artist repeatedly transfers an original image from one prepared surface to another.
7. A series of identical prints made from the same plate.
8. A technique of capturing optical images on light-sensitive surfaces.
9. Surrounded on all sides by space.
10. Sculpture in which forms project from a flat background.
11. The image viewers can easily identify in a work of art.
12. Art that has no recognizable subject matter.

Reviewing Art Facts

Answer the following questions using complete sentences.

1. Name the elements of art.
2. List the principles of design.
3. Name at least four of the most popular media used in drawing.
4. What are the three basic ingredients common to all paints?
5. What three basic steps are used in the printmaking process?
6. What printmaking process is best suited to printing on fabric?
7. Name a subtractive process an artist can use to create a sculpture.
8. Select a work of art in this chapter and name the subject.
9. Read the credit-line information of an artwork from any chapter and list the figure number, the title, the year the work was created, and the medium.
10. In what way do you think increasing your perception skills will enrich your everyday experiences?

Thinking Critically About Art

1. **Analyze.** List all the art media you have used. Which media do you prefer? Write a brief paragraph including two or more reasons for your personal preference.
2. **Compare and contrast.** Study Figures 1.15, 1.16, and 1.17 on page 19. List the similarities you find in all three paintings. Then identify the qualities that make each of the paintings unique and different.
3. **Analyze.** Compare Figure 1.19 on page 21 to Figure 11.27 on page 297. List the similarities and differences. Find at least two facts in the credit lines of the two works that account for the similarities. Explain the importance of these facts.

Making Art Connections

1. **Science.** In addition to being a master artist, Leonardo da Vinci was a man of many other talents. He designed machines that could not work during his time because things such as the internal combustion engine had not been invented yet. Hold Figure 1.5 up to a mirror and transcribe some of the notes he wrote. Find someone who can translate the notes and discover what Leonardo was communicating in his sketchbook.
2. **Music and Dance.** Find out how the arts of music and dance communicate without words. Is there a language of music? Is there a language of dance? Look up these art forms in the library or interview an expert such as your music teacher or a dance instructor. Write a report in which you discuss the "words" and "grammar" of either of these art forms.

Art Criticism and Aesthetic Judgment

INTRODUCE

CHAPTER OVERVIEW

Chapter 2 explains the importance of art criticism and introduces students to the sequential procedures of art criticism. It then examines the three aesthetic theories of art—Imitationalism, Formalism, and Emotionalism.

CHAPTER SUPPLIES

For a list of the materials you will need for the Activities in this chapter, refer to the "Art Supplies Grid" in the Teacher's Manual.

FINE ART RESOURCES

Transparencies
- Balthus (Balthasar Klossowski). *Girl at a Window*
- Gabriele Münter. *Breakfast of the Birds*
- Dorothea Tanning. *Guardian Angels*
- Sharon Hardin. *Camouflage*

Fine Art Prints
- Jan Steen. *The Dancing Couple*
- Peggy Flora Zalucha. *Map Still Life with Carnation, Keys, and Glasses*

FIGURE 2.1 Cassatt is famous for the inventive way she created paintings and prints on one theme: the relationship between mother and child. She presented them in everyday settings without making them look sentimental or trite.

Mary Cassatt. *Baby Reaching for an Apple*. 1893. Oil on canvas. 100.3 × 65.4 cm (39½ × 25¾"). Virginia Museum of Fine Arts, Richmond, Virginia. Museum purchase with funds provided by an anonymous donor.

24

RESOURCES FOR CHAPTER 2

Application Activities 3, 4
Artist's Profiles 2, 25, 41
Cooperative Learning Activities 3, 4
Cultural Diversity in Art
Enrichment Activities 3, 4

Reteaching Activities
   Study Guide 2
   Concept Map 2
Chapter 2 Test

Art Criticism and Aesthetic Judgment

Have you ever been so involved in watching a movie that you felt as if you were part of the action? Have you ever watched a favorite movie so many times that you knew the dialogue by heart? If so, you have been deeply involved with a work of art.

After you see a new TV program, you probably discuss it with your friends. You might recommend that they watch the next episode—or advise them not to waste their time. In either case you are judging the show and making decisions about why it was a failure or success. You are acting like a critic.

There are professional critics who appear on television and write reviews in newspapers or magazines. They tell you about new movies, TV shows, videos, and books. They tell you something about the plot, the quality of the acting and directing, and their opinion of the work as a whole. You don't always agree with their opinion because your **criteria**, or *standards of judgment,* may be very different from those of the professional critics.

In this chapter you will learn about **art criticism**, *an organized system for studying a work of art.* You will also learn about **aesthetics** (es-**thet**-iks), *the philosophy or study of the nature of beauty and art.* After you have learned the steps of art criticism, you will be able to criticize works of art yourself. When you have learned the different aesthetic theories for judging the merits of an artwork, you will be able to form your own opinions about works of art with self-confidence.

FIRST IMPRESSIONS

Mary Cassatt belonged to a group of painters called Impressionists. They painted outdoors to capture the effects of sunlight on their subjects. What do you see in Cassatt's painting (Figure 2.1) that indicates it was painted outside? Look for areas of the painting in which the artist shows the effects of sunlight. How has she used brushstrokes to give the impression of filtered light? Notice the way the woman is holding the child. What does this say to you about the relationship between the woman and the child?

Objectives

After completing this chapter, you will be able to:

- Explain the purpose of art criticism.
- Use the steps of art criticism.
- Begin to criticize works of art yourself.
- Explain the aesthetic theories of art: Imitationalism, Formalism, and Emotionalism.
- Know what to look for when judging functional objects.

Words to Know

aesthetic experience
aesthetics
analysis
art criticism
criteria
description
design qualities
Emotionalism
expressive qualities
Formalism
Imitationalism
interpretation
judgment
literal qualities

25

WHY STUDY ART CRITICISM?

What do you think of when you hear the word *criticism*? Do you think it means saying something negative? This is not true. A criticism can be a positive statement. When you shop for clothes, you try on many things. You act as a critic using personal criteria to determine which pieces of clothing look good on you and which pieces do not suit you. You have developed your own criteria for choosing clothing through personal experience.

When you look at Nancy Graves's *Rheo* (Figure 2.2) you may be confused. You may not have had enough experience to develop a set of criteria to judge this work. If you are like most people, you don't know what to say. You may be afraid that you will say the wrong thing.

Art criticism is not difficult. In fact, it can be a lot of fun. At the very least, it can make the study of art less mysterious and more logical.

Art criticism is an organized system for looking at and talking about art. Anyone can do it. You do not need to be an expert on art. All you really need are your eyes to see and a brain to think about what you are seeing.

If you look at art without thinking, nothing can happen. If you think carefully about what you see, however, you will build your perceptual skills and learn a great deal.

Your own life experiences will help you understand each work of art. No one has done or seen exactly the same things you have, so no one will see exactly what you see in a work of art. No one can think exactly the way you think. You may see ideas in a work of art that were never dreamed of by the artist. This does not mean that you are wrong; it simply means that the work of art is so powerful that it has a special meaning for everybody.

Learning art criticism will help you interpret a work of art. It will give you the confidence to discuss a work of art without worrying about what other people might think. It will help you to organize your thoughts. You will develop the courage to speak your mind and make sound aesthetic

Nancy Graves. *Rheo.* 1975. Acrylic, oil, and gold leaf on canvas. 162.5 × 162.5 cm (64 × 64"). National Museum of Women in the Arts, Washington, D.C. Gift of Wallace and Wihelmina Holladay. © Nancy Graves/VAGA 1994.

L O O K I N G
C L O S E L Y

FIGURE 2.2   At first glance this seems to be a painting of simple shapes, lines, and color. Look again. What kind of shapes do you see? What sizes are they? What colors do you see? Where are they? There are different kinds of lines. Describe them and tell what colors they are. What kinds of textures are painted on the small shapes? Do they remind you of anything? Notice how the small shapes are arranged. They seem to be floating over the others and yet there are no shadows. Can you discover how Graves created this illusion?

judgments. It will help you develop a better understanding and appreciation for all types and styles of art.

As you learn the language of art, you will be able to "dig deeper" into each art object. The deeper you dig, the more important your feelings for that work of art will become. This will make your **aesthetic experience**, or your *personal interaction with a work of art*, more meaningful and memorable. The work will then become a permanent part of your memory. From that point on it will affect the way you react to other visual images.

 Testing Personal Responses

1. Applying Your Skills.   Show the painting of the cat in Figure 2.3 to at least three people outside of class. Ask each person to think about and interpret this work of art. Then ask how he or she feels about cats. Did the judgment each one made match his or her feelings about cats?

2. Further Challenge.   Record the responses you received. Ask those people who did not think this work of art was aesthetically pleasing to give you their reasons. Report your findings during the class discussion.

FIGURE 2.3   If you are a cat lover, you will have a positive reaction to the tiger cat resting luxuriously on the cushion. If you do not like cats, however, you will probably have a completely different response to this work.

Théophile-Alexandre Steinlen. *Winter: Cat on a Cushion*. Date unknown. Color lithograph. 50.8 × 61 cm (20 × 24"). The Metropolitan Museum of Art, New York, New York. Gift of Henry J. Plantin, 1950.

How to Criticize a Work of Art

Critiquing an artwork is like playing detective. You must assume the artist has a secret message hidden within the work. Your job is to find the message and solve the mystery.

In this chapter you will learn a special four-step system that will help you find the hidden messages in art. The four steps, which must be taken in order, are **Description, Analysis, Interpretation**, and **Judgment**. By taking these steps you will be able to answer the following questions:

■ What do I see? (Description)
■ How is the work organized? (Analysis)
■ What is the artist saying? (Interpretation)
■ Is this a successful work of art? (Judgment)

As you go through the steps of *description* and *analysis*, you will collect facts and clues. When you get to *interpretation*, you will make guesses about what you think the artist is trying to say. Finally, during *judgment*, you will make your own decisions, both personal and objective, about the artistic merit of the work.

Step One: Description (What do I see?)

In the first step in art criticism, **description**, you carefully *make a list of all the things you see in the work*. This step is meant to slow your pace. Slowing down helps you notice things you might otherwise miss. It keeps you from making a judgment before you have studied all the details.

Every description should include the size of the work and the medium used. You will find these facts in the credit line. This information will help you visualize the real size and the look of the work. Notice that Figure 3.31 on page 62 and Figure 3.36 on page 67 are about the same size in this book. Read the credit line to see which work is the larger.

GUIDED PRACTICE
(continued)

 Testing Personal Responses

1. Applying Your Skills. Instead of sharing results singly, one student might collect responses and make a chart to record the relationship of people's responses to their feelings about cats.

2. Further Challenge. As with the preceding activity, responses collected by students could be made into a chart or quickly recorded on the board for general discussion. Ask students to extend their observations about the relationship between subject and viewer responses to include speculation about how colors, textures, media, and so on, might affect a person's reaction to a piece of art.

Promoting Discussion
Have students mentally picture the school cafeteria or other common room. Agree on a single vantage point from which the room is being pictured. Ask them to write down a detailed description of what is seen from that viewpoint. Read the descriptions aloud. Discuss the similarities and differences. Why do some people see details that others miss?

Using Art Criticism
Select a large, clear reproduction of a fine art print that shows plenty of detail. Ask students to write down two or three descriptive phrases about the artwork. Then, using their sketchbooks, have them sketch the artwork. Ask them to list items in their sketchbook that they only noticed after sketching the work. Did they see details that they initially overlooked? Discuss the importance of careful observation in art criticism.

MEETING SPECIAL NEEDS

Visually Impaired   Understanding the complicated interplay between form and content is challenging for the sighted person, but for the blind or visually impaired student, the struggle is even greater. You and your students can help the visually impaired student understand the aesthetic qualities of artworks by offering detailed descriptions of colors, light, textures, shapes, and sizes. Rich metaphors will enhance your descriptions and allow the student to visualize with greater success. As a demonstration of empathy, you might have sighted students attempt to create an artwork, or understand your description of one, while they are blindfolded.

Promoting Discussion

When discussing *The Visitation*, inform students that new bronze has a shiny, gold color. When it is exposed to weather, it develops a green patina. Ask: What brings about the change in color?

Practicing Description

1. Applying Your Skills.
If students work on this activity during class, tape two minutes of a sports program beforehand to show during class time. Play the tape several times so students can write a description of the action they have observed.

2. Further Challenge.
If this activity is part of a class exercise, provide copies of sports magazines and allow students to sketch from the magazines' pictures. If your supply of magazines is limited, make several photocopies of good action pictures and keep them in your picture file.

Using Art Criticism

Ask students to study the artwork in Figures 2.4 or 2.5, and choose one to examine closely. In their sketchbooks, have them write five questions about the artwork for each of the following categories: Who? What? When? Where? Why? Encourage them to sketch the work in their sketchbooks and experiment with the layout of the design on the page. Discuss the questions they posed about the artwork as well as possible responses. Tell them that this method is another way to address the steps of art criticism. For example, "What are the boys doing?" is an interpretation question about Figure 2.5.

Look at the sculpture by Sir Jacob Epstein called *The Visitation* (Figure 2.4). Notice that the figure is 66 inches, or 5 feet 6 inches (167.6 cm), tall. How does that compare to your own height? If you were standing on the same level as the sculpture, how would the level of the woman's eyes relate to yours?

The medium of the sculpture is cast bronze. Do you know what bronze looks like when it is new? Do you know what happens to bronze when it is exposed to weather?

During the description step you must be objective. You must list only the facts. For example, if you are describing Figure 2.1 on page 24, *Baby Reaching for an Apple* by Mary Cassatt, you can say that you see a woman holding a child. Do not say that you see a mother holding her own child. That would be a guess. You do not know if the woman is the child's mother. Save your guesses for the

FIGURE 2.4 Imagine standing next to this figure. How would it look? What do you think your first reaction would be?

Sir Jacob Epstein. *The Visitation.* 1926. Bronze. 165.3 × 53.1 × 47.9 cm (65⅛ × 20⅞ × 18⅞"). Hirshhorn Museum and Sculpture Garden, Smithsonian Institution, Washington, D.C. Gift of Joseph H. Hirshhorn, 1966.

interpretation step. If you see distant figures and you cannot tell whether they are women or men, simply list them as people.

Look at Figure 2.2 on page 26. It is difficult to identify objects in this work. This is a nonobjective work. In this work the elements become the subject matter.

Practicing Description

1. Applying Your Skills. Watch a sports program on television. Pretend you are an explorer from another planet and do not know anything about the game. Describe in writing what the athletes are doing, but remember you know none of the terms related to the sport or the people. Read your description to the class. Can your classmates guess what kind of game you were watching?

2. Further Challenge. Sketch two figures participating in a popular sport. Do not show any uniforms or equipment that would give away the name of the sport. Try to capture the gestures and action that describe the sport. Can your friends guess what sport you are describing with figures alone?

Step Two: Analysis
(How is the work organized?)

During Step Two you are still collecting facts. Now, however, you will pay attention to the elements and principles, which you read about in Chapter 1. In **analysis** you *discover how the work is organized.* This is where the artist creates the secret message, the mood or idea, by the way he or she organizes the elements using the principles.

For example, look again at Figure 2.4. Notice the *shape* of the figure; the *lines* formed by the folds in the skirt; the surface *texture* of her hair, skin, and fabric; and so on. Shape, lines, and texture are elements of art. Look for other elements. In this step you will list the way the artist has used all the elements. You will also note the way the elements are organized using rhythm, movement, balance, proportion, variety, emphasis, and unity. Of course, you will learn more about both the elements and principles later in this book.

Building Self-Esteem Just as this woman shown in Epstein's *The Visitation* appears to be visited by an otherworldly power, some artists feel a relationship between their creativity and divine inspiration. Consider James Hampton's *Throne of the Kingdom of Heaven* in Figure 8.28, page 208. He believed that the Lord was telling him to make it.

Such a sense of "calling" can give people extraordinary strength and drive. Some people believe that individuals with disabilities have special gifts; for example, persons who are blind can hear better. However, most persons with disabilities prefer to be treated just like ordinary people, not special.

FIGURE 2.5   What is your interpretation of this painting? If you were to show it to others, do you think their interpretations would be the same as yours?

Leo Twiggs. *The Blue Wall.* 1969. Batik painting. 61 × 76.2 cm (24 × 30″). Private collection.

Step Three: Interpretation
(What is the artist saying?)

During Step Three you will answer the question "What is the artist saying to me?" In **interpretation** you will *explain or tell the meaning or mood of the work.* It is here that you can make guesses.

Interpretation can be the most difficult step in art criticism, because you must dare to be different. It can also be the most creative and the most rewarding step.

You must use your intelligence, imagination, and courage. You must not be afraid to make an interpretation that is different from someone else's. After all, you are different from other people. Your interpretation will depend on what you have experienced and seen in your life.

Your interpretation must be based on the facts and clues you collected during your first two steps. Your interpretation can be based on your feelings, but your feelings must be backed up by observation of what you actually see in the artwork.

 Interpreting a Work

1. Applying Your Skills.   Show *The Blue Wall* by Leo Twiggs, Figure 2.5, to three people outside of class. Ask them what they think is the meaning of this painting. Tell them it doesn't matter whether they like the work or not. You just want to know what they think it means. Then write a few sentences telling what each person said. Compare your results with those of your

AT THE MUSEUM

The Art Institute of Chicago (Chicago, Illinois) Experience 250 masterworks from the Art Institute of Chicago on a computer-driven laserdisc called *With Open Eyes,* co-developed with and published by the Voyager Company. The laserdisc was made especially for children and teenagers. This laserdisc enhances a viewer's experience of the full-color detailed art with poems, sound effects, and narration. The works span many different cultures, media, and periods ranging from ancient African tribal masks to Picasso's modernist masterpieces. An easy touchscreen system provides rapid choice of artworks to explore.

GUIDED PRACTICE
(continued)

Using Art Criticism

Be very sure that students understand that interpretation is much more than storytelling. Literature students must interpret and generalize from the given data. This process is also required in art if they are to perceive more than superficial qualities. During step three, each student must go beyond storytelling to generalize, to find the metaphor or allegory in the work. To say that Figure 2.5, *The Blue Wall,* is about two boys by a wall is not enough. Study the relationship between the two boys. Notice that even though the boys look away from each other as if they are angry or frightened, their bodies touch ever so slightly. Ask students what the touching means. They must see the touching and sense the relationship between the boys.

 Interpreting a Work

1. Applying Your Skills. To save time, one student might make a chart depicting the types of responses.

2. Further Challenge. The responses to this activity will vary. Encourage students to be creative and expressive in their writing.

INDEPENDENT PRACTICE

Enrichment

Ask students to share any experiences they have had where listening to others or learning new ideas helped them develop new or different standards of judgment. Ask: How can learning about art help them make more informed judgments about art in its many forms?

(pages 30–35)

- Aesthetic Theories and Qualities of Art
- Art Criticism: Getting Started
- Students Practice Art Criticism

GUIDED PRACTICE

Critical Thinking

A critical-thinking strategy called "Cubing" can be helpful when teaching the concept of criticism. The name of this strategy comes from the six steps of the process, which are likened to the six sides of a cube. They are as follows:

1. Describe it: Look at the subject closely and describe what you see—colors, size, shapes, and so on.
2. Compare it: To what is it similar? From what is it different?
3. Associate it: What comes into your mind when you look at it? Let your mind make any associations it wants to.
4. Analyze it: Tell how it is made, or how you *think* it's made.
5. Apply it: Tell what you can do with it and/or how it can be used.
6. Argue for or against it: Take a stand—use any logic you desire, whether rational, silly, or anywhere in between.

These steps move a student's thinking from sensual description to higher levels of critical judgment and evaluation, parallel to the four steps of art criticism.

classmates. Are there any similar answers? Do adults see different meanings than people your age?

2. Further Challenge. When you decide on your own interpretation of the work, write a story about the boys that explains the message you have received from the work. What happened before this scene, what are they thinking at the moment depicted in this painting, and what will happen next? Explain why the wall is important in their lives.

Step Four: Judgment (Is this a successful work of art?)

In Step Four you will judge whether or not the work is successful. In **judgment** you *determine the degree of artistic merit.* This is the time to give your opinions. No one can ever tell you what to like or dislike. You must make up your own mind. To make a good judgment, you need to be honest with yourself. You need to know why you feel the way you do. For example, look back at Figure 2.3 on page 27. How do you feel about this picture? The artist loved cats. Do you? How do you think the way you feel about cats might affect your reaction to this work?

The chief goal of aesthetics is to answer the question "What is successful art?" In their search for an answer, aestheticians have put forth different views on what is important in a work of art. These ideas, or schools of thought, on what to look for in works of art are called aesthetic theories.

You can also make an objective judgment that does not depend entirely on your personal feelings. You can turn to aesthetic theories to answer the question "Is this a successful work of art?" This is an aesthetic question.

AESTHETIC THEORIES AND QUALITIES OF ART

The aesthetic qualities that are discussed most often by aestheticians are the literal qualities, the design qualities, and the expressive qualities. These are directly related to the properties of art that were discussed in Chapter 1 on page 17: subject,

composition, and content. The **literal qualities**, are *the realistic qualities that appear in the subject of the work.* For instance, if the artist depicts a realistic figure of a man on a horse, the literal quality of the work is the image of a man on a horse. The **design qualities**, or *how well the work is organized,* are found when you look at the composition of the work. Does it look balanced; is there a rhythmic quality; is there variety? Has the artist made a unified work of art? The **expressive qualities**, or *those qualities that communicate ideas and moods,* are those you notice when you study the content of a work. Is there something in the work that makes you feel a certain emotion or conveys an idea to you? The three aesthetic theories are most commonly referred to as Imitationalism, Formalism, and Emotionalism.

Imitationalism and Literal Qualities

Some critics think that the most important thing about a work of art is the realistic presentation of subject matter. It is their opinion that a work is successful if it looks like and reminds the viewer of what he or she sees in the real world. People with this point of view feel that an artwork should imitate life, that it should look lifelike before it can be considered successful. This aesthetic theory, called **Imitationalism**, *focuses on realistic presentation.*

Formalism and Design Qualities

Other critics think that composition is the most important factor in a work of art. This aesthetic theory, called **Formalism**, *places emphasis on the design qualities,* the arrangement of the elements of art using the principles of design.

Emotionalism and Expressive Qualities

This theory is concerned with the content of the work of art. Some critics claim that no object can be considered art if it fails to send a message to the viewer. The expressive quality is most important to them. Their theory, called **Emotionalism**, *requires a strong communication of feelings, moods, or ideas* from the work to the viewer.

Look at Margareta Haverman's painting *A Vase of Flowers* (Figure 2.6). You may like it because the

---

MEETING SPECIAL NEEDS

Building Self-Esteem Some students with disabilities or retardation may always remain in the scribbling stage or in an early stage of representation. Help them to see the beauty in formal and design qualities and in emotional expression. Much of the world's great art does not imitate outer appearances. Art by untaught artists can have as much power as that by artists who have extensive training. Show your students examples of powerful artwork by untaught or "primitive" artists to show the truth in that observation. Praise such non-realistic features as "the pleasing use of repeated pattern" and "the strong feeling that the lines give."

LOOKING
C L O S E L Y

Margareta Haverman. *A Vase of Flowers.* 1716. Oil on wood. 79.4 × 60.3 cm (31¼ × 23¾").
The Metropolitan Museum of Art, New York, New York. Purchase, 1871.

FIGURE 2.6 There is much more to this painting than its obvious realistic beauty. Notice that the flower at the top of the painting is a tulip, which blooms in the spring. The flowers in the center are summer flowers. Observe how the roses near the bottom are fading and drooping. At the lower edge of the painting you see autumn fruits. This painting is a *vanitas* painting. The word *vanitas* is a Latin word meaning vain and empty. These paintings are meant to remind people that time passes and things change, and that people shouldn't put too much emphasis on material things.

LOOKING
C L O S E L Y

Have students study Figure 2.6. Tell students that the vanitas paintings were started as secular reminders of moral issues. Even though the artists were no longer painting religious works, the moral lesson about the possession of material objects was continuously taught through the vanitas still lifes.

Sparking Creativity

Want students to think creatively about visual perception? Suggest this: Layout is an art form. Magazine designers and book designers arrange blocks of print, pictures, and headlines to pull your eyes to the page and entice you to read. Try being a layout editor. From an outdated magazine, cut several photos, illustrations, headlines of different sizes and typefaces, and columns of "copy." Try several page layouts before you decide to glue your pieces. Think about balance, organization, and readability.

---

artist has painted everything very realistically (Imitationalism). You can see drops of water sparkling on the leaves and a snail crawling on a leaf in the lower-left corner. Someone else may like this painting because of the arrangement of the flowers and how light is used to sweep from the top flower to the grapes at the bottom (Formalism). A third person may like the painting simply because he or she likes flowers (Emotionalism).

You can judge art using just one aesthetic theory or more than one, depending on the type of art and your own purposes. If you limit yourself to using only one theory, however, you may miss some exciting discoveries in a work. Perhaps the best method is to use all three. Then you will be able to discover as much as possible about a particular piece of art.

Judging Functional Objects

You can use art criticism to make aesthetic judgments about functional objects as well as objects of fine art. The object in Figure 2.7, on page 32, is an example. In criticizing functional objects, you follow the first two steps, description and analysis, as described earlier. During interpretation you must consider the purpose of the object as its meaning. In the judgment phase you consider how the object

Using Art Criticism

Bring some functional objects to class, such as cookware, a chair, eating utensils, or a drinking glass. Then ask the students to criticize the object. As they begin interpretation, remind them that they must try it out. At the judgment stage they must make two decisions: Is the object aesthetically pleasing? Does it function properly?

CURRICULUM CONNECTION

Science   While appreciating a painting such as Margareta Haverman's *A Vase of Flowers,* students interested in botany might be inspired to research the identification of the flowers in the painting. In doing so, they should pay attention to the date of the painting and, if possible, know where the artist painted the artwork. Specific species might be extinct today or might be common to limited geographical areas. Identification of flowers or animals in a work of art could give clues to its degree of realism. Ask students to consider how a scientist researching plant or animal life through paintings could use this information in his or her studies.

GUIDED PRACTICE
(continued)

Using Art Criticism

Present this analogy: Use the four steps of art criticism to study one of your favorite possessions. Does this change your perception of that familiar object? If so, how? Now look at the painting in Figure 2.1, page 24. Cassatt has taken a familiar, everyday event and created a work of art. Do you feel that common, everyday objects and events are suitable subjects for an artwork?

Classifying Aesthetic Theories

1. Applying Your Skills. Responses will vary. Use the information gathered by students to discuss the reasons why people might have diverse responses to artwork.

2. Further Challenge. Again, responses will vary.

Sparking Creativity

Want students to think creatively about aesthetics? Suggest this: We need a critical eye and aesthetic judgment in many aspects of our daily life. Skim through a catalog for furniture and housewares to see the many different tastes it shows. Test your own aesthetic sense. Cut out from catalogs the furnishings of what you consider a well-designed living room, bedroom, or den. Look for furniture, drapes, bedspreads, rugs, lamps, and decorative pieces. Cut out shapes for each room and arrange them on a sheet of paper. Then share your ideas with classmates.

FIGURE 2.7 Sitting on this beautiful chair would make you feel as if you were sitting on a pedestal, but the chair would not be considered a well-designed chair unless you were comfortable.

Eero Saarinen. *Armchair.* 1957. Molded plastic reinforced with fiberglass; painted aluminum base. 81.3 cm (32") high. Collection, The Museum of Modern Art, New York, New York. Gift of Knoll Associates, Inc.

works when it is used. A chair may look beautiful, but if it is not comfortable to sit in, it does not function properly and you must judge it to be unsuccessful.

Someone may buy a car based on looks alone. Someone else may buy a piece of clothing without regard for the way it looks on his or her body. Neither person is making a wise choice. When judging functional objects, attention must be given to function as well as aesthetic qualities.

Judging Your Own Work

Art criticism will help you analyze your own works of art. The four steps of art criticism will help you be as honest and unbiased as possible. The analysis step may be the most useful. It will help you perceive how you have organized the elements using the principles of design. By looking carefully at each element and reviewing how you have used it, you will see your work in a new way. By observing how you have organized the elements, you will gain insight into your decision-making process. When you apply all four of the steps of art criticism to your work, you should find out why your work either needs improvement or is a success.

Classifying Aesthetic Theories

1. Applying Your Skills. Select one large work of art in this book. Show the picture to at least three people outside of class. Ask them whether they like the work. Then ask them to tell you why they like or dislike the work. Classify their answers according to the three aesthetic theories of art: Imitationalism, Formalism, or Emotionalism.

2. Further Challenge. Find a work that fits each of the aesthetic theories in this chapter. List the title of each work, the theory that best applies to the work, and why you think that theory is most applicable.

ART CRITICISM: GETTING STARTED

There is only one way to learn art criticism: by doing it. This is why you will be given many opportunities throughout *ArtTalk* to develop your criticism skills.

At the end of each chapter you will be given questions to help you criticize a work of art. The evaluation questions at the end of each major Studio Lesson will also take you through the art-criticism steps to help you study your own artworks.

To help you begin, we will look at and criticize *Christina's World* by Andrew Wyeth (Figure 2.8).

Description

Look at the credit line below Figure 2.8. Record the size of the painting and the medium. Imagine the size of the work as if it were hanging on a wall in front of you.

CULTURAL PERSPECTIVES

Explain to students that aesthetics is a branch of western philosophy that focuses on the fundamental nature and value of art. Tell students that people who study and write about aesthetics include philosophers, art historians, art critics, and cultural anthropologists. Have students examine the professional role of cultural anthropologists, whose goal when conducting ethnographic research, is to learn about a contemporary culture by living in it for a year or more. They learn the language, participate in daily activities, and record the lifestyles and art of that culture. (Some cultures do not even have the word *art* in their vocabulary.)

GUIDED PRACTICE
(continued)

Critical Thinking

When students approach *Christina's World,* ask them to stop and list everything they see in the picture. Have them work separately, or, because this is their first critical attempt, have them work as a group. One student can write the class's findings on the board. Then when they begin interpretation, refer back to the clues collected during the first two stages.

Understanding Art History

To help students further appreciate the life and times of Andrew Wyeth, assign *Artist's Profile 41* in the TCR.

Using Art Criticism

Encourage students to keep an open mind when observing a work of art. In the history of art, historians have often disagreed about the importance of particular styles of art. For example, art from third world countries has been traditionally assigned to exhibits in natural history museums, rather than art museums. Now art historians are more knowledgeable about the cultures from which these artworks come. They agree that an open mind is essential to developing an appreciation of all styles of art.

Using Art Criticism

Allow students to choose an artwork from the book. Then have them discuss their responses to these questions: What do you think was the inspiration for this work? What do you think the artist saw, felt, or thought about before beginning this artwork? How do you think the artist reacted to that experience?

FIGURE 2.8   Andrew Wyeth. *Christina's World.* 1948. Tempera on gesso panel. 81.9 × 121.3 cm (32¼ × 47¾"). Collection, The Museum of Modern Art, New York, New York. Purchase.

Now look at the reproduction of the painting very carefully. List everything you see. Try to be objective. Don't make guesses, and don't let your feelings about the work influence you during this step. Write down every fact you can observe, even the small details.

When you finish describing the work, read through the following questions and statements. They will show you the details you might have missed. Don't feel upset if you missed some of the details. Remember, this is your first attempt at art criticism.

What facts about the female's dress did you list? Did you notice the faded pink quality? Does the dress look new? Do you think the fabric is heavy or light? Look at the folds. What do they tell you about the fabric? What does the belt look like? What color is it?

What matches the belt color? Her hair. Look at her hair. Notice all the individual hairs? Does the way she fixes her hair match the style of her dress? What about those strands of hair flying loosely around her head?

Next, notice her shoes. What do you think was used to make them? Is there any sign of wear on the bottom of the shoes? Look closely at her legs. What color are they? Is the color quality the same as that of her arms? Do you notice anything unusual about her arms and her hands? Look carefully at her left hand. Is it at the same level as the rest of her body?

Imitate her posture. Study the picture closely as you do this. Where is all your weight resting?

Where is the female located? What facts can you gather by studying the ground and the rest of the background? What colors do you see? Notice the

GUIDED PRACTICE
(continued)

Understanding Art History

Have students look at all artworks in the chapter and choose one from each of three time periods: one that is over two hundred years old, one from the nineteenth century, and one from the last thirty years. Then have them write five descriptive adjectives about each of the selected works. Next, make a list of the three time periods on the board and ask students to call out the artworks and adjectives from their sketchbooks. What general statements can be made concerning the ways artistic expression was used at different times in the history of art?

Using Art Criticism

Remind students that aesthetic judgment often reflects a personal outlook on art. For example, a person who prefers art that shows actual people, places, or events will probably not be inclined to judge a nonobjective piece of art as very successful. It is natural for people to have particular aesthetic views. Ask each student to state what he or she feels is most important in a work of art.

Promoting Discussion

It is very important that you not impose your own interpretation upon the students. Both you and they may confront the same visual facts, but you bring experiences and values to your interpretation that may vary greatly from theirs. This does not mean that you should totally avoid sharing your ideas with them, but you must respect their opinions. As long as a student's interpretation is backed up by visual facts, it is valid, even if you disagree with it.

individual blades of grass. Do they bend in a special direction? What is the difference between the area where she is located and the top of the hill? Did you see the road? Did you notice what kind of a road it is?

How many buildings do you see? How are they different? What material was used to build them? What color are they? Do you see the birds flying around one building?

What color is the sky? From what direction is the light coming? Let the shadows help you. How much of the picture is sky and how much is ground? Was the artist looking down from above or up from below the scene?

Try to avoid making guesses. Save your written clues to help you during interpretation.

Analysis

This is the step that reveals the artist's message, or idea. For now we will move on to interpretation. Later, when you know more about the language of art, come back and look at *Christina's World* again. You will uncover many clues about the work that you may have missed at this point.

Interpretation

Review the clues you have collected. What do you think the artist is trying to say about the relationship between the female and her environment?

Hold a ruler along the left slope of the roof of the largest building. Do you see how that line leads your eyes to the woman? Notice how she is straining toward the house. She is wearing faded colors, and the house looks unpainted and weathered. What does that tell you about her and the house? Why do you think so much of the space in the work is taken up by the ground? Why has the artist shown separate blades of grass? When you acted out the woman's pose, did you feel pressure on your arms and hands? Did you feel the tension? Did you notice that your legs were not carrying any weight?

Have you guessed what the artist is trying to say about the relationship between the woman and the house? Did you sense any special feelings?

Other than the title that has been given, can you think of a word or phrase that describes this work? What title would you give it?

Try to go beyond the events that appear to be taking place in this painting. Search for the general idea, or theme, that you believe the artist was trying to express. If you add the facts you discovered during description to your personal ideas, you will discover what the painting means to you.

Remember, your interpretation may be different from your classmates'. You may all have collected the same facts from the work, but the memories of life that you bring to this experience are uniquely your own. The message that this work communicates to you is influenced by your own life experiences.

Judgment

Now you are ready to make an aesthetic judgment about *Christina's World*.

Would an aesthetician who embraces the theory of Imitationalism judge this to be a successful work? Why or why not?

Would an aesthetician who believes Formalism is the correct theory consider this a successful work? Has Wyeth done a successful job of organizing the elements of art using the principles of design? Why or why not?

Would an aesthetician who believes Emotionalism to be the most important theory consider this work a success? Has the work communicated a message to you, the viewer? Why or why not?

What do *you* think? Does the painting make you think? Would you like to be able to look at it every day? Why or why not?

Do you think one of the three aesthetic theories is more important in judging this work than the others? Explain your answer.

STUDENTS PRACTICE ART CRITICISM

Look at *Dawn* by Louise Nevelson (Figure 2.9 on page 36).

Students studying art criticism have written about this work. During description they noticed that the work is very large, almost 8 feet (2.4 m) tall, and that it was made of wood painted gold. It is made of forty-nine rectangular boxes. At first

COOPERATIVE LEARNING

A successful method for getting students to participate in critical activities is peer teaching. Divide the class up into small groups. Balance each group with students both below- and above-average academically. Groups of three to five students are a good size. Give each group one large print or one full page illustration from the text to study.

Ask each group to select a secretary to keep notes as they discuss the work together. Then, at the end of the class period, give each group a few minutes to report their findings to the class. The group can elect a representative speaker, or each person might report on a different part of the study.

FIGURE 2.8A Andrew Wyeth. *Christina's World.* (Detail) 1948. Tempera on gessoed panel. 81.9 × 121.3 cm (32¼ × 47¾"). Collection, The Museum of Modern Art, New York, New York.

they thought it was nonobjective, but as they studied it they saw pieces of recognizable objects in the boxes such as banisters, gun stocks, baseball bats, rolling pins, musical instruments, carved leaves, dumbbells, and bedposts. They also observed both free-form and geometric shapes in the work.

During interpretation each student had different ideas. One said "This work is about people. The total work looks static, with free-form shapes in their own individual containers. The space seems crammed full of things. This makes me think of society. The geometric shapes represent the normal, everyday people. The free-form shapes are the eccentric, rebellious people in life. The many individual compartments are the many individual social groups of today."

Another student commented, "It shows the bad and good of human nature, all existing in the same world. The guns and bats represent violence. The musical instruments and the finely carved pieces of furniture seem to express education and culture. No two people are alike, but all are united in one world represented by the unified boxes in this sculpture."

A third student felt this work was very nostalgic. "I think that this work should be called 'America.'

The rifle stock reminds me of being out in the wilderness hunting with my grandpa. The banisters make me think of my house and how important our houses are to us in America. The rolling pin reminds me of Mom and my grandma cooking in the kitchen on a hot summer day and of eating under the shade tree at the picnic table."

Although this work has many strong formal qualities, when the students reached the judgment step, many of them felt that this work evoked powerful emotional responses!

"I like this work because it evokes emotions in me about how I think America should be, not the reality of how it really is."

"I like this sculpture because it uses Emotionalism, because it gives me certain feelings about society."

"It looks very emotional. It has too many feelings crammed into one piece of art!"

These students were not afraid to reveal their thoughts and feelings during interpretation and judgment. Now it is your turn to study Nevelson's *Dawn.* Even though you have read what other students said about this work, study it yourself. Turn the page. You may see things they never noticed.

CURRICULUM CONNECTION

History   After Franklin Delano Roosevelt became President of the United States in 1932, he began the Works Progress Administration (WPA) under his New Deal program. The program sponsored artists of all races, genders, and artistic forms—ceramics, painting, crafts, furniture design, metalwork, textiles, wood-carving, glassware, and architecture.

For many artists in the program, such as Jackson Pollack, Alice Neel, and Louise Nevelson, the program supported them through the turbulent years following the Great Depression. By the middle of 1943, all WPA projects were phased out, although many local buildings and works of art still remain.

INDEPENDENT PRACTICE

Study Guide
Distribute and have students complete *Study Guide 2* in the Reteaching booklet. Have students use the guide to review key concepts.

Enrichment
- Assign *Enrichment 3* and *4* in the TCR.
- You might take the class to a furniture store on a field trip. Perhaps a store representative could explain how to recognize the quality of something like a sofa. Ask each student to select a chair that looks good and then criticize it. Before the trip, set up some criteria for interpretation and judgment. When discussing shape and form, consider the inner structure of the object. They should look for quality construction as well as aesthetic quality.

Keeping a Sketchbook
Remind students that familiar sights and objects often serve as inspiration for works of art. By learning to observe their environments, they sharpen their abilities to notice the smallest of details as well as the largest of scenes. Encourage them to keep a record of sketches and ideas as resources for future works.

Extension
To help students further understand how to be aware of their critical perceptions, show a music video to the class. Then have them identify and list the techniques and methods used in the video. Next, ask them to evaluate how the methods and techniques in the video affect their impressions of the video.

INTRODUCTION

In this chapter, students were introduced to art criticism using Andrew Wyeth's realistic painting. Now they are asked to use the steps of art criticism to study a nonobjective work of art. There are objects in this work, but they are placed in the work as shapes and forms. In the comparison artwork, students are brought back to realism by comparing *Dawn* to a panel from *Gates of Paradise* by Ghiberti.

CRITIQUING THE WORK

1. **Describe** Since this work is almost 8 feet (2.4 m) tall and more than 6 feet (1.8 m) wide, it would cover a classroom wall, but it probably would be close to the ceiling. The work is composed of forty-nine rectangular forms on a rectangular base. There are pieces of wooden objects arranged in the rectangle: baseball bats, dumbbells, pieces of musical instruments, and lots of wood scraps that have both free-form and geometric shapes. Some pieces are placed close to the viewer, and some are in the back of the boxes, behind other shapes.
2. **Analyze** All of the different found pieces of wood have been organized inside matching rectangular boxes. Everything is painted gold. The work looks very crowded.
3. **Interpret** Answers will vary.
4. **Judge** Answers will vary.

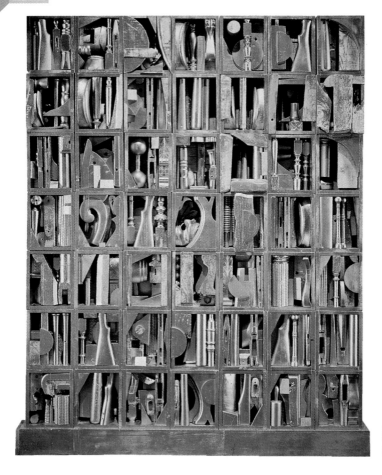

FIGURE 2.9 Louise Nevelson. *Dawn*. 1962. Wood painted gold. 323 × 240 × 19 cm (127 × 94½ × 7½"). The Pace Gallery, New York, New York.

CRITIQUING THE WORK

1. **Describe** Read the credit line and record the important information. Would this work fit on a wall in your classroom? Look over all the small parts and list the things you find.
2. **Analyze** How is the work organized? What has Louise Nevelson done to make the different found objects look like they belong together? Does the work look crowded or empty? What affect does the use of a single color have on the piece?
3. **Interpret** What kind of message is the artist making about your world with this sculpture? Write a paragraph explaining your interpretation. Then create a new title for the work that fits your interpretation.
4. **Judge** You have now had a "conversation" with a work of art that does not convey an obvious story. Do you feel more comfortable with nonobjective art? Do you think this is a successful work? Which of the aesthetic theories would you use to judge this work?

36

RESOURCES BEYOND THE CLASSROOM

Other Works By . . . Louise Nevelson
Sky Cathedral
Atmosphere and Environment
Mirror Shadow II

Other Works By . . . Ghiberti
Biblical Stories of Joseph
The Sacrifice of Isaac

Similarities: Both artworks are relief sculptures and have only one color—shiny gold.

Differences: *Gates of Paradise* is a realistic representation of people in a realistic setting. Ghiberti imitates the textures of the objects represented. The work has the illusion of deep space through the use of perspective, even though the raised part of the relief is very shallow. *Dawn* is nonobjective. There is no attempt to imitate reality. Although the sculpture has depth, there is no illusion of deep space. Even though Nevelson has painted the whole work with an even coat of gold paint, the textures of the different pieces of wood show through. In some places the texture is very smooth, in other places the grain of the wood is obvious.

EXTENSION

- Have students read the "Meet the Artist" feature on the following page.
- Assign *Artist's Profile 2* in the TCR.

Art Is Everywhere

To foster students' awareness of artistic expression in everyday life, suggest this: In Figure 2.9, we see how Louise Nevelson made a visual metaphor of dawn. Listen to Claude Debussey's *La Mer* which expresses in music the sun rising over the ocean, or Ferde Grofe's *Grand Canyon Suite* in which you hear sunrise in the canyon. Discover more about poets Robert Stern and e. e. cummings who wrote poems about the beauty and mystery of dawn.

FIGURE 2.10 Lorenzo Ghiberti. *Gates of Paradise.* (Detail). 1425–52. Gilt bronze. Baptistry of Florence, Italy.

COMPARING THE WORKS

Look at *Dawn* (Figure 2.9) and the panel from the *Gates of Paradise* by Lorenzo Ghiberti (Figure 2.10). Identify the similarities and differences between the two works. Compare your interpretation of the Nevelson wall to the theme of the Ghiberti panel. Do you find a connection between the two themes? Explain. Decide which of these works you find more interesting. Use one or more of the aesthetic theories to defend your judgment in a class discussion.

FYI Nevelson joined the brand-new Pace Gallery in 1964. The director, Arnold Glimcher, believed in her and did a good job of presenting her work to collectors. By 1967 she had become financially secure. She appreciated wealth for the obvious reasons, but she also saw it as an indication of the value of her work. In 1969 she told a *Houston Chronicle* reporter that she enjoyed the fact that a woman artist in America could collect wooden scraps from the street, put them together, and sell them to the Rockefellers for one hundred thousand dollars.

37

MORE ABOUT . . . LORENZO GHIBERTI

Ghiberti, a sculptor, was best known for the work he produced for the Baptistry of the Florence Cathedral, which was built in the twelfth century and dedicated to St. John the Baptist. Ghiberti entered his design for the Baptistry doors in a contest sponsored by the city. After being declared the winner of the contest, Ghiberti spent the next twenty-one years of his life completing all twenty-eight panels in the door. Earlier panels reflect a Gothic influence, while panels for another Baptistry door draw upon Renaissance styles. Michelangelo declared the doors worthy of being the gates to heaven. Consequently, they have been called "The Gates of Paradise."

- On a separate sheet of paper have students complete "Building Vocabulary" and "Reviewing Art Facts" on page 39.
- Assign *Application 3* and *4* in the TCR to evaluate students' comprehension.

ANSWERS TO BUILDING VOCABULARY

1. criteria
2. art criticism
3. aesthetics
4. aesthetic experience
5. description
6. analysis
7. interpretation
8. judgment
9. literal qualities
10. design qualities
11. expressive qualities
12. Imitationalism
13. Formalism
14. Emotionalism

ANSWERS TO REVIEWING ART FACTS

1. The courage to speak your mind and make sound aesthetic judgments.
2. Description, analysis, interpretation, judgment.
3. Description.
4. Imitationalism, Formalism, Emotionalism.
5. Formalism.
6. How the object works when it is used.

MEET THE ARTIST

LOUISE NEVELSON

Born in Kiev, Ukraine
American citizen, 1899–1988

Louise Nevelson was the glamorous, fascinating person that everyone imagines an artist should be. Art was the dominating force in her life. She claimed that by the time she was seven she knew she would be a sculptor.

In 1920 Nevelson moved to New York City. By 1929 she was a full-time student at the Art Students' League, seriously studying with some of the best teachers of the time. She knew she was destined to spend the rest of her life creating art. Inspired by Cubism, pre-Columbian art, and the creative drive within herself, Nevelson continued her studies in Europe.

During the 1940s she experimented with all art media. She lived near a neighborhood that was being renovated, and the discarded wood scraps from the demolished buildings inspired her first three-dimensional assemblage, or assembled sculpture.

Nevelson painted each assemblage a solid color. She started out painting all her work black. Later she experimented with solid white. She even painted a few pieces, like *Dawn*, gold.

In the 1970s she experimented with new media such as Cor-ten steel, Lucite, and aluminum. These strong materials enabled her to produce gigantic outdoor pieces.

Today there is a square in New York City named for Louise Nevelson. It contains seven of her mammoth, freestanding, steel sculptures that are about 90 feet (30 m) high. Like many other great artists, she led a very self-centered life, but she has left the world a magnificent collection of uniquely powerful sculptures.

MORE PORTFOLIO IDEAS

Collect small found objects. Arrange them in a small box, no larger than a shoe box, in the manner of Nevelson. You may create nonobjective shapes with scraps of cardboard to help your composition. Glue your final arrangement into the box. Paint everything one color.

Select a story or poem as a theme for your box. Do the above activity, but collect objects to fit your theme. You may have to create some objective shapes as well as nonobjective shapes to enhance your theme.

Select five objects at random from clip art. Arrange them in an interesting manner inside a rectangle, adding geometric shapes to the composition. Use only one hue to color all the shapes, but change the intensity or value of the hue to indicate depth.

38

DEVELOPING A PORTFOLIO

Choosing a Project   Learning to isolate problem areas in an artwork can help the student decide whether or not the project should be included in a portfolio. Show them how a series of critical questions will help make a decision about the piece. First, they should determine if the project meets the specific requirements given. If not, what adjustments are necessary? Second, have they remained focused on their individual goals for the project? If not, what direction can they take in order to meet their goals? Then have them apply the four steps to critiquing their work. Lastly, they should ask themselves if the artwork is a worthy example for their portfolio.

CHAPTER 2 REVIEW

Building Vocabulary

On a separate sheet of paper, write the term that best matches each definition given below.
1. Standards of judgment.
2. An organized system for studying a work of art.
3. The philosophy or study of the nature of beauty and art.
4. Personal interaction with a work of art.
5. The art-criticism step in which you make a list of all the things you see in a work.
6. The art-criticism step in which you discover how the work is organized.
7. The art-criticism step in which you explain or tell the meaning or mood of the work.
8. The art-criticism step in which you determine the degree of artistic merit of the work.
9. The realistic qualities that appear in the subject of the work.
10. The qualities that indicate how well the work is organized.
11. The qualities that communicate ideas and moods.
12. The aesthetic theory that focuses on realistic presentation.
13. The aesthetic theory that places emphasis on the design qualities.
14. The aesthetic theory that requires a communication of feelings, moods, or ideas.

Reviewing Art Facts

Answer the following questions using complete sentences.
1. What will learning the steps of art criticism help you develop?
2. Name the four steps of art criticism in the order in which they must be followed.
3. In which step would you list the size of the work and the medium used?
4. Name the three aesthetic theories.
5. If the organization of an artwork is most important to an art critic, which aesthetic theory would he or she hold?

6. When criticizing functional objects, what must you consider during interpretation besides beauty?

Thinking Critically About Art

1. **Apply.** Select something from your home that is used solely for aesthetic purposes. Critique it using the four steps of art criticism. When you are finished, ask yourself if the object seems different than it did before. Has your opinion of the object changed?
2. **Analyze.** Find a movie critic's review of a current film in a newspaper or magazine. Read it carefully. Try to find statements that fit each of the four steps of art criticism.
3. **Extend.** Do you think you can appreciate the qualities of a work of art even though you don't like it? Explain your conclusions.

Making Art Connections

1. **Mathematics.** Look at the art of M. C. Escher. It utilizes geometric concepts to convey its messages. Pay attention to the use of literal qualities in unusual settings. Do the literal qualities and design qualities play equally important parts in Escher's work? Critique an Escher work using the four steps of art criticism.
2. **Science.** Some say that the four steps of art criticism parallel the four steps of the scientific method. Research information about the scientific method. Do you think the two methods are similar or different? Explain your conclusions.
3. **Social Studies.** Research the work of Mexican Muralists such as Diego Rivera and David Alfaro Siqueiros. Much of their art focused on the social struggles of the Mexican working class and was meant to bring about social change. Can you identify the aesthetic theories in this chapter that apply to art movements that concern social protest? Bring your findings to class for discussion.

EVALUATE

- Have students complete the *Chapter 2 Test* in the TCR.
- Alternative Assessment teaching strategies are provided below or in the Testing Program and Alternative Assessment booklet.

RETEACHING

- Have students complete *Concept Map 2* in the Reteaching booklet.
- Ask students to apply the four steps of art criticism to Figure 2.1, Mary Cassatt's *Baby Reaching for an Apple* on page 24.

EXTENSION

Challenge students to assume the role of an artist or a person whose job requires him or her to make value judgments about a work of art (for example, a museum curator or art critic). Allow each student to select an artwork from the textbook that he or she likes personally. Ask each student to discuss the artwork from the point of view of the person they have chosen to be. Finally, have them write a brief summary of their evaluation of the artwork.

CLOSE

Ask each student to briefly state what he or she thinks is most important in a work of art. Ask: Can one aesthetic viewpoint express your personal criteria?

ALTERNATIVE ASSESSMENT

To reinforce art-criticism concepts, assign this activity: Select one of the following art processes and media discussed in Chapter 1. During a six-week period attend three gallery shows or museum exhibitions that focus on this particular art process. After viewing each exhibition, write a two-page review about one of the artworks on display there. In your review, follow the four steps of art criticism. Keep your three reviews in a portfolio. At the end of the six-week period, reread your reviews. What accounts for any difference(s) between the review you wrote at the beginning of the period with the one you wrote at the end?

Art History

INTRODUCE

CHAPTER OVERVIEW

Art history is the record of art from past to present. Chapter 3 explains how art historians follow a four-step system to learn about a work of art.

Also in Chapter 3, students learn about the relationships between cultures, world events, and the creation of art.

CHAPTER SUPPLIES

For a list of the materials you will need for the Activities in this chapter, refer to the "Art Supplies Grid" in the Teacher's Manual.

FINE ART RESOURCES
Transparencies
- Yoruba peoples, Nigeria. *Male Figures (ere ibeji)*
- Thailand. *Amulet Necklace*
- Maria Martinez and Popovi Da of San Ildefonso. *Plate*
- *Stone Lintel* Yaxichilian.

Fine Art Prints
- Pieter Bruegel. *The Tower of Babel*
- Joseph Mallord William Turner. *Burning of the Houses of Parliament, 1834.*

FIGURE 3.1 Hayden's self-portrait is symbolic rather than realistic. He tells us about his life without telling us what he really looked like. Hayden exhibited his work in the Harmon Foundation shows; he also worked as a janitor in the Harmon Foundation's office building to support himself. The Foundation was an organization that promoted and supported the work of African-American artists from the 1920s through the 1960s.

Palmer Hayden. *The Janitor Who Paints*. c. 1937. Oil on canvas. 99.4 × 83.5 cm (39⅛ × 32⅞"). National Museum of American Art, Washington, D.C.

RESOURCES FOR CHAPTER 3
Application Activities 5, 6
Artist's Profile 3, 17, 22, 23, 31, 32
Cooperative Learning Activities 5, 6
Cultural Diversity in Art
Enrichment Activities 5, 6

Reteaching Activities
   Study Guide 3
   Concept Map 3
Chapter 3 Test

Art History

Ever since there have been human beings, there has been art. The need to create has always been a part of human nature. Before people kept written records, they made paintings, drawings, sculpture, and objects to adorn their bodies, and they decorated functional objects with attractive designs.

You can look at visual images from the past to learn what the people who lived before us were like. The art they made reveals a great deal about their feelings, their beliefs, their ideas, and the way they lived. Someday in the future people will learn about our lives by studying the art objects we are producing now.

Art history is the record of art from past to present. Art historians look at changes that occur in the field of art over time. They also look at differences in the way art is made from place to place.

The history of visual art is as broad and complex as the history of the world. This chapter is just a peek into the treasure chest that makes up your visual heritage. It will help you understand how works of art are related.

Objectives

After completing this chapter, you will be able to:

- Explain the value of art history.
- Use a four-step system to learn about a work of art.
- Understand how historical events influence artists' work.
- Briefly discuss movements in the history of art, from prehistoric through modern times.

Words to Know

Baroque
Byzantine
Cubism
dynasty
Expressionism
Gothic
Impressionism
linear perspective
mobile
Realism
Regionalist
Renaissance
Rococo
Romanesque
style
Surrealism

FIRST IMPRESSIONS

What is your first impression of the three people in *The Janitor Who Paints* by Palmer Hayden (Figure 3.1)? Can you use the visual clues to collect information about that artist and his world? How does he support himself? Can you guess when this work was painted by looking at the objects in the room and at the people's clothing? Can you guess where this room might be located?

41

TEACH

(pages 42–45)
• Learning About Works
  of Art
• Art of Earliest Times

GUIDED PRACTICE

Understanding Art History

Refer students to the section titled "Artists and Their Works" in the back of their student text. Tell them this resource is available for their reference throughout the course. It lists the name of the artist, his or her birth and death dates, and other works of art by the artist which are featured in this program. Ask them to study the list and identify two other artists who worked during the same time as Palmer Hayden, whose painting is shown on page 40.

Exploring Aesthetics

Encourage students to discuss the definition of the term *work of art*. Ask: How do you know if an object is a work of art? What is an example of an object that most people would agree is a work of art? Why? What object might people disagree on? Why? How can learning about the properties of artworks help you understand and evaluate specific works? Now ask students to again study Palmer Hayden's painting in Figure 3.1. What makes this painting a work of art?

Exploring Aesthetics

Ask each student to look through the chapter and choose an artwork that he or she would like enough to purchase. Ask: Why do you find this artwork appealing? As a patron, would you expect the artwork to increase in value? Why or why not?

LEARNING ABOUT WORKS OF ART

In the last chapter you learned the four steps of *art criticism*, an organized system for getting information from a work of art. There is also a four-step system for organizing the way you gather information about the history of a work of art. The labels for these four steps are the same: Description, Analysis, Interpretation, and Judgment. This time, however, there are different definitions for the terms, and different questions to be answered.

■ When, where, and by whom was the work done? (Description)
■ What is the style of the work, and does the work fit into an art movement? (Analysis)
■ How did time and place affect the artist's style and subject matter? (Interpretation)
■ Does the work of art make an important contribution to the history of art? (Judgment)

Step One: Description

During this step you are collecting facts, just as you did during art criticism. This time you are looking for information *about* the work of art. You want to know who did it, when, and where it was done. If you were looking at an original work of art, you would look for the artist's signature and the date on the work. In this book, since the works have been reduced in size, you probably will not be able to see the artist's signature or date on the work itself. You will find the name of the artist and the date the work was created, however, in the credit line. If you look at the credit line for Figure 3.1, you will discover that the name of the artist is Palmer Hayden, and that the work was painted sometime between 1930 and 1940. To learn where it was painted, you can look back to the section called Artists and Their Works on pages 366–370. There you can find Hayden's nationality as well as the time he lived.

Step Two: Analysis

During analysis you will be looking for the artist's style. Style is like handwriting: No two people have exactly the same handwriting, and no two artists have exactly the same style. Individual **style**

is *the artist's personal way of using the elements of art and principles of design to express feelings and ideas.* To analyze the style of one artist, you will need to see several works by the same artist. Look at *Marisol* by Alice Neel (Figure 3.2). Notice the blue lines that outline the figure and the chair. Observe that the clothing is painted in rough, loose brushstrokes but the face and hands are modeled carefully with a heavy buildup of paint. Study the intense expression of the eyes. The blue lines and the concentration on the intensely expressive hands and face are part of Neel's unique style.

FIGURE 3.2 In this portrait Neel communicates her feelings about her friend as well as what Marisol looks like. Notice the posture of the sculptor. Her torso is as rigid as one of her sculptures. See Figure 6.1, page 118.

Alice Neel. *Marisol.* 1981. Oil on canvas. 107 × 61 cm (42 × 24"). Collection of the Honolulu Academy of Art. Hawaii, Robert Miller Gallery, New York, New York. © The estate of Alice Neel.

MORE ABOUT . . . ALICE NEEL

Alice Neel painted only people in whom she was interested. She called her works "painting of people" and did not like them to be called portraits. She thought that portraits had to be flattering, and she did not want to lie. During her entire career she struggled against fads and trends in art to become a collector of personalities. Never doubting the ability of her own work, she knew that she was doing the right thing by remaining true to herself. Neel was not recognized by the art establishment until she was in her mid-seventies. She lived to enjoy acclaim and financial success.

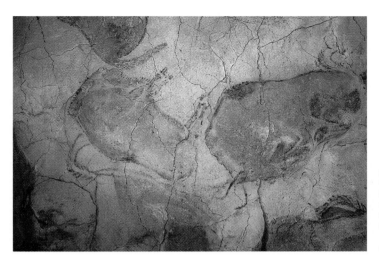

FIGURE 3.3 An amateur archaeologist excavated in this low-roofed cave for four years before his daughter, who was small enough to stand up straight in the cave and look up, discovered these paintings of sleeping, galloping, and crouching animals.

The Hall of the Bulls. c. 15,000 B.C. Altamira Caves, Spain.

Step Three: Interpretation

In order to do the interpretation step, you will need to do some research to find out how time and place have affected the artist's style and subject matter. An art historian would tell you that Alice Neel was an American artist who painted only people in whom she was interested. The rise of an abstract art style after World War II left her on the outside. Neel believed that the abstract elements were important, but she felt strongly that people and psychological truths were even more important. She remained independent of all styles and movements, and her work was not recognized by the Establishment until 1970.

Step Four: Judgment

Once again you must turn to research to find out this work's importance in the history of art. Did the work introduce a new style, or is it an outstanding example of an existing style? When you check the date it was painted and the birth date of Neel in Artists and Their Works on page 366, you find that it was painted when Neel was eighty-one years old and at the height of her career. As you read you will find out that historians consider her a great American portrait painter. You will also learn that *Marisol* is a portrait of an important American sculptor. Since this work was done at the height of Neel's career, you can conclude that it is an outstanding example of her unique style.

Now that you have become familiar with the system for gathering information about the history of a work of art, we will take a journey back into time. As early as 15,000 B.C. artists were drawing pictures reflecting their life and times.

ART OF EARLIEST TIMES

The art presented in this section was produced over a period of many thousands of years. The artworks produced during those ancient times tell us a great deal about the earliest cultures and civilizations of our world.

Prehistoric Cultures

Prehistoric means before history, or before written records were kept. That is why the art and artifacts from that period are so important. They are all that remains to tell us about the people who lived during those times.

Figure 3.3 is one of many paintings left by Stone Age cave dwellers. The colors are so bright and the animals so realistic that, for a long time, experts refused to believe paintings such as these were really created by prehistoric artists.

To this day no one knows the purpose of the paintings. They were found deep inside caves, far from the entrances and living areas. Because of

---

CULTURAL PERSPECTIVES

Humans produced their first pictures in cave paintings such as those shown in Figure 3.3. It was another seventeen millennia before the art of writing evolved, primarily out of a practical need. The population of Mesopotamia, now modern Iraq, was made up largely of shepherds and farmers, which explains why the oldest writing samples are clay tablets that show agricultural accounts from the Sumerians. Other later tablets preserve information about Sumerian life—religion, interest on money-lending, even tablets that have a teacher's text on one side and the pupil's text on the other.

GUIDED PRACTICE
(continued)

Interdisciplinary: Geography

Have students locate a map of the world. Working in pairs or small teams, have them identify and trace the location of the major river valleys discussed in this section. Then have them name the major cities found along the rivers' banks. Ask them to imagine they are traveling by boat on any one specific river from its source to its end. From the map, what land formations would they see? What do they speculate about the climatic conditions? What do they already know about each specific river and the country surrounding it?

Sparking Creativity

Want students to think creatively about art history? Suggest this: The artist has his or her finger on the pulse of time. As you survey all these art forms, think about the kind of world in which each artist lived. Many new buildings have cornerstones containing objects representing the time of construction and are intended to be opened in the future. What would you want to put into one today? Imagine your world of the twenty-first century. Write about or draw what you will see, how you will travel, and what will be happening to you and to the world around you. Gather all the writings and sketches and bind them into a twenty-first century almanac.

FIGURE 3.4 Notice how the sculptor has followed the rules of Egyptian art, showing each part of the body from the most visible view. The symbols around the figures are hieroglyphs, picture symbols that stand for words.

Methethy with His Daughter and a Son. c. 2450 B.C. Polychromed limestone relief. 143 × 76 cm (56¼ × 30″). Nelson-Atkins Museum of Art, Kansas City, Missouri. Purchase, Nelson Trust.

their location, we know they were not created for decoration. Some people believe the paintings were part of a hunting ritual. They may have been created by a shaman, or medicine man, who believed that the magical image of the animal could help hunters capture the animal. The paintings may also have been visual prayers for animals to appear during the next hunt. Another theory is that the paintings were created by cave dwellers to celebrate a successful hunt.

Ancient River Valleys

The ancient civilizations of Egypt, Mesopotamia, China, and India each developed in a river valley. Each civilization had a monarchy and a religion based on nature.

Egypt. Ancient Egypt developed along the banks of the Nile River more than three thousand years before the birth of Christ. The Egyptian civilization continued for almost three thousand years after that. The arts of Ancient Egypt express the endurance and solidity of that culture.

Religion influenced every part of Egyptian life. The *pharaohs,* or rulers, were worshiped as gods and held complete authority over the kingdom. Egyptians believed in life after death and preserved bodies of the dead in preparation for the afterlife. The famous pyramids of Egypt were built as the tombs of the pharaohs.

Egyptian artists who decorated temples and tombs had to follow very strict rules set forth by the rulers. The rules required that each part of the body be shown from the most visible angle. Thus, in relief wall sculpture and painting, figures were represented in an unusual way. Look at Figure 3.4. You can see that the heads, arms, legs, and feet are shown in profile. The shoulders and eyes are seen from a frontal view.

We have learned a great deal about life in Egypt from the paintings found on the walls inside the tombs. Scenes from the life of the person buried in the tomb were depicted. These scenes were intended to remind the spirit of its life on earth.

Mesopotamia. The culture of Mesopotamia was more the culture of a region than of a people. The region was the fertile crescent of land between the Tigris and Euphrates rivers. The people lived in city-states, and each city had its own monarch. Today this land is shared by Syria and Iraq.

The first important group to dominate the area were the Sumerians. They were the first people to have a system of writing. Called *cuneiform,* this writing system was made up of wedge-shaped characters. Sumerian artwork was more realistic than that of the Egyptians. In Figure 3.5 you see a small sculpture showing details of dress and facial features. Other cultures that later became important in this valley were those of Babylon and Assyria.

China. The Yellow River valley was the site of the ancient Chinese civilization. This civilization

FIGURE 3.5   This figure was placed in the temple as a substitute for the worshiper. The large eyes, hands clasped in prayer, and realistic detail are typical of Sumerian sculpture.

Statua di Donna. c. 2700–2600 B.C. Marble. The Iraq Museum, Baghdad, Iraq.

FIGURE 3.6   This vessel was used in a ceremony to ensure harmony with the spirits of deceased ancestors. Notice the large eyes and beak of an owl on the lower part of the vessel. Can you find other animals in the designs that cover this container?

Ancient China. *Ritual Wine Container.* Shang dynasty. Thirteenth century B.C. Bronze. 76.4 × 31 × 31.8 cm (30 × 12⅛ × 12½"). Arthur M. Sackler Gallery, Smithsonian Institution, Washington, D.C.

still exists today. It boasts the oldest continuous culture in the history of the world.

The history of China, until modern times, was divided into dynasties. A **dynasty** was *a period of time during which a single family provided a succession of rulers.* Dynasties are named for ruling families.

The first of these was the Shang dynasty. The lasting achievement from that time period was the cast-bronze work. The ritual wine vessel in Figure 3.6 is an example of the beautiful work done at that time: the thirteenth century B.C.

India. The culture of ancient India remained a legend until modern times. In 1865 railroad workers laying track in the Indus River valley discovered a hill of crumbling fired-clay bricks near the city of Harappa. The bricks date back to 2500 B.C.

In 1922 a second city was found in the same area. Its name is Mohenjo-Daro. The architectural remains of the city indicate that it was a major commercial center. Wide, open streets divided the city into large blocks, multistoried houses of fired brick and wood, and elaborate drainage systems (Figure 3.7 on page 46). Other ancient sites have also been uncovered in India.

MORE ABOUT . . . SUMERIAN ARTWORK

The Sumerians constructed ziggurats in the belief that mountaintops were the dwelling places of their gods. Lacking real mountains on the Mesopotamian plain, the Sumerians had to create their own artificial ones to provide a suitable home for their gods. The cult statues placed inside the ziggurat temple were believed to embody the deities that they depicted. Sumerians also made statues of worshipers to send prayers and messages to the gods in their places.

(pages 46–50)
• Art of Asia
• Art of Greece and Rome

GUIDED PRACTICE

Interdisciplinary: Social Studies

Turn students' attention to a world map and point out the lands of India, China, and Japan. Ask students to note the dates of artworks represented by each region and consider the distances on the map between each of the cultures represented. Do they imagine that the peoples of these ancient lands had contact with one another, or were they isolated from each other as their individual art styles developed? As students read about the different artworks and locations in the remainder of this chapter, refer them back to the world map.

Exploring Aesthetics

Guide students in discussing the sculpture of Vishnu, the Preserver in Figure 3.8. Ask: What message or mood do you think this sculpture was intended to communicate?

Developing Studio Skills

Have students study the Chinese scroll painting in Figure 3.10 to understand the artist's approach to space, giving a sense of distance with mountains, and moving into the middle ground and foreground detail. Point out the brush and ink technique most often used in scroll paintings. Tell students that every brushstroke counts and that the Chinese painters used long scrolls to represent a continuous viewing of a scene. Have students plan and execute a drawing like this to detail a nature scene.

FIGURE 3.7 Mohenjo-Daro is an early example of urban planning. The city was a center of commerce and trade and is believed to have had a population of 35,000 people.

Mohenjo-Daro, India. c. 2500 B.C.

FIGURE 3.8 Vishnu, the Preserver, holds his symbols: a discus, a conch shell, a mace, and a lotus.

South Indian. *Standing Vishnu.* Early Chola period, tenth century. Bronze. 85.7 × 35.6 cm (33¾ × 14″). The Metropolitan Museum of Art, New York, New York. Purchase, 1962. Mr. and Mrs. John D. Rockfeller gift.

FIGURE 3.9 The layout of this temple was designed to create a solar calendar by which the summer and winter solstices and the spring and fall equinoxes could be fixed. Why was this important in an agricultural society?

Southeast Asia. Temple at Angkor Wat, Kampuchea (Cambodia). 1113–50.

CULTURAL PERSPECTIVES

Scholars have discovered that Neolithic people venerated a Goddess-Mother Creator whose body was the universe itself. Artifacts describing this goddess religion have been found in the Near East, the Mediterranean area, and in all parts of Europe. Tracing its origin back to Paleolithic times, the goddess religion taught that the goddess was the source of life, that humans were a part of nature, and that the goddess's power could be felt in nature. Many of the geometric forms on Neolithic pottery, once thought to be mere designs, are now believed to represent parts of the goddess's body and animals associated with her powers.

ART OF ASIA

The cultures of India, Indochina, China, and Japan have all produced exciting art forms. One way in which the art of these cultures is different from European art is that it is based on different philosophies and religious beliefs.

India

The art of India has been strongly influenced by the Hindu and Buddhist religions. Buddhism had a strong influence over the country from the third century B.C. to the sixth century A.D. After that time Hinduism became dominant. Hinduism combined several different beliefs and practices that developed over a long period of time. In Hinduism there are three primary processes in life and in the universe: creation, preservation, and destruction. The three main Hindu gods reflect this belief. They are Brahma, the Creator; Vishnu, the Preserver (Figure 3.8); and Shiva, the Destroyer. In Hinduism both humans and animals are believed to have souls. Reincarnation is a purification process in which the soul lives in many bodies in many lifetimes until it becomes one with Brahma, the great soul.

India exported its religions to the rest of Asia. In Cambodia many temples were built of stone in the Indian style. The temple at Angkor Wat (Figure 3.9) was originally a Hindu temple built between the years 1113 and 1150. Dedicated to Vishnu by its builder, it represents the Hindu view of the universe.

China

China adopted Buddhism during the Han dynasty, which lasted from 206 B.C. to A.D. 220. Buddhism and the other Chinese religions stressed the oneness of human beings with nature. Chinese artists found that long periods of meditation enabled them to perceive the beauty of an object or a scene. This made them better able to capture the beauty of the subject in their painting. (See Figure 3.10.) Many Chinese paintings were made on a scroll. The scroll is a long roll of parchment or silk. Some were hung on walls; others were meant to be unrolled a little at a time and read like a book.

FIGURE 3.10   Notice how small a space on the scroll is taken up by the people. The hut blends into the natural setting. The fine handwriting in the upper right corner is an important part of the composition. The busy lines of the writing balance the busy lines of the autumn leaves below.

Hua Yen. *Conversation in Autumn.* 1762. Ink and color on paper. 115.3 × 39.7 cm (45⅜ × 15⅝″). The Cleveland Museum of Art, Cleveland, Ohio. The John L. Severance Fund.

The Chinese also produced sculpture for religious purposes and to the honor the dead. During the Sung dynasty porcelain objects were made of fine-grained white clay called kaolin. Work in porcelain reached its highest point during the Ming dynasty. Today tombs full of clay sculptures are being discovered.

Exploring Aesthetics

Have students study *Discobolus* (*Discus Thrower*) in Figure 3.12. Point out the way the ribs and muscles are clearly defined. Have students consider the position of the figure, and ask whether this contributes to a feeling of movement. Next, ask students to compare the work with Figure 3.13 and ask which sculpture is more detailed. Point out that these details help make *Discus Thrower* seem more realistic. Have students proceed through the section, examining artworks in terms of attention to detail and its role in realism.

Exploring Aesthetics

Help students discuss the portrait sculpture shown in Figure 3.13 and compare it to the copy of a Greek sculpture shown in Figure 3.12. Ask: What do you see when you look at this Roman sculpture? Who is the subject of the work? How does this subject compare with the athlete shown in the Greek sculpture? What mood or message does the Roman portrait sculpture communicate to you? How is that mood or message different from the one communicated by the Greek sculpture?

Critical Thinking

Have students work with partners or in small groups to examine portrait sculptures of Roman emperors: For which emperors did portrait sculptures survive? What does each sculpture seem to say about that emperor? Have each group select one emperor depicted in sculpture, discuss what kind of ruler they expect him to have been, and then read about his life and reign.

FIGURE 3.11 The woodcut print has long been a work of art that even the poorest person could afford. The printmaker is able to make many inexpensive original works from the wooden printing plates. In this print the great pine tree of Karasaki is seen in a drenching rain. The artist, Hiroshige, was a great landscape print artist.

Andō Hiroshige. *Evening Rain on the Karasaki Pine* (from the series Eight Views of Omi Province). Nineteenth century. Woodblock print. 26 × 38.1 cm (10¼ × 15″). The Metropolitan Museum of Art, New York, New York. H. O. Havemeyer Collection. Bequest of Mrs. H. O. Havemeyer, 1929.

Japan

Japan also adopted Buddhism as its major religion. Until the end of the ninth century, Japanese artists copied the art styles of China and other Asian countries. Then Japanese artists began to develop a style uniquely their own. Many different subjects are shown in Japanese painting and printmaking. Some of the subjects are stories of war, everyday scenes, court life, and nature. The demands for artwork were great. To meet those demands, Japanese artists perfected a technique that had been invented in China—woodblock printing. Using this technique the artist could produce many inexpensive prints of one image (Figure 3.11).

ART OF GREECE AND ROME

Greece was the birthplace of Western civilization. The influence of ancient Greek culture can still be seen today. Almost every city in our country has at least one building with features that resemble the architecture of the classic Greek temple.

The Greeks built temples in honor of their gods. The most outstanding example is the Parthenon in Athens. Inside was a huge statue of the goddess Athena in ivory and gold.

The Greeks believed in a logical, harmonious world. They sought perfect proportions in buildings, sculpture, and music by following formulas. Their artists produced statues that represented the Greek ideal of a perfect body. According to one story, athletes used these statues, like the one shown in Figure 3.12, as models for building up their own muscle structure.

When they were new, Greek temples and statues were not the pure white they are today. The Greeks loved color, and they painted their buildings and sculpture various hues. Time has since worn the paint away.

Even though the Romans conquered Greece in 146 B.C., they did not conquer Greek culture. The Romans adopted Greek culture and changed it to suit their own needs. Greek sculptors, painters, architects, philosophers, and teachers had a great influence on the Roman Empire.

Earlier, the Romans had absorbed the culture of the Etruscans in Italy. Two outstanding Etruscan developments that the Romans adopted were a system of drainage and an improved use of the arch in the construction of buildings. What we call Roman art is a blend of the ideal Greek and the practical Etruscan arts.

The Romans added much to what they adopted. They used the arch and concrete to build large-scale structures, including huge vaulted and domed inner spaces. The Romans also developed beautiful interior decoration, excellent roads, and realistic rather than idealized portrait sculpture (Figure 3.13).

Before the fourth century, Christians were not allowed to practice their religion in public. After the Roman emperor Constantine legalized Christianity, the Christians were able to build their own churches. Their churches were based on Roman design, and the interiors were decorated with mosaics. These were pictures made by arranging small pieces of colored glass. The pieces of glass were set unevenly into the wall so that they glittered in the reflected light of church candles.

FIGURE 3.13   The Romans were not concerned with the Greek ideal of human perfection. They wanted accurate, realistic portraits that looked like the people they represented. Notice the wrinkles and loose skin of the man in this portrait.

Greco-Roman. *Man of the Republic.* c. 50 B.C. Terra cotta. 35.7 cm (14″) high, face 18 cm (7″) long. Courtesy of the Museum of Fine Arts, Boston, Massachusetts. Contribution, purchase of E. P. Warren.

FIGURE 3.12   Many of the original sculptures by the great Greek artists have been lost. This is a copy made by a Roman sculptor.

Myron. *Discobolus (Discus Thrower).* c. 450 B.C. Roman copy of a bronze original. Life-size. Italy. Palazzo Vecchio, Florence, Italy.

In the eastern part of the Roman Empire, a new style of art developed. This style thrived around the city of Constantinople (now Istanbul) and spread to towns such as Ravenna in Italy. Named after the city of Byzantium, **Byzantine** art used *very rich colors and figures that were flat and stiff* (Figure 3.14 on page 50). These artworks blended Greek, Roman, and Asian styles and usually had a religious theme.

 Analyzing Architecture

1. Applying Your Skills.   Find a building in your community that uses the style of one of the ancient cultures discussed on the previous pages. Write the location, the culture from which the style was adopted, the purpose of the building, and anything else you can learn about it.

GUIDED PRACTICE
(continued)

ACTIVITY   **Analyzing Architecture**

1. Applying Your Skills. As an alternative activity, have students work in small groups to prepare a class presentation about architectural styles.

2. Further Challenge. Students might also enjoy sketching the building in a completely different style. If they find that idea too complex, ask them to work in groups to brainstorm new designs for famous buildings.

3. Computer Option. If your students have access to computer art programs, suggest the following activity: Design arches, columns, and pediments, creating the façade of a building.

Discuss the types of columns (Doric, Ionic, and Corinthian). Using the Straight Line tool and the Brush or Pencil tool, design a column. Select the column and then use the Copy and Paste commands to repeat the column shape creating the front to a temple or great building. Add a pediment, arches, sculpture, or landscape to complete the façade. Vary line thickness. Save and Title.

INDEPENDENT PRACTICE

Enrichment

Have students design a group mural in the manner of Figure 3.14 on page 50. First they will need to decide on a subject. Have students study the stylistic features and use tempera on a sheet of white paper. Colors should typify those of the Byzantine palette. Students can use metallic pigments to imitate gold leaf and apply glitter to the background.

- Art of the Middle Ages in Europe
- Art of the Renaissance in Europe
- Art of Islam
- Art of Native Americans

GUIDED PRACTICE

Interdisciplinary: Music

Play a recording of canticles used in the Orthodox church for your students. Although relatively little is known about Byzantine music, many of the ancient hymns are known to have survived in altered form into the present, and even the modern versions can be helpful in creating an atmosphere in which to appreciate Byzantine art.

The Gothic Style

1. Applying Your Skills.
Two excellent references for information about Cathedrals in the Gothic style are *The Horizon Book of Great Cathedrals* published by the American Heritage Publishing Company and *Cathedral: The Story of Its Construction* by David Macaulay.

2. Further Challenge.
Display a chart on a bulletin board showing a diagram of a cross section of a Gothic cathedral. If students have trouble copying the picture, supply a small diagram and have them study the large poster and label all the parts. You might have them color each section with specific colors and use the same colors to write each label.

2. Further Challenge.   Make a sketch of the same building in your sketchbook. List the ancient culture and describe the features that match the style of the ancient culture.

ART OF THE MIDDLE AGES IN EUROPE

The Middle Ages began with the conquest of Rome in A.D. 476 by invaders from the north and lasted about one thousand years. This period of time was also called the *Age of Faith* because the Christian religion was such an important force. Monasteries, or buildings that housed persons under religious vows, grew in number, and the monks who lived in them created finely decorated religious manuscripts. Churches grew in size and political importance.

At the beginning of this period, new churches were built in western Europe. The style of architecture, named after the Roman style, was called **Romanesque** and *featured massive size; solid, heavy walls; wide use of the rounded Roman arch; and many sculptural decorations.*

In the twelfth century, more and more European people moved from the countryside into towns. Workers such as stone carvers and carpenters organized into craft guilds (unions), and apprentices learned their craft from the masters in these guilds. A wealthy new middle class, city pride, and religious faith led to the building of huge cathedrals. Two developments—the pointed arch and the flying buttress—brought about changes in architecture. This new style, called **Gothic**, *featured churches that soared upward*, like the cathedral shown in Figure 3.15. The Gothic cathedrals became the world's largest architectural structures since the Egyptian pyramids.

By using stained-glass windows, Gothic builders changed the light that entered the churches into rich, glowing color. Gothic sculpture and painting took on less stylized, more realistic qualities. Religious scenes were painted on church altarpieces with egg tempera paint and gold leaf.

FIGURE 3.14   This painting is a good example of the Byzantine blending of Western realism and Asian decorative patterns. The heads and graceful hands are shaded to give the illusion of roundness. The Oriental influence is seen in the flat bodies and the patterns of the gold lines.

Byzantine. *Madonna and Child on Curved Throne*. 1480. Tempera on wood. 81.5 × 49 cm (32¼ × 19⅜"). National Gallery of Art, Washington, D.C. Andrew W. Mellon Collection.

The Gothic Style

1. Applying Your Skills.   Find a book in the library about cathedrals built in the Gothic style. List the names of three of the cathedrals in your sketchbook and tell where and when they were built.

2. Further Challenge.   Draw a diagram in your sketchbook of the cross section of a Gothic cathedral. Identify and label the pointed arch and the flying buttresses.

FIGURE 3.15 Notice the use of pointed arches, stained-glass windows, and realistic sculptures in this Gothic cathedral.

Reims Cathedral. Reims, France. 1225–99.

ART OF THE RENAISSANCE IN EUROPE

By the beginning of the fifteenth century, the Middle Ages were waning. The invention of the printing press and the European exploration of the Americas and the Pacific were two factors that indicated the beginning of a new era. As you would expect, the art of Europe also went through many changes.

Renaissance (**ren**-uh-sahns) is a French word that means "rebirth." In Italy the fifteenth century brought new interest, a rebirth, in the philosophy and art of ancient Greece and Rome. The **Renaissance** is *the name given to the period of awakening at the end of the Middle Ages.*

The Renaissance in Italy, and later in northern Europe, was much more than a rebirth of ancient ways. It was a complete change in human awareness. People became more aware of the world around them and realized that each person had an important part to play in it. Kings and church leaders had to make way at the top of the power structure for bankers and merchants.

During the Middle Ages artists had worked not for themselves but for the Church. They had been members of the working class. During the Renaissance, however, great artists such as Leonardo da Vinci (**vin**-chee), Michelangelo (my-kel-**an**-jay-loh), and Raphael (**rah**-fah-yell) mingled socially with nobles and kings.

In both painting and sculpture the solid, realistic appearance of people and objects became very important (Figure 3.16 on page 52). To show people and objects accurately, Italian artists studied the classical art of Greece and Rome as well as the natural world around them. Leonardo studied many subjects in depth. He left more than 120 notebooks filled with observation drawings and notes on subjects that range from human anatomy to plans for machines.

An architect named Filippo Brunelleschi (fee-**leep**-poh brew-nell-**less**-key) developed a technique called **linear perspective,** *a graphic system that creates the illusion of depth and volume on a flat surface.* Perspective provided a set of rules that

MORE ABOUT . . . MODERN DRAWING

Modern drawing techniques have their roots in the Italian Renaissance. The media of choice during that period included silverpoint (the forerunner of the lead pencil), pen, charcoal, and chalk. The common pencil is still the most often used medium for drawing. Drawing pencils come in seventeen degrees of hardness; they are made of graphite, carbon, or charcoal. Colored pencils are also widely used. Wax crayons are another popular choice for students and amateur artists. They come in a wide variety of colors and sizes, and can be used the way paints are used.

GUIDED PRACTICE
(continued)

Understanding Art History

Inform students that because early Islamic artists could not depict the figures of humans or animals, they developed a style of flat, abstract designs to be used in a variety of works. The most familiar form is arabesque, which comes from the Italian word meaning "Arab-like." These swirling, interlaced designs are apparently based on plant shapes, but the forms of leaves, branches, and vines have been transformed into scrolls, spirals, and curves. Such arabesque designs were first used during the 900s in all Muslim countries. Arabesques and other geometric designs have been used to decorate the walls of buildings, tiles, rugs, metalware, and other craft objects.

Developing Perceptual Skills

As students study Figure 3.18, tell them that the artists of many cultures were less interested in exploring the psychological aspect of the subject and more interested in their symbolic, historical, or spiritual meanings. Ask them to find other artworks in the textbook that make use of stylized facial expressions instead of faces that describe the feelings of that person.

Developing Vocabulary

Have students examine the prefix in the word *pre-Columbian*. Ask volunteers to explain the meaning of *pre-* and suggest a few other words in which the prefix is used. Ask: Based on your understanding of the use of the prefix and the definition in the dictionary, how would you define the word *pre-Columbian*?

FIGURE 3.16 Notice how realistically Michelangelo carved the features of this head of the Virgin Mary. You will find the full sculpture in Figure 11.37, page 309.

Michelangelo. *Pietà.* (Detail) c. 1500. Marble. 174 cm (5′ 8½″) high; base 195 cm (6′4⅝″) high. Vatican, St. Peter's Basilica, Rome, Italy.

enabled artists to show figures and objects in space. The rules of perspective made the placement of objects, and the depiction of their mass, measurable and exact. This gave an exciting illusion of reality to works of art.

The changes in painting seen in Renaissance Italy came later to northern European countries such as Flanders and Germany. Northern artists like Jan van Eyck (yahn van ike) concentrated mainly on symbols and the surface details of objects (Figure 7.42, page 187). The invention of oil painting (usually credited to van Eyck) allowed artists to work on fine details while the paint was still wet. Later, northern artists combined this attention to detail with an emotional style.

ART OF ISLAM

One thousand years earlier in the Middle East, an event took place that had a major effect on both the religious beliefs and the art of the area. Muhammad was born in Mecca in A.D. 570. He grew up and became an Arab merchant, and he believed that he received personal revelations that challenged him to change the current religion of the Arabs who worshiped many idols. He taught

that there was only one god, Allah, and his followers were called Muslims. Muhammad became their prophet, and after his death his teachings were assembled into the Koran, the holy scripture; and Islam was the name given to the religious faith of the Muslims.

Islamic art, the art of the Muslim world, is decorative. The interior of a mosque, a Muslim place of worship, was decorated with ornate calligraphy (beautiful writing), geometric patterns, and stylized plants and flowers. Art depicting people or animals was not permitted in mosques.

Book illustrators, however, were not limited by the same restrictions. They depicted people and animals in everyday scenes such as banquets, hunting scenes, and incidents inspired by popular romantic stories. They filled their illustrations with beautiful, decorative patterns. The illustration shown in Figure 3.17 was completed in 1525, just

FIGURE 3.17 This is a scene from a book about court life in Iran.

Nizami. *Khamseh: Bahram Gur and the Chinese Princess in the Sandalwood Pavilion on Thursday.* 1524–25. Colors and gilt on paper. 32.4 × 22.2 cm (12¾ × 8¾″). The Metropolitan Museum of Art, New York, New York. Gift of Alexander Smith Cochran, 1913.

TEACHER TALK

Planning Coursework If you take time before the first day of each term to prepare a thorough syllabus, you might save yourself misunderstanding later on, as well as provide your students with timely information. Indicate the minimum requirements for a passing grade and extra-credit projects. Be specific about due dates and your, or the school's, policy regarding late work. When you assign a project that will have a significant bearing on students' progress, a well-written assignment sheet given to each student will underscore your seriousness about the project. Students who find it difficult to keep up with class work may be more successful if allowed to finish work at home.

twenty-five years after Michelangelo created *Pietà*, shown on page 309. Only eight years earlier, Christopher Columbus left on a trip that was to culminate in an unexpected discovery.

ART OF NATIVE AMERICANS

The people of North, Central, and South America had well-organized civilizations by the time the Europeans arrived on these continents in 1492. Any culture before the Europeans arrived is considered pre-Columbian, or prior to Columbus. There were over twenty million people living in two thousand different groups. Each group had its own unique language, traditions, rituals, and art forms. Some groups remained hunters, some became farmers, and some built and lived in complex

FIGURE 3.19   This mask was woven with corn husks. What does that tell you about the people who used the mask?

Iroquois. *Corn Husk Mask.* Ontario, Canada, Grand River Reservation. c. 1900. Woven corn husks. 31 cm (12″). Milwaukee Public Museum, Milwaukee, Wisconsin.

cities. The arts were an integral part of their sacred rituals and daily living.

The statue in Figure 3.18 comes from pre-Columbian Mexico and represented a participant in an elaborate ritual that was carried out in the manner of a ball game.

The corn-husk mask shown in Figure 3.19 was worn by the Iroquois of North America during ceremonies in which bountiful crops were predicted in the year to come. The men's leggings shown in Figure 6.5 (page 121) and Figure 6.6 (page 121) also come from North America. The glass beads used to decorate the leggings tell us that they were made after the arrival of the Europeans.

FIGURE 3.18   This figure represents a participant in a game that served as a religious ceremony. The player had to bounce a ball off the band that encircled his waist and into a hoop on a wall. The winners received many gifts from the audience, while the losers were sacrificed to the gods.

Gulf Coast, Mexico. *Figurine (Ballplayer).* Late Classic period, c. A.D. 900. Hollow, mold-made ceramic. Height 17 cm (6¾″). Width, 7.6 cm (3″). Albany Museum of Art, Albany, Georgia.

ART OF EUROPE IN THE SEVENTEENTH THROUGH THE NINETEENTH CENTURY

The European world was growing through exploration and scientific discoveries. Both the telescope and the microscope were changing the way people saw the universe. The new worldview was reflected in the arts.

AT THE MUSEUM

Dallas Museum of Art (Dallas, Texas)   At the Dallas Museum of Art, visit the Museum of the Americas, the world's first museum to showcase art from all the cultures in the Western Hemisphere, from Canada to South America. The Museum of the Americas spans over 3000 years and includes over 2000 works of art. Special wall labels show maps, city plans, and diary entries from certain time periods. These provide information about the art and the cultures that created it. Through art, the Museum of the Americas tells the story of civilizations now living in the Western Hemisphere. The Dallas Museum of Art also houses collections of European, African, Asian, and contemporary art.

The Seventeenth Century

By the beginning of the seventeenth century, artists were creating dramatic, theatrical works that seemed to burst with energy and strong emotions. The art style that developed was called **Baroque** and *emphasized movement, strong value contrast, and variety.*

The forms and figures in Baroque art turn, twist, and spiral into space. Baroque artists refined perspective to the point where they could make figures seem to move off the canvas toward the viewer. They opened up space in the distance toward infinity. In addition to all this movement, they added dramatic lighting effects using dark, mysterious shadows and brightly lit areas. (Figure 3.20).

The Eighteenth Century

In the eighteenth century, Baroque art evolved into a more relaxed style called **Rococo**, which *stressed free graceful movement, a playful use of line,*

FIGURE 3.20 Judith Leyster was a Dutch woman who dared to break rules. Women artists of her time were expected to paint delicate still lifes, but Leyster chose to do portraits and subjects from everyday life.

Judith Leyster. *Self-Portrait.* c. 1635. Oil on canvas. 72.3 × 65.3 (29⅜ × 25⅝"). National Gallery of Art, Washington, D.C. Gift of Mr. and Mrs. Robert Woods Bliss.

and delicate colors. Rococo art was used to decorate the homes of the French aristocracy, and their luxurious and carefree life was often depicted in the paintings.

The Nineteenth Century

The industrial and democratic revolutions of the late eighteenth century brought about a new, faster way of life. Change was the only thing that was certain. New styles of art developed quickly as a rebellion against the styles of earlier artists.

Neoclassicism. The French Revolution abandoned the Rococo style because it mirrored the life of the aristocracy. Academies, which replaced the old apprentice system, taught a new style of art that better suited the new society. This style was based on the look of Greek and Roman art and was called *Neoclassic* ("new classic"). The Neoclassic style was severely realistic and unemotional. An outstanding artist of this style was Jacques Louis David (zjahk loo-**ee** dah-**veed**). See *Death of Socrates* by David (Figure 5.40, page 115).

Romanticism. *Romanticism* was a reaction to the unemotional Neoclassic style. The Romantic artists disliked the many rules and lack of emotion in the Neoclassic style of art. Romanticists such as Rosa Bonheur painted emotional scenes of action with brilliant colors. (See *The Horse Fair*, Figure 9.4, page 224.) The Romanticists believed that the artist's personal impression of an event was more interesting than an accurate, historical report.

Realism. Another group of artists felt that they should portray political, social, and moral issues. They rejected the rules of Neoclassicism and the

FIGURE 3.21 Eakins was so concerned with learning to draw realistically that he left the Pennsylvania Academy of Fine Arts, where students drew from plaster casts, and attended classes at a medical school to learn anatomy.

Thomas Eakins. *Baseball Players Practicing.* 1875. Watercolor. 27.6 × 32.7 cm (10⅞ × 12⅞"). Museum of Art, Rhode Island School of Design, Providence, Rhode Island. Jesse Metcalf and Walter H. Kimball Funds.

drama of Romanticism. They believed that peasants and factory workers shown in a realistic style were suitable subjects for artistic study. This style, called **Realism**, *presented familiar scenes as they actually were.* In Spain, the art of Francisco Goya (fran-**seese**-koh **goh**-yah) took a realistic turn as he recorded the ugly truth of war during the Spanish Revolution. American artists such as Thomas Eakins also painted everyday subjects realistically (Figure 3.21).

Impressionism. The Realists had taken a hard look at the real world. Another group of artists also were interested in the world outside the studio and, in fact, did much of their painting outdoors. Scientific discoveries about light and color led this group to emphasize the effects of sunlight on objects. They concentrated on reflected light rather than on the form of objects. These artists broke up solid forms and blurred edges by applying paint to the canvas in small dabs of pure color. The dabs were blended together in the eye of the viewer. The style, **Impressionism**, *captured everyday subjects and emphasized the momentary effects of sunlight.* If you stand too close to an Impressionist's painting, all you will see are colorful dabs and dots. You have to step back to allow your vision to blend the colors. In Figure 3.22 on page 56 the camera has done the blending for you.

Post-Impressionism. Gradually some artists who had started as Impressionists became dissatisfied. They wanted to produce something more meaningful. Some wanted to express feelings, intuitions, and ideas. Others wanted to show more structure and form in their work, like that shown in the house depicted in Figure 3.23 on page 56. The most outstanding of these *Post-Impressionists* were Paul Cézanne (say-**zahn**), Vincent van Gogh (goh), and Paul Gauguin (goh-**gan**). Each expanded his style to create something so unusual that the styles themselves led to important developments in the art of the twentieth century.

 Analyzing a Style

1. Applying Your Skills. Choose one of the styles of the nineteenth century. Find a picture of an artwork in that style in another chapter of this book. Tell the class why you think your example represents that style.

2. Further Challenge. Find a book about Impressionism in the library. List at least four Impressionist works of art, each one painted by a different artist. Select one of the four works. Use the four steps of art history to write about the work.

 Analyzing a Style

GUIDED PRACTICE
(continued)

1. Applying Your Skills.
If desired, have students work on this activity in small groups and have them find an example of each nineteenth-century style.

2. Further Challenge.
Students do not have to be limited to Impressionism for this activity, especially if resource material is scarce. Some titles to consider as research sources are as follows: *The Academy and French Painting in the Nineteenth Century* by Albert Boime; *Modern Art: Impressionism to Post-Modernism* by David Britt; *Romanticism* by Hugh Honour; and *The French Impressionists and Their Century* by Diane Kelder.

3. Computer Option.
If your students have access to computer art programs, suggest the following: Explore the use of light and colors that fascinated the Impressionists. Draw simple objects or shapes on the screen with the drawing tools of your choice. Add a variety of complex colors and patterns. Experiment with the Fatbits or Zoom-in/Zoom-out tool. Select an area. Observe the changes as you Zoom-in several times to get maximum magnification. You will be looking at the individual pixels. Step back from the computer and look at the screen from a distance. How is the screen similar to an Impressionist's painting? Alter the colors of several pixels. Zoom-out. Can you detect the changes? Use a magnifying glass to look at color comic strips or observe the dot matrix or an ink jet printer as it is printing in color.

TEACHER TALK

Classroom Management   A way to help students become more familiar with artists is to set aside one small bulletin board as an "Artist of the Week" board. At first, you can provide the display. Later, responsibility for the bulletin board might be assigned to one student or a team of students. There are several ways to plan displays. You might decide which artists you want to feature and assign the artist as you assign the group. Or you might have a list of artists you wish to include during the year, and allow each student or group to select one from your list. A third method might be to allow each student or group to freely choose an artist with your approval.

GUIDED PRACTICE
(continued)

Understanding Art History

Remind students that Impressionist painters favored casual, everyday themes for their subjects. Ask students to identify any time in art history when such subjects were not favored.

Developing Studio Skills

Ask students to bring to class a photo of themselves or of people they like. If they were asked to paint the same subject matter in the style of the Impressionists, how would they plan the assignment? (Later, in Chapter 10, they will be asked to do this in a Studio Lesson.) Ask them to first write a description of their intended portrait in their sketchbooks. Next, have them make a sketch of the design.

Understanding Art History

To help students further appreciate the life and times of Claude Monet, whose work is shown in Figure 3.22, assign *Artist's Profile 23* in the TCR.

Understanding Art History

To help students further appreciate the life and times of Paul Cézanne, whose work is shown in Figure 3.23, assign *Artist's Profile 22* in the TCR.

FIGURE 3.22   In this work, Monet dissolves all edges and lines in variations of color. The buildings and the water seem to melt together into dabs and dots of flickering violet and blue.

Claude Monet. *Palazzo da Mula, Venice.* 1908. Oil on canvas. 62 × 81.1 cm (24½ × 31⅞"). National Gallery of Art, Washington, D.C. Chester Dale Collection.

FIGURE 3.23   Cézanne was concerned with the structure of objects. He used small brushstrokes like little building blocks to make forms look like geometric solids. Notice how the foliage looks as solid as the rocks.

Paul Cézanne. *Le Chateau Noir.* 1900–04. Oil on canvas. 73.7 × 96.6 cm (29 × 38"). National Gallery of Art, Washington, D.C. Gift of Eugene and Agnes E. Meyer.

MEETING SPECIAL NEEDS

Building Self-Esteem   Academically gifted students often pursue library research with minimal guidance. Encourage self-motivated students to type reports into a computer and generate an art newsletter. Students particularly interested in art may like to form an art club or attend art activities. Creating artworks is just one manifestation of giftedness in art. Other ways are to write about art or to help others to appreciate it. Since some gifted students feel like outsiders, involve them in the teaching process. For example, an older student might give a report to younger students.

ART OF AFRICA

The huge continent of Africa has a population of millions that is subdivided into about one thousand culture groups. The arts are as varied as the peoples. Africa has hundreds of ancient Neolithic rock painting sights. The paintings and rock engravings are more recent than those found in Europe, but they have the same subject matter. They depict humans, animals, and nonobjective symbolic designs.

Most of the African art you see in museums today has been made within the last century. Older wooden or fabric pieces have been destroyed by the damp climate and by insects such as the wood-eating white ant. As early as the sixteenth century, however, artists of the Benin kingdom produced metal sculptures that displayed an outstanding command of metal-casting techniques (Figure 6.45, page 146).

The arts of Africa were, and still are, interwoven into the religious and everyday lives of the many nations, kingdoms, and culture groups on that continent. Africans do not see art as a separate activity unrelated to their everyday lives. Everything, from the paintings that women apply to the mud walls of their homes (Figure 7.30, page 172) to the ancestral figure made by the Bamum peoples of Cameroon (Figure 3.24), serves a practical function. Ceremonial canes, combs for the hair, stools, chairs, pipes, and spoons are carved with the same care and craftsmanship as an ancestral mask.

Weaving is widespread. Traditionally women weave everyday fabrics, while the ceremonial weavings such as Kente cloth was reserved for men alone (Figure 9.11 page 228, and Figure 9.29 on page 242).

Sculpture is regarded as one of Africa's greatest contributions to the world's cultural heritage. It inspired the development of Cubism in Europe at the beginning of the twentieth century. African wood carvings include figures and masks. The figures are ancestral figures, power figures, and funeral figures. They all have proportions that reflect cultural concepts rather than realism and an enlarged head to indicate its importance as the center of reason and wisdom. See the wood carving shown in Figure 3.25 on page 58.

FIGURE 3.24   As trade with Europeans increased, African artists incorporated new materials into traditional art. The imported glass beads used to decorate the surface of this royal figure denote wealth and power.

Bamum peoples, Fumban, Grassfields region, Cameroon. *Male Figure*. 1908 or earlier. Wood, brass, glass beads, cowrie shells. Height, 160 cm (63″). National Museum of African Art, Smithsonian Institution, Washington, D.C. Gift of Evelyn A. J. Hall and John Friede.

AT THE MUSEUM

The Baltimore Museum of Art (Baltimore, Maryland)   Watch African masks being danced with and listen to stories of their origin and meaning on an interactive touchscreen video created by the Baltimore Museum of Art. This twelve-minute video highlights four masks in the museum's permanent collection. To add depth to viewers' understanding, the video uses sound and visuals to show the importance of dancing with masks in the African culture. The video's quick-access feature is enjoyed by visitors who want to learn more about a certain mask and by docents to emphasize an important feature in the video for their tour group.

FIGURE 3.25 This sculpture represents a magician who can travel between the spirit world and the real world. Notice how his posture, with his shoulders back and his chest thrust forward, captures the dignity and pride of a man who speaks with spirits.

Africa, Ivory Coast, Senufo Tribe. *Equestrian Figure.* Nineteenth to twentieth centuries. Wood, patination. 32.5 × 7.3 × 22.3 cm (12¾ × 3 × 8¾"). Dallas Museum of Art, Dallas, Texas. Gustav and Franyo Schindler Collection. Gift of the McDermott Foundation in honor of Eugene McDermott.

THE BEGINNING OF THE TWENTIETH CENTURY

During the first half of the twentieth century, the range of art styles grew, and the speed at which changes occurred increased. The influence of rules and the Academy were dead. Artists were free to experiment and explore. It became impossible to separate artists into neat categories. Increased travel and new ways of communication helped artists compare ideas. One individual or group could influence another. Some artists who lived a long life, such as Matisse and Picasso, changed their own styles several times.

European Art

In general, art in Europe moved in three major directions. One direction was primarily concerned with expressing emotions. Another emphasized structure, or composition. Still another stressed imagination and dreamlike inventions. Artists experimented with subject matter as well as with composition and style.

At the beginning of the twentieth century, a group of young French painters expressed emotion by creating works that exploded with brilliant colors, bold distortions, and loose brushstrokes. They were called *Fauves*, which is French for "wild beasts." The Fauves continued the expressive ideas of Vincent van Gogh and Paul Gauguin. The leader of this group, Henri Matisse (ahn-**ree** mah-**tees**), was concerned with expressing the feeling he had for life. He insisted that his work had but one purpose: to give pleasure.

A different sort of feeling characterized the work of the German artists. A movement began that was called **Expressionism,** in which *artists tried to*

FIGURE 3.26 Kollwitz devoted her art to describing the plight of the poor and denouncing the atrocities of war. She was concerned with the human condition and believed she could best express this concern through printmaking.

Käthe Kollwitz. *Self-Portrait.* 1921. Etching. 21.6 × 26.7 cm (8½ × 10½"). National Museum of Women in the Arts, Washington, D.C. Museum Purchase: The Member's Acquisition Fund.

MORE ABOUT . . . GERMAN EXPRESSIONISM

The term German Expressionism refers to several art movements that formed in the early modern period. Ernst Ludwig Kirchner was one of the founding members of Die Brucke ("The Bridge") in 1905, which was opposed to most movements of the day. Kirchner created the Brucke Manifesto, a philosophical statement printed by hand from a carved wood block. The manifesto holds that the young and new should replace the old and established, and that art should be first and foremost about life. Other Expressionist groups formed soon after, each with different theories about the goals of modern art.

FIGURE 3.27 Picasso has changed the traditional view of the human form using a style known as Analytical Cubism. We see hints of geometric shapes with transparent openings through which colors melt and flow. Can you see how the atomic theory of matter in motion has influenced this stage of Picasso's work?

Pablo Picasso. *Nude Woman.* 1910. Oil on canvas. 187.3 × 61 cm (73¾ × 24″). National Gallery of Art, Washington, D.C. Ailsa Mellon Bruce Fund.

communicate their strong emotional feelings and which stressed personal feelings rather than composition. The German Expressionists experienced the terrible economic and social conditions in Germany before and after World War I. Their emotional subjects ranged from fear and anger to concern with death. Käthe Kollwitz (**kah**-teh **kohl**-vits) (Figure 3.26) was one Expressionist who was concerned with poverty and war. She produced many moving images of mothers grieving for dead children. Her work was based on personal experience: She lost her eldest son during World War I.

Another group of artists created work that went in a different direction. **Cubism** is *a style that emphasizes structure and design.* Three different things influenced the Cubists. The first was an idea: All shapes in nature are based on geometric solids. The second was a scientific discovery: All matter is made up of atoms that are constantly in motion. The third was art from another culture: the structure of African sculpture that had recently been brought to Paris. The Cubists tried to paint three-dimensional objects as if they could be seen from many different points of view at the same time. The painting in Figure 3.27 is an early Cubist work.

A group of Italian artists, the *Futurists,* took Cubism a step farther. They placed lines and shapes in a composition to suggest motion. Their paintings and sculpture seem to come to life. (See Figure 9.24 on page 236.)

In Holland, an artist named Piet Mondrian created nonobjective art using only vertical and horizontal black lines; black, white, and gray rectangles; and the three primary colors. His style was the exact opposite of Expressionism. (See Figure 7.35, page 176.)

A third group of artists introduced fantasy into their subject matter. Fantasy has always been a part of art. It can be traced back to Greek mythology and to the monsters and gargoyles of the Middle Ages. After World War I, the *Dadaists* used fantasy to take aim at the culture they thought had failed them. Their works featured strange objects such as fur-lined teacups.

Another movement offered a slightly saner version of the Dada philosophy. **Surrealism** was *a style in which dreams, fantasy, and the subconscious served as inspiration for artists.* Surrealists presented very realistic, almost photographic images but

MORE ABOUT . . . CUBISM

Cubism is the first truly twentieth-century artistic style. Heralded by Picasso's 1907 work *Demoiselles d'Avignon,* Cubism involved entirely new approaches to the treatment of pictorial space and to the representation of emotions and states of mind. Cubists broke away from the two major features of Western art since the Renaissance: the classical model of rendering the human figure, and the spatial illusionism of one-point perspective. The result was not only the reduction of body parts to geometrical forms and the loss of a normal scale of human proportion, but also a means of suggesting three-dimensional relationships that did not hinge on the convention of illusionistic, one-point perspective.

GUIDED PRACTICE
(continued)

Critical Thinking

While discussing the artists of specific periods, ask students to suggest why artists working in the same time period under similar conditions might develop radically different artistic goals. Ask students if they think this phenomenon is the result of personal preference or whether there are other factors to consider. What are those other factors?

Developing Studio Skills

Have students create a variety of geometric forms such as a cube, a cone, or a cylinder, using stiff white paper and transparent tape. Have students work in groups and agree on a still-life arrangement of these objects. Then, working individually, have students make drawings of the arrangement as seen simultaneously from various perspectives.

Exploring Aesthetics

Divide the class into two groups and ask them to debate this statement: Cubism is a successful intellectual approach to art, rather than an emotional approach.

Exploring Aesthetics

Explain to students that the modern notion that art should be original began with the Dadaists and the Surrealists. Then divide the students into debating teams. One side should defend the proposition that originality in art is important. The other side must provide counter-arguments that great art can be produced without necessarily being entirely new or a unique act of self-expression. Encourage students to refer to specific works that have been discussed in class to support their conclusions.

Using Art Criticism

Have students imagine they are art critics assigned to write a review of Dali's painting in Figure 3.28. Ask them to begin writing notes that would eventually become their published review. Remind them to incorporate information from the four steps of art criticism.

Developing Studio Skills

Remind students that the Armory Show of 1913 played a significant part in the introduction of European art to Americans. Tell students that the class will produce a similar show for other teachers, parents, and interested students. To begin, have students create a piece of art or select samples of original works with which they are pleased. Have them arrange the works in a way that showcases their creative efforts. On a given date, allow visitors to attend the show and have students take turns acting as docents. Tell students that they should be prepared to answer any questions that viewers might ask about their artworks or their training.

Critical Thinking

When discussing Regionalist art, ask students to share their travel experiences. Ask: What subject matter did they choose to photograph while on vacation? Why? If they were painters, would they want to paint the same subjects they photographed? If so, what choices about media and processes would they make in order to paint the subject in the style of the Regionalists? If they chose not to paint the same subjects, why not?

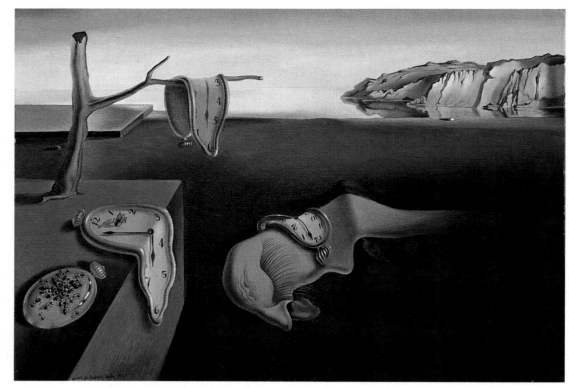

FIGURE 3.28 Dali has created a strange world in which metal objects that should be firm seem to melt. Realistic details, such as the ants, add to the nightmare quality of the scene. Can you recognize the object lying on the ground in the center of the picture?

Salvador Dali. *The Persistence of Memory.* 1931. Oil on canvas. 24.1 × 33 cm (9½ × 13″). Collection, The Museum of Modern Art, New York, New York. Given anonymously.

combined objects that didn't belong together. Figure 3.28 is an example. The work of the Surrealists is strange and dreamlike. Some paintings are like nightmares, some are funny, and some are mysterious and frightening. No Surrealist work is supposed to make sense to the viewer, however.

North American Art

At the beginning of the twentieth century, a group of young artists in the United States turned to the harsh realities of the city for subject matter. They called themselves The Eight and organized an exhibition in 1908. Their original name was forgotten when they were quickly labeled the Ashcan School by critics who were shocked by the subject matter of their work: stark tenement buildings, crowded city streets, and poor working people.

An even greater impact on the American art world was made when the Armory Show of 1913 was held. This show introduced Americans to the new art being created in Europe. Most of the American public was confused by what they saw, but many artists were challenged by the daring exhibition and took their first steps toward making modern art in America.

However, there was one group of artists with whom Americans felt comfortable. The **Regionalists** were *artists who painted the farmlands and cities of America realistically,* as in Figure 3.29. Each artist had a slightly different style, but their messages were more upbeat than the messages of the Ashcan

---

COOPERATIVE LEARNING

In groups of four or five, have students discuss clues that they see in an artwork selected from previous chapters that tell them, if possible, the period in history that the work depicts. Have them pretend that they do not have the credit line information. Encourage them to look at hairstyles and clothing of the figures. Look at their surroundings, furniture, roads, tools, and so on. Look at their gestures. What are they doing? After they finish their investigation and discussion, have them choose two speakers from the group who will give a verbal report of their findings to the class.

LOOKING CLOSELY

FIGURE 3.29 Benton painted his American scenes larger than life. His subject was a nation filled with restless people, surging industrial forces, and landscapes full of a barely controllable power. This mural was a combination of biographical and historical information blended with artistic invention. Can you identify the musical instruments depicted in this mural? How many sources of country music can you find? What other clues can you find that reveal the time and place portrayed in this mural? How did Benton achieve the vitality conveyed by the work?

Thomas Hart Benton. *The Sources of Country Music.* 1975. Acrylic on canvas. 1.8 x 3 m (6 x 10'). The Country Music Hall of Fame and Museum, Nashville, Tennessee. © T. H. Benton and R.P. Benton Testamentary Trusts/VAGA, New York 1994.

School. They focused on the vast expanse, beauty, productivity, and abundance of America. The people in their paintings were shown as happy and hardworking.

Most sculptors at this time worked with traditional materials using traditional methods. A few then began experimenting with the new materials of the twentieth century. The most exciting step was taken by Alexander Calder (Figure 9.26, page 237), who made sculpture move by arranging wire and sheet metal into a balanced arrangement that stayed in motion. He called these moving sculptures *mobiles* (**moh**-beels).

The twentieth century also saw big changes in architecture. New materials and new demands led to the development of skyscrapers. Functional structures with steel frames that emphasized simplicity of form replaced heavy, decorated structures. Frank Lloyd Wright believed that form should follow function, and he designed buildings that were in harmony with the environment (Figure 3.30 on page 62).

MORE ABOUT . . . THOMAS HART BENTON

Thomas Hart Benton (1889–1975) was born in Neosho, Missouri, and based his most popular paintings on familiar Midwestern life. Benton briefly studied with avant-garde artists in Paris, but he abandoned modernism around 1920 and began creating pictures that satirized city life and glorified rural life in the Midwest and the South. Benton was a member of the Regionalist painters' movement and became its spokesperson, speaking out against urban industrial civilization and what he called the sickly nature of modernist art. He continued to defend Regionalism and became one of its only remaining advocates in the 1940s, when abstract painting gained prominence.

GUIDED PRACTICE
(continued)

Exploring Aesthetics

Tell students that Thomas Benton studied traditional painting techniques and usually worked in egg tempera, which he finished in glazes that brought out the depth of his colors. Using the four steps of art criticism, have students evaluate Benton's painting in Figure 3.29.

Interdisciplinary: Language Arts

American literature, like American art, can boast of writers who captured the charm and uniqueness of specific areas of the country. These Regionalists focused on the activities, dialect, appearance, and customs of the characters they created, as well as the environment in which they lived. To appreciate the literary contribution of American Regionalists, encourage students to research more about writers such as Sarah Orne Jewett, Samuel Clemens, Bret Harte, Kate Chopin, and Hamlin Garland.

LOOKING CLOSELY

Have students study Figure 3.29 and answer the questions in the caption. The instruments depicted are as follows: two violins being held and played as fiddles, a guitar, human voices, and a dulcimer. The sources of music are a choir, folk singers, a cowboy playing his guitar, a man playing a banjo, fiddlers playing music for the dancers, the train and the showboat bringing traveling musicians, and in the distance, a church which represents religious music.

GUIDED PRACTICE
(continued)

Understanding Art History

Ask students to work in small groups and research other buildings designed by Frank Lloyd Wright. Have each group present its findings along with pictures of the buildings studied.

Understanding Art History

To help students further appreciate the life and times of Frank Lloyd Wright, whose work is shown in Figure 3.30, assign *Artist's Profile 32* in the TCR.

Using Art Criticism

Divide the class into small groups and have them apply the steps of art criticism to the building shown in Figure 3.30. Have a volunteer from each group share the findings as a lead-in to a discussion about the aesthetics of architecture.

Cooperative Learning

Remind students that the murals of Orozco and other Mexican muralists are part of a long tradition of narrative art. Divide the class into small groups and instruct each group to decide on a particular story or event they wish to narrate visually, using newsprint, pencils, and pastels. When groups have completed their projects, have them use spray fixative to keep the work looking fresh. Display the works and ask students to try to identify the story without being informed about its theme. Ask students to discuss the criteria for judging narrative art. Ask: Should the criteria be any different from that used for other kinds of art? If so, in what way(s) should it be different?

FIGURE 3.30   Frank Lloyd Wright designed this house to be functional as well as to blend in with the environment.

Frank Lloyd Wright. *The David Wright House.* Scottsdale, Arizona. 1951.

The strong emotions of the time were also revealed in the art of a group of Mexican artists. As the twentieth century started, Mexico was deeply troubled. The tension erupted into the Mexican Revolution. Some Mexican artists developed a style with which to express their feelings about the plight of the people. They were referred to as the *Mexican Muralists*, because they covered walls and ceilings with their murals about Mexican history, the suffering of the peasants, and the immoral behavior of the ruling class (Figure 3.31). They combined the solid forms of ancient Mexican art with the powerful colors of European Expressionism. The work of José Clemente Orozco shown in Figure 3.31 is an example of the vigorous style and social-protest subject matter protrayed by the Mexican Muralists.

FIGURE 3.31   Orozco captures the raw emotion of the Mexican peasants fighting to hold their position. Notice how the artist has exaggerated the muscles to show how the men are tensed for combat.

José Clemente Orozco. *Barricade.* 1931. Oil on canvas. 140 × 114.3 cm (55 × 45″). The Museum of Modern Art, New York, New York. Given anonymously.

MEETING SPECIAL NEEDS

Physically Disabled   When taking students with disabilities to a museum, be sure to tell the museum educational director of your students' special needs. Extra chaperons can help make the event go more smoothly. Urge docents to include ways for the students to interact verbally and kinesthetically with the art, either through treasure hunts or by acting out scenes in paintings. Postcards or slides depicting some of the museum's works are useful for orientation or follow-up lessons. Encourage your docent to come to the school, for discussion before or after the students' visit.

Analyzing a Style

1. Applying Your Skills. Choose one of the styles from the beginning of the twentieth century. Find a picture of an artwork in that style in another chapter of this book. Tell the class why you think your example represents that style.

2. Further Challenge. Go to the library and find a book about one of the artists who worked during the first half of the twentieth century. Select one work of art in that book and use the four steps of art history to write about it.

FROM THE FIFTIES TO THE FUTURE

After World War II the European art world was disorganized. Paris was no longer the center of creativity. Many artists who had fled Hitler's Germany settled in New York City. They began teaching there, and by the 1950s they and their students established a new center for the arts.

What happened next took place with breathtaking speed. During the last fifty years there have been more changes in artistic style and technique than there have been since prehistoric times. To begin with, a variety of art forms once considered minor art found a place as equals to painting and sculpture, and their creators are exploring new frontiers. These arts include printmaking, weaving, ceramics, and jewelry.

There are also more artists working today than ever before, all over the world. With new developments in travel and communication, no place is far from the mainstream of art. Artists in mainland China are creating oil paintings in the style of the old European masters. Sculptors in Africa who have studied art history are creating individual sculptures that are not tied to community traditions. Because of increased opportunity and changing attitudes, more women and minority artists have been able to study, exhibit, and gain recognition.

The following is a brief description of some of the major movements that have occurred.

Abstract Expressionism

Abstract Expressionism was the first new style to arrive on the scene in New York in the years following World War II. It was *abstract* because it emphasized the elements and principles of art as its subject matter. It was *expressive* because it stressed feelings and emotions rather than planned design (See Figure 3.32, page 64).

Pop and Op Art

During the early 1960s artists turned to the mass media, and especially to advertising, for subject matter. *Pop* artists portrayed images of popular culture, such as Coke bottles, soup cans, Brillo boxes, giant hamburgers, and comic strips, in a variety of art forms. Sculptors worked with the neon tubing of signs. These artists made people take a new look at everyday objects. (See Figure 12.28, page 336.)

People have always been fascinated by illusions. They enjoy looking at pictures that fool the eye. *Op*, or optical art, uses scientific knowledge about vision to create optical illusions of movement. Op art has hard edges and smooth surfaces, and every element is carefully planned. (See Figure 7.6, page 158.)

Color-Field Painting

Color-field painting is concerned only with flat fields of color. It is done without the precision of Op art, and it is without emotion. It is color for the pure sensation of color. One example is the work of Mark Rothko. His color areas have hazy edges that seem to float in space. (See Figure 7.20, page 166.)

New Realism

Americans have a love for realism, and some American artists continue to portray subjects in a realistic style. Andrew Wyeth, whose work you studied in Chapter 2, is one example. Sculpture made by Duane Hanson is so real that it once

GUIDED PRACTICE
(continued)

 **Analyzing a Style**

1. Applying Your Skills. If your students work well together, you might have them form small groups and find an example of each style discussed in the section. An alternative approach is to have each group find multiple examples of one specific style. Just be sure that each style is chosen by a group.

2. Further Challenge. If sending students to the library for research is not practical or if there is not enough time for them to adequately complete the activity, you might bring books to the classroom and allow students to use them in class.

Exploring Aesthetics
Have students study the painting by Hans Hofmann in Figure 3.32 on page 64. Then ask them to respond to these questions: What hues do you find? Do you see primaries, secondaries, or intermediates? Where are the areas of pure hue? Do you see areas of low-intensity color? Where are the lightest values? Where are the darkest values? How are color contrasts at work in this painting?

Exploring Aesthetics
Have pairs of students show Figure 3.32 to at least three people who are unfamiliar with Abstract Expressionist art and ask their interpretation. Students should compare the various responses and categorize them according to the three main aesthetic theories. Conclude with a discussion of whether people's opinions correlated with their age, gender, or personality.

GUIDED PRACTICE
(continued)

Understanding Art History

Tell students that Abstract Expressionists have been labeled "action painters." This name came from the tendency of Abstract Expressionists to concentrate more on the act of painting than on the subject matter. Ask students to find out more about other artists associated with this movement, such as Jackson Pollack, Arshile Gorky, James Brooks, and Helen Frankenthaler.

Critical Thinking

Point out to students that the Abstract Expressionist movement brought with it an expanded definition of art. There was a sense that art is as much the act of creation as the object resulting from that act. Have students work in small groups to discuss this idea, specifically as it applies to Figure 3.32.

Understanding Art History

Ask students to read about Andy Warhol, the best-known American Pop artist. Remind them that he is famous for his declaration that everyone should be famous for fifteen minutes. Ask students to research the unknown people that he made famous through his art.

Critical Thinking

Using Duane Hanson's sculpture as a source of inspiration, have students suggest ideas for a sculptural group that represents the student population of their school. Ask: How would the design be arranged? How would models be chosen? Describe their appearance. What objects or props do you feel are essential?

FIGURE 3.32 Hofmann came to New York from Germany and opened an art school. He was the father of the Abstract Expressionist style that grew in New York. He is best known for his heavy use of brilliant colors. In this work, two sharply-defined rectangles seem to float over a background of loosely brushed but heavily built-up colors, which suggest water and flowers.

Hans Hofmann. *Flowering Swamp*. 1957. Oil on wood. 122 × 91.5 cm (48⅛ × 36⅛"). Hirshhorn Museum and Sculpture Garden, Smithsonian Institution, Washington, D.C. Gift of the Joseph H. Hirshhorn Foundation, 1966.

fooled a gallery security guard (Figure 3.33). One of Hanson's motionless, seated figures looked so real that the guard thought it was ill and called for an ambulance. This style has several names: *Photo-Realism*, *Hyper-Realism*, and *Super-Realism*.

Other Styles

Minimalists reduced their works to a minimum of elements. Sculpture was reduced to a minimum of geometric forms; paintings were reduced to one color. Some artists created gigantic earthworks that made the public more aware of the environment. Today critics are calling some artists *Postmodern*.

The art world is changing so fast that you need to look at a current monthly art magazine to know what the newest movements are.

Directions in Architecture

As with every other visual form, architecture has not followed just one direction. Some buildings, like the glass and metal boxes that fill the cities, are still being designed for function. Some buildings are shaped to take advantage of solar power. Architects are also designing buildings that are asymmetrical and decorative (Figure 3.34). Landscape

MORE ABOUT . . . HANS HOFMANN

Hofmann explained his theory about the use of space in his paintings as a "push-pull" theory of movement. He said that Italian perspective is all wrong. He felt that the illusion had only one direction in depth, and that nothing came back. However, he said that in his paintings space goes in and it comes back. The tensions he creates show shapes that are constantly moving in and out. In his paintings we can see the hints of many styles: Abstract Expressionism, Cubism, Color Field, and Op Art.

architects are teaming up with city architects and planners to create cities that help solve urban-living problems. Other teams are redesigning the centers of cities to make them more attractive places to live in and to visit.

Applying the Steps

1. Applying Your Skills.   Look through this book to find five paintings that were created since 1950. For each, list the name of the artist, the title of the work, and the style in which the work was painted.

2. Further Challenge.   Select a work of art, other than a painting, that was created since 1950. Use the four steps of art history to write about the work. You may have to go to the library to find the information you need.

FIGURE 3.33   Hanson's sculpture is an example of the New Realism. If you observed this figure in an art gallery, would you mistake him for a real person?

Duane Hanson. *Traveler with Sunburn*. 1986. Bronze, oil paint, and mixed media. Life-size. Private collection.

FIGURE 3.34   Spear says that her firm seeks to capture the spirit of time and place in its architecture. This building is a center for the development of innovative technology and software production. Do you think the form, which seems to defy the forces of gravity, fits the purpose of the building?

Laurinda Spear of the architectural firm of Arquitectonica International, Miami. *Centre for Innovative Technology*. Fairfax and Louden counties, Virginia.

ART CRITICISM IN ACTION

INTRODUCTION

The purpose of this feature is to review the art-criticism process that was introduced in Chapter 2. *Lady with a Bowl of Violets* was selected to be compared to another portrait of a woman from a different period of time, *Ginevra de' Benci* by Leonardo da Vinci. The different styles and expressive qualities of the works illustrate how time and place affect the look of an artwork.

CRITIQUING THE WORK

1. **Describe**   The woman is sitting very straight. She holds her head up proudly. She is wearing a negligee decorated with lace. Her hairstyle is from the turn of the century. She is looking out above and beyond the artist with a dreamy expression. She is sitting on a bench, next to a fireplace. There is a glass bowl of violets on the mantle. Behind the woman's head we see a framed work of art.

2. **Analyze**   There are many different blues in the woman's dress. The wall is a dull yellow and a blue that matches the dress. The mantle of the fireplace looks like blue and violet marble. The unusual lighting is the glow of warm light from the fireplace. Short brushstrokes of yellows and whites give the dress its luminous quality.

3. **Interpret**   Answers will vary. Some may see the mood as sad and lonely. (Some may see this pose as a reflection of the idle rich.) The dreamy look on the face of the woman will influence interpretations.

FIGURE 3.35   Lilla Cabot Perry. *Lady with a Bowl of Violets*. 1910. Oil on canvas. 102 × 76.2 cm (40¼ × 30″). National Museum of Women in the Arts, Washington, D.C. The Holladay Collection. Gift of Wallace and Wilhelmina Holladay.

CRITIQUING THE WORK

1. **Describe**   Study the painting *Lady with a Bowl of Violets* by Lilla Cabot Perry (Figure 3.35). Read the credit line. Notice the size of the painting and the medium. Now describe everything you see in the painting. Observe the woman's clothing, her hairstyle, her posture, and the expression on her face. Notice the furniture and the objects in the background. Collect facts and clues only.

2. **Analyze**   Look at the colors. Do you see any unusual lighting effects? What has the artist done to create the luminous quality in the subject's dress?

66

RESOURCES BEYOND THE CLASSROOM

Other Works By . . . Lilla Cabot Perry
Lady in Evening Dress
Haystacks, Giverny
The Old Cobbler
Reminiscences (four volumes of poetry)
Other Works By . . . da Vinci
Anatomical Studies

The Last Supper
Annunciation
Mona Lisa
The Adoration of the Magi
Lady with an Ermine
St. John the Baptist

FIGURE 3.36 Leonardo da Vinci. *Ginevra de' Benci*. c. 1474. Paint on wood. 38.8 × 36.7 (15¼ × 14½"). National Gallery of Art, Washington, D.C. Ailsa Mellon Bruce Fund.

3. **Interpret** Now it is time to express your own opinion. Add the facts you have collected to your own personal ideas and decide what theme or mood this painting communicates. Write a paragraph explaining your interpretation. Then write a new title for the work that sums up your interpretation.

4. **Judge** Now you are ready to make an aesthetic judgment. Do you think this is a successful work of art? Use one or more of the three aesthetic theories explained in Chapter 2 to defend your judgment.

COMPARING THE WORKS

Look at *Lady with a Bowl of Violets* (Figure 3.35) and *Ginevra de' Benci* (Figure 3.36) by Leonardo da Vinci. List the similarities and differences between the two works. How does each artist use the sitter's eyes to communicate an emotion to the viewer? How does each use color and light? Which of the two works would you prefer to hang in your room? Why? Note the year in which each work was completed. Do you find the styles in which one of the portraits was painted more appealing than the other? Why? Share your ideas in a class discussion.

67

MORE ABOUT . . . LEONARDO DA VINCI

Leonardo da Vinci was the first artist to systematically study the structure of the human body. One of his means of investigation was dissection, a practice he developed to an unprecedented degree. Dissection helped Leonardo to learn how arms and legs bend and how muscles shift as the body moves. He was especially interested in the head, particularly how the eye sees and the mind reasons. He searched for the part of the brain where the senses meet, believing that this was where the soul would be found. Despite his fascination with the human form, da Vinci did not approve of artists who exaggerated musculature in their art.

CHECKING COMPREHENSION

- Have students complete "Building Vocabulary" and "Reviewing Art Facts" on page 69.
- Assign *Application 5* and *6* in the TCR.

ANSWERS TO BUILDING VOCABULARY

1. style
2. dynasty
3. Byzantine
4. Gothic
5. Renaissance
6. linear perspective
7. Baroque
8. Impressionism
9. Expressionism
10. Surrealism

ANSWERS TO REVIEWING ART FACTS

1. Description, Analysis, Interpretation, Judgment.
2. Analysis.
3. Answers will vary.
4. Heads, arms, legs, and feet were shown in profile; eyes shown in frontal view.
5. The Greeks sought perfect proportion in buildings and sculpture.
6. Realistic appearance of people and objects became very important.
7. Mosques were decorated with calligraphy, geometric patterns, and stylized plants and flowers. Book illustration included people and animals.
8. Similarity: Both painted familiar subjects. Difference: Realists' style was realistic; Impressionists broke up solid forms and blurred edges to show the effect of sunlight.
9. The suffering of the peasants and the immoral behavior of the ruling class.

*M*EET THE ARTIST

LILLA CABOT PERRY
American, 1848–1933

Lilla Cabot Perry was a late nineteenth-century artist who captured the atmosphere of the genteel world of turn-of-the-century Boston.

She was born in 1848 to the socially prominent Cabot family, the first of eight children. Encouraged by her parents, she was an exceptional student who was interested in literature, language, poetry, music, and especially visual art. At age twenty-six she married the noted scholar Thomas Perry.

Perry's husband was supportive of her desire to pursue a career in art, and they moved to Paris in 1887, where she attended classes at a French academy. As part of her training, she spent hours copying old masters at the Louvre. The turning point for Perry's art came in 1889 when she saw the work of Claude Monet (kload moh-**nay**). The family spent that summer, and many more, in Germany near Monet's famous home and gardens. The Perrys became close friends with the Monets, and Perry embraced the Impressionist style. Monet did not accept students on a formal basis, but he reviewed her work as a friend and offered suggestions to improve her painting techniques.

When the Perrys returned home, Lilla used her social influence to introduce and promote Impressionism in Boston. She painted portraits and landscapes, merging the lessons of Impressionism with her academic training.

Her career spanned half a century, and she was very successful. Near the end of her life she was able to turn down portrait commissions and devote herself to painting landscapes.

In her poem "Requiescat in Pace" (Rest in Peace), published in 1898, Perry summarized the many roles she had juggled throughout her career: "Artist and woman, daughter, mother, wife." Perry was painting on the day she died.

MORE PORTFOLIO IDEAS

Focusing on the eyes and how they communicate different moods, cut out and arrange faces of different sizes into an interesting composition that displays a variety of expressions. Use acrylic paints to fill in the background. You may modify the faces using paints, but do not cover the eyes.

Give the women in Perry's and da Vinci's paintings each a name. Choose a theme such as love or child care, and write a dialogue between these women. Let each woman's statements reflect the mood in her eyes.

68

DEVELOPING A PORTFOLIO

Presentation Inform students that the purpose of a portfolio is to exhibit their competence as artists. It is most effective when it showcases their strengths while minimizing their weaknesses; thus, they will need to pay close attention to the selection and order of the pieces they include. When assembling the contents, students should keep in mind that the portfolio reflects pride in their work. It should never be incomplete, presented late, or carelessly put together. A student's sincere concern with the formalities of presentation and attention to detail could influence the overall impact of their portfolio on evaluators.

CHAPTER 3 REVIEW

Building Vocabulary

On a separate sheet of paper, write the term that best matches each definition given below.

1. The artist's personal way of using the elements of art and principles of design to express feelings and ideas.
2. A period of time during which a single family provided a succession of rulers.
3. A style of art that used rich color and flat, stiff figures and blended Greek, Roman, and Asian styles.
4. A style of architecture in which churches soared upward, used pointed arches, and had stained-glass windows.
5. The name given to the period of rebirth, or awakening, at the end of the Middle Ages.
6. A graphic system that creates the illusion of depth and volume on a flat surface.
7. A seventeenth-century art style that emphasized movement, contrast, and variety.
8. An art style that captured everyday subjects and emphasized the momentary effects of sunlight by using broken brushstrokes.
9. An art style that stressed personal feelings rather than composition.
10. A style of art in which dreams, fantasy, and the subconscious served as inspiration.

Reviewing Art Facts

Answer the following questions using complete sentences.

1. Name the four steps used by art historians to gain information about a work of art. List them in the order in which they must be followed.
2. In which step would you examine the style of the work and decide if it fit into an art movement?
3. Select a painting shown in this chapter and list three characteristics of the artist's style.
4. Describe the rules that Egyptian artists were required to follow when painting or sculpting a relief figure.

5. How did the ancient Greek belief in a logical, harmonious world affect the art that was produced?
6. What effect did the Renaissance rebirth of interest in the classical art of Greece and Rome have on the art of that period?
7. Describe the difference between the art forms used in an Islamic mosque and in Islamic book illustration.
8. Name one similarity and one difference between the artworks created by the Realists and the Impressionists.
9. Describe the subject matter chosen by the Mexican Muralists.

Thinking Critically About Art

1. **Explain.** In Chapter 2 you learned how to use the four steps of art criticism. In this chapter you have learned the four steps of art history. Both of these systems are useful in learning about a work of art. Explain the difference between the two systems.
2. **Compare and contrast.** You can look at visual images from the past to learn what the people who lived before us were like. Compare two of the self-portraits in this chapter, Figure 3.1 on page 40 and Figure 3.20 on page 54, and explain how these two artists are similar and how they are different.

Making Art Connections

1. **Music.** Listen to a piece of music by a Baroque composer. In what way is the style of the music related to Baroque art?
2. **Science.** We know the cave paintings were created between 15,000 and 10,000 B.C. and that the bricks of Harappa were made in 2500 B.C. Scientists use a system known as carbon 14 dating that proves how old certain materials are. Go to the library and research carbon dating. Find out why it is possible and how it is done.

EVALUATE

- Have students complete the *Chapter 3 Test*.
- Alternative Assessment teaching strategies are provided below or in the Testing Program and Alternative Assessment booklet.

RETEACHING

- Have students complete *Concept Map 3* in the Reteaching booklet.
- Have students work in small groups to write and present a skit that illustrates how an art historian properly identifies the artist of a previously unidentified work of art.

ENRICHMENT

Provide each student with a blank time line that begins with prehistoric times and concludes with the current year. As work on this chapter is completed, ask students to place two of their favorite works on the time line. Repeat after each chapter. Encourage students to also include artists' birth dates, major historic events, and so on. Instruct students to take note of trends. Where are many of their favorite works clustered? What significant events happened at the same time? What connection do they see between art and the world scene?

EXTENSION

Invite an art historian or museum curator to class to discuss the training and education necessary to qualify for the position that he or she has.

ALTERNATIVE ASSESSMENT

In groups of four, have students create a ten-page special section for an art magazine about one of the art periods studied in this chapter. Each student in the group could write one article. In group meetings, students should choose the period they want to focus on, assign one article for the magazine section to each student, discuss possible research sources for the articles, and decide how the articles will be arranged. The special section should also include visuals to accompany each article. Students may find it helpful to find models in art magazines.

When each group has completed its special section, display them in class and review the work.

CLOSE

Have students state which culture or artistic period they would most like to live in. Ask them to explain why they chose it and what they would hope to contribute to it.

Careers in Art

CHAPTER OVERVIEW

Chapter 4 introduces students to the opportunities for art careers in various fields. In particular, the areas of business and industry, environmental planning and development, entertainment, and education and cultural enrichment are examined.

CHAPTER SUPPLIES

For a list of the materials you will need for the Activities in this chapter, refer to the "Art Supplies Grid" in the Teacher's Manual.

FINE ART RESOURCES

Transparencies
- Maya Ying Lin. *Vietnam Veterans Memorial*
- *Advertising Poster*
- *High Museum of Art*
- Christine Merriam. *Charm Necklace*

Fine Art Prints
- Mattie Lou O'Kelley. *Sundown on the Snow*
- Henri de Toulouse-Lautrec. *Au Moulin Rouge*

FIGURE 4.1   For forty-seven years Rockwell captured the look of America in his paintings that appeared on the covers of *The Saturday Evening Post.* He worked seven days a week to create the covers, advertisements, and many private commissions.

Norman Rockwell. *Triple Self-Portrait.* 1960. Oil on canvas. 113 × 87.2 cm (44½ × 34½"). The Norman Rockwell Museum, Stockbridge, Massachusetts. Norman Rockwell Family Trust.

70

RESOURCES FOR CHAPTER 4

Application Activities 7, 8
Artist's Profile 4
Cooperative Learning Activities 7, 8
Cultural Diversity in Art
Enrichment Activities 7, 8

Reteaching Activities
    Study Guide 4
    Concept Map 4
Chapter 4 Test

Careers in Art

Now is an exciting time to consider a career in the visual arts. There are many possibilities from which to choose. Every year more challenging and rewarding positions are becoming available in art-related careers. People who can perform art and design jobs are needed in schools, museums, galleries, small businesses, and large corporations.

In the distant past, a young person who wanted to be an artist would pay a master artist for permission to work as an *apprentice* in the master's studio. These apprentices learned as they observed and assisted the masters. Today students can develop their skills by taking courses in high school and postsecondary schools. Vocational schools and professional art schools provide the education for some art careers. Other careers may require four- or five-year college degrees.

In this chapter you will learn how to find out whether or not you might be suited for a career in art. You will also get a taste of the many different types of art careers from which you can choose. If you have been thinking that you might enjoy a career in art, this chapter should help you move closer to a career decision. If you have never considered an art career, this chapter may open the door to some exciting career possibilities.

Objectives

After completing this chapter, you will be able to:
- Name many fields in which an art career is possible.
- Name some of the skills artists need for various jobs.
- Make a meaningful decision about your own interest in a career in art.

Words to Know

animation
architect
industrial designer
interior designer
landscape architect
layout
logos
photojournalist
storyboards

FIRST IMPRESSIONS

Norman Rockwell had a very successful career as an illustrator. Look at his painting *Triple Self-Portrait* (Figure 4.1). Does the picture on the white canvas match the image in the mirror? Do you know anything about the small pictures taped to the right corner of the canvas? They do not look like Rockwell. Why are they there? What has Rockwell done to the background to help you concentrate on all the objects that make up the subject of the work?

FIGURE 4.2   Graphic designer working at a computer.

ART-RELATED CAREERS

You are probably beginning to consider ideas about your own future. If you have talent and art is something you enjoy, this chapter will open your mind to some exciting career possibilities. In addition to the major categories mentioned here, there are many careers within each field. As you read, think about each career and keep those that interest you in mind. You will be surprised at how many different opportunities exist.

BUSINESS AND INDUSTRY

Today the business world needs the skills of an art specialist in many areas. Company reports, publications, and advertising are all designed by someone with training in the visual arts. Some of this design work is done by company staff. Other, more complex projects are given to outside design or advertising firms with many different kinds of artists on staff. Following are descriptions of some of the areas in which artists work.

Graphic Design

The early Christian monks who illustrated religious writings were artists. After the invention of the printing press in the fifteenth century, the craftspeople who arranged type and illustrations were what we now call *graphic artists*. They had to plan the **layout**, *the way items were arranged on the page*, before a page could be printed. It was slow work because it all had to be done by hand. Today graphic designers use computers, laser scanners, and many other machines that work at speeds never before thought possible.

Computer Graphics. Using a computer, designers create images that can be moved, changed, erased, duplicated, shrunk or enlarged, colored, and textured. The designer works with tools such as electric-light pens on electronic tablets, as shown in Figure 4.2. With these tools, designers may draw and color images.

Software programs also exist that enable the user to design a page layout and insert artwork. Electronic equipment merely speeds up this design process. Some systems let the artist see the finished work in a variety of color and size arrangements. Computers can also be used to send images along telephone lines to customers all over the world.

There are also computer programs being developed that are interactive. These programs give the user many different ways of exploring a large database of information. Some interactive programs are very simple. Others combine information in written form; graphic images including animation and motion pictures; and sound, including music and sound effects. The viewer can use the mouse

MORE ABOUT . . . NORMAN ROCKWELL

Rockwell's life often reflected the same gentle humor and irony that he presents in his paintings. For example, the helmet shown in the painting in Figure 4.1 on page 70 has special significance. On one of Rockwell's trips to Paris, he saw the helmet in an antique shop. He was sure that it was ancient and valuable. Excitedly, he walked into the store, found that the price was right, and purchased his prize. On his way back to his hotel, he stopped to watch Parisian firefighters. They were all wearing the same helmet as the one Rockwell had under his arm. He hung it on his easel to remind himself that anyone can be fooled.

control to switch back and forth between the various kinds of information, following his or her own path to in-depth learning. Each segment of these complex interactive programs must be planned. One person may develop the overall concept, another may create the images, still others may integrate the various parts of the program.

Advertising Art. Graphic artists may be employed by corporations to design promotional material, by outdoor-advertising agencies to create billboards, and by advertising agencies to work on ad campaigns (Figure 4.3). Advertising agencies employ artists of many kinds. These artists work together as a team, and their work is coordinated by the art director. Graphic designers also create **logos,** or *identifying symbols,* such as the CBS eye or McDonald's golden arches.

Publishing Design and Illustration. Newspaper, magazine, and book publishers employ graphic designers. A designer created the look of this book. The size of the type, the length of the lines, the layout of the text and artwork, and the length of the columns were all carefully planned. Computers were used to type the manuscript, and the information was stored on a disk and given to the typesetting company. The typesetter then followed the design provided by the book designer.

In addition to the type and the paintings you see in this book, there are drawings by commercial illustrators, such as the viewing frame on page 351 of the Handbook. Some illustrators specialize in one area, such as fashion, medical, or technical illustration. Others accept assignments in many areas.

Cartoonists submit their work for publication in magazines and newspapers. They may choose to draw individual cartoons or comic strips. Editorial cartoonists must be interested in politics. They present complex ideas in a simple drawing that usually makes a humorous point. Editorial cartoonists try to make people think about current issues. They also try to influence public opinion.

Film and Video Graphics. Artists who work in film and video graphics design such things as stage sets, the graphic symbols and pictures that introduce sports programs, and the animated graphics in commercials. Video manufacturers use graphic artists to design the box covers for their tapes, set up photo shoots, and help produce the advertising campaigns that introduce the new product.

Industrial Design

Industrial designers *design the products of industry.* They plan everything from tools, home appliances, furniture, and toys to automobiles. They must be familiar with production processes as well as the characteristics of the different materials used

M A R A T H O N

FIGURE 4.3   A poster advertising a marathon.

GUIDED PRACTICE
(continued)

Analyzing Design

1. Applying Your Skills.
Answers will vary depending on students' favorite cars and their familiarity with car features. All students should recognize that the Avanti is as aerodynamic as modern cars.

2. Further Challenge.
In advance of this exercise, prepare a poster with logos familiar to students.

3. Computer Option.
Suggest that students begin with a geometric shape. Then using the Pencil, Brush, Line, or Text tool, create the logo by drawing and filling in the shape. Several colors and patterns may be included. Have students make variations and changes to the logo by moving or changing sizes, colors, and textures. As an alternative, students might begin with the Text tool and choose interesting fonts, sizes, colors, or patterns, or arrange the letters to create an interesting logo. Save. Print.

Critical Thinking

Bring to class a manufactured product you use everyday, such as a hair dryer or a toothbrush. Ask students to study the object, then think of one change in the product's design that would make it easier to use or more aesthetically pleasing.

Understanding Art History

If students are interested in the evolution of fashion design, suggest that they study at least three different historical periods that are widely separated. Encourage students to find any similarities among the three groups, using categories such as fabrics, accessories, and styles.

FIGURE 4.4 Look closely at this Avanti. Like many of today's aerodynamic cars, it has no grill. How do you think this design might affect the car's performance?

Raymond Loewy. *Avanti.* 1963.

in those processes. Industrial designers plan a product based on three requirements. First, it must do the job for which it was designed. Second, it must look like it can do the job. Third, it must be visually pleasing.

Package designers produce boxes, tubes, bottles, shopping bags, and other kinds of containers. They use shape and color to make every package unique and appealing. Package designers must also consider package function. For example, when pill bottles first came on the market, the caps were so easy to remove that children were able to open them. Designers had to come up with a cap that was childproof but could be opened by an adult.

Industrial designers usually specialize in one industry or product, such as machinery, furniture, medical equipment, or cars. The design of an automobile is a team effort. Special designers plan the outer form or body. Then other specialists who work with fabrics and plastics create new interiors to go with the body. Computers help ensure that all the parts fit together correctly.

Raymond Loewy is credited with making many advances in industrial design. He is best known for his automotive designs. The 1953 Starlight Coupe was chosen for exhibition at The Museum of Modern Art in New York because of its unique design quality. The Avanti (Figure 4.4) is a luxury sports car that was made between June 1962 and December 1963. It has such an unusual design that it was produced and sold until 1992. The Smithsonian Institution has the car on display as an outstanding example of industrial design.

Analyzing Design

1. Applying Your Skills. Compare the 1963 Avanti in Figure 4.4 with one of your favorite sports cars sold today. List any similarities or differences you find.

2. Further Challenge. Design a logo for your school, your favorite club, or your community.

3. Computer Option. Use any tools or options available on your computer software and design a logo for yourself, your family, or your school.

Fashion Design

Fashion designers plan and create clothing, hats, handbags, shoes, jewelry, and sportswear. They must know the appropriate materials to use for the articles being designed. High-fashion designers create one-of-a-kind originals that are very

RESOURCES BEYOND THE CLASSROOM

Professional Contacts If you bring in resource people during the time that careers are being studied, the material will be more meaningful. Even though you may know more about the subject than the resource person, students will be interested in listening to someone new. If you live in an urban area, it will not be difficult to find people who work at some of these careers. Even the smallest newspaper in a rural area needs a layout person. The local television station will also employ someone who fits one of the categories. Other workers to consider are florists, cosmetologists or hairstylists who can show how hair styles complement face shape.

expensive (Figure 4.5). Fashion designers also work for manufacturers who make clothes everyone can afford. All clothing designers are supported by a team of patternmakers, cutters, tailors, and people who work in the factories that produce the clothes.

Photography

Figure 1.11 on page 15 in this book was created by Dorothea Lange. She captured the despair of a migrant mother and her children during the Great Depression.

Photojournalists are *visual reporters.* They work for newspapers and magazines and tell their stories through their photographs. Photojournalists understand design, know how to develop and print their own work, and have an eye for what is interesting to look at (Figure 4.6). Other photographers may be able to work in the comfort of a studio, but photojournalists must go where the news events are occurring.

Other careers in the field of photography include fashion, product and food photography, architectural photography, fine-art photography, and moving-picture photography for television, videos, and film.

FIGURE 4.5 Fashion designers must come up with fresh, new ideas every season. Anyone considering a career in this area must be able to work under intense pressure to meet deadlines.

FIGURE 4.6 Photojournalists covering a game.

MORE ABOUT . . . MOTION PICTURES

The first motion pictures truly seemed like magic. Pioneers such as George Melies experimented with the new technique. Melies accidentally invented the "jump cut" when his film suddenly jammed while he was filming a busy street in Paris. After developing the footage, he discovered that he had captured a bus suddenly turning into a hearse! In 1902 he made a five-minute film titled *A Trip to the Moon,* a fantasy that would later inspire *Star Wars.* In another piece, titled *The Man with the Rubber Head,* he combined forms into what he called "artificially arranged scenes."

ENVIRONMENTAL PLANNING AND DEVELOPMENT

The first environmental designers were the prehistoric cave dwellers who eventually moved out of their caves and into the countryside. They learned to build huts for protection and became the first architects. Today there are many kinds of designers who plan environmental space. Their jobs involve making homes, work space, and the surrounding landscape attractive and functional.

Architecture

An **architect** must *design buildings that are well constructed, aesthetically pleasing, and functional.*

To function properly a building must do what it was planned to do. Private houses and apartments must serve as comfortable homes for people. Office buildings, schools, and factories must also be comfortable, safe, efficient, and aesthetically pleasing. The aesthetic effect of a building is extremely important. The structure must fit the surrounding environment and improve the community. Because modern technology is so complex, architects

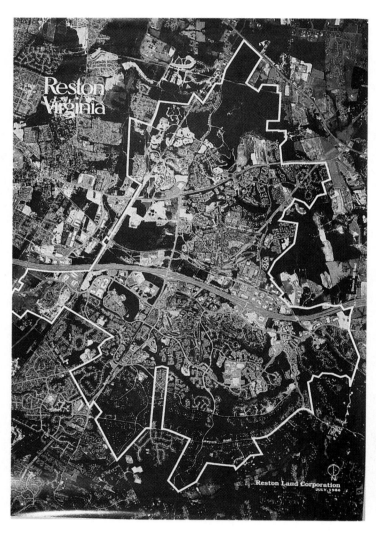

FIGURE 4.7   Reston is a planned community founded in 1962, with completion expected in the mid-1990s. About 40 percent of the total area has been planned for open space and public use. People can work, shop, attend school, and participate in a variety of leisure activities without leaving the community.

Aerial view of Reston, Virginia, a planned city. Courtesy of the Reston Land Corporation, Reston, Virginia.

FIGURE 4.8   Frederick Law Olmsted designed New York City's Central Park in 1858. He was the first person to call himself a landscape architect. He tried to create a calm, natural place in the center of America's largest city.

Courtesy of the Central Park Conservancy.

usually specialize in a particular type of building such as skyscrapers, shopping malls, or homes.

An architect must be knowledgeable about such things as building materials, ventilation, heating and cooling systems, plumbing, stairways, and elevators. In addition, an architect must be creative, be able to make accurate mechanical drawings, have a strong background in mathematics and drafting, and be able to deal with customers.

City Planning

City planners are trained as architects, but they are mainly concerned with the care and improvement of city environments. Every major American city has a city planner. This person helps control the growth and development of the city. Some of the responsibilities of the city planner are land use, urban renewal, and the development of harbors, city parks, and shopping malls. Reston, Virginia, shown in Figure 4.7, is a planned community.

Landscape Architecture

Landscape architects *design playgrounds, parks, and outdoor areas around buildings and along highways.* They work closely with architects and other planners to use and improve the natural setting so that it is easy to maintain and beautiful to look at. They create designs using flowers, plants, trees, shrubs, rivers, ponds, lakes, walks, benches, and signs, as shown in Figure 4.8.

Landscape artists work with architectural firms, government agencies, individual home owners, and facilities such as golf courses.

Interior Design

An **interior designer** *plans the design and decoration of the interior spaces in homes and offices.* Successful designers use styles and materials that blend with the architecture and that please the client.

Interior designers must understand decorating styles and materials. They must be able to look at an empty room and visualize the finished area. They must know the latest trends and developments in wallcoverings, carpets, furniture, appliances, and lamps.

Since interior designers spend as much time with clients as they do at the drawing board, they must have patience and the ability to make a client feel comfortable. Some designers work for individual home owners, while others plan and coordinate the interiors of department stores, offices, and large hotels.

Exhibit and Display Design

Exhibit designers work for trade shows, department stores, showrooms, galleries, and museums. They plan presentations of collections, temporary exhibits, and traveling shows of all types. They

TEACH

(pages 78–79)
• Entertainment

GUIDED PRACTICE

Exploring Aesthetics

Direct each student to evaluate a comic strip using the following guidelines: Describe the comic strip in terms of the elements and principles of art. What is the focus of the strip? What makes it humorous? How is the comic strip aesthetically appealing? What does the artist do to make this comic strip different from others?

Promoting Discussion

If available, show the video *Mona Lisa Descending a Staircase* distributed by Pyramid Film and Video. Available in VHS format, it shows masterpieces of art evolving through periods of art history. The evolution is achieved through clay painting and special effects. The video is not only amusing, but it helps students follow the changes in art styles through the ages.

Sparking Creativity

Want students to think creatively about art-related careers? Suggest this: Any career in the arts needs a person with *ideas*. Test and stretch your readiness to risk new ideas. Don't let the fear of failing hold you back. Often the best ideas grow from the wild ones that seem too far out to be practical. Think of ten ways to (1) design the letter "A"; (2) build a tree house; (3) use a pair of chopsticks; (4) take out the garbage; or (5) decorate your room.

decide which things should be grouped together and how they should be lit.

Displays attract customers and help persuade them to buy. The display designer is an important member of the sales team. The way the designer makes the merchandise look in a store window helps draw customers into the store.

ACTIVITY   Using Design for Display

1. Applying Your Skills.   Think of one room in your school that looks as if it needs an interior designer. List some of the things you would like to change. Then describe how you would change them. Think in terms of color, traffic flow, furniture, and so on.

2. Further Challenge.   Create a display of art objects for a display window in your school, or one of flat artwork for a bulletin board. Invent a title for your display, letter it neatly, and include it in the arrangement.

ENTERTAINMENT

The entertainment industry provides opportunities for artists with a wide range of skills. Motion pictures, TV shows, stage plays, and dance performances all use designers and artists to create the magic we see.

FIGURE 4.9   Artist working with storyboard.

Animation

Animation, *the art of moving cartoons,* was invented for film, but it is used on television as well. Animation needs more visual artists than any other art-career area.

When artists create an animated film, they first select a story. They decide what styles of architecture and dress fit the story. Then they develop the story by drawing **storyboards,** *a series of still drawings that show the story's progress* (Figure 4.9). They draw approximately sixty sketches for each board. A short film needs three storyboards, and a full-length film needs more than twenty-five. The storyboards look like comic strips. They provide the outline for the development of the film.

Layout artists are responsible for the overall look of the film. Background artists paint the settings from the layout artist's sketches. To create action, animators draw the major poses of each character, then other artists fill in the many drawings required to complete each movement. Every second of film requires twenty-four drawings to make the movement look smooth.

Special Effects Design

Training for the field of special effects artist may require that you attend a school that has an art department as well as take courses in film production and technology. Many people who create the magic illusions we love in film and television have come up through the ranks. Today, however, there are

---

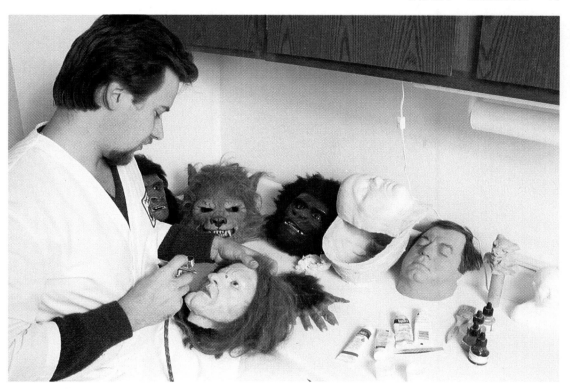

FIGURE 4.10 Special effects artist.

large universities with cinema departments that offer courses in many aspects of film production.

Special effects artists require the skills of a painter, sculptor, and engineer. They have the ability to imagine and create fantasy scenes or imaginary creatures that look real (Figure 4.10). They can make you believe you are watching a dinosaur driving a car or a battle scene in a galaxy light-years away. In their work they use papier-mâché, plaster, plastic molds, paint, makeup, trick photography, and computers.

Art Direction for the Performing Arts

In the theater the *art director* works with stage, costume, and lighting designers, as well as makeup artists and hairstylists, to bring all elements of the show together (Figure 4.11 on page 80). Art directors know art history as well as the special techniques of their craft. If a play is set in the past, the setting, furniture, costumes, and hairstyles must correctly reflect that period of history.

Art directors also coordinate all the visual elements involved in the production of a movie or a TV program. They work with set and costume designers, graphic artists, property designers, and location planners.

 Critiquing Animation

1. Applying Your Skills. Watch several animated programs on television. Notice the differences in quality. Then list the programs you watched in order, from best to worst. How did the backgrounds compare? Describe the quality of the movement. Did the programs with the best movement have the best backgrounds?

2. Further Challenge. Create a character for a new animated film. Draw your character and list the specific qualities of this animated personality. Make at least three sketches showing the character in action.

COOPERATIVE LEARNING

As a cumulative activity for this chapter, have students work in pairs or small groups to select career fields in which they are interested. Have them work with school guidance counselors and librarians to find what educational requirements are necessary and what schools would be appropriate for them. Instruct students to make worksheets that show how much their education will cost and what kinds of employment are available to them once they have graduated as well as an estimate of the cost of living in specific areas of the country where they might work. As a final event, host a ten-year reunion where students share information about their education and career paths.

TEACH

(pages 80–81)
- Education and Cultural Enrichment
- Thinking About an Art Career

GUIDED PRACTICE

Interdisciplinary: History

Working with a history teacher, assign each student this project: Research an artist or group of artists whose work influenced history in a significant way. As examples, remind them of the artists' guilds that formed during the Middle Ages, giving rise to labor unions in later centuries, and as a specific example, the cartoons of Thomas Nast which brought attention to political corruption in America's infancy.

Understanding Art History

Have students select contemporary artists that interest them and research their lives through biographies. In particular, ask students to look for information about how the artists make their livelihoods and how they promote their works. As a contrast, have students research the role that art patrons held when artists were once unable to make a living from their art. How does patronage differ from modern methods of support such as endowments and grants?

Promoting Discussion

Instruct students to write down three decisions that are important to a person who wants to pursue an art-related career. Ask volunteer students to share their lists and use their responses to discuss some specific steps a person should take if he or she intends to work in such a career.

FIGURE 4.11 Art directors must make backgrounds, costumes, and other visual elements work together. They coordinate the tasks of all the creative people who work in the theater.

EDUCATION AND CULTURAL ENRICHMENT

There are careers that combine an interest in art and in education. Teachers, art therapists, and people who work in museums all use their training in different ways.

Art Education

People who like to share their knowledge and skills and have a strong interest in art may choose to teach. Teachers work in elementary, middle, or high schools as well as colleges (Figure 4.12). They help students learn to make aesthetic judgments and to develop their artistic skills and talents.

Art therapists, who are also teachers, use art to help people with emotional and physical problems. They help patients change their behavior in a positive manner. They work in psychiatric hospitals, community centers, drug and alcohol treatment centers, and prisons.

Museums house collections of paintings, sculpture, crafts, costumes, books, jewelry, and artifacts from ancient cultures. People with training in art history organize, assemble, and display these collections. Others lead groups through the displays, providing information to the viewers. Some museums publish books that contain pictures of the objects in their collections. Many museums have stores that sell books and reproductions. Visiting a museum will open your eyes to art forms you may never have seen before.

CULTURAL PERSPECTIVES

Quilting is an art form that touches the core of American life. Quilt designs are the product of women who made necessary covers for their family beds. Often using the scraps left from clothing they made for family members, they planned designs that represented nature, animals, flowers, family traditions, Biblical stories, symbols of love, and so on.

Quilts from all over the country form a history of the lives of families and communities. Some closely knit communities, such as the Amish and the Pennsylvania Dutch, have traditional designs that have been carried through many generations. Because quilters often have no formal training in design, the quality of their work is all the more remarkable.

Fine Arts and Crafts

Some people choose to work on their own as painters, sculptors, printmakers, weavers, jewelers, and so on. They are committed to making art. Many of these artists need a second job to help pay their living expenses. In the visual arts, as in the performing arts, the opportunities for stardom and large incomes are rare. Some artists work in the commercial art fields to supplement their income. Many teach in schools and colleges. Leo Twiggs (Figure 2.5, page 29, and Figure 5.1, page 88) is the head of the Art Department at Orangeberg State College in South Carolina. Larry Smith (Figure 6.44, page 144) teaches in a middle school in Georgia. Some, like Jacob Lawrence (Figure 5.39, page 114, and Figure 9.27, page 238), continue teaching even after they have become financially comfortable, because they feel that the ongoing interaction with art students enhances their creative thinking.

If you are driven to paint, sculpt, make prints, weave, or create other art forms and want to make a commitment to the arts, you must realize that you may have to consider taking a second job.

FIGURE 4.12 In addition to enjoying art, teachers must enjoy working with people and sharing their knowledge.

T HINKING ABOUT AN ART CAREER

Are you suited for a career in the art world? It may be too soon for you to make a final decision about your future. However, if you have talent and art is something you enjoy, then an art career may be right for you.

Ask yourself the following questions. The more "yes" answers you give, the better your chances of being happy in the art field.

▨ Do you find yourself noticing things that your friends may miss, such as the colors of autumn leaves or the shapes of clouds?
▨ Are you curious?
▨ Do you like to solve problems?
▨ Do you keep an open mind about new and unusual forms of art?

▨ Do you like to draw or make things with your hands?
▨ Do you like to experiment with new materials and techniques?
▨ Do you get "lost" in an art project and lose track of time?
▨ When a work of art turns out wrong, are you willing to throw it out and start again?
▨ Do you keep at a project until it is finished?
▨ Can you meet deadlines?

If you decide you want a career in art, you should begin working toward that goal in high school. In the meantime, practice your skills on your own. Study the great artists. Ask teachers for advice. If you really want a career in art, it will be there for you!

 Thinking About Careers

1. Applying Your Skills. Select a question from the list that is difficult for you to do. Write your own list of at least five ways in which to improve your performance in that area.

2. Further Challenge. From the visual art careers listed in this chapter, choose one that interests you. Through personal interviews or library research, write a brief biography of one person (famous or not so famous) who has had experience in this career.

GUIDED PRACTICE
(continued)

ACTIVITY Thinking About Careers

1. Applying Your Skills. Responses to this activity will vary.

2. Further Challenge. Through personal contacts in the art community, find professional and amateur artists who are willing to attend class and speak to your students. If field trips are possible, a visit to an artist's studio would be worthwhile.

INDEPENDENT PRACTICE

Study Guide
Distribute and have students complete *Study Guide 4* in the Reteaching booklet.

Enrichment
• Assign *Enrichment Activities 7* and *8* in the TCR.
• Invite a personnel director to speak to the class about ways to prepare for job interviews.

Art Is Everywhere

To foster students' awareness of the use of technology in art-related fields, suggest this: Today the artist's media include computers, lasers, video technology, chemicals, calculus, plastics, new metals, light, solar and artificial heat energy, and power machinery. Artists reshape acres of land, even wrap whole buildings and bridges with cloth. They also construct vast buildings on the screen of their computer, visualizing them in three dimensions, turning them around, shifting walls, enlarging, and reducing. A whole new world is open to the artist.

RESOURCES BEYOND THE CLASSROOM

Sources of Career Information Remember that teachers and school officials, especially guidance counselors, often receive catalogs from institutes of higher education that might be of interest to your students. If possible, arrange to get copies of these catalogs when discussing art-related careers. A map of the United States, even of the world, could be used to indicate the locations of colleges, universities, and schools that might be of interest to students interested in pursuing art careers. Students could be encouraged to research more about a specific institution and present the findings to the class, using the catalog, the map, and possibly interviews with alumni.

INTRODUCTION

For this chapter, a commercial art piece was selected to show students that the same steps of art criticism can be applied to commercial art. The cover of *A Wrinkle in Time* is a familiar one to students who have read the book. For comparison, Goya was selected as a fine artist who worked for a patron just as commercial artists work for employers.

CRITIQUING THE WORK

1. **Describe** The original artwork was 19¹⁄₁₆ × 13 inches (48.4 × 33 cm), probably larger than the final size of the cover. The purpose of this dust jacket is to interest readers in the content of the book.

   There are many forms and shapes in the artwork including a large dark figure, a boy, small figures silhouetted in black, a monster, a dragon, clouds, geometric shapes, a large black tear, and so on. There is a large dark rectangle that fills most of the picture. The top of this shape is plain black; that is where the publishers put the title of the book.

2. **Analyze** The colors are cool blues and greens, low intensity browns, black, and white. There are several geometric shapes and several decorative patterns. There are stars in the sky above the boy and behind the dark figure in the circle.

3. **Interpret** Answers will vary. The book is a science fiction fantasy.

4. **Judge** Answers will vary. Students will probably cite Formalism and Emotionalism.

FIGURE 4.13 Leo and Diane Dillon. Book cover illustration for *A Wrinkle in Time*. 1979. Watercolor and pastel on paper. 48.4 × 33 cm (19¹⁄₁₆ × 13″). Private collection.

82

RESOURCES BEYOND THE CLASSROOM

Other Works By . . . Leo and Diane Dillon
Why Mosquitos Buzz in People's Ears: A West Africa Tale (illustrations)
Ashanti to Zulu: African Traditions (illustrations)
Other Works By . . . Goya
The Family of Charles IV
The Duchess of Alba

The Giant
Black Paintings
Los Desastres de la Guerra
The Marquesa de Pontejos
Clothed Maja
The Third of May, 1808

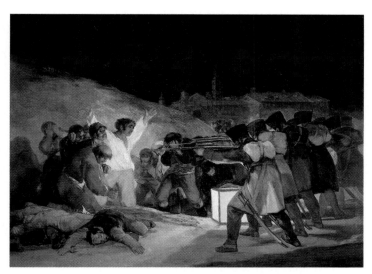

FIGURE 4.14 Francisco Goya. *The Third of May, 1808*. Oil on canvas. Approximately 2.64 × 3.43 m (8′8″ × 11′2″). The Prado, Madrid, Spain.

CRITIQUING THE WORK

1. **Describe** Look at the dust jacket for *A Wrinkle in Time* in Figure 4.13. Read the credit line. List the size and media of the work. What is the purpose of this graphic design? Now look at the work and list and describe all the people, objects, and shapes you see.

2. **Analyze** What kinds of colors do you find in this cover? How many geometric shapes can you locate? Describe them. Identify the decorative patterns that you find and explain where they are located.

3. **Interpret** Can you tell into what category the book *A Wrinkle in Time* fits? What kind of idea or mood does this book cover express? Does the cover design make you curious about the story?

4. **Judge** Do you think this graphic design makes a successful book cover? Which of the three aesthetic theories would you use to judge this work?

COMPARING THE WORKS

Look at the book cover for *A Wrinkle in Time* (Figure 4.13) and the painting *The Third of May, 1808* (Figure 4.14) by Francisco Goya. Both the Dillons and Goya earned their living as artists. The Dillons work for publishers, ad agencies, and different companies that hire them to do a specific job. Goya painted portraits of nobles and others who paid him for his work.

The Dillons were paid to create this book cover. Do you think someone paid Goya to paint *The Third of May, 1808*? Why or why not?

Identify the similarities and differences you find in the two works. Look at the elements of art as well as the subject matter in your comparison. Notice the difference between the people in the Dillons' cover and the people in the Goya painting. Both works show strong contrast between black and white. How is the use of white light different? What are the themes of the two works? What, if anything, do the two works have in common?

The Dillons' work is calm; the people are very still. The people on the left of the Goya work are very agitated. The soldiers on the right are all in the same, slightly active, pose. The book cover is a fantasy. Even the evil monster with the many faces is moving in a horizontal, calm direction. The Goya work is an extremely disturbing depiction of the ugliness of war.

Both works use similar color schemes. Black and dark values dominate in both. In the Dillons' work the light is used as a border to the work. There is very little contrast in the heart of the book cover. In the Goya work, light has been used to emphasize the horror of the people being shot.

Both works tell stories. Goya tells about the horrors of war. The Dillons tell about a fantasy in which children move through time to defeat a danger to the universe.

EXTENSION

- Have students read the "Meet the Artist" feature on the following page.
- Assign *Artist's Profile 4* in the TCR.
- Suggest this Computer Option as an alternative for "More Portfolio Ideas" on the following page: In pairs or small groups, have students select a story to illustrate together using a draw or paint program. The first person begins by drawing the main character or object in the story. Each person in the group takes turns adding to the illustration until the illustration has been completed. Follow these simple rules: No one may erase what another person has drawn. Every group member must participate.

MORE ABOUT . . . FRANCISCO GOYA

Goya was born in Saragossa, Spain. As a young man he traveled to Italy, but he was not impressed by the Renaissance masterpieces and soon returned home. There he worked as a portrait painter, flattering the members of the Spanish ruling class who were his subjects. In 1786 he was named personal painter to King Charles IV. An illness four years later left the artist deaf. Instead of despairing, he used his handicap to fuel his imagination. When war broke out in 1808, he painted a series of prints depicting a view of war that had no heroes or acts of glory. Instead, he focused on the senseless acts of waste and brutality.

*M*EET THE ARTIST

LEO AND DIANE DILLON

American, both b. 1933

Many long-married couples finish each other's sentences, but Diane and Leo Dillon finish each other's drawings. Married more than thirty-six years, they have achieved an award-winning career in graphic arts.

Their combined talents produce what they call "the third artist," one who creates something neither would do alone. They feel that the collaboration, which they compare to jazz improvisation, keeps their work fresh. When one gets stuck, the other comes up with a solution. When one gets tired, the other takes over. They never divide up an assignment. They think of each other as equals.

Before beginning an illustration for a book cover, the Dillons read the book carefully. They often research information in the book and look for additional photographs or images to help them better understand the book. One picture book the Dillons illustrated, *Ashanti to Zulu: African Traditions,* took three months to research. The artwork took only one month to complete.

The Dillons have won many awards for their graphic design. They won the Caldecott Medal two years in a row for *Why Mosquitos Buzz in People's Ears: A West African Tale* by Verna Aardema, and *Ashanti to Zulu: African Traditions* by Margaret W. Musgrove. They have also received the Hamilton King Award and the Hugo Award.

The Dillons' dedication to craftsmanship has given them more control over the reproduction of their work than most graphic artists have. Some publishers have even allowed them to design the type and layout for their cover illustrations, which is rare. The Dillons prove that it is possible to work within the limits of commercial realities and still produce art that meets the highest aesthetic standards. Their body of work is varied and impressive.

MORE PORTFOLIO IDEAS

Read *A Wrinkle in Time* by Madeleine L'Engle. Identify and explain the symbolic meaning of each of the people, creatures, and shapes on this book cover. Can you guess why there is a large area of black at the top of the design?

Select a story you have read recently. Design a book cover for the story.

DEVELOPING A PORTFOLIO

Presentation When making decisions about the appearance of artworks in a portfolio, encourage students to pay attention to important concerns such as the mounting for paintings and protective jackets for pastels and chalk drawings. Remind them to label individual pieces sufficiently to avoid loss. Use slides for projects too large to include and show multiple viewpoints of three-dimensional artworks. When photographing a work of art, tell them that the investment in quality film and careful lighting is worthwhile as it will enhance the finished slide. Use examples from the text to illustrate this point.

CHAPTER 4 REVIEW

Building Vocabulary

On a separate sheet of paper, write the term that best matches the definition given below.
1. The way items are arranged on a page.
2. Identifying symbols.
3. One who designs the products of industry.
4. A photographer who is a visual reporter.
5. Designer of buildings that are well constructed, aesthetically pleasing, and functional.
6. Designer of playgrounds, parks, and outdoor areas around buildings, and along highways.
7. One who plans the design and decoration and design of the interior spaces in homes and offices.
8. The art of moving cartoons.
9. Series of still drawings that show a story's progress.

Reviewing Art Facts

Answer the following questions using complete sentences.
1. How did young people who wanted to be artists receive their training before there were art schools?
2. When did the field of graphic design begin? What invention made it possible?
3. List four ways in which the use of a computer can speed up the design process for a graphic artist.
4. Select a logo of a well-known product and describe how the artist has symbolized the product.
5. Name three characteristics of an editorial cartoon.
6. What elements of art do package designers use to make every package unique and visually appealing? What else must they consider?
7. What is the subject of Figure 1.11 on page 15? What do you think is the theme or message of this photograph?

Thinking Critically About Art

1. **Analyze.** Norman Rockwell earned his living as an illustrator and graphic artist. He is most famous for his magazine covers for *The Saturday Evening Post.* His work is so famous that today the term *Rockwell* is synonymous with nostalgia, as in "a Rockwell Christmas." Organize a debate in your class to discuss whether the work of Norman Rockwell is as important as the work of Andrew Wyeth and other artists from the same time period.
2. **Extend.** The Surrealist painter René Magritte has had a strong influence on commercial art. The CBS eye and a certain TV commercial are based on two of his famous works. Look for a book about his work in the library and search for the paintings that inspired the commercial. Write a paragraph taking a position that commercial artists should or should not use the works of other artists.
3. **Extend.** Contact someone who works in a career area mentioned in this chapter. Find out what kind of schooling and/or training this person needed to prepare for his or her career. Bring your findings to class.

Making Art Connections

1. **Photography.** Try out photography as a career. Decide whether you want to be a fine-art photographer such as Ansel Adams, a commercial photographer, or a photojournalist. Take a series of photos that qualify as fine art or as photojournalism. Select your best photo and mount or mat it.
2. **Literary and Art Awards.** Do some research on the Caldecott Medal, the Newbery Medal, the Hugo Award, and the Hamilton King Award. Write a report telling what each award is given for and what specific criteria are used in the judging for each award.

THE ELEMENTS OF ART

UNIT OVERVIEW

Unit 2 focuses specifically on the individual elements of art. Because the elements of art are the basic visual symbols in the language of art, students are encouraged throughout the unit to recognize the presence of the elements in the world around them.

In Chapter 5, students explore the expressive qualities of line and how to use lines to make contour, gesture, and calligraphic drawings. In Chapter 6, students examine the elements of shape, form, and space in two- and three-dimensional artworks. Chapter 7 concentrates on the properties of color—hue, value, and intensity, and students examine various color schemes. In Chapter 8, students recognize the difference between real and simulated textures.

UNIT PLANNING GUIDE

The following chart shows the number of class periods suggested for each chapter.

	9 wks.	18 wks.	36 wks.
Ch. 5	6	9	13
Ch. 6	7	9	15
Ch. 7	7	9	19
Ch. 8	5	7	18

Claude Monet. *Poplars.* (Detail.) 1891. Oil on canvas. 81.9 × 81.6 cm (32¼ × 32⅛″). The Metropolitan Museum of Art, New York, New York. Bequest of Mrs. H. O. Havemeyer, 1929. The H. O. Havemeyer Collection.

86

RESOURCES FOR UNIT 2

Unit 2 Test
ArtTalk Fine Art Transparency
• Petroglyphs

ArtTalk Fine Art Print
• John James Audubon. *The Mocking Bird*

THE ELEMENTS OF ART

CHAPTER 5
Line

CHAPTER 7
Color

CHAPTER 6
Shape, Form, and Space

CHAPTER 8
Texture

The next four chapters are devoted to the elements of art. These elements are *line, value, shape, form, space, color,* and *texture.*

In each chapter you will learn to recognize, identify, and describe the elements. You will also learn to use the elements to express ideas and feelings in your own works of art.

You will start by examining the elements as concrete, familiar things in your environment and then become acquainted with the more abstract, expressive qualities of the elements. After finishing a chapter, you will be able to use the element you have studied to uncover the mystery of the meaning in a work of art created by a master artist.

You will learn to recognize and use the elements one at a time. After completing Unit 2, however, you will have a full understanding of all the elements. You will have made a giant step toward learning the language of art and how to communicate your ideas.

87

CHAPTER OVERVIEW

Chapter 5 examines the element of line. Students become aware that line is common to both the natural and the manufactured environment. Additionally, students study and practice techniques of drawing with lines.

CHAPTER SUPPLIES

For a list of the materials you will need for the Activities in this chapter, refer to the "Art Supplies Grid" in the Teacher's Manual. In addition, have on hand the following special items: camera and film, small found objects, record or tape player, bamboo brushes, quill pens.

FINE ART RESOURCES
Transparencies
- Katsushika Hokusai. *Dancing Man*
- Rosalind Ragans. *Self-Portrait*
- Jaune Quick-to-See Smith. *Indian Drawing Lesson*

Fine Art Print
- Frank Stella. *Hockenheim*

FIGURE 5.1 This work is painted with the materials of batik, hot wax and dye, in a very untraditional manner. Twiggs must think backwards like a printmaker. First he blocks in the white lines and areas. Then he brushes on the lightest dyes. When the dye dries, he blocks in areas that must stay light and adds more dye with a brush. This process is repeated more than ten times before the work is finished.

Leo F. Twiggs. *East Wind Suite: Door*. Hugo Series. 1989. Batik: Dyes and wax resist on cotton. 61 × 51 cm (24 × 20″). Private collection.

RESOURCES FOR CHAPTER 5

Application Activities 9, 10
Artist's Profiles 5, 26, 35, 37
Cooperative Learning Activities 9, 10
Cultural Diversity in Art
Enrichment Activities 9, 10

Reteaching
  Study Guide 5
  Concept Map 5
Studio Lessons 1, 2
Chapter 5 Test

Line

Lines are everywhere. You write words, numbers, and symbols with the help of lines. You use lines to draw pictures. You read lines of printed words. The lines on a map help you find the best route from one place to another. Have you ever had to stand in line to get into the movies or to pay for merchandise in a store?

How many times a day do you see lines? What about the bare winter trees making lacy line patterns against the sky? Have you ever felt the lines of the grain in a piece of wood? Did you ever interrupt a line of ants parading from a piece of food to the anthill?

The photos in Figure 5.2 on the next page show just a few examples of lines in our environment. How many lines can you find in each picture? In this chapter, you will learn to use line in your artwork to create expressive qualities, to capture movement, and to control value change.

FIRST IMPRESSIONS

Look at *East Wind Suite: Door* from the Hugo Series by Leo Twiggs (Figure 5.1). Twiggs lives near the coast of South Carolina. To what event does he refer to when he calls a set of works the *Hugo Series?* Notice in the credit line that this work was painted in 1989. To what does the "East Wind" refer?

This particular work is called *Door.* Do you see a door or any part of a door? Look at the dark shape near the center of the painting. What kinds of lines outline the left side of the shape? What kind of line do you see on the right side of the shape? Why are they different? What kinds of lines define the shape of the door frame? What does that imply? What do the light horizontal lines and dark horizontal streaks suggest? How does the artist's use of line affect the mood of this painting?

Objectives
After completing this chapter, you will be able to:
- Observe the lines in your environment more closely.
- Name the different kinds of lines.
- Tell the five ways lines can vary in appearance.
- Understand the expressive qualities or meanings of different lines in works of art.
- Use lines to make contour, gesture, and calligraphic drawings.
- Use lines to change values.

Words to Know
calligraphy
contour line
crosshatching
dimension
gesture
implied lines
line
outline
static
value

89

FOCUS

INTRODUCING THE CHAPTER
To help students become aware of the need for words that can define line types, ask one student to describe the lines in one of the photos in Figure 5.2 on page 90 without naming anything in the photo. Then let the others try to guess which photo is being described.

VOCABULARY PREVIEW
Have students preview the list of vocabulary words on this page. Also, acquaint them with these words that will appear in the chapter: vertical lines, horizontal lines, diagonal lines, curved lines, zigzag lines, and active (lines).

USING FIRST IMPRESSIONS
Tell students that Leo Twigg's *East Wind Suite: Door* was made in response to the force of hurricane Hugo. "East Wind" refers to the wind coming in from the ocean. Encourage them to see that curved lines outline the left side of the shape; a strong, straight line defines the right side of the shape. The curved lines represent a group of people huddled together in the doorway; the straight line shows that they are partly inside the door. The door frame is defined with diagonal lines, which indicate the pull of the wind on the buildings. The streaks suggest the pull of the wind. The lines show how the hurricane winds pull on people and the buildings.

(*pages 90–99*)
• What Is Line?
• Kinds of Line
• Line Variation
• What Different Lines
  Express

GUIDED PRACTICE

**Developing
Perceptual Skills**

Have students look slowly
around the classroom and list
the lines they see. Then ask
them to identify and describe
the lines. For example, they
might list the straight, blue
lines on their writing paper
or the wrinkles around their
knuckles. Ask them to identify lines that they only now
became aware of as a result of
this exercise.

Developing Vocabulary

Ask students to brainstorm
words that they associate
with the word *line*. Examples
are *direction, path, road,
straight, narrow, row,* and *curve.*

Art Is Everywhere

To foster students'
awareness of line in everyday life, suggest this: Look
for lines in your world—
the meandering lines
of a vine, the sway of
telephone lines from pole
to pole, the organic lines
of wood grain, or the lines
of sorrow, anger, laughter,
and age in faces. Find
dynamic diagonal lines,
rigid verticals, quiet horizontals, and flowing
curves. Follow the lines
of the movement of birds,
the converging lines of
railroad tracks, or the
squiggly lines of a plate
of fettucini. Line is alive!
Watch the lines of a
dancer's movements or
the swinging arms of a
rollerblader.

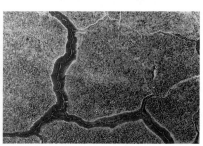

FIGURE 5.2   What lines do you see around you?

MEETING SPECIAL NEEDS

Physically or Learning Disabled   Students with
disabilities may be helped in doing an analysis by
taping a sheet of acetate over a large art reproduction. Then the students can trace over certain types
of lines with a colored marking pen. They can
mark all those lines which are vertical with one
color, all the horizontal lines in another color, and
the circular forms in another color. In this way,
students can see how artists carry design elements throughout an artwork and vary them to
add interest.

WHAT IS LINE?

In geometry, *line* is defined as an endless series of dots. In drawing, a **line** is *a mark drawn with a pointed, moving tool.* You can draw a line on paper with a pencil or scratch a line into wet clay with a stick.

Artists use lines to control your eye movement. Lines can lead your eyes into, around, and out of visual images, as in the painting in Figure 5.3.

A line has width as well as length, but the width of a line is always very small compared with its length. In fact, a line is thought of as being one-dimensional. Its one dimension is length. **Dimension** means *the amount of space an object takes up in*

LOOKING CLOSELY

FIGURE 5.3 In this painting Grant Wood uses the artificially smooth road to pull you into and through this picture story. Notice the dots of light on the top of a hill in the upper right corner. Now notice where the road begins at the top of that hill. The dark road comes leaping into the painting, and as it crests each hill it seems to get lighter. Now stop at the first house. The windows are lit with a yellow glow and there are at least three figures dressed in white standing in the roadway. What are they doing? Notice how each house that has been passed by Revere is lit and has people outside. Where the lights stop you see our hero riding into the dark ahead. Notice the house in the lower left corner. There is someone leaning out the window but the lights have not been lit yet. The smooth line of the road has pulled you into, through, and out of this enchanted memory of an American legend.

Grant Wood. *Midnight Ride of Paul Revere.* 1931. Oil on masonite. 76.2 × 101.6 cm (30 × 40″). The Metropolitan Museum of Art, New York, New York. Arthur Hoppock Hearn Fund, 1950. © Estate of Grant Wood/VAGA, New York 1987.

TEACHER TALK

Class Discussions Research demonstrates that teachers tend to dominate discussions. When class discussions are called for, such as with the "Looking Closely" feature above, be careful that the discussion does not become a monologue. Don't be afraid of silence. Give the students time to think and shape language for their responses. Also watch out for the bright, verbal student who loves to talk and might intimidate less aggressive students. One technique that some teachers use to get all the students to participate in discussions is to assign a question by calling out a name from the roll. You might reserve one section of your roll book for the purpose of recording names of students who answer questions.

one direction. You will learn more about dimensions in the next chapter when you study shapes, forms, and spaces.

As mentioned in Chapter 1, line is one of the elements of art. Artists like to think of a line as the path of a dot through space. This definition is a good one to remember, because it reminds you that it takes movement to make a line. When you

FIGURE 5.4 What edges do you see?

FIGURE 5.5 Student work. How have the edges on this picture been created?

see a line, your eyes usually follow the movement of the line.

Of course, the world is full of lines that were not drawn with a tool. Some thin, solid objects look like lines. Examples are flower stems, yarn, spiderwebs, and wires. These items look like lines because length is their most important dimension.

Some lines that we think we see in nature really do not exist. For instance, when you look at the edges of shapes, you think of lines. In the photo of the dogwood blossom (Figure 5.4), notice that there are no black lines around the outside of each petal. However, in a drawing of that same blossom in Figure 5.5, lines are used to show the edges of each shape. *A line that shows or creates the outer edges of a shape* is an **outline.**

Look at Figure 5.6 on the next page. The series of white dots representing car headlights creates lines that pull your eyes up into the picture. At first the dots are widely spaced, but as you follow them, they get closer and closer together until the line is almost solid. These are called *implied* lines. **Implied lines** are *a series of points that the viewer's eyes automatically connect.* Implied lines are only suggested; they are not real. A dotted line, a line of machine stitches, or a trail of wet footprints can create an implied line. A group of shapes arranged in a row can also create an implied line.

 Creating Lines

1 Applying Your Skills. Draw a rough plan of your school building with a pencil and ruler. Use a felt-tip pen to make a line that marks the path you follow from room to room on an average day. Invent symbols to mark the locations of the lunchroom, math class, main entrance, principal's office, and so on.

2. Further Challenge. If you have a camera that can make a time exposure, try this experiment. Mount your camera on a tripod and record the movement of car headlights that pass your house during the night. Try different effects with a variety of lens openings and exposure times.

3. Computer Option. Choose the round Pencil tool. Do not hold down the mouse button as you draw. Simply click on it frequently to create an implied line. Choose a different drawing tool and repeat. Create a design using only implied lines.

Cooperative Learning

Divide students into small groups and give them this assignment: As a group, select one of the kinds of line described on this page. Each group should appoint a recorder who will write down all the visual examples of the line type that the students can name in five minutes. For example, for curved lines, they might list sagging telephone wires, an eyebrow, and the trail that a snake leaves in the sand. The purpose of the exercise is to have students generate as many ideas as possible without censoring their responses. At the end of the time limit, each group will read its list to the rest of the class. Duplications are likely; allow students to generate as many examples as possible. Encourage students to realize that generally, collaborative efforts are often more productive than individual efforts.

FIGURE 5.6   Can you identify two examples of implied line in this painting?

Yvonne Jacquette. *East River Drive*. 1976. Pastel on paper. 47.6 × 58.4 cm (18¾ × 23″). The Metropolitan Museum of Art, New York, New York. Purchase. Friends of the Department gifts and matching funds from the National Endowment for the Arts, 1978.

KINDS OF LINES

There are five basic kinds of lines: vertical, horizontal, diagonal, curved, and zigzag.

Vertical lines (Figure 5.7, page 94) move straight up and down—they do not lean at all. A vertical line drawn on a piece of paper is perpendicular to the bottom edge of the paper. It is also perpendicular to the horizon (the line where earth and sky seem to meet). When you stand up straight, your body forms a vertical line.

Horizontal lines (Figure 5.8, page 94) are parallel to the horizon. They do not slant. When you lie flat on the floor, your body forms a horizontal line.

Diagonal lines (Figure 5.9, page 94) slant. Diagonals are somewhere between a vertical and a horizontal line. Diagonals look as if they are either rising or falling. Imagine you are standing straight up; then, with your body stiff, you fall to the floor. At any point during your fall, your body forms a diagonal line.

Curved lines (Figure 5.10, page 94) change direction gradually. When you draw wiggly lines, you

Sparking Creativity

Want students to think creatively about lines? Suggest this: Exaggerated lines make caricatures. Look for cartoons that exaggerate features of famous people. Try some of your own. Look for the strongest, or weakest, feature in someone's face or body. Then draw it with exaggeration. Exaggerate gestures to express what your character is saying or feeling. Think about the *quality* of line you need—thick or thin, nervous or strong, rough or smooth. Caricature a friend on rollerblades, someone overeating, showing off on a skateboard, and so on.

MEETING SPECIAL NEEDS

Learning Disabled   Sometimes we take for granted what might pose a challenge for another person. Different types of lines may challenge some students with mental retardation. Some may be able to make scribbles with little order. Others can conceive of and depict circularity. Still others can show verticality and horizontality. Others will be able to draw circles, squares, and triangles. Some students find satisfaction in being able to make a wavy or zigzag line. Some students with mild retardation will take delight in figuring out how to draw such a complicated form as a five-pointed star.

GUIDED PRACTICE
(continued)

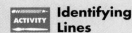

Identifying Lines

1. Applying Your Skills. To explain this activity, place a large print on the board, cover it with acetate, then demonstrate how to find the different lines.

2. Further Challenge. Rather than take new photographs, students might collect old snapshots to use for this activity. Another option would be to cut photos out of magazines or newspapers and label them.

3. Computer Option. As an alternative exercise, have students draw five equal-sized rectangles. In these frames, they can use the Line tool to create a series of drawings to illustrate each of the five line types. Vary the widths and lengths. Students may also choose to work in color or use patterns for the lines. Label each drawing with the line type.

Understanding Art History

One fascinating way to learn about line is to learn more about Japan's Zen gardens. Explain to students that Zen Buddhism is a religion that emphasizes meditation. Kyoto, Japan, is an important Zen center and the home of more than 2,000 shrines and temples. One of these is the Ryoanji Temple, famous for its garden made entirely of rocks. The garden rocks are raked into straight lines. Zen Buddhists feel that this garden of lines facilitates meditation.

An interesting activity for students is to bring to class large, shallow boxes with a layer of sand in the bottom. Allow students to use old combs or hairbrushes to sculpt lines in the sand in the manner of the Zen gardens.

94

FIGURE 5.7   Vertical lines move straight up and down.

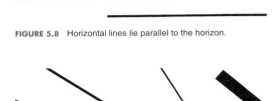

FIGURE 5.8   Horizontal lines lie parallel to the horizon.

FIGURE 5.9   Diagonal lines slant.

FIGURE 5.10   Curved lines change direction gradually.

FIGURE 5.11   Zigzag lines are combinations of diagonals.

are putting together a series of curves. Other kinds of curved lines form spirals and circles.

Zigzag lines (Figure 5.11) are made from a combination of diagonal lines. The diagonals form angles and change direction suddenly.

Identifying Lines

1. Applying Your Skills. Choose one of the following paintings from this chapter: Figure 5.1, 5.17, 5.22, 5.23, or 5.24. Diagram the lines of the painting. Use green for verticals, blue for horizontals, red for diagonals, and violet for curves. Place your diagram on display. Can your classmates identify the painting you represented by looking at the colors?

2. Further Challenge. Take a series of photographs to illustrate each of the five line types. Mount and label the photos with the type of line each illustrates.

3. Computer Option. Use the Line tool to create a series of drawings to illustrate each of the five line types. Vary the widths and lengths of your lines. You may also choose to vary patterns and colors. Label each drawing's line type.

LINE VARIATION

Lines vary in appearance in five major ways:

- **Length.** Lines can be long or short (Figure 5.12).
- **Width.** Lines can be wide or thin (Figure 5.13).
- **Texture.** Lines can be rough or smooth (Figure 5.14).
- **Direction.** Lines can move in any direction, such as vertical, horizontal, or diagonal (Figure 5.15).
- **Degree of curve.** Lines can curve gradually or not at all, become wavy, or form spirals (Figure 5.16).

These five variations can be combined in many, many ways. You can make long, wide lines; rough, short lines; and smooth, curved lines. The list is almost endless.

TECHNIQUE TIP

Students should learn to make a ruler bridge to keep from smearing their work. The materials needed include one ruler, three nickels, and some masking tape.

1. Place the three nickels on the back of the ruler, spaced equally apart.
2. Tape each coin in place.
3. Place the ruler on the work, nickel-side down. The nickels will keep the ruler from touching the work and smearing it.
4. Hold the ruler bridge steady with your free hand while you make paintbrush or marker lines.
5. When you have drawn the line, lift the ruler carefully so you don't make a smear.

FIGURE 5.12   Lines can be long or short.

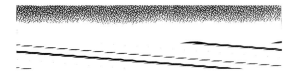

FIGURE 5.13   Lines can be wide or thin.

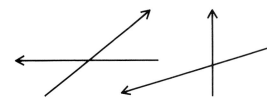

FIGURE 5.14   Lines can be rough or smooth.

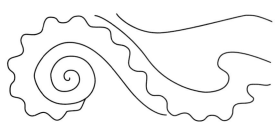

FIGURE 5.15   Lines can move in any direction.

FIGURE 5.16   Lines can curve gradually, follow reverse curves, or turn inward to form spirals.

The media, tools, and surfaces used to make lines affect the way a line looks. As with the combination of various line types, a multitude of possible effects can be created.

Some common materials used by artists to make lines are graphite, chalk, crayon, ink, and paint. The material is applied by using a tool. Some tools used for making lines include pencils, markers, pens, brushes, and scissors. A line drawn with chalk on a chalkboard looks smoother than a line drawn with chalk on a sidewalk.

Artists use different tools and materials to create different types of lines. Some artists have discovered very unusual ways of using a line, as shown in Figures 5.17 and 5.18 on page 96.

 **Creating Varied Lines**

1. Applying Your Skills.   On a sheet of paper, do a close-up line drawing in pencil (Figure 5.19 on page 96) of one of the following:

- Bare twigs on the limb of a tree
- Pine needles on the end of a branch
- A patch of uncut weeds
- The cracks in one square of pavement
- The feathers of a bird
- The bark of a tree
- The bristles of a toothbrush

2. Further Challenge.   Look carefully at a bicycle and think of it as an object made of thin and thick lines. Notice the difference between the thickness of the spokes and the thickness of the handlebars. On a large sheet of paper, make a pencil line drawing of the bicycle. Your drawing should use different line widths (Figure 5.20 on page 96) to show the different thicknesses of the parts.

3. Computer Option.   Use the Line, Pencil, and Brush tools to create a wide variety of lines. Make line variations that are long, short, wide, thin, rough, smooth, vertical, horizontal, diagonal, and curved.

GUIDED PRACTICE
(continued)

Developing Studio Skills

Collect as many different media and tools as you can for students to experiment with in making lines. After they have experimented, challenge them to go home and find at least one different way to create a line. Ask them to bring the results to school the next day.

Creating Varied Lines

1. Applying Your Skills. Demonstrate how to use the sharp point of the pencil for thin lines and the side of the pencil for wide lines.

2. Further Challenge. This activity requires some expertise in perception drawing. If your students lack confidence in their ability to draw, you can help. Bring a bicycle into the room. When they complain that it is too hard to draw, agree with them. Then ask if anyone can draw a circle. Ask someone to point out the circles on the bike. Have them find vertical, horizontal, and diagonal lines on the bike. Now challenge the students to forget that this object is a bike and to think of it as a combination of lines. They can draw the bike by drawing the various lines.

3. Computer Option. Students also might view a natural object such as a seed pod, leaf, sea shell, or bark with a magnifying glass. Instruct them to observe the varying thicknesses of the natural lines in these objects. Using the Pencil or Brush tool, have students draw what they see. Also, they can try the Calligraphic Brush tool as it varies the thickness and shapes of the lines as they draw.

MEETING SPECIAL NEEDS

Building Self-Esteem   Drawing a dense pattern of lines is the type of challenge which gifted students can rise to. Challenge their skills in elaboration by urging them to include intricate patterns. While elaboration is a key element in creativity, others are fluency, flexibility, and originality. Drawing a dense pattern of lines may need to be simplified for some students with disabilities. For example, the feathers of a bird can be conceived in a schematic way, which communicates the idea of feather just as much as does a realistic feather drawing. It is a sufficient challenge for some students to visually conceive of and draw a single object.

GUIDED PRACTICE
(continued)

Understanding Art History

Inform students that Georges Rouault was associated with the Fauves (see Chapter 3, page 58). As such, he was less interested in painting scenes that depicted happiness and pleasure than he was in showing the more sorrowful side of life. He used his art to point out injustices and problems in the world. Probably because he was apprenticed to a stained-glass maker as a young boy, his style reflects the heavy lines that are similar to the lines of solder that join pieces of stained glass. If possible, show other examples of his works such as *The Old King* and *The Italian Woman*. Ask students to discuss the similarities between his paintings and examples of stained glass.

Developing Perceptual Skills

Try to provide a variety of pencil hardness and a variety of pens for the students to experiment with. Even if you can only get a few of each kind, students can share them so that they can discover the effects they can create with different pens and pencils.

Developing Studio Skills

Have students work in pairs or small groups to list at least five adjectives that describe moods or activities. For example, playful, sad, mysterious, puzzled, and disagreeable. Then have students independently draw a line that expresses each adjective. Encourage them to use the kinds of lines described in this chapter. Have students select one example to share with the rest of the class.

FIGURE 5.17 When Rouault was a boy he was apprenticed to a maker of stained glass. The thick black lines surrounding bright colors in his paintings remind the viewer of stained-glass windows.

Georges Rouault. *Christ and the Apostles.* 1937–38. Oil on canvas. 64.3 × 99.4 cm (25¼ × 39⅛″). The Metropolitan Museum of Art, New York, New York. The Jacques and Natasha Gelman Collection.

FIGURE 5.18 How many different line directions and line variations can you find in Curnoe's painting?

Greg Curnoe. *Mariposa 10 Speed.* 1973. Watercolor over graphite on paper. 101.1 × 181.4 cm (39⅞ × 71⅜″). National Gallery of Canada, Ottawa, Canada. © Estate of Greg Curnoe/VAGA, New York 1994.

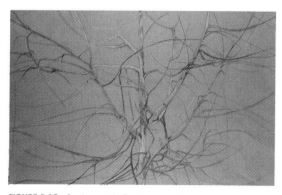

FIGURE 5.19 Student work. Close-up line drawing.

FIGURE 5.20 Student work. Using thin and thick lines.

RESOURCES BEYOND THE CLASSROOM

Involving others in your art program is invaluable to its success. Both within the school and the community, teachers find it worthwhile to establish communication and interaction with people and organizations, who are interested in maintaining the art programs for students. Just as sports programs often have a booster club, art programs would benefit from a similar organization. Why not organize a support group? Even if you don't hold meetings, work with the journalism instructors to send out newsletters designed by students advising people of art shows, awards, and general student progress in your program.

WHAT DIFFERENT LINES EXPRESS

Depending on its direction, a line can communicate, or express, different ideas or feelings. This is why lines are an important part in the language of art. Vertical lines can make certain objects look taller. For example, vertical lines on wallpaper can make low ceilings seem higher. Clothing designers use vertical lines to make short people look taller and heavy people look thinner.

Vertical lines are **static**, or *inactive*. They appear to be at rest. For this reason, they express stability. Vertical lines can also give an impression of dignity, poise, stiffness, and formality, as shown in Figure 5.21.

Horizontal lines are also static. They express feelings of peace, rest, quiet, and stability, as in Figure 5.22, page 98. Horizontal lines make you feel content, relaxed, and calm. Modern, casual furniture uses horizontal lines to create a soft, comfortable look.

Unlike vertical and horizontal lines, diagonal and zigzag lines are *active* lines. They communicate action and movement because they seem to be pulled one way or the other. They are not at rest.

Diagonals express instability, tension, activity, and excitement, as shown in Figure 5.23, page 98. Since they can appear to be either falling or rising, they sometimes make a viewer feel uncomfortable. Artists use them to add tension or to create an exciting mood. However, when two diagonals meet and seem to support each other, as in the roof of a house, they appear more stable.

FIGURE 5.21 What do the lines tell you about the sound of the chant that this painting represents? Is it loud and wild, or quiet and dignified? How many different line directions can you find? What is the predominant line movement? How does that affect the mood of this work? How many line variations can you find? What do you think the different lines represent?

Dan Namingha. *Blessing Rain Chant.* 1992. Acrylic on canvas. 198 × 305 cm (78 × 120″). Niman Fine Art, Santa Fe, New Mexico.

AT THE MUSEUM

Minneapolis Institute of Arts (Minneapolis, Minnesota) At the Minneapolis Institute of Arts, visitors have their choice of three touch-screen interpretive multimedia programs. Each program is related to the objects in the gallery it is located in. One section of "The Art of Japan" program is a computer-simulated tour of a Japanese house with objects from the Japanese gallery placed throughout the house. The second program, "From Silver to Silica," is about the history of photography and is located in the photo gallery. The African art program is positioned in their African art gallery and is in the form of a "video jukebox."

GUIDED PRACTICE
(continued)

Developing Perceptual Skills

Discuss how the line type affects the expressive quality of each work. To help the student grasp the idea of expressive line qualities, refer to the pull of gravity. Vertical lines are in balance with gravity. When you are standing upright, gravity is pulling through the center of your body. When you are horizontal, you are totally at rest. You are lying flat and gravity is pulling evenly on all parts of your body. However, anyone in a diagonal position must be supported. A diagonal looks as if it is falling or rising; it seems to be in motion.

If your students are not too inhibited, ask them to act out the line directions—to stand straight as a vertical, for example—and then ask them how they feel.

Art Is Everywhere

To foster students' awareness of art in everyday life, suggest this: Listen to the melodic line of a musical composition. Try to move your hand in its pattern. Compare several musical works to find a flowing melody, a staccato melody, a heavy one, or a light one. Look at music scores and see if the linear movement created by the notes tells you something about the sound. Listen to an orchestral work to hear the interplay of many melodic lines. Watch the hand movement of an orchestra conductor and see how he or she "draws" the linear movement of the composition and signals cues to individuals or groups of musicians.

GUIDED PRACTICE
(continued)

Understanding Art History
To help students further appreciate the life and times of Edward Hopper, whose work is shown in Figure 5.22, assign *Artist's Profile 35* in the TCR.

Developing Studio Skills
Have students make a pencil drawing of a person engaged in an activity and use straight lines in the composition to lead the viewer's eye toward the focal point of action.

Using Art Criticism
Divide the class into four groups and assign each one to assume the role of one of the following: art educator, consumer, art patron, and art critic. Then have them brainstorm a list of reasons why their particular person would, or would not, purchase a painting like Hopper's *Early Sunday Morning*. List the reasons on the board and discuss the results.

Exploring Aesthetics
After students have studied Thomas Hart Benton's painting *I Got a Girl on Sourwood Mountain*, guide them through the steps of art criticism by asking the following questions: What painting media did Benton use? What do you see in the painting? How has Benton used lines to create a sense of excitement and liveliness? How many horizontal or vertical lines do you see? What is happening in the scene? What is the artist trying to say in the painting? How might a critic respond to the painting?

FIGURE 5.22 Strong horizontal lines create a sense of calm on this empty street. As you look at this painting, you get the feeling that everyone is sleeping peacefully. How many real and how many implied horizontal lines can you find in this painting?

Edward Hopper. *Early Sunday Morning*. 1930. Oil on canvas. 89.2 × 152.4 cm (35 × 60″). Collection of Whitney Museum of American Art, New York, New York.

Zigzag lines create confusion. They are extremely active and evoke feelings of excitement and nervousness, as in Figure 5.24. The degree of intensity is indicated by the direction of the zigzag. Zigzags that move horizontally, such as those across the top of a picket fence, are less active than the irregular zigzags of a streak of lightning.

Because curved lines change direction, they too express some activity. How much activity they express depends on the type and direction of the curve. The less active the curve, the calmer the feeling. Whatever the amount of activity, all curved lines are graceful. Curved lines are often used in interior decoration to suggest a feeling of luxury, as in Figure 5.25, page 100. Spiral curves wind around a central point. They are hypnotic and draw the eye to their center.

FIGURE 5.23 In this print every line that should be static is diagonal. Look at the window, the lamp, the rug, the floor planks, and the fiddler's bench. The diagonal lines fill the work with a sense of excitement. Not only the people but also every corner of the room seems to be alive and dancing to the music of the fiddler.

Thomas Hart Benton. *I Got a Girl on Sourwood Mountain*. 1938. Lithograph. 31.7 × 23.4 cm (12½ × 9¼″). Courtesy of the Library of Congress, Washington, D.C. © T. H. Benton and R. P. Benton Testamentary Trusts/VAGA, New York 1994.

COOPERATIVE LEARNING

Collaborative learning is tailor-made for the art teacher who wants to reinforce the steps of art criticism. When students work in groups, they are usually less inhibited and therefore more likely to be original with their ideas. For example, when studying how Benton and Hopper use line to convey mood, suggest that students form small groups and pretend to be explorers from another galaxy who are trying to understand something about our civilization from its artworks. Encourage playful, creative responses that ultimately incorporate the steps of art criticism. Group members might discuss the first two steps together, then each student could write his or her interpretation and judgment.

FIGURE 5.24   Sheeler uses diagonal lines to indicate the houses are sliding into the flood waters. Notice how the houses in the background are beginning to lean.

Charles Sheeler. *Catastrophe No. 2.* 1944. Tempera on panel. 43.2 × 35.5 cm (17 ×14″). Wichita Art Museum, Wichita, Kansas. The Roland P. Murdock Collection.

 Using Lines Expressively

1. Applying Your Skills.   Choose two words from the following list:

swimming	burning	praying
rocking	flowing	jumping
marching	running	growing
dancing	crawling	laughing
wagging	writing	flying

On separate sheets of paper, illustrate the words you have chosen by using line movement only (see Figure 5.26 on page 101). Do not draw objects. Choose the medium you think will work best. When you have finished, write the word on the back of each paper. Ask your friends to look at the lines and guess which words you have illustrated.

2. Further Challenge.   Make two line drawings of crowded city buildings. Use static lines in one to express calm stability. Use active lines in the other to express the rush and confusion of a crowded city. Choose the medium you think is most effective for depicting each cityscape.(See Figure 5.27 on page 101.)

3. Computer Option.   Make two drawings using lines, not objects. Let one drawing illustrate quiet, calm piano music, and let the other illustrate music produced by the loudest rock group you can imagine.

ART ON A SHOESTRING

Students' capacity to appreciate works of art or architecture that contain an abundance of fine or intricate detail, such as Figure 5.25 on page 100, can be enhanced by displaying the works as slides or overhead transparencies. A common, but often overlooked, source of such material is vacation slides and photographic negatives that can be processed into slides at a nominal cost. Also, museum gift shops often sell high-quality slides of their major artworks. Prior to lesson time, assemble slides, either from your own collection or from other teachers, friends, and relatives.

FIGURE 5.25 Many of the decorative elements in this luxurious bedroom seem to swirl with curves. How do you think you would feel living in a room like this? Would you be comfortable?

Italian, Venice. Bedroom from the Sagredo Palace. c. 1725–35. The Metropolitan Museum of Art. New York, New York. Rogers Fund, 1906.

CONTOUR DRAWING

A **contour line** *defines the edges and surface ridges of an object.* A contour line also creates a boundary separating one area from another. Contour drawing will add to your drawing skills as well as to your ability to observe and understand objects. See the examples in Figure 5.28 on page 101 and in 5.29 on page 102.

When you are drawing contours, do not lift the pencil from the paper. Let your eyes follow the contour of the object you are drawing, and move your pencil at the same speed as your eyes. The line should be continuous. Draw the line slowly and with care. Concentrate in order to draw accurately. See the Technique Tip on page 349 in the Handbook for help in making contour drawings.

 Using Contour Lines

1. Applying Your Skills. Using a felt-tip or ball-point pen, make a series of five contour drawings of your hand or bare foot on a single sheet of paper. You can indicate roundness by showing the curve of the wrinkles on your fingers or toes. Change the position of your hand or foot for each drawing. Then, on a second sheet of paper, do a contour drawing of your hand or foot from memory only.

2. Further Challenge. Use a water-based felt-tip or ballpoint pen and one sheet of paper to make a series of five contour drawings of a single object, such as a pair of scissors, a key, a shoe, or a hairbrush. Change the position of the object for each drawing. Then, on a new sheet of paper, draw the object from memory.

TECHNIQUE TIP

When making contour drawings of a still-life arrangement, be sure to place the arrangement high on a counter or table so that it can be seen by everyone in the class. This may require that you rearrange the seating. Some students may need to lean on drawing boards or sit upon countertops or tabletops so that they can see the arrangement. You will not have discipline problems if you insist upon quiet concentration while drawing is going on. Sometimes playing music on the radio helps students concentrate. The choice of music is up to you. Some prefer classical or easy-listening, while others will want pop and rock. Be sure to get permission from your administrators before you bring a radio into the room.

FIGURE 5.26   Student art. Which word fits this art?

FIGURE 5.28   Andrews indicates that this scholar is concentrating deeply by accenting the head with lines to indicate the wrinkles of thought. He leaves the rest of the scene, except for the book, very simple.

Benny Andrews. *The Scholar.* 1974. Pen and ink on paper. 30 × 23 cm (12 × 9″). Private collection.

FIGURE 5.27   Student art. What contrasting moods do these two scenes express?

GUIDED PRACTICE *(continued)*

Developing Studio Skills

Ask students to do contour drawings as a homework assignment. Have them sketch a pet, an animal at the zoo, objects in their homes, and so on.

ACTIVITY   Using Contour Lines

1. Applying Your Skills. To help students be successful with this activity, have them sit sideways in their chairs and tape the drawing paper to the table. Instruct them to place the drawing hand on the paper but look only at the other hand to draw. This will force students to think about the contours of the hand or foot. (You will easily tell if any student is not doing a contour drawing.) Remind students that contour drawings never look good at first, but with practice, the quality of students' drawings, as well as the quality of their perceptual skills, will improve.

2. Further Challenge. The purpose of this activity is to show students that contour drawings help improve their perception skills. After students have completed the contour studies, their memory of the object should be sharp.

3. Computer Option. Students who are unfamiliar with the technique of using a mouse might at first be discouraged or frustrated when trying to complete this activity. Encourage them to be patient and experiment with the controls on the mouse and the way it moves. If other students have more experience, ask them to demonstrate the use of the mouse to computer novices and ask them to share any practical advise they might have.

TEACHER TALK

Classroom Management   Set small still-life arrangements around the room in various places so that every student can see one clearly. You might have to place one on each table. Limit the arrangements to three objects each. Try to include one plant in each arrangement. Ask the students to make contour drawings. First, have them point to the objects and draw them in the air. Get them to notice that the bottom of round things, like pots and cylinders, usually curve. Observe when they draw in the air that they are drawing on a flat picture plane and not in depth.

GUIDED PRACTICE
(continued)

Developing Perceptual Skills

Encourage students to practice gesture drawing as it makes use of the whole arm not just the hand. Encourage students to practice this method often, using the same object each time. After several attempts, ask them to evaluate their progress by examining the rough sketches in the order that they were made.

Developing Studio Skills

Have students make chalk gesture drawings using photographs of action figures from sports or fashion magazines. They should then put the photograph away and turn the gestures into a different scene of the student's choice. For example, the gestures of a basketball player could turn into those of a dancer. Make these sketches into finished works using oil pastels or paints.

Capturing Motion

1. Applying Your Skills. The best way to help students understand gesture drawing is to demonstrate it for them. Have a model pose, point out the position to the students, and explain that you are going to draw only the position and not the details of the model. Before you draw, show them that you are observing the curve of the back or the diagonal lines of one leg. Then quickly demonstrate.

Have a second model pose, point out the different lines of the body, and then ask students to draw quickly. Give them 30 seconds. (Most of them won't finish.) Then show the students what you see and let them correct their sketches.

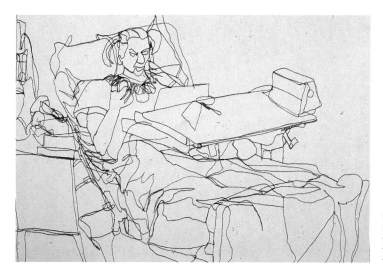

FIGURE 5.29   Student work. Notice how the line flows through this hospital scene. Look at the difference between the busy zigzag lines that describe the wrinkles in the sheet and the few lines that define the person's face.

GESTURE DRAWING

A **gesture** is *an expressive movement.* The purpose of drawing gestures is to capture the feeling of motion. A gesture drawing does not use a lot of detail (Figure 5.30).

Lines showing gestures are quickly drawn. They should be sketched freely and loosely, almost in a reckless manner in order to capture movement. Unlike contours, they represent the interior of an object. Your drawing of gestures may look like scribbles at first, but this is acceptable. Concentrate on showing position and movement.

   Capturing Motion

1. Applying Your Skills.   Make a series of gesture drawings. (See the Technique Tip on page 349 in the Handbook.) Classmates should take turns posing for

FIGURE 5.30   Tintoretto describes the gesture and bulk of this figure with just a few rough lines. You can sense the movement of the figure through the looseness of the quickly drawn lines.

Jacopo Tintoretto. *Standing Youth with His Arm Raised, Seen from Behind.* Black chalk on laid paper. 36.3 × 21.9 cm (14¼ × 8⅝"). National Gallery of Art, Washington, D.C. Ailsa Mellon Bruce Fund.

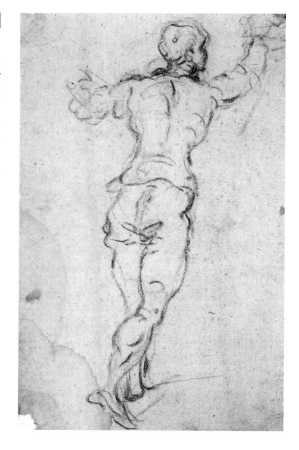

TEACHER TALK

Classroom Management   Because the art room is more often used for noisy production activities, classroom arrangement should lend itself to quick manipulation. It is hard to space young people around the room at tables and still keep their attention during a lengthy discussion. Even though you must crowd students together or ask them to move chairs from work stations to a discussion area, some provision must be made so that they can gather, facing the teacher. Consider the need for an area where quiet activities take place—films, slide presentations, lectures, and discussions. It can also serve as a reading/study center where books and prints are available.

FIGURE 5.31   Student work. Gesture drawing.

one another. Start with thirty-second poses. Shorten the time by five seconds for each pose until you are down to ten seconds. Since the poses are so short, ask the model to be active. Have her or him twist, turn, bend, and kick, trying to avoid doing the same thing twice. (See Figure 5.31.)

2. Further Challenge.   Play "musical gestures." You will need a record or tape player and a recording of your favorite music. Choose at least two people to be models and one to be a disc jockey. The DJ is in charge of starting and stopping the music and must face away from the models. When the music starts, the models dance; when it stops, the models freeze. As soon as the music stops, the artists draw the models in the positions in which they have frozen, using the same sheet of paper. The DJ may let a pose last from ten to thirty seconds. When the music starts again, the artists stop drawing, and the models resume dancing. This exercise can be repeated as many times as desired. Change crayon or pen color with each pose and feel free to overlap figures.

3. Computer Option.   Choose a round, medium-size Brush or Pencil tool. Sit at the computer station, turn sideways, and look at other students who are modeling for gesture drawing. They will be changing positions every twenty or thirty seconds. Try to capture the feeling of motion, not detail. Change color each time the model changes positions. Some of your drawings will overlap.

CALLIGRAPHIC DRAWING

The word **calligraphy** means *beautiful handwriting.* Calligraphy is often thought of in connection with Oriental writing and art. In China and Japan, calligraphy is used to form *characters* that Oriental writers use in much the same way we use the alphabet. Chinese and Japanese characters are more like pictures, however. They can represent a complete idea, object, or verbal sound. They are more than just a letter. The Chinese and Japanese use the same types of calligraphic lines and brushstrokes in their paintings (Figure 5.32, page 104). In fact, in the Chinese language, the words *writing* and *painting* are represented by the same character.

Calligraphic lines are usually made with brushstrokes that change from thin to thick in one stroke. To make a very thin line, use the tip of the brush. As you press on the brush and more of it touches the paper, the line becomes wider. (See the Technique Tip 3 on page 349 in the Handbook.)

 Thick-to-Thin Lines

1. Applying Your Skills.   Practice making calligraphic lines with ink or watercolor paint. Use round, pointed brushes, both thin and thick. Also, try bamboo brushes.

2. Further Challenge. Before the game starts, it would be wise for you to be the DJ and show students how to work the equipment. Then you might have students take turns playing both DJ and models so that everyone does some drawing. Having more than one model helps everyone see at least one model well. It is also a chance for the student who finished quickly to have a second model to look at. Insist that students change colors as they work or everything will look like a gigantic scribble.

3. Computer Option. Students will have to work quickly. Encourage them to capture the feeling of motion and energy by selecting a different brush color each time the model changes position. They might also overlap their drawings.

**Developing
Perceptual Skills**

Display several examples of calligraphic and typeset texts and ask students to distinguish between the two. Help students become sensitive to the minute variations in form and rhythm that are a part of the charm of calligraphic work.

 Thick-to-Thin Lines

1. Applying Your Skills. Bring in other examples of Oriental calligraphy. Read over Technique Tip 3 directions found on page 349 and study the photographs with the students to help them see how they can gain control over their brushes. This activity will be more successful if you have some nylon sable brushes for them to use.

CULTURAL PERSPECTIVES

The Chinese tradition of artistic training dictated that students study and copy the works and styles of ancient masters. They valued this ability to copy the masters. Tung Ch'i'ch'ang (1555–1636) declared, "It is ingenious to be able to conform to the model: it is divine to be able to depart from it." So, in his eyes the truly gifted artist was the one who could breathe new life into an old tradition. Tung succeeded in bringing this innovative flavor to both his famous landscape paintings and his calligraphy.

LOOKING
CLOSELY

Have students study Figure 5.32 and answer the questions in the caption. Help them see that every mark in this work has been made with a single brushstroke. Even the short, wide leaves in the lower left were made with a single stroke. There is not a sketchy line in the work. The lines that define the rocks and the lines of the water look fuzzy because they were made with a dry brush.

2. Further Challenge.
If you have plants in the room, place at least one on each table. Tell students to choose one that can be easily seen for their studies. Another option would be to bring some large weeds to class for these studies. Each student could place one on the table near his or her paper. Be careful not to bring in allergy-causing plants such as ragweed.

3. Computer Option.
A program's selection of fonts and styles gives students additional options for this activity. Encourage students to use the options on their programs that they are least familiar with, thereby expanding their knowledge.

Developing Perceptual Skills
Encourage students to view a dollar bill with a magnifying glass. Ask the same questions of the lines in the paper money that are asked of Dürer's work in Figure 6.23 on page 134.

LOOKING CLOSELY

FIGURE 5.32 Gu Mei was a famous singer, poet, and painter of landscapes and ink orchids. She created this long handscroll containing three different sections depicting orchids and rocks. Notice how the long curving lines have been made with one brushstroke. Where else can you find lines that seem to have been painted with one brushstroke? Notice how the calligraphic Chinese writing is an integral part of the design.

Gu Mei. *Orchids and Rocks.* 1644. Ming dynasty. Detail of handscroll. Ink on paper. 27 × 170.8 cm (10⅝ × 67¼"). Arthur M. Sackler Gallery, Smithsonian Institution, Washington, D.C. Arthur M. Sackler Collection.

2. Further Challenge. Use a watercolor brush and ink or watercolor paint to make a series of five calligraphic studies of one natural object, such as a leaf or vegetable (Figure 5.33).

3. Computer Option. Research either Egyptian hieroglyphics or Southwestern pictographs to gain information about "picture writing." Create a picture writing by making up your own symbols. Use any computer tools and options available. Remember that the Cut and Paste options are helpful when you want to repeat a symbol without redrawing it.

FIGURE 5.33 Student work. A drawing made with calligraphic lines.

MEETING SPECIAL NEEDS

Learning Partners Students who may have difficulty following directions or discussion topics may benefit from a learning partner. Choose a partner based on the nature of a student's difficulty, such as hearing, vision, language proficiency, or comprehension. Allow time for partners to confer whenever the partner needing help feels it is necessary.

Encourage students to develop an ongoing method of self-directed learning. For example, students with limited English proficiency might routinely make a list of terms that are particularly difficult. They can then ask their learning partners to work with them to clarify the meanings of those terms.

LINE AND VALUE

Value is *the art element that describes the darkness or lightness of an object.* Value depends on how much light a surface reflects. A surface has a dark value if it reflects little light. It has a light value if it reflects a lot of light. Because value is closely related to the way every element and principle of art works, it will be mentioned throughout *ArtTalk.*

Every time you make a pencil mark on a piece of white paper, you are creating a line with a certain value. The harder you press, the darker the value. A series of closely placed lines can create areas of dark value. The lines may be parallel or they may cross one another. **Crosshatching** is *the technique of using crossed lines for shading.* You will learn more about crosshatching in Chapter 6.

The values that line groups create depend on many things: the number of lines, the size of the spaces between the lines, the media, and the tools. A soft pencil (2B, 4B) makes a wide, dark line. A hard pencil (2H, 4H) makes a thin, gray line. A crayon stroked over a rough surface makes a broken line. A crayon stroked over smooth paper makes a solid line.

Look at the Dürer etching in Figure 6.23 on page 134. Use a magnifying glass to study the way Dürer has used a variety of line combinations to create dark and light values. What method did he use in the lightest areas? How did he create the darkest values? How many different kinds of line combinations can you find? How many different uses does Dürer make of line in this one work?

FIGURE 5.34   Student work. Using lines to create values.

Using Line to Create Value

1. Applying Your Skills.   Create a crosshatched value scale using a medium HB pencil on white paper. First, draw a long, thin rectangle using a ruler. Divide the rectangle into seven parts. Leave the section on the far left blank. The section on the far right should be as black as you can make it. Crosshatch the middle section so that it is a middle gray. Now crosshatch the other squares so the values move in gradual steps from white to black.

2. Further Challenge.   Fold a small sheet of white drawing paper into nine squares. In each square use a different combination of parallel or crosshatched lines to create a different value (Figure 5.34). Try a variety of pencils, from hard 2H to soft 4B lead. Try quill pens, ballpoint pens, and felt-tip pens. Think of some other tools and materials to use.

3. Computer Option.   Use the Line tool to draw three diagonal lines from screen edge to screen edge. This will divide your screen into six or seven sections. Fill each section with lines. Vary the spacing of the lines by placing them close together in one section and farther apart in another. Lines can be crosshatched. You can choose the Patterns palette and fill the sections by using the Fill Bucket tool or create your own pattern. Use only black and white. Notice that the value of the area darkens as lines are placed close together and lightens when lines are farther apart.

GUIDED PRACTICE
(continued)

ACTIVITY Using Line to Create Value

1. Applying Your Skills.
To save time, prepare photocopies of rectangles so that students can concentrate on the crosshatching. Emphasize that crosshatching must be controlled—it is not scribbling quickly. Crosshatching requires carefully placed, controlled marks.

2. Further Challenge.
To facilitate this activity, set out a variety of pencils and pens with which students could shade the squares. Suggest that students experiment on scrap paper before they work on the final paper.

3. Computer Option.
As an alternative computer activity, have students draw a large three-dimensional box. Fill in each of the sides using lines. Vary the thicknesses and distances between lines or use crosshatching. Each side should have a different value. Also, students can choose from the Pattern palette or create their own pattern.

INDEPENDENT PRACTICE

Study Guide
Distribute and have students complete *Study Guide 5* in the Reteaching booklet.

Enrichment
- Assign *Enrichment Activity 9* and *10* in the TCR.
- Ask students to choose works from Chapter 3 and analyze how the artists' use of line communicates something about the culture in which the artwork was created.

Studio Lessons
To expand students' familiarity with the concept of line, Studio Lessons are available in the TCR.

TEACHER TALK
Computer Classrooms The students presently in your classrooms are no strangers to the keyboard, mouse, and monitor. When you combine their comfort level with the art programs available commercially, you have the potential for significant creative responses in the art classroom. Computers speed up the process of creating artworks and allow for manipulation of the text. Consequently, students can test an idea or design then alter all or part of it as they revise their thinking. Importantly, the time saved by the efficiency of the computer can be directed to even more creative efforts.

Yarn Painting

FIGURE 5.35 Artist unknown. Huichol Indian, Santa Caterina, Jalisco, Mexico. *Sacrifice to the Mother of the Eagles*. 1991. Braided yarn embedded in vegetable wax on wood. 40 × 49.5 cm (15¾ × 19½"). Private collection.

FOCUS

OBJECTIVE

Design and create a yarn painting using a realistic or nonobjective theme and simple shapes.

MOTIVATOR

Review how symbolism is used in a work of art. (See Chapter 1, page 6.) As an example, Surrealists Salvador Dali and René Magritte used ordinary objects in their paintings to represent certain meanings or emotions. Ask students to volunteer other examples of symbolism in art.

TEACH

GUIDED PRACTICE

Developing Studio Skills

When working with yarn and glue, suggest that students pre-measure and cut small amounts of yarn before applying glue to the individual strands of yarn. When covering the larger areas of the picture, it may be less messy to apply individual lines of glue to the cardboard, then place each strand of yarn into the glue.

Exploring Aesthetics

Provide examples of medieval tapestries such as the *Bayeux Tapestry*. Compare and contrast the yarn paintings of the Huichol with the tapestries of the Middle Ages. How are they similar? How are they different?

Supplies
- Pencil and sketchbook
- Heavy cardboard
- Scissors and white glue
- Yarns of various colors and textures
- Toothpicks or paper clips
- Damp sponge and towels

A Huichol Indian from Mexico created the yarn painting shown in Figure 5.35. Although the Huichol do not sign their artwork, other artists in the area can identify the creator of the work by examining the drawing style and the kinds of materials used by the artist. Notice the simple drawing style and how the braided yarn is laid in careful rows within the outlined figures. The colors of the yarn are bright and clear, and the picture tells a story. This work was created as an offering to please a goddess in the hope that she would send much-needed rain for the crops. The Mother of the Eagles in the center of the work can be identified by her wings. There are other symbols in the picture. Can you find them?

This work has been made with great care. Notice that the entire surface of the work was covered and that each figure was given a contrasting border to define the shape.

Select a theme for your yarn painting and decide on the symbol you will include. Design and create the painting using realistic or nonobjective shapes. After gluing yarn to the outlines of the shapes, fill in the shapes with strands of yarn. Use a variety of line directions, colors, and textures. Cover the entire surface so that no board shows.

106

SAFETY NOTE

Vapor or fumes from permanent markers can be harmful. Always use water-base markers. Also, avoid using rubber cement and airplane glue for projects. Both contain solvents that are harmful if allowed to remain on the skin too long. Remember that students with disabilities are at risk because their systems may not be as robust. In using certain art materials, urge students to wash their hands frequently and to avoid putting their fingers into their mouths. One safety precaution is to make students aware of the dangers of, and potential lethality of, inhaling aromatic hydrocarbons from typewriter erasure fluid, nail polish, hair sprays, and aerosol spray cans, such as artist's fixative.

FOCUSING

Study the Huichol yarn painting. Read the information about the work and discuss the meaning of the symbols in the painting. Notice that the outlines of the figures, flowers, candles, and rain lines were made first. Then study how the artist used lines of yarn to fill in the outlines.

CREATING

Decide whether you want to create a realistic or nonobjective design. Sketch several ideas for your yarn painting in your sketchbook. Keep the design simple, using just a few large shapes. Do not go into detail. Select your best design and draw it on the cardboard.

Plan the colors and types of yarn you will use. Collect all the materials you will need, including the yarn. Before you start gluing, cover your work space with newspaper and find a flat surface on which your work can be stored to dry.

Outline the major shapes on the cardboard by squeezing a thin line of glue over your pencil line and pressing one strand into the glue.

Spread the glue over the area inside the outline. Use the nozzle as a spreader. Then press the yarn firmly into the glue with toothpicks or unbent paper clips. Fill each area with sets of touching parallel strands. One shape may be filled with a vertical pattern. Other shapes may be filled with horizontal lines or with a spiral. Do not leave any spaces between the yarn lines. Be sure to cover the entire surface of the cardboard.

If your fingers or your pressing tools get sticky, use the damp sponge to clean off the glue. Between sessions, be sure to store the work on a flat surface, uncovered, so nothing sticks to the glue.

Mount or mat the finished work for display. (See Technique Tip 27 on page 363 in the Handbook.)

FIGURE 5.35A   Student work.

C R I T I Q U I N G

Describe   What kind of shapes did you choose for your design, realistic or nonobjective? Did the Huichol yarn painting influence your decision? How did you prepare your finished work for display?

Analyze   Did you create outlines around the shapes? Describe the line directions you used to fill in the shapes and the spaces between them. Which yarn colors and textures did you use for the outlines, the shapes, and the background? Did you cover the entire surface of the board?

Interpret   Did you select a realistic or a nonobjective theme? How do the line directions, the outlines, the colors, and the yarn textures affect the mood? Give your work a title.

Judge   Is your work successful? Did the line directions, the outlines, the colors, and the yarn textures create the effect you planned? Is there anything you would change to make the work more successful? Which aesthetic theory fits your work?

107

Enrichment

Tell students that the arts of many cultures are rich in abstract symbols. For example, the written language of Asian countries is not a series of sound symbols like our alphabet. Each character represents an object or an idea—tree, rain, fields, fear, love, and so on. Sign language is another form of communication based on a system of symbols expressing ideas. Encourage students to learn more about cultural symbols. Then, with a brush have them make up symbols of their own to use with their yarn painting.

Keeping a Portfolio

Remind students that the preliminary sketches and the final artwork for this Studio Lesson are likely considerations for their portfolios.

ASSESS

CRITIQUING

Have students apply the steps of art criticism to their own artwork using the "Critiquing" steps in the text.

CLOSE

Have students list as many concepts about line as they can remember. Ask them to sketch a design using as many line types as possible, including a variety of techniques and media.

MEETING SPECIAL NEEDS

Visually Impaired   Some students with disabilities may reject the idea of contour drawing, because things do not look "right." Students with retardation may have difficulty in conceiving the idea of an edge that cuts across a form and they may also have difficulty in portraying it. Encourage students with partial vision to draw on a black background with a bottle of white glue (it now also comes in colors). The glue, when dry, will leave a raised edge that the artist can feel, and the shapes can then be filled in. Another technique for students who are blind is to draw into a styrofoam meat tray, leaving an embossed line, which can be felt.

Contour Wire Sculpture

OBJECTIVE

Design and create a three-dimensional contour sculpture based on a series of contour drawings of a single object.

MOTIVATOR

Show large photos of wire sculptures and mobiles by Alexander Calder. Show students how he used line to define shape in space.

GUIDED PRACTICE

Developing Studio Skills

When making contour drawings for ideas, begin by making initial drawings of a variety of objects before choosing one to draw and sculpt.

Also, if a jeweler's jig is available, students may benefit by using it to bend the wire. This tool can provide a variety of bends and angles for the wire. To provide a nice finish, students may want to sand and apply varnish to the block of wood before mounting the sculpture.

Developing Perceptual Skills

Remind students that since the sculpture is three-dimensional, they should keep turning the sculpture to view it from all sides as they work on it. A successful sculpture should look interesting from every point of view.

STUDIO LESSON: CONTOUR WIRE SCULPTURE

FIGURE 5.36   Alexander Calder. *Varese*. 1931. Wire. 34.2 × 34.9 × 31.1 cm (13½ × 13 ¾ × 12¼″). Whitney Museum of American Art, New York, New York.

Supplies

- Sketchbook and pencil
- Needle-nose pliers
- Wire cutter
- Pliable wire

Optional:

- Small block of wood
- Staple gun or staple nail and hammer
- String

SAFETY NOTE

Wear safety glasses when working with long pieces of wire.

As a child, Alexander Calder made spiral-wire jewelry for his sister's dolls. Both his parents were artists, and Calder grew up in their studios. The path that led to his invention of the mobile sculpture and wire-line sculptures such as *Varese* (Figure 5.36) began in this family atmosphere of creativity.

While attending the Art Students' League in New York City, Calder and his fellow classmates would go out into the streets and rapidly sketch people as they passed by. He was well known for his skill in capturing a sense of movement with a single, unbroken line. In these simple contour drawings, he captured the essential characteristics of his subjects.

Eventually Calder began to experiment with wire sculptures. His new figures became three-dimensional forms drawn in space by wire lines. He made animals inspired by his childhood fascination with the circus, and he created portraits of people such as *Varese*. Many of his wire drawings were humorous, and each was interesting to look at from every angle.

Try your hand at wire sculpture and discover what kind of lively and interesting three-dimensional figure you can create.

Design and create a three-dimensional sculpture that defines space and shape through the movement of a wire line through space. Make this three-dimensional contour wire sculpture look interesting from every point of view. Base this sculpture on your own series of contour drawings of a single object. Prepare your finished work for display.

108

MORE ABOUT . . . ALEXANDER CALDER

Alexander Calder is most noted for his wind mobiles. These mobiles were made from rods, wires, and delicate shapes made of sheet metal and wire hung from a single point. Air currents set the mobiles in motion, treating the viewer to constantly changing patterns of colors and shapes. Many of Calder's mobiles are based on natural forms—animals, birds, fish, or plants—and the motions were carefully planned to imitate the movement of the subject. His later works show that he became more interested in shapes and movements that had little to do with natural objects.

FIGURE 5.36A Student work.

FOCUSING

Brainstorm with classmates to identify objects for this project. Some possibilities are a houseplant, a bicycle, an animal, a person, or a head. Choose something that is interesting to you and that you can observe. Do not use a photograph. Study the photos of Calder's wire sculpture. Notice how the wire is used.

CREATING

Make a series of three or more contour studies of the object. Make each drawing from a different point of view.

Collect your materials and experiment with some scrap wire. Practice using the tools to bend, twist, loop, and cut the wire so that you understand the way the wire behaves.

Create your wire sculpture based on the drawings you have made. As you work, keep turning the sculpture so that every side looks interesting.

To prepare your work for display, you may staple or nail it to a small block of wood, hang it with string from a support, or invent your own method to show the finished piece.

CRITIQUING

Describe Name the object you chose as the subject of your wire sculpture. How many contour line drawings of the object did you make? List the contour line variations you used to create the outlines and ridges of your sculpture. How did you prepare your finished work for display?

Analyze Do the lines of your work follow the contours and ridges of the object you chose? Is the work interesting from every side and angle?

Interpret What kind of mood is created by the use of line in three-dimensional space? Describe the difference between the look of the two-dimensional contour line drawings and the three-dimensional wire sculpture. Give your work a title.

Judge Have you created a contour sculpture that is three-dimensional and interesting from all sides and angles? Is your work successful? Is there anything you would change to make the work more successful? Which aesthetic theory would be the best to judge your work?

109

GUIDED PRACTICE
(continued)

Understanding Art History

To help students further appreciate the life and times of Alexander Calder, whose work is shown in Figure 5.36, assign *Artist's Profile 26* in the TCR.

INDEPENDENT PRACTICE

Enrichment

As an optional activity, have students create a non-objective wire sculpture by bending the wire in different directions to create movement and rhythm. Encourage them to think about how they feel as they bend the wire. They can reflect this emotional reaction in the sharp edges, smooth curves, and straight lines of the sculpture. The final artwork can be freestanding or attached to a base.

Keeping a Portfolio

Remind students that the preliminary sketches and the final artwork for this Studio Lesson are likely considerations for their portfolios.

ASSESS

CRITIQUING

Have students apply the steps of art criticism to their own artwork using the "Critiquing" questions on this page.

CLOSE

Ask each student to display both the sketch for the design and the wire sculpture. Encourage each student to briefly explain how the sculpture defines space with line.

COOPERATIVE LEARNING

Activities such as the Studio Lesson above lend themselves to collaborative sessions, especially in the planning stage. Often, students have difficulty conceiving an idea when called to do so. Working in groups, students hear the ideas of other students which in turn promotes more ideas. Teachers who have had an opportunity to recognize which students have no problem generating creative ideas are wise to place these students into groups with students who have difficulty. That way, their ideas benefit others. Another approach to brainstorming sessions is to provide examples of previous student work to small groups and instruct them to use the sample as a discussion model for their own designs.

FOCUS

OBJECTIVE

Create an imaginary landscape using torn paper stencils to make the edges of land masses. Imagine living things and objects that belong in the landscape and add them to the design.

MOTIVATOR

Ask the students to look for lines in their environment that define edges. If necessary, refer to the discussion of contour lines on pages 100–101. Also, take the students outside and ask them to describe the surrounding horizons. What do they see? Mountains? Trees? Flat plains? Buildings and skyscrapers? What kind of lines are created where the sky appears to meet the horizon? What sort of edges and lines do they see between them and the horizon? Tell the class to keep in mind what they've just seen and described when making their stencils and creating their landscapes.

TEACH

GUIDED PRACTICE

Developing Studio Skills

Some techniques for holding the paper towel may include a pushing or pulling method. Also, the towel may be held between the fingers and pulled across the color or it may be wrapped around the finger to rub. Tortillions may be used, but this could get expensive.

FIGURE 5.37 Carolyn Clive. *Amplitude.* 1987. Oil paint used with stencil brush and torn paper stencil on paper, 61 × 46 cm (24 × 18″). Collection of the artist.

Supplies

- Sketchbook
- Oil pastels
- Large sheet of white paper
- Paper towels
- Newspaper for tearing into stencils
- Scissors (optional)

Look at *Amplitude* (Figure 5.37) and turn your imagination loose. What might this landscape be? Do you see misty mountains? Are there surging waves and an angry sky? What does the sphere in the rectangle represent, and how has the artist used line to create this landscape?

Carolyn Clive was driving through the Georgia countryside one bleak fall day. "The leaves had fallen and the crops were in. I looked out over the land and told myself, 'I don't know what I'm going to do, but I'm going to capture the spirit of this land.'"

Clive developed her own stenciling technique for working with oil paints and used line and value changes to create her abstract landscape. Notice how she has combined geometric shapes with

---

CULTURAL PERSPECTIVES

Visual elements are the ingredients of art. Explain to students that the elements have been analyzed, organized, and used in many ways, but they are not the inventions of artists. They are natural elements that artists have learned to use as an alternative language. For example, Carolyn Clive "translated" the spirit of her photographs into a visual design with a unique medium. Emphasize that the use of visual elements is common to all cultures. Helping students to understand the elements, in this case, line, will give them new methods of applying them and new ways to perceive the environment and the environment of others.

flowing, overlapping waves of color. Observe how she has brought parts of the design outside the image area to provide added interest.

Experiment with Clive's stenciling technique to capture the spirit of the land and then create your own imaginary landscape.

Use torn paper stencils to form the edges of land masses. After you have made the land-mass edges, imagine what objects and living things belong in this landscape. Add these to your scene.

FOCUSING

Study the stencil painting by Carolyn Clive. Notice how the edges of the shapes are dark on one side and light on the other. This was done by holding a stencil in place and pulling oil color gently from the edge of the stencil into the shape with a stippling brush.

CREATING

First, practice the following technique in your sketchbook. Tear a 9 × 6 inch (23 × 15 cm) piece of newspaper to create a rough, curving edge that will be your stencil. Draw a heavy line of oil pastel along the rough edge of the stencil. With one hand, hold the stencil firmly on a page of your sketchbook. With the other hand, use a piece of paper towel to pull the color from the stencil onto paper. Experiment with different techniques until you feel comfortable. Try mixing colors. Compare your results with those of your classmates. Discuss the different effects you have created. For variety, try cutting the edge of your stencil with scissors.

Based on your findings from the experiments, make some rough plans in your sketchbook for the final work. Choose your best idea. Now you are ready to create your landscape.

Using newspaper or other scratch paper, tear or cut stencils for your finished work. Choose the colors you will use. In order to keep from smudging the pastel lines, work from the top of your page toward the bottom edge. Draw a very heavy line of oil pastel along the edge of your first stencil. Hold the stencil firmly in place and

FIGURE 5.37A   Student work.

pull the oil pastel color from the stencil onto the large sheet of paper. Repeat this step until you have created the land masses you want.

Study this work and imagine what objects and living creatures belong in your landscape. Add them using oil pastels. Give your work a title. Mount or mat your finished work for display.

C R I T I Q U I N G

Describe   Tell what kind of a landscape you have created. What creatures and objects have you added to the land masses?

Analyze   How did you create your stencils? What kinds of lines make up the edges of your land masses? How did the technique you used to pull the color from the stencil to the paper affect the look of your work?

Interpret   Describe the mood of your imagination landscape. Did the stencil technique you used contribute to the mood?

Judge   Which aesthetic theory would be best to judge your work? Do you think this work is successful? Is there anything you would change to make it more successful?

111

Exploring Aesthetics

Experiment with different types and thicknesses of paper for varied edges. Cutting the paper with scissors will give a sharp edge. Torn thick, soft paper will result in a rough, yet, softer edge.

INDEPENDENT PRACTICE

Enrichment

Encourage students to create a second version of their imagination landscape, this time using a different medium than the first attempt. For example, they might try colored markers, crayons, or watercolors. When finished, ask them to write a brief evaluation of the media used for the two works. Ask them to consider which medium worked best mechanically for this project. Which was more aesthetically pleasing? What else might they change about the activity that would change the quality and appeal of the finished product?

Keeping a Portfolio

Remind students that the preliminary sketches and the final artwork for this Studio Lesson are likely considerations for their portfolios.

ASSESS

CRITIQUING

Have students apply the steps of art criticism to their own artwork using the "Critiquing" questions on this page.

CLOSE

Ask each student to express what they learned about the stenciling technique while making this landscape.

MEETING SPECIAL NEEDS

Learning Disabled   Students with retardation may have difficulty conceiving a landscape with the method prescribed in this Studio Lesson. The student may find more satisfaction in a less abstract subject for representation. Use the smear technique on a stencil of a simple or familiar object, such as an animal's outline shape. For even more clarity of conception (a worthwhile goal for students with retardation who are in an early stage of representation), few media surpass painting with a half-inch brush and poster paint on a large sheet of paper.

STUDIO LESSON: DRAWING EXPRESSING MOVEMENT

FIGURE 5.38   William H. Johnson. *Jitterbugs IV.* 1939–40. Gouache and pen and ink with pencil on paper, 32.7 × 26.9 cm (12⅞ × 10⁹⁄₁₆″). National Museum of American Art, Smithsonian Institution, Washington, D.C. Gift of the Harmon Foundation.

Supplies

- Sketchbook, pencil, and eraser
- Large sheet of white paper
- Colored pencils or crayons
- Watercolor paints
- Variety of watercolor brushes

In *Jitterbugs IV* (Figure 5.38), William H. Johnson used diagonal lines to provide high-action, energetic movement. Although his dancers are abstract, simple figures, they *move.* For contrast he used vertical and horizontal lines to show stable, unmoving objects.

Johnson is considered a major African-American artist. He integrated the customs and cultures of New York, Europe, and North Africa into his African-American heritage, finally settling on the abstract forms and limited color palette you see here. In *Jitterbugs IV* Johnson used line and simple shapes to show the expressive movements of the jitterbug dance craze of the 1940s.

CURRICULUM CONNECTION

Language Arts   Inform students that in addition to the flowering of art during the Harlem Renaissance, significant contributions were made to American literature. Have them research the works of Jean Toomer, Countee Cullen, and Langston Hughes. Although these three writers were known for their poetry, they were truly Renaissance men. Toomer wrote essays on religion and philosophy; Cullen published books for children; and Langston Hughes wrote drama, fiction, popular songs, and movie screenplays.

Create a drawing that expresses the linear movement of people involved in energetic action. Emphasize the lines that express movement. Base the figures on the gesture drawings you made while observing real people in action. If you wish, you may create contrast between the active figures and the background by using static lines for the background objects.

FOCUSING

Study the painting by William H. Johnson. Notice how he has represented two dancing people with a few geometric shapes and many diagonal lines. Can you find the floor, the drum, and the drumsticks? Observe how the lines of the floor under the dancers are diagonal, while the rest of the floor remains vertical and static.

CREATING

Think of an energetic activity you could represent using active lines. Ask a friend to act out the movement of the activity so that you can make several different gesture drawings in your sketchbook.

Study your sketches. Decide which line directions will best express the movement of the activity. Will you use diagonals and zigzags, or curved lines? Simplify the figures in your gesture drawings using the lines you have chosen.

Decide which objects you will use for the background. Remember that you may use static lines for these objects. Sketch your finished plan on white paper.

Go over the lines of your composition with colored pencils or crayons. Press hard to make the colors bright. Vary the lines. Emphasize the action lines by drawing them wide and using bold colors. Make the other lines thinner with softer colors.

Color the shapes between the lines and the spaces around the figures with watercolor paints. (See Technique Tip 12 on page 353 in the Handbook for using watercolors.) Mount or mat the finished work for display.

FIGURE 5.38A Student work.

CRITIQUING

Describe Which energetic action did you choose as the subject of your drawing? Did you make gesture drawings of a real person acting out that movement? How many gesture drawings did you make? How many figures did you put in your finished work? Did you use any objects for the background?

Analyze Which line directions did you choose to express the action? Which line directions did you choose for the background objects? Which lines did you emphasize and how did you emphasize them?

Interpret Does your work express the action you were trying to capture? Give your work an expressive title. Do not use the name of the action your figures are doing.

Judge Have you created a drawing that expresses the movement of people involved in energetic action? Is there anything you would change to make the work more successful? Which aesthetic theory would be best to judge this work?

113

GUIDED PRACTICE
(continued)

Developing Studio Skills
Have students who are less confident with their creative abilities draw with three or more pencils taped together. This method will create a multiple-line drawing which should automatically loosen the students' fears and apprehensions about drawing.

Developing Studio Skills
As an alternative medium, have students use watercolor markers rather than watercolor paints, which give a nice wash when brushed with clear water.

INDEPENDENT PRACTICE

Enrichment
Have students make life-sized or larger gesture drawings on butcher paper. Suggest that they use colored chalk on dark paper as it creates a nice effect.

Keeping a Portfolio
Remind students that the preliminary sketches and the final artwork for this Studio Lesson are likely considerations for their portfolios.

ASSESS

CRITIQUING
Have students apply the steps of art criticism to their own artwork using the "Critiquing" questions on this page.

CLOSE

Have students write a paragraph in their sketchbooks explaining what they learned about themselves or the element of line while completing this activity.

MEETING SPECIAL NEEDS

Learning Disabled If the class is drawing for a posed student model, easily discouraged students with behavioral disorders may be inclined to yell out, "Hold still" and "He ruined mine when he moved." Tell this student that it is just the gesture, the essence, the feeling, that is to be captured. Help the student who says, "I messed up," by assisting the student in diagnosing one particular area that is wrong and in coming up with a way to try to fix it. To foster integration, include students with disabilities as models; figures in wheelchairs are particularly good to challenge drawing skills.

INTRODUCTION

Jacob Lawrence's work was chosen for this chapter because of his strong use of hard edges and line movement. Students will be able to apply what they have learned about lines during the critical study of this work. Not only the real lines, but the active linear movements of the racers' bodies are important. David's *Death of Socrates* was selected to compare with *Study for the Munich Olympic Games Poster* because of the contrast in movement. The people in David's painting are very still and static, while Lawrence's figures are extremely active. Students will be able to see how artists use different line directions for different expressive purposes.

CRITIQUING THE WORK

1. **Describe** Point out that gouache is an opaque watercolor medium, very similar to school tempera. There are five men running on a race track in what appears to be a relay race. There is grass on the sides of the track and in the background there is another track. Only men and the ground are seen; there is no sky. The faces show great stress. We can see the finish line in the foreground of the picture.

2. **Analyze** Every object has sharp edges so every shape makes a line when it meets another shape. There are some outlines on the figures as well as white and gray outlines on the tracks. Lawrence uses some contour lines on the men. There are black lines that indicate straining muscles in their necks,

FIGURE 5.39 Jacob Lawrence. *Study for the Munich Olympic Games Poster.* 1971. Gouache on paper. 90.1 × 68.6 cm (35 ½ × 27″). Seattle Art Museum, Seattle, Washington. Purchased with funds from P.O.N.C.H.O.

114

RESOURCES BEYOND THE CLASSROOM

Other Works By . . . Jacob Lawrence
Builders 1980
Tombstone's
War Series: Another Patrol
Toussaint L'Overture Series
The Migration of the Negro
Pool Parlor

Other Works By . . . Jacques David
The Death of Marat
Napoleon in His Study
The Oath of the Horatii
Brutus and His Dead Sons
Intervention of the Savine Women
Coronation of Napoleon

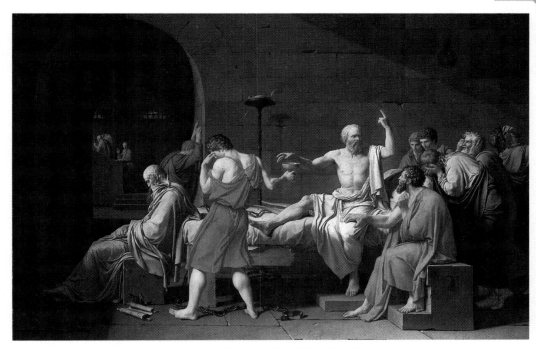

FIGURE 5.40 Jacques Louis David. *Death of Socrates.* 1787. Oil on canvas. 129.5 × 196.2 cm (51 × 77¼"). The Metropolitan Museum of Art, New York, New York. Wolfe Fund, 1931. Catharine Lorillard Wolfe Collection.

CRITIQUING THE WORK

1. **Describe**   Look at Jacob Lawrence's *Study for the Munich Olympic Games Poster.* Read the credit line for information about the work. Then list and describe everything you see in the work.

2. **Analyze**   Do you see lines where the edge of one shape meets the edge of another? Do you see outlines? Can you find any contour lines? Can you find line variations? Are the lines active or static? Which kinds of lines seem to dominate the painting? Does Lawrence use value contrasts?

3. **Interpret**   Remember that interpretation is more than telling a story about the subject matter. You must express your own opinion about the meaning or the mood of the work based on the facts you collected during the first two steps. Write a paragraph explaining your interpretation.

4. **Judge**   Now it is time to make an aesthetic judgment. Do you think this is a successful work of art? Use one or more of the three aesthetic theories you studied in Chapter 2 to defend your judgment.

COMPARING THE WORKS

Look at *Study for the Munich Olympic Games Poster* by Jacob Lawrence (Figure 5.39) and the *Death of Socrates* by Jacques Louis David (Figure 5.40). Compare the way each artist uses line to create the expressive quality in each work. In which work are the line directions static? In which work are they active? Compare the way the two artists use value for expressive effect. Notice the facial expressions on the figures in each work. List all the other similarities and differences you find between the two works.

115

legs, and arms. A few contour lines indicate the strain in the men's faces. Line variations show in the contours. He uses calligraphic, flowing lines that vary from thin to thick in the contours. The lines around the track are wide and smooth. The lines in the men's clothes are thin and smooth. The finish line is a thin, curved, smooth line. All of the lines are either curved or diagonal.

3. **Interpret**   Answers will vary. Encourage students to look for symbolism and metaphors when they interpret works of art.

4. **Judge**   Answers will vary.

COMPARING THE WORKS

David uses static line direction to give a calm mood to a very dramatic occurrence. Socrates is about to drink the poison hemlock, and he is surrounded by his friends. There are some diagonal lines, but they are not very strong. Lawrence uses active diagonals to express the energy and excitement of the Olympic races.

In David's work the figures are lighter in value than the dark background. The main figure, Socrates, seems to be lit by a spotlight. He is the focus of this work. The dark figures in Lawrence's work contrast against the light background. This is to emphasize the dark skin of the athletes, and perhaps to show how African-American men, as a group, are succeeding in the Olympics.

MORE ABOUT . . . JACQUES DAVID

Jacques Louis David (1748–1825) spent five years studying in Rome, where he devoted most of his efforts to the study of ancient art. The *Oath of Horatii* was his first masterpiece. In 1792 he was elected to France's national convention and voted for the death of King Louis XVI. He painted several paintings depicting the martyrs of the French Rev-

olution; the most familiar of these is *The Death of Marat.* After Robespierre was put to death, David was sent to prison for a time. After his release, he was a supporter of Napoleon and became his principle painter. Following Napoleon's exile, David left France and spent the rest of his life in Belgium where he produced no major works.

EXTENSION

- Have students read more about Jacob Lawrence in the "Meet the Artist" feature on the following page.
- Assign *Artist's Profile 5* in the TCR.

- On a separate sheet of paper have students complete "Building Vocabulary" and "Reviewing Art Facts" on page 117.
- Assign *Application 9* and *10* in the TCR to evaluate students' comprehension.

ANSWERS TO BUILDING VOCABULARY

1. line
2. dimension
3. outline
4. implied lines
5. static
6. contour line
7. gesture
8. calligraphy
9. value
10. crosshatching

ANSWERS TO REVIEWING ART FACTS

1. Answers will vary but can include such examples as a trail of wet footprints or any other series of points that a viewer's eyes would automatically connect.
2. Vertical, horizontal, diagonal, curved, zigzag. Vertical, horizontal, and diagonal lines do not change direction. A curved line changes direction gradually. A zigzag line changes direction suddenly.
3. Length, width, texture, direction, and degree of curve.
4. Contour line.
5. Vertical and horizontal lines.
6. Diagonal lines.
7. Gesture drawing.
8. Number of lines; size of the spaces between the lines; media; and tools.

MEET THE ARTIST

JACOB LAWRENCE
American, b. 1917

The story of Jacob Lawrence's life is an American success story: he achieved success and fame before he was twenty-four. Lawrence was born in Atlantic City, New Jersey, in 1917. When he was twelve, his family moved to Harlem in New York City. The year was 1929, and it was the beginning of the Great Depression, which brought hard times upon all Americans.

Growing up in Harlem in the thirties was an important factor in Lawrence's development as an artist and in government support of the arts. The Harlem Renaissance of the twenties had attracted black intellectuals, artists, and musicians from all over the world, and many remained there during the thirties. The people of that community were Lawrence's role models.

Lawrence learned about art from many sources. He listened to the artists as they talked in their studios. The 135th Street Public Library, which he visited often, always had pieces of African sculpture on display. His many trips to The Metropolitan Museum of Art gave him a strong background in art history. He would walk sixty blocks to the museum and spend hours admiring all the works.

Lawrence became fascinated with black history and its heroic figures. His first subject was Toussaint L'Ouverture, the hero of Haiti, whose story was so interesting to Lawrence that he made a series of paintings to tell everything about L'Ouverture. For Lawrence could not always express all he wanted to say in just a single picture. He continued to make paintings in series. Some of his other subjects were Harriet Tubman and Frederick Douglass. Throughout his life he painted the everyday scenes of Harlem.

MORE PORTFOLIO IDEAS

Both Lawrence and David used line to create a specific feeling in their work. Select a magazine photograph of a scene in which static lines seem to predominate. Cut out the photo and paste it onto a page in your sketchbook. Redraw the scene, changing all the static lines to active lines. How does this change the mood of the scene?

Make a sketch of your home in your sketchbook. Copy that sketch, changing all the vertical and horizontal static lines to active diagonal lines. Compare the two sketches. How does changing the line directions affect the look of the house?

116

DEVELOPING A PORTFOLIO

Self-Evaluation Ultimately, students must come to terms with the limitations set on the number of artworks included in a portfolio; they cannot submit everything they have done. Consequently, they learn to be qualitatively sensitive about their work. Stress the value of setting standards, especially through informed judgments, that is, developing the ability to assess their own work on the basis of accepted criteria. Through self-evaluation, students take control of decision-making and feel increasingly responsible for the quality of their work.

CHAPTER 5 REVIEW

Building Vocabulary

On a separate sheet of paper, write the term that best matches each definition given below.

1. A mark drawn with a pointed, moving tool.
2. The amount of space an object takes up in one direction.
3. A line that shows or creates the outer edges of a shape.
4. A series of points that the viewer's eyes automatically connect.
5. The quality of being inactive.
6. A line that defines the edges and surface ridges of an object.
7. An expressive movement.
8. A term meaning beautiful handwriting.
9. The art element that describes the darkness or lightness of an object.
10. The technique of using crossed lines for shading.

Reviewing Art Facts

Answer the following questions using complete sentences.

1. Give an example of an implied line.
2. Name the five basic kinds of lines. Tell which three do not change direction, which kind changes direction gradually, and which kind changes direction suddenly.
3. Name five major ways in which lines can vary.
4. Tell which kind of line you would use to represent the surface of ridges in an object.
5. Name two kinds of lines that give the impression of stability.
6. Name the kind of line that conveys tension, instability, and action.
7. Tell what kind of drawing can be done quickly to capture movement.
8. What are the four factors that affect the value of a group of lines?

Thinking Critically About Art

1. **Analyze.** Study Figure 5.1 (page 88) by Twiggs, Figure 5.21 (page 97) by Namingha, Figure 5.24 (page 99) by Sheeler, and Figure 5.35 (page 106) by a Huichol Indian. What is the common thread that links the four works? The four works can be divided into two pairs, with each pair related to the other. How would you pair them, and what is the relationship in each set?
2. **Synthesize.** Explain why the four related works, Figures 5.1, 5.21, 5.24, and 5.35, belong in a chapter devoted to the concept of line.
3. **Compare and contrast.** In what way are Grant Wood's *Midnight Ride of Paul Revere* (Figure 5.3 on page 91) and Yvonne Jacquette's *East River Drive* (Figure 5.6 page 93) similar? In what ways are they different? Consider the element of line and the subject matter of each composition in your comparison.

Making Art Connections

1. **Music.** Investigate the importance of the element of line in music. Interview your school's music teacher or a friend who is studying music.
2. **Social Studies.** Jacob Lawrence arrived in Harlem near the end of the Harlem Renaissance. Find out when the Harlem Renaissance occurred, what caused it, and what was so important about that period in the history of American culture.
3. **History.** Neoclassicism was inspired by the discovery of Pompeii and Herculaneum. What and where were they? Why were they unknown before the mid-eighteenth century? Why was their discovery important? What did we learn from them? How did they affect the arts?

EVALUATE

- Have students complete the *Chapter 5 Test* in the TCR.
- Alternative Assessment teaching strategies are provided below or in the Testing Program and Alternative Assessment booklet.

RETEACHING

- Have students complete *Concept Map 5* in the Reteaching booklet.
- Stimulate perception by playing a "spelling bee"-type game based on the element of line. Divide the class into two teams. Each person must name and describe the location of a different line in a selected artwork. Do not allow anyone to point. The others guess which line it is. Encourage the use of adjectives that help to identify the line in question.
- To help students remember the names of the lines, use flash cards on which you have drawn the line types. Call the students by name, hold up a card, and ask them to name the types of lines. Then have students point to illustrations in the book that exemplify the line.

EXTENSION

Have students find a book on Oriental brush painting. After they have learned to make some of the brushstrokes, have them demonstrate the technique to the class.

CLOSE

Have students choose two illustrations from this chapter and compare how the artists use the element of line.

Shape, Form, and Space

CHAPTER OVERVIEW

Chapter 6 examines the close relationship between the elements of shape, form, and space. It helps students become more perceptive of the fact that every object has a shape or form.

CHAPTER SUPPLIES

Refer to the "Art Supplies Grid" in the Teacher's Manual. In addition, have on hand the following special items: small found objects, newspaper, cardboard tubing, and small boxes.

FINE ART RESOURCES
Transparencies
- Carolyn F. Sollman. *Shadow Assortment*
- Van Gogh. *La Mousme*
- Winslow Homer. *A Good Pool, Saquenay River*
- Antonio Ruiz. *The Bicycle Race*

Fine Art Prints
- Allan Houser. *Prayer Song*
- Alice Neel. *Mother and Child*

FIGURE 6.1 In the 1960s, Marisol was a star of the Pop art movement. She made assemblages that used humor to make viewers think about the materialistic attitude of the time. Today, her work uses the same media and has a similar purpose, but it is presented in a serious mood.

Marisol. *Poor Family I.* 1987. Wood, charcoal, stones, plastic doll. 198 × 396 × 213 cm (78 × 156 × 84"). Sidney Janis Gallery, New York, New York. © Marisol/VAGA, New York 1994.

RESOURCES FOR CHAPTER 6
Application Activities 11, 12
Artist's Profile 6, 13, 14, 16, 33, 39, 43
Cooperative Learning Activities 11, 12
Cultural Diversity in Art
Enrichment Activities 11, 12

Reteaching Activities
  Study Guide 6
  Concept Map 6
Studio Lessons 3, 4, 5
Chapter 6 Test

Shape, Form, and Space

You live in space, in a world full of objects. Each object—whether it be a car, an apple, this book, or you—has a shape or form. Often it is by their shapes or forms that you recognize objects. You identify a stop sign in the distance by its shape long before you can read the word *stop* on it. You identify a friend in the distance long before you see his or her face.

Shape, form, and space are all closely related to one another. They are elements of art, and artists use their knowledge of how these elements work together to speak the language of art. In this chapter you will learn how to "read" the meaning of these elements and how to use them to express your own ideas and feelings.

On the following pages you will begin to understand how artists create shapes, forms, and space in their artworks. You will learn how to use perspective to give depth to your drawings and paintings and how to use shapes, forms, and space to create a variety of expressive qualities. Your work will spring to life as you learn how to depict three dimensions on a two-dimensional surface.

FIRST IMPRESSIONS

Look at *Poor Family I* (Figure 6.1). Notice how Marisol has used flat areas to create the illusion of depth in some areas of her assemblage, while she has carved some three-dimensional forms and attached them to the flat surfaces in other areas. Can you find the realistic three-dimensional forms? Can you find the flat surfaces that have been altered to look three-dimensional? What effect has the artist created by placing the figures so close together? Why has she left a wide space between the figures and the rocks? Why are the rocks included in this work?

Objectives

After reading this chapter, you will be able to:
- Explain the difference between shapes and forms.
- Create two- and three-dimensional works of art.
- Observe more carefully the shapes and forms in the space around you.
- Understand point of view and perspective.
- Use point of view and perspective to create drawings and paintings.
- Understand the expressive qualities, or meanings, of shapes, forms, and spaces in a work of art.

Words to Know

chiaroscuro
form
free-form shapes
geometric shapes
highlights
holograms
perspective
shape
space

119

FOCUS

INTRODUCING THE CHAPTER

Ask students to think about shapes that can be made without drawing outlines. You can stimulate their thinking by naming a few examples, such as spilled paint or cutting a shape with scissors.

MOTIVATOR

Ask students to look around the space in which they are sitting and write a description of three shapes in this space. Encourage them to describe the shape without naming the objects.

VOCABULARY PREVIEW

Have students preview the list of vocabulary words on this page. Also, acquaint them with these words that will appear in the chapter: figure, ground, freestanding, bas relief, high relief, point of view, picture plane, foreground, background, middle ground, atmospheric perspective, linear perspective, and vanishing point.

USING FIRST IMPRESSIONS

Have students study Figure 6.1 and answer the questions in the box on this page. Help them see that two heads are carved from wood while all the others are drawn on flat surfaces. The broken plastic doll and the two dogs are three-dimensional. Several of the feet are partially carved and attached to the drawn, flat part of the foot. All the other people have been drawn with charcoal and shaded to look as if they have depth.

TEACHER TALK

A Success Story   As supervisor of art for the Somerville Public Schools, Elaine McMichael is instrumental in organizing and managing the yearly All-City Art Fair for all elementary, middle, and secondary students. Students design and create invitations and direct hands-on activities in addition to producing quality art for the show. For three days, local high schools host the show while students gallery sit, sell caricatures, demonstrate animation, make photo buttons, and sell crafts. Most of all, students prove to the community that creativity is alive and well in Somerville!

TEACH

(pages 120–128)
- Shapes
- Forms
- Space and Its Relationship to Shape and Form

GUIDED PRACTICE

Developing Perceptual Skills

Ask volunteers to bring in geometry texts. Then have students look for examples of shapes in the textbook. If possible, borrow charts or other visual material from the math teacher.

It is important that they understand that although free-form shapes do not have specific names, such as "circle" or "square," they may have object names such as "tree" or "dog."

Understanding Art History

To help students further appreciate the life and times of Marisol, assign *Artist's Profile 43* in the TCR.

Developing Perceptual Skills

One type of shape is the silhouette, which originally meant a profile portrait that looked like a solid shadow. Now it is used to describe any two-dimensional, shadow-like shape. Using a slide or overhead projector, have students make hand shadows. Project the light onto a large piece of white paper. Have one student trace the silhouette on the paper while another "poses" the hand. To take this even further, use a slide projector and trace the silhouettes of full-length figures. Remind them although they are using outlines, they are concerned with the concept that one object can have many different silhouettes.

120

SHAPES

A **shape** is *a two-dimensional area that is defined in some way.* A shape may have an outline or a boundary around it, or you may recognize it by its area, such as the shadow in Figure 6.2. For instance, if you draw the outline of a square on a sheet of paper, you have created a shape. You could also create the same shape without an outline by painting the area of the square red.

You see many two-dimensional shapes every day. They are found in most designs, which in turn can be seen on many flat surfaces. Look for shapes on such things as floor coverings, fabrics, and wallpapers. Floors and walls are two-dimensional shapes; so are tabletops, book pages, posters, and billboards.

All shapes can be classified as either *geometric* or *free-form*. **Geometric shapes** are *precise shapes that can be described using mathematical formulas* (Figure 6.3). The basic geometric shapes are the circle, the square, and the triangle. All other geometric shapes are either variations or combinations of these basic shapes. Some of the variations include the oval, rectangle, parallelogram, trapezoid, pentagon, pentagram, hexagon, and octagon.

FIGURE 6.2 Shadow is the shape of darkness.

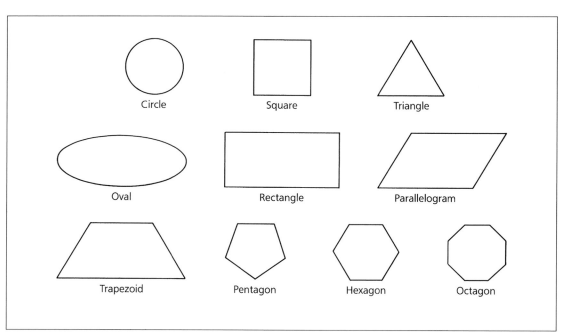

Circle Square Triangle

Oval Rectangle Parallelogram

Trapezoid Pentagon Hexagon Octagon

FIGURE 6.3 Geometric shapes.

AT THE MUSEUM

Museum of Fine Arts, Houston (Houston, Texas) How would your students like to give tours of a museum to their teacher and parents? That's what they could do if they joined the junior docent program at the Museum of Fine Arts in Houston. Students give tours after school and help out with the various education programs. As trained volunteers, they learn how to speak in front of large and small groups, learn about the works of art in the museum, and gain experience in how to approach museum visitors. The Family Night, the highlight event where the student docents educate their families and teachers, is a very special reversal of roles.

Geometric shapes are used for decoration, uniformity, and organization. Road signs, for example, must be uniform. The same kind of sign must always have the same shape. Do you know the shape of a stop sign? Which shape is used for "Yield"? Which shape is used for TV screens? Why do you think ceiling tiles and window panes have geometric shapes?

Free-form shapes are *irregular and uneven shapes* (Figure 6.4). Their outlines may be curved, angular, or a combination of both. They often occur in nature. Free-form shapes may be silhouettes of living things, such as animals, people, or trees. Notice the decorative quality of the geometric shapes in the beadwork on the leggings shown in Figure 6.5. Geometric designs on white backgrounds were often used by the Blackfeet women. Now compare those designs to the free-form shapes on the leggings in Figure 6.6. These Chippewa formal leggings are an example of the refined floral style used by the Woodlands peoples. Which do you prefer?

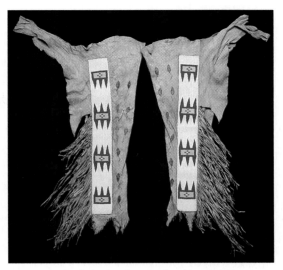

FIGURE 6.5   The Native Americans produced formal clothing decorated with bead embroidery for social dances and formal events in the late nineteenth century.

Montata. *Blackfeet Man's Leggings.* Montana. 1880. Buckskin, glass beads, pigment. 101 × 49 cm (39¾ × 19¼"). Buffalo Bill Historical Center, Cody, Wyoming.

FIGURE 6.4   Free-form shapes.

FIGURE 6.6   The Chippewa women incorporated the free-form flower shapes they saw in the European decorative arts of the nineteenth century into their own designs.

Chippewa Man's Leggings. Minnesota. c. 1890. Cotton velveteen, polished cotton, glass beads, wool twill. 74.6 × 28 cm (29¾ × 11"). Detroit Institute of Arts, Detroit, Michigan. Founders Society purchase.

CULTURAL PERSPECTIVES

To extend the concept of free-form shapes, tell your students about the bronze animal sculptures created primarily during the Shang dynasty (eighteenth–twelfth centuries B.C.). These free-form animal sculptures are believed to have been used in religious rituals to promote the relationship between people and the natural world. Art historians believe the sculptures were placed in tombs to give the person that died some of the animal's believed qualities. For example, the elephant's strength, the bird's soaring skills, or the lion's courage. These beautiful stylized sculptures often took the form of real animals— tigers, birds, owls, cats, and so on.

GUIDED PRACTICE
(continued)

Interdisciplinary: Science

Direct students to look at a drop of water through a microscope and sketch the free-form shapes they see. Encourage them to discuss the activity with their science teachers who may make other suggestions for sources of free-form shapes from the scientific point of view.

Developing Studio Skills

On a sheet of white paper, instruct students to draw a light pencil line from the upper right corner to the lower left corner. Then have them cut out a variety of large and small geometric shapes from colored magazine illustrations. Arrange these shapes along the diagonal line by placing the smaller, more intensely colored ones nearest the line. The remaining shapes should become gradually larger and duller as they are placed further and further away from the line. Study the finished composition and add as many new shapes as necessary to make it more unified and visually appealing. Overlap shapes so that no white paper shows.

Sparking Creativity

Want students to think creatively about shapes? Suggest this: Put a spoonful of cooking oil and a few drops of food coloring in a shallow dish of water. Use a stick to move the oil and watch the shapes it takes. Try putting small quantities of oil, water, and color in a sealed plastic bag and place it on an overhead projector. Gently move the bag and watch the projected shapes change.

GUIDED PRACTICE

(continued)

 Exploring Shapes

1. Applying Your Skills.
This activity is a design problem that can be achieved successfully by all students.

Be sure to point out the difference between contour and outline. Contour drawings define all the lines on an object, the interior as well as the outlines. Outlines are like a fence around a shape—they define the area of a shape. In this activity, they will be drawing pure outlines.

The activity will be more interesting if students place their own possessions on the projector. However, you should have a few things handy to start the activity. For instance, you might place several different keys on the projector and then ask the students to describe verbally the differences in their outlines.

2. Further Challenge.
Have students share and compare their cut-paper designs.

3. Computer Option.
Students might vary this exercise by flipping, inverting, rotating, or nudging as they fill the page. Sometimes, an arrangement may create a new shape. This shape or unit may be copied and pasted to form larger units. Suggest that they try varying solid colors, patterns, and gradients. Do not overlap. Another alternative is to draw an irregular shape using the Brush or Pencil tool. Select the shape, then use the Copy and Paste commands to repeat the free-form shape. Arrange each shape. Fill the page. Use the Bucket Flood-fill tool to fill the shapes with a solid color, pattern, or gradient. Try altering the colors, patterns, and gradients on some of the shapes. Use the Bucket Flood-fill tool to fill in the spaces between the irregular shapes. Do not overlap.

ACTIVITY Exploring Shapes

1. Applying Your Skills. Search your pockets or purse for objects small enough to fit on an overhead projector. Place the objects, one at a time, on the projector. Project the silhouette of the object on a screen or blank wall. Then draw only the outline of each object on a piece of white paper. After you have drawn several shapes, cut them out carefully. Arrange and glue them on a dark background.

2. Further Challenge. Using the printed areas of a newspaper, make two cut-paper designs. Make one design by measuring and cutting precise geometric shapes. Make the second design by tearing free-form shapes. Arrange the shapes and glue them on a sheet of black construction paper. Use a white crayon to print the words *free-form* and *geometric* on the appropriate design. Try to make the letters for *geometric* look geometric, and the letters for *free-form* look free-form.

3. Computer Option. Use the Shape tool to draw four different geometric shapes. Draw them spaced apart so you will be able to select them later. Make each of these shapes a solid color. Use the Select tool and the Copy and Paste options to repeat each of these shapes several times on your screen. When your screen is half filled with solid, geometric shapes, draw free-form shapes in between the geometric shapes. Use the Fill Bucket tool to fill the free-form shapes with a pattern. Do not overlap shapes.

FORMS

Although the words *shape* and *form* are often used interchangeably in everyday language, they have different meanings in the language of art. **Forms** are *objects having three dimensions.* Like shapes, they have both length and width, but forms also have depth. *You* are a three-dimensional form; so is a tree or a table.

Two-dimensional shapes and three-dimensional forms are related. The end of a cylinder is a circle. One side of a cube is a square (Figure 6.7). A triangle can "grow" into a cone or a pyramid.

Like shapes, forms may be either geometric (Figure 6.8) or free-form (Figure 6.9). Geometric forms are used in construction, for organization, and as parts in machines. Look around you. What forms were used to build your school, your church, your home? Look under the hood of a car. What forms were used to build the motor? Did you know that common table salt is made of a series of interlocking cubes? You can see these cubes when you look at salt through a microscope.

Free-form forms are irregular and uneven three-dimensional objects such as stones, puddles, and clouds. Your own body and the bodies of animals and plants are free-form forms.

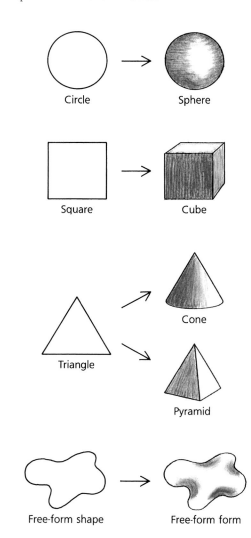

Circle → Sphere

Square → Cube

Triangle → Cone / Pyramid

Free-form shape → Free-form form

FIGURE 6.7 Do you see a relationship between two-dimensional shapes and three-dimensional forms?

MEETING SPECIAL NEEDS

Visually Impaired For students who are blind, cut shapes from a stiff paper such as oak tag. Keep the outline simple. Students will then be able to feel the outline and form a mental image of the shape. The student can sort the different shapes into categories and then trace around them onto a styrofoam meat tray which will leave an indented line. This tracing could then be printed to make greeting cards or note cards.

FIGURE 6.8 This is one of Smith's earliest stainless steel geometric sculptures. It is made of steel plates joined to form rectangular solids. Smith insisted that his monumental sculptures were made to sit in nature, not in buildings. Because the smooth steel reflected light like chrome on a car, he burnished the surface to diffuse the light and so the surface would take on the colors of the natural environment.

David Smith. *Cubi IX.* 1961. Stainless steel. 268 × 149 × 111.4 cm (105⅝ × 58⅝ × 43⅞"). Walker Art Center, Minneapolis, Minnesota. Gift of the T. B. Walker Foundation, 1966. © Estate of David Smith/VAGA, New York 1994.

 Creating Forms

1. Applying Your Skills. Find a geometric object that is three dimensional. Use a pencil and ruler to draw its contours. Next, find a three-dimensional free-form object. Using brush and ink, draw it with flowing, calligraphic contour lines.

2. Further Challenge. Make a flat sheet of construction paper into a three-dimensional paper sculpture by using cutting and scoring techniques. (See Technique Tip on page 356 in the Handbook.) Give your sculpture a minimum of five different surfaces. Do not cut the paper into separate pieces. Use only slots and tabs if you wish to join any parts. Experiment with scratch paper before you construct your final paper sculpture.

3. Computer Option. Use the Oval shape to draw an oval shape on the screen. Draw another oval and use the Fill Bucket tool to fill it with a gradient. This will make it appear rounded and represent a form. Repeat this procedure using additional geometric and free-form shapes. Some software programs have both Uniform Gradient Fill and Gradient Fill to Shape options.

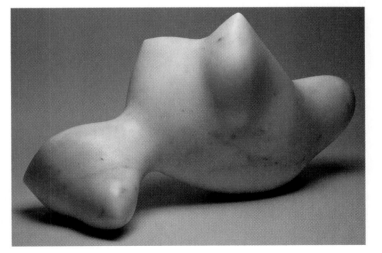

FIGURE 6.9 Arp always created sculpture that was free-form and organic looking. He never named his sculpture until it was finished. Can you see why he gave this form a title related to water?

Jean (Hans) Arp. *Aquatique.* 1953. Marble. 34 × 64.3 × 23.3 cm (13½ × 25⅜ × 9⅛"). Walker Art Center, Minneapolis, Minnesota. Gift of the T. B. Walker Foundation, 1955.

GUIDED PRACTICE
(continued)

 Creating Forms

1. Applying Your Skills.
This activity requires perception. Notice that it calls upon skills learned in Chapter 5—contour drawing and making calligraphic lines.

2. Further Challenge.
Students are always surprised that they can make curved forms from flat paper.

3. Computer Option.
Students who wish to draw a cylinder might try this: Draw an oval high on the screen. Select it, then Copy and Paste another oval, placing the second one directly below the original but some distance apart. Connect the two ovals using two straight lines. Erase the top half of the lower oval to make a solid-looking cylinder. Use the Gradient Fill to cover the top and side of the cylinder. Use a common light direction.

To draw a cube or box try this: Draw a square high on the screen. Select it and make a copy below the first one, overlapping the first square but placing the second square slightly to the left or right. Use the Straight Line tool and three lines to connect the two squares on the top from corner to corner and one side corner. Erase the unnecessary lines to make a cube or open box. Using the Gradient Fill and a common light source, fill in the shapes to create a form.

To draw a pyramid they might try this: Draw a large triangle. Use the Straight Line tool to draw two lines, one slanting down from the top corner and the other slanting up from a bottom corner. Connect these two lines. Use the Gradient Fill to cover the top and side of the pyramid with a gradient. Use a common light direction.

SAFETY NOTE

Be sure to emphasize safety if you let students use sharp blades to score paper. If you use construction paper, the scoring can be done easily with the point of a pair of scissors. The purpose of scoring is to weaken the paper along one line and make it thinner so it will give when bent.

If you have never tried scoring before, do so before you work with the class. You need to discover how much of a curve you can score before it gets too tight to bend without wrinkling the rest of the paper. If you wish to make a semicircular curve, you will have to make a cut from the open side of the curve to that edge of the paper.

GUIDED PRACTICE
(continued)

Promoting Discussion

It is important for students to realize that every bit of empty space around them is negative space. Someone in the class is bound to argue that this space is full of air. You can explain that we are talking about visual space and, therefore, we are concerned only with things that can be seen.

Developing Studio Skills

Almost everyone has seen the figure/ground, vase/face design shown in Figure 6.10. You can have students create their own. Fold a small piece of paper in half. On one side of the fold have the students draw a profile with a pencil. It can be accurate or distorted. Go over the line of the profile with a dark crayon, pressing heavily to lay down a heavy layer of wax. Then fold the paper again and rub heavily over the area of the profile line to transfer it to the other half. Unfold the paper and go over the transferred line. Then have some students color in the center shape and others color in the two outside shapes. Display these so that the class can see how the different designs keep reversing as students look at them.

Exploring Aesthetics

Ask students to look through the text for examples of two-dimensional works that (1) illustrate obvious distinctions between figure and ground, (2) make negative space as important as the positive, and (3) reverse the figure and ground.

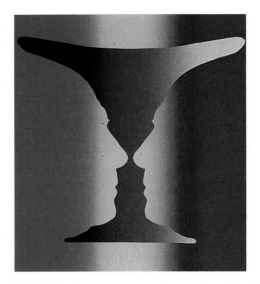 

FIGURE 6.10   Do you see a vase or do you see two profiles of Picasso? Johns has deliberately organized this lithograph as a visual puzzle to confuse the viewer. One minute the faces are very clear and they seem to be the figure while the space between the profiles is the ground. The next moment the vase between the profiles becomes the figure and the space around the vase becomes the ground.

Jasper Johns. *Cups 4 Picasso*. 1972. Lithograph. 57 × 82 cm (22½ × 32¼"). The Museum of Modern Art, New York, New York. Gift of Celeste Bartos. © Jasper Johns/VAGA, New York 1994.

SPACE AND ITS RELATIONSHIP TO SHAPE AND FORM

Shapes and forms exist in **space**, which is *the element of art that refers to the emptiness or area between, around, above, below, or within objects.* All objects take up space. You, for example, are a living, breathing form moving through space.

Shapes and forms are defined by the space around and within them. They depend on space for their existence. This is why it is important to understand the relationship of space to shapes and forms.

Positive and Negative Spaces

In both two- and three-dimensional art, the shapes or forms are called the *positive space* or the *figure.* The empty spaces between the shapes or forms are called *negative spaces* or *ground.* Look at Figure 6.10 and read the caption for an example of figure and ground. In a portrait, the image of the person is the positive space; the negative space is the area surrounding the person (Figure 6.11).

The shape and size of negative spaces affect the way you interpret positive spaces. Large negative spaces around positive spaces may express loneliness or freedom. When the positive spaces are crowded together, you may feel tension or togetherness (Figure 6.12, page 126). The full meaning of a work depends on the interaction between the positive and negative spaces.

It is not always easy to tell which are the positive spaces and which are the negative spaces in two-dimensional art. Sometimes it is hard to find any negative space. This is because some artists give equal emphasis to both the figure and the ground.

Some artists even try to confuse the viewer. They create positive and negative spaces that reverse themselves while you are looking at them. These visual puzzles fascinate some viewers (Figure 6.13, page 127).

MEETING SPECIAL NEEDS

Learning Disabled   One concrete way to clarify the concept of three dimensions for students who have learning disabilities is to use a cardboard box. Color each set of parallel lines on the box form with different colors. Label one set "length," the second set "width," and the third set "depth." Show them how length and width just outline a flat shape, but when you add the dimension of depth, the box takes up space.

Lavinia Fontana. *Portrait of a Noblewoman.* c. 1580. Oil on canvas. 115 × 89.5 cm (45¼ × 35¼"). National Museum of Women in the Arts, Washington, D.C.

LOOKING
CLOSELY

FIGURE 6.11 Notice how the negative space affects the look of the subject. There is more negative space on the woman's right than on her left, and both spaces have different shapes. The spaces between her arms and her dress are very different. Fontana's style of painting the background flat black forces the viewer to pay attention to the details in the positive space.

The light color of the sleeves pulls your eyes down to her hands. You can easily see what she is petting with her right hand. Do you know what she is holding in her left hand? Notice that it has a jeweled head and is attached to her waist with a chain.

LOOKING
CLOSELY

Have students study Figure 6.11 and answer the question in the caption. Help them to see that the black negative space allows the viewer to concentrate on the subject. If the background were busy, we would not notice all the fine details of the clothing and jewelry. In her left hand she is holding a marten skin, often seen in portraits of upper-class women. These skins were worn to draw fleas away from their bodies and clothes.

**Understanding
Art History**

To help students further appreciate the life and times of Lavinia Fontana, whose work is shown in Figure 6.11, assign *Artist's Profile 16* in the TCR.

 **Experimenting
With Space**

1. Applying Your Skills.
Warn the students not to glue down any pieces until they are satisfied with the arrangement of shapes and space. Emphasize that the shapes will not change, but the negative space must vary, and that the negative space will control the final look of the design.

2. Further Challenge.
Part of this exercise is to set up objects so that the negative spaces are interesting.

3. Computer Option.
Encourage students to experiment with the space on the screen by using black and white, colors, patterns, and/or gradients.

 **Experimenting
with Space**

1. Applying Your Skills. Cut a large geometric shape from a sheet of black paper. Then cut the shape into nine or more separate pieces. Re-form the pieces into the original shape on a large sheet of white paper. Expand the shape by gradually sliding the pieces apart. Experiment by creating different amounts of space between the pieces, then glue down the best arrangement. You may not add or subtract any pieces from the original number, and the original shape must be recognizable. Shapes may touch the edges.

2. Further Challenge. Select a group of objects to draw. Make an arrangement with a variety of negative spaces between the shapes. Draw the arrangement lightly with pencil or chalk. Finish the work by (a) coloring only the negative spaces with crayons or paint, or (b) filling the negative spaces with closely drawn sets of parallel lines. Leave the positive spaces empty. What shapes did the negative spaces take?

MEETING SPECIAL NEEDS

Learning or Physically Disabled Some students with disabilities may not have the patience to hold shapes together for several minutes while the glue sets. Quick-tack glue, masking tape, straight pins, and paper clips will help to facilitate the attaching. The teacher might use a hot-melt glue gun for especially problematic joining operations. Cutting the bases of tubes to fit onto other curved surfaces can also be very challenging for students with some types of disabilities. Having some precut shapes will be useful. Some students may have difficulty in conceiving an attractive form in abstract designs. Perhaps they will prefer to make some kind of animal or a robot.

GUIDED PRACTICE
(continued)

Using Art Criticism

Have students study Figure 6.12 and apply the four steps of art criticism to it. If preferred, have students work in pairs or small groups. Because the painting has a strong emotional impact, you may want to first allow students to offer their reactions to the subject matter before they proceed with the critical analysis.

Developing Perceptual Skills

To help students comprehend space in three-dimensional art, bring in a few examples of three-dimensional works, if possible. Have students study the objects from all sides and analyze the use of space. In discussing three-dimensional art forms, ask students to name specific objects that they have seen or used. Include manufactured objects, such as pots, dishes, vacuum cleaners, and so on. Ask students to speculate about how these functional objects must be designed for specific uses. For example, a vacuum cleaner is usually stored inside a closet, pots and pans are used on a stove top, and dishes are used to serve food.

Critical Thinking

Direct students' attention to the interior space of your classroom. Remind them that this interior volume is defined by the room's walls. Encourage a discussion about how the feel of the space would change if the walls were placed at different angles or at different points in space. Challenge students to consider the effect a room's interior space might have on individuals who live and work there.

126

FIGURE 6.12 Garcia has created the feeling of a prisoner confined in a small space by eliminating almost all the negative space and filling the picture with the head of the woman. You can feel her sense of confinement because she is crushed by the edges of the picture.

Rupert Garcia. *Political Prisoner.* 1976. Pastel on paper. 122 × 91.5 cm (48 × 36″). National Museum of American Art, Smithsonian Institution, Washington, D.C.

3. Computer Option. Use the rectangle shape tool to draw a 2 x 3-inch (5 x 7.6-cm) solid rectangle in the middle of the screen. Use the Selection tool to select and then move part of the rectangle away from the original. Repeat until the rectangle has been broken into many smaller parts with varying spaces in between. Continue selecting and moving until you have created an interesting composition by the addition of space within the form.

Space in Three-Dimensional Art

Over, under, through, behind, and *around* are words that describe three-dimensional space. Architecture, sculpture, weaving, ceramics, and jewelry are three-dimensional art forms. They all take up real space. You can walk around, look through, look behind, peer over, and reach into three-dimensional art.

Architects shape space. They design structures that enclose a variety of spaces for people. They

ART ON A SHOESTRING

If you are planning an art project that involves styrofoam containers or empty food cartons, you might investigate organizations that bring food to elderly and confined people, such as the "Meals on Wheels" program. They may be able to supply you with clean, recyclable supplies. Also, ask students and parents to send in unneeded mail-order catalogs to use for collages. The slick paper used in these catalogs usually makes them nonrecyclable, but in the art classroom, they still have some life left in them!

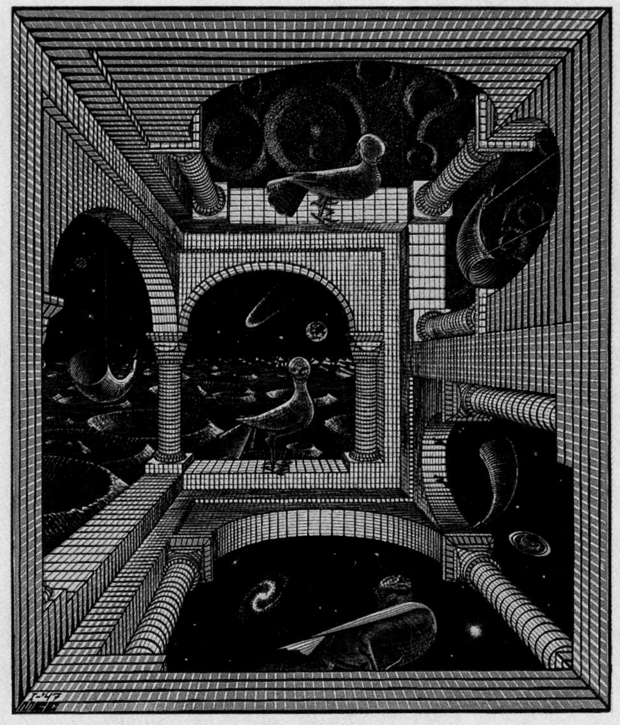

M. C. Escher. *Other World*. 1947. Wood engraving in three colors. 31.8 × 26 cm (12½ × 10¼").
National Gallery of Art, Washington, D.C.

LOOKING
CLOSELY

FIGURE 6.13 Escher uses two forms, the bird and an architectural structure, and presents them in an unusual distortion of reality. Look at the lower third of the picture. Where is the viewer in relation to the bird? Now look at the bird in the middle of the picture. Where is the viewer now? Then study the top third of the picture. Now what happened to the position of the viewer with relation to the bird? Can you figure out how Escher made this visual puzzle look logical?

create large spaces for group activities, such as the one you see in Figure 6.14 on page 128. They also create small spaces for privacy. Landscape architects and city planners are also involved in planning spaces for people to use.

Negative areas in three-dimensional art are very real. Most three-dimensional works are meant to be *freestanding*, which means they are surrounded by negative space (Figure 6.15, page 128). The viewer must move through this negative space to see all of the different views of a three-dimensional work.

Relief sculpture is not intended to be freestanding. It projects out from a flat surface into negative space. You can find relief sculpture on ceramic pots and plaster ceilings. When the positive areas

project slightly from the flat surface, the work is called *bas relief*, or *low relief* (Figure 6.16, page 129). When the positive areas project farther out, the work is called *high relief* (Figure 6.17, page 129).

Most jewelry is planned as relief sculpture to decorate human surfaces. The inside of a ring or the back of a pendant is smooth. It is not meant to be seen; it simply rests on the person's surface.

Today many artists are experimenting and changing traditional art forms. Printmakers are creating relief prints. Some printmakers are molding relief designs in handmade paper. Painters are adding a third dimension to the painted surface. Some painters are cutting or tearing real negative spaces in two-dimensional surfaces.

MEETING SPECIAL NEEDS

Learning Disabled A good material for students with disabilities to use to experience subtractive sculpture is discarded sand cores from a metal casting foundry. Call a foundry and inquire if they have any sand cores or ask parents if they have

knowledge of places where sand cores may be acquired. Students can shape the material with a butter knife or shape it by grinding it down on an asphalt or concrete sidewalk.

GUIDED PRACTICE
(continued)

LOOKING
CLOSELY

Have students study Figure 6.13 and answer the questions in the caption. Help students to see that in the lower third of the picture, the viewer is looking up from below the bird and the wall. In the middle third of the picture, the viewer is looking straight ahead at the bird. In the top third of the picture, the viewer is looking down on the bird. Notice how the negative space changes in each third. In the lower third the viewer sees the night sky in the negative space. In the middle third the viewer sees the ground at eye level, with crater ridges showing on the ground. In the top third the viewer is looking down on the ground, and the shadows and highlights made by the craters are visible.

Escher has made this scene look possible because he has used only one vanishing point for all three views. If you photocopy the print, you can use a ruler and trace the edges of the walls. You will see that the vanishing lines for all three scenes meet at a point slightly to the left of the head of the center bird. To keep the work more interesting, Escher has placed the vanishing point a little to the right of the center arch.

Understanding Art History

To help students further appreciate the life and times of M. C. Escher, whose work is shown in Figure 6.13, assign *Artist's Profile 39* in the TCR.

GUIDED PRACTICE
(continued)

 ### Using Three Dimensions

1. Applying Your Skills.
Unless students do this activity at home, it will be wise to start collecting cardboard tubes and boxes about a week before they construct their forms. The paint is not necessary, but it enhances the forms.

2. Further Challenge.
At home any lamp will serve as a light source to create the shadows as long as the other lights in the room are dim. In school, students might have to share the light, so they might select one of the pieces in the group to draw.

3. Computer Option.
Using the same steps, students can draw a cylinder, cube, or pyramid. Use the Gradient Fill to make the form appear three-dimensional. Use the Copy and Paste commands to make multiple copies. The sizes of each copy can be varied by using the Scale Selection or Resize tool. An environment with three or more dimensional forms can be arranged in the same manner by storing the original copies in the Scrapbook. The invisible Clipboard saves a copy when you use the Copy and Paste commands, but it only holds one image at a time.

INDEPENDENT PRACTICE

Keeping a Sketchbook

Have students draw a building or a motor using a pencil and mechanical drawing tools, such as a ruler, compass, and protractor. Remind them to make a diagram of the main geometric forms they see and avoid drawing small details.

FIGURE 6.14 The architect designed this auditorium to seat representatives from every country in the world. It was designed to look as if it could hold all of the world's people. Notice the ways in which line and implied line have been used to emphasize the feeling of space in this auditorium.

Wallace Kirkman Harrison. United Nations Buildings. Assembly Building, Main Auditorium. New York, New York. 1949. Photo by Sendak, Inc.

Weaving also has gone in new directions. It started as a practical craft, with weavers making two-dimensional fabrics for clothing, and has evolved into an art form. Today hand weavers are creating relief hangings and three-dimensional woven sculptures.

Photographers are creating **holograms,** *images in three dimensions created with a laser beam.* Sculptors are making *kinetic,* or moving, sculpture.

 ### Using Three Dimensions

1. Applying Your Skills. Make a freestanding, three-dimensional design that projects into negative space on all sides. Using pieces of cardboard tubing and small boxes, join the design pieces with glue and tape. Paint the finished work in one color to emphasize its form.

2. Further Challenge. Set up a spotlight on one side of your freestanding sculpture from the above activity. In your sketchbook draw the contours of the sculpture and the shape of the shadow it casts. Move the spotlight to another angle. Draw the sculpture and its shadow. Notice how the changing light changes the shape of the shadow.

3. Computer Option. Draw a cube so that the top, side, and front are visible. Fill each surface with a different color or texture. Use the Select tool and the Copy and Paste options on the cube. Begin pasting the cube high on the page. Continue by pasting it repeatedly in the middle and lower portion of the screen. Notice that the cubes pasted low and last appear closer. Resize the cube that you are pasting or draw a smaller cube. Use the Copy and Paste options to add smaller cubes to the design. You will create an illusion of three-dimensional space. Imagine a small animal walking through the spaces and climbing over the cubes.

FIGURE 6.15 The negative shapes that pierce the shell of this form are as important to the structure as the solid bronze. They create the feeling of a person.

Barbara Hepworth. *Figure for Landscape.* 1960. Bronze. 269.2 × 128.3 × 67.3 cm (106 × 50½ × 26½"). Hirshhorn Museum and Sculpture Garden, Smithsonian Institution, Washington, D.C. Gift of Joseph H. Hirshhorn, 1966.

MEETING SPECIAL NEEDS

Learning Disabled Some students with mental retardation may have difficulty conceiving of effects of light on form. A more ability-appropriate objective for them would be to conceive of an object's basic outline shape, then reproduce it using large marking pens. If gray or tan paper is used, the student can go back into the drawing with white and black chalk after the outline has been drawn.

FIGURE 6.16   Student work. An example of low relief.

FIGURE 6.17   Notice how far out the animals and the decorative columns protrude from the surface of this building. There is a strong shadow behind the salamander over the arch that indicates how far it is raised from the surface. How many other examples of high relief can you find on the façade of this building?

Berenice Abbot. *Façade, Alwyn Court, 174–182 West 58th Street.* August 10, 1938. Museum of the City New York, New York. The Berenice Abbott Collection, #283-A. Federal Arts Project "Changing New York."

How We Perceive Shape, Form, and Space

Look up from this book to an object across the room to see if you can feel the movement of your eye muscles. If you didn't feel anything, try again until you become aware that your eyes are working to refocus.

You have just taken a trip through visual space. Your brain measured the amount of space between you and the object and sent a message to your eye muscles to adjust. The muscles then refocused your eyes so that you could clearly see the object.

Perceiving Depth

Your eyes and brain work together to enable you to see in three dimensions—*length*, *width*, and *depth*. Each eye sees an object from a slightly different angle. The brain merges these two separate and slightly different views into one, creating a three-dimensional image.

To see how this works try the following experiment. Close your right eye. Point to a specific spot in the room. Without moving your pointing finger, open your right eye and close your left eye. It will appear you have moved your finger, even though you know you have not.

Point of View

The shapes and forms you see depend on your *point of view*. Your point of view is the angle from which you see an object. Another person at another location will see the same shape or form differently. For example, a person looking down on a circle drawn on the sidewalk sees a round shape. If that person lies on the ground beside the circle and looks at it, the circle will appear to have an oblong shape. A person looking at the front end of a car will see a form different from the one seen by a person looking at the side of that same car. Figure 6.18 on page 130 shows three different views of a sculpture.

You can learn about points of view by doing the following experiments. Place your hand flat on the desk and spread your fingers apart. The shape and form you see are the shape and form you would probably draw. They are part of the mental image you have of the object "hand." Now lift your hand

TEACH

(pages 129–139)
• How We Perceive Shape, Form, and Space
• How Artists Create Shapes and Forms in Space

GUIDED PRACTICE

Promoting Discussion

To help students understand that they have stereoscopic vision, try to bring in an example of stereography (three-dimensional photography) and the special glasses required to merge the two pictures into one.

Check with your optician to see if there is anything like a "stereopticon" (an old-fashioned, two-image viewer) available to show your class.

Critical Thinking

Help students understand depth perception by following each step of the directions to this experiment carefully:
• Cover your right eye. Point with your finger to a specific spot in the room. Note the position of the spot now.
• Without moving your pointing finger, cover your left eye. Note how the spot looks now.
• Again, without moving your pointing finger, uncover both eyes and focus on the tip of your finger.
• Describe exactly what you saw in each step of this experiment. Based on your experience, what can you conclude about someone who is blind in one eye? Can this person function as well as someone with two good eyes? Can he or she drive a car? Explain your conclusions.

MORE ABOUT . . . BINOCULAR VISION

No photographic technique has been able to duplicate the human brain and eyes in creating images of objects in space. Stereoscopic photography captures some of the illusion, but this photography is limited. The principle of binocular vision has also been used to design optical range finders for map-making and tank gunnery.

Double-image (or 3-D) movies are produced by making one print of the film in warm colors and one print in cool colors. These prints are shown side-by-side. The audience is given glasses that filter out the warm colors for one eye and cool colors for the other eye. The brain lays one image on top of the other so that viewers see a third dimension, depth.

GUIDED PRACTICE
(continued)

Interdisciplinary: Physiology

Place several small objects on a table top. Ask one student to stand by the table with closed eyes. Then ask the student to open just one eye and pick up an item that you name. Be sure to call on a student who does not object to being laughed at, since he or she will probably not be able to pick up the object.

You need to explain that people with one eye can adjust to the three-dimensional world. Somehow the brain learns that only one eye is operating and it adapts.

Exploring Aesthetics

After students have studied Kurelek's painting in Figure 6.19, ask them to discuss the effects of line. Ask: What types of line are predominant? How does Kurelek define space with line?

Sparking Creativity

Want students to think creatively about our perception of shapes and forms? Suggest this: Look at the shapes in a mountainous landscape. Mountains are not triangles. They flow in a range of shapes. The science of topography shows that land contours were formed as the earth buckled, folded, and eroded. Arrange a sweater or a large piece of cloth on a table in a heap. Draw the shapes you see. Then turn your drawing into a landscape. Use your imagination to add your own details of roads, lakes, and tree clusters.

FIGURE 6.18   Notice how the feeling expressed by this ceramic sculpture changes as your point of view changes. You must view sculpture from all angles to truly understand it. Can you find the warrior's face and the bird's head?

Bob Owens. *Warrior with Carnivorous Helmet.* 1986. Ceramic. 53.3 cm (21″). Private collection.

FIGURE 6.19   In this painting the viewer can see all the tabletops easily. All the serving dishes and the food in them are clearly visible. Can you tell what kind of a party this is? Why was this point of view a good one for this painting?

William Kurelek. *Manitoba Party.* 1964. Oil on Masonite. 121.9 x 152.6 cm (48 × 60″). National Gallery of Canada, Ottawa, Canada.

COOPERATIVE LEARNING

Select a group of four to six students to set up a composition outside to be viewed through a viewing frame. The viewing frame may be set up on a pole, fence, or other structure. Place one student far in the background, one closer in the middle ground, and one in the foreground. The person in the foreground or middle ground should stand so that part of his or her body partially blocks the view of, or overlaps part of, someone else. A variation is to have a person wearing bright colors stand the same distance away from the viewer as another wearing dull light colors. After each student has had the opportunity to look through the viewing frame, review the concepts of creating the illusion of depth.

and let your fingers relax. Notice how the shape and form of your hand change. Turn your hand and watch what happens. Your hand is still the same hand. Only its shape and form are different.

Next, look at a rectangular table. What shape does the top have when you are sitting at the table? Look at the top through a rectangular viewing frame. Are the edges of the table parallel to the edges of the frame? You know the top is a rectangle, but does it really look rectangular now? What shape does the top seem to take if you are sitting across the room from it? What would the shape look like if you viewed it from the top of a tall ladder? Do you think the shape you see will change if you lie on the floor directly under the table?

When you looked at your hand, your eyes stayed in the same place, but your hand moved. When you studied the table, it remained in one place, but you moved. In both cases, what you saw changed because your relationship to the object changed. Your point of view depends on where you are and where the object is. Look at Figure 6.19. Where is the artist's point of view in relation to the tables in that picture?

 Shape and Point of View

1. Applying Your Skills. Look through magazines for three or more different views of one type of object. Look for TV sets, sofas, spoons, toasters, cars, or shoes. Cut out the objects and mount each one on a sheet of white paper. Emphasize the changes in shape by drawing around each outline with a crayon or marker.

2. Further Challenge. Study the three photographs of a baseball glove in Figure 6.20. Each picture looks different because the relationship between the camera and the glove changes. Using a pencil, make a contour drawing of each view of the glove. Go over the outline of each drawing of the glove with a crayon or watercolor marker to emphasize shape changes.

3. Computer Option. Use the Line tool to draw three cubes, each from a different point of view. Use the Fill Bucket tool to fill each front with one color or texture. Fill the sides with a second color or texture. Use a third color or texture for each top and a fourth for each bottom.

FIGURE 6.20 How does your perception of the glove change in each view?

GUIDED PRACTICE
(continued)

Understanding Art History

Three years after Henri Matisse created *Beasts of the Sea*, he created another collage titled *The Snail*. Because he was ill and bedridden at this time, he could no longer stand at an easel. In spite of his physical limitations, he found this period of his art liberating, saying "Cutting paper permits me to draw with scissors." He often used such strong colors that his doctors advised him to wear dark glasses to avoid damage to his failing eyes.

Point out that the white spaces, which some students might regard as "blank," are also shapes. How do the individual shapes combine to form a lively, balanced whole? How does Matisse use the element of line to enhance the shapes and colors of the collage?

Understanding Art History

To help students further appreciate the life and times of Henri Matisse, whose work is shown in Figure 6.21, assign *Artist's Profile 33* in the TCR.

Using Art Criticism

After students have studied Figure 6.21, have them cut photographs of geometrically-shaped objects from magazines. For example, look for cans, boxes, tires, and gears and arrange the shapes to create a mechanical creature. Instruct students to glue the design onto paper then draw or paint a mechanical, geometric environment for the creature. Have them use the four steps of art criticism to evaluate their work individually, then work in groups to critique each other's creation.

HOW ARTISTS CREATE SHAPES AND FORMS IN SPACE

Shapes and forms can be classified as *natural* or *manufactured*. Natural shapes and forms are made by the forces of nature. For instance, animals, plants, and stones are natural forms. Manufactured forms are those created by people, whether mass-produced by the thousands in factories or made by hand.

Artists use many materials and techniques to make shapes. They concentrate on both outline and area. Some artists outline shapes in drawings and paintings. Others may paint shapes by placing brushstrokes together without using even a beginning outline. They cut shapes and print shapes as well (Figure 6.21).

Like shapes, forms can be made in many ways. Artists model clay forms, mold metal forms, and carve forms from wood or stone. They use glass, plastics, bricks, and cement to make forms as well as shapes.

The Illusion of Form

Artists can create the illusion of three-dimensional form on a two-dimensional surface. They can give the impression of depth and solidity by using changes in value. Figure 6.22 is an example of this illusion.

The *arrangement of light and shadow* is called **chiaroscuro** (**kyah**-roh-**skoo**-roh). In Italian *chiaro* means "bright," and *oscuro* means "dark." Chiaroscuro was introduced by Italian artists during the Renaissance. Figure 3.36, page 67, is an example. Later it was used for dramatic lighting effects by Baroque artists (Figure 12.5, page 317). Through careful observation, artists have learned how light is reflected off of three-dimensional forms. They have learned how to represent shadows realistically. Today, chiaroscuro is often called *modeling* or *shading*.

Look, for instance, at an object with angular surfaces, such as a cube. You will see a large jump in value from one surface of the cube to the next. One surface may be very light in value and the next very dark. Now look at an object such as a baseball. The curved surfaces of spheres and cylinders show gradual changes in value.

FIGURE 6.21   Matisse cut the shapes for this work directly from sheets of paper that he had colored with paint. He did not use anything to draw the shapes before he cut. Some of the shapes to look for in this work are fish, sea animals, sea plants, and coral.

Henri Matisse. *Beasts of the Sea.* 1950. Paper on canvas. 295.5 × 154 cm (116⅜ × 60⅝"). National Gallery of Art, Washington, D.C. Ailsa Mellon Bruce Fund.

The area of a curved surface that reflects the most light is, of course, the lightest in a drawing. **Highlights** are *small areas of white used to show the very brightest spots*. Starting at the highlights, the value changes gradually from light values of gray to dark values of gray. The darkest values are used to show areas that receive the least light. An area that is turned completely away from a light source is almost black. Look at Figure 6.23 on page 134 to see the ways an artist has created the illusion of form.

COOPERATIVE LEARNING

Point out that, although the practice of modeling figures in light and shadow was certainly a hallmark of Baroque art (the word *chiaroscuro* was itself coined in 1686), the technique had its roots in works of art as early as the Renaissance. Divide the class into research committees and ask them to choose one of the following topics as the basis for an oral presentation: (1) the origins of chiaroscuro (i.e., who coined the term?); (2) the history of chiaroscuro in art; and (3) different color models (e.g., process color, the RGB model) and their role in gradations of light and dark. Set aside time for committees to present their findings.

FIGURE 6.22 Giotto was the first artist to break away from the flat look of Byzantine painting. He studied the human form and used gestures and expressions that showed human qualities. Giotto's figures are so solid that they seem to be carved from rock.

Giotto. *Madonna and Child.* 1320–30. Paint on wood. 85.5 × 62 cm (33⅝ × 24⅜"). National Gallery of Art, Washington, D.C. Samuel H. Kress Collection.

 **Using Shading**

1. Applying Your Skills.
Try to set up a still life in the classroom as described in this activity. Turn off as many of the overhead lights as you can, and place a strong spotlight on one side of the still life. Before students start to draw, help them analyze the values they perceive by finding the darkest and lightest areas. Help them see the difference between gradual changes of value on rounded forms and jumps in value on angular surfaces. Insist that they use all of the values from white to black in their works. Many students try to stay in the safe gray areas of value and need to be pushed to go to black.

2. Further Challenge.
This activity will probably be easier to do as homework unless you can collect enough mirrors for the entire class. One way to control the lighting in your room is to turn off overhead lights and open the shades or blinds on one side of the room only. If you don't have windows, try to bring in enough lamps, which can be placed on one side of the room.

3. Computer Option.
Suggest this activity: Use any drawing tool or shape to design a large vase. If the Brush Symmetry command is available, use it to ensure a symmetrical shape. Determine the direction of the light source. Experiment with the Pencil, Airbrush, Gradient Fill, Brush, or Line tools to shade in the vase leaving highlighted areas. Add the shadow cast by the vase.

 Using Shading

1. Applying Your Skills. Set up an arrangement of geometric forms. Use boxes, books, balls, and cylindrical containers. Study the way light reflects off the surfaces of the objects. Draw the arrangement. Give the shapes in your drawing the illusion of three dimensions by using the medium and shading technique of your choice. Use values that range from black to white, and employ many value steps in between.

2. Further Challenge. Using yourself as the model, make a shaded drawing of a face (Figure 6.24, page 135). Sit facing a mirror. Set up a lamp to light your face from one side. Study the lights and shadows that fall on your face. Notice that there appears to be no edge to the side of your nose. It is a form with a rounded surface. Then, using the medium and shading technique that you prefer, model shadows and highlights. Avoid drawing contour lines. This drawing does not have to look like you.

3. Computer Option. Several computer tools can be used for shading objects. Experiment with the Pencil, Brush, Line, Gradient Fill, and Air Brush tools. Some software programs have a Smudge tool that also can be used for shading. Small Pencil and Brush tools can be used with shading techniques like those used when working with pen and ink.

COOPERATIVE LEARNING

Tell students that still–life painting began in the Baroque period. With the highly developed techniques of oil painting and the dramatic effects of chiaroscuro, artists looked for subject matter in everything around them. Acceptable still–life materials were fruits, vegetables, fish, elaborate containers, bowls and candlesticks, even dead birds and animals fresh from the hunt. Suggest that students work in small groups and arrange objects for a still–life arrangement on a draped cloth. Have them consider heights, shapes, overlapping, and the flow of the drapery. Suggest they darken the room so that the spotlight will be most effective, and have them draw the still life using black ink and a brush.

GUIDED PRACTICE
(continued)

Understanding Art History

Remind students that while most of Albrecht Dürer's contemporary German artists, such as Matthias Grünewald, were following the Gothic style, Dürer turned instead to the ideas and styles of Renaissance artists. (See Grünewald's *The Small Crucifixion* in Figure 11.24 on page 295.) Consequently, Dürer's artworks demonstrate the properties of perspective and proportions typical of Italian paintings of this time. His style also reflects his early training in printmaking, which he learned as an apprentice when he was fifteen years old.

Understanding Art History

To help students further appreciate the life and times of Albrecht Dürer, whose work is shown in Figure 6.23, assign *Artist's Profile 14* in the TCR.

Developing Studio Skills

Have students cut out seven magazine photos of objects that are all related to each other, such as animals, food, cars, shoes, furniture, and so on. Each object should be of a different size. Instruct students to arrange the cutouts on a dark sheet of paper using overlapping, differing sizes, placement, varying detail, and color to create the illusion of depth. Remind students that they can blur details and lighten colors in a magazine photograph by rubbing it lightly with an eraser. Have students share their work in small groups and explain how their choices create the illusion of depth.

FIGURE 6.23   Notice how Dürer has created the illusion of form using hatching and cross-hatching. Which side of the robe is getting more light, and which side is darker? How can you tell?

Albrecht Dürer. *An Oriental Ruler Seated on His Throne.* c. 1495. Pen and black ink. 30.6 × 19.7 cm (12 × 7¾"). National Gallery of Art, Washington, D.C. Ailsa Mellon Bruce Fund.

CULTURAL PERSPECTIVES

There are many different ways of organizing space in works of art. Show students examples of how other, non-Western cultures show depth in their works of art. For example, in some Asian and African art, both front and side views of an object or figure are shown at the same time. Asian artists often show distance by using parallel lines to divide an area in the foreground, middle ground, and background. Ancient Egyptian wall paintings found in Egyptian tombs are divided into geometric areas, often to allow the important figures to be drawn larger. Entire stories can be told in an Egyptian painting with each part presented in a horizontal panel.

FIGURE 6.24   Student work. A self-portrait.

The Illusion of Depth

In their paintings artists often create the illusion of depth. When you look at these paintings, you see objects and shapes, some of which seem closer to you than others. You seem to be looking through a window into a real place (Figure 6.25). This idea—that a painting should be like a window to the real world—has dominated traditional Western art since the early Renaissance.

There are several terms that will help you as you talk about and create depth in a painting or drawing. The surface of a painting or drawing is sometimes called the *picture plane*. The part of the picture plane that appears nearest to you is the *foreground*. The part that appears farthest away is the *background*. The area in between is called the *middle ground*.

FIGURE 6.25   Everything is carefully placed within the frame of this scene. In the foreground, figures dressed in bright robes kneel before the Christ Child. Beyond the human activity there is a background of calm, rolling, green hills. Notice how the artist tries to focus your attention on the Child. After reading about perspective, see if you can find examples of each of the six devices used for creating perspective in this painting.

Sandro Botticelli. *The Adoration of the Magi.* c. 1481–82. Tempera on wood. 70.1 × 104.1 cm (27⅝ × 41″). National Gallery of Art, Washington, D.C. Andrew W. Mellon Collection, 1937.

Perspective is *a graphic system that creates the illusion of depth and volume on a two-dimensional surface.* In the following pages are techniques artists use to give their paintings and drawings perspective.

Overlapping. When one object covers part of a second object, the first seems to be closer to the viewer, as in Figure 6.26.

Size. Large objects appear to be closer to the viewer than small objects, as in Figure 6.27. The farther an object is from you, the smaller it appears. Cars far down the road seem to be much smaller than the ones close to you. If you stand at the end of a long hallway and raise your hand, you can block your view of a whole crowd of people. You know that each is about your size, but at a distance the crowd appears to be smaller than your hand.

Placement. Objects placed low on the picture plane seem to be closer to the viewer than objects placed near eye level. The most distant shapes seem to be exactly at eye level (Figure 6.28).

Detail. Objects with clear, sharp edges and visible details seem to be close to you (Figure 6.29). Objects that lack detail and have hazy outlines seem to be farther away. Look closely at your own hand. You can see very tiny lines clearly. Now look at someone's hand from across the room. You have trouble seeing the lines between the fingers. All the details seem to melt together because of the distance between you and what you are seeing.

Color. Brightly colored objects seem closer to you, and objects with dull, light colors seem to be farther away (Figure 6.30). This is called *atmospheric* perspective. The air around us is not empty. It is full of moisture and dust that create a haze. The more air there is between you and an object, the more the object seems to fade. Have you ever noticed that trees close to you seem to be a much brighter green than trees farther down the road? You have probably been coloring mountains blue-gray since first grade, but of course they really aren't blue-gray.

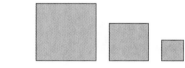

FIGURE 6.26 Overlapping.

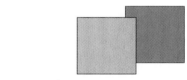

FIGURE 6.27 Size.

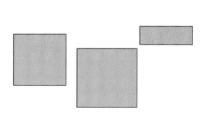

FIGURE 6.28 Placement.

FIGURE 6.29 Detail.

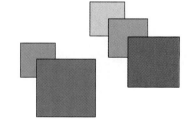

FIGURE 6.30 Color.

Converging Lines. *Linear* perspective is one way of using lines to show distance and depth. As parallel lines move away from you, they seem to move closer together toward the horizon line (Figure 6.31). When you look at the highway ahead of you, the sides of the road appear to move closer together. You don't worry, though, because you know this is an illusion. You know that the sides of the road ahead of you actually are just as far apart as they are in your present position.

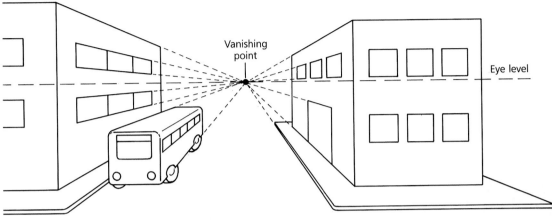

FIGURE 6.31 In this drawing the lines gradually come together and meet at one point in the distance. This is one-point linear perspective.

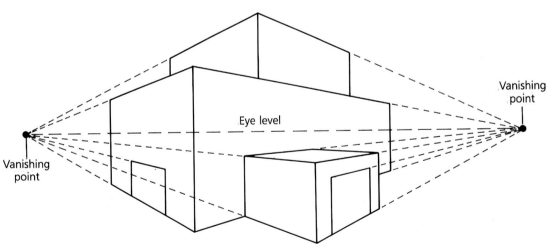

FIGURE 6.32 In this drawing the lines come together and meet at two points. This is two-point linear perspective.

GUIDED PRACTICE
(continued)

Understanding Art History

Instruct students to find out more about the development of linear perspective by Filippo Brunelleschi during the Renaissance. Ask them to write a brief summary of the way linear perspective was used by Renaissance artists in their paintings and drawings. Students should indicate that they understand the strict mathematical rules used to calculate perspective. Encourage them to analyze the difference between one-point and two-point perspective.

Exploring Aesthetics

Have students find a newspaper or magazine photograph of rectangular solids, such as the exterior of buildings or interior rooms of a building. Instruct students to use tracing paper to trace the main shapes in the photograph. Then, using a ruler and pencil, extend any parallel lines that recede into the distance. Ask them to identify the vanishing point(s) and the horizon line.

Computer Option

If your illustration program contains an extrude feature or some other command for adding perspective to an object, have students practice "assigning" perspective to a variety of simultaneously displayed objects so that they share a vanishing point. Ambitious students may want to create landscapes, making use not only of linear perspective but of aerial perspective. Ask students to describe how they went about choosing colors for near and distant objects.

CULTURAL PERSPECTIVES

Because linear perspective is fundamental to our understanding of art, we often take it for granted. Our familiarity with complex computer graphics could make us forget that earlier cultures did not understand the concept. Does the lack of linear perspective in the art of earlier generations diminish its significance? Ask students to choose an illustration from an earlier chapter and sketch the same subject using linear perspective to create the illusion of depth; for example, an Egyptian hieroglyphic, a frieze from the Parthenon, or a Byzantine painting.

GUIDED PRACTICE
(continued)

Creating Depth

1. Applying Your Skills.
Accurately measured linear perspective is not a subject of this course. It is, however, very important that students recognize and identify that perspective is always mathematical.

2. Further Challenge.
Remind students to look at Shading Techniques on page 350 of the Handbook to help them shade their forms to have the illusion of three dimensions. To further challenge them, ask them to plan a light source and then draw shadows on the ground.

3. Computer Option.
Students can create a simple landscape by choosing the Pencil or Brush tool to draw overlapping lines representing mountains, hills, and fields. Use the foreground, middle ground, and background space on their screen. Add winding roads or roaming streams and fences that change size and direction as they move higher on the picture plane. Draw trees, houses, barns, bridges, animals, or other details. Use the Copy and Paste commands and Scale Selection or Resizing tool to repeat these shapes in varying sizes, overlapping occasionally. Add color and patterns using the Bucket Flood-fill tool.

INDEPENDENT PRACTICE

Keeping a Sketchbook

Have students sketch at least ten manufactured shapes and forms in their environments. Encourage them to look for both mass-produced and handmade objects. With each sketch, have them write a description of how they think the objects were made.

138

Sometimes lines appear to meet at a point on the horizon line called the *vanishing point.* In one-point linear perspective, all receding lines meet at a single vanishing point. In two-point linear perspective, different sets of parallel lines meet at different vanishing points (Figure 6.32, page 137). Because two-point perspective creates more diagonal lines in a painting, it seems more active. Renaissance artists used strict mathematical formulas to calculate perspective. Most of today's artists rely on visual perception rather than mathematical formulas. Notice the ways in which Doris Lee has used perspective to show depth in her busy kitchen scene (Figure 6.33).

ACTIVITY Creating Depth

1. Applying Your Skills. Create three different designs on three separate sheets of paper. Each design should contain five shapes. Use the same five shapes in each design as follows:

■ Draw all of the items as close to the foreground as possible.

■ Draw one item close to the foreground and make the others look as if they are slightly farther back.

■ Draw one item close to the foreground, one far in the background, and the other three in the middle ground.

FIGURE 6.33 Can you find the six perspective techniques in this scene?

Doris Lee. *Thanksgiving.* 1935. Oil on canvas. 71.4 × 101.6 cm (28 × 40″). The Art Institute of Chicago, Chicago, Illinois. Mr. and Mrs. Frank G. Logan Prize Fund, 1935.

▌CURRICULUM CONNECTION▐

Math   Renaissance fascination with mathematics and with representation led artists into devising mathematical approaches to drawing. Leon Battista Alberti (1404–72), an Italian artist, published the first written account of the system of perspective. From this, mathematicians developed projective geometry.

German artist Albrecht Dürer (1471–1528) experimented with perspective by looking at his subject through a pane of glass and seeing how receding lines seemed to angle inward and narrow. Think of the glass as the *picture plane* and the depth you show as the *picture space.* The point where your eye rests in the distance is the *vanishing point.*

2. Further Challenge.   Do the same exercise using three-dimensional forms instead of shapes.

3. Computer Option.   Use the Brush or Pencil tool and the Fill Bucket tool to create a simple landscape. Divide the land into the background, middle ground, and foreground. Draw one or two small trees in the middle ground. Draw at least one large tree in the foreground. It can overlap those in the middle ground if you wish. Add other details. Keep in mind the methods for creating the illusion of depth that were discussed in this section.

WHAT DIFFERENT SPACES, SHAPES, AND FORMS EXPRESS

Shapes, forms, and spaces in art communicate certain feelings. This is possible because you associate them with similar shapes, forms, and spaces in real life. When you see a certain shape or form in a work of art, you may think of an object from real life. Any feelings you have about that object will affect your feelings about the artistic work. Artists use this relationship between art and your environment to communicate with you.

Outline and Surface

The outline of a shape and the surface of a form carry messages. Artists often use free-form shapes and forms to symbolize living things. When they want to please and soothe viewers, they use shapes and forms with smooth, curved outlines and surfaces (Figure 6.34). Forms that remind us of well-worn river rocks or curled-up kittens tempt us to touch them. These forms are comfortable. They appeal to us through our memories of pleasant touching experiences.

Angular shapes with zigzag outlines and forms with pointed projections remind us of sharp, jagged things (Figure 6.35, on page 140). We remember the pain caused by broken glass and sharp knives. We would never carelessly grab a pointed, angular form. If we were to touch it at all, we would do so very carefully.

Geometric shapes suggest mechanical perfection. It is impossible to draw a perfect circle freehand. The special appeal of geometric shapes and forms has been felt throughout the ages. Their lines, contours, and surfaces are clean and crisp. This appeals to people's sense of order.

As used by modern artists, geometric shapes and forms express less feeling than other types. They are unemotional; in fact, they may express a total lack of feeling. Geometric forms in artworks appeal to viewers' minds rather than to their emotions (Figure 6.36, page 140).

FIGURE 6.34   "William," this round, roly-poly hippo, has such an appealing shape that he has become the unofficial mascot of The Metropolitan Museum of Art in New York City.

Egyptian. *Figure of Hippopotamus.* XII dynasty (1991–1786 B.C.). Ceramics-Faience. Meir, Tomb of Senbi. 11 × 20 cm (4⅓ × 7⅞"). The Metropolitan Museum of Art, New York, New York. Gift of Edward S. Harkness, 1917.

GUIDED PRACTICE
(continued)

Developing Vocabulary

Students often confuse the terms *density* and *texture*. This point will be discussed further in Chapter 8, but it is important that students realize now that hard and soft are properties of shape and form, while texture is a surface quality.

Understanding Art History

Tell students that Ben Shahn, like many artists of his time, was employed through government programs during the Depression years. Between 1934 and 1938, he was commissioned under the Farm Security Administration to capture images of rural poverty with his paintings and photographs. After World War II, he turned to easel and poster painting, then was a Charles Eliot Norton Professor of Poetry at Harvard University in 1956–1957 where he published several essays. He is also famous for his illustrations of books about Jewish festivals and Hebrew script.

Exploring Aesthetics

Have students study Figure 6.36 then explore their emotional reactions to the sculpture. Ask: What do you think the sculpture feels like? Why? How does the artwork make you feel? How has the artist manipulated the elements and principles of art to create that feeling? Why would the artist have chosen this particular medium to portray the subject matter? What shapes do you see in the sculpture? What do you imagine the sculpture looks like from other angles? Does the shape of the sculpture successfully convey the conventional image of a man's torso? Why or why not?

140

FIGURE 6.35 This painting shows contrast between the static, solid form of the man and the active movement of the stems and thorns. This is a moment of tension. The viewer can imagine the pain that will occur when the blind botanist moves his hands to study the plant.

Ben Shahn. *The Blind Botanist.* 1954. Tempera on Masonite. 132 × 78.8 cm (52 × 31"). Wichita Museum of Art, Wichita, Kansas. The Roland P. Murdock Collection. © Estate of Ben Shahn/VAGA, New York 1994.

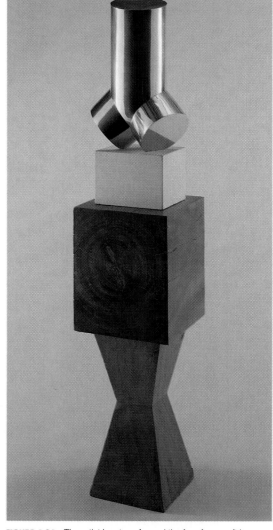

FIGURE 6.36 The artist has transformed the free-form, soft human torso into a metallic, dense, geometric abstraction.

Constantin Brancusi. *Torso of a Young Man.* 1924. Polished bronze on stone and wood base. 45.7 × 27.9 × 17.8 cm (18 × 11 × 7"). Hirshhorn Museum and Sculpture Garden, Smithsonian Institution, Washington, D.C. Gift of Joseph H. Hirshhorn, 1966.

Density

The *density* of an object refers to how compact it is. Dense materials are solid and heavy. Granite and lead, for example, are very dense. They are so solid and firm that you cannot make a dent on their surfaces when you press on them. Dense forms seem unyielding. They resist impact. For this reason, you may associate them with the idea of protection. In two-dimensional art, you can depict dense objects by using shading techniques and hard-edge contours.

Soft, fluffy forms are less dense. When you press on them, you can make a dent. These forms have air inside them, and they look more comfortable than denser forms. In two-dimensional art, you can depict soft forms by using shading techniques and curved contours.

CURRICULUM CONNECTION

Language Arts Just as the visual arts are concerned with shape and form, certain language arts are based on specific forms as well. For example, poetry has a long tradition of precision in its composition. The sonnet is always fourteen lines of iambic pentameter; the ballad is four lines of iambic verse alternating tetrameter and trimeter; the Spenserian stanza is eight lines of iambic pentameter followed by one of iambic hexameter. Free verse is unrhymed iambic pentameter; the haiku is based on exact syllable count. Often, students of literature are so familiar with poetic forms that they can identify the type of poem by looking at its shape on the printed page!

Openness

An open shape or form appears inviting. It seems to say, "Come in." You can see into or through it. An armchair is an open form that invites you to sit. An open door invites you to enter. An empty cup invites you to fill it. Transparent objects, such as a glass wall, invite you to look inside (Figure 6.37). When you extend your hand to invite someone to join you, the form of your outstretched hand is an open form.

Open spaces in sculpture invite your eyes to wander through the work. Weavers leave openings in fabrics and hangings to let you see through them. If you remove an oak table from a room and replace it with a glass table, the room will seem less crowded. Architects use glass walls to open small spaces. Windows open up a building and bring in the outdoors.

Closed shapes and forms look solid and self-contained. Windowless buildings look forbidding. Closed doors keep people out; closed drapes and shades keep light out. When you make a tight fist, your hand is a closed form that seems to say, "Keep away." Folding your arms tightly to your body closes you off from others. Open arms invite people to come closer to you. The woman shown in Figure 6.38 has wrapped her robes around herself, creating a closed form to repel any contact. She tells you that she wants to be alone without saying a word. Her body language says it all.

FIGURE 6.37 The openness of the transparent glass walls of this house invites you to look inside, but when you are inside, the transparent walls invite you to look out at the beauty of the natural surroundings.

Phillip Johnson. *Johnson House.* 1949. New Canaan, Connecticut. View: exterior of glass house.

FIGURE 6.38 Notice how the artist has indicated the extreme feeling of isolation one experiences at the loss of a loved one. She has created this effect by using a closed form to represent the grieving person.

Marie Apel. *Grief.* 1940. Bronze. 51 × 17.8 × 15.2 cm (20 × 7 × 6"). National Museum of Women in the Arts, Washington, D.C. Gift of the artist's daughter.

GUIDED PRACTICE
(continued)

Cooperative Learning

Have students work in pairs or small groups to find examples of active and static shapes and forms in other chapters of the text. Have them make a list that is divided into two columns, one for active and the other for static. Challenge them to find as many examples as possible in a specific length of time, such as fifteen minutes. Then ask each group to identify their examples and the category where each is placed. A volunteer student could write the figure numbers or titles on the board. Review the list to see how many examples were repeated in the same category. Look for any that were listed in both categories. Choose one or more of these examples to discuss more closely with the entire class.

Understanding Art History

Remind students that artists are a product of the historical, cultural, and aesthetic contexts in which they live and work. By understanding more about these areas, students will have a greater understanding and appreciation for any particular artist's style.

 Active and Static Shapes

1. Applying Your Skills.
To make this project work, the different parts must look like they belong together. It is important that students do not glue any shapes to the background until all shapes are cut and arranged.

2. Further Challenge.
The purpose of this activity is to show how the same shapes and colors will look different when just the edges are changed from sharp to fuzzy.

142

Activity and Stability

You have already learned about active and static lines. Shapes and forms, also, can look as if they are about to move or as if they are fixed in one place.

Active shapes and forms seem to defy gravity. They slant diagonally, as if they are falling or running. In Figure 6.39 notice how the back of the wave and all the horse forms are arranged in diagonal, active positions.

Static shapes and forms are motionless, or stable. Their direction is usually horizontal (Figure 6.40). However, if two diagonal shapes or forms are balanced against each other, a static shape results. For instance, if an equilateral triangle rests on a horizontal base, the two diagonal edges balance each other.

Because static shapes and forms are firmly fixed in position, they evoke quiet and calm feelings. For instance, in landscape paintings the land forms are horizontal and the trees are vertical. They look very peaceful. This is probably why so many landscape paintings are chosen for people's homes.

FIGURE 6.39 The diagonal push of the back of the wave creates an unstable, active feeling. The wave is caught at the moment before it will collapse.

Anna Hyatt Huntington. *Riders to the Sea.* c. 1912. Bronze. 47 × 61 × 53 cm (18½ × 24 × 21"). Collection of the Newark Museum, Newark, New Jersey. Gift of the estate of Mrs. Florence P. Eagleton, 1954.

FIGURE 6.40 This figure expresses a stable feeling because of the long horizontal base and the vertical position of the mother's torso.

Henry Moore. *Reclining Mother and Child.* 1974–76. Plaster. 132 × 216 × 105 cm (51¹⁵⁄₁₆ × 85⅛ × 41¼"). Dallas Museum of Art, Dallas, Texas. Lent by the Henry Moore Foundation.

COOPERATIVE LEARNING

Reinforce the concepts in this chapter by dividing the class into five groups. Assign each group one of the following artworks: *Figure for Landscape* (Figure 6.15, page 128), *Beasts of the Sea* (Figure 6.21, page 132), *Madonna and Child* (Figure 6.22, page 133), *The Adoration of the Magi* (Figure 6.25, page 135), and *Thanksgiving* (Figure 6.33, page 138). Have students look for evidence of the following in their assigned artwork: positive and negative space, shapes, three-dimensional form, realism, humanism, solidity of form in two- and three-dimensional paintings, shapes in free-form, perspective in space, and unique techniques. Ask each group to select a spokesperson who will present the group's findings.

ACTIVITY   Active and Static Shapes

1. Applying Your Skills. Cut out pictures of free-form objects from magazines. Arrange them to create a living fantasy creature (Figure 6.41). Use parts of people if you wish, but include other shapes as well. Glue your creature on a large sheet of paper. Draw or paint an environment full of free-form shapes for this fantasy creature.

2. Further Challenge. Make a simple design with geometric shapes. Lightly draw it with pencil on a small sheet of watercolor paper. Repeat the same design on another sheet of watercolor paper of the same size. Next, paint the first design precisely. Use a pointed brush to make sure that all of the edges are clearly defined (Figure 6.42). Wet the second sheet of paper by sponging it with water. Using exactly the same colors, paint the second design while the paper is wet so that the edges of the shapes run and look soft (Figure 6.43). Mount the two designs, side by side, on a sheet of black paper. Label the first "hard-edged" and the second "soft-edged."

3. Computer Option. Use the Rectangle shape tool to draw several solid black rectangles. Arrange them on the screen to create a static feeling. Use the Line tool to add static black lines to the design. On a new screen, draw several solid black triangles of various sizes to create an active feeling. Use the Line tool to add active black lines to the design. Label the designs either "stable" or "active." The Line tool can be constrained to draw a straight horizontal, vertical, or diagonal line in many software programs by holding down the shift key while drawing with the mouse.

FIGURE 6.42   Student work. Hard edges.

FIGURE 6.43   Student work. Soft edges.

FIGURE 6.41   Student work. A living fantasy creature.

Drawing an Outdoor Scene

OBJECTIVE

Draw an outdoor scene that creates the illusion of three-dimensional depth by using shading techniques.

MOTIVATOR

If possible, take the students on a field trip to a state or national park for a day of drawing. Otherwise, a trip outside or a travel video might provide inspiration. Encourage students to see the values, forms, and composition of the landscape.

GUIDED PRACTICE

Developing Studio Skills

To help students understand the value of the viewing frame, instruct them to be sure that the shape and proportions of the viewing frame are the same as that of the paper they are using.

Understanding Art History

Discuss the works of Georges Seurat, particularly his use and invention of pointillism as a method of creating the illusion of solid form and structure in compositions. Ask students to compare Seurat's style to Larry Smith's use of stippling to create shadows in his landscape. Other artists who worked with landscapes to consider for discussion might include photographer Ansel Adams, painter Thomas Eakins, and painter Andrew Wyeth.

STUDIO LESSON: DRAWING AN OUTDOOR SCENE

FIGURE 6.44 Larry Smith. *North Georgia Waterfall.* 1993. Pen and ink on paper. 66 x 61 cm (26 × 24"). Collection of the artist.

Supplies

- Sketchbook
- Large sheet of white drawing paper
- Drawing board and tape
- Pencils and erasers
- Viewing frame

Larry Smith is an artist in love with the land. Born and raised in Georgia, he has committed his professional life to capturing its majestic scenery on paper. In this view of Tallula Falls (Figure 6.44), he shares his impression of water cascading down the rocks and collecting in the lake below.

Smith uses a realistic style to create his artwork. Regionalists such as Winslow Homer (Figures 1.7 and 1.8, page 12) and Edward Hopper (Figure 5.22, page 98) inspired him to preserve the historical significance of a building, a landscape, or an environmental treasure. Smith likes to use pencil, colored pencils, or pen and ink to draw the scenes that represent his local environment. He is concerned with capturing light, and in this landscape he has used stippling for the shadows and has left the white of the paper to represent the white froth of the foaming falls.

Observe the different ways in which Larry Smith has created three-dimensional forms and depth in his landscape. Watch how your drawing springs to life when you use shading to create three-dimensional forms and perspective techniques to show deep space.

Remind students that landscape art, such as the example in Figure 6.44 is common to all cultures. To encourage an appreciation for the diversity of styles of landscape art, divide students into small groups and ask them to browse through art books with reproductions of landscapes from various countries. Instruct each group to find at least five examples that represent different cultural groups. They should consider whether each artist tried to create a mirror of the natural world, or tried to evoke a sense of the landscape without copying it. Allow time for each group to share their examples with the class and discuss the styles.

Make a drawing of an outdoor scene that is interesting to you. This scene should have a foreground, middle ground, and background. Create the illusion of three-dimensional forms in the scene by using a variety of shading techniques. Use values that range from black to various grays to white. Create the illusion of deep, three-dimensional space by using one or more perspective techniques. Mount or mat the finished work for display.

FOCUSING

Larry Smith chooses scenes from his local environment to record for others to enjoy. Find an outdoor scene that is important to you and that you think is important enough to record for the future. Think of the view from your window, a country or park scene, or a view of boats in a harbor. Do not use a photograph or another drawing.

CREATING

Make a viewing frame and use it to help select the exact view you wish to draw. (See Technique Tip on page 351 in the Handbook.) Be sure to include a large shape in the foreground. All parts of the large shape do not have to fit in the picture. Take time to study the relationship of each shape and form to the frame. Each shape and form will have the same relationship to the edges of the paper as it does to the edges of the frame. Make some rough sketches of the scene in your sketchbook.

Now look through the frame at the objects in the scene and write notes in your sketchbook about how they are arranged. Pay attention to overlapping, placement, size differences, details, values, and receding parallel lines.

Tape your paper to the drawing board and lightly draw in the shapes, paying careful attention to the placement of the major objects on the page. Shade the shapes using a value scale that includes black, white, and all the grays in between. Use a variety of shading techniques to

FIGURE 6.44A Student work.

create the illusion of flat and rounded three-dimensional forms.

Give your work a title that expresses the mood or meaning of the work. Mount or mat your work for display.

C R I T I Q U I N G

Describe What scene did you choose as the subject of your drawing? Tell why you selected this scene. How did the use of the viewing frame affect your work? How did you prepare the work for display?

Analyze Which shading techniques did you use to create three-dimensional forms? Which perspective techniques did you use to create the illusion of depth?

Interpret What kind of a feeling does this drawing express? Does the title you chose express the mood or meaning of the work?

Judge Which aesthetic theory would you use to judge your work? Do you think the work was successful? What would you change to improve it?

145

TECHNIQUE TIP

The viewing frame technique tip mentioned above is important. Students will be asked to use a viewing frame many times during drawing activities. They do not have to hold the viewing frame all of the time while drawing. The purpose of the frame is to limit the field of vision and to help make

decisions about which part of a larger area will be the subject. When students first begin drawing outside, the expanse of landscape may be overwhelming. The viewing frame helps students tame the visual environment.

GUIDED PRACTICE
(continued)

Developing Perceptual Skills

To reinforce the concept of perspective for students who are having difficulty, instruct them to draw three or four geometric and organic shapes on white drawing paper. Then show them how to draw converging lines to a vanishing point. Remind them to overlap shapes and forms to create the illusion of depth.

INDEPENDENT PRACTICE

Keeping a Portfolio

Remind students that the preliminary sketches and the final artwork for this Studio Lesson are likely considerations for their portfolios.

Extension

Give each student an apple or pear as they finish the Studio Lesson. Direct them to eat the fruit but leave the core intact. Instruct students to draw the core by using the shading techniques learned in this chapter.

ASSESS

CRITIQUING

Have students apply the steps of art criticism to their own artwork using the "Critiquing" questions on this page. In addition, ask the following: What interested you most about the scene that you chose? How did you incorporate that interest in your scene? Did you use a variety of values ranging from black to white? How does the composition of your piece effect the mood of your drawing? Did the use of a viewing frame improve your ability to concentrate and draw better?

145

FOCUS

OBJECTIVE

Use high and low relief to create a clay plaque depicting a current event.

MOTIVATOR

Ask students to suggest contemporary issues and events. Event topics could relate to current studies in social studies, or they could be drawn from world, national, state, local, or family history. Discuss why artists might be inspired to create artworks based on contemporary issues and events.

TEACH

GUIDED PRACTICE

Understanding Art History

Remind students that there is little information on the past of the African nations because of the absence of a written history. However, students may be interested in studying the influences by the people of Africa on colonial Europeans. Likewise, students may also enjoy learning about various artists such as Picasso and Matisse who were influenced by African art.

Critical Thinking

Encourage students to choose background patterns that reflect the culture or period represented by the figures they choose. Ask volunteers to describe their methods of deciding how a visual pattern represents a culture or period.

STUDIO LESSON: CLAY PLAQUE WITH HIGH RELIEF

FIGURE 6.45 *Warrior Chief, Warriors, and Attendants.* Plaque. Nigeria, Edo. Court of Benin. Sixteenth to seventeenth centuries. Brass. Height 48 cm (18⅞"). The Metropolitan Museum of Art, New York, New York. Gift of Mr. and Mrs. Klaus G. Perls, 1990.

Supplies

- Sketchbook and pencil
- Clay
- Clay tools and equipment
- Newspaper and scissors
- Slip and brush
- Large plastic bag
- Kiln
- Glaze or acrylic paints and brushes (optional)

The brass plaque shown in Figure 6.45 was one of many that decorated the walls of the palace of the Oba, the divine ruler of the Benin kingdom (now the capital of Nigeria's Bendel state). *Warrior Chief, Warriors, and Attendants* depicts ceremonies and rituals that were carried out in the court. In fact, because the plaques so accurately documented the costumes, ornaments, hairstyles, weapons, and musical instruments employed in these ceremonies, they were often used in later centuries to answer questions about court procedures.

The technique of high and low relief, shown here, indicates a person's rank. Notice how the most important figure, located in the center of the plaque, is larger and in higher relief than the others. People of less importance are placed to the side and are shown smaller and in low relief. Many detailed objects are added to the surfaces and are used to fill the spaces in between.

Create a clay plaque depicting an event from current events or history that you find interesting. Using high and low relief, include

---

MORE ABOUT . . . THE BENIN KINGDOM

The Benin kingdom exists today as a part of modern Nigeria's Bendel State, with Benin City serving as the capital of the state. It is located in the tropical rain forest of southern Nigeria, on a sandy coastal plain west of the Niger River. The people are known as Edo, which is the name also given to their language. Outside of the city, people live as they have always lived in small villages with an average population of four to five hundred people. The villagers are farmers who grow yams, timber, and rubber trees.

three or more people and the necessary objects to illustrate the scene. In the style of the Benin plaque, the most important person should be the largest and in the highest relief.

FOCUSING

Study the Benin plaque. What can you learn about the people by observing their relative sizes and the degrees of relief? Brainstorm ideas for your plaque with your classmates. Once you have selected a topic, do some visual research.

CREATING

Do research sketching. Draw examples in your sketchbook of clothing, the setting, and the objects related to the event. Make detail sketches of the most important items. These do not have to be complete drawings. Think of them as visual note taking.

If you have not worked with clay, take time to become familiar with clay and the proper clay-joining techniques. (See Technique Tips on page 354 in the Handbook.)

Make a complete plan for your plaque in your sketchbook. First, sketch the figures using the Benin style of making the most important figure the largest. Then add objects and a natural setting, if necessary. Finally, plan the shape of the plaque.

Draw a pattern for the shape of the plaque on a sheet of newspaper and cut it out. Roll out a slab of clay approximately ½ inch (1.3 cm) thick. Trace the shape of the plaque pattern onto the slab and cut the slab into the shape of the pattern.

Model the figures and objects you have designed for the plaque. Add the figures and the objects to the plaque using scoring and slip. Notice how the Benin plaque has details added to the main figures as well as details that are carved and stippled into the work. Use clay tools to add details to your plaque.

Punch holes into the slab for hanging the plaque. Make sure they are more than ½ inch (1.3 cm) from every edge of the slab.

FIGURE 6.45A Student work.

When the clay is bone dry, fire it in the kiln following your teacher's instructions.

CRITIQUING

Describe What is the subject matter of your plaque? Describe the event and identify the people you have included. Did you use proper clay-modeling procedures? Did the clay stay joined, and did it come through the firing process successfully? Which option did you choose to finish the work?

Analyze Did you follow the style of the Benin relief by making the most important figure larger and in higher relief than the others? What kind of a shape did you make the background slab? Did you fill the negative space with patterns?

Interpret Can the viewer recognize the event by just looking at your work? What is the mood you were trying to convey? Have you caught the mood of the occasion?

Judge Were the viewers able to understand the event you were illustrating? Which aesthetic theory would you use to judge this work?

147

Understanding Art History

The plaque shown in Figure 6.45 had decorated the walls of the palace of the Oba, the divine ruler of the Benin Kingdom. It is one of many rectangular plaques that depict the ceremonies and rituals that were carried out in the daily life of the court. The plaques were used as references when questions about court procedures came up. They were like an etiquette book for the rulers to consult.

INDEPENDENT PRACTICE

Keeping a Portfolio

Remind students that the preliminary sketches and the final artwork for this Studio Lesson are likely considerations for their portfolios.

Extension

Ask students to research the culture and government of the Benin Kingdom. Have them compare and contrast the Benin Kingdom with another African kingdom that flourished at the same time. Students might also be interested in learning more about Oba Eweka II who was crowned king after his father's death in 1914.

ASSESS

CRITIQUING

Have students apply the steps of art criticism to their own artwork using the "Critiquing" questions on this page. In addition, ask the following: How did you choose the subject matter for your plaque? Did you choose a theme close to your personal beliefs or something that you feel strongly about?

MORE ABOUT . . . LOST WAX METHOD

In the lost wax process, an exact model of the object to be produced is made in wax. Skillful modeling and scratching enable the artist to make works with fine surface details. After modeling, wax extensions called sprues are added to provide space for the metal to flow into the mold and the gases to escape. The entire wax model is covered with a layer of fine clay, then further layers of increasingly coarse clay are added. The mold is heated. This fires the outer clay and melts the inner wax. When the wax is poured out it leaves an empty space which is filled by pouring in molten brass. After the metal hardens, the clay mold is broken, revealing a brass object identical to the original wax model.

Landscape Using
Surreal Space

FOCUS

OBJECTIVE

Create a surreal still life, landscape, or cityscape using positive and negative spaces.

MOTIVATOR

Ask students to suggest phrases that represent contraries, such as "expect the unexpected," or "achieve the impossible." Likewise, discuss how Magritte could claim to make invisible things visible. Because this activity is challenging as a concept, you might try to push the initial discussions as far as your students' imaginations will go.

TEACH

GUIDED PRACTICE

Interdisciplinary: Language Arts

Some of Magritte's paintings could be referred to as a visual paradox. Instruct the students to research the meaning of *paradox* as it relates to literature. Ask them to bring examples of literary paradox to class. Also instruct them to make up examples of their own visual paradox. Examples could include a light bulb bearing the weight of a human being or a fish swimming in the desert sand.

STUDIO LESSON: LANDSCAPE USING SURREAL SPACE

FIGURE 6.46 René Magritte. *The Blank Signature.* 1965. Oil on canvas. 81 × 65 cm (32 × 25½"). National Gallery of Art, Washington, D.C. Collection of Mr. and Mrs. Paul Mellon, 1985.

Supplies
- Sketchbook and pencil
- Sheet of tracing paper
- Two large sheets of white paper
- Yellow chalk and soap eraser
- Oil pastels

René Magritte was a Belgian Surrealist who loved to create visual puzzles. He began his career as a graphic artist, and by the time he was forty, he was able to give up commercial art and work full time as a painter.

While French Surrealists were exploring fantasy, psychology, and the subconscious mind to find subjects for their art, Magritte worked with ordinary images from the real world. His painting style was very realistic, and his ideas were powerful because the images he used were familiar and lifelike.

In the painting *The Blank Signature* (Figure 6.46), Magritte was trying to find a way to express the visible and the invisible. He said, "Visible things can be invisible. When someone rides a horse in the forest, first you see her, then you don't, but you know that she is there . . . the rider hides the trees and the trees hide her."

Look at Magritte's painting to see how he created his surreal landscape. See if you can turn your painting into a visual puzzle.

148

MORE ABOUT . . . RENÉ MAGRITTE

Magritte did not like to talk about his work. Finding subjects to paint, and then titles for the finished pieces, was a game that was played by Magritte and the Brussels Surrealists. His paintings can be interpreted differently by each person who sees them. Magritte felt that the image should speak for itself and the titles "protect" the paintings. The titles never explained the images. He said that the titles were an extra protection to discourage any attempt to reduce pure poetry to a trivial game. When he was asked what he painted and why, he would answer, "Life obliges me to do something, so I paint."

Using oil pastels on white paper, create a surreal seascape, landscape, or cityscape in which the positive shapes and negative spaces are interwoven into a reversal of the visible and invisible, as in Magritte's painting *The Blank Signature* (Figure 6.46).

FOCUSING

Brainstorm with your classmates about ways that you can create Magritte's visible/invisible effect. Trees, a network of branches, or haystacks might divide the positive and negative in a landscape. Signposts, lampposts, or buildings with big windows can divide the space in a cityscape.

Design the realistic scene as a whole first. What makes Magritte's work so successful is that every object looks realistic. To make your scene work, choose a subject with which you are familiar. First, make rough sketches in your sketchbook and then organize them into a good composition on a sheet of white paper. Plan to use colors in the realistic scene that are different from and contrast with the color of the dividing scene, as Magritte used greens and blues for his scenery and purple and brown for the woman and her horse.

Place a sheet of tracing paper over the realistic composition. On the tracing paper, sketch the second drawing into which you will weave your first scene.

Using yellow chalk, lightly copy your realistic scene onto the other large sheet of white paper. Then sketch the dividing drawing over the first using another light chalk color. Now decide which scene will be visible in each area. Use the soap eraser to remove the chalk lines that will be invisible.

Apply color lightly until you have all the positive and negative areas worked out. Then apply the oil pastel color heavily, blending colors when necessary to build up layers of color.

Give your work a title that helps viewers to understand your work. Mount or mat your work for display.

FIGURE 6.46A Student work.

CRITIQUING

Describe Explain how you have created a surreal scene by telling what realistic scene you chose for the subject matter. Then, explain what device you have used to divide the scene so that the visible and invisible are reversed.

Analyze Explain how you managed to create a reversal of visible and invisible through your arrangement of positive and negative space. Describe how you used contrasting colors to help the viewer see the two different scenes.

Interpret Describe the emotional effect you have achieved in your work. Does the title you gave your piece help the viewer understand your work?

Judge Was your attempt to create a surreal space successful? Which aesthetic theory would you use to evaluate this work?

149

149

INTRODUCTION

Since *Spirits Soaring* is a three-dimensional work of art, we have shown three different views of the sculpture so that students can understand that a sculpture looks different from different points of view. For comparison, *Nike of Samothrace* has been presented as a contrast, to show how the philosophies of different cultures can be expressed in their art.

CRITIQUING THE WORK

1. Describe *Spirits Soaring* is done in bronze. It is 20 inches (51 cm) tall. A male figure wears a leather skirt and leather moccasins. His body is bent into a zigzag direction. The man's face is hidden by a headdress that looks like the feathers and beak of an eagle's head. Notice that the headdress has no eyes. Wings made of eagle feathers are attached to his arms, which seem to blend softly into the wings. From the back, the sweep of the wings make a sweeping "S" curve. His feet barely touch the ground. Only his toes make contact. The skirt flares out to indicate his movement.

2. Analyze This is a three-dimensional form. It is free-form. The body looks dense but the feathers soften the look of the work. Because the feet barely touch the ground, the sculpture seems to be floating. This is in real space. The form looks open, and it is active because of the zigzag movement of the feet, legs, torso, head, and arms.

ART CRITICISM IN ACTION

FIGURE 6.47 Michael Naranjo. *Spirits Soaring.* 1985. Bronze. Height 51 cm (20″). Private collection.

150

RESOURCES BEYOND THE CLASSROOM

Other Works By . . . Michael Naranjo

Spirit Mother
Devil Dancer
The Eagle's Song
Grasshopper
Room for One More

Good Medicine
Grey Fox
Spirit Maiden
Little Cloud
Woman with Towel
Joy

CRITIQUING THE WORK

1. **Describe** Notice the photographs of *Spirits Soaring* in Figure 6.47. Each is a different view of the same work. If you were looking at the real sculpture, you would be able to walk around it and look at it from every point of view. Since it is in a book, we have given you more than one point of view to study. Read the credit information. What material did the sculptor use to create this work? How tall is it? Study the three views of the work. Describe what you see.

2. **Analyze** Is *Spirits Soaring* a shape or a form? Is it geometric or free-form? Does it look dense or soft? Does it look heavy or light? How has the artist used space? Is it real or an illusion? As you look at the three views, do they look open or closed? Does the work seem to be active or static? Explain by describing the parts that make it look active or static. Do you see many intricate details, or are the details simplified? What color is the work?

3. **Interpret** What kind of mood is the artist creating with this sculpture? Review the clues you have collected during the Analysis step. Now let your own feelings combine with the facts. Write a paragraph explaining your personal interpretation of the work. Then write a new title for the work that sums up your interpretation.

4. **Judge** Do you think this is a successful work? Use one or more of the aesthetic theories of art to defend your judgment.

COMPARING THE WORKS

Look at *Spirits Soaring* (Figure 6.47) and *Nike of Samothrace* (Figure 6.48). In what way are the two works similar? In what ways are they different? Notice the amount of detail, the posture of each figure, the costumes, and the interaction between positive and negative space. What is the difference in the relationship between wing and body in each work? Nike is the

FIGURE 6.48 *Nike of Samothrace.* c. 190 B.C. Marble. Approx. 2.4 m (8′). The Louvre, Paris, France.

Greek goddess of victory. The nickname for this work is "Winged Victory." Based on the rest of the work, what do you think her head and arms would look like? Would they be similar to or different from those in *Spirits Soaring?* What would she be doing with her arms and hands? What position would her head hold? In what way does each work accentuate the difference between the philosophies of the cultures from which they come?

151

3. **Interpret** Answers will vary. They may think of the relationship of people to other inhabitants of the earth.

4. **Judge** Answers will vary. All three aesthetic theories can be applied to this work.

COMPARING THE WORKS

Similarities: Both are sculpture, and both depict people with wings. Nike's wings seem to grow out of her body. Her arms that are missing would be separate from the wings. Naranjo's figure is wearing his wings on his arms. Even though they seem to blend together, the wings do not grow on his body. In Naranjo's work the details are blurred. The details of Nike's feather and the folds of her flowing dress are clearly defined. Nike's dress is elaborate; it covers the entire body. Naranjo's figure wears only a skirt and moccasins.

Differences: The posture of *Nike* is proud. She stands tall, feet planted firmly on the prow of a ship, leaning against the winds, and she seems to conquer all before her. This reflects the Greek philosophy of man conquering the world. In Naranjo's sculpture, the figure dances lightly on the earth, barely touching the ground with his toes. His knees are bent and his torso leans toward the ground. Even though the dancer represents the proud eagle, he seems to be one with the earth, reflecting the philosophy of the Native Americans.

EXTENSION

- Have students read more about Michael Naranjo in the "Meet the Artist" feature on the following page.
- Assign *Artist's Profile 6* in the TCR.

MORE ABOUT . . . NIKE OF SAMOTHRACE

Perhaps next to *Venus of Melos*, this sculpture is the most famous incomplete statue in all of Western art. It was found in 1875 on a hillside near the town of Samothrace in Greece, headless, armless, and in 118 pieces. The sculptor is unknown, but art historians have determined that the statue once stood on a pedestal made to look like the bow of a war ship, where it celebrated a naval victory. Today, the statue holds a place of honor at the grand staircase in the Louvre, Paris, where it welcomes visitors to the museum.

ASSESS

CHECKING COMPREHENSION

- On a separate sheet of paper have students complete "Building Vocabulary" and "Reviewing Art Facts" on page 153.
- Assign *Application 11* and *12* in the TCR to evaluate students' comprehension.

ANSWERS TO BUILDING VOCABULARY

1. shape
2. geometric shapes
3. free-form shapes
4. forms
5. space
6. holograms
7. chiaroscuro
8. highlights
9. perspective

ANSWERS TO REVIEWING ART FACTS

1. Geometric and free-form; geometric.
2. Forms have depth; shapes do not.
3. By the space around them.
4. Positive and negative space.
5. Positive space.
6. The eyes see an object at slightly different angles. The brain causes these two separate and slightly different views to merge into one.
7. By using shading to show a change in value.
8. Overlapping, size, placement, detail, color, converging lines.
9. Atmospheric and linear.
10. Active shape would be one that had diagonal lines. It looks as if it is falling or rising.
11. A rectangle resting on a horizontal surface. Horizontal lines look stable and static.

MICHAEL NARANJO
Native American, b. 1944

Just like every other sculptor, Michael Naranjo feels the need to study the works of other artists. When he looks, however, he sees with his hands. In 1968, while serving in the army, he was blinded by a grenade in Vietnam.

Naranjo has always been interested in art. He was born near Santa Fe, New Mexico, a Tewa Indian of the Santa Clara Pueblo. His mother was a potter, and he has pleasant memories of helping her mix the white clay with the brown by stepping on it. Mixing clay was like a dance, a rhythmic stepping.

Michael was drafted in 1967 and was sent to Vietnam for active duty. While there, he was caught on his hands and knees in an ambush. A grenade exploded, lifting him up in the air. When he awoke in a hospital, he found his right arm damaged and his sight gone. In a hospital bed in Japan he began modeling a piece of clay. In a hospital in Denver he made an Indian whipping a horse across the plain.

He gets ideas from the things he saw in the past. He has to visualize the image in his mind. That takes a long time. Then he models his idea in wax or carves it from stone. Wax carving is easier, because he can correct mistakes. He has to keep the whole of the image in his mind so he knows how much he has taken away. Because Naranjo works in a three-dimensional art form with challenging media, he only produces a few sculptures a year.

MORE PORTFOLIO IDEAS

Tape a piece of white paper to the table. Put on a blindfold. Think about an object you know very well—something you use every day. Visualize it in your mind. Using a pencil, make a contour drawing of the object with the blindfold in place. Remove the blindfold. Can you see what your mind was telling your eyes to draw?

Using the blindfold again, visualize your own face and head in your mind. Think about what you have seen in the mirror. Model your face and head in clay using only your fingers and nails as tools. You may touch your own face and head as you work to check proportions and details. Keep a damp sponge nearby to clean your fingers before you touch your face.

DEVELOPING A PORTFOLIO

Self-Evaluation Peer review helps students establish priorities for revision of their work through feedback from other students. When expected to articulate responses to the work of others, basic concepts are reinforced, and a student learns to trust his or her artistic insights. Often a cooperative environment encourages a mutual exchange of ideas that help students progress at an accelerated rate. Peer review is also a source of ongoing reflection that refines judgment. Students often see the relationship between ideas and design in another's work more easily than in their own; likewise, suggestions from peers are sometimes less intimidating.

CHAPTER 6 REVIEW

Building Vocabulary

On a separate sheet of paper, write the term that best matches each definition given below.

1. A two-dimensional area that is defined in some way.
2. Precise shapes that can be described using mathematical formulas.
3. Irregular and uneven shapes.
4. Objects having three dimensions.
5. The element of art that refers to the area between, around, above, below, or within objects.
6. Images in three dimensions created with a laser beam.
7. The arrangement of light and shadow.
8. Small areas of white used to show the very brightest spots.
9. A graphic system that creates the illusion of depth and volume on a two-dimensional surface.

Reviewing Art Facts

Answer the following questions using complete sentences.

1. Name the two basic types of shapes and tell which is more often used for decorative purposes.
2. What is the difference between shapes and forms?
3. By what are shapes and forms defined?
4. Name the two kinds of space found in art.
5. Using a portrait as an example, name the kind of space the subject occupies.
6. Explain how the eyes and brain enable us to see in three dimensions.
7. Explain how an artist is able to create the illusion of three-dimensional form on a two-dimensional surface.
8. Name the six devices for creating perspective in drawing.
9. Name two kinds of perspective.
10. Give an example of an active shape and tell what makes it look active.
11. Give an example of a static shape and tell what makes it look motionless, or stable.

Thinking Critically About Art

1. **Explain.** Matisse started his artistic career as a painter. He made important contributions to the field of painting. Do some research on Matisse at the library. Find out what his contributions were. Then find out why he created *Beasts of the Sea* (Figure 6.21, page 132) by cutting shapes with scissors. Write a brief paper explaining your findings.
2. **Compare and contrast.** Look at *Johnson House* by Philip Johnson (Figure 6.37, page 141) and *Falling Water* by Frank Lloyd Wright (Figure 12.21, page 330). Evaluate the architects' use of forms and space. In what ways are these two houses similar? In what ways are they different? Explain.
3. **Analyze.** Look at *Other World* by M.C. Escher (Figure 6.13, page 127) and *The Blank Signature* by René Magritte (Figure 6.46, page 148). Both artists used optical illusions. Look for information about each artist in the library. Are they both from the same art movement? Do they have the same philosophy? Explain your findings in a brief paragraph.

Making Art Connections

1. **Science.** Research the theory of Gestalt psychology. Explain the Figure/Ground theory in gestalt psychology to your classmates. Make a poster or chart to help explain your findings.
2. **Social Studies.** Choose a manufactured object such as a telephone, coffee pot, ship, airplane, TV set, sewing machine, shoe, radio, or something else that interests you personally. Research the history of its form and function. Use the library, an encyclopedia, or interview a grandparent. Make a chart showing how, when, and why the form changed. Was it changed because of improved technology, for the convenience of the user, or for some other reason? Explain your findings to your class.

153

ALTERNATIVE ASSESSMENT

Have students draw an imaginary scene, either of an interior or exterior location, that uses as many of the six techniques for creating the illusion of depth discussed in this chapter as possible. Students should make several preliminary sketches to help them place the images they create. They may use any of the various media studied in this textbook. Have them give their works titles that express the mood or convey the meaning of the works. Next, students should critique the finished drawing or painting, using the four-step process.

Color

CHAPTER OVERVIEW

Chapter 7 focuses on the element of color. Students learn about the importance of color in art and its complexity.

CHAPTER SUPPLIES

For a list of the materials you will need for the Activities in this chapter, refer to the "Art Supplies Grid" in the Teacher's Manual. In addition, have on hand the following special items: fabric scraps and earth pigments.

FINE ART RESOURCES
Transparencies
- Tommye Scanlin. *Carolina Lily*
- Henri de Toulouse-Lautrec. *At the Moulin Rouge*
- Lucas Samaras. *Mosaic Painting #6*
- Elizabeth Murray. *Web*

Fine Art Prints
- Georges Seurat. *Sunday Afternoon on the Island of La Grande Jatte*
- Henri Matisse. *Pianist and Checker Players*

FIGURE 7.1 Gauguin gave up a successful career as a stockbroker to devote his time to art. He traveled around the world to find freedom from traditions. In Tahiti he produced art that was simplified and full of brilliant colors.

Paul Gauguin. *Faaturuma (The Dreamer)*. c. 1891. Oil on canvas. 95 × 68.6 cm (37½ × 27"). Nelson-Atkins Museum of Art, Kansas City, Missouri. Museum purchase, 1938.

154

RESOURCES FOR CHAPTER 7
Application Activities 13, 14
Artist's Profiles 7, 23, 27
Cooperative Learning Activities 13, 14
Cultural Diversity in Art
Enrichment Activities 13, 14

Reteaching Activities
  Study Guide 7
  Concept Map 7
Studio Lessons 6, 7, 8, 9
Chapter 7 Test

Color

Color is exciting! We are so sensitive to color that it appeals directly to our emotions. Color is the most expressive element of art and most of us have a favorite color, but it is also the most difficult element to talk about. Try to imagine how to describe the difference between red and orange to a blind person. It is almost impossible to describe color without also talking about other colors.

Colors stand for ideas and feelings. You use color symbolically when you say, "I feel blue," "She's green with envy," or "He's a yellow coward."

You may remember a time when you mixed some beautiful, bright colors into a muddy, dull gray mess. Color can be very frustrating. Sometimes it acts like a wild thing, but it *can* be tamed. In this chapter you will learn how to speak with color in the language of art.

FIRST IMPRESSIONS

Look at the bright colors in this painting (Figure 7.1). This Tahitian woman has golden skin but in the four areas where you can see her skin you see four different colors. What is the difference between the colors used for her face, her right hand, her left hand, and the exposed foot? She is wearing a red robe, yet look at the varieties of red with which Gauguin has painted that robe. What color did he use in the shadows? How many different blues can you find in the wall? What colors has he used on the foot? How many greens are there inside the picture frame? How many colors can you find on the wooden rocking chair? Notice how he has even used color to enhance the white handkerchief.

Objectives

After completing this chapter, you will be able to:

- Understand how your eyes see color.
- Name the properties of color and the colors of the spectrum.
- Identify different color schemes.
- Mix your own paints using different pigments and vehicles.
- Use color as the expressive element in creating two- and three-dimensional artworks.
- Recognize the expressive qualities of color that artists use to create meaning.

Words to Know

analogous colors
binder
color
color spectrum
color wheel
complementary colors
dyes
hue
intensity
monochromatic
pigments
shade
solvent
tint

155

TEACH

(pages 156–170)
• How We See Color
• Color Schemes

GUIDED PRACTICE

Interdisciplinary: Language Arts

Have students research the symbolic meanings people have given to various colors. What cultural factors, if any, influence these different meanings? Have them ask their English teacher how poets and writers use color in different ways.

Understanding Art History

To help students further appreciate the life and times of Paul Gauguin, whose work is shown in Figure 7.1 on page 154, assign *Artist's Profile 27* in the TCR.

Interdisciplinary: Physical Science

Tell students that in 1665, Isaac Newton was grinding lenses for a telescope when he found that one of his lenses made blurred rims of color around the edge. He stopped working on lenses and began his study of color.

Developing Perceptual Skills

The most effective way to illustrate the relationship between light and color and to explain the spectrum is to use a prism. Science labs will have one if you do not. If you cannot take the students outside, you can use the strong light from a slide projector to demonstrate the spectral colors. You will not always get all six colors evenly spaced as they are shown on charts. If you play with the prism and turn it slowly you can demonstrate how the color spread occurs.

How we see color

Color is *an element of art that is derived from reflected light* (Figure 7.2). You see color because light waves are reflected from objects to your eyes (Figure 7.3). White light from the sun is actually a combination of all colors.

When light passes through a wedge-shaped glass, called a prism, the beam of white light is bent and separated into bands of color, called the **color spectrum**. The colors of the spectrum always appear in the same order: red, orange, yellow, green, blue, and violet.

A rainbow is a natural example of a spectrum. Rainbows occur when sunlight is bent by water, oil, or a glass prism. You can find rainbows in the sky, in the spray from a garden hose, or in a puddle of oil in a parking lot.

Objects absorb some waves of light and reflect others. A red apple looks red because it reflects red waves and absorbs the rest of the colors (Figure 7.4). Special color receptors in your eyes detect these red light waves, and your mind then reads the light as being a certain color. The light enters your eye and travels to a membrane of nerve tissue, called the retina, at the back of your eyeball. There, two types of cells react to the light. One type receives impressions of lightness and darkness. The other type receives color.

FIGURE 7.2 Can you imagine how dull and drab our world would be without color?

FIGURE 7.3 These colors glow as daylight shines through the stained-glass window.

Bronislaw M. Bak. *Holocaust.* 1969. Stained-glass windows (detail). Whole window: 3 × 9.1 m (10 × 30'). Temple Emanu-El, Chicago, Illinois.

MORE ABOUT . . . COLOR

For many artists, color has been essential both to the experience of life and to the creation of art. This importance of color has led painters to discuss and write about the subject. During a trip to Tunisia, Paul Klee felt nearly overwhelmed by the intense light. He wrote, "Color has taken possession of me. No longer do I have to chase after it; I know that it has hold of me forever. That is the significance of this blessed moment. Color and I are one. I am a painter."

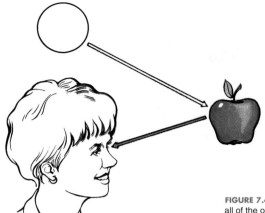

FIGURE 7.4   The red apple reflects the red light waves and absorbs all of the other colors. This is why we see the apple as red.

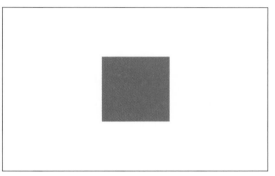 

FIGURE 7.5   What color do you see when you shift your gaze from the red to the white area? Your eyes can fool you about color.

Colors really don't change, but your ability to distinguish between them does. That is why your eyes have trouble seeing colors in dim light, whether the light is from the sun or a lamp.

Some people are color-blind. There are many different types of color blindness. Some people cannot tell the difference between red and green, and others see only black, white, and gray. Many animals have limited color vision. Others—birds and bees, for example—see light waves that are invisible to humans.

When you are looking at colors, your eyes can sometimes fool you. For instance, stare at the bright red shape in Figure 7.5 for thirty seconds; then quickly shift your gaze to the white area next to it. Did you see a green shape on the white surface? This is called an *afterimage*. It occurs because the receptors in your eyes retain the visual stimulation even after it has ceased.

The afterimage of a color is the opposite of that color. Green is the opposite of red. The afterimage of black is white, and the afterimage of blue is orange. Don't expect an afterimage to be a strong color—it is only the ghost of a color. Your brain creates the afterimage as a reaction to the color you stared at originally. Some artists make use of the

AT THE MUSEUM

The Philadelphia Museum of Art (Philadelphia, Pennsylvania)   Go back to the time of knights and shiny armor at The Philadelphia Museum of Art's Medieval Gallery. Feel like a medieval craftsman with the museum's five hands-on kits used to demonstrate medieval and Renaissance craft techniques to school children and family groups. Groups are introduced to one of the following crafts: the methods and materials of stone-masonry and sculpture, stained glass, manuscript illumination, egg tempera painting, and carpet knotting. The hands-on kits are also part of an outreach program to people in residential facilities, hospitals, and community centers.

Exploring Aesthetics

Have students choose one hue, then look through magazines and cut out examples of all the variations of that hue they can find. Classify the colors into five groups: (1) pure hue, (2) dull tint, (3) dull shade, (4) bright tint, and (5) bright shade. Glue them to a small sheet of white paper and label each group.

Developing Perceptual Skills

Impress upon students that the facts about hue are extremely important. Students must know the primary hues and the order of the spectrum before they can control color. This information is as basic to working with color as simple addition is to mathematics.

Critical Thinking

While discussing *Orange Crush* (Figure 7.6), ask students to stare at one dot. After a few seconds the dot will appear to begin moving no matter how they try to stop it. That will explain the relationship between the work and the image of musical notes that Larry Poons was trying to create. Of course no afterimage exercise will work unless the students make the effort to concentrate.

Building Vocabulary

To strengthen students' familiarity and their usage of the terms associated with hue, have them work in pairs and prepare five flash cards on which they write one of the following terms: *hue, primary, secondary, intermediate,* and *color wheel.* On each of five other cards they should write the definition for each of the terms. Then let the partners use their cards to quiz each other on the definitions.

FIGURE 7.6 This painting is named for the soft drink that has an unnatural, man-made color similar to the orange of this painting. The blue-green dots seem to have no order, but they were carefully planned. The dots are meant to suggest musical notes. As you stare at this work, the afterimage of the dots creates the feeling of dancelike movements. Try to make the dots remain still!

Larry Poons. *Orange Crush.* 1963. Acrylic on canvas. 203.2 × 203.2 cm (80 × 80″). Albright-Knox Art Gallery, Buffalo, New York. Gift of Seymour H. Knox, 1964. © Larry Poons/VAGA, New York 1994.

way your eyes work when they create optical illusions of color and movement (Figure 7.6).

Understanding the three properties of color will help you work with color. The properties are *hue, value,* and *intensity.*

Hue

Hue is *the name of a spectral color*, such as red, blue, or yellow. Red, yellow, and blue are the *primary* hues. You cannot make primary hues by mixing other hues together. By combining only the three primary colors and black and white, however, you can produce almost every other color.

The *secondary* hues are made by mixing two primary colors (Figure 7.7). Red and yellow make orange; red and blue make violet; and blue and yellow make green. Orange, violet, and green are the secondary hues.

The six *intermediate* colors are made by mixing a primary color with its secondary color. For example, red and orange make red-orange, red and violet make red-violet, blue and violet make

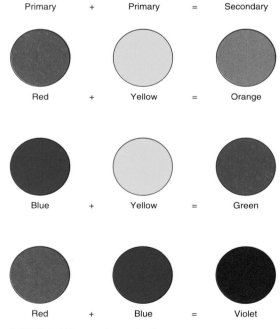

Primary	+	Primary	=	Secondary
Red	+	Yellow	=	Orange
Blue	+	Yellow	=	Green
Red	+	Blue	=	Violet

FIGURE 7.7 Primary and secondary hues.

Learning Disabled Working with color intensities demands that students remember the order of the color wheel. They cannot remember opposites unless they remember what goes where. The colors of the spectrum are pure hues. Explaining the relationships of the complements to the three primaries clarifies the concept for students who have difficulty understanding these concepts. If you start with red, you have blue and yellow left. They combine to make green, and green is the opposite, or complement, of red. This works even with intermediate colors. The opposite of blue-green is the opposite of blue (orange), plus the opposite of green (red) or red-orange.

blue-violet, and so on. You can, of course, make many additional variations by combining the newly created intermediate colors.

A **color wheel** is *the spectrum bent into a circle.* It is a useful tool for organizing colors. The color wheel in Figure 7.8 is a twelve-color wheel showing the three primary, three secondary, and six intermediate hues.

ACTIVITY Making a Color Wheel

1. Applying Your Skills. Make a color-wheel collage. Draw a circle and divide it into twelve equal parts. Collect colors from construction paper, magazine photographs, and fabric scraps and fill each section with a combination of the proper colors. Cover the entire area. Do not let the background show through.

2. Further Challenge. Design your own unique color wheel (Figure 7.9). Show the correct color relationships. Use only primary paint colors to mix the secondary and intermediate colors. The wheel does not have to be perfectly round, nor does it even have to be a circle. Be creative. Plan some way to indicate the differences among primary, secondary, and intermediate colors.

3. Computer Option. Use the tools of your choice to design your own unique color wheel. Show the correct color relationships. The color wheel does not have to be round, nor does it have to be a circle. Be creative. Plan some way to indicate the differences among primary, secondary, and intermediate colors. Choose and mix your colors carefully.

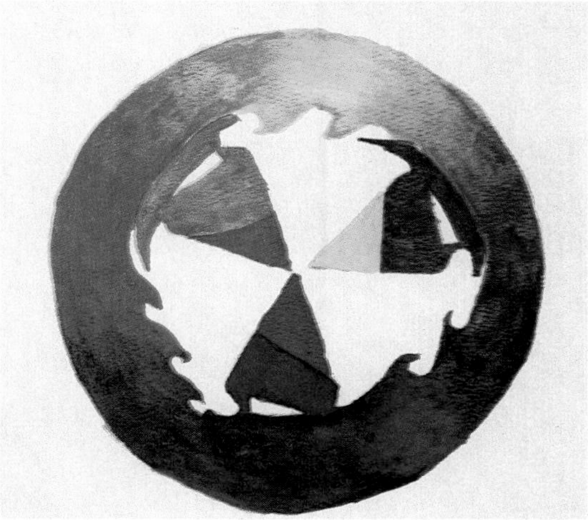

FIGURE 7.9 Student work. Creative color wheel. Sailboats.

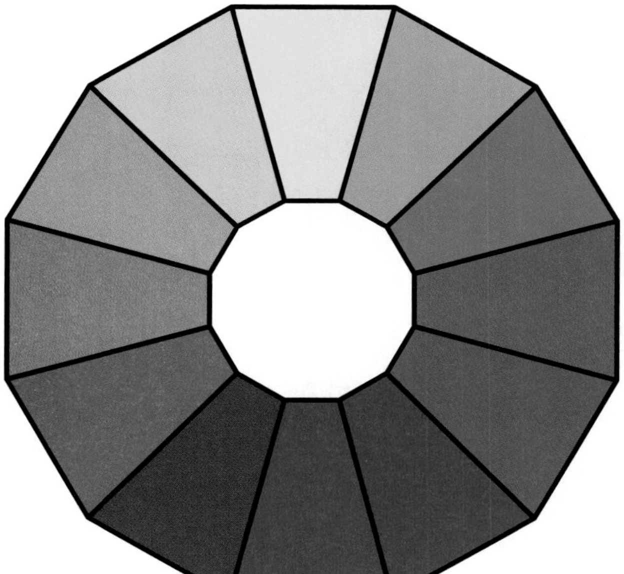

FIGURE 7.8 The color wheel.

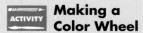

ACTIVITY Making a Color Wheel

1. Applying Your Skills. This activity encourages perceptive rather than creative skills.

2. Further Challenge. This activity is a creative solution to a rather dull color-wheel exercise. The two student examples are evidence that this activity can be exciting. There is no limit to the kinds of objects that the students can use for their wheels.

An alternate activity for less creative students, which will help them memorize the order of the spectrum, is to make a picture of whatever they like using the colors of the spectrum in the correct order. The results can be anything from a scene with a rainbow in the sky to an eighteen-wheeler truck decorated with color stripes.

3. Computer Option. Use the Brush, Pencil and/or Shape tools to design a manufactured, imaginary, or natural shape. This shape will be used to create a unique color wheel; therefore, the size should be somewhat small so that twelve copies of this shape can be used on a full page. When a satisfactory shape has been made, use the Lasso Selection tool to tightly select the object. Then choose the Copy command from the Edit menu to make a duplicate on the Clipboard. Use the Paste command to successively copy twelve editions of the shape. These shapes should be arranged without overlapping to form a continuous, but not necessarily a circular, design. Experiment with flipping and reversing some of the shapes. After achieving an interesting arrangement of space with the shapes, assign each shape the appropriate primary, secondary, and intermediate colors using the Bucket Flood-fill tool.

CURRICULUM CONNECTION

Journalism Show examples of both color and black-and-white photographs from newspapers and magazines. Also, have students study Figure 1.11 on page 15, and any of the photographs that accompany the Meet the Artist feature in each chapter. Ask these questions: How is any one photograph different from the others? Is there more or less emotional content? Why or why not? What considerations must a photographer make regarding the color, or the absence of it, in the final product? How does the photographer's angle, type of film, and viewpoint affect the story being told with the photograph?

Value

As you have already learned, value is the art element that refers to darkness or lightness. Color value is related to the amount of light a color reflects. Not all hues of the spectrum have the same value. Yellow is the lightest hue, and violet is the darkest.

Black, white, and gray are neutral colors (Figure 7.10). When white light shines on a white object, the object reflects all of the color waves and does not absorb any. As a result, you see the color of all the light, which is white. A black object absorbs all of the color waves. Black reflects no light; black is the absence of light. Gray is impure white—it reflects an equal part of each color wave. The more light that gray reflects, the lighter it looks; the more it absorbs, the darker it looks.

You can change the value of any hue by adding black or white (Figure 7.11). *A light value of a hue* is called a **tint**, and *a dark value of a hue* is called a **shade**. The term *shade* is often used incorrectly to refer to both tints and shades.

FIGURE 7.10   Neutral colors: black, gray, and white.

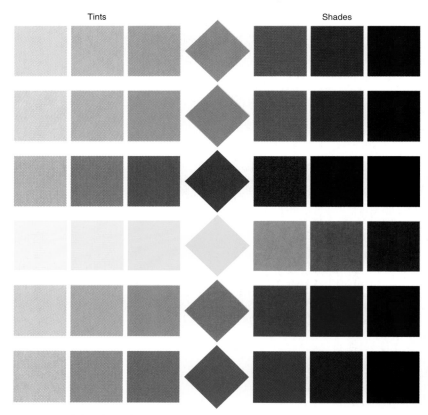

FIGURE 7.11   Color value scales.

When artists want to show a bright, sunny day, they use tints (Figure 7.12). Paintings having many tints are referred to as *high-key* paintings. Monet's *Ice Floes* is an example of a high-key painting. *Low-key* paintings have shades, or dark values, which are used when the artist wants to represent dark, gloomy days, nighttime, and dusk (Figure 7.13). Dark values can add a feeling of mystery to a work. They can also be used to create a sense of foreboding or danger.

If the change in value is gradual, the design produces a calm feeling. If the values take large leaps up and down the scale, from almost white to almost black, the artwork has an active, even nervous effect.

FIGURE 7.12   The tints of blue used in this painting gives the impression of a cold, icy day.

Claude Monet. *Ice Floes.* 1893. Oil on canvas. 66 × 100 cm (26 × 39½"). The Metropolitan Museum of Art, New York, New York. Bequest of Mrs. H. O. Havemeyer, 1929. The H. O. Havemeyer Collection.

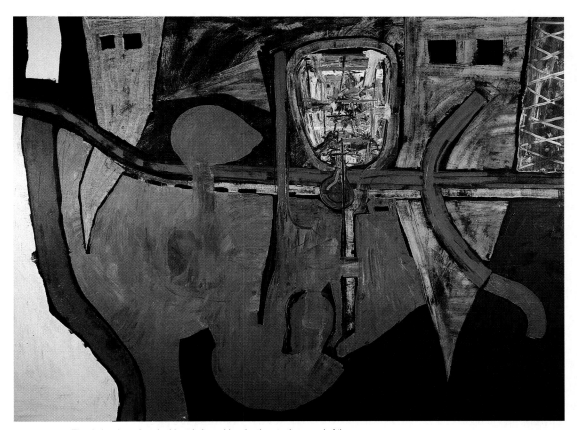

FIGURE 7.13   The dark color values in this painting add to the threatening mood of the work. Do you see any shapes that add to this mood?

Harold Town. *Night Riders.* 1960. Oil and lucite on canvas. 204 × 274.5 cm (80½ × 108"). Collection of the Art Gallery of Nova Scotia, Halifax, Nova Scotia, Canada. Gift of the Barling Company, Toronto, Ontario, Canada, 1987.

MEETING SPECIAL NEEDS

Emotional Disability   Students with emotional disturbance or who are experiencing unhappiness and suicidal thoughts might use dark colors. The art teacher may be among the first to notice such corroborating color cues shown by depressed students. Other visual art cues of depression might show in the themes portrayed, such as barren broken trees, hanging ropes, and lonely figures. The art teacher is neither trained to be nor expected to be an art therapist, but nevertheless can give emotional support to such students. Be a friend to them, someone they can talk to.

GUIDED PRACTICE
(continued)

 **Creating Values**

1. Applying Your Skills.
Remind students that it takes just a drop of hue to turn white to a light value of the hue.

2. Further Challenge.
The seven-step value scale in this activity is easier to make using opaque paints than with transparent watercolors. Some teachers prefer that students mix colors on the palette; others prefer that students mix paint on the paper until it looks just right.

3. Computer Option.
Use the full page of the computer program or draw a large rectangle, circle, or square frame that covers most of the page. Select the Brush tool to draw a curved line that connects one side of the paper or frame to the other. Choose the Line tool. Draw a straight line from the curved line to one side of the page or frame. Draw a zigzag line. Draw a wavy line. Add a thick line. Draw a dotted line. Repeat one of the previous lines two more times. Draw one circle, two squares, and three triangles. Thicken some of the lines for contrast. Add or repeat whatever is necessary to complete the composition. Now choose a monochromatic color scheme. Using the color palettes of the software program, choose the hue and at least one tint and one shade of the color. Flood-fill the individual spaces of the composition with alternating colors of the selected monochromatic color scheme. If the program allows mixing white or black to the hue, students will be able to make more variations. Continue to fill all the spaces with a hue and its tints and shades until no white remains. Print.

 Creating Values

1. Applying Your Skills.
Select a hue. Draw a row of three equal shapes. If you are using an opaque paint, such as tempera, add only a small amount of the hue to white. Fill the first shape with the light value. Paint the pure hue in the second shape. Add a small amount of black to the hue to create a dark value, and paint this in the third shape.

If you are using transparent watercolor paint, make a light value by thinning the paint with water to let more white paper show through. Make a hue darker by adding a small amount of black. Fill the three shapes as in the above directions.

2. Further Challenge.
Make a seven-step value scale for one hue (see Figure 7.11, page 160). Select a hue, then draw a row of seven equal shapes, one for each step. Make the first step almost white; make the fourth step the pure hue; and make the seventh step almost black. The second step should be a very light tint of the hue, and the third step should be a little darker. The fifth step needs a small amount of black; the sixth, a little more.

Safety Note. When paints are called for, use watercolors, liquid tempera, or acrylics if possible. If you must use powdered tempera, wear a dust mask and work away from other class members.

Remember to check the safety labels on your paints. All materials used in the classroom should be properly labeled. You should know the following safety codes:

AP—Approved Product
CP—Certified Product
HL—Health Label

AP and **CP** labels assure you that the product contains no materials in sufficient amounts to be dangerous or toxic. The **CP** label further assures you that the art materials meet certain quality standards. An **HL** label can indicate that the art materials contain toxic ingredients.

FIGURE 7.14 Intensity scale. This scale shows how the intensity of one hue changes as you add its complement to it. The first box is pure, high-intensity green. Each time you add more red, the green becomes duller. Eventually the even mix of green and red creates an interesting, low-intensity gray.

FIGURE 7.15 Sets of complements.

TEACHER TALK

Classroom Management Remind students that when mixing tempera colors and white to create a variety of tints, they can conserve paint by starting with several blobs of white. Clean the brush, wipe it on the edge of the water container, and blot it on a towel. Then take a brush dipped in the hue they have chosen and drop one dot of color on the first, two dots of color on the second, and three on the third. Wash, wipe, and blot the brush. Mix color in the first dot, move to the second and mix, then on to the third. The brush can be scraped against the edge of a pan to remove excess paint, but doesn't have to be cleaned.

Intensity

Intensity is *the brightness or dullness of a hue* (Figure 7.14). If a surface reflects only yellow light waves, for example, you see an intensely bright yellow. A pure hue is called a *high-intensity color*. Dull hues are called *low-intensity colors*.

Complementary colors are *the colors opposite each other on the color wheel*. The complement, or opposite, of a hue absorbs all of the light waves that the hue reflects (Figure 7.15). Red and green are complements. Red absorbs blue and yellow waves and reflects red waves. Green absorbs red waves and reflects blue and yellow waves.

Mixing a hue with its complement dulls the hue, or lowers its intensity. The more complement you add to a hue, the duller the hue looks. Eventually, the hue will lose its own color quality and appear a neutral gray.

The hue used in the greatest amount in a mixture becomes dominant. For this reason, a mixture might look dull orange or dull blue, depending on the amount of color used. Orange and blue mixtures usually yield brownish results.

Hue, value, and intensity do not operate independently. They rely on one another to create the variety of colors that you see around you. When you observe colors, you will see dull tints and bright tints, dull shades and bright shades. When you can classify types of colors, you will understand color.

 Working with Intensity

1. Applying Your Skills.   Create a seven-step intensity scale for a primary color. Paint the first step with the pure primary color. Dull the paint for the second step with a small amount of that color's complement. Add more of the complement to the paint for the third step and continue to the seventh step, which should be a neutral, grayish color.

2. Further Challenge.   Contrary to what you may have thought, tree trunks are not really brown. They reflect a variety of light and dark low-intensity grays. Draw seven or more bare trees on a large sheet of white paper (Figure 7.16). Use real trees as models, if possible; if not, find photographs. Combine varying amounts of one primary color and its complement as well as white and black to create a number of different, low-intensity light- and dark-valued colors. Then use these colors to paint each tree a different color from the others.

3. Computer Option.   Design a simple motif using only two solid colors. Use the Select tool and the Copy and Paste options to make five copies of the motif. Use the Fill Bucket tool to fill each motif with one primary color or intermediate color and its complement. If your software has the capabilities, mix the two complements together to get a dull intensity of each. Label each set of complements and mixture sets.

FIGURE 7.16   Student work. Notice the range of intensity.

GUIDED PRACTICE
(continued)

**Developing
Perceptual Skills**

Have students collect color-sample charts from local paint stores and art supply stores. Have them work in groups to classify the commercial colors and the artists' paints according to hue, value, and intensity. For example, yellow ocher is a yellow hue of light-middle value and low intensity.

 **Working
with Intensity**

1. Applying Your Skills.
This exercise works best with opaque colors, but it can also be done with transparent watercolors. Students must be careful to control the amount of water used so that the values are consistent.

2. Further Challenge.
This activity is a creative application of low intensities. It does not need to be limited to trees.

3. Computer Option.
Design a simple motif using two or three geometric shape tools and any type of line. Choose a Selection tool to select the motif. Use the Copy and Paste commands to make six copies. Using the Bucket Flood-fill tool, assign a primary or secondary color for each motif. Now choose the complement for each color and fill in each motif with the combination. If your software has the capabilities, students can mix the two complements to get a color with low intensity. Or, if your program has an Opaque and Transparent Paint option, choose to work with transparent colors, overlapping some of the complementary colors as the shapes of the motif are filled in.

GUIDED PRACTICE
(continued)

GUIDED PRACTICE
(continued)

Promoting Discussion

The value of understanding color schemes is in knowing how they may be used for specific purposes. Discuss the attributes of various color schemes. Ask students to analyze colors such as the colors they would like to use to decorate a room in their home and the colors they would choose for a car. Would they choose the same color scheme for a family sedan as for a sports car? Would they wear the same colors to a formal prom as to a beach party? What color scheme would they use to paint a battle scene, a scene of children playing, or an old couple sitting together on a park bench? Name a color scheme and let the students suggest a scene that would be effective painted in those colors.

Exploring Aesthetics

Another activity that will help students see the effects of different color schemes would be to have each student find one reproduction in *ArtTalk* that fits one of the color schemes described in this section. Make a rough sketch of the reproduction and then color it using oil pastels or crayons in a different color scheme.

Critical Thinking

Ask students if they have noticed that during one season a certain color scheme seems to be emphasized by fashion designers. Whether the clothes are high-fashion or mass-produced, there seems to be a dominant color scheme. Then, by the next year at the same time, the color scheme may be completely different. Ask the class to suggest reasons why this happens.

164

COLOR SCHEMES

Single colors are like musical instruments. Each instrument has its own special sound. When you hear an instrument in an orchestra, the sound you hear is affected by the sounds of the other instruments. When the musicians tune up before a performance, you hear confusing noises. When they play together in an organized way, they can make beautiful sounds. Unplanned colors can be as confusing to your eyes as unplanned sound is to your ears. Color without organization can look like a visual argument.

When two colors come into direct contact, their differences increase. A yellow-green surrounded by a green looks yellower. A yellow-green surrounded by yellow seems greener. Grayish green will brighten when it is placed against a gray background (Figure 7.17).

A color scheme is a plan for organizing colors. Someone may tell you that certain colors go together or that certain colors clash. These are merely statements of personal likes and dislikes. Some years ago it was considered poor taste to put pink and orange together. Today color combinations are used more freely. The following are some of the most frequently used color schemes.

Monochromatic Colors

Monochrome means one color. A **monochromatic** color scheme is *a color scheme that uses only one hue and the values, tints, and shades of that hue.* Because this is such a limited scheme, it has a strong, unifying effect on a design. (See Figure 7.18.) It is very easy to organize furniture or clothing using monochromatic colors. The major problem with a monochromatic color scheme is that it can be boring.

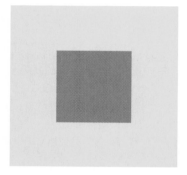

FIGURE 7.17 Your perception of any color is affected by the colors that surround it. This effect is called simultaneous contrast.

FIGURE 7.18 Hartley was fascinated with the mysterious solitude of "Dogtown." To capture this feeling, he eliminated details, painted with bold brushstrokes, and limited his colors to a monochrome of reds. The wide range of values prevents monotony.

Marsden Hartley. *Blueberry Highway, Dogtown.* 1931. Oil on canvas. 47 × 61 cm (18½ × 24″). High Museum of Art, Atlanta, Georgia. Purchase with bequest of C. Donald Belcher, 1977.

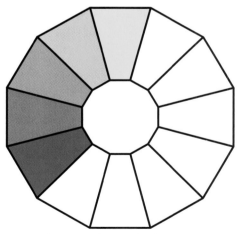

FIGURE 7.19 Analogous colors are related.

Analogous Colors

Analogous colors are *colors that sit side by side on the color wheel and have a common hue* (Figure 7.19). Violet, red-violet, red, red-orange, and orange all have red in common. A more narrowly related scheme would be limited to only three hues, such as violet, red-violet, and red.

Analogous colors can be blended to create a design that ties one shape to the next through a common color (Figure 7.20, page 166). Because of their common hue, these colors are easy to organize.

Complementary Colors

The strongest contrast of a hue is produced by complementary colors. When a pair of high-

GUIDED PRACTICE
(continued)

Building Vocabulary

Have students research both the Greek and French etymologies of the word *analogous.* What are the differences and similarities? Ask students to suggest other uses of the word in different fields. How does the word relate to similar words such as *analog, analogue,* and *analogy?* Ask them to give examples of analogies and explain the parallels between analogous statements and colors.

Using Art Criticism

Divide the students into small groups and assign to each group a painting from this chapter. Each group should choose a secretary and a spokesperson. Instruct students to write down as many single words or phrases that come to mind within a prescribed period of time, perhaps five minutes. When the time is up, ask each group to rearrange their lists into categories with these titles: describe, analyze, interpret, and judge. Using these categories and lists as starting points, have each group compose a paragraph about their artwork. Conclude by having the spokespersons share the groups' findings.

Developing Perceptual Skills

Ask students to design a new color scheme for a specific area of the school—hallways, classroom doors, cafeteria, health office, front office, and so on. Using scale model drawings of the selected areas, have students create new color and/or graphic schemes. When they are finished, have them give rationales for the way(s) the new scheme would affect students, faculty, staff, and visitors.

MORE ABOUT . . . COLOR PRESERVATION

Art conservators are sometimes forced to transfer a painting from its original surface to a better one, especially when a poor quality of canvas or wood panel has begun to deteriorate. Environmental factors such as excessive dryness, humidity, or cold might also cause paint to crack or pull away from a surface. The transfer of a painting is a serious process that is only used after all preventative measures have been taken. Sometimes the results are futile. For example, paintings have been transferred from wood to plastic surfaces that reacted poorly with the paint composition. There are occasions when conservators have to be content with the damaged original, rather than take dangerous risks.

FIGURE 7.20 Rothko limited the colors in this painting to an analogous scheme of yellow and orange. He uses soft edges and colors that blend so that the painting seems to have no borders or edges. The yellow and orange float against a ground that glows mysteriously. Standing in front of this work, which is almost 8 feet (2.4 m) high, the viewer can have an intense visual experience.

Mark Rothko. *Orange and Yellow.* 1956. Oil on canvas. 231.1 × 180.3 cm (91 × 71″). Albright-Knox Art Gallery, Buffalo, New York. Gift of Seymour H. Knox, 1956.

intensity complements are placed side by side, they seem to vibrate. It is difficult to focus on the edge where the complements touch. Some artists use this visual vibration to create special effects. They make designs that sparkle, snap, and sizzle as if charged with electricity. (See Figure 7.21.)

Complementary color schemes are exciting. They are loud, and they demand to be noticed. They are frequently used to catch the viewer's attention. How many ways do people use the red-and-green color scheme? Where else have you seen complementary color schemes used to grab attention?

Not all color schemes based on complements are loud and demanding. If the hues are of low intensity, the contrast is not so harsh. Changing the values of the hues will also soften the effect of the design.

Color Triads

A color triad is composed of three colors spaced an equal distance apart on the color wheel. The contrast between triad colors is not as strong as that between complements. The primary triad is composed of red, yellow, and blue. The secondary triad contains orange, green, and violet (Figure 7.22 on page 168).

A high-intensity primary triad is very difficult to work with. The contrast between the three hues is so strong that they might make people uncomfortable. A triad can be made more comfortable to the

---

MORE ABOUT . . . ENDOWMENT FOR THE ARTS

During the Depression, the government established a program, called *The Federal Arts Projects*, to help artists. The program created jobs for artists in all the arts: theater, dance, music, and the visual arts. The artists were able to support themselves and their families on the $23 a week they were receiving. Many artists survived the Depression through this government support. Some of them were Ben Shahn, Alice Neel, Louise Nevelson, Mark Rothko, Stuart Davis, and Jackson Pollack. Some artists painted murals in post offices, some created drawings and paintings that recorded what the country looked like at that time, and some were employed as teachers in community art centers.

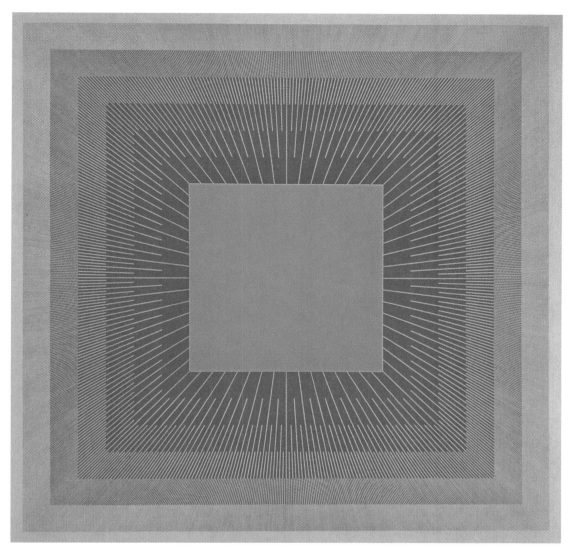

FIGURE 7.21   This painting is an experiment with the effects of high-intensity, complementary colors. The well-defined squares have been created by precise lines, evenly placed. Notice how the red ground changes color according to the density of the alternating blue and green lines. Stare at this painting. Do the afterimages affect your perception?

Richard Anuszkiewicz. *Iridescence*. 1965. Acrylic on canvas. 152.4 × 152.4 cm (60 × 60″). Albright-Knox Art Gallery, Buffalo, New York. Gift of Seymour H. Knox, 1966.

TEACHER TALK

Classroom Management   Since the visual environment is an important consideration in art education, the art room itself should be aesthetically pleasing—orderly and interesting. As a classroom exercise in color aesthetics, have students sketch the classroom then choose a new color scheme that they feel would be more pleasing.

Even if you have no control over the wall color or carpeting in the room, organization will enhance the aesthetics of the environment. Organize your supplies and label shelves where they should be stored. Students should learn where to find certain materials that they use frequently and should be expected to return them to their proper places.

Promoting Discussion

Invite students to volunteer their knowledge of, and experience with, fashion and cosmetic colors that are classified as "warm," "cool," and "neutral." Ask students to explain the differences between the categories and how a person goes about finding out which category is right for him or her.

Developing Studio Skills

Have students select an object in the classroom with a single solid color, such as a wastebasket or a storage cabinet, and make three separate pencil sketches of it. With colored pencils or watercolors, have them select three hues from the color wheel and color one sketch a hue and its complementary colors. A second sketch should be another hue and its analogous colors. The final sketch should be the third hue and its split complement.

Ask students to exchange sketches among themselves and challenge them to identify the position on the color wheel of each of the hues used.

Exploring Aesthetics

Have students study *Relational Painting #93* in Figure 7.23. Then ask these questions: How does Fritz Glarner create interest in the painting by his use of the element of color? What sense, feeling, or mood does he communicate through his use of line? What message do you think he intends to convey? What roles do line, shape, and color play in conveying the painting's message?

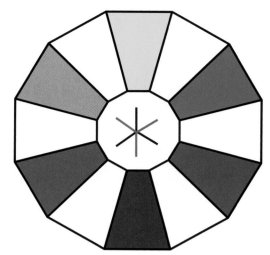

FIGURE 7.22 Color triads.

FIGURE 7.23 Even though this painting is based on the primary triad, it is very comfortable to view. What has the artist done with the colors to make this painting easy to look at?

Fritz Glarner. *Relational Painting #93*. 1962. Oil on canvas. 169.9 × 111.8 cm (66⅞ × 44"). Albright-Knox Art Gallery, Buffalo, New York. Gift of the Seymour H. Knox Foundation, Inc., 1966.

viewer by changing the intensity or values (Figure 7.23). A triad of secondary colors is less disturbing.

Split Complements

A *split complement* is the combination of one hue plus the hues on each side of its complement (Figure 7.24). This is easier to work with than a straight complementary scheme because it offers more variety. For example, start with red-orange. Check the color wheel to find its complement, blue-green. The two hues next to blue-green are blue and green. Red-orange, blue, and green form a split-complementary color scheme.

Warm and Cool Colors

Sometimes the colors are divided into two groups, called *warm* and *cool* (Figure 7.25). Warm colors are red, orange, and yellow. They are usually associated with warm things, such as sunshine or fire (Figure 7.26). Cool colors are blue, green, and violet. They are usually associated with cool things, such as ice, snow, water, or grass (Figure 7.27, page 170). Warm colors seem to move toward the viewer and cool colors seem to recede, or move away.

The amount of warmth or coolness is relative. Violet on a red background appears much cooler than violet alone. However, the same violet on a blue background seems much warmer than the violet alone.

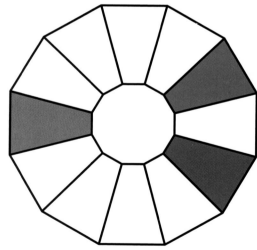

FIGURE 7.24 Split complement.

Using Color Schemes

1. Applying Your Skills. Make a chart to demonstrate the effects of colors on one another. Select a sheet of construction paper of a primary hue. Cut the paper into sixteen equal rectangles. Mount each small

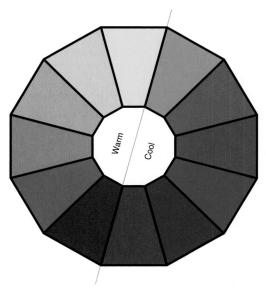

FIGURE 7.25 Warm and cool colors.

rectangle on a different-colored background. Use a variety of materials for the backgrounds. Try colored photos, painted areas, fabric samples, construction paper, and tissue paper. Group the color pairs according to color scheme or degree of contrast. Can you think of other ways to group them?

2. Further Challenge. In your sketchbook, write your initials or the letters of your name. Draw several squares and arrange the letters in a design in one of the squares. The letters must touch the four edges of the square. Do several different designs using the remaining squares. Play with the letters—turn them upside down, twist them out of shape, make them fat, or overlap them. Consider the letters as shapes. They do not have to be readable.

When you find a design you like, reproduce it on four squares of white paper. Now paint each design using one of the following color schemes: monochromatic, analogous, complementary, triad, split-complementary, warm, and cool. How do the color arrangements affect the design? (See Figures 7.28 and 7.29, page 171.)

3. Computer Option. Draw the initials or letters of your name into a design on the computer screen. The letters must touch the four edges of the screen. Play with the letters—turn them upside down or twist them out of shape. Try making them fat or overlapping them. Use only solid color areas and solid lines, since you will

FIGURE 7.26 The warm colors in this painting tell us the mood the artist is trying to create.

Rufino Tamayo. *Toast to the Sun.* 1956. Oil on canvas. 80 × 99 cm (31½ × 39″). Wichita Art Museum, Wichita, Kansas. The Roland P. Murdock Collection.

GUIDED PRACTICE *(continued)*

 **Using Color Schemes**

1. Applying Your Skills. Give everyone in the room a small square of the same piece of construction paper. Let each one take the square home and find a larger square of color on which to glue the small one. (You can dictate a specific size if you wish). Encourage students to use different materials, such as construction paper, wrapping paper, fabric, paper towels, small pieces of wood, and leather for the larger square. When students bring the squares to class mounted on unique backgrounds, have them glue the squares onto a large sheet of poster board or cardboard. When the color collage is complete, ask them to write a few sentences describing unusual combinations within the collage.

2. Further Challenge. The purpose of this activity is to show students how changing a color scheme can change the look of a design.

3. Computer Option. Make a design with the initials or letters of your name. Begin by drawing one letter at a time. Use a Selection tool and experiment with some of the options on your software application. Vary the thickness of each letter and try overlapping. The letters do not need to be recognizable. Choose a geometric shape to frame the letters. Save the most satisfying design and label it "Basic Design." Now, begin to make multiple editions (seriations) of the chosen design by opening the original design and using the Bucket Flood-fill tool to colorize each copy. Use the Save As command to label and save each rendition. Represent the various color schemes. Print. Evaluate your results and choose your personal preferences.

MORE ABOUT . . . WATERCOLOR PAINTING

Paints made with water and gum arabic have been used since ancient times. One form of water paint was used on the illuminated manuscripts of the Middle Ages. Albrecht Dürer used another form of water paint as a wash. Watercolor, as we know it today, did not develop until the late eighteenth century. The medium became especially popular in Great Britain, where several outstanding landscape artists painted with watercolor. Remember that watercolor is a difficult medium to work in; inexperienced students might easily become frustrated because it must be put down quickly and should not be reworked. Stress to them that artists practice for many years to obtain the desired visual effect.

GUIDED PRACTICE
(continued)

LOOKING
C L O S E L Y

Have students study Figure 7.27 and answer the questions in the caption. Encourage them to see that the treetops look like cones with the points rounded. There is light green in the sky. Carr used it to tie the large area of sky to the forest. She has used blue-violet to represent the darker sky. We see touches of yellow and dark orange (brown). She has used white and black.

Carr may have used solid forms to represent the dense foliage, or to represent the strength of the forests.

INDEPENDENT PRACTICE

Enrichment

Divide the students into small groups and assign each group one of the concepts discussed in the first part of Chapter 7, such as the spectrum, hue, the color wheel, value, intensity, complementary colors, and so on. Each group is responsible for finding, or making, examples of the concept and presenting them to the class, using their visual examples as part of their presentation.

Extension

If you know a photographer who prefers black-and-white film to create aesthetic (as opposed to journalistic) photographs, invite him or her to visit the class and explain the process. Before the visit, help students prepare meaningful questions to ask.

Emily Carr. *Above the Trees.* c. 1939. Oil on paper. 91.2 × 61 cm (36 × 24″). Vancouver Art Gallery, Vancouver, British Columbia, Canada.

LOOKING
C L O S E L Y

FIGURE 7.27 Notice how Carr has used cool colors to represent the moisture-laden atmosphere of the forests of Victoria. The foliage of the trees has been portrayed as solid forms. What forms do they look like? The curves in the sky seem to echo the forms of the trees. Look at the light values in the sky near the top of the painting. What light hue has Carr used in addition to blue? Why do you think she used that color? What color has she used to represent the darker sky in the bottom right corner?

Besides blue and green, what other hues can you find? Which neutral colors have been used?

Why do you think Carr has painted the forms of the foliage as if they are solid?

need to fill them with new colors as you progress through the assignment. Consider the letters as shapes. They do not have to be readable. You may use any tools or options available on your computer software. Resize and Distort options would be useful.

When you find a design you like, label it "Basic Design" and save it. Use the Fill Bucket and other tools to fill in all the shapes, lines, and spaces with each of the following color schemes: monochromatic, analogous, complementary, triad, split-complementary, warm, and cool.

Label and save each color scheme as you finish it. When you finish all the color schemes, evaluate their effect on the basic design. Also evaluate your personal preferences in the use of color schemes.

SAFETY NOTE

Natural dyes are not as safe to use in school as you might imagine. The dye material itself is safe, but many of the mordants are poisonous. Check all the directions carefully, and check out the nature of the chemicals before you bring anything into your classroom. Also note that some of the author's experiments with natural coloring materials yielded some horrible aromas, so be careful before you boil them inside the school building. A safe mordant to use when making your own dye is iron. If you boil onion skins in an old iron kettle, the iron acts as a mordant.

FIGURE 7.28   Student work. Designing the letters of a name.

FIGURE 7.29   Student work. Designing the letters of a name.

COLOR IN PIGMENTS

Artists' **pigments** are *finely ground, colored powders that form paint when mixed with a liquid.* Pigment colors cannot match the purity and intensity of the colors of light.

Artists' paints are sometimes named according to the mineral from which the pigment powder is made. For example, cadmium yellow is made with the mineral cadmium sulfide. Sometimes the pigment gets its name from the place where it was discovered. Burnt sienna, for instance, is made with clay found in the soil in Siena, Italy.

Before you buy paint, look at the manufacturer's color chart to find out what the color looks like. You will see that ultramarine blue, cobalt blue, cerulean blue, and thalo blue all look different.

Paint

All paints used in art are made up of three basic ingredients: pigment, binder, and solvent. The **binder** is *a liquid that holds together the grains of pigment* in a form that can be spread over some surface. Linseed oil is the binder for oil paints. Wax is the binder for encaustic paint. Gum arabic is the binder for watercolor paints. Acrylic polymer is the binder for acrylic paints. A chemical emulsion is used to make school tempera paint. Many professional artists mix pure pigments with egg yolk for a translucent tempera paint. The **solvent** is *the liquid that controls the thickness or the thinness of the paint.* The solvent for oil paints is turpentine. Water is the solvent for watercolors and tempera. Acrylics can be thinned with water or acrylic medium while wet, but once acrylic paint dries, it is waterproof.

Paint pigments do not dissolve—they remain suspended in the medium. When applied to a surface, the pigments stay on top of the surface and they dry there. *Pigments that dissolve in liquid* are called **dyes.** Dyes do not remain on the surfaces as paints do. Dyes sink into the fabric to which they are applied and color the fabric by staining it.

The pigment, the binder, the solvent, and the surface to which the paint is applied all affect the color you see. Wet colors look brighter and darker than dry ones. Tempera and watercolor paints always look lighter and duller after they dry. Oil paints glow even when dry because of their oil vehicle. If diluted with turpentine, oil paints dry to a dull finish.

The density and color of the surface receiving the paint affects the way the light waves will be

Developing Studio Skills

Tell students that prehistoric artists used their hands, fur, bark, twigs, moss, and leather to achieve various textures and colors when they used natural pigments. Discuss the advantages and disadvantages of a color palette that uses only earth pigments. Encourage students to make a sketch of an object. Then using only earth tones, color the sketch in a way that makes it interesting and aesthetically pleasing.

Exploring Aesthetics

The sky in Figure 7.31 was created by mixing natural beige pigment with some school acrylic paint. All of the other colors are pure earth pigment. Ask students to read the question in the caption and discuss their responses.

Art Is Everywhere

To foster students' awareness of expressions of color in everyday life, suggest this: Poets use color in their poetry, sometimes to describe objects but also as metaphors of feelings, moods, or scenes. For example, Matthew Arnold wrote vivid descriptions of Dover Beach, England, at night. Look in *Bartlett's Familiar Quotations* for literary references to each color. You will find under *red*, for example, a reference to Percy Bysshe Shelley's "Ode to the West Wind." Find a copy of the poem and locate his description of autumn leaves. Write your own color metaphors.

reflected back to your eyes. Have you ever applied wax crayon to colored paper? The crayon lets light through to the paper, and the colored paper absorbs some of these light waves and reflects the rest. Only white paper allows the true color of the crayon to show, because it reflects all the light.

Have you ever tried to match colors that are on two different surfaces? A fuzzy brown sweater can

FIGURE 7.30 This Soninke woman is applying a paste of ground natural pigment and water to the mud wall. All the paints are made from materials found in the local environment. The scratch lines on the unpainted wall are the outlines for the paints that will be applied.

Photo from *African Canvas* by Margaret Courtney-Clarke. Rizzoli, 1990.

ART ON A SHOESTRING

Be resourceful when designing lesson plans and remember that it never hurts to ask. For example, a natural pigment source that is easy and safe to demonstrate is onion skins. Ask the produce manager of a grocery store to save onion skins for you the next time the bins are cleaned out. Boil them in water to obtain a golden yellow-orange color. Red onions will provide yet another natural pigment. Elaborate formulas have been developed for using natural dyes and making them permanent, but even without a mordant to set the colors, they can be brushed on paper.

never truly match a brown leather bag. A shiny green polyester shirt looks brighter than green knit pants even though the same dye is used. Shiny, dense surfaces always look brighter because they reflect more light.

Sources of Pigment

In the past, pigments came from animals, vegetables, and minerals. A kind of beetle and the root of a certain plant were both sources for red. Another plant produced a deep, transparent blue. Ultramarine blue was made by grinding a semiprecious stone. The color ocher is natural clay colored by iron rust. Prehistoric people made paint from natural minerals. They ground different-colored pieces of earth and combined them with animal fat to make paint.

Today synthetic (artificially made) pigments have been developed by scientists. The synthetics are brighter and more permanent than natural pigments, but some artists still prefer to use natural colors (Figure 7.30). Many weavers color their yarns with natural dyes. Andrew Wyeth is a modern artist who uses only natural earth pigments.

FIGURE 7.31 Student work. Earth pigments were used to create this painting. What would be the result if the student painted the same scene with synthetic paints?

 Mixing Colors

1. Applying Your Skills.   Collect and grind three of your own earth pigments (see Technique Tip 11 on page 353 in the Handbook). Mix them with a binder and solvent and experiment with them. Try using a variety of brushes and surfaces. Finally, paint a design that shows all the colors you can obtain from the pigments. (See Figure 7.31.)

2. Further Challenge.   Experiment by applying a variety of paint media to many different surfaces. Collect as many paints and surfaces as possible and cut the surfaces into regular, matching shapes. Try every paint on every surface. What conclusions can you make about paints and surfaces?

3. Computer Option.   Mixing colors with light on a computer is very different from mixing colors with pigment. If your computer software has the capabilities, practice making secondary and intermediate colors. Also mix tints, shades, and intensity changes. Fill a variety of geometric shapes with all the new colors you have made, and show off your work by filling your screen with repeated shapes.

How Artists Use Color

You have studied the facts of color. Now you need to look at how artists use color in the language of art. There are many ways to communicate with color, and realistic representation is only one of them.

Optical Color

Sometimes artists reproduce colors as they see them. Until the late nineteenth century, this was

FIGURE 7.32 Monet was one of the first artists to take his paints and canvases outdoors. He realized that the colors of the scene changed as the time of day changed, so he carried several canvases. As the light changed, he moved on to another painting.

Claude Monet. *Poplars.* 1891. Oil on canvas. 100 × 65.2 cm (39½ × 25¹/₁₆″). Philadelphia Museum of Art, Philadelphia, Pennsylvania. Bequest of Anne Thomson as a memorial to her father Frank Thomson and her mother Mary Elizabeth Clarke Thomson.

the way all Western artists painted. For example, in an automobile dealer's showroom, the color of a blue car is affected by light and other factors surrounding it. The car may sparkle as it reflects the showroom lights. Shadows on the car may look dark blue or blue-violet. The red from the car next to it may cause a red-violet reflection on the blue surface.

A painter who is trying to show the car in its setting will use all the colors involved. He or she will make use of *optical color,* the color that results when a true color is affected by the atmosphere or unusual lighting. Optical color is the color that people actually perceive. Compare the two paintings by Claude Monet shown in Figures 7.32 and 7.33 to see how the time of day affects color.

The Impressionists were deeply involved with optical color. They tried to express the sensation of light and atmosphere with their unique style of painting. They applied dots and dabs of spectral colors and did not mix black with any colors. They made gray, low-intensity colors by putting complements together instead of mixing just black and white. These low-intensity grays, such as dull blue and dull green, are much richer and look more natural in landscapes than do grays made by mixing black and white.

Arbitrary Color

When artists use color to express feelings, they usually ignore the optical colors of objects. They choose the colors *arbitrarily,* which means they make their choices on the basis of personal preference. They choose arbitrary colors rather than optical colors because they want to use color to express meaning (Figure 7.34, page 175). In abstract art, color is teamed with the other elements to become the subject as well as the meaning of the work (Figure 7.21, page 167, and Figure 7.35, page 176).

Bright colors are loud. Light, bright colors can create happy, upbeat moods. Cool, dark colors can express mysterious or depressing themes. Warm, low-intensity earth tones are very comfortable and friendly and are often used to decorate rooms in which people gather. A unique light value of red-orange has been used to calm people and has even been successful in calming violent prisoners. Bright yellow is stimulating; blue soothes; and red excites.

MORE ABOUT . . . CLAUDE MONET

Born on November 14, 1840 in Paris, France, Claude Monet is best known for his paintings of flowers, especially water lilies. However, he also painted trees, steam engines, churches, mountains, the sea, and people. Because he loved sunlight and was fascinated by the effect it had on the color of objects, he tried to capture a special moment in his paintings. He wanted his paintings to shine, sparkle, and come alive on the canvas. Monet, along with other artists such as Picasso, Renoir, Sisley, and Morisot, were called Impressionists by enraged critics who viewed their style with contempt. However, Impressionism has had a lasting influence on the course of art history.

FIGURE 7.33   This painting shows the cool shadows of late afternoon.

Claude Monet. *Poplars.* 1891. Oil on canvas. 81.9 × 81.6 cm (32¼ × 32⅛″). The Metropolitan Museum of Art, New York, New York. Bequest of Mrs. H. O. Havemeyer, 1929. The H. O. Havemeyer Collection.

Artists today have put their knowledge of color psychology to work to develop unusual methods for using color. Many of their choices are personal—they make color say what they wish to express.

Space

The placement of warm and cool colors can create illusions of depth. Warm colors advance toward the viewer, and cool colors seem to recede and pull away. The French artist Paul Cézanne was the first to use warm and cool colors to create depth. He painted a cool, blue outline around the shape of a warm, round orange. The fruit seemed to be pushed forward by the surrounding blue.

FIGURE 7.34   Marc developed his own personal scheme for the symbolic meaning of color. To him, blue represented the spiritual. Red represented matter, and in this work he used it to represent the land. Yellow represented comfort, and green served to set off red. The combination of the abstract, curved forms of the horses and the blue spiritual color reveal Marc's philosophy that animals have a purer relationship with the earth than human beings do.

Franz Marc. *The Large Blue Horses.* 1911. Oil on canvas. 106 x 181 cm (41⅝ × 71¼″). Walker Art Center, Minneapolis, Minnesota. Gift of the T. B. Walker Foundation, Gilbert M. Walker Fund, 1942.

GUIDED PRACTICE
(continued)

Understanding Art History

Inform students that Franz Marc, whose painting is shown in Figure 7.34, is remembered as one of the founders of Der Blaue Reiter along with Wassily Kandinsky and Alexei von Jawlensky. His passionate interest in the spiritual nature of animals is reflected in his work. Often he used symbolic colors that were not natural to the animals because he wanted to depict them as we see them, not as they are. His paintings became more abstract as he fell under the influence of the Cubists and Futurists at the beginning of World War I. Perhaps as a foreshadowing of the tragedy that would become the war, his last paintings portrayed a world on the edge of destruction. Marc's life and art were cut short when he died in action during the war.

Promoting Discussion

Give students this challenge: How many ways can they say this sentence, "I really want to go now"? Encourage them to use voice inflections and body language to accent their delivery. Now tell them that artists use color in order to achieve the same type of impact. Ask them to choose an artwork from the book and describe its use of color with voice inflections that mirror the impact of color on the viewer.

ART ON A SHOESTRING

If your art program participates in a school or community art show, use the following idea to create inexpensive, handmade calendars to sell. Make photocopies of blank calendar pages or, if you have access to computers, print them using a computer program that has a selection of calendar forms. (Do not use any decorative additions either from the original that is photocopied or that are available on the computer program.) Have students use watercolors, tempera, or permanent markers to decorate the calendars in the style of a specific artist. For example, a Monet calendar could include Impressionistic scenes, even a few facts about the artist. Staple or bind the pages at the top. Encourage originality.

GUIDED PRACTICE
(continued)

Exploring Aesthetics

Call students' attention to Figure 7.18 on page 165, Hartley's monochrome. Ask them what effect the changes in value have on the work. Ask them to compare that work to the one by Mondrian in Figure 7.35. Which one has larger jumps in value? Which one is calmer?

Using Color for Effect

1. Applying Your Skills.
The purpose of these activities is to show how different uses of color arrangements can change the look of a painting.

2. Further Challenge.
As with the Applying Your Skills activity, encourage students to be creative with their designs.

3. Computer Option.
Use the Brush or Pencil tool to sketch a leaf or a tree. Try Brush Symmetry, if available. Either select the object and resize it to fill the page, or select it and make multiple overlapping copies to fill the page. Save and label as "Basic Design." Use the Bucket Flood-fill tool. Choose from available colors and the Mixing, Blending, Transparent, and Gradient options to illustrate one of the following: true color, optical color, arbitrary color that expresses personal feelings, warm and cool colors to show depth, movement through value, and tonality. Use the Save As command to label the work. Open another copy of "Basic Design." Choose and create another edition using a different color scheme. Use the Save As command to label work. Complete three editions. Have students evaluate the results of this series of artworks.

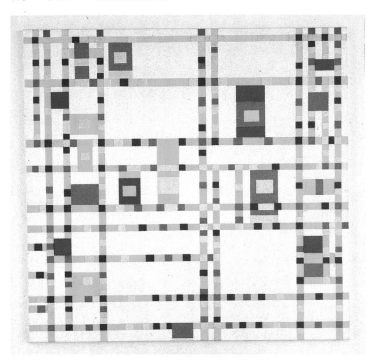

FIGURE 7.35 In this painting you feel the syncopated beat of the Boogie Woogie as your eyes bounce along the paths created by the squares and rectangles of yellow, red, blue, and gray. All of this is painted against a white background. The jumps in value from very light grays and light yellows to darker blues and reds create a sense of movement similar to the beat of the dance.

Piet Mondrian. *Broadway Boogie Woogie.* 1942–43. Oil on canvas. 127 × 127 cm (50 × 50"). Collection, The Museum of Modern Art, New York, New York.

Movement

Color can create a sense of movement. When the values in a work jump quickly from very high key to very low key, a feeling of excitement and movement is created (Figure 7.35). When all the values are close together, the work seems much calmer. Today's artists use color to create movement and depth in abstract art.

When you work with color to create movement, remember to use values of pure hues as well as those of tints and shades. You will need to remember, for instance, that the pure hue yellow is much lighter than red or blue.

Tonality

Sometimes an artist lets one color, such as blue, dominate the work. In such a case, the work is said to have a blue *tonality*. (See Figure 7.36.) The painting does not have to be monochrome—there may be other colors present. The overall effect of the work, however, is an impression of blueness. Tonality has a unifying effect.

 Using Color for Effect

1. Applying Your Skills. Create three small sketches of trees with leaves. Use a simple color medium such as crayon. Color each sketch to illustrate one of the following: true color; arbitrary color; or tonality.

2. Further Challenge. Make three drawings of trees with leaves. Use a simple color medium such as crayon or oil pastel. Color each sketch to illustrate one of the following: optical color; depth through the use of warm and cool colors; or movement through value.

3. Computer Option. Using the tools of your choice, draw and label six sketches of trees with leaves. Let each sketch illustrate one of the following: true color; optical color; color that expresses personal feelings; depth through the use of warm and cool colors; movement through value; or tonality.

Evaluate the results of your work. Develop your favorite into a finished drawing.

MEETING SPECIAL NEEDS

Visually Impaired   If you have students who are blind, rather than shy away from talking about color, be aware of the need for complete descriptions when talking about color. Instead of avoiding references to the subtleties of color, use creative and natural analogies, such as "a light delicate purple color like lilac flowers," or "reds, yellows, and oranges like the color in flames of fire." The age of the onset of blindness governs how many visual memories the person retains. Monet did his greatest paintings while experiencing yellowing of the cornea. El Greco is reported to have had an astigmatism, a condition that caused him to see and draw figures stretched out.

LOOKING CLOSELY

FIGURE 7.36 The blue tonality of this work conveys the cool impression of water. The jellyfish are in the inlet and swimming close to the rocks. They are spots of contrast in the blue water.

This is not a monochrome. Hassam has used other hues. What are they? Where do you see the brightest blue? Where do you find the darkest area of blue? Can you find light gray-blue, gray-blue, and dark gray-blue? Where are they?

There is no sky. What point of view has the artist taken? How has he divided the composition?

Childe Hassam. *Jelly Fish*. 1912. Oil on canvas. 51.4 × 61.6 cm (20¼ × 24¼″). Wichita Art Museum, Wichita, Kansas. The John W. and Mildred L. Graves Collection.

GUIDED PRACTICE
(continued)

LOOKING CLOSELY

Have students study Figure 7.36 and answer the questions in the caption. Encourage them to see that Hassam has used greens, yellow, and touches of light red. The brightest blue is near the top of the work. The darkest area of blue is within the triangular cove cutting into the rocks, in the lower left area. The different values of blue-gray are on the rocks. The artist is looking down on the scene. He has divided the composition using a zigzag type line that separates the water from the rocks.

INDEPENDENT PRACTICE

Study Guide
Distribute and have students complete *Study Guide 7* in the Reteaching booklet. Have students use the guide to review key concepts in the chapter.

Enrichment
• Assign *Enrichment Activity 13 and 14* in the TCR.
• Have students make a painting, collage, or mural design that focuses on major events in their lives. Instruct them to use color to indicate the emotional connection they have with each specific event.

Studio Lessons
To expand students' familiarity with the concept of color, Studio Lessons are available in the TCR.

COOPERATIVE LEARNING

When planning peer review sessions, remember that students often benefit from a short feedback form that lists the criteria for the activity and a way to streamline their comments. With this technique, students confine their comments and assessment to specific areas that are relevant to the activity and are useful to the student who receives them. For example, while working on this chapter, a feedback form might take the shape of a grid that lists criteria for consideration, such as *intensity, depth of color*, and *movement* in the far left column. Additional columns to check off for each criteria might be "Yes," "No," and another titled "Suggestions for Improvement."

FOCUS

OBJECTIVE

Use cut-out shapes from black-and-white magazine and newspaper photographs to create a composition in the manner of Romare Bearden.

MOTIVATOR

Bring to class examples of African masks so that students can see the relationship between the masks and the faces in the painting. Display the masks and discuss them before you begin this lesson.

TEACH

GUIDED PRACTICE

Developing Studio Skills

Provide magazines that are popular for their photography, such as *Life, National Geographic,* and *Vogue.* Fashion and sports magazines are great sources for facial and body parts. Avoid weekly news magazines unless you are doing current events. Students can also bring their own magazines from home. If a color photograph is desirable, use it. However, it will photocopy in black and white.

Interdisciplinary: Music

Music, particularly jazz, has always been important to Bearden; the theme of music appears often in his artwork. Have students find examples of various forms of jazz and listen to the variations. Then find recordings of African music and find the essence of jazz in them.

FIGURE 7.37   Romare Bearden. *Prevalence of Ritual: Baptism.* 1964. Photomechanical reproduction, synthetic polymer, and pencil on board. 23.2 x 30.5 cm (9⅛ × 12"). Hirshhorn Museum and Sculpture Garden, Smithsonian Institution, Washington, D.C. Gift of Joseph H. Hirshhorn, 1966.

Supplies

- Sketchbook and pencils
- Magazines and newspapers
- Envelope and scissors
- 6 x 9″ (15 x 23 cm) white paper
- White glue, damp sponge, paper towels
- Photocopy machine
- Crayons
- Oil pastels
- Colored pencils
- Acrylic paints, gloss medium, and brushes
- Felt-tip fine-line marker

R omare Bearden's collage looks deceptively simple. If you look closely, however, you will see an unusual mixture of media and color. Bearden's art was influenced by his experience as an African-American, but his goal was to create a universal art. He said, "I am trying to explore, in terms of the particulars of life I know best, those things common to all cultures."

Figure 7.37 is one of Bearden's many collages. In this example, he combined many different pieces to complete the picture. To compose the figures and background, he used photographs of textiles, water, cloth, wood, leaves, grass, metal, and people. He made his faces by cutting details from pictures of African masks, marbles, animal eyes, and mossy vegetation. For this work he had his small, original works enlarged photographically. Finally, he added paint to complete the colorful collage you see here.

For Bearden, any meaningful art had to have a subject. He once said, "All painting is a kind of talking about life."

MORE ABOUT . . . ROMARE BEARDEN

In 1936, Bearden enrolled at the Art Students League in New York City. There he met and studied under the German Expressionist, George Grosz. Because Bearden wanted to make a social statement about his African-American heritage, Grosz introduced him to the work of Daumier, Goya, and Kollwitz, and led him to study composition through the analysis of Brueghel and the great Dutch masters. Grosz also pushed Bearden to refine his draftsmanship by studying the work of Ingres, Dürer, and Holbein. In 1938, Bearden left the Art Students League, but he continued to paint while working at the New York City Department of Social Services.

Choose a theme that interests you. Cut out objects and shapes from black-and-white magazine and newspaper photographs. On a small background approximately 6 x 9 inches (15 x 23 cm), arrange the shapes and recut them as necessary to create a composition in the manner of Bearden's work. Using a photocopy machine, enlarge your work as much as possible. Paint your enlarged work with a color scheme that best expresses the theme of your work. Use any combination of the following: crayons, oil pastels, colored pencils, and school acrylics.

FOCUSING

Study Bearden's collage. Notice how the faces take on a masklike quality because they are made of parts that do not necessarily match.

FIGURE 7.37A Student work.

Notice how the entire space is filled. Select a theme related to people to use in your work.

CREATING

Collect magazines and newspapers. Cut small pieces from the photos that you might use. Remember that the first step of the finished product will be small, so keep your pieces small. Put the cut pieces into the envelope for storage. You may combine color with black and white, since the photocopy machine will produce a black-and-white product. You must consider how the values of the colors will reproduce in the photocopy.

Arrange and rearrange the cut pieces until you are pleased with your composition. Do not leave any negative space. Every area must be filled. When you are satisfied with your composition, glue it down.

When your work is dry, enlarge it using the photocopy machine. Make more than one copy so you can experiment with one or more and use the final one as the finished product.

Choose a color scheme that is appropriate for your theme. Use crayons, oil pastels, colored pencils, school acrylics with gloss medium, and brushes, or any combination of the mentioned color media.

CRITIQUING

Describe Tell the theme you chose and explain how you carried it out. Did you have to create most of the shapes you needed or were you able to find them in photographs?

Analyze Did the shapes you arranged carry out the effect of your theme? What color scheme did you choose?

Interpret Did your work express the mood of the theme you selected? Does your title enhance the expressive effect?

Judge Is your work successful? Does it have the look of the Bearden collage style? Which aesthetic theory would be best to judge this work?

179

TECHNIQUE TIP

To help students complete this activity without complication, make these suggestions: Some copy machines will handle thicker drawing paper if it is hand fed. When using watercolors, the students may find it necessary to tape the edges of their paper to the table to help prevent rolling and wrinkles. Also, vary techniques when using watercolor. Dampen areas of your paper where you wish to create a wash effect. Use a dry brush for stipple and sharp line effects. For watercolor techniques, see page 353 in the Handbook.

FOCUS

OBJECTIVE

Enlarge a reproduction of a master artwork and create individual rectangles that stand alone as a nonobjective artwork.

MOTIVATOR

Encourage a class critique of Steir's *A Vanitas of Style*. Ask the students to study each panel as a separate piece. Magnifying glasses may be necessary for a true detailed search of the reproduction in the book. Ask them to list all of the various art styles that they can find in the painting. Remind them to use the vocabulary terms they have learned since Chapter 1, especially those associated with the elements and principles of art.

TEACH

GUIDED PRACTICE

Building Vocabulary

Ask students to look up the definitions for the word *appropriation*. Have them explain how the word is an accurate description of Pat Steir's process.

Understanding Art History

Have students locate books on the Brueghels, Rembrandt, Bosch, and Rubens. Ask the students to research and discuss these artists' works. Begin a session in which the students discuss similarities and differences in these artists' works.

STUDIO LESSON: PHOTO ENLARGEMENT

FIGURE 7.38 Pat Steir. *The Brueghel Series (A Vanitas of Style).* 1982–84. Oil on canvas. Sixty-four panels, each 72.4 × 57 cm (28 ½ × 22½"); total dimensions approximately 5.8 × 4.6 m (19 × 15′). Courtesy of Robert Miller Gallery, New York, New York.

Supplies

- Reproduction of a master- piece
- Ruler, pencil, soft eraser, and scissors
- Large rectangles of white paper
- Sketchbook
- Acrylic paints, brushes

Pat Steir was looking for a unique way to express her vision of the history of painting.

Pat Steir had studied art history, and as a painter she had practiced the styles of the masters. She explored the colors and brushwork of Rembrandt, Bosch, Rubens, and the Brueghels. To practice, she used what she called *appropriation:* the themes and styles of the masters. The subject for her painting-about-painting was a reproduction of a sixteenth-century still life by Jan Brueghel (**broi**-gul) the Elder called *Flower Piece in Blue Vase.*

180

TEACHER TALK

An alternate method of managing a studio lesson such as the Photo Enlargement, above, is to let the whole class work on one large reproduction, or set up smaller groups to work with smaller reproductions. To get the whole piece finished, one or two students may have to work on more than one rectangle. You might precut and number the rectangles so that the students do not know which reproduction is being used. Alternately, you may wish to decide the ratio of enlargement since the size of the finished work depends on the available space and available materials. Have the students place the works on the floor for viewing. They may be glued to a large paper background, then later cut up.

After laying grids over the reproduction to divide it evenly into rectangles, Steir painted each panel as an homage to one of the great artists of history.

Study a work of art by *appropriating* it in the manner of Pat Steir. Working in a group, divide a reproduction of a master work into rectangles using a grid. Distribute the pieces among the group members. Enlarge your individual rectangle using a grid. (See Technique Tip 8 on page 352 in the Handbook for instructions on how to enlarge a work using a grid.) Paint your individual rectangle using colors that are the complements of the original colors.

FOCUSING

Study Steir's *Brueghel Series (A Vanitas of Style)*. Notice how each rectangle is painted in a different style.

FIGURE 7.38A Student work.

CREATING

Using a ruler and pencil, divide the back of the reproduction evenly into rectangles. Number them in order and then cut them apart.

Follow directions on page 352 to draw a grid on the face of your rectangle and a matching grid on your large sheet of white paper. Using the grid as a guide, enlarge your section of the reproduction onto the white paper. You do not have to erase the grid lines. They are part of your work.

Paint your enlarged composition using complements of the original colors. For example, if one shape was red-orange in the reproduction, you will paint it blue-green. Keep the values the same. If the shape was a light red-orange, paint it a light blue-green.

Join all the finished works back together using the numbers as a guide.

CRITIQUING

Describe What is the name of the artwork your group appropriated? Describe the look of your individual rectangle. Is it realistic or nonobjective? When you join your work with that of the rest of your group, can you recognize the original subject?

Analyze Describe the lines, shapes, and colors in your individual panel. When you join the group's panels together, do they fit? Do the shapes and lines match? Have you all interpreted the color complements the same way? Do the colors match?

Interpret Has changing the colors to their complements affected the expressive quality of the whole work? Do the individual styles affect the look of the work?

Judge Which aesthetic theory would you use to judge your individual panel? Would you use the same theory to judge the whole group's work?

TECHNIQUE TIP

When cutting the individual rectangles of paper for the panels, make certain that each piece of paper is exactly cut the same size. Even a slight variance can affect the final assemblage of the whole work. In some cases it may be necessary to use the neutrals, black and white, when the values are adversely affected by a color's complement. As the students progress, you might advise them to paint beside those who are painting adjacent panels. By doing this, students can compare colors and placement of objects that cross from one panel to another. It will also be helpful to begin each class by putting the entire painting together for a brief critique of matching panels.

Enrichment

Students may be interested in doing a similar project in which only neutrals are used to create an array of values. Also, try this lesson with monochromatic or warm and cool color schemes.

Keeping a Portfolio

Remind students that the preliminary sketches and the final artworks for this Studio Lesson are likely considerations for their portfolios. Encourage them to label their work, evaluate the process, and make any notes that will help them make meaningful choices when they prepare a portfolio for evaluation.

Extension

Ask students to research various artists and the variety of jobs they held to support their creative efforts. For example, inform students that Pat Steir worked as a model and art director. Norman Rockwell worked as an extra at the Metropolitan Opera. Sculptor David Smith worked as a welder in an automobile factory and Robert Rauschenberg designed window displays.

ASSESS

CRITIQUING

Have students apply the steps of art criticism to their own artwork using the "Critiquing" questions on this page.

CLOSE

Allow each group to exhibit their finished artwork and explain how colors and styles work together to form a unified composition.

Using Color to Create an Expressive Statement

FIGURE 7.39   Jaune Quick-To-See Smith. *Spotted Owl*. 1990. Oil and beeswax on canvas, wood panels, and axes. 203 x 294.6 cm (80 × 116″). Courtesy of the Steinbaum-Krauss Gallery, New York, New York. Collection of the artist.

FOCUS

OBJECTIVE

Use color and symbols to create a drawing that expresses a personal concern and emphasizes the issue.

MOTIVATOR

Ask students what values, beliefs, traditions, and other influences from their childhood molded and shaped their world today. Ask students to recall from memory a speech, poem, or song that made an impact on them in a similar way that television commercials concerning the environment made an impact on so many.

TEACH

GUIDED PRACTICE

Promoting Discussion

Tell students to collect images and articles from magazines and newspapers concerning the environment. Generate a class discussion based on the subjects of these clippings. Ask students to discuss other issues that are important to them. The issues may be political, religious, environmental, educational, and so on. Ask them to explain why an artwork might be an appropriate vehicle for expressing their concerns.

Supplies

- Sketchbook and pencil
- Large sheet of white paper
- Crayons and chalk
- Acrylic paints and assorted brushes
- Scissors and nontoxic rubber cement
- Large sheets of colored poster board

Jaune Quick-To-See Smith was born in St. Ignatius, a small town on the Flathead reservation of the Confederated Salish and Kootenai tribes of southwestern Montana. Her Shoshone grandmother gave her her name: *Jaune*, French for "yellow," relates to her French-Cree ancestors; Quick-To-See was an insightful prediction of her life's work.

Drawing came easily to Smith, who wanted to be an artist from childhood. Her hunger for learning took her on a long journey out of the Flathead valley, but the things she learned there are still a part of everything she does. In 1980 she received a master's degree, and in her work she combines her university training with her tribal heritage. She draws deeply from her own life experiences as well as from mainstream modern art to communicate her concern for the vanishing West.

In *Spotted Owl* (Figure 7.39), Smith focuses on the new West. This work symbolizes the current concern over endangered species, and she uses neutral color and visual symbols to convey her message

182

MORE ABOUT . . . JAUNE QUICK-TO-SEE SMITH

Although she lives in New Mexico, Smith still maintains close ties to the people and the landscape of the Flathead Reservation. She draws deeply from her own life experiences, traditional Indian heritage, historical western landscape, as well as the mainstream modern art to communicate her concern for the vanishing west. In her new body of work, she quotes from Chief Seattle's visionary speech given in 1854. The environmental concerns that he addressed are as relevant today as they were nearly 130 years ago. Her paintings insist that all living things must co-exist and that no single life form controls another. Jaune Quick-to-See Smith's work is her plea to each of us to save the earth.

that all living things must coexist. Her paintings are a plea to each of us to save the earth.

Jaune Quick-to-See Smith expresses her concerns in her paintings. Choose an issue that is personally important to you. Create a shaped painting, without words, that expresses your concern. Use visual symbols and color contrast to emphasize your point.

FOCUSING

Select an issue. Discuss your concerns with your classmates. This may help you think of ways to express your ideas visually. Your subject may be as personal as your relationships with friends or family. It may be about school issues such as rules or teacher-student relationships. Your subject could be a world issue such as politics or the environment.

Write about your issue in your sketchbook. List words and concepts. Make several small sketches for your painting. Use crayons to plan your color scheme. The shape of your finished work does not have to be rectangular. You may choose a circle, a free-form shape, or the shape of an object that is part of your idea. Things may protrude from the edges of the shape for emphasis.

Discuss your sketches with a small group of classmates and share composition ideas. For example, you might want to make the people larger, or make the negative spaces larger than the positive shape to emphasize loneliness. Try painting everything in warm colors except a calm area. Express the calmness with a cool color.

CREATING

Draw your final idea on a large sheet of white paper with beige or yellow chalk. Paint with acrylics before you cut out the final outline. Remember to use color contrast for emphasis.

Cut out your finished piece. Test your work on several different colors of poster board before you choose the final background color. Certain colors could change the message of

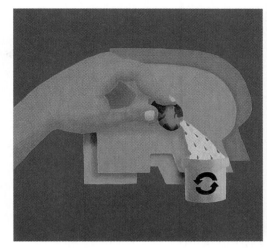

FIGURE 7.39A   Student work.

your painting while others may enhance it. Mount your painting on the poster board. Make up a title for your work that incorporates a reference to the issue.

CRITIQUING

Describe   Name the issue that is the subject of your painting. Tell which visual symbols you selected to illustrate your idea and explain why you chose them.

Analyze   How did you use color contrast to make your point? Which other elements did you emphasize to express your ideas? Explain.

Interpret   Did your work convey your message without words? Were your classmates able to understand your visual symbols?

Judge   Which aesthetic theory would you use to judge this work? Was it successful? If you were to do it over, what would you change?

183

INDEPENDENT PRACTICE

Enrichment

Get permission from your principal for the students to paint nature scenes on the school's trash cans. Messages or slogans about recycling could be incorporated into the designs.

Keeping a Portfolio

Remind students that the preliminary sketches and the final artworks for this Studio Lesson are likely considerations for their portfolios. Encourage them to label their work, evaluate the process, and make any notes that will help them make meaningful choices when they prepare a portfolio for evaluation.

ASSESS

CRITIQUING

Have students apply the steps of art criticism to their own artwork using the "Critiquing" questions on this page. In addition, ask the following: Is the issue chosen one that is of personal importance? Is it one of public importance? Do the symbols adequately represent the issue? What shape was chosen for the painting? Does it have any symbolic meaning? Was the design planned and thought out? Did the plan change during the process? If so, how?

CLOSE

Display the finished artworks. Ask each student to study the work of another student. (If necessary, assign artworks randomly). Have each student write a brief explanation of what he or she believes to be the theme of the work. Ask volunteers to read their analyses.

CULTURAL PERSPECTIVES

Enhance your students' awareness of art from other cultures by arranging "art pals." First, establish contact with an art teacher in another country whose students are the same age or level as your own. If international connections are difficult, a different part of the United States will suffice since geographical areas often represent subcultures. Have the students from both cultures initiate contact by writing, or drawing, an introduction of themselves. Throughout the semester or school year, have the students exchange artworks created for class assignments and allow time to discuss the similarities and differences between the work they send and the work they receive.

OBJECTIVE

Design and paint an imaginary creature using found
objects.

MOTIVATOR

Begin this lesson by decorating and assembling objects
in the room into temporary
works of art. Objects to be
transformed into objects d'art
could include chairs, tables,
desks, cups, pencil sharpen-
ers, and so on. Materials for
decorating could include
crepe paper, masking tape,
yarn, colored paper, art tissue, colored wire, chenille
stems, and so on. Items could
be stuffed, taped, tied, and
wrapped to produce a decorative effect.

GUIDED PRACTICE

Promoting Discussion

Students may be interested
in learning about various folk
artists in their region or state.
A folk artist is one who creates art, yet has no formal
schooling in art. Like most
artists, they are influenced by
their background and environment. Ask students to
volunteer their familiarity
with folk art and folk artists.

Critical Thinking

Ask students to explain the
difference between an artist
and a craftsperson. What
kinds of works does each
create? Then ask students to
explain the relationship between a craftsperson and
applied art.

184

STUDIO LESSON: CREATING A RAINBOW CREATURE

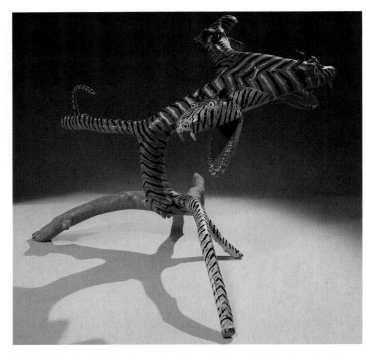

FIGURE 7.40 Miles Burkholder Carpenter. *Root Monster.* 1968. Carved and painted tree roots, rubber, metal, and string. 57.5 × 72.7 × 71.7 cm (22⅝ × 28⅝ × 28¼"). The National Museum of American Art, Washington, D.C. Gift of Herbert Waide Hemphill, Jr. and Museum purchase made possible by Ralph Cross Johnson.

Supplies
- Sketchbook, pencil, and crayons
- One large found object that will be the main body of your creature
- White glue, nontoxic rubber cement, and masking tape
- String, rubber bands, straight pins, and other joining materials
- Small found objects
- Acrylic paints, brushes

Miles Burkholder Carpenter is a folk artist; he just started carving without any training. He says, "There's something in
there under the surface of every piece of wood."

Carpenter was also an experienced lumberman. He collected
fallen branches and exposed roots, and he cut trees into thick planks
for his carvings. The wood of poplar trees, which grew near his
home in Waverly, Virginia, was his favorite because it was soft but
solid and almost grainless.

When he found the piece of root shown in Figure 7.40, his imagination quickly began working. He saw legs and the hint of a tail, so
he made rubber ears and carved separate jaws and teeth for the three
heads of his "root monster." Then he attached strings and rubber
hands so the teeth could clack when someone pulled the string.

Look at *Root Monster* for ideas. Then search for a found object that
can serve as the basis for your rainbow creature.

Bring a natural or manufactured found object to class. Transform
the object into a rainbow creature by adding to or subtracting from

MORE ABOUT . . . FOLK ARTISTRY

Art critics are sometimes divided on the issue of
applied and fine arts, and depending on where you
stand, examples of applied arts belong either in art
museums or a natural history museum. Folk art
is a further refinement of the applied arts category
and includes artworks created by artists or craftspeople untutored in concepts of design and critical
judgment. Included in this category would be objects such as shop signs, pottery, whirligigs, carvings, quilts, weathervanes, and toys. *Root Monster*
in Figure 7.40 is an excellent example of folk art
and serves as a tribute to the natural creative talent
of Miles Carpenter.

the original form. Paint your creature using the hues of the rainbow. The hues on the main body of the creature must be arranged in spectral order.

FOCUSING

Study Carpenter's *Root Monster*. Notice the humor he has added to his work by attaching the rubber ears and the clacking jaws. Brainstorm with your classmates for ideas about what kind of found objects to look for. Some natural things you might find outdoors are branches, roots, rocks, pebbles, twigs, pine needles, pinecones, feathers, and dried leaves. In addition to the buttons and plastic forks, manufactured objects might include pieces of broken furniture, bottle caps, crushed cans, beads, broken costume jewelry, broken toys, empty pill bottles, cardboard tubes, pencil stubs, hangers, and boxes of all sizes. Remember that you need one large object to serve as the body of your creature.

CREATING

Identify the found object that will serve as the main body of your rainbow creature. Study it. Make rough sketches of it in your sketchbook. Draw it from different points of view. Then make some drawings showing what you will add or carve away. Don't forget that you are working with three dimensions and you must keep turning your object as you organize your ideas. Design your arrangement of colors in your sketchbook using crayons. Try to devise a way to give your creature humor and movement. Give it a name.

Join all the parts. If you are gluing a piece that is hanging down, you can keep it from falling off by using tape to hold it in place until the glue sets. You may have to paint over the tape, so add it neatly. If you are adding parts that will move, plan them carefully so that the paint won't get in the way of the movement.

Paint your creature. Make sure that you have the colors in correct spectral order. Add yarns, silk flowers, or articles of clothing if they are appropriate.

Prepare the creature for display. Include a name card in the display.

FIGURE 7.40A   Student work.

C R I T I Q U I N G

Describe   Explain how you made the creature. Tell what found objects you used, and how you joined them together. Are there any moving parts? Explain what they do. How did you prepare your creature for display?

Analyze   Describe what you have added to or subtracted from the original form to change it. Can you recognize the original form? Describe the colors you added. How many spectral colors did you use? Did you repeat them?

Interpret   What mood does your finished creature convey? Did the final display improve the mood or take away from it?

Judge   Which aesthetic theory would you use to judge this work? Do you think this project was successful? If you wanted to improve it, what would you change?

185

Computer Option

If computers are available to your students, suggest this activity: If your software has a Symmetry tool, encourage students to use it to create an imaginary creature. The Symmetry tool provides choices: vertical, horizontal, or diagonal symmetry. Sometimes this option is called Mirrors. After they have completed a satisfactory design, instruct them to save and label it. Now choose the Bucket Flood-fill option to color the design with rainbow colors. Try rainbow Gradients or rainbow Color options. Have them use the Save As command to save and label their best work.

INDEPENDENT PRACTICE

Enrichment

Have students write a science fiction or fantasy story about the creature they designed in this lesson.

Keeping a Portfolio

Remind students that the preliminary sketches and the final artworks for this Studio Lesson are likely considerations for their portfolios.

ASSESS

CRITIQUING

Have students apply the steps of art criticism to their own artwork using the "Critiquing" questions on this page.

CLOSE

Have students display and demonstrate their rainbow creatures.

CURRICULUM CONNECTION

Social Studies   Ask students to research the folk arts and crafts of European countries and early American colonists. Ask them to notice the various European influences on colonial American folk art. Before our world became so busy and filled with technology, people had more time to devote to crafts. They also had to adapt their resources to necessary chores. In Scandinavian countries and in other colder climates throughout the world, people used their long stretches of winter time to create highly decorative functional items. Such items include beautiful rugs, tapestries, and furniture. Weather vanes, hope chests, and tools often bore elaborate designs as well.

ART CRITICISM IN ACTION

INTRODUCTION

The work of Elizabeth Murray was selected because of her use of intense hues. The comparison of her work with that of Jan van Eyck shows students that contemporary art is related to works from the past. The elements have not changed, only the way artists manipulate them.

CRITIQUING THE WORK

1. Describe This work is almost 10 feet (2.9 m) tall and almost as wide. It protrudes from the wall more than 2 feet (71 cm). It would not fit in most classrooms. The shape of the canvas represents an ordinary dress that is torn across the waist, with a gaping round hole in the middle of the waist. There is a neck opening, and the canvas is formed to make sleeve openings. The dress looks like it has a yellow apron-like center over the blue-violet dress.

2. Analyze Blue and yellow dominate, but there are reds on the edges of the yellow shapes. The yellow areas and drops are the lightest. The darkest values are in the shadows of the skirt; they look black. Drips of white and black show on the unpainted edges of the forms.

3. Interpret Answers will vary.

4. Judge The most important aesthetic theory is Formalism. Some students may see Realism in the dress form, while others may use Emotionalism to defend their opinion.

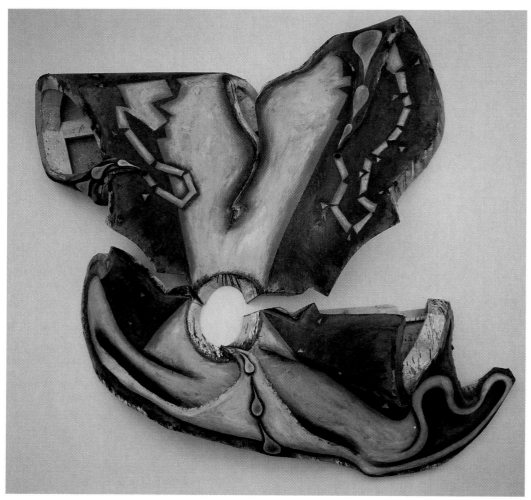

FIGURE 7.41 Elizabeth Murray. *Things to Come.* 1988. Oil on canvas. 292 × 287 × 71 cm (115 × 113 × 27″). Paula Cooper Gallery, New York, New York. Private Collection, San Francisco. California.

RESOURCES BEYOND THE CLASSROOM

Other Works By . . . Elizabeth Murray
Join
Popeye
Sail Baby

Other Works By . . . Jan van Eyck
Adoration of the Lamb

Man in a Red Turban
Giovanni Amolfini and His Bride
The Madonna of Chancellor Rolin
The Madonna with Canon van der Paele

CRITIQUING THE WORK

1. **Describe** Read the credit line under Figure 7.41. Notice the dimensions. How high is the painting? How wide? How far does it protrude from the wall? This is not a typical rectangle or oval shape. This is an abstract work in which the shape represents something. Describe what you see.

2. **Analyze** What hues do you see? Where do you find light values? Where are the dark values? Do you see any neutral colors? Are the colors predominantly of high or low intensity? Is all of the work that is visible to the viewer covered carefully with paint?

   How does the artist use space in this work? Is it easy to tell the difference between the three-dimensional areas and the dimensions? Are the shapes geometric or freeform?

3. **Interpret** Based on the clues you collected and your own personal ideas, what communication do you receive from this work? What is the mood of the work? Write a paragraph explaining your interpretation.

4. **Judge** Do you think this is a successful work? Use one or more of the aesthetic theories of art explained in Chapter 2 to defend your judgment.

COMPARING THE WORKS

Look at *Things to Come* by Elizabeth Murray (Figure 7.41) and *The Annunciation* by Jan van Eyck (Figure 7.42). At first glance, you might think there is no possible way these two works could be related. In what style is the van Eyck painted and what style did Murray use? How does van Eyck use space in his work? How does Murray use space in her work? Are there symbols in the van Eyck? Has Murray used symbols? What color scheme does each painter use? In what way does each work represent the culture of its time?

FIGURE 7.42 Jan van Eyck. *The Annunciation.* 1434–36. Oil on wood transferred to canvas. 90.2 × 34.1 cm (35⅜ × 13¾″). National Gallery of Art, Washington, D.C. Andrew W. Mellon Collection.

The style of Figure 7.42 is very realistic. Van Eyck uses perspective to depict the inside of a church. Murray seems to combine Cubism and Abstract Expressionism. Van Eyck uses accurate perspective and shading to create the illusion of three-dimensional forms. Figure 7.41 takes up real space, but in some areas Murray uses shading to create the illusion of form. The negative spaces in *Things to Come* are important.

The Annunciation is full of religious symbols such as the white dove, the white lilies, the three windows behind Mary, and wings that suggest an angel. Even the scenes on the floor tiles represent scenes from the life of Christ. Murray also uses symbols. The dress, the hole in the center, the tear drops, and the black heart are all symbols of ideas. Both artists use a primary triad color scheme. Van Eyck uses more neutral colors and darker values than does Murray; therefore, Figure 7.42 does not look as bright as Figure 7.41.

Van Eyck's work represents a culture that was still centered in religion. Murray's work represents the rapid changes in our society. Her work symbolizes a transition from traditional art toward something new for the next century.

EXTENSION

- Have students read more about Elizabeth Murray in the "Meet the Artist" feature on the following page.
- Assign *Artist's Profile* 7 in the TCR.

MORE ABOUT . . . JAN VAN EYCK

In addition to Jan van Eyck's lasting contribution to the technique of oil painting, his life and work is popular with art historians because it poses so many questions. Most art historians will agree that his most lasting contribution is the altarpiece in Ghent. What remains in controversy, however, is the inscription on the altarpiece that states the work was initiated by "Hubert van Eyck, than whom none was greater" and completed by "Jan, second in art." Verification of a brother named Hubert is inconclusive; some historians believe him to be nonexistent. The issue is complicated even further by the general agreement that the altarpiece was not the work of two artists.

- Have students complete "Building Vocabulary" and "Reviewing Art Facts."
- Assign *Application 13* and *14* in the TCR.

ANSWERS TO BUILDING VOCABULARY

1. color
2. color spectrum
3. hue
4. color wheel
5. tint
6. shade
7. intensity
8. complementary colors
9. monochromatic
10. analogous colors
11. pigments
12. binder
13. solvent
14. dyes

ANSWERS TO REVIEWING ART FACTS

1. Light waves are reflected from objects to your eyes. The light hits the retina where cells receive the color images.
2. An opposite color image that remains after viewing a shape or object.
3. Hue, value, intensity.
4. Red, orange, yellow, green, blue, violet.
5. Related to the amount of light a color reflects.
6. By adding its complementary color.
7. Monochromatic, analogous, complementary, triad, split-complementary, warm, and cool.
8. Colors located opposite each other on the color wheel. When placed side by side they seem to vibrate.
9. When the artist uses color to express feelings and ignores optical color.

188

MEET THE ARTIST

ELIZABETH MURRAY

American, b. 1940

Elizabeth Murray is an American artist who was born in Chicago in 1940 and grew up in small towns in Michigan and Illinois.

She always loved to draw, and her parents encouraged her dream of becoming an artist when she grew up. As far back as elementary school she sold drawings of elephants, cowboys, and stagecoaches to her classmates for twenty-five cents a piece. She was lucky to have a high school teacher who recognized her talent and created a scholarship for Murray at the Art Institute of Chicago. Murray blossomed in Chicago. For the first time in her life she found students her own age who liked the same things she did. She took classes in figure drawing, landscape painting, and traditional techniques. To get to her classes she had to walk through the exhibit halls of the museum of the Art Institute. The masterpieces she saw every day changed her life; they gave her the drive to become a painter.

When she was told in the 1960s that painting was dead, she refused to listen and kept painting. She developed a style that combines painting and sculpture and is now considered a master of the shaped canvas.

She says that she loves and respects traditional painting, but she is fascinated with relief—with the possibilities of two dimensions becoming three. She is always trying to devise a new way of painting and redefining the structure of things. Her work is famous because of her creative compositions and her daring adventures into unknown territory.

MORE PORTFOLIO IDEAS

Change a flat, two-dimensional shape of paper into a three-dimensional form. Use the paper sculpture techniques explained in Technique Tip 20 on page 356 in the Handbook. You may cut into the paper, but do not cut it into two pieces. Use markers to emphasize the edges of the forms where they overlap and to decorate some of the surfaces with line patterns.

Create a three-dimensional form from a sheet of paper following the directions given above. This time paint the surfaces before the final gluing. Try to create optical illusions as Murray does in her work. Shade some flat areas so they look rounded and paint some joined areas in one color so that they look flat.

188

DEVELOPING A PORTFOLIO

Self-Reflection A well-maintained art journal or sketchbook provides a permanent record of personal and creative growth. Students who routinely write about their work in a journal and use a sketchbook to practice designs have more insights into their progress. These impressions, responses, thoughts, and efforts provide students with a means of understanding how willing they are to be challenged, as well as recognizing those areas that need improvement. A regular five-minute writing exercise at the beginning or the end of each class gives students the opportunity to reflect on changes and refinements of their artistic skills.

CHAPTER 7 REVIEW

Building Vocabulary

On a separate sheet of paper, write the term that best matches each definition given below.
1. An element of art that is derived from reflected light.
2. Bands of color produced when white light passes through a prism and is broken into separate wavelengths.
3. The name of a spectral color.
4. The spectrum bent into a circle.
5. A light value of a hue.
6. A dark value of a hue.
7. The brightness or dullness of a hue.
8. The colors opposite each other on the color wheel.
9. A scheme that uses only one hue and the values, tints, and shades of that hue.
10. Colors that sit side by side on the color wheel.
11. Finely ground, colored powders that form paint when mixed with a liquid.
12. The liquid that holds together the grains of pigment.
13. The liquid that controls the thickness or thinness of the paint.
14. Pigments that dissolve in liquid.

Reviewing Art Facts

Answer the following questions using complete sentences.
1. Explain how the eye sees color.
2. What is an afterimage? Why is it always a weak color?
3. Name the three properties of color.
4. What are the colors of the spectrum? Name them in the correct order.
5. What is color value?
6. Tell how to dull, or lower the intensity of, a hue.
7. Name the seven different kinds of color schemes.
8. What are complementary colors? How do complementary colors affect each other?
9. What is arbitrary color?

Thinking Critically About Art

1. **Synthesize.** Tamayo's *Toast to the Sun* (Figure 7.26, page 169) and Carr's *Above the Trees* (Figure 7.27, page 170) use very different color schemes. Compare the two works. List the similarities and differences in their style and use of color. Look up each artist in Artists and Their Works on pages 366–370. Then explain why each work appropriately represents the climate of the country in which the artists worked.
2. **Interpret.** Look at Town's *Night Riders* (Figure 7.13, page 161). The artist has used a color scheme of dark values to create a specific mood. Study the lines and shapes in this work. Note the positive and negative spaces. Do the shapes suggest some images you can recognize? Does the title add to the mood? Based on the clues you have collected, write a brief interpretation of this painting.

Making Art Connections

1. **Social Studies.** Paul Gauguin left his family and his work in France to live on a tropical island. It was in Tahiti that he found the freedom to create great masterpieces. Research the lifestyle of a stockbroker in France in the late nineteenth century and the lifestyle of the people of Tahiti during the same time period. Why might the first lifestyle inhibit an artist, and why might the second inspire him? Report your conclusions to the class.
2. **Science.** Consult the science teacher or do some research in the library to find out the difference between mixing color with pigments and mixing the colors of light. If you have a theater department at your school, ask the teacher in charge to help you set up a demonstration of mixing light colors.

189

Texture

INTRODUCE

CHAPTER OVERVIEW

Texture is an element of art that refers to how things feel, or look as though they might feel, if touched. The viewer perceives this element of art with two senses—both sight and touch.

CHAPTER SUPPLIES

For a list of the materials you will need for the Activities in this chapter, refer to the "Art Supplies Grid" in the Teacher's Manual. In addition, have on hand the following special items: textured fabric and acetate squares.

FINE ART RESOURCES
Transparencies
- Bing Davis. *Urban Mask #8*
- Kuba peoples, Zaire. *Helmet Mask (Mashamboy)*
- Max Ernst. *The Barbarians*
- Elena Bonafonte Vidotto. *Eggs*

Fine Art Prints
- Chuck Close. *Fanny/Fingerpainting*
- Deborah Butterfield. *Woodrow*

FIGURE 8.1 This feather bonnet was created for a ceremonial dance. All of the materials used to create the bonnet, except one, came from the immediate environment, the Northwestern Plains. Do you know which one was not native to the area?

Northwestern Plains Indian. *Feather Bonnet.* c. 1890. Rooster hackles, wood rods, porcupine hair, ermine skins, horsehair, buckskin, glass beads. 84 × 68.6 cm (33 × 27″). Buffalo Bill Historical Center, Cody, Wyoming. Chandler-Pohrt Collection.

190

RESOURCES FOR CHAPTER 8

Application Activities 15, 16
Artist's Profiles 8, 18, 24, 28, 32, 42
Cooperative Learning Activities 15, 16
Cultural Diversity in Art
Enrichment Activities 15, 16

Reteaching Activities
  Study Guide 8
  Concept Map 8
Studio Lessons 10, 11, 12
Chapter 8 Test

Texture

Every surface has a texture. **Texture** is *the element of art that refers to how things feel, or look as if they might feel if touched.* No one needs to teach you about texture—you know what is rough and what is smooth. There are certain textures you enjoy touching, and there are certain surfaces you avoid because you do not like the way they feel.

Textures play an active part in many of the decisions you make about the clothes you wear. Think how often fabric textures have influenced your choices. Would you buy skintight pants made from rough burlap? Clothing manufacturers consider textures when they decide what fabrics to use. Why do you think they put silky linings inside winter coats and jackets? Which are more comfortable—prewashed jeans or stiff, scratchy new jeans?

The textures of foods influence what you eat. Think about the smoothness of ice cream, and consider how different it is from the angular roughness of potato chips. Would grilled steak taste the same if it were ground up in a blender?

Objectives

After completing this chapter, you will be able to:

- Understand how texture is perceived through the senses.
- Describe various textures.
- Reproduce textures by changing values.
- Use texture as the expressive element in creating two- and three-dimensional works of art.
- Understand how artists communicate by means of textures.

Words to Know

appliqué
collage
decalcomania
frottage
grattage
matte surface
texture
visual texture

FIRST IMPRESSIONS

Look at the headdress in Figure 8.1 on the opposite page. This feather bonnet was made to be worn during special dance ceremonies. Try to determine your reaction to the overall design before looking closely at the details. What is your evaluation of the artist's selection of textures? Look at the media listed in the credits and try to identify the materials with the roughest and the smoothest textures.

191

FOCUS

INTRODUCING THE CHAPTER

Write the following items on the board: rock, bark, cotton, silk, feather, marbles, staples, keys, and so forth. Have students classify the objects according to the way they feel.

MOTIVATOR

Have students work with partners. Give each pair of students a bag containing a scrap of material. Ask the partners to take turns feeling the material inside the bag, describing it as fully as possible, and then trying to identify it.

VOCABULARY PREVIEW

Have students preview the list of vocabulary words on this page. Also, acquaint them with these words that will appear in the chapter: simulated, invented, and trompe l'oeil.

USING FIRST IMPRESSIONS

Have students study Figure 8.1 and answer the question in the box on this page. Explain that this headdress was worn by the Native Americans of the Northwestern Plains. Have students read the credit line and identify rough textures: wood rods, porcupine hair, ermine skins; and smooth textures: glass beads and buckskin. Discuss how descriptive adjectives help us perceive texture. Answers will vary on opinions. The roughest texture is the feathers, and the smoothest texture is the buckskin. The beads are smooth individually, but as they are woven together they create a bumpy surface.

TEACHER TALK

A Success Story Audrey Komroy of Akron Central High School in Akron, New York, spends a great deal of her time organizing student art shows. At the high school, she puts on a huge art show in collaboration with the music department. Also, she arranges an art sale where all two-dimensional work is matted and judged! Because Audrey is a firm believer in raising awareness and standards of student work, she brings student work to the community through the art shows, art sales, even a show at the Albright Knox Art Gallery in November, 1993.

GUIDED PRACTICE

Promoting Discussion

To help students become aware of texture, promote a discussion about the textures of food and clothing. Have them use adjectives to describe the textures. Some possibilities include: rough, coarse, and slick.

Building Vocabulary

If possible, devote a large section of classroom wall space to a "Wall of Words." On the wall, list the elements and principles of art. As you study each chapter, put up the specific vocabulary terms listed on the chapter opening page. Especially in Chapter 8, students will encounter several unusual words that need to be reinforced as they progress through the lessons. As students discuss and critique artworks, remind them to look at the "Wall of Words" and use the terms properly in their discussions.

Interdisciplinary: Science

Challenge students to think about how much they depend upon their sense of touch. Have them make a list of ten daily activities that involve their sense of touch. Then have them describe how the touching sensation affects their activity. For example, can they identify a food they like or dislike because of its texture? Think about walking. Their sense of touch works every time they put their foot down on the ground. They don't have to look down; they feel the ground with their foot, and without thinking, they allow that foot to support all of their weight.

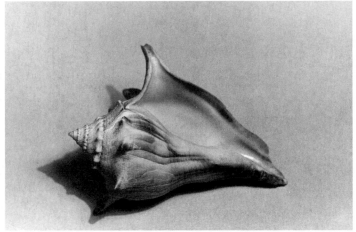

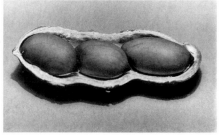

FIGURE 8.2   What textures are represented in these photographs?

ART ON A SHOESTRING

Ask students to bring in textured materials from home to complete the exercises in this chapter. You might prepare a list of suggested materials, which could include the following: aluminum foil, plastic wrap, wrapping paper, ribbons, wax paper, paper napkins, paper towels, tree bark, sandpaper, screening, styrofoam plates, paper plates, loose sand (in a bag), scrap fabrics, gum wrappers, grasses, pine straw, and so on.

How You Perceive Texture

You perceive texture with two of your senses: touch and vision. Infants learn about things by touching them and by putting them into their mouths. Toddlers, who cannot keep their hands off anything, are visually attracted to all objects within their reach. In a way you still use your sense of touch when you look at surfaces. Your eyes tell you what something would feel like if you were to touch it. (See Figure 8.2.)

When you actually touch something to determine its texture, you experience real texture. When you look at a photograph of velvet, leather, concrete, or ice, you see surface patterns of light and dark that bring back memories of how those objects actually feel. When this happens, you are experiencing **visual texture**, *the illusion of a three-dimensional surface.* If you touch visual textures, you do not feel what your eyes told you to expect.

There are two kinds of visual texture: *simulated* and *invented.* Simulated textures imitate real textures. Plastic tabletops can be made to look like wood. Some vinyl flooring is made to look like ceramic tile or stone. Manufactured fabrics imitate natural leather and fur. Figure 8.3 is an example of simulated texture in a painting.

Invented textures are two-dimensional patterns created by the repetition of lines or shapes. These textures do not represent any real surface qualities, but the patterns of light and dark stimulate your

FIGURE 8.3 Vigée-Lebrun was one of the most highly paid portrait painters of her time. She always showed her subject at his or her best. She was able to manipulate the paint to show off the rich fabrics and fine jewels of her sitter. How many different kinds of textured surfaces can you identify in this painting?

Élisabeth Vigée-Lebrun. *Self-Portrait.* c. 1781. Oil on canvas. 65 × 54 cm (25½ × 21¼"). Kimbell Art Museum, Fort Worth, Texas.

MORE ABOUT . . . ÉLISABETH VIGÉE-LEBRUN

Maria Louise Élisabeth Vigée-Lebrun (France 1755–1842) is one of history's most celebrated women artists. Before she was twenty, she had studied in a convent and had received private art lessons from colleagues of her artist father. She also painted portraits of important members of the French aristocracy. By the age of twenty-five, she was employed by Queen Marie-Antoinette, whose portrait she painted some twenty times. On the night the queen and king were arrested, Vigée-Lebrun escaped from Paris. The French Revolution did not stop her career, however. She continued to work in other European capitals and was flooded with commissions.

Creating Textures

1. Applying Your Skills.
This activity involves rubbings and designs. In the student example you can see that a variety of colored crayons were used. This works well with wax crayons, but oil pastels do not make good rubbings. You might want to limit the number of colors used, or you might wish to eliminate color and just use a pencil.

This activity also requires drawing skills. It may seem to be too demanding for some students, but it is not. Ask the students to study the rubbings for repetition of lines, dots, or small shapes. A magnifying glass can help them analyze the rubbings more easily. When the activity is finished, display the rubbings and the drawings made from them in a random manner, and then ask the students to match the drawings to the rubbings. Of course a student may not choose his or her own to match.

2. Further Challenge.
Before assigning this activity, challenge students to brainstorm a list of unusual textural surfaces.

3. Computer Option.
As an alternative computer option, give these directions: Select a Shape tool and a black line for the foreground with white or clear as the fill (background) color. Draw a series of eight to twelve shapes. Using the Bucket Flood-fill tool, fill each shape with a different pattern.

Experiment. Create your own patterns or alter existing preprogrammed ones. Which textures look rough or smooth? How does the varying amount of pixels (the individual dots used to collectively create line, thickness, shape, and color) affect perceptual changes in the invented textures?

FIGURE 8.4 In this print the artist has invented textures by attaching textured materials to the printing plate. Looking closely, you can see areas that appear to be wrinkled fabrics and paper. If you look at the work as a whole, the textures remind you of rocks and layers of earth.

Hedi Bak. *Grand Canyon #2*. 1980. Collograph print. 49.5 × 75 cm (19½ × 29½"). Private collection.

memories of actual textures. The purpose of invented texture is to create decorated surfaces that evoke memories of unusual textures (Figure 8.4).

 Creating Textures

1. Applying Your Skills. Make a collection of texture rubbings. To make a rubbing, place a sheet of thin paper against a rough surface. Hold the paper in place with one hand. Use the flat side of an unwrapped crayon or the side of a pencil lead to rub over the paper (Figure 8.5). Always rub away from the hand holding the paper. Never rub back and forth because the paper or object may slip. Examine the rubbings closely, paying special attention to the lines, dots, shapes, and values (Figure 8.6).

2. Further Challenge. Make a small dream landscape by cutting shapes of visual textures out of magazines and arranging them on a background sheet of paper. Try to get a variety of textures from different objects. Turn your imagination loose. Concentrate more on the textures than on the shapes. Look at a large photograph of a piece of chocolate cake. Consider the visual texture of a picture of dog food. What can you do with the texture of hair? Of a rug or of tree foliage (Figure 8.7)?

3. Computer Option. Use a Pencil tool, or Brush tool, or Shape tool to create several unfilled objects. Fill each object with a different preprogrammed texture from the pattern menu and, if the application you are using permits, blend the objects. Identify which objects and blends look rough to the touch and which do not (Figure 8.8).

MEETING SPECIAL NEEDS

Visually Impaired Students who are blind enjoy feeling textures and telling what it reminds them of. In addition to the usual visual stimulation material brought to the lesson by the art teacher, tactile motivational materials can supplement each lesson. For example, still-life materials need not just be looked at, they can be passed around, handled, and discussed. Also, when germane to the topic, materials which can be smelled, such as cinnamon, charred wood, and perfume, enrich lesson motivations as do audiocassettes. Multisensory materials are especially helpful for students who learn through sharing their personal responses and who learn through their senses.

FIGURE 8.5 Rub the surface with the flat side of the crayon.

FIGURE 8.6 Student work. A page full of texture rubbings.

FIGURE 8.7 Student work.

FIGURE 8.8 Student work. Textures done on a computer.

Developing Studio Skills

It may seem unnecessary to include a photograph of a rubbing, but most students do not know how to achieve a clear rubbing. Most of them rub the crayon back and forth across the surface of the paper, and sometimes this succeeds. More often, rubbing back and forth moves the paper and ruins the rubbing. Students do not need any special dexterity, so they should not be afraid to change hands during the procedure. Refer students to the photograph and review the procedure for rubbings.

Developing Perceptual Skills

Have students assemble the rubbings made in the Activity on page 194 or make new rubbings if they wish to have more. Instruct them to assemble the rubbings and make a collage.

Art Is Everywhere

To foster students' awareness of texture as sound in everyday life, suggest this: Listen to the textures of a variety of musical instruments. Often they imitate the human voice. The legendary jazz musician Louis Armstrong had a deep gravelly voice. He made his trumpet imitate his voice by using a mute placed into the bell of the trumpet. Skilled violinists create a vibrato, a textural sound much different from the slender sound of the violin. Cellos have a mellow texture. Oboes sound like satin. Listen to each instrument of an orchestra and think of a texture simile for it.

ART ON A SHOESTRING

One way to save time in the art classroom is to work smaller. Another way is to divide responsibilities. When assigning an exercise in which students are asked to show one design using various textures, for example, you can save time by dividing the class into groups. You can then assign one texture to each group, put all the finished works on display, and ask the students to discuss the similarities and differences. When multiple choices are called for in an exercise, assign only one, or divide the class and assign a different problem to each group. Students could have the opportunity to work on the remaining choices as extra credit or enrichment.

GUIDED PRACTICE
(continued)

Promoting Discussion

It is important to help students realize that textures may have more than one characteristic. For example, rough and smooth can be either matte or shiny. Sandpaper and aluminum foil are good examples. Pull a piece of foil out of a box. It is smooth. Crinkle it up. It is still shiny but it is no longer smooth. Ask students to share other examples.

Developing Studio Skills

Have students bring to class various small objects with different textures. Have them glue these objects to a large sheet of tag board. After you and your students have assembled a wide range of objects, shine a light on the anchored objects and have students draw the different textures. Move the source of light and repeat the activity as many times as you can.

Sparking Creativity

Want students to think creatively about textured surfaces? Suggest this: Make a texture collage that a blind person can enjoy. Find fabric, papers, yarn and twine, sandpaper, and mesh. Think about cutting shapes that will lead the fingers on a path through your design. Glue fabrics into folds. Test your design as you work by feeling without looking. Make it a pleasant "trip" with your fingers. Think about making a texture book with each page offering a new experience. Find a braille typewriter and have someone write your message or story in braille. Punch holes and sew your pages together.

FIGURE 8.9 Even though you can't touch the real texture, your eyes recognize the irregular patterns of light and dark. As a result, you can guess what this surface would feel like.

FIGURE 8.10 These apples reflect light evenly. The shadows you see are caused by the spherical forms.

TEXTURE AND VALUE

The look of a surface depends on the manner in which it reflects light. Every surface is an arrangement of light and dark values.

Rough and Smooth Textures

The roughness or smoothness of a texture can be determined by looking at the shadows. A rough surface reflects light unevenly (Figure 8.9). Rough textures show irregular patterns of light and shadow. Look at a shag rug, an orange, tree bark, or a patch of bare ground. Notice how the high places catch the light, creating shadows of different sizes and shapes.

A smooth texture reflects light evenly (Figure 8.10). Look at a sheet of paper, an apple, or a new,

FIGURE 8.11 The soft, white, downy fiber of the cotton plant has been lit with bright light, but you see no highlights. Even though the fibers are not smoothly arranged, they reflect light evenly. The cotton has a matte surface.

CULTURAL PERSPECTIVES

Fabric, like paint, has texture, and no fabric matches the smooth, rich quality of silk. Chinese legend says that the Goddess of Silk is Lie Zu (Lady Xiling), the wife of the mythical Yellow Emperor (ca. 3000 B.C.). It was believed that she was responsible for the discovery of silk, the rearing of silkworms, and the invention of the loom. Archae-ologists unearthed a small ivory cup carved with a silkworm design, thought to be between 6000 and 7000 years old. From other archeological sites along the Yangtze River, researchers have uncovered items such as spinning tools, silk threads, and fabric fragments that are even older than the ivory cup.

FIGURE 8.12 The irregular pattern of dark and light tells you that this rock is far from smooth, but the streaks, or white highlights, tell you that this surface is also shiny.

unmarked desktop. Your eyes glide across these objects, uninterrupted by shadows, just as your fingers would glide across them, uninterrupted by bumps and dents.

Matte and Shiny Textures

A **matte surface** is *a surface that reflects a soft, dull light*. It absorbs some light and reflects the rest. Matte surfaces, such as paper, denim, unfinished wood, and your skin, have a soft, dull look (Figure 8.11).

A shiny surface is the opposite of a matte surface. A shiny surface reflects so much bright light that it seems to glow (Figure 8.12). Shiny surfaces also have highlights. Some surfaces reflect bright sunlight with such intensity that you have to squint your eyes. Window glass is shiny; so is a new car, a polished brass candlestick, and the surface of a calm pool of water.

Matte and shiny surfaces can be rough or smooth. Sandpaper is matte rough, and a freshly ironed pillowcase is matte smooth. Aluminum foil is shiny and smooth until it gets crumpled up; then it becomes shiny and rough.

ACTIVITY Creating Contrasting Textures

1. Applying Your Skills. Make a series of small drawings and paintings of objects that have different textures. Try to reproduce both smooth and rough textures (See Figure 8.13, page 198). You may use a different medium for each drawing. Study the lights and shadows on each object before you choose the medium. For example, you might examine a hairbrush, an old work shoe, weathered wood, a wig, a fuzzy slipper, or a satin slip, then select a medium for each texture.

2. Further Challenge. Make a texture collage on a small piece of heavy paper or cardboard by pasting various two-dimensional materials onto the surface. Place contrasting textures next to each other to make an interesting design (Figure 8.14 on page 198).

3. Computer Option. Draw the texture collage from the preceding activity using the Pencil or Brush tool on the computer. First, sketch your shapes; then copy the texture of each shape using dots, lines, and value blending. Concentrate on the shadows, lights, and highlights of each different texture.

GUIDED PRACTICE
(continued)

ACTIVITY Creating Contrasting Textures

1. Applying Your Skills. This activity is a perception drawing problem and does not require students to focus on the composition. Instead, students can concentrate on rendering various textured surfaces one at a time.

2. Further Challenge. This activity requires students to organize textured surfaces into a collage. It is important that students consider the other elements while they arrange the texture. They need shapes that vary in size, and they need to limit colors so that the color does not detract from the texture. At the same time, they must consider lines, shapes, and color as they organize the total design.

3. Computer Option. Students who wish to continue this activity at another level might try this: Choose the Rectangular shape tool and a Fill pattern you have altered, created, or have available to you. Fill either half or the whole page with the chosen pattern. Use one color and a variety of invented patterns. Print several sheets. More textured papers can be created as needed, either printing from the computer or making additional copies on a copy machine. On a stiff piece of construction paper or cardboard, sketch a simple still life, landscape, or imaginary animal. Cut out the shapes from your textured papers and glue them onto the sketch using a glue stick or other adhesive that won't stretch and wrinkle the computer paper. After all the shapes have been collaged with texture, use colored pens, pencils, or inks to add shadows, shading, and highlights.

COOPERATIVE LEARNING

Divide the class into two groups. Have one group work together to identify objects around their classroom and school that effectively represent textures with a matte texture. Ask them to identify words that describe the texture. Ask the other group to locate objects that effectively represent a shiny texture. Have them also develop a list of terms that describe the shiny texture. Ask students to compare their lists of adjectives and find works of art in this text that use the different types of textures.

GUIDED PRACTICE

Exploring Aesthetics

Remind students that they were first acquainted with Janet Fish's work in Chapter 1. Have them keep a finger in this page while they find Figure 1.2 on page 7. Ask: How does the texture in *Fallen Vase* compare with the texture in *Jonathan and Lorraine?* Do they notice any consistency of style in regards to texture? If so, how would they describe her style. If not, what is the difference between them?

Sparking Creativity

Want students to think creatively about painting tools? Suggest this: You can get interesting textures of paint by using different tools. Experiment with tempera paint, acrylic, and watercolor to see how many textures you can achieve. Use soft wash brushes and stiff bristle brushes. Try brushing, stippling, and twisting them as you paint. Work with both wet and dry brushes, using very little water. Use a twig or a palette knife or the edge of a piece of cardboard to apply your paint. Cut lines through wet paint. Use your fingers as van Gogh often did. Lay threads into the paint. See what a sponge can do. Start with an exciting blend of colors. Try painting on many different textures of paper or on fabric, even burlap.

FIGURE 8.13   This artist likes to be referred to as a perceptual realist. Notice how she captures the image of light reflecting from various surfaces. What is the difference between the way she paints the light on Jonathan's arm and the light on the red vase? Study the way she has used paint to make the yellow platter, the red vase, the green pitcher, and the transparent red bowl all look different.

Janet Fish. *Jonathan and Lorraine.* 1988. Oil on canvas. 163 × 185 cm (64 × 72¾"). Grace Borgenicht Gallery, New York, New York.

FIGURE 8.14   Student work. A texture collage.

MORE ABOUT . . . TEXTURE

Two senses—vision and touch—are responsive to the sensation of texture. Point out to students that careful observation of detail, through whatever means available to them, is the hallmark of any successful artist. They can work at improving their perceptual powers—and in doing so, improve their abilities to draw and paint—by examining under magnification any objects whose surfaces give different textural "readings" to the eyes and fingers. As an example, display samples of fabrics that appear coarse but are, in fact, quite smooth. Ask a local fabric merchant or a parent who is familiar with fabrics to help you.

How artists use texture

The texture of surfaces is important to every form of visual art. Our minds are full of texture memories. Artists use both visual and real textures to make you remember those texture experiences.

The artist Pierre Auguste Renoir (ren-**wahr**) painted young people with healthy, glowing complexions (Figure 8.15). Another artist, Ivan Albright, was concerned with the wrinkles of old age (Figure 8.16, page 200). In their works, both of these artists have imitated human skin. In one the skin is appealing; in the other it is repulsive

because of the excessive attention to detail. Both artists try to control your reactions to the people in the paintings through the use of visual texture.

In the past many painters reproduced the color and value patterns of textures. Look, for instance, at the paintings by Judith Leyster (Figure 3.20, page 54) or Rembrandt van Rijn (ryne) (Figure 12.5, page 317). These artists were experts at suggesting textures such as soft velvet, shiny satin, delicate lace, and fluffy feathers. When you look closely at their paintings, you discover that these artists do not paint every texture in photographic detail. They use a few brushstrokes to suggest the texture from a certain distance.

FIGURE 8.15 Renoir started his career as an artist in a porcelain factory. His job was to copy famous portraits of beautiful women onto the porcelain plates. Renoir spent the rest of his life painting beautiful people. Notice how he uses his brushstrokes to create texture.

Pierre Auguste Renoir. *Madame Henriot.* 1876. Oil on canvas. 66 × 50 cm (26 × 19⅞"). National Gallery of Art, Washington, D.C. Gift of Adele R. Levy Fund, Inc.

MORE ABOUT . . . PIERRE AUGUSTE RENOIR

Pierre Auguste Renoir was born in 1841. His artistic talents became apparent early. By the age of 13, he was already making a living as an artist in a porcelain factory. His job was painting scenes on pieces of china. His earnings helped pay for his education at a Paris art school, the Ecole des Beaux-Arts. It was at school that Renoir met two other

young artists, Claude Monet and Alfred Sisley. The three soon became friends and began experimenting together by making paintings outdoors in natural sunlight. Their goal was to give objects a shimmering, sunlit quality. At first, their works were scorned by critics. Today they are among the most admired in the history of art.

GUIDED PRACTICE
(continued)

LOOKING
CLOSELY

Have students study Figure 8.16 and encourage them to notice carefully the textures in the artwork. Responses will vary as students identify different objects or areas to discuss. As it is an independent thinking problem, encourage each student to use precise vocabulary terms from this chapter and the preceding ones as well.

Exploring Aesthetics

Remind students that when looking at the works of Albright and van Gogh, they should remember that photographs and reproductions can never duplicate the experience of seeing the originals. The aesthetic quality of these works is largely dependent on the thick, rich textures of paint that can never be fully appreciated until seen in the original.

Developing Studio Skills

If cost is not a problem, give students some thick acrylic paints to manipulate. There is a satisfaction in working with thick paints that cannot be realized just by looking at two-dimensional reproductions.

Developing Perceptual Skills

All of Albright's paintings have the same quality of age and decay. He renders them by using minute details that take a long time to complete. Have students refer to the credit line and notice that the work took over two years to complete. Instruct them to study the work with a magnifying glass.

Ivan Albright. *The Farmer's Kitchen*. 1933–34. Oil on canvas. 91.5 × 76.5 cm (36 × 30″). National Museum of American Art, Smithsonian Institution, Washington, D.C.

LOOKING
CLOSELY

FIGURE 8.16 Ivan Albright's painting contains many textured surfaces—too many to take in with a casual glance. Find an object or small area that intrigues you. Look closely at the surface pattern you see. Try to determine how the artist gave that area its unique texture. Analyze the technique he used to produce the visual quality you see and experiment with that technique in your sketchbook.

FIGURE 8.17 At times van Gogh became so impatient with the progress of his work that he squeezed the paint directly from the tube onto the canvas. Then he used anything that was handy, including his fingers, to move and swirl the globs of paint around.

Vincent van Gogh. *Landscape at Saint-Rémy (Enclosed Field with Peasant)*. 1889. Oil on canvas. 73.6 × 92 cm (29 × 36¼″). © 1993, Indianapolis Museum of Art, Indianapolis, Indiana. Gift of Mrs. James W. Fesler in memory of Daniel W. and Elizabeth C. Marmon.

SAFETY NOTE

It has been suggested that the paint chemicals from Vincent van Gogh's hands may have found their way into his body and injured his health. Oil paints contain cadmium, chrome, lead, and numerous other metal compounds, which are harmful if they get into one's internal organs. Artists and hobbyists need to be aware of the dangers in the materials and processes they use and to read carefully and heed warning labels. Wear gloves or wash hands as soon as possible after exposure to potentially harmful solvents and chemicals.

FIGURE 8.18 Schapiro invented the word *Femmage* to describe her collages. Rather than scraps of discarded paper, she used pieces of embroidered, appliquéd, and crocheted fabrics, that were created by women, to add real textures to her work. In this way she connected her work to the traditional women's arts of the past.

Miriam Schapiro. *Yard Sale.* 1993. Acrylic and fabric on canvas. 208 × 228 cm (82 × 90″). Courtesy of the Steinbaum Krauss Gallery, New York, New York.

The *trompe-l'oeil* (French for "fool the eye") painters were masters of visual texture. See Figure 6.13 on page 127. All of the objects were depicted in sharp focus with great care. Every color and value pattern of every surface was copied exactly. In these works the appearance of the objects is so realistic that, for a moment, you think you can touch what you see.

Many painters add real textures to their paintings. Vincent van Gogh (goh) used such thick paint on his canvas that his swirling brushstrokes created a rough surface (Figure 8.17). The surface ridges of the thick paint actually make the paint look brighter. The ridges catch more light and reflect brighter colors to the viewer.

Some painters add real textures to their work by attaching various materials to the work's surface. Some artists add sand and other materials to the paint. In some cases, artists create what is called a **collage** (kul-**lahzh**), in which *bits and pieces of textured paper and fabric have been pasted onto a painting.* Folk artists have used this technique for centuries. Miriam Schapiro added bits of fabric, lace, and thread to her paintings to enrich the surfaces (Figure 8.18).

Architects use a variety of materials to create interesting surfaces in buildings. You can find stucco, brick, wood, stone, concrete, metal, and glass in modern buildings (Figure 8.19). Interior designers select textures for rugs, drapes, furniture, pottery, and sculpture that complement different wall textures (Figure 8.20 on page 202).

FIGURE 8.19 The colors, forms, and textures of this building were planned so that Taliesin West would blend into the colors, forms, and textures of its desert setting. Wright believed that a building should be in harmony with its environment.

Frank Lloyd Wright. *Taliesin West.* Near Phoenix, Arizona.

MORE ABOUT . . . TROMPE-L'OEIL

Skilled artists who master the technique of trompe-l'oeil can make a viewer believe that a two-dimensional object is real. During the Classical age in Greece, famous painters amused themselves, and others, with the technique. According to legend, Giotto di Bondone (ca. 1267–1337) slyly painted a fly on the nose of a subject in a painting that his master, Cimabue, was working on. The image was so real that Cimabue tried several times to brush the fly away from the painting, not realizing he was the victim of a practical joke.

GUIDED PRACTICE
(continued)

Critical Thinking

Call students' attention to the caption of Figure 8.18 that explains the origins of Schapiro's invented word *Femmage.* Ask them to think about a new word that would describe their personal interests. Additionally, what would they include to add real texture to a collage designed to call attention to their interests in the way Schapiro uses fabrics created by women?

Promoting Discussion

Have students read the credit line for Figure 8.18. Have volunteers mark off the size of the canvas so that students will have a better sense of the painting's dimensions. Ask them to guess the sizes of some of the textured fabric in the artwork.

Understanding Art History

Tell students that the following quotation is credited to Frank Lloyd Wright: "No house should ever be *on* any hill or *on* anything. It should be *of* the hill, belonging to it, so hill and house could live together, each one happier for the other." Ask students to volunteer their evaluation of his quotation and the building they see in Figure 8.19. Ask: In your opinion, has Wright designed *Taliesin West* to be *of* the hill? In what way(s) are the hill and house interrelated?

Encourage students to find other examples of Wright's architecture and apply the same questions to them. To start, have them look again at *The David Wright House* (Figure 3.30 on page 62) then look ahead to *Falling Water House* in Figure 12.21 on page 330.

LOOKING
C L O S E L Y

Have students study Figure 8.20 and answer the questions in the caption. Encourage them to notice how Hoover uses smoothly curving lines and rounded shapes. The lines flow from one shape to the other.

Interdisciplinary: Language Arts

Allow students to work in pairs or small groups and write an imaginative history of the wood carving shown in Figure 8.20. Encourage them to use any literary form they wish: prose, poetry, or drama.

Exploring Aesthetics

Point out that like most Native American artists, the Aleuts used whatever materials happened to be at hand to create their art. Have students first find other materials commonly used by this cultural group, then design a chart listing some of these materials and the types of objects or artworks most often made from the materials.

Interdisciplinary: Language Arts

Have students imagine that they have just become best friends with someone who has been blind since birth, and they want to share their visual world with this person. To do so they must talk about how things feel, their textures, and describe how the objects look. Have them describe clouds, blue sky, the first light of dawn, or the glow of sunset.

John Hoover. *Loon Song*. 1990. Cedar and natural pigments. 152 × 61 cm (60 × 24″). Glenn Green Galleries, Scottsdale, Arizona.

LOOKING
C L O S E L Y

FIGURE 8.20   John Hoover is an Aleut sculptor. He uses the folklore of his people as subject matter, but he has developed a style that is not traditional. Notice how he lets the texture of the cedar wood show through the paint. He uses only natural pigments. Can you identify the colors? What kinds of lines and forms did he use to give texture to the work? How does he use the elements of art to link the human heads and the loons? Do you see the hinges? This work can be closed like a box. If it were closed, you would see a symbolic design on the back.

CURRICULUM CONNECTION

Geography   On a geographic or topographical map of Asia and North America, have students locate the Aleutian Islands. Ask them to trace the most logical path early migrating tribes would have taken across the Bering Strait into present-day Alaska. Ask them to speculate about what cultural influences would have remained, especially in the arts. After studying John Hoover's work, above, do they see any familiar use of the elements of art that might suggest an ancient influence? Encourage them to learn more about the geographical conditions of the Northwest Coast region that have an impact on daily life in this area.

Sculptors must be aware of texture as they work because the texture of each surface must fit the whole. Some sculptors imitate the real texture of skin, hair, and cloth, while others create new textures to fit new forms (Figure 8.21).

Weavers control texture through the use of fibers and weaving techniques (Figure 8.22). Potters change textures by pressing different objects into wet clay. They can also change surfaces by applying glazes. Some glazes are shiny, and others have matte finishes (Figure 8.23). Feathers, river

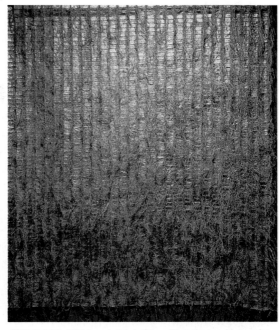

FIGURE 8.22 Which materials in this wall hanging would never be used by a traditional weaver who was creating cloth to be made into clothing?

Olga de Amaral. *Alquimia XIII*. 1984. Woven hanging. Cotton, linen, rice paper, gesso, paint, and gold leaf. 180 × 75 cm (71 × 29½"). The Metropolitan Museum of Art, New York, New York. Gift of Olga and Jim Amaral, 1987.

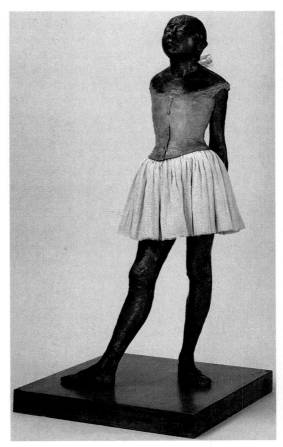

FIGURE 8.21 What an unusual combination of textures! The figure of the young dancer is cast in bronze. Even the vest and the ballet shoes she wears are bronze. To that Degas added a skirt made of gauzelike fabric and a satin hair ribbon. Why do you think he added real textures to the metal figure?

Edgar Degas. *Little Fourteen-Year-Old Dancer*. 1880, cast 1922. Bronze, cotton skirt, satin ribbon. 104.5 cm (41½") high. The Metropolitan Museum of Art, New York, New York. Havemeyer Collection, bequest of Mrs. H. O. Havemeyer, 1929.

FIGURE 8.23 To create the shiny surface, Tafoya rubs his clay with a smooth river rock before it is fired. After he has planned his design, he gently carves away the areas where he wants a matte surface. The turquoise is added after the work is fired.

Juan Tafoya of San Ildefonso Pueblo. *Seed Pot*. 1992. Black-on-black pottery with turquoise. 8.9 x 7 x 7 cm (3½ × 2¾ × 2¾"). Private collection.

CULTURAL PERSPECTIVES

Invite students to explore the ways texture is used by artists from different cultures. They can accomplish this task by researching the following topics: Native American pottery and blankets, Spanish lace, African sculpture, and Japanese woodcuts. Have them compare the similarities and differences and the effects that texture has on artworks from different cultures. Encourage students to record their findings, along with original pencil illustrations, in an art journal or sketchbook.

GUIDED PRACTICE
(continued)

Promoting Discussion

Have students form small discussion groups and consider this issue: What techniques have the artists used to emphasize texture in the four artworks shown on these two pages. Since all are three-dimensional works, what special considerations, if any, should critics and art collectors make regarding the success of the artworks?

Understanding Art History

Have students research what subject matter Degas typically painted. List the results on the board. Then discuss how an art historian might use this information.

Art Is Everywhere

To foster students' awareness of the texture of sculpting media, suggest this: Textures in sculpture come from the medium and the tools the sculptor uses. Stone is chipped off and leaves a rough granular surface that can be polished smooth. Because wood is cut with gouges, a sculptor often will leave a surface of smooth grooves. Clay is shaped with fingers or tools and will take any shape that is pressed into it. Ancient Sumerians wrote in soft slabs of clay, pressing their cuneiform shapes into it with small wedges. Copper sheets can be hammered into three-dimensional forms with every hammer stroke making a texture. Bronze sculptures are cast from molds made of clay or wax. Compare examples of sculpture materials that you find in your environment.

GUIDED PRACTICE
(continued)

Inventing Textures

1. Applying Your Skills. Words written in cursive and repeated over and over, line after line, make very interesting invented textures.

2. Further Challenge. This activity is a little expensive, but well worth the result. The students place large lumps of thin, creamy paint on the white paper. Then they place the transparent acetate over the paint. This way they can see the colors as they pull them around under the acetate. This gives the student some control over the colors. It is best to have a partner when pulling the two surfaces apart. One person pulls the top surface and the other holds down the bottom surface so that the paint textures aren't damaged. Then both people hold all four corners of the work while placing it on a piece of heavy paper or a thick layer of newspapers to dry.

3. Computer Option. As an alternative activity, use these instructions: Explore the tools and menus on your software program to create visual textures or patterns. Use a gradient or pattern as the Brush to draw images with varying textures or values. Select Shape tools, automatically filled with pattern. Create your own patterns and use them. Draw empty shapes and fill them using the Bucket Flood-fill tool. Explore the Spray Can or Airbrush tool; if available, alter the settings. Add shading, shadows, and highlights. If your application allows, create your own gradients. Flood-fill large portions of the screen with pattern and then draw into the area with an eraser, changing size if possible. Save your results for future reference or collages.

rocks, seashells, seeds, bones, and teeth have been used to make jewelry and hair ornaments (Figure 8.24).

Today, the true textures of paint, stone, and fibers are more important to some artists. They feel that the media contribute textural qualities that enhance the work. Some painters brush on paint and do not try to smooth out the brushstrokes (Figure 8.25).

Painters and printmakers invent textures to enrich their works. Max Ernst used three unusual techniques—*frottage*, *grattage*, and *decalcomania*—to create his fantasies. In **frottage** (froh-**tahzh**), Ernst placed *freshly painted canvas right-side-up over a raised texture and scraped across the surface of the paint*. The paint that remained created a pattern that was an image of the texture below. The texture rubbings you made earlier in this chapter are another form of frottage. To create **grattage** (grah-**tahzh**) effects, Ernst *scratched into wet paint with a variety of tools, such as forks, razors, and combs*. Finally, Ernst squeezed wet blobs of paint between two canvas surfaces and then pulled the canvases apart (Figure 8.26). In this technique, called **decalcomania**, *paint is forced into random textured patterns*. Using the random patterns as a basis, Ernst elaborated on the design. The patterns inspired him to create fantasy landscapes (Figure 8.27, page 206). The textures created with these techniques contributed to the surface interest and created varied patterns and values to the work.

Inventing Textures

1. Applying Your Skills. On a small piece of white paper, draw nine shapes of different sizes with a pencil or felt-tip pen. Have some shapes touch the edges of the paper. Fill each shape with sketches of a different texture. The textures should be invented. For instance, you could put lines of writing close together in one shape, or you could try repeating small shapes in another. Try line patterns, stippling, or smooth shadow.

2. Further Challenge. Experiment with decalcomania by using two different surfaces: white drawing paper and small squares of acetate. Place large lumps of thick, creamy paint on the white paper. Then place the transparent acetate over the paint. Work with a partner to pull the two pieces apart. One person pulls the top surface while the other holds down the bottom surface so the paint textures are not damaged. Then both people lift the work, holding all four corners, and place it on a heavy piece of paper or thick stack of newspapers to dry.

3. Computer Option. Use the Pencil or Brush tool to create three shapes. Select a preprogrammed texture from the pattern menu to fill the first shape. Repeat with the second shape, selecting a different texture. Invent a texture for the third shape, giving it a three-dimensional look.

FIGURE 8.24 The forest Indians of Ecuador use brilliant, tropical bird feathers to create ornaments. These ornaments were created to decorate ears and hair.

South American Indian. *Featherwork Ornaments.* Collected in 1938 by E. Erskine. National Museum of the American Indian, Smithsonian Institution, Heye Foundation, New York, New York.

MEETING SPECIAL NEEDS

Learning Disabled Students with mental retardation who may be in the scribbling stage usually enjoy creating pictorial texture through frottage, grattage, and decalcomania. Teachers should be mindful that, in all likelihood, they will have to provide the link between two steps. First, have students experiment with textures and techniques for the sake of the experience and skill alone. Second, use the result of their practice in a creative activity. For example, having scraped with a comb into green paint to create a grass-like effect one day, during the next class meeting students could cut this up to use in their landscape representations.

FIGURE 8.25 Joan Mitchell remained an Abstract Expressionist throughout her entire painting career. This work refers to the snow and cold of her Chicago childhood. Notice how she uses the brushstrokes to show the excitement and tension of a snowy day in the city. What kinds of lines do you find in the brushstrokes?

Joan Mitchell. *Dirty Snow.* 1980. Oil on canvas. 220 × 180 cm (86¼ × 70⅞"). National Museum of Women in the Arts, Washington, D.C. Gift of Wallace and Wilhelmina Holladay.

FIGURE 8.26 Decalcomania technique.

AT THE MUSEUM

Country Music Hall of Fame and Museum (Nashville, Tennessee)   Explore the history, personalities, and styles of America's musical heritage at the Country Music Hall of Fame and Museum with a guided, hands-on tour. Play traditional stringed instruments, look like a country music star by trying on costumes worn on the Grand Ole Opry stage, and view legendary music stars on rare vintage films. Also, visit RCA's Studio B where you can learn how musicians, engineers, and producers create the music we hear on the radio.

GUIDED PRACTICE
(continued)

Understanding Art History

Tell students about Jackson Pollack, an American painter who is popular for his technique of spattering paint on a large canvas. The technique results in unusual colors, shapes, and textures which blend to make a successful work. If possible, show examples of his work. Students could try this technique by spatter-painting the bottom of differently sized boxes.

INDEPENDENT PRACTICE

Study Guide

Distribute and have students complete *Study Guide 8* in the Reteaching booklet.

Keeping a Sketchbook

Have students work in pairs, each student taking a turn identifying a specific textual quality while the other person sketches an object that exhibits that quality.

Enrichment

- Assign *Enrichment 15* and *16* in the TCR.
- Have students photograph, sketch, or write notes about different kinds of textures, both natural and manufactured. Ask them to save their photographs, sketches, or notes to use as references for future artworks.

Extension

Have students interview an interior designer to learn more about the role of texture in design.

Studio Lessons

To expand students' familiarity with the concept of texture, Studio Lessons are available in the TCR.

Fantasy Landscape

FOCUS

OBJECTIVE

Create a fantasy painting using Max Ernst's techniques to produce textured areas.

MOTIVATOR

Have students offer suggestions of various objects that might be included in a fantasy landscape. If possible, ask them to identify sketches in their sketchbook that might be used in this activity.

Students may enjoy practicing the three techniques of frottage, grattage, and decalcomania. Set up three stations in the room, one for each technique. Allow students to move from station to station to practice each technique. Students should carry the same piece of paper from each station to the next so they will have a sample of each technique.

TEACH

GUIDED PRACTICE

Developing Studio Skills

In adding cut-out objects to the collage, it is important to stress skill in cutting. Also indicate to students that the shape of the object must fit into the work. Students should not cut out a rough shape and glue it down without considering the area on which it is to be placed. Any details being painted or glued onto the textured background must be planned so that the shapes relate to the background. If needed, students could blend the shapes into the background by painting over the edges.

206

STUDIO LESSON: FANTASY LANDSCAPE

FIGURE 8.27   Max Ernst. *The Eye of Silence.* 1943–44. Oil on canvas. 108 × 141 cm (42½ × 55½"). Washington University Gallery of Art, St. Louis, Missouri.

Supplies

- Acrylic paints and assorted brushes
- One sheet of heavy paper or canvas
- Scratch paper for practice
- Wax paper
- Scratching and rubbing tools such as combs or rulers
- Magazine clippings
- Scissors and white glue

Max Ernst was among the artists, philosophers, and writers who formed the Surrealist movement in the mid-1920s. Surrealists searched for a new reality—one that rejected the long-established rules of composition and logic. They believed that this reality could be found in the subconscious mind, and they created paintings that took on the look of dreams or nightmares. Salvador Dali (Figure 3.28, page 60) and René Magritte (Figure 6.46, page 148) were members of this movement.

Ernst used three unusual techniques—*frottage, grattage,* and *decalcomania*—to bring his fantasies to life. Ernst then elaborated on the design. Sometimes he cut the textured pieces into forms with which he created collages. Sometimes he painted over areas such as the sky in *The Eye of Silence* (Figure 8.27).

206

MORE ABOUT . . . DADA

After World War I, Max Ernst joined with several other artists and writers to form the Dada movement. This group was angry about the terrible destruction that the war had brought, and they believed that the civilized world was destroying itself. Writers created nonsense poetry by cutting individual words from printed pages and dropping the words onto a sheet of paper. The Dadaists tried to shock the public into awareness. The word *Dada* is the French word meaning "hobby horse." It was chosen as the name of the group because it made no sense. Because of the rebellious nature of this group, the movement did not last long.

Create a fantasy painting using Max Ernst's techniques to produce textured areas. You may cut and rearrange the textured area to make new shapes. Add details and contrasting shapes using paint, oil pastels, markers, and collage. The work should be unified. One object must blend into the next without empty spaces separating them. When you are finished, the work must look like a Surrealist's dream.

FOCUSING

Study Ernst's painting (Figure 8.27). Notice that the woman's face has been cut from another picture and pasted on. Notice also how the realistic sky has been painted up to the edges of the textured areas. Can you guess which shapes have been cut and attached to the surface of the canvas? Can you tell where he has brushed on paint and where he has used decalcomania, frottage, or grattage?

CREATING

Using scratch paper, experiment with Ernst's three techniques. For decalcomania, try placing translucent wax paper over the blobs of paint so that you can see the way the paint moves as you gently push the colors around. With a little practice you can control the shapes and the blending of colors. Don't let the paint dry before you separate the sheets of paper. You will need a partner to hold the bottom paper down while you quickly pull the top paper off the surface.

Apply blobs of color to your large sheet of paper. Place the second painting surface over the first and use gentle pressure to push the paints around. Then pull the surfaces apart quickly. Rub or scratch the wet surfaces if you wish. Let the paint dry. Save both surfaces.

Study the textured shapes you have made and let them give you ideas for your fantasy picture. Do you see land or animal forms among the shapes and textures? Do you want to cut up one of the surfaces and glue it on the other? Do you need to paint out some parts?

Release your imagination. Add details using paint, oil pastels, markers, and collage. If you glue on shapes cut from magazine pictures, you may need to paint over the edges of the added shapes with a color that unifies them with the background.

Mount or mat your finished copy for display.

FIGURE 8.27A Student work.

C R I T I Q U I N G

Describe Identify the subjects of the fantasy scene you created. List and explain the techniques you used to create visual textures in your fantasy scene.

Analyze How did the visual textures affect the look of your work? Did you attach any textured shapes or magazine cutouts? What color scheme did you use? How did it affect the work? Are the shapes predominantly geometric or free-form? How does that affect the look of the work?

Interpret What kind of mood does your work express? Give it a title that sums up your feelings about the meaning of this work.

Judge Which aesthetic theories would be the most important in judging this work? Do you think your work is successful? If you were to do it over, is there anything you would change to improve it?

207

GUIDED PRACTICE
(continued)

Developing Perceptual Skills
While viewing reproductions as closely as described in the "Focusing" step of the directions, students may need magnifying glasses to look for details. In students' designs, there may be a need for separation in some areas of the composition to create a sense of depth. Other techniques such as size, color, and overlapping of shapes can create the illusion of depth.

INDEPENDENT PRACTICE

Keeping a Portfolio
Remind students that the preliminary sketches and the final artworks for this Studio Lesson are likely considerations for their portfolios. Encourage them to label their work, evaluate the process, and make any notes that will help them make meaningful choices when they prepare a portfolio for evaluation.

ASSESS

CRITIQUING
Have students apply the steps of art criticism to their own artwork using the "Critiquing" questions on this page. In addition, ask the following: What influenced your decision about the subject of the fantasy? Was it a choice based on rebellion, or was it a decision based on a strong feeling? Was one technique for creating texture preferred over another?

CLOSE
Have each student respond to this question: How is texture used in his or her fantasy landscape?

TEACHER TALK

Classroom Management In an art classroom, open shelves stocked with storage containers remind students that there is logic in storing supplies neatly. Coffee cans, large ice cream containers, shoe boxes, wooden or plastic crates, and so on, are available from sources within the community. The open shelves remind students that someone has to clean up. Consequently, clutter is less likely to build up. A closed cupboard or closet door tempts students to hide away a mess in hopes that someone else will take care of the routine maintenance.

Assemblage

FIGURE 8.28 James Hampton. *The Throne of the Third Heaven of the Nations' Millennium General Assembly.* c. 1950–64. Aluminum and gold foil over wood furniture, plastic, paper, and glass. 3.2 × 8.2 × 4.2 m (10½ × 27 × 14'). National Museum of American Art, Washington, D.C.

FOCUS

OBJECTIVE

Design and create a throne with a theme by assembling and joining found objects. If space, materials, and time do not allow students to create life-sized thrones, miniatures or models will successfully meet the objectives of this lesson.

MOTIVATOR

Ask students to bring in examples of art and craft objects made by friends and family members. Ask them to find out if there are any artists in their family's history.

TEACH

GUIDED PRACTICE

**Understanding
Art History**

Some visionary artists claim to have visions that tell them what and why to create. For example, in North Georgia, the Rev. Howard Finster has created a beautiful and fantastic garden composed of what most people would call junk. He also paints visions and messages from God. Eddie Martin, also known as St. EOM, built and painted colorful walls, sculptures, and architectural pieces in his yard. Italian tile setter Simon Rodia used ceramic tile, broken glass, dishes, and other found objects to create the Watts Towers in Los Angeles. Students may want to research and study other visionary artists. Ask students to speculate about the sources of inspiration for these artists. Are they driven by an inner purpose?

208

Supplies
- Sketchbook and pencils
- Materials that will serve as a base for the throne
- Found objects such as boxes, tubes, lightbulbs, and small spice jars
- White glue, nontoxic rubber cement, masking tape, duct tape
- String, rope, wire
- Scissors and utility knife
- Aluminum foil, foil wrapping paper, sequins

208

Vases, lightbulbs, jelly glasses, and used furniture may seem like unusual art media to you, but not to James Hampton. These are a few of the objects he used to create his unique assemblage (Figure 8.28).

Hampton, a soft-spoken African-American, was born in 1909 in a small South Carolina community. Around 1950 he rented an unheated, poorly lit garage near the boarding house where he lived. By November 4, 1964, the day he died, Hampton had built in that garage *The Throne of the Third Heaven of the Nations' Millennium General Assembly,* a collection of 180 glittering objects.

Hampton believed that God and his angels regularly visited him in the garage to direct him in creating *The Throne.* Each night, upon returning from his janitorial job around midnight, Hampton would work on the project for five or six hours. Although Hampton never studied art, he had a natural sense of design. Notice how the throne at the center of the rear line of objects serves as the heart of the assemblage. Bordering both sides of the throne are matching pairs of objects. He used old furniture and discarded objects, such as cardboard tubes and insulation board, to construct the major pieces. He joined the pieces with strips of cardboard or metal cut from coffee cans. Glass vases, lightbulbs, and jelly glasses completed the tops and corners of objects. Upholstery tacks, small nails, and straight pins held everything together. Finally, all of the objects were covered with recycled foil of various colors. Some of his foil came from store displays, some from gift wrap, and some was ordinary aluminum foil.

After Hampton's death, the massive construction was moved to the National Museum of American Art in Washington, D.C.

MORE ABOUT . . . *THE THRONE*

James Hampton used his imagination to collect and transform the discarded materials he used to construct *The Throne.* All of the objects in the throne are covered with different kinds of gold and aluminum foils. In addition to wooden furniture, Hampton used layers of insulation board and hollow cardboard tubes from rolls of carpeting, jelly glasses and light bulbs covered with foil, while construction paper and cardboard are the foundations for decorative forms such as stars and wings. The edges of tables are sometimes trimmed with tubes of electrical cable camouflaged with gold foil. Rows of small knobs are made of balls of crumpled foil or newspaper covered with foil.

Design and create a small throne with a theme by assembling and joining found materials. Working individually or in small groups, symmetrically join the found materials to make a chairlike structure. Then, as James Hampton did, alter the look of the work by changing the surface texture: cover the entire structure with foil and foil wrapping paper.

FOCUSING

Brainstorm with classmates for themes for your throne. Think of school subjects such as math, science, or history. Think of activities you do after school and create a skating throne, movie throne, auto throne, food throne, or music throne. Let your imaginations loose and come up with outer-space themes, underwater themes, or time-period themes. How about a throne for your favorite hero? Decide on a theme for your group.

CREATING

Working in a small group, design a chair-shaped object that will serve as the base for your throne. Collect small discarded objects and pieces of heavy cardboard that can be used to construct and decorate the throne.

Each person should look at the objects collected and make sketches of his or her ideas for the throne structure and the decorations that will go on it. Then, as a group, study all the sketches and select the best ideas. Each member of the group should make one final drawing of the combined ideas.

Join your found objects, organizing them symmetrically. If necessary, cut shapes out of heavy cardboard. Before you cover the finished work with foil, decorate the surfaces with rope and wire, buttons, and layers of cardboard to create raised surfaces and various textures. Be sure everything is joined securely. You may even add words or phrases with raised block letters or rope that imitates cursive writing.

Change the surface by covering everything with shiny foil. You may glue paper-backed foil to smooth surfaces, or press aluminum foil

FIGURE 8.28A   Student work.

tightly to irregular surfaces. Some aluminum foil may be left smooth, and some may be crumpled up. Sequins and other shiny objects can be attached with pins or glue. Give your throne a poetic title.

C R I T I Q U I N G

Describe   Describe the way you constructed the basic form of the throne. Name the theme. Identify the objects and shapes you attached to the main form and explain how they represented the theme.

Analyze   What kinds of materials did you use to create your throne? Did you use symmetry to organize your decorative objects? How did the addition of shiny foil change the surface quality of the structure?

Interpret   Can your classmates recognize the theme? Did your group find a poetic title that reflects the theme?

Judge   Which aesthetic theories would you use to judge this work? Do you think your throne is successful? If you were going to do it over, what would you change?

209

MORE ABOUT . . . ASSEMBLAGE ART

The roots of assemblage art were established during the first decade of the twentieth century. Dadaists and Cubists had profound effects on assemblage art fifty years later when it was defined and recognized as its own genre. While it may at first seem nonsensical, assemblage sculpture is a natural medium for affecting an audience. Using common objects that have not been designed for artistic purposes, the artist effectively bridges the gap between the viewer's world and the artistic world. When the viewer sees an everyday object in the context of art, he or she is forced to consider its place in the artwork and in society.

FOCUS

OBJECTIVE

Design and create a three-dimensional, freestanding, imaginary paper creature using a variety of strong papers. Alternative media might include feathers, foil paper, ribbons, yarn, sequins, glitter, mylar, or papers with contrasting colors on each side.

MOTIVATOR

Distribute photos and prints of various animals and creatures for students to study. Ask students to choose a creature, then describe it to the class without revealing it's identity. They should describe both its behavioral and physical characteristics. The rest of the class should try to guess what type of creature is being described.

TEACH

GUIDED PRACTICE

Exploring Aesthetics

Remind students that many Mexican towns are famous for producing a certain type of art or craft, such as pottery, jewelry, glassware, hand-woven clothing, and handbags. Also, Mexico is famous for the magnificent murals that adorn its city's buildings. Mexican painters often express the pride of the Mexican people by rendering images of traditional folklore, daily life, and political history. Encourage students to study other arts and crafts of Mexico, as well as other artists such as Frida Kahlo, Diego Rivera, and José Clemente Orozco.

FIGURE 8.29   Artist unknown. Mexico. *Bird*. 1988. Tin and gold paint. 28 × 22 × 17.8 cm (11 × 8½ × 7").
Private collection.

Supplies

- Sketchbook and pencil
- Colored construction paper
- Variety of other papers to decorate the surface, such as wallpaper samples, shiny wrapping papers, and paper ribbons
- Scissors, ruler, and sharp knife
- Pointed tool for piercing, such as compass point
- Transparent tape, white glue, straight pins
- Cardboard tubes and containers for internal support

Visit Mexico and you can see beautiful traditional tinwork pieces such as frames, lanterns, sconces, candleholders, chandeliers, crosses, and trinket boxes. Using flat sheets of tin, craftspeople cut, score, and pierce the tin to form three-dimensional works of art that are used to decorate their homes and churches.

This bird was made by a craftsperson in Mexico just a few years ago. However, the techniques used by the artist are the same as the tinwork processes that have been used in Mexico for more than two hundred years. The decorative processes used by the tinsmiths are part of a long tradition of surface decoration practices developed in Spain and brought to Mexico by the Spaniards.

These surface decorations, which produce highly textured real and visual effects, are made by using processes of cutting, piercing, stamping, scoring, and soldering. Another method of joining, tab-and-slot construction, is also used.

As you study the tin bird in Figure 8.29, you can see how the artist used these processes to create a three-dimensional form. Many

MEETING SPECIAL NEEDS

Physically Disabled   Punching designs through tin with a hammer and nails can be a very satisfying experience for many students with disabilities, especially those with neurological or orthopedic handicaps and those with behavioral disorders. Though the noise could be a problem, the sheer physicality and manual challenge of the hammering and the resistance of the materials are very satisfying. Some teachers freeze a soda can full of water to make a hard surface into which students pound nails. Another easy hammering exercise is pounding large nails into molded styrofoam packing forms, a project which can be related to African nail fetish figures.

of these same processes are used to create forms with paper sculpture.

The back has been scored and is bent into a curve. The textural effects of the feathers have been created by layers of fringe that have been curled. Notice the contrast obtained by using fringes of different lengths. The fringes on the head and around the eyes are short. The wing areas have short and long fringes. The longest fringes are cut from a long strip and shaped into a spiral to create the round tail. The breast of the bird is decorated with oval shapes that have been applied to the form in a repeated, overlapping pattern.

Try to use many forms of decoration to give your paper sculpture varied textures. Design a creature that is interesting from every point of view.

After studying the photo of the Mexican bird and practicing paper sculpture techniques, design and create a three-dimensional, freestanding, imaginary paper creature using a variety of strong papers. Cover the surface with a variety of interesting textures using fringing, cutting, curling, and scoring. This sculpture should look interesting from every point of view.

FOCUSING

Study the paper sculpture techniques on page 356 in the Handbook. Practice them all using construction paper. Study the tin bird to see what techniques you think were used to construct that sculpture.

CREATING

Make several sketches in your sketchbook to plan the sculpture you will make. Select your best design. Make some sketches showing different views of the sculpture. List the materials and techniques you will use to construct your three-dimensional creature and those you will use to create surface textures.

Collect the materials you will need. Construct your sculpture based on the drawings you have made. You may change your plan as

FIGURE 8.29A Student work.

you go along. If your creature is too heavy and does not stand up, support it on the inside with cardboard tubes and containers.

Place the finished sculpture on a firm base for display. Glue or pin it to the base.

C R I T I Q U I N G

Describe List the materials and paper-sculpture techniques you used to create your sculpture. Did the practice session with paper-sculpture techniques help you in planning your final project? How did you prepare it for display?

Analyze What form did you create for your sculpture? Describe the different textures you created. Is the work interesting from every point of view?

Interpret What kind of mood or idea does your finished sculpture express? Give your work a title that expresses the mood.

Judge Have you created a freestanding, three-dimensional, fantasy creature? Is your work successful? Is there anything you would change to make the work more successful? Which aesthetic view would be best to judge this work?

211

If computers are available to your students, suggest this activity: Use paper sculpture techniques to create a three-dimensional box using sturdy paper or cardboard. Each of the six sides should measure 6 × 6" (15.2 × 15.2 cm). Next, you will create a square motif on the computer that can be printed six times and applied to the cube to observe the changes in a design motif when it is transferred from a two-dimensional to a three-dimensional form.

INDEPENDENT PRACTICE

Keeping a Portfolio

Remind students that the preliminary sketches and the final artworks for this Studio Lesson are likely considerations for their portfolios.

ASSESS

CRITIQUING

Have students apply the steps of art criticism to their own artwork using the "Critiquing" questions on this page. In addition, ask the following: What types of papers and materials were used? Were various textures and patterns created? How?

CLOSE

Have each student display his or her paper sculpture creature from all sides.

CULTURAL PERSPECTIVES

The ancient cultures in West Mexico did not demonstrate the trademark architectural achievements or stone sculpting skills of the Aztecs. However, they established a remarkable artistic culture that shows its influence on Mexico's contemporary art, such as the tin bird shown in Figure 8.29. Ancient artists presented humans and animals in typical situations, not as gods or supreme spiritual powers as the Mayans often did. These animals sing, hug, and play instruments and are most often found depicted in a natural, plump state.

Stitchery and Appliqué

FOCUS

OBJECTIVE

Design and create an appliqué work selecting an ordinary object from your early life as the subject matter.

MOTIVATOR

Ask students to bring in any Japanese artifacts or collectibles from home that have examples of appliqué or stitchery on them. Suggestions are dolls, kimonos, or smoking jackets. Ask the students to share any stories associated with their items. Next, discuss the design of each piece.

TEACH

GUIDED PRACTICE

Understanding Art History

Students may be interested in learning more about how art forms recorded the day-to-day lifestyles of the Japanese family prior to World War II. They may want to investigate any changes in traditions caused by the war.

Developing Studio Skills

When stitching, an embroidery hoop might be helpful for keeping the fabric flat. The hoop can also be used as a practical frame for a round design. Use a backing fabric such as burlap on the finished appliqué to give the piece more body. Layering pieces of fabric by stitching will be easier if completed before the backing is attached.

212

STUDIO LESSON: STITCHERY AND APPLIQUÉ

FIGURE 8.30 Ayako Miyawaki. *The Red Crab*. 1981. Fabric and thread. 29.5 × 57.5 cm (11¾ × 22⅝″). The future Toyota Municipal Museum of Art, Aichi, Japan.

Supplies

- Sketchbook and pencil
- One large piece of fabric for the background
- Variety of scraps for appliqué
- Embroidery threads, yarns, and other fibers
- Pins, needles, tapestry needles, and a pincushion
- Sharp fabric scissors
- Envelope for storing cut pieces
- Dowel or other straight rod for hanging

SAFETY NOTE

Use a pincushion or a container to hold your pins as you remove them from the work. Never put them in your mouth.

212

Many Japanese kimonos and banners are decorated using appliqué. **Appliqué** is *an art form in which cutout decorations are fastened to a larger surface to create a new design.* This technique enables the artist to use an assortment of fabrics with varying textures to create contrast and emphasis in the design.

Ayako Miyawaki is a Japanese artist who uses appliqué. She began her work after World War II. Having no formal art training, she created her own designs and modeled them after objects she observed in her everyday life—objects such as fish, fruit, vegetables, and flowers (Figure 8.30).

Miyawaki has a unique style, cutting her fabrics freely without patterns and applying them boldly, creating the effect of bright splashes of pigment on canvas. She collects brightly colored fabrics and those decorated with Japanese designs. Sometimes she stitches the fabrics to the background as she has done in this work, and sometimes she uses glue to hold her pieces in place. She also uses fibers and threads as lines in her compositions.

Design and create an appliqué work selecting an ordinary object from your daily life as subject matter. Starting with a large piece of fabric for the background, cut and apply a variety of contrasting fabrics, using different fibers and stitches. Emphasize the elements of color and texture for contrast.

ART ON A SHOESTRING

When planning for Studio Lessons such as the Stitchery and Appliqué on these pages, a teacher needs to collect fabric scraps from local seamstresses and teachers who sew before beginning this project. Another method of obtaining interesting, even special, material samples is to encourage students to bring in a scrap of fabric from a favorite piece of clothing or an old worn blanket. Also, ask students who have other means of access to fabrics and fibers to bring in extra material to share with the class.

212

FOCUSING

Study Miyawaki's appliqué *The Red Crab*. Notice the contrasts of the complementary red and green colors. Observe the contrast between the smoother weave of the crab fabric and the rougher weave in the background. Can you find where the artist created line using only thread?

CREATING

Collect and bring to class fabric scraps that have a variety of textures and colors and fibers such as sewing threads, yarns, dried grasses, and pieces of thin rope.

Study the fabrics using your imagination. What ordinary, everyday objects do the fabrics and the patterns on the fabrics suggest to you? Discuss your ideas with classmates. Give each other suggestions.

Select the fabrics you will use to make the objects. Then select a large piece for the background that will provide a contrast in color and texture.

Plan your composition before you start cutting. Make notes and sketches in your sketchbook. Cut a sample of each fabric you will use and tape it to the page, noting how it will be used. If your background shape is some variation of a rectangle, your work will be easy to hang, but you may choose another shape.

Cut all the pieces you will need before you do any stitching. Keep all your cut fabrics in an envelope so they won't get lost before you begin sewing. Arrange and rearrange the cut pieces on the background until the composition looks right to you. Pin your final composition to the background.

Study the embroidery stitches in the Handbook on page 357. Practice on extra scraps if necessary. Use a variety of stitches to appliqué your fabrics to the background. Stitch your signature or initials on your finished work.

Turn the edges of your background fabric under at least 1/4 inch (6 mm) and sew them down using a running stitch or a hemstitch.

FIGURE 8.30A Student work.

Add loops to the top of your fabric so that it can be hung on a dowel rod, or invent some other way to display your work. Give your work a creative title.

C R I T I Q U I N G

Describe Tell what subject matter you selected for your appliqué and explain why. Did you tape fabric swatches in your sketchbook and make notes explaining how they were to be used? What kinds of stitches did you use to attach your fabrics? Did you use fibers as an addition to your design or were they just used to attach fabrics?

Analyze Describe the contrasting colors and textures you used in the work. Did the printed designs on your fabric help you think of objects to make?

Interpret Is your subject matter obvious or is it hard to recognize? What is the mood of your work? Does the title you gave your appliqué enhance the feeling of the work?

Judge Which aesthetic theories would you use to judge this work? Are you satisfied with your finished product? If you were going to redo it, what would you change?

213

INTRODUCTION

Tell students that Sandy Skoglund is a twentieth-century artist who works in an unusual mix of media. In this feature, students will be applying the steps of art criticism to her photograph *The Green House*. Next, they will be asked to compare this contemporary artwork to *Daniel in the Lions' Den*.

CRITIQUING THE WORK

1. Describe Students should realize that Skoglund created the entire setting for *The Green House*. The dogs are modeled from clay, fired, then painted. The furniture was collected then covered with artificial grass and painted. The floor, walls, and ceiling are also covered with grass. Anything not covered with grass has been painted a matte green. The only color that is not artificial is the skin and hair of the people. The size in the credit line refers to the size of the photo; the setting is life-size, since people fit into it.

2. Analyze Texture is the dominating factor in the work, but students should note that most surface texture is unnatural. Students should be aware of the strong contrast between the unnatural cool color scheme of blue and green and the warm skin tones of the people. The forms of the subjects are realistic; most are free-form while a few are geometric.

3. Interpret Most likely, students will tie meaning to the "greenhouse" effect.

4. Judge Answers will vary.

214

ART CRITICISM IN ACTION

FIGURE 8.31 Sandy Skoglund. *The Green House*. 1990. Cibachrome photograph. 127 × 178 cm (50 × 70″). Skoglund Art Gallery, New York, New York.

CRITIQUING THE WORK

1. Describe Study the photograph *The Green House* by Sandy Skoglund (Figure 8.31). Describe exactly what you see in this work.

2. Analyze What kind of color scheme was used by the artist? Notice the color of the people. How did she use texture? Did she use real or visual textures? Did Skoglund reproduce textures as she saw them or did she invent her own? Locate and describe rough, smooth, matte textured surfaces. Do you see different degrees of texture?

3. Interpret When the artist created *The Green House*, she selected various elements and positioned them in unusual ways. Does the photograph convey a mood, feeling, or idea to you? How did Skoglund use texture to enhance her work? How does the color of the people affect your interpretation of the work? Write a paragraph explaining your interpretation. Then write a new title for the work. Your title should sum up your interpretation.

214

RESOURCES BEYOND THE CLASSROOM

Other Works By . . . Sandy Skoglund
Radioactive Cats
Revenge of the Goldfish

Other Works By . . . Peter Paul Rubens
Lion

The Raising of the Cross
The Assumption of the Virgin
Hélène Fourment with Two of her Children
Descent from the Cross
The Elevation of the Cross
Marchesa Brigida Spinola-Doria

FIGURE 8.32 Peter Paul Rubens. *Daniel in the Lions' Den.* c. 1615. Oil on linen. 224.3 × 330.4 cm (88¼ × 130⅛"). National Gallery of Art, Washington, D.C. Ailsa Mellon Bruce Fund.

4. Judge Do you think this is a successful work of art? Use one of the theories of art explained in Chapter 2 to defend your answer.

COMPARING THE WORKS

Look at *The Green House* (Figure 8.31) and *Daniel in the Lions' Den* by Peter Paul Rubens (Figure 8.32). Identify the similarities and differences between the two works. What idea is communicated in *The Green House*? Is a similar idea conveyed by the painting *Daniel in the Lions' Den*? How does each artist use animals in communicating the idea or message to the viewer? How does each use texture? Decide which artwork you find more interesting and share your reaction in a class discussion.

FYI This painting by Rubens hung for many years in the boardroom of an English business firm. People assumed it was only a copy of a work by the master. When it was finally purchased by an art lover who had admired it for years, the painting was authenticated as being a lost original by Rubens himself.

215

Although the two works of Rubens and Skoglund were created 375 years apart using different media and styles, they are both dependent on the element of texture as it is related to subject matter for meaning. Skoglund uses texture to shock. The texture in her work is part of the meaning of the piece. Rubens imitates real textures in his painting. He uses imitated textures to convince the viewer that this story from the *Old Testament* was true.

EXTENSION

- Suggest this Computer Option as an alternative for "More Portfolio Ideas" on page 216: Draw a still life or landscape using the Pencil, Brush, and Shape tools. Add a "surprise" element— an object that normally would not appear in the composition. This form or shape should be selected and repeated using the Resizing and Turn, Flip, or Rotate tools. Choose a monochromatic color scheme, a hue (color) plus tints and shades, and the Bucket Flood-fill tool to add color. Consider gradients and thoughtful placement of colors to create a sense of depth. Think about how the intensity or value of a color affects its appearance. Fill in all the areas and shapes except the "surprise" element. Select a different monochromatic color scheme for filling in the "surprise" elements. Try adding shading and shadows with the Airbrush, Spray Can, or Gradient tools. How is your work similar or different from Skoglund's work?

MORE ABOUT . . . PETER PAUL RUBENS

Of all the European artists of the seventeenth century, Peter Paul Rubens most completely captured the exciting spirit and rich effects of the Baroque style. While still a young man, he spent eight years in Italy. There he came to know sixteenth-century Italian painting and the works of Caravaggio. When he returned to his native Antwerp, he set up a studio that soon became the busiest in Europe. Assisted by many helpers, Rubens turned out portraits, religious pictures, and mythical scenes. He also gained fame as a diplomat and as a man of learning.

ANSWERS TO BUILDING VOCABULARY

1. texture
2. visual texture
3. matte surface
4. collage
5. frottage
6. grattage
7. decalcomania

ANSWERS TO REVIEWING ART FACTS

1. Touch and vision.
2. When you actually touch something you are experiencing real texture. When you look at a photograph of textures and remember how they feel, you are experiencing visual texture.
3. Simulated textures imitate real textures. Invented textures do not represent any real surface qualities but stimulate memories of real textures.
4. Rough, smooth, matte, and shiny.
5. The manner in which it reflects light.
6. The shadows or values.
7. Rough.
8. Smooth.

*M*EET THE ARTIST

SANDY SKOGLUND
American, b. 1946

Sandy Skoglund is a contemporary American artist who works in an unusual mix of media. She builds installations, working with found materials and strangely colored animal sculptures. Her installations often are intricate reproductions of everyday environments, like a lawn or a living room, being overrun by nature in the form of brightly colored animals. She does the photography of these works herself, and the prints she produces are considered as much a part of the work as the installation itself.

Each installation Skoglund creates takes an average of six months to complete. She constructs the environment using found materials, and she hand sculpts the animals that appear in her work. Each is like a movie set that is then painted in a single color and filled with objects to create a fantastic and absurd scenario. Each conveys a symbolic message. The title of *The Green House* provides a clue to the message of this work. Just as the man and woman in the photograph seem unaware that they are literally living in a green house and are surrounded by blue and green dogs, many people are unaware of their own relationship to nature. The title also suggests the dangers that man can create for nature. The "greenhouse effect" is a global warming created by pollution. The artist may be pointing out that the modern technologies that cause pollution are out of control, and many people, like those in the picture, do not notice or care.

MORE PORTFOLIO IDEAS

Create a tabletop model of a staged environment that juxtaposes unexpected objects. Plan a theme and title for the scene. Using a large carton open at the front, bring found objects in to fill the "room" and carry out the theme. Select a compatible color scheme and photograph the finished project.

Write a poem or story from the point of view of the dog on the mantle in Skoglund's photograph.

Create a still life or landscape using variations from an all-blue palette to create depth and interest. To begin, draw several objects with closed paths, including a large rectangle to serve as a backdrop. Move and resize the foreground objects to create a visually pleasing design.

DEVELOPING A PORTFOLIO

Self-Reflection   The success of a portfolio as a indication of a student's artistic competency is enhanced by the continual awareness of the process of personal development. Students who are encouraged to reflect often on the stages of growth of their work are less mystified by the process of learning. Their education, then, is not limited to the class period; they become active participants in their growth. Ask them frequently to evaluate their personal development. For example: How do you measure the success of your artwork? What have you learned about art that helps your talent grow? What have you learned about yourself as an artist? What new areas do you wish to explore?

CHAPTER 8 REVIEW

Building Vocabulary

On a separate sheet of paper, write the term that best matches each definition given below.
1. The element of art that refers to how things feel, or look as if they might feel if touched.
2. The illusion of a three-dimensional surface.
3. A surface that reflects a soft, dull light.
4. An artwork onto which bits and pieces of textured paper and fabric have been pasted.
5. A method of producing textures by rubbing crayon over paper placed over a rough-textured surface, or scraping across a freshly painted canvas that has been placed over a similar surface.
6. The technique of scratching into wet paint with a variety of tools to create texture.
7. A technique of creating random texture patterns by applying thick paint to two surfaces, pressing them together, and then pulling them apart.

Reviewing Art Facts

Answer the following questions using complete sentences.
1. With what senses is texture perceived?
2. What is the difference between real and visual texture?
3. What is the difference between simulated and invented texture?
4. Name the four types of textures.
5. What determines how a surface looks?
6. How can the roughness or smoothness of a texture be determined?
7. What kind of a surface reflects light unevenly?
8. What kind of texture reflects light evenly?

Thinking Critically About Art

1. **Describe.** Look at the photographs in Figure 8.2 on page 192. Describe three of these photographs without naming any of the objects in them. Describe only the lines, shapes, spaces, values, and textures in the photographs. From your description have classmates guess the photograph you are describing.
2. **Analyze.** Which kinds of visual textures are shown in Figure 8.4 on page 194? Which surfaces in this print appear to be rough? Which appear to be smooth?
3. **Analyze.** How would you describe the different surface textures in Figure 8.17 on page 200? How were the different effects created?
4. **Compare and contrast.** Compare the ways Vigée-Lebrun (Figure 8.3, page 193), Renoir (Figure 8.15, page 199), and Albright (Figure 8.16, page 200) have used texture in the representation of women's clothes.
5. **Compare.** Compare the texture in Figure 3.32 (page 64) and Figure 8.17 (page 200). What purpose does it serve in each?

Making Art Connections

1. **Music.** Hedi Bak created many textures in *Grand Canyon #2* (Figure 8.4, page 194) that resemble the walls of the gorge in northern Arizona. Listen to a recording of Ferde Grofé's *Grand Canyon Suite*. Does the music convey the magnitude of the Grand Canyon? Can you detect any *audible* color or texture?
2. **Literature.** Rubens's painting *Daniel in the Lions' Den* (Figure 8.32, page 215) illustrates a biblical story. Read this story for a deeper understanding of the relationship shown between Daniel and the lions. Write your own version of this story.
3. **Technology.** At about the same time Edgar Degas was completing *Little Fourteen-Year-Old Dancer* (Figure 8.21, page 203), three developments in electricity were taking place. Research the incandescent lightbulb, steam power for generating electricity, or electric streetcars and share your findings with the class.

EVALUATE

- Have students complete the *Chapter 8 Test* in the TCR.
- Alternative Assessment teaching strategies are provided below or in the Testing Program and Alternative Assessment booklet.

RETEACHING

- Have students complete *Concept Map 8* in the Reteaching booklet.
- Have students collect three examples of each of the four types of textures: rough, smooth, matte, and shiny. Have them cut out a small shape from each example and organize the shapes into four groups. Glue the shapes on a small sheet of paper and label each group properly.

ENRICHMENT

- Point out to students that the artist Picasso was an innovator of the twentieth century. Although students may not think a collage seems very unique today, Picasso was the first artist to use collage as fine art. Have students research how many firsts can be attributed to Picasso.
- Have students layer various colors of paper by gluing them at the edges, one on top of another. Next, students can cut shapes through the layers of paper by using a hobby knife. This will reveal the colors below. This activity can be kept simple or developed into a complex design similar to the molas of South America.

ALTERNATIVE ASSESSMENT

In Chapter 8, students learned that many artists used the collage technique to create exciting and innovative textures in their artworks. Have students research the use of collage and write a three-page paper about the technique. Instruct them to include an analysis of one unfamiliar collage they discovered in their research. In writing their analyses, they should include the four-step process of description, analysis, interpretation, and judgment. Remind them to include a copy of the collage that is the subject of their papers. In small groups, have them discuss their collages as well as their research techniques.

CLOSE

Have students open their textbooks and randomly select an artwork. Encourage them to describe how texture is used in the artwork.

THE PRINCIPLES OF DESIGN

UNIT OVERVIEW

Unit 3 completes this course by focusing on the principles of design. These principles are guidelines by which artists organize the elements for specific effects.

Chapter 9 introduces students to the five types of rhythms and how they are used to add a sense of movement to artworks. In Chapter 10, students learn why balance is important in art and how visual weight is created. Chapter 11 focuses on the principle of proportion. Students learn about the Golden Mean, the two kinds of visual scale, and human proportions. Chapter 12 explains how artists use variety, emphasis, and harmony to express ideas and feelings. Also in this chapter, students appreciate that the elements and principles are not isolated characteristics that exist in an artistic vacuum. Rather, it is the interplay between the elements of art and the principles of design that makes an artwork unified.

UNIT PLANNING GUIDE

The following chart shows the number of class periods suggested for each chapter.

	9 wks.	18 wks.	36 wks.
Ch. 9	—	8	18
Ch. 10	—	7	19
Ch. 11	—	9	20
Ch. 12	—	11	25

Miriam Schapiro. *Master of Ceremonies.* (Detail.) 1985. Acrylic and fabric on canvas. 228.6 × 365.7 cm (90 × 144"). Courtesy Steinbaum Krauss Gallery, New York, New York.

218

RESOURCES FOR UNIT 3

Unit 3 Test
ArtTalk Fine Art Transparency
• Edward Hopper. *Two on the Aisle*

ArtTalk Fine Art Print
• Frederic S. Remington. *A Dash for the Timber*

UNIT 3

$\mathcal{T}$HE PRINCIPLES OF DESIGN

CHAPTER 9
Rhythm and Movement

CHAPTER 10
Balance

CHAPTER 11
Proportion

CHAPTER 12
Variety, Emphasis, Harmony, and Unity

Putting art together is the purpose for learning the principles of design. In this unit of *ArtTalk* you will learn about the principles of design. They are *rhythm, balance, proportion, variety, emphasis, harmony,* and *unity.*

Understanding the principles of design will help you understand how art objects are organized. It will also help you create successful works of your own. You will learn to recognize each principle in your natural environment and in works of art. You will then see how artists use a principle

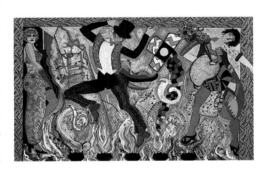

to express their feelings and ideas. At the same time, you will work to develop a skillful use of that principle in your own art.

As you did with the elements in Unit 2, you will learn one principle at a time. At the end of each chapter you will add this new principle to your accumulated knowledge of elements and principles. After completing Chapter 12, you will have all the "words" and "grammar" you need to speak the language of art. You will be able to communicate your own artistic ideas in creative and exciting ways.

219

219

Rhythm and Movement

CHAPTER OVERVIEW

Chapter 9 calls students' attention to the presence of rhythm around them. It helps them see that visual rhythm is a part of their environment. They learn that rhythm and repetition are interrelated and that there are five different types of rhythm. Finally, they learn that artists use rhythm to create a sensation of movement in artworks.

CHAPTER SUPPLIES

For a list of the materials you will need for the Activities in this chapter, refer to the "Art Supplies Grid" in the Teacher's Manual. In addition, have on hand fabric scraps.

FINE ART RESOURCES

Transparencies
- Agnes Tait. *Skating in Central Park*
- Paul Gauguin. *Still Life With Three Puppies*
- Rosalind Ragans. *Firebirds*

Fine Art Print
- Miriam Schapiro. *Master of Ceremonies*

FIGURE 9.1 The woman who made this story cloth currently lives in Providence, Rhode Island. Her people fought beside the Americans during the Vietnam conflict. This picture tells the story of her flight from Laos, across the Mekong River, to an American refugee camp in Thailand. The story starts in the upper right corner. Can you follow her as she moves toward safety?

Chaing Xiong. *Hmong Story Cloth*. 1987. Pieced and embroidered polyester, cotton blend. 140.3 × 145.4 cm (55¼ × 57¼"). Wadsworth Atheneum, Hartford, Connecticut. Florence Paull Berger Fund.

220

RESOURCES FOR CHAPTER 9

Application Activities 17, 18
Artist's Profiles 9, 20
Cooperative Learning Activities 17, 18
Cultural Diversity in Art
Enrichment Activities 17, 18

Reteaching Activities
  Study Guide 9
  Concept Map 9
Studio Lessons 13, 14, 15
Chapter 9 Test

Rhythm and Movement

Rhythm is a hand-clapping, toe-tapping musical beat. Rhythm is the throb of bass notes booming out of stereo speakers. It is the steady strumming on a guitar.

Rhythm is the synchronization of a marching band and a drill team making snappy moves.

Rhythm is the flashing lights and wailing sounds of fire engines.

Rhythm is the coming and going of the moon.

Rhythm is the steady beating of a heart.

Rhythm is tempo.

Rhythm is beat.

Life is full of rhythmic events. People crave the dependable rhythms of life. Rhythms are comforting. There is a rhythmic cycle to the seasons. Spring always follows winter, and when it comes, people feel like celebrating. When you go to bed at night, you expect the next day. You are sure the earth will turn, the sun will rise, and day will follow night. The rhythmic routines of daily living give your life a sense of stability and security.

Objectives

After completing this chapter, you will be able to:

- Identify rhythms occurring in the world around you.
- Understand how rhythm adds a sense of movement to a work of art.
- Identify and explain motif and pattern.
- Name and identify the types of rhythm.
- Use the principle of rhythm to create your own works.

Words to Know

kinetic
module
motif
movement
pattern
rhythm
visual rhythm

FIRST IMPRESSIONS

Look at Figure 9.1 and read the caption. To tell this story the artist uses many different kinds of rhythmic repetition. Can you find the steady beat of a regular rhythm? Can you find objects that are repeated in a random manner? Can you find a flowing rhythm that moves your eye through the picture? Can you find the repetitions of the family, starting from when they fled the village until they crossed the river and reached the Americans? What other repetitions can you find?

INTRODUCING THE CHAPTER

Ask volunteers to recite nursery rhymes they remember from childhood. Discuss the way these verses use rhythmically constructed phrases. Tell students that in this chapter, they will learn about the principle of art that has the same effect in a visual way.

MOTIVATOR

Ask each student to make a list of six events that are a part of his or her own daily rhythm, such as eating a meal. In small groups, have them compare lists.

VOCABULARY PREVIEW

Have students preview the list of vocabulary words. Also, acquaint them with these words: random, regular, alternating, flowing, progressive, and dynamism.

USING FIRST IMPRESSIONS

Have students study Figure 9.1. Help them see that the blue triangles that border the picture are arranged in a regular rhythm. The plants and trees are repeated randomly. The white lines of the river create a flowing rhythm. There are about six repetitions of families leaving the villages and walking toward the river. We see three different boats crossing the river, as well as individual people swimming across it. Finally, in the bottom right corner of the work, we see the family coming out of the river and being met by the American soldiers. Other repeated objects are mountains, clouds, buildings, and cars.

TEACHER TALK

A Success Story When students at Chaffin Junior High School in Fort Smith, Arizona, had Becky Shopfner as their art teacher, they were in for a special learning opportunity. What began as a single idea—learn about art through the rhythms and patterns of life—soon involved interdisciplinary studies, a quilt-making project, even visits to elderly members of the community. Students learned about the patterns of history, and how human life is cyclical. Importantly, they have a better understanding of how art is alive and dynamic, and how it reflects human nature in more dimensions than they had ever imagined.

221

TEACH

(pages 222–226)
- How We Perceive Visual Rhythm
- Repetition

GUIDED PRACTICE

Developing Perceptual Skills

Ask students to look around and identify five visual rhythms that they see every day. Instruct students to list the rhythms and describe the images that create the positive beats. Then describe the negative space that acts as the rests between the beats. Discuss their findings.

Developing Perceptual Skills

Bring in some natural objects such as leaves, acorns, small round pebbles, or shells. Demonstrate the feeling of movement by asking students to arrange them in a row across a table top. Give different groups of objects to different groups of students and ask them to make patterns that move the viewers' eyes across the table. Some students may see that these regular rhythms are implied lines. Point out that the elements and principles of art are all interwoven, and in real life, it is hard to separate them.

Promoting Discussion

To emphasize how we perceive visual movement, bring to class a painting of flowers and a stop-action photograph of an athlete. Ask students to explain how the painting demonstrates visual movement while the photograph does not. (The painting may cause your eyes to jump from one flower shape to the next, while the stop-action photograph may have frozen the movement in such a way that your eyes hardly move.)

HOW WE PERCEIVE VISUAL RHYTHM

Rhythm is *the principle of design that indicates movement by the repetition of elements.* The principle of rhythm is used in every art form.

In music, rhythm is created by the measure of time between musical sounds. There is a beat followed by a rest. **Visual rhythm** is *rhythm you receive through your eyes rather than through your ears* (Figure 9.2). Visual rhythm is created by repeated positive shapes separated by negative spaces. The positive areas are the "beats." Each beat is separated by negative spaces, which are the "rests." Look at Figure 9.3 for an example of visual beats and rests.

FIGURE 9.2   Visual rhythms can be both natural and manufactured.

FIGURE 9.3   This artist saw the meaning of existence in the changes of weather and seasons. He uses rhythms to express the living force in the natural environment. The elements in this painting seem to dance the dance of life.

Charles Burchfield. *October Wind and Sunlight in the Woods.* c. 1962–63. Watercolor on paper. 101.6 × 137.2 cm (40 × 54″). Georgia Museum of Art, University of Georgia, Athens, Georgia. University purchase.

Everywhere you look you can see visual rhythms. Sometimes, without even thinking, you note the beats and the spaces between the beats. The books in a bookcase and the cars in a parking lot show visual rhythms. A line of people in the cafeteria has visual rhythm. Each person is a positive beat, and the space between each person is the negative area.

A beat may be one element or a combination of elements. Look at the photograph of the lily pads in Figure 9.2. The strongest beats are the round shapes that vary in size. Each round shape has one split from its center to its edge. Each split is turned in a slightly different direction. Since this is a black-and-white photograph, you cannot see the colors of the round shapes, but you can see the value changes. Some leaves are very light—almost white. Most have a middle-gray value, and some are almost as dark as the negative spaces. Look closely and you will see a second, less noticeable beat: the thin curving and diagonal lines of the stems linking the lily pads.

The negative space between the beats varies greatly. Some shapes touch or overlap, and in other areas the space between the shapes is wide. The value of the negative space varies from dark gray to black. The lightest areas of negative space are on the left side and at the bottom of the photograph.

Visual rhythms create a sensation of movement as the viewer's eyes follow the visual beats through a work of art. Visual movement is different from real action, which involves a physical change in position. For example, a ball bouncing across a room is real action. Round shapes separated by negative spaces in a picture can create the same visual sensation as the movement of the ball because your eyes bounce from one round shape to the next. Artists use this type of visual movement to control the way the viewer looks at a work of art (Figure 9.4 on page 224).

Using Visual Beats

1. Applying Your Skills.   Look through newspapers and magazines for two advertisements that use rhythm to create visual movement. Circle the positive beats with a crayon or a marker.

2. Further Challenge.   Bonheur creates a sense of movement through her work by repeating the horses in Figure 9.4 on page 224. The horses are the major beat in the rhythm, and the men are the secondary beat in her composition. Create a composition of your own in which trees in a forest are the major beat that leads the viewer's eyes through the work. Then add a secondary

---

GUIDED PRACTICE
(continued)

Exploring Aesthetics

Ask the students to look for the repetition of all elements in Figures 9.3 and 9.4 on page 224. Have students demonstrate how the paintings are similar to, and different from, each other.

Using Visual Beats

1. Applying Your Skills. This activity requires the visual perception of positive beats. If students have trouble finding advertisements that show rhythms, refer them to fashion magazines such as *Vogue*.

2. Further Challenge. Let students discuss where the trees are located and what would be in the composition to create the second beat. Some ideas might be animals, flowers, branches, joggers, or bicycle riders.

3. Computer Option. As an alternative, have students follow these directions: Choose a black line (foreground) color and white or clear for the fill (background) color. Use the Brush, Pencil, or Shape tools to create an organic or geometric, real or imaginary shape. After you have designed a satisfying unit, use a Selection tool and the Copy and Paste commands to repeat the shape. Arrange each one, remembering to use overlapping and the transformation options—Flip, Turn, Rotate, Slant, or Resize—to create variety and a sense of depth. Save and title it "Basic Design." Choose a color scheme to reinforce the rhythm you have created. Use the Bucket Flood-fill option to add color. Also decide on a color to use that will add a secondary beat or accent to enhance the sense of movement. Experiment.

CURRICULUM CONNECTION

Music   Collect sticklike objects that can be used for rhythm instruments. Use a utility knife to notch ¹⁄₂-inch (1-cm) dowel rods to use as rasps. Make drum surfaces by stretching circles cut from wide inner tubes over the open end of a coffee can. Find objects at home that can be used as sound and rhythm instruments.

Then compose rhythm patterns that can be played on the instruments. Listen to the sound that each of your found or made instruments makes. You will hear different *timbres*, or tone qualities. Play the sounds together to hear orchestration. Then add vocal sounds such as scat singing.

GUIDED PRACTICE
(continued)

Exploring Aesthetics

Ask students to think of implied lines when they look at *The Horse Fair*. Where do they see an implied line? How does Bonheur control the movement of the viewer's eyes in this work?

LOOKING CLOSELY

Have students study Figure 9.4 and answer the questions in the caption. Help them to see that the horses are the beats of the rhythm. They are all horses, but they all move differently, and they are different colors and sizes. We know by the way they are placed that there is space between them, but they all overlap so that we do not see any negative space between them. The movement starts in the center of the left side with the white horse that is pulling up. The artist pulls us from center left toward the foreground in the center and then back up to the right where the horses turn to pass before the men who are sitting on the hill. This is done as we follow the movement of the horses. The white highlights lead us to the white horses in the center and then lead us up to the right and around the hill. The men make up the counterpoint of beats. The trees move along with a steady beat. They start out small in the distance on the left and get progressively larger as they move to the right.

LOOKING CLOSELY

FIGURE 9.4 What are the beats of the rhythm that move your eyes through this painting? Are the beats all the same? Can you see any negative spaces between the beats as in the photograph of the lily pads? Where does the movement start? Which way has the artist pulled you through the work? How has she accomplished this? Are there any other objects in this painting that make up a counterpoint of beats? Can you find a steady beat that moves along in the same direction as the more active beats? How do they help create the rhythmic movement?

Rosa Bonheur. *The Horse Fair.* 1853–55. Oil on canvas. 244.5 x 506.7 cm (96¼ × 199½"). The Metropolitan Museum of Art, New York, New York. Gift of Cornelius Vanderbilt, 1887.

beat that enhances the sense of movement. Be creative in what you decide to use for the secondary beat.

3. Computer Option. Choose the Line tool of your computer program and draw one straight, wide line. Make several exact copies of this line by using the Select, Copy, and Paste options. Choose the Circle tool and draw one circle using a *cool color* with *no pattern*. Make several exact copies of this circle by using the Select, Copy, and Paste options. You will create rhythm as you place each line and circle. Additional smaller circles may be added. If your monitor is monochrome, make your lines solid and put patterns in the circles. Remember that you can add, rearrange, or remove elements easily when drawing with the computer.

REPETITION

Rhythm results from repetition. *Motif* and *pattern* are often used to talk about repetition in art.

A **motif** is *a unit that is repeated in visual rhythm.* Sometimes every motif is an exact duplicate of the first unit, and sometimes the repetitions vary from the original (Figure 9.5).

Look around and you will find examples of motif and repetition. In a marching band, one band member is a motif, even though each band member carries a different instrument. On a grocery store shelf full of canned goods, one can is a motif. In a herd of cattle, one cow is a motif.

MORE ABOUT . . . ROSA BONHEUR

Rosa Bonheur came from an unusual family, a fact that surely contributed to both her pursuit of the arts and fondness for animal subjects. Bonheur's father belonged to a sect known as the St. Simonians, who believed in the complete equality of women and men and a feminine element in God. The St. Simonians anticipated the coming of a female messiah and wanted a society based on love, with no war or class distinctions. The French government eventually forced the St. Simonians to disband, but Bonheur and her family continued to support these ideals. Bonheur's fondness for animal subjects may have stemmed in part from her family's habit of keeping animals in the household.

FIGURE 9.5   See if you can identify one or more motifs in this design.

Mantle. Coastal Huari (Tiahuanaco), Peru. 600–1000. Cotton and wool. 103.5 × 50.5 cm (40¾ × 19⅞"). The Metropolitan Museum of Art, New York, New York. The Michael C. Rockefeller Memorial Collection, bequest of Nelson A. Rockefeller, 1979.

In sculpture and architecture *a three-dimensional motif* is sometimes called a **module**. Modular furniture is composed of standard matching units.

Pattern is a word used to describe a decorative surface design. **Pattern** is *a two-dimensional decorative visual repetition.*

You have seen a pattern of lines decorating fabric or a pattern used in construction (Figure 9.6).

FIGURE 9.6   This elevator grill is a delicate pattern of lines and round forms. It was once part of a large bank of elevators in the 1893 Chicago Stock Exchange. The building was torn down in 1972, but parts of it, such as this grill, have been saved and housed in various museums.

Louis Sullivan. *Elevator Grille.* 1893–94. Bronze-plated cast iron. 185.4 × 78.7 cm (73 × 31"). High Museum of Art, Atlanta, Georgia. Carroll Crawford Collection, 1982.

In some complex patterns, finding motifs is hard to do, but if students study each other's clothes, it will be easy. Ask them to find the exact areas that are being repeated. It would be also helpful if you wore clothes with obvious motifs and brought fabric samples that showed motifs clearly.

Developing Perceptual Skills

Let students know that the difference between pattern and rhythm can be difficult to see clearly. In fact, artists do not always agree, and many use the terms interchangeably. Pattern is flat and decorative, like the design on fabric and wallpaper. Rhythm is a repetition that causes a viewer's eyes to move around a composition. Ask students to look through the textbook and find examples of patterns and rhythms.

Building Vocabulary

Have students look up definitions of the word *module*, as well as its variations. Ask students to practice using *module* or any other form of the word in sentences. As an alternative exercise, have them sketch a three-dimensional drawing of the word *module*, then decorate it with rhythmic designs.

Understanding Art History

If you have students who are interested in architecture, suggest that they find out more about Louis Sullivan. Ask them to make a presentation to the class that includes biographical information, as well as a description of his style and examples of his work.

MORE ABOUT . . . LOUIS SULLIVAN

Known for his motto "Form follows function," Louis Sullivan combined decorative elements of his work to create functional buildings that please the eye. After studying at the Massachusetts Institute of Technology, he trained in the United States and Paris until he found his own practice in Chicago. There he became one of the founders of the Chicago School of Architecture. The Chicago Fire of 1871 had created a need for many new buildings, and the price of land dictated the need for taller buildings. At the same time, steel frames and electric elevators became practical. Sullivan's work in designing functional, yet aesthetic, skyscrapers has influenced the work of modern architects.

Motifs and Patterns

1. Applying Your Skills.
If magazines are scarce, you might photocopy patterns from books and let students color one motif.

2. Further Challenge.
To help students who may have difficulty understanding verbal instructions, show them some photographs of houses similar to those they might find in their neighborhoods and point out the types of rhythms they might expect to find.

3. Computer Option.
As an alternative activity, have students follow these directions: Select two of the geometric Shape tools: square, circle, triangle, hexagon, oval, diamond, and so on. Combine the two shapes. Add a straight, curved, or zigzag line. Select the motif and make copies using the Copy and Paste commands. As you paste each copy, arrange the motifs in a row. When the row is complete, it can be selected, copied, then pasted directly below or shifted a half space to the right. Fill the page. Use the Bucket Flood-fill tool to add color and/or patterns.

INDEPENDENT PRACTICE

Enrichment

Have students make a design using shapes and lines to illustrate the difference between a 3/4-time waltz rhythm and a 4/4-time march rhythm. As an alternative exercise, have students listen to various types of music: rock, waltzes, marches, or music from other cultures. After each listening session, they should create designs using lines that visually match the beat of the music.

226

Some of these patterns are functional; others are used only as decoration. They tend to be stiff and rather dull. If you remember that rhythm is a repetition intended to create the feeling of movement, and that pattern is intended to be flat and decorative, you will have no trouble telling the difference between the two.

Motifs and Patterns

1. Applying Your Skills. Make a collection of decorative patterns. You may use photographs, clippings from magazines, scraps of fabric, and so on. Identify the motif in each pattern by drawing a circle around one. Organize your pattern collection into a poster, a bulletin board, a booklet, or some other kind of presentation.

2. Further Challenge. Find a house in your neighborhood that has interesting visual rhythms. Make a pencil drawing of it, emphasizing the rhythmic areas. For example, you might draw the outer shape with a light line and then darken any rectangular shapes. Or, starting with a light line drawing, you might use a colored marker to accent vertical repetitions.

3. Computer Option. Start with a rectangle and design a simple motif. Use three colors or three original textures in black and white. Create a variety of patterns with that motif. Print your patterns. If your printer is black and white, you can add color with other media such as colored pencil after the design is printed out.

TYPES OF RHYTHM

Different visual rhythms are created with different arrangements of motif and space. There are many ways to combine motifs and space. Each way gives a different character to the rhythm depicted.

Random

A motif repeated in no apparent order, with no regular spaces in between, creates a *random* rhythm. One example is autumn leaves that cover the ground. Cracks in mud and splashes of paint are two more examples of random rhythm.

FIGURE 9.7 The potter who created this bowl made an aesthetic decision to splash the ware with vegetable juices to create a random pattern of round shapes and lines.

Bowl. Sundi group, Kongo peoples. Congo, Zaire, and Angola. Before 1910. Fired clay and natural pigment. 11.3 × 15.6 cm (4½ × 6¼"). National Museum of African Art, Smithsonian Institution, Washington, D.C. Purchased with funds provided by the Smithsonian Collections Acquisition Program, 89–13–31.

Crowds often create random rhythms—think of holiday shoppers, rush-hour commuters, and students in the halls between classes. A large group of people pushing into a subway train is full of rhythm. The motif is one person. Every person is different, and every space is slightly different.

The Sundi woman who created the bowl shown in Figure 9.7 deliberately splashed the bowl with vegetable juices immediately after pulling it from the fire to create the random pattern of round shapes that decorate the surface. If she had dipped it into the liquid, the bowl would have had an even brown hue. The vegetable liquid applied while the clay is still hot makes it able to resist the heat of the cooking fire. The bowl can be used over an open fire without shattering. In some parts of Africa, the marks left by the vegetable juices are interpreted as proof of the thermal strength of the vessel.

Using Random Rhythm

1. Applying Your Skills. Make a stamp motif and print it in a random rhythm (Figure 9.8).

2. Further Challenge. Choose one letter of the alphabet. Look through newspapers and magazines for large examples of that letter. Neatly cut out twenty or more. Arrange them on a piece of colored paper in a random pattern (Figure 9.9). If you have trouble finding

---

MEETING SPECIAL NEEDS

Learning Disabled Students with disabilities may enjoy cutting out a collection of patterns, large letters, or examples of different types of rhythm. They can find these patterns in magazines and then put them into envelopes or paste them into a notebook. All students will enjoy exercising their perceptive skills by looking around the room to locate examples of patterns of repetitive rhythm (in ceiling tiles, air conditioner grids, chairs in a row) and alternating rhythms (perhaps in designs on sweaters or other clothing). Students can become attuned to the idea of flowing rhythm by moving their arms or bodies to a flowing musical selection.

large letters, you can add some neatly drawn letters of your own to your design.

3. Computer Option. Depending on your computer program capabilities: (1) design a motif, (2) choose a stamp, (3) edit a stamp, or (4) edit a brush. Use the resulting motif in a random manner. You can use Flip, Rotate, Size Change, and Color options if your program has them.

FIGURE 9.8   Student work.

FIGURE 9.10   This fern shows the regular rhythm found in nature.

Regular

Regular rhythm has identical motifs and equal amounts of space between them (Figure 9.10). Regular rhythm has a steady beat.

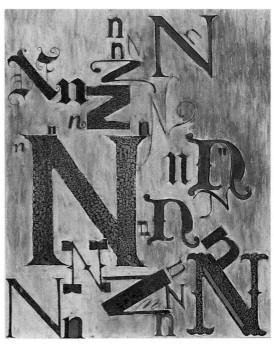

FIGURE 9.9   Student work. Random arrangement of letters.

Exploring Aesthetics

Ask students to carefully study the Asante weaving in Figure 9.11. Tell them that at the conclusion of this chapter, they will have an opportunity to create a similar weaving. Ask them to look at Figure 9.29 in the Studio Lesson and compare the patterns in the two photographs. Ask: How are they similar? How are they different? Tell students that these Asante weavings are made on special looms that are treated with respect. (You might read the information in your Teacher's Wraparound Edition at the bottom of page 242.) Ask: How does this knowledge influence your appreciation of the Asante weavings?

To foster students' awareness of rhythm in everyday life, suggest this: Listen to the rhythms of your day, beginning with the alarm clock. Stop to hear the beat of your heart during gym class, the sound of feet between classes, the pattern of traffic, or the rumble of a train. Musicians often transform the sounds they hear around them into music. Johann Strauss drove through the Vienna woods in a horse-drawn carriage. He heard the birds singing, leaves rustling, and hunters' horns signaling. He combined these sounds with the rhythm of the horses' hooves and the rumble of the carriage to compose the famous waltz *Tales from Vienna Woods*. Find contemporary music that you feel captures the rhythm of a specific place.

Regular repetitions are used to organize things. Parking spaces and office mailboxes are laid out with regular rhythm. Stores organize merchandise into regular stacks and rows. This makes it easier for you to find things, and it also makes the displays more attractive than if items were arranged in a random fashion.

A grid is based on regular rhythm. It is a regular arrangement of parallel lines. A football field is laid out in a grid, as is a checkerboard. Windows form a grid pattern on the side of a skyscraper. The artist who created the cloth in Figure 9.11 had a grid pattern in his mind as he wove the long, narrow strips of cloth. Later he cut and sewed the strips together to make the wide cloth you see. Notice the regular repetition of the various motifs.

Regular rhythm can be boring if it is overdone. One note played on a piano over and over again is an example. Pop artist Andy Warhol used regular rhythm to make a social-protest statement (Figure 9.12). How would you describe the effect of this regular rhythm? What do you suppose Warhol intended to convey with this repeated motif?

Alternating

Alternating rhythm can occur in several ways. One way is to introduce a second motif. Another way is to make a change in the placement or content of the original motif. A third way is to change the spaces between the motifs. Sometimes alternation is created simply by changing the position of the motif. For example, the motif may be turned upside down. The Japanese artist who painted the wave design on the bowl shown in Figure 9.13 created the feeling of movement by alternating the placement of the wave shapes. The Native American who embroidered the shoulder bag in Figure 9.14 on page 230 made the design interesting by changing the sets of motifs several times.

Bricks are often laid in an alternating pattern. As a child, did you ever play with interlocking blocks? You had to use an alternating pattern to join the blocks.

An alternating rhythm using two motifs can still be very repetitive. Your eyes keep returning to the first motif even after the second motif joins the design, but the alternation does create interest and relieve monotony.

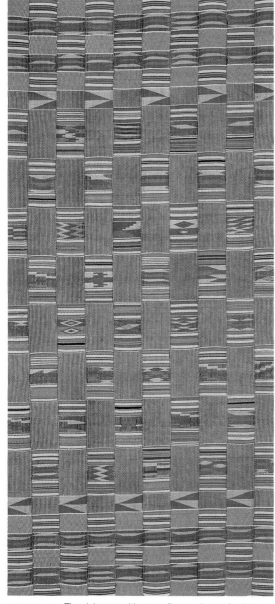

FIGURE 9.11 The elaborate grid pattern fits together perfectly because the weaver has memorized the whole plan through many years of practice.

Wrapper. Asante peoples, Ghana. Date unknown. Cotton and rayon plain weave with supplementary rayon weft. 190 × 83 cm (74⅞ × 32¾"). National Museum of African Art and National Museum of Natural History, Washington, D.C. Purchased with funds provided by the Smithsonian Institution. Collection Acquisition Program, 1983–85.

CULTURAL PERSPECTIVES

Tell your students about the rich, indigenous textile tradition which exists in West Africa. Adire cloths are indigo home-dyed "country cloths" and are impressive because of their large number and variety. They are created in what is present-day Nigeria. Every individual pattern has a name. Traditional designs are used in village ceremonies.

Many motifs are governed by Yoruba (located in the western part of Nigeria) mythology and folklore. Stylized designs on a variety of themes such as lizards, turtles, snakes, birds, trees, and even human beings can be found. These designs are created in praise of Oduduwa—the creator of the world.

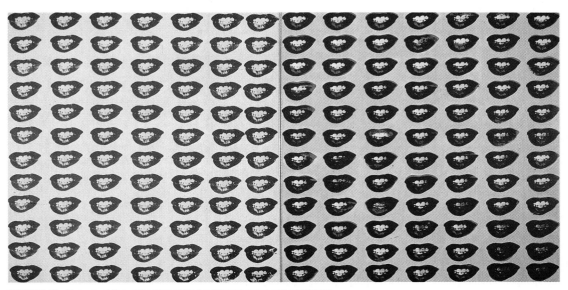

FIGURE 9.12 One pair of lips on the face of Marilyn Monroe would be beautiful and appealing. What has Andy Warhol done to them by repeating them in a regular rhythm?

Andy Warhol. *Marilyn Monroe's Lips*. 1962. Diptych. Synthetic polymer, enamel, and pencil on canvas. Left: 210.7 × 204.9 cm (82¾ × 80¾"). Right: 210.7 × 209.7 cm (82¾ × 82⅜"). Hirshhorn Museum and Sculpture Garden, Smithsonian Institution, Washington, D.C. Gift of Joseph H. Hirshhorn, 1972.

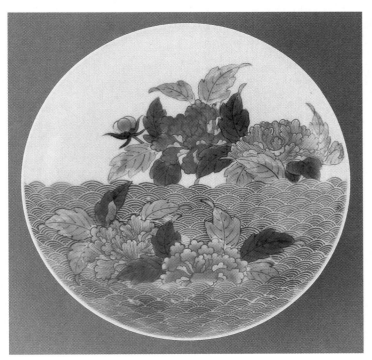

FIGURE 9.13 The artist who painted this dish used an alternating pattern of sets of blue curved lines to symbolize waves of water.

Footed Dish. Japanese, Nabeshima ware. 1700–50. Porcelain with underglaze blue and overglaze polychrome enamel decoration. 5.4 × 20 cm (2⅛ × 7⅞"). Nelson-Atkins Museum of Art, Kansas City, Missouri. Purchase: Nelson Trust.

GUIDED PRACTICE
(continued)

Exploring Aesthetics

After students have studied the arrangement of motifs in Figure 9.14, ask them to use their knowledge about the elements of art to describe how the elements are used in the bag. For example, what types of lines are evident? What color schemes? What type of balance is used? How is shape, space, and form used?

 Alternating Rhythm

1. Applying Your Skills. This would be a good opportunity to have students practice measuring and using a ruler correctly.

2. Further Challenge. If some students are not able to measure or hold a ruler because of disabilities, you might prepare photocopied pages with checkerboard grids already drawn.

3. Computer Option. As an alternative activity, have students follow any of these directions:

A. Design two geometric motifs, similar in size, using a minimum of two shapes and one line. If available, use the Grids and Rulers option to help measure size and align motifs. Save and title "Basic Units." Make copies by using a Selection tool and the Copy and Paste commands. Arrange both motifs in an alternating pattern. Fill the page. Use the Save As command and retitle the work.

B. Open the File titled "Basic Units." Begin again, this time choose patterns to fill some of the areas of the motifs. Make copies, repeating the motifs to create an alternating pattern. Try the Flip, Rotate, or Turn commands to explore many possibilities. Fill the page.

FIGURE 9.14 How many sets of motifs can you find embroidered on this Creek shoulder bag? How many different ways has the artist alternated the motifs?

Shoulder Bag. Creek. Georgia or Alabama. 1810–30. Wool fabric, cotton fabric and thread, silk ribbon, glass beads. Strap: 135 × 18.7 cm (53¼ × 7⅜"). Bag: 19.4 × 10 cm (7⅝× 4"). The Detroit Institute of Arts, Detroit, Michigan. Founders Society Purchase with funds from Flint Ink Corporation.

 Alternating Rhythm

1. Applying Your Skills. Draw a checkerboard grid and create an alternating rhythm using one motif. Turn the motif upside down in every other box (See Figure 9.15).

2. Further Challenge. Draw a checkerboard grid and create an alternating rhythm using two motifs (Figure 9.16).

3. Computer Option. Design two motifs using the tools of your choice. Use the Select tool and the Copy and Paste options to create an alternating rhythm using both motifs. On a new screen, create an alternating

TEACHER TALK

One way to enhance students' appreciation of contemporary Native American art is by creating a well-stocked classroom library of Native American audiovisual and print resources. If you have a video cassette recorder at your disposal, you might purchase one or more of the several available outstanding videotapes about Native American artists, such as *Daughters of the Anasazi*, which traces the life and work of potter Lucy Lewis, and *Maria*, which deals in like fashion with Maria Martinez and her son, Papovi Da. You might also consider subscribing to periodicals such as *American Indian Art* and *Southwest Art*, as well as obtaining brochures from appropriate art galleries.

FIGURE 9.15   Student work. Alternating rhythm with one motif.

FIGURE 9.16   Student work. Alternating rhythm with two motifs.

rhythm using only one motif. In this design, you can change the placement of the motif; for example, turn it upside down or change the spaces between the motifs. Label and save both designs.

Flowing

Flowing rhythm is created by repeating wavy lines. Curved shapes, such as rolling hills or ocean waves, create flowing rhythms (Figure 9.17 on page 232). Your eyes glide along a curving path that changes direction gradually (Figure 9.18 on page 232). There are no sudden breaks in the movement of a flowing line.

Flowing rhythm is all upward swells and downward slides. You might think of the upward moves as the beats and the downward moves as the rests. Allan Houser has used flowing rhythms symbolically in his sculpture *Coming of Age* (Figure 9.19

GUIDED PRACTICE
(*continued*)

C. Open the File titled "Basic Units." Continue exploring new arrangements by using the Flip, Turn, or Rotate commands and changing the spacing between the motifs. Turning each copy of one motif, a quarter of a turn each time it is pasted, will create a unit or network. Add color and/or pattern. Use the Save As command to save and title your final copy. If limited to black and white, color can be added after printing with colored pencils, pens, or crayons. Mount and display all examples together.

Developing Perceptual Skills

If possible, find a Chinese scroll painting to show to your students. Remind them that the scrolls were read like books, with only 24 inches (61 cm) of the scroll exposed at a time. The reader would begin at one end and slowly "read" the scroll while rolling it toward the other end. This way, the viewer was able to journey through the entire painting from one scene to another. Often, the scenes on the scroll were designed to inspire a viewer, rather than tell a dramatic story. As you demonstrate this technique, direct students to observe how the artist of the scroll used the principle of rhythm to maintain interest and flow to the scenes. Ask them to specifically look for evidence of flowing rhythm.

Critical Thinking

Have each student create a grid with the types of rhythm listed down the left column. List music, literature, math, language arts, and so on, across the top. Have them work in groups to complete the grid, showing how each area of study demonstrates characteristics of rhythm.

■ CURRICULUM CONNECTION ■

Music   Many audio stores offer recordings on compact discs or tapes that feature natural sounds of the environment. In most cases, the natural sounds are blended with instrumental music, creating an interplay of sounds that is both delightful and calming. Play a few of these selections for students and have them identify the natural rhythms created by waves crashing, birds chirping, or a breeze blowing. As a group project, students may want to record, edit, and produce their own tape.

GUIDED PRACTICE
(continued)

Exploring Aesthetics

Point out that often, bronze sculptures such as Allan Houser's *Coming of Age* (Figure 9.19 on page 233) are parts of a series of castings with between five and seven "editions." Arrange a debate in which students argue the relative value of sculptures that have been reproduced in multiples. Ask: Is it important to destroy a mold after a certain number of reproductions have been made? Is the aesthetic value of a work diminished if that piece is reproduced?

Exploring Aesthetics

Have students study Houser's sculpture in Figure 9.19. Encourage them to visualize the work from all sides. Ask: Can you see how the artist introduced a sense of action? How did he achieve this sense of action?

Art Is Everywhere

To foster students' awareness of rhythm and sound in everyday life, suggest this: Russian composer Modest Mussorgsky wrote *Pictures at an Exhibition* to capture the rhythm of his visit to a museum. In "Promenade," you hear the rhythm of his heavy footstep (he was a very big man). "Gnome" picks up the spry, jerky movements and dragging steps of the gnome. In "Tuileries" you can hear the beat of chattering children and anxious nurses against the soft rustle of the park trees. "Ballad of the Unhatched Chicks" is a lively musical sketch of chicks chirping, bouncing, and pecking inside their shells. Listen and enjoy the whole suite.

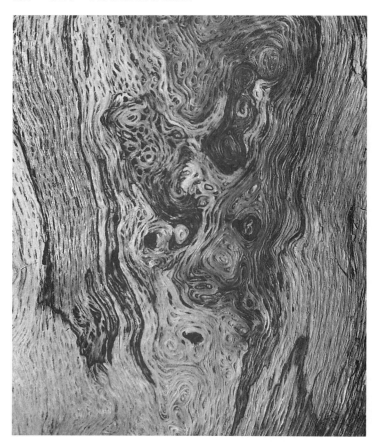

FIGURE 9.17   The natural curves in this tree bark create a flowing rhythm.

FIGURE 9.18   Student work. Relief design with flowing rhythm.

AT THE MUSEUM

Cleveland Museum of Art (Cleveland, Ohio) Remember drawing on your sidewalk with chalk as a child? At the Cleveland Museum of Art, you can draw on the walls and pavement of the museum during their annual Chalk Festival. This unique program invites the public to create "big chalk murals" similar to a tradition dating back to sixteenth- century Italy when artists colored scenes on the village sidewalks. The museum sells squares to families and groups, who submit their design and learn street-chalking techniques from the museum staff before they create their own chalk murals for the pleasure of everyone to see.

FIGURE 9.19   This sculpture, with its upturned head and flowing hair, was created to celebrate feminine youth and beauty. The upturned head symbolizes the girl's desire to run to the four directions of the earth. The small shape above her forehead represents an abalone shell, a fertility symbol. The feather worn in her hair signifies a long life.

Allan Houser. *Coming of Age.* 1977. Bronze, edition of 12. 19 × 39.4 × 17.8 cm (7½ × 15½ × 7″). Denver Art Museum, Denver, Colorado.

above). The work expresses the symbolic union of nature and feminity. The thick, rhythmically flowing strands of her hair suggest motion and the act of running. They also suggest the movement of the wind, of water, or even the blazing motion of flames.

 Using Flowing Rhythm

1. Applying Your Skills.   Look through magazines and newspapers for pictures that feature flowing rhythms. Be sure to look at all the advertisements as you search for the flowing rhythms. Mount and label the best examples that you find.

2. Further Challenge.   Create a relief design showing flowing rhythm. Cut strips of construction paper 1/2 inch (1.3 cm) wide. Glue them on edge to a small piece of poster board. Use analogous colors for the strips and a complement of one of the colors for the background. Curl the strips so that they will hold their curve after you have glued them. Arrange the strips in sets of almost parallel ridges.

GUIDED PRACTICE
(continued)

ACTIVITY **Using Flowing Rhythm**

1. Applying Your Skills. Flowing rhythms may not be obvious. Have students go over the flowing lines in the magazine pictures with a dark marker if they experience difficulty with this activity.

2. Further Challenge. The strips will stay in place if students curl and arrange the flowing movement before applying glue. You cannot force the glue to hold a curve, because white glue takes so long to dry. Be sure that there is a flat place to put these works while they dry. If they slant, the glue will drip and the strips may not stay in place.

3. Computer Option. As an alternative activity, have students follow these directions: Create a flowing rhythm by using line. Choose the Brush or Pencil tool. First, explore by drawing a curvy, wavy line that goes from one side of the page to the other, not necessarily in a direct horizontal or vertical movement. Vary the curves or waves. Using a Selection tool and Copy and Paste commands, repeat this line. Experiment. Create a flowing rhythm design by changing the space between the lines and/or overlapping. Try varying the direction and thickness of the line. Fill the page. Save and title "Basic Line Rhythm." Explore colors, patterns, and gradients using the Bucket Flood-fill tool to color the design and enhance the sense of movement. Choose a color scheme to express movement. Use the Save As command to save the compositions you like. Print. Display all examples together.

MORE ABOUT . . . ALLAN HOUSER

Chiricahua Apache sculptor Allan Houser (1914–), is credited with developing the modern style of Native American sculpture almost single-handedly. Raised on a farm near Fort Sill, Oklahoma, Houser could not afford formal art training and worked in a rubber plant and on a farm to support himself. By 1948 he was seriously thinking of becoming a house painter, when his design for a statue commemorating Native American servicemen killed in World War II was selected by the Haskell Institute in Lawrence, Kansas. After creating this monument, he was determined to pursue a career as a professional artist.

Exploring Aesthetics

Have students discuss the painting shown in Figure 9.20. Direct them to consider how line, color, texture, shape, form, and space are used. What principles of art emphasize those elements? What message or idea do they think Balla was trying to convey in this painting?

LOOKING
CLOSELY

Have students study Figure 9.20 and answer the question in the caption. Help them to see that the V lines may have been used to symbolize the spreading out of the light as it moves away from the lamp. They also resemble white moths, clustering around the warm light.

Sparking Creativity

Want students to think creatively about rhythm and movement? Suggest this: Rhythm in dance is found in the movements of the dancers. Try to see it and give it a visual form. Ask one or two students to dance and draw their movements rather than their bodies. Try a slow graceful dance and then a rock rhythm. Compare your drawings. Think about colors that will suit each movement. Choose a medium that will suit each rhythm. Try pastels used on the side to get wider lines. Use india ink and a brush, paint and a sponge, or oil pastels. Each different tool and medium will affect the rhythm of your design.

3. Computer Option. Draw a modified S shape using the Pencil or Brush tool. Use the Select tool and Copy and Paste options to repeat this curved shape, covering most of the screen. Have shapes touch or overlap. Pay attention to the negative shapes created as you paste positive shapes. Save your work. Experiment by pouring colors into the shapes. Make all the connected shapes one color and one original shape a different color. Pour a gradient or a rainbow of colors into the connected shapes. Save the experiments you like. The designs you have created use flowing rhythm. Create another flowing rhythm design without cutting and pasting.

Progressive

In *progressive* rhythm there is a change in the motif each time the motif is repeated. It is like the number series *x plus 1, x plus 2, x plus 3.*

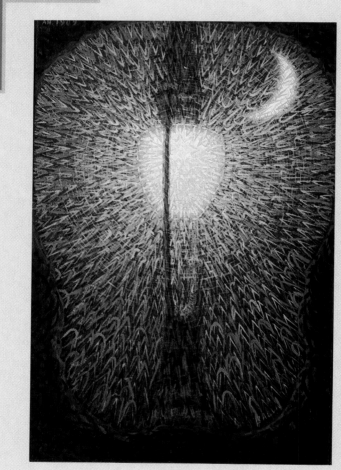

Giacomo Balla. *Street Light.* 1909. Oil on canvas. 174.7 × 114.7 cm (68¾ × 45¼"). Collection, The Museum of Modern Art, New York, New York. Hillman Periodicals Fund.

LOOKING
CLOSELY

FIGURE 9.20 The light glowing from the street lamp is represented by a progressive rhythm of both line and color. Notice how the light close to the lamp is white and yellow in color and is created with thin, small V-shaped lines. The light that is farther from the source gradually changes into mostly reds and lavenders, and the V-shaped lines are wider and larger. Why do you think the artist has used the V lines to represent the movement of light from the lamp out into the darkness?

MORE ABOUT . . . FUTURISTS

Umberto Boccioni (Italy, 1882–1916) was one of the leading artists of the Futurist movement, which began as an extension of Cubism. The emphasis of Futurism was on the dynamic quality of life. As one Futurist wrote, "The splendor of the world has been enriched by a new form of beauty, the beauty of speed."

The Futurists announced the end of the art of the past and the beginning of the art of the future. In 1910, Boccioni and other Futurists published a manifesto that included this statement: "All things move and run, change rapidly, and this universal dynamism is what the artist should strive to represent."

FIGURE 9.21   Student work. Progressive rhythm.

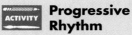

FIGURE 9.22   Student work. Progressive rhythm.

A progressive rhythm may start with a square as its motif. The size of the square may be changed by making it slightly smaller each time it is repeated, or each square may be made a different color of the spectrum or a different step on the value scale each time it is repeated. Shapes can be progressively changed. The sides of a square can be gradually rounded until the square becomes a circle. (See Figure 9.20.)

ACTIVITY   **Progressive Rhythm**

1. Applying Your Skills.   Starting with a simple geometric shape such as a square for your motif, create a progressive rhythm by gradually changing the square into a free-form shape (Figure 9.21).

2. Further Challenge.   Begin by drawing a picture using simple shapes. Change the shapes gradually, using progressive rhythm, to tell a visual story. (See Figure 9.22.)

3. Computer Option.   Use the tools of your choice to create a simple motif such as a circle or a free-form shape. Gradually change this motif in six or seven steps to create a progressive rhythm. You may change the size, the value, or the color of the motif to create progression. Tip: After finishing each step, make a copy of it and place it next to the one you just finished. You will have the starting point for the next step of your progression.

How Artists Use Rhythm to Create Movement

In Figure 9.23 on page 236, a photograph of the Golden Gate bridge in San Francisco, nothing is really moving. Everything is frozen in time, but your eye is pulled to the right side of the photograph by the repetition of diagonal lines. **Movement** is *the principle of art used to create the look and feeling of action and to guide the viewer's eyes throughout the work of art.* Notice how the upper lines of the bridge structure slant downward to the right. Even though the supports are vertical, the active sweep of the diagonal lines carry the eyes into the distance. The photographer who took this picture decided to photograph it from an angle that emphasizes the sweeping lines.

What memories does the picture of this bridge arouse for you? A trip to a large city? Fresh air and summer vacations? The rhythm of the diagonal lines creates the excitement here.

Artists use rhythm in a work of art just as they use the elements and other principles of art—to communicate feelings and ideas. As your eyes follow the visual beats through a work of art, you experience the sensation of movement. Is the movement slow and easy, or quick and excited? Does it soothe you or make you nervous? An artist uses rhythm to create these feelings.

One group of artists tried to do more than control the way in which viewers looked at works of

1. Applying Your Skills. Show students some Escher metamorphosis designs to inspire them.

2. Further Challenge. Ask students to continue their creative efforts in this activity by writing a story that accompanies their visual stories.

3. Computer Option. As an alternative activity, have students follow these directions: Choose a black line (foreground) color and a white or clear fill (background) color. Begin by creating a geometric motif using a combination of Shape tools and lines. If available, use the Grids and Rulers option to guide size and placement. Save and title the motif as "Basic Design." Now add color and use the Save As command to retitle the motif. Use a Selection tool and the Copy and Paste commands to repeat the command to retitle any work in progress. Close the page. Open the original motif. Make a change in the motif by varying one element: line, shape, pattern, or color. Use the Save As command to label the new motif. Select and use the Copy and Paste commands to place a copy on the Clipboard. Close the page. Open the work in progress and make a second row by pasting copies of the second motif from the Clipboard. Save. Close page. Begin again, opening the basic design motif. Make another change and repeat the steps, using the Save As command to retitle new editions when necessary. Continue until the page is full; try to make six or seven rows. Save and print your final arrangement.

MORE ABOUT . . . MOVEMENT IN ART

Artists are particularly aware of the importance of movement as it allows the artist to direct the observer's eye. For example, Gothic architecture uses vertical movement to draw our eyes heavenward. We perceive horizontal movement to be safe.

Diagonal movement gives us a sense of action, as evident when we see flowers bending in the wind or an athlete running. Spiral movement gives us a sense of depth and space.

GUIDED PRACTICE

GUIDED PRACTICE
(continued)

Understanding Art History

Although the Futurist movement lasted only a short time, the artists were important because they tried to express movement on non-moving surfaces using rhythmic effects. They took the philosophy of Cubism a step farther. Figure 9.24 is an example of visual rhythm used to create the effect of movement. Ask students to analyze how Giacomo Balla created this illusion.

Developing Perceptual Skills

Find copies of Marcel Duchamp's *Nude Descending a Staircase* and Umberto Boccioni's *Dynamism of a Cyclist*. Ask students to compare these two reproductions with Balla's work in Figure 9.20. Help students to analyze the movement in each painting.

Sparking Creativity

Want students to think creatively about movement? Suggest this: Have someone pose for you in an action position and cut a silhouette of his or her figure. Then move your figure around on a large sheet of paper and plan a continuous action for it. Start tracing the figure into a strobe light of pattern, either in contour, drawing the whole figure every time, or overlapping, drawing figures behind other figures. Glue your model figure into the design when you are finished. Watch a person move in a dark room with a strobe light flashing on him or her. It will look just like your design.

236

FIGURE 9.23 Your eye is drawn through this photograph by the repeated diagonal lines.

FIGURE 9.24 The many repetitions of the legs, feet, tail, and chain in this work give it the appearance of actual movement.

Giacomo Balla. *Dynamism of a Dog on a Leash*. 1912. Oil on canvas. 89.9 × 109.9 cm (35⅜ × 43¼"). Albright-Knox Art Gallery, Buffalo, New York. Bequest of A. Conger Goodyear and gift of George F. Goodyear, 1964.

COOPERATIVE LEARNING

Tell students that *mobile* is a fairly new term invented to describe sculptures that move. The work for which Calder is most noted is wind mobiles. These mobiles were made from rods, wires, and delicate shapes made of sheet metal and wire hung from a single point.

Many of Calder's mobiles are based on natural forms—animals, birds, fish, or plants—and the motions were carefully planned to imitate the movement of the subject. His later works show that he became more interested in shapes and movements that had little to do with natural objects. Have students work in small groups to create a free-standing mobile based on natural forms.

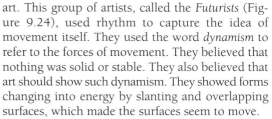

FIGURE 9.25   McKelvey's repetition of lines and forms that swirl out from the neck of her pot create the illusion of movement. The intricate sandpainting design along the graceful curve of a vessel is the hallmark of a McKelvey pot.

Lucy Leuppe McKelvey. *Whirling Rainbow Goddesses*. Ceramic container. 18 × 30 cm (6¾ × 12″). Keams Canyon Arts and Crafts, Keams Canyon, Arizona.

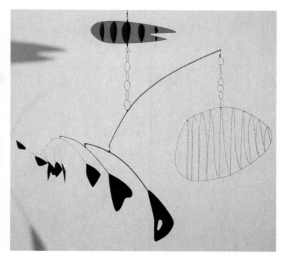

FIGURE 9.26   Look closely at the places where the rods are joined by a carefully planned set of loops. Calder's works are so carefully balanced that the slightest movement of air will set the sculpture in motion. Watching a Calder sculpture is like watching a graceful dancer.

Alexander Calder. *Lobster Trap and Fish Tail*. 1939. Hanging mobile. Painted steel wire and sheet aluminum. About 2.6 × 2.9 m (8′ 6″ × 9′ 6″). Collection, The Museum of Modern Art, New York, New York. Commissioned by the Advisory Committee for the stairwell of the museum.

art. This group of artists, called the *Futurists* (Figure 9.24), used rhythm to capture the idea of movement itself. They used the word *dynamism* to refer to the forces of movement. They believed that nothing was solid or stable. They also believed that art should show such dynamism. They showed forms changing into energy by slanting and overlapping surfaces, which made the surfaces seem to move.

When you look at the modern Navajo pottery by Native American artist Lucy McKelvey, you will also find rhythmic repetitions of shapes and lines that seem to move across the surface. The designs are inspired by traditional Navajo sandpaintings. McKelvey says that her grandfather, who was a medicine man, told her she could use the designs as long as she did not reproduce one of the sacred

sandpainting figures exactly as it was depicted in a ritual ceremony. She always changes the original and adds something different. (Figure 9.25.)

You can also see movement in the visual art of Alexander Calder (**call**-dur). He was a mechanical engineer, but his father was a sculptor. Calder believed in what the Futurists were doing. In his work he repeated abstract shapes and he put them into real motion. He did this using the real forces of air currents and gravity. Calder's creations were dubbed **kinetic** sculpture, because *they actually move in space.* (Figure 9.26.)

Artist Marcel Duchamp gave Calder's moving sculptures another name, *mobiles,* which you read about in Chapter 3. Moving sculptures of this kind have been called mobiles ever since.

MORE ABOUT . . . ALEXANDER CALDER

Perhaps the most famous American sculptor of this century, Alexander Calder's fanciful, witty, and ingenious work reflects his training as an engineer and illustrator. Born into a family of artists, Calder began sculpting at the age of five with bits of wire and wood. In 1924 he landed his first job as an artist, illustrating for the *National Police Gazette.*

After spending several years in Paris creating miniature circus figures, he began working on mobiles in 1931. During his lifetime he played a significant role in defining contemporary art and culture. Two of his more widely known ventures included a campaign poster for George McGovern and a design that appeared on Braniff jets in the mid-1970s.

GUIDED PRACTICE
(continued)

Interdisciplinary: Engineering

Remind students that Calder was an innovator. His mobiles seem to float in the air like dancing forms. Most students have made imitations of mobiles by tying strings to rods. Ask them to study the engineered joints of *Lobster Trap and Fish Tail* closely to see how Calder made them move so gracefully. If possible, ask a professional engineer to come to class and discuss the engineering problems an artist might face when designing a mobile.

INDEPENDENT PRACTICE

Study Guide

Distribute and have students complete *Study Guide 9* in the Reteaching booklet. Have students use the guide to review key concepts in the chapter.

Enrichment

• Assign *Enrichment Activity 17* and *18* in the TCR.

• Have students work in pairs and use small found objects to make various patterns. Let the partners share each of their patterns with another pair of students. Ask the students who are viewing: What rhythm does each pattern create? How does it create that rhythm?

Studio Lessons

To expand students' familiarity with the concept of rhythm and movement, these Studio Lessons are available in the TCR:

• Modular Sculpture
• Printing a Rhythmic Fabric Design
• Clay Coil Pot

OBJECTIVE

Create a painting expressing rhythmic movement.

MOTIVATOR

Involve students in some
type of rhythmic activity such
as dancing, clapping, or
drumming. Ask them to
share their own interpretations of rhythm.

GUIDED PRACTICE

Promoting Discussion

Encourage students to
select an activity they like,
then think about the movements inherent in that activity. Are the movements light
and bouncy as in soccer, or
are they the heavy, thudding
movements of football? Take
time to discuss the different
movements and how they can
be expressed in rhythms.

**Understanding
Art History**

Jacob Lawrence is famous
for his paintings of African-
American leaders such as
Harriet Tubman and Frederic
Douglas. He also has painted
subjects such as the migration of the Negro. (Inform the
students that "Negro" was a
term of respect used when
referring to African-Ameri-
cans prior to the late 1960s.)
In addition he painted inner
city street scenes and images
of construction workers and
carpenters. Lawrence was
also the first African-American artist to be represented
by a major New York gallery.

STUDIO LESSON: PAINTING WITH A RHYTHMIC ACTIVITY

FIGURE 9.27 Jacob Lawrence. *Parade.* 1960. Egg tempera on fiberboard. 60.6 × 76.3 cm (23¾ × 30⅛").
Hirshhorn Museum and Sculpture Garden, Smithsonian Institution, Washington, D.C. Gift of Joseph H.
Hirshhorn, 1966.

Supplies

- Sketchbook and pencils
- Large white paper
- Yellow chalk
- Acrylic paints and a variety
  of brushes

When Jacob Lawrence arrived in Harlem as a young boy, he
had never seen such crowded city streets. The shapes of the
tall buildings, the windows full of excited people, and the fire es-
capes that zigzagged down the outside walls fascinated him. He
loved the excitement that filled the neighborhood.

To tell a story, Lawrence painted series of pictures. In 1940–41 he
painted sixty paintings in a series called *The Migration of the Negro,*
which depicts the southern Negroes coming north to find work.
This was familiar subject matter, because the people in his neighborhood were part of that migration. These paintings brought him
fame and success, and in 1942–43 he painted thirty paintings about
the neighborhood itself and called it, simply, *Harlem Series.*

MORE ABOUT . . . JACOB LAWRENCE

Jacob Lawrence (United States, born 1917) is an
African-American painter who first became famous
during the Harlem Renaissance of the 1920s and
1930s.

Lawrence produced graphic images of urban life.
As a Social Realist, he has used his art as a means of
expressing his social values. Major themes in his
work include violence and injustice. The uprooted-
ness of African Americans is the subject of a series
of paintings entitled *The Migration of the Negro*
(1940–41). There are sixty individual works in this
series.

However, that was not the end of his paintings about Harlem. He returned to the subject many times. The painting *Parade* in Figure 9.27 depicts the neighborhood during one of its happiest times. People are dressed in their best clothes, and everyone is having a good time. Observe the many ways Lawrence has used rhythm in his painting, and think of ways you can use it in your painting.

Create a painting expressing rhythmic movement. Show one or more groups of people involved in rhythmic activity. Base the figures in your work on your own sketches of people in action. As in Lawrence's *Parade*, use more than one motif. Strengthen the rhythmic quality of your work by using four of the five kinds of visual rhythm described in this chapter. Use repetition to accent the visual rhythms. Choose a color scheme that will help to express the mood of the rhythms in your work.

FOCUSING

Brainstorm with your classmates for ideas of rhythmic activities. Think of marching bands, sports, cheerleaders, dancers, joggers, or children on a playground.

Select the rhythmic activities you will use in your painting. Do visual research by making gesture sketches in your sketchbook of active people involved in the activities.

CREATING

Select your best gesture drawings. In your sketchbook, make rough plans of how to organize the figures into a composition emphasizing rhythmic movement that will pull the viewer's eye through the painting. As in Lawrence's *Parade*, you may create several different rhythms by using more than one motif. Be sure to use rhythmic repetition.

Choose your best rhythmic composition and sketch it on a large sheet of white paper using yellow chalk. Press lightly with the chalk so it will disappear when you paint over it. Chalk marks should not remain.

FIGURE 9.27A Student work.

Before you start painting, plan how you will repeat the elements of line, shape, space, and color to accent the visual rhythms in your painting. Also plan a color scheme that will express the mood of the rhythms in your work. Make notes with crayons or colored pencils in your sketchbook.

Paint your work, covering the entire surface of the paper.

Mount or mat your work for display.

CRITIQUING

Describe Tell which rhythmic activities you chose. Describe how you did your visual research. How many motifs did you use?

Analyze Explain how and where you repeated the elements of line, shape, space, and color. What color scheme did you choose? Which kinds of rhythm did you use? Explain how and where you used them.

Interpret What is the expressive mood of your work? Which elements helped to create that mood?

Judge Which aesthetic theories would you use to judge this work? Were you satisfied with the finished work? If you were to do it over, what, if anything, would you change to improve it?

239

GUIDED PRACTICE
(continued)

Developing Studio Skills

Spend time practicing gesture drawing. Timed sessions set to music will help motivate students. Ask volunteers to take turns posing. If any are willing, they might dance or march to music in front of the class while the gesture drawings are being made. Students could freeze in mid-action and the rest of the class could begin drawing their pose.

Developing Studio Skills

If it is desirable for lines to show through the painting, instruct students to sketch with a soft pencil such as an 8B instead of the yellow chalk. Heavy graphite lines will show through transparent acrylic colors. Tell students to notice how Lawrence has used bold colors to create a festive mood. If they use repeated colors, this effect will add another element to the rhythm of the painting.

INDEPENDENT PRACTICE

Keeping a Portfolio

Remind students that the preliminary sketches and the final artwork for this Studio Lesson are likely considerations for their portfolios.

ASSESS

CRITIQUING

Have students apply the steps of art criticism to their own artwork using the "Critiquing" questions on this page.

CLOSE

Ask each student to describe the kinds of visual rhythm used in his or her painting.

TECHNIQUE TIPS

Remind students that gesture drawing is a way of capturing movement in a sketch; there are no outlines or details. Suggest the following guidelines and see page 349 in the Handbook for more about gesture drawing:

• Use the side of the drawing tool. Do not hold the medium as if writing.

• Find the lines of movement that show the direction in which the figure is bending. Draw the main line showing this movement.

• Use quickly drawn lines to build up the shape of the person.

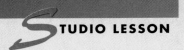
OBJECTIVE

Create a collage in the Persian style by presenting more than one point of view.

MOTIVATOR

Display as many examples of Islamic art as possible, such as woven rugs and wall hangings, metalwork, and pottery. Wooden carvings, glassware, and architecture are important areas of the art of Islam. Ask students to bring to school any Middle Eastern artifacts that they may have at home and share any information that they may have about the objects.

GUIDED PRACTICE

Understanding Art History

Students may be interested in knowing why the teachings of Mohammed prohibited the production of images of living things. It was believed that the people might regard these images as idols or objects of worship. Artists who produced such images were condemned in the afterlife. Consequently, floral images and geometric patterns were widely produced. As mentioned in the text, calligraphy was used, primarily for copying the Koran. Two types of Arabic calligraphy are Kufic and Neskhi. Kufic, a more geometric style, was first used for copying the Koran. Later, Neskhi was used for writing text, and Kufic was used to title chapters in the Koran.

STUDIO LESSON: A PATTERN COLLAGE

FIGURE 9.28 'Abd Allah Musawwir. *The Meeting of the Theologians.* c. 1540–49. Colors on paper. 28.4 × 19 cm (11⅜ × 7½"). Nelson-Atkins Museum of Art, Kansas City, Missouri. Purchase: Nelson Trust.

Supplies

- Sketchbook and pencils
- Ruler, scissors, and white glue
- One large sheet of paper or poster board
- A variety of patterned fabrics and papers
- Colored pencils, watercolors, or acrylics
- Assorted brushes
- Small pieces of white paper for figures

Persian miniature paintings such as the one shown in Figure 9.28 are book illustrations. The primary purpose of these illustrations is to tell stories about sacred religious events and depict the exploits of heroes who accomplished superhuman feats.

Persian painters used pattern, rhythmic designs, and brilliant colors enhanced with gold to create pages that looked like jewels. Artists created many of the pigments used in these paintings by grinding minerals such as gold, silver, lapis lazuli, and malachite. They filled every available space with a rhythmic pattern. Notice how each pattern is filled with intense colors. This emphasis on pattern compresses space. Everything seems to lie flat against the picture plane.

The style of Persian art is not like Western realism. More than one point of view appears in the composition, allowing the artist to portray several events in the same picture.

The Meeting of the Theologians (Figure 9.28) takes place in a religious school, where a young man is seated with a teacher and seven other bearded men. In the doorway a theologian approaches while two beggars hold out their hands begging for alms. This artwork was one page of an illustrated book. Look at it closely and see how the colors, patterns, and calligraphy have been merged to make the story easy to read and visually interesting.

Create a collage in the Persian style by presenting more than one point of view. In this way you can show different aspects of one event in the picture. Organize your work so every shape and space is filled with brightly colored patterns. Create the background shapes using patterned fabrics and papers. People and other objects can be made by drawing and painting them on white paper and cutting them out. The finished composition should not have any feeling of three-dimensional form or space.

MORE ABOUT . . . ISLAMIC STYLE

Because early Islamic artists could not depict the figures of humans or animals, they developed a style of flat, abstract designs to be used in a variety of works. Best known is the arabesque, which comes from the Italian word meaning "Arab-like." These swirling, interlaced designs are apparently based on plant shapes, but the forms of leaves, branches, and vines have been transformed into scrolls, spirals, and curves. Such arabesque designs were first used during the 900s in all Muslim countries. Arabesques and other geometric designs have been used to decorate the walls of buildings, tiles, miniature paintings, rugs, metalware, and other craft objects.

FOCUSING

Brainstorm with classmates about complex events that would be appropriate subjects for this project. Think of an event that can be best explained by showing several scenes. For example, a play involves auditions, rehearsals, costume fittings, and performing.

After the group discussion, choose a situation from your personal experience to illustrate. Think it through by listing the different incidents of this event in your sketchbook. Make some rough sketches. Choose the scenes that you would like to illustrate.

CREATING

Now sketch a plan for dividing your composition into shapes of different sizes and decide where to place your figures. Using the ruler and pencil, lightly draw the dividing lines on a large sheet of paper.

Before you add figures, fill all the rectangles with patterns. Measure each shape and cut out patterned fabrics and papers to fit each shape. As you select each pattern for the background, consider how one will look next to another. Use contrasting patterns so you can see the distinction between each shape. If you wish, you may draw and color patterns in some of the spaces. Glue the fabrics and papers to the background.

On the small pieces of white paper, draw and paint figures and objects to place in different shapes. Consider the pattern you will place each figure against so that the figure will contrast. Cut out the drawn figures and objects and glue them onto the design.

Mount or mat your finished work for display.

FIGURE 9.28A Student work.

CRITIQUING

Describe Identify the event you chose to illustrate. Describe the different scenes. What kinds of patterned materials did you use for your background spaces?

Analyze How did you organize your background spaces? How did you arrange the figures? Did you fill the background with patterns? Is there contrast between patterns and between the figures and the background? Does everything look flat?

Interpret What mood does your finished product express? Give your work an expressive title.

Judge Which aesthetic theories would you use to judge this work? Is it successful? If you were going to do it over, what, if anything, would you change?

241

Developing Studio Skills

Before dividing the paper into rectangles, talk to students about methods of creating visual balance. If you wish to preview balance, refer to pages 252–262 in the text. Also, be aware that white glue will work in this activity, but stitchery tape or a hot glue gun may be desirable for attaching fabric to the paper.

INDEPENDENT PRACTICE

Keeping a Portfolio

Remind students that the preliminary sketches and the final artwork for this Studio Lesson are likely considerations for their portfolios.

Extension

Students may enjoy studying writing in Arabic calligraphy or creating miniature paintings to illustrate a favorite book.

ASSESS

CRITIQUING

Have students apply the steps of art criticism to their own artwork using the "Critiquing" questions on this page. In addition, ask the following: What events were portrayed in the collage? Was every space and shape filled? How? What colors and patterns were chosen to fill the background? What types of people and objects were put into the composition?

CLOSE

Allow time for students to walk around the room and survey the finished designs. If time allows, have volunteers show their collages while other students critique them using the four-step process.

COOPERATIVE LEARNING

Persian miniature paintings are richly colored illustrations. To keep the flat effect that works well with Islamic calligraphy, these artists used several composition devices. One was to build upward in the picture plane instead of using perspective to move back into space. The figures in the back are the same size as those in the foreground but are placed higher in the picture. Another device is the combination of several planes into one—outside and inside spaces. Study Figure 9.28.

Work in small groups to plan a miniature-style painting of the inside and outside of a home, placing people in both spaces.

241

Weaving with a Pattern

FOCUS

OBJECTIVE

Create a strip of kente-type weaving using cardboard frames.

MOTIVATOR

Display a variety of weavings. Generate class discussion based on students' knowledge of weaving. Look for examples of woven clothing that the students might be wearing.

TEACH

GUIDED PRACTICE

Understanding Art History

Ask students to research the history of weaving, including types of looms, types of fibers, and the names of those civilizations known for weaving. Types of looms include the back strap, floor, and primitive. Traditional fibers include cotton, silk, and wool. Today fiber artists weave with just about every material imaginable.

Developing Studio Skills

Alternative media for this lesson might include beads, ceramic pieces, and various objects that can be attached to the weavings. Nontraditional weaving materials for the Extension activity could include torn strips of fabric, wire, torn strips of painted canvas, gauze and bandage strips, grasses and long weeds, wild flowers, twigs, feathers, plastics, stockings, any variety of papers, and so on.

STUDIO LESSON: WEAVING WITH A PATTERN

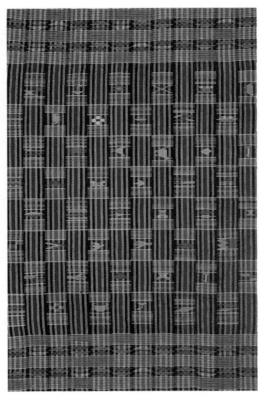

FIGURE 9.29 *Wrapper.* Ewe peoples, Volta region, Ghana. 1972. Cotton and rayon plain weave with cotton and rayon supplementary weft. 201 × 125 cm (79¼ × 49"). National Museum of African Art, Smithsonian Institution, Washington, D.C.

Supplies

- Sketchbook and pencils
- Ruler, scissors, and tape
- Heavy cardboard, 6 x 20 inches (15 x 50.8 cm)
- Ball of strong, thin crochet thread
- Yarns and fibers that vary in color and texture
- Tapestry needle and comb
- Bag to hold materials

In the court at Kumasi, fine textiles were one of the symbols of leadership among the Asante people. The cloth identified the rank and purpose of the wearer. This cloth in Figure 9.29 is commonly known as *kente.*

It is woven on a portable, horizontal treadle loom in strips of cloth 2 to 6 inches (5 to 15 cm) wide. The treadles enable the men to weave elaborate patterns into the strips of cloth. The length of the strips may be a few yards or several hundred yards. When the single strip is finished, it is cut into pieces and sewn together, edge to edge, to make a wider cloth.

Weavers begin as apprentices to master weavers. By the time they become a master weaver, they have memorized the patterns they will weave and the length of each motif. They know what the finished product will look like before they begin. The simplest warp stripes are called *ahwepan.* The most complex, and therefore most costly, weft designs are called *adweneasa,* which means "my skill is exhausted."

Create a narrow strip of kente-type weaving, in the manner of the Asante weavers, using a cardboard loom as a frame. Work with a group of four or five classmates and coordinate your colors and designs. Create a repeat pattern by using one of five techniques. The strip should be 3–4 inches (7.6–10 cm) wide. You can control the length of the strip by the length of your loom. Sew the four or five strips together to make a piece of cloth.

FOCUSING

Confer with your weaving team. Keep visual and verbal notes from the conference in your sketchbook. Decide which of the following weaving techniques you will use to create repeating patterns: (1) Change weft colors to create rectangles; (2) insert weft threads that deflect the ground threads; (3) embroider shapes on the rectangles; (4) change weaving techniques to alter texture; (5) add supplementary weft threads; (6) appliqué shapes on the

---

MORE ABOUT . . . ASANTE WEAVING

The West African narrow-strip loom consists of three or four upright poles to hold the pattern heddles and horizontal elements to control the path of the weaving thread. Warp threads are fastened at one end to a bar, or breast beam, next to the weaver. At the other end the warp is attached to a heavy dragstone, which keeps the necessary tension on the threads so they can be worked. It is this tensioning device, along with the narrow width of the finished cloth strip, that distinguishes the West African men's loom from other looms. African weavers work outside and rarely leave the loom outside when not in use. They take the loom apart and store it with the unfinished cloth.

rectangles. Choose the color scheme, the length of the repeat in the pattern, and the length of the woven strip. See Technique Tip 23 on page 358 in the Handbook.

CREATING

To make your loom, hold the ruler along the top edge of your cardboard. With the pencil, mark off every 1/4 inch (6 mm). Using the scissors, make a cut about 1/2 inch (13 mm) deep at each mark. Do the same thing along the bottom of your cardboard.

Tape the end of your thread to the back of the cardboard. Bring the spool to the front, passing the thread through the top left notch. Pull the spool down to the bottom of the loom. Pass the thread through the bottom left notch to the back. Move one notch to the right. Pull the thread through and up the front of the loom. Keep working until you reach the last notch. Bring the spool to the back. Cut the thread and tape the end of it to the back.

Collect the yarns and fibers that your team selected. Keep all materials in a bag.

Thread one of your thinner yarns through the eye of the tapestry needle. Start to weave at the bottom of your loom. Move the weft thread across the warp, passing over one thread and under the next. When you reach the end of the warp, reverse direction. If you wove over the last thread you must weave under it when you start the second line of weft. Do not pull the weft tightly. Curve it slightly as you pull it through the warp. This is called *ballooning*, and it will prevent the strip from getting narrower as you weave.

After weaving a few rows, pack the weft threads tightly with the comb. The tighter the weft, the stronger the fabric will be. Tight weft will be easier to match with your team. Weave 1 inch (2.5 cm) of tabby before you start making designs.

Be sure to end with another inch of thin, tightly packed tabby weave. Join your strip with those of the other members of your team by sewing them together.

FIGURE 9.29A   Student work.

Prepare your fabric for display. You may mount it on a flat board or hang it from a dowel.

C R I T I Q U I N G

Describe   Explain the procedures your team used to make decisions about the kente-type cloth and list the decisions your team made. Which weaving techniques did you use? How did you display the finished product?

Analyze   What kind of rhythmic pattern did you create in your own strip? What kind of a pattern did you create as a team? Describe the color scheme in your strip. Describe the color scheme of the team's cloth.

Interpret   Considering the colors, textures, and patterns, what useful function could the team's cloth have if it were larger? What mood does it convey?

Judge   What aesthetic theories would you use to judge this work? If you were to do the whole project over, what would you change to improve the finished product?

Developing Studio Skills

To enable everyone in the group to work out the color scheme, suggest that students use colored pencils for their initial sketches. The colored sketches also serve as reference tools for placement of colors in the designs. It will help to make identical sketches of the patterns to attach to the cardboard looms to ensure exact placement of the design from each member of the group. Remind students that it is important to pack the weavings tightly. When the weavings are removed from the looms, it will be easy to make adjustments to match patterns.

INDEPENDENT PRACTICE

Keeping a Portfolio

Remind students that the preliminary sketches and the final artwork for this Studio Lesson are likely considerations for their portfolios.

Extension

Encourage students to weave with various nontraditional materials. Any variety of loom choices can be made.

ASSESS

CRITIQUING

Have students apply the steps of art criticism to their own artwork using the "Critiquing" questions on this page.

CLOSE

Have students critique their work with other students on their team. Then ask each group to answer this question: Which visual element is used most successfully in this weaving?

MEETING SPECIAL NEEDS

Physically and Learning Disabled   Some students with neurological/orthopedic disabilities, learning disabilities, or retardation may be challenged to keep in mind the alternating rhythm of over and under. Large diameter yarn and a warp made of thick rope, even in alternating colors, can help them to achieve success. To help students conceive of alternating over and under, try a body movement exercise in which half the class stands in a row like slalom posts, and the other students weave through them alternating sides. When through, the weaving students become the new posts, and the other students weave through them.

Coil Baskets

OBJECTIVE

Design and create a coil basket form that has a functional or decorative purpose.

MOTIVATOR

Ask students to bring baskets from home. Display as many sizes and varieties as possible.

GUIDED PRACTICE

Promoting Discussion

Generate discussion about the purposes of baskets. Discuss how some baskets are designed for specific purposes. Start some friendly competition by dividing the class into research teams. Tell them to search for books and magazines on basketry. Reward the group or groups who find the following: the oldest basket in existence; the biggest variety of basketry techniques; and the most unusual baskets.

Developing Studio Skills

To make this studio experience more satisfying, students may need to know the following: When cutting the coiling core by using the taper method mentioned in the directions, the cut should be made at an extreme angle. Whenever beginning, ending, or joining cords in the basket, use the taper method. For a tightly stitched basket, wrap around the previous coil every third or fourth stitch. If a looser design is desired, do not stitch as often.

S TUDIO LESSON: COIL BASKETS

FIGURE 9.30 Louisa Keyser (Dat So La Lee). *Basket.* c. 1917–18. Willow, redbud, braken fern. 30 × 41.2 cm (12 × 16¼"). Philbrook Art Center, Tulsa, Oklahoma. Clark Field Collection.

Supplies

- Core material for the warp
- Fibers for the weft: colored yarns, raffia, or natural fibers
- Tapestry needle
- Sharp scissors
- Masking tape
- Sketchbook, pencil, and crayons

T he basket shown in Figure 9.30 was created by Louisa Keyser (Dat So La Lee). She belonged to a small Native American tribe known as the Washoe. They were hunters and gatherers who ranged through the territory around Lake Tahoe, California, following the seasons. The Washoe women made many types of baskets for carrying possessions as the tribe moved between the lakes, mountains, hills, and valley floors in their yearly gathering circuit. Washoe basketry is woven primarily from willow, which was found in the valleys. The Washoe used the coiling technique to make large storage baskets, watertight cooking baskets, and *degikups,* which were small spherical baskets for ceremonial use.

This basket is one of Keyser's variations of the *degikup* form. It rises gradually from a narrow base until it reaches a maximum width at three-quarters of its height. This design is called the scatter

Louisa Keyser was free to experiment with aesthetic concerns because she had a patron, Abe Cohn. He provided Louisa and her husband Charlie with food, clothing, and medical care. He even built them a house next to his own home. Secure from economic concerns, Louisa was free to develop her art. Louisa designed larger baskets, and developed finer stitching. She created a new color scheme based on the contrasting colors of black (mud-dyed, bracken-fern root) and red (redbud branch). The result was her variation of the *degikup,* a fabric sculpture without utilitarian function and without precedent in traditional Washoe basketweaving.

pattern. It consists of a series of stepped triangles arranged vertically. In this basket the artist has increased the size of the triangles to match the form of the basket. Then she has diminished the design as the form curves inward. She has used the progressive rhythm of the design to emphasize the form of the basket. She created an illusion of perspective in which the exaggerated curve of the design mirrors the form of the basket, unifying the basket with its design.

Study Louisa Keyser's basket to see how she used rhythm in her design and then plan your own coil basket.

To prepare for this lesson, practice the coil method of basket making until you have satisfactorily started and completed a simple flat coaster using the "lazy squaw" stitch in a regular rhythm. When you have mastered the technique, design and create a unique coil basket form that has either a functional or decorative purpose. Organize arrangement of the colors of the weft into a random, regular, alternating, or progressive rhythm.

FOCUSING

Study the directions for the coil method of basket making in Technique Tip 24 in the Handbook, page 360. Following those directions, use about 2 feet (61 cm) of core material to make a small coaster using the "lazy squaw" stitch. If the center of your coaster does not look right the first time, undo it and start over. This is the most difficult part of making the basket. Finish the coaster using the taper method.

CREATING

Draw several plans in your sketchbook and select your best plan. Choose your color scheme and note the materials and colors you will use to make the weft. Decide whether you will use regular, alternating, or progressive rhythm to organize your colors. Note your decision in the sketchbook and color the design to indicate how you will use the colors.

FIGURE 9.30A   Student work.

Construct the basket form based on your design. You will control the position of the warp coils by holding them in position as you sew the stitches that connect the coils. You can position them to go up vertically or to slant in or out. Finish your basket using the taper method.

CRITIQUING

Describe   Explain the procedures you followed to create your basket, including the practice coaster.

Analyze   Describe the form of your basket. Tell what color scheme you used and explain which type of rhythm you used to organize your colors.

Interpret   Did you create a functional or decorative basket? Explain. How did your use of color and pattern affect the feeling of your basket?

Judge   Which aesthetic theories would you use to judge this work? If you were to make another basket, what, if anything, would you change? Explain.

TECHNIQUE TIPS

If students have not worked with clay recently, they may need to feel the way the clay works before they can plan how to use it. Students might begin by squeezing and shaping the clay into forms from their own imagination. Have a variety of clay tools available for them to experiment with modeling techniques. Remind them of the following guidelines or see pages 354 and 355 in the Handbook:

• Dip one or two fingers in water.
• Spread the moisture from their fingers over their palms.
• Never completely dip their hands in water as too much moisture turns clay to mud.

INTRODUCTION

Janet was chosen because it is one of the earliest color works done by Close after the illness that paralyzed him. The subject of the painting is a photograph of his artist friend, Janet Fish. (See Figures 1.2 on page 7, and 8.14 on page 198.) Close has always painted from his photographs, using a grid to copy one square at a time.

Vermeer's work was chosen as a comparison piece because both are paintings of a woman's head. Once again, students should realize that there are similarities between two works that, at first, look completely different.

CRITIQUING THE WORK

1. Describe This is a portrait of a woman wearing glasses. The head takes up most of the composition. The bottom third of the work shows the woman's neck and the beginning of her shoulders.

2. Analyze The work is full of implied lines, such as the black dashes of her glasses and the plaid-like pattern in the background.

The background is darker, but it has red between the black and blue lines, and is not as warm as the positive area. The texture is definitely that of the brushstrokes.

The background is primarily an alternating rhythm; it almost looks woven. Across the face are progressive color and value movements. The repetition of brushstrokes to create a rhythm gives this work a sparkling effect.

FIGURE 9.31 Chuck Close. *Janet.* 1989. Oil on canvas. 91.4 × 76.2 cm (36 × 30″). Photo by Bill Jacobson. Courtesy of the Pace Gallery, New York, New York.

CRITIQUING THE WORK

1. Describe Read the credit line for Figure 9.31 to find out the size of the work and the medium with which it was created. Now describe the subject of this painting. What do you see?

2. Analyze Before you study Close's use of rhythm, look at the way he has used the elements. Do you see any lines? Where? What kind? How has he used shape and space? Is there any illusion of three dimensions in the work? How has he used color? What kinds of color dominate the work? Has he imitated the texture of the subject or has he emphasized the texture of the paint itself?

What kinds of visual rhythms do you see? Can you find any examples of random, regular, alternating, flowing, and progressive rhythm? How does Close's unusual use of rhythm affect the look of this work?

3. Interpret Based on the clues you collected and your own personal experience, write a brief paragraph explaining your interpretation of the painting *Janet*. What type of

RESOURCES BEYOND THE CLASSROOM

Other Works By . . . Chuck Close
Robert / 104, 072
Other Works By . . . Vermeer
The Love Letter
Woman Holding a Balance
The Astronomer
The Geographer

Christ in the House of Mary and Martha
The Artist's Studio
Allegory of Faith
Little Street
Diana and Her Companions

FIGURE 9.32 Jan Vermeer. *The Girl with the Red Hat.* c. 1665. Oil on panel. 23.1 × 18.1 cm (9⅛ × 7⅛"). National Gallery of Art, Washington, D.C. Andrew W. Mellon Collection.

person do you think Janet is? How does she make you feel? Write a new title for this work that sums up your interpretation.

4. Judge Do you think this is a successful work of art? Why or why not? Use one or more of the aesthetic theories explained in Chapter 2 to defend your opinion.

COMPARING THE WORKS

Look at *Janet* by Chuck Close (Figure 9.31) and *The Girl with the Red Hat* by Jan Vermeer (Figure 9.32). At first you may think there are no similarities between the two works. Look, however, at the subject matter, the colors, the contrast of dark and light values, and the relationship of positive and negative space. What did you discover? In what ways are the two works different? You have analyzed Close's use of rhythm. How did Vermeer use rhythm in the organization of his work?

COMPARING THE WORKS

Both artworks have the same subject; they are paintings of the head and shoulders of a woman. Close's color scheme is warm, and even though Vermeer paints the woman's shawl with a blue, it is a warm aqua, giving *The Girl with the Red Hat* a warm feeling to it as well. There is a contrast of dark and light in *Janet*. The background is darker than the face, and areas of the face show shadows. Vermeer uses light like a spotlight. He highlights one spot of the woman's face, a bit of her shawl, and the top of her hat. The background in Figure 9.31 is a low-intensity yellow and black. In both works, the woman is the positive shape, and the background is the negative space. The greatest difference is the use of realism: Vermeer paints in a very realistic style, imitating the textures of skin, satin, and wood, while Close is concerned with the quality of brushstrokes. Vermeer's rhythms are much more subtle than Close's. The rhythms in Figure 9.32 are in the repetition of the flowing diagonal of the edge of the red hat, and the flowing diagonal lines in the fold of the shawl.

EXTENSION

- Have students read more about Chuck Close in the "Meet the Artist" feature on the following page.
- Assign *Artist's Profile 9* in the TCR.

247

MORE ABOUT . . . JAN VERMEER

In Vermeer's world, artists did not receive the high social position that was enjoyed by such Italian Renaissance artists as Raphael. Dutch artists of Vermeer's time were considered craftspeople, and their financial success was in the hands of the new wealthy middle class. This new class wanted artworks that showed scenes of everyday life rather than religious scenes. Paintings of this type became known as "genre" paintings. Soon even innkeepers and picture framers were art dealers and regulated the prices that artists could get for their works.

ASSESS

CHECKING COMPREHENSION

- On a separate sheet of paper have students complete "Building Vocabulary" and "Reviewing Art Facts" on page 249.
- Assign *Application 17* and *18* in the TCR to evaluate students' comprehension.

ANSWERS TO BUILDING VOCABULARY

1. rhythm
2. visual rhythm
3. motif
4. module
5. pattern
6. movement
7. kinetic

ANSWERS TO REVIEWING ART FACTS

1. By the measure of time between musical sounds.
2. By repeated positive shapes separated by negative spaces.
3. The viewer's eye follows the visual beats through a work of art.
4. Rhythm is repetition intended to create the feeling of movement. Pattern is intended to be flat and decorative.
5. With different arrangements of motif and space.
6. A motif is repeated in no apparent order, with no regular spaces.
7. By using identical motifs and equal amounts of space between the motifs.
8. A second motif is used, the placement or content of the original motif is changed, or the spaces between the motifs are changed.
9. Repeating wavy lines are used.
10. A steady change is made in the motif each time it is repeated.

248

CHUCK CLOSE
American, b. 1940

Chuck Close is not a portrait painter in the traditional sense. He does not paint portraits of people, he creates paintings based on photographs that he has taken of people. For twenty years he was known as a leading Photo-Realist. He painted black-and-white, exact imitations of photographs and he was very successful.

Then in the late 1980s he suffered an illness that left him partially paralyzed. During his recovery he was determined to get back to painting, although he could use only his arms—his hands didn't work.

Sitting in a wheelchair, Close paints using a device that straps around the middle of his forearm, his wrist, and his fingers and thumb. At first, he needed help getting the brush in and out of the brush holder. Gradually, he developed a technique for accomplishing this with his teeth. He also has a forklift that raises him to the top of his gigantic paintings.

Close feared that others would pity him as a disabled artist. When the Museum of Modern Art bought the first large painting he made after he was dismissed from the hospital, however, he was encouraged. He knew the Museum of Modern Art did not buy art just to make someone feel better.

His new work is no longer photo-realistic, but he still works with a grid from photographs. His new works, in color, have been widely praised by the critics for their abundance of color and light.

MORE PORTFOLIO IDEAS

Take a small school photograph of yourself and make a copy of it on a photocopier. The copy will be black and white. Make a grid and copy the photo on a piece of white paper. Shade the work to match the values in the photocopy.

Use an old, small, colored school photograph of yourself. Draw a grid on the photo and then draw a grid double the original size on a sheet of white paper. Working directly with paint and brush, use dabs and shapes of color in the style of Close's *Janet* to make a loose color copy of the photo.

248

DEVELOPING A PORTFOLIO

Personal Style The success of a portfolio is somewhat based on the ability of the student to impress evaluators with his or her style. Personal talents are showcased in the portfolio, but can only be effective when students learn to set long-term aims and sustain projects that eventually meet those goals. Ask them to regularly evaluate their constructive efforts toward the complete portfolio. How aware is each student of his or her style? What do they know about their style that will help them strengthen the portfolio's presentation? Have they chosen pieces that emphasize their style?

CHAPTER 9 REVIEW

Building Vocabulary

On a separate sheet of paper, write the term that best matches each definition given below.
1. The principle of design that indicates movement by the repetition of elements.
2. Rhythm you receive through your eyes rather than through your ears.
3. A unit that is repeated in visual rhythm.
4. A three-dimensional motif.
5. A two-dimensional decorative visual repetition.
6. The principle of art used to create the look and feeling of action and to guide the viewer's eyes throughout the work of art.
7. A kind of sculpture that actually moves in space.

Reviewing Art Facts

Answer the following questions using complete sentences.
1. How is rhythm created in music?
2. In general, how is visual rhythm created?
3. How does rhythm add a sense of movement to a work of art?
4. What is the difference between rhythm and pattern?
5. In general, how are different rhythms created?
6. How is random rhythm created?
7. Tell how regular rhythm is created.
8. Describe how alternating rhythm is created.
9. How is flowing rhythm created?
10. Tell how progressive rhythm is created.

Thinking Critically About Art

1. **Compare and contrast.** Study the subject matter of the *Hmong Story Cloth* (Figure 9.1 on page 220) and *Parade* (Figure 9.27 on page 238). List the similarities and differences you find. Are the themes of the two works similar or different? Explain.
2. **Extend.** The *Elevator Grille* in Figure 9.6 on page 225 was designed by the architect Louis Sullivan for a building he designed. Find information about Louis Sullivan in the library. Discover what contributions he had made to the field of architecture in the late nineteenth and early twentieth centuries. Give a brief report to the class about the importance of Louis Sullivan in the history of American architecture.
3. **Synthesize.** Use a tape recorder to collect nonmusical rhythmic sounds. Try to find sounds that match the various types of visual rhythm: random, regular, alternating, progressive, and flowing. Bring your tape to class and share the sounds with your classmates.

Making Art Connections

1. **Language Arts.** Write a poem or paragraph to express the differences between the rhythms of today's technological world and the pace of horse-and-buggy days gone by. Use rhythm in your language.
2. **Science.** Make a chart illustrating the life cycle of a plant or animal. Emphasize the rhythmic quality of that cycle.
3. **Music.** Discuss the principle of rhythm with your music teacher. Find out if musicians use the same types of rhythms as visual artists do. Try to find a work of music to illustrate at least two of the visual rhythms or create a musical rhythm to match at least two of the visual rhythm types.
4. **Language Arts.** To tell her story in the *Hmong Story Cloth* (Figure 9.1, page 220), Chaing Xiong used repetition and movement to carry you through her story. Can you find an example in literature where the author used repetition to help create the mood of the story? Write a brief paragraph about the author's use of repetition and how you think it affected the mood or theme of the work.

ALTERNATIVE ASSESSMENT

Ask students to work in pairs or small groups and design, create, then display an artwork that reflects what they have learned about rhythm and movement. One idea is a poster that uses the same motif with each of the five types of rhythm. Another idea is to plan an art display of the artworks created in the activities in this chapter. Each section of the display would have a group of artworks that the students consider to be most successful in demonstrating the objectives of the activity. Remind students that they will be evaluated on the material selected for the display as well as the overall aesthetic value of the display itself.

Balance

CHAPTER OVERVIEW

Chapter 10 examines balance as a principle of design as well as a principle of life, and it helps students understand the different types of balance. They expand their knowledge by exploring the expressive qualities of balance in art.

CHAPTER SUPPLIES

Refer to the "Art Supplies Grid" in the Teacher's Manual. In addition, have on hand the following special items: found objects for a still life, magazines, newspapers, and fabric pieces.

FINE ART RESOURCES

Transparencies
- Stephen Bayless. *Freight Doors*
- *Face of Glory (Kirttimukha)*
- Minnie Lacy. *Basket Tray*
- Ma Wan. *Spring Landscape*

Fine Art Prints
- John Sloan. *Red Kimono on the Roof*
- Milton Avery. *Seated Blonde*

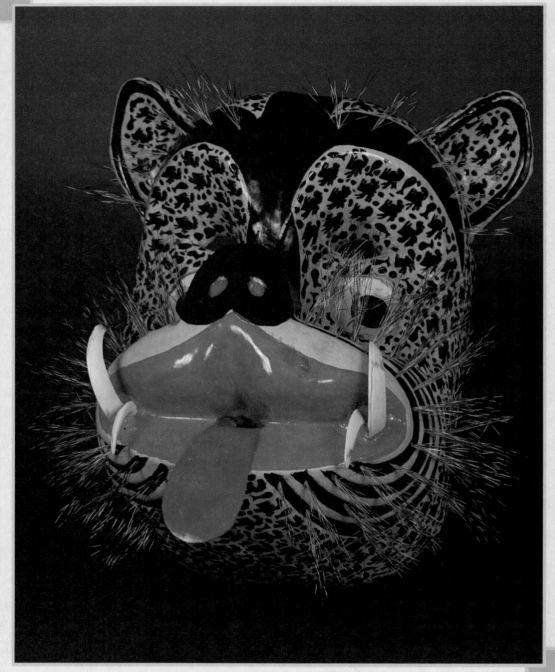

FIGURE 10.1 This mask was made to be worn during a ceremony called the Dance of the Jaguar. It was carved from wood and then painted.

Artist unknown. *Jaguar Mask*. Mexico. Papier-mâché, enamel paint, straw.

RESOURCES FOR CHAPTER 10

Application Activities 19, 20
Artist's Profiles 10, 19, 34, 35, 36, 37, 40
Cooperative Learning Activities 19, 20
Cultural Diversity in Art
Enrichment Activities 19, 20

Reteaching Activities
 Study Guide 10
 Concept Map 10
Studio Lessons 16, 17, 18
Chapter 10 Test

Balance

Balance is a principle of life. Every animal must balance breathing in and breathing out. The earth stays in orbit because the pull of the sun is balanced by the earth's revolution around the sun. Without balance we feel uncomfortable. Artists use this feeling to communicate with us.

We all need to use balance to function from day to day. It is hard to keep your balance when you are standing up in a moving train or bus. It is also hard to balance a stack of books you are carrying to your locker. Because of your ability to balance, you can stand erect and walk on two limbs instead of four.

Have you ever watched a toddler wobble, fall, and struggle to get back up? The toddler learns to use leg muscles and shifts in weight to overcome the effects of gravity. He or she learns to balance the force of gravity with the force of muscle.

As you read this chapter, you will begin to understand how artists use the elements of art to create different kinds of balance in their works. You will learn why balance is important in both two-dimensional and three-dimensional art, and you will discover techniques for creating balance in your own artworks.

Objectives

After completing this chapter, you will be able to:

- Understand why balance is important in a work of art.
- Explain how visual weight is created and produce it in your own work.
- Describe the types of balance and use them in your own work.
- Tell what different types of balance can mean in a work of art.

Words to Know

balance
central axis
formal balance
informal balance
radial balance
symmetry

FIRST IMPRESSIONS

Do you know what kind of balance was used to organize the features of this mask shown in Figure 10.1? Notice that the black spots of the fur represent small creatures. Can you recognize the shapes? What other features do you notice that contribute to the impact of this jaguar mask?

251

FOCUS

INTRODUCING THE CHAPTER

Have students make a list of at least five objects they use or see every day that have balance. Ask them to imagine what the objects would be like if they did not have balance. Tell them that in this chapter they will learn about another principle of design—balance.

MOTIVATOR

If you have or can borrow a two-sided balance scale, bring it to class. Another method that will achieve the same results is to balance a sturdy ruler or piece of board over a square block, flat cup, or even the palm of your hand. Challenge students to place small, unlike objects on the sides of the scale, or the ends of the ruler. Coach them in rearranging, adding, or subtracting objects to make the sides balance.

VOCABULARY PREVIEW

Have students preview the list of vocabulary words on this page. Also, acquaint them with these words that will appear in the chapter: imbalance and asymmetrical.

USING FIRST IMPRESSIONS

Have students study Figure 10.1 then answer the questions in the box on this page. Help them notice that the mask is organized with formal balance. The small shapes are black spots that form the shapes of fish, birds, and small animals. Answers to the last question will vary.

TEACHER TALK

A Success Story Each autumn, Carlyne Seegraves, Elementary Art Consultant for the East Grand Rapids Public Schools in Grand Rapids, Michigan, prepares a lesson plan that she knows will be a big success. First, students complete a biographical study of van Gogh's life and his artistic style. Next, they study a large bouquet of real sunflowers for inspiration and direction regarding color, shape, balance, and so on. On large pieces of black construction paper, students use contrasting hot and cool colors of sunflowers to make startling images of color. According to Carlyne, students and parents alike are so thrilled that many of the final artworks have been professionally framed!

(pages 252–263)
• Visual Balance

GUIDED PRACTICE

Critical Thinking

Ask students to think about balance in sports. If possible, borrow a balance beam from the physical education teacher. Invite students to walk the beam, then ask them to describe how they felt trying to maintain their balance. Relate this to how a young child feels when learning to walk. Ask students to discuss specific events that require good balance in sports. If possible, have them demonstrate.

Interdisciplinary: Dance

If you have ballet dancers in the class who can dance on point, ask them to discuss the training. Ask for a demonstration of the technique.

Developing Perceptual Skills

To help the students understand the concept of the axis that divides a work, first show them how the axis works in Figures 10.3 and 10.4 on this page. Ask them to look through other chapters to find works where the axis is obvious and where the axis can only be sensed.

Developing Studio Skills

Challenge students with this exercise: Using formal balance, create a composition that presents the image of something that you think is very important. Make several sketches with pencil and paper. Be sure that you have drawn the object you are presenting very accurately. Choose your best design. Draw it large and paint it with tempera paint.

FIGURE 10.2   This building is known throughout the world, not because of its beauty or because the architect is well known, but because it leans. The many diagonal lines tell the viewer that this building must either straighten up or fall down. Because it remains off balance, defying gravity, it is famous.

Bell Tower of the Cathedral at Pisa (The Leaning Tower of Pisa). Begun in 1174.

VISUAL BALANCE

A work of art must contain balance. **Balance** is *the principle of design concerned with equalizing visual forces, or elements, in a work of art.* Visual balance causes you to feel that the elements have been arranged just right.

A visual *imbalance* creates a feeling of uneasiness. It makes you feel that something isn't quite right. You feel a need to rearrange the elements, just like you might feel a need to straighten a picture on the wall (Figure 10.2).

In the real world a balance scale can be used to measure equal weights. In visual art balance must be *seen* rather than weighed. The art elements become the visual forces, or weights, in an art object. A **central axis** is *a dividing line that works like the point of balance in the balance scale.*

Many works of art have a central vertical axis (Figure 10.3) with equal visual weight on both sides. Artists also use a horizontal axis. In works with a horizontal axis, the weight is balanced between top and bottom (Figure 10.4).

There are basically two types of balance: formal and informal. They differ in how elements are arranged around the axis.

Formal Balance

Formal balance occurs *when equal, or very similar, elements are placed on opposite sides of a central axis.* The axis may be a real part of the design, or it

FIGURE 10.3   (at left) With a vertical axis, there is equal visual weight on both sides.

FIGURE 10.4   (at right) Artists also use a horizontal axis, arranging the balance between top and bottom.

Physically Disabled   Students with neurological or orthopedic disabilities may have physical problems with balance; some will use wheelchairs, canes, or walkers. Thus, in discussing balance, it may be sensitive to also discuss the occasional advantages of being a little off-balance, such as falling into new exciting circumstances and meeting new people. In as much as a study of symmetry (bilateral and quadrilateral) has analogies to orthopedic disabilities, some terminology may be helpful: paraplegia affects either both arms or both legs; hemiplegia affects the arm and leg on one side of the body; and quadriplegia affects all four limbs.

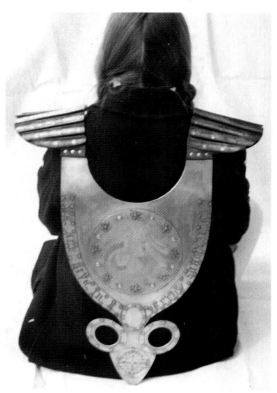

FIGURE 10.5 This unusually large nose ornament was designed using formal balance to fit the balance of the human face. It was fitted to the pierced septum by the clips at the middle of the top edge. The beast heads on either side rise up over the cheekbones.

Loma Negra, Peru. *Nose Ornament*. Moche period, first to third century. Silver, gold, inlays of shell. Width: 20.8 × 12.3 cm (8⅜ × 4⅞"). The Metropolitan Museum of Art, New York, New York. The Michael C. Rockefeller Memorial Collection. Bequest of Nelson A. Rockefeller, 1979.

may be an imaginary line, such as that in Figures 10.3 and 10.4.

Formal balance is the easiest type of balance to recognize and to create (Figure 10.5). After you find the axis, all you have to do is match objects on each side and place them equally distant from the center.

Symmetry. Symmetry is *a special type of formal balance in which two halves of a balanced composition are identical, mirror images of each other* (Figure 10.6). Another term for this is *bilateral* symmetry.

The strong appeal symmetry has for us may be related to the bilateral symmetry of the human body. Things closely associated with our bodies, such as clothing and furniture, are usually symmetrical. Most traditional architecture, especially public architecture, is symmetrical (Figure 10.7 on page 254).

Symmetry is very stiff. Artists use it to express dignity, endurance, and stability. Because formal balance is so predictable, however, it can be dull. Many artists avoid boring the viewer by using approximate symmetry, which is *almost* symmetrical.

Approximate symmetry has the stability of formal balance (Figure 10.8, page 254). Some small differences make it more interesting than perfect symmetry. If you look carefully in a mirror, you may discover that your face has approximate symmetry. The two sides do not match perfectly.

FIGURE 10.6 This body adornment is symmetrical to match the symmetry of the human body. The symmetry communicates dignity, which was the expressive intent of the artist who designed the adornment.

Leslie Mims Tichich. *Body Adornment*. c. 1970. Copper, brass, and leather with decorative ornaments applied. Private collection.

 Using Symmetry

1. Applying Your Skills.   Using shapes cut from construction paper, create a symmetrical design on a small sheet of paper. Organize both sides into accurate mirror images of each other before you glue them down on the sheet of paper.

2. Further Challenge.   Arrange a symmetrical still life and make a pencil drawing of the arrangement on a small sheet of paper (Figure 10.9 on page 255). Then rearrange or change the objects slightly to create approximate symmetry (Figure 10.10, page 255). Make a drawing of the second arrangement. Mount the drawings side by side on a sheet of construction paper and label each drawing. Which one do you prefer? Survey your friends to find out their preferences.

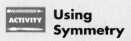

COOPERATIVE LEARNING

To help students remember the different types of balance, divide the class into small groups. Write the following terms on cards: *symmetry, approximate symmetry, radial balance,* and *informal balance.* Turn the cards over so the words are hidden; then have one student from each group choose a card. Each group is to pose in a tableau to illustrate the type of balance on the card. Give the groups about five minutes to plan their design. They may use props found in the classroom if they wish. For example, each member of one group may hold a book, but the way that the book is held may add to the pose. When they are ready, have them act out the scenes.

GUIDED PRACTICE
(continued)

Interdisciplinary: Physics

Borrow a balance scale with weights from the science department to help students grasp the concepts of balance and imbalance.

Bring in an assortment of objects of varying densities, such as paper clips, styrofoam forms, a baseball, a leather football, a foam football, a large feather, an acorn, a live plant in a pot of soil, an arrangement of silk flowers in a basket, pebbles, corks, a plastic cup, a stoneware mug, and so on. Try to find more objects that are the same size but different weights, such as the leather and foam balls. Allow students time to experiment with the scales to discover that size and weight are not always equal.

Use the scales to demonstrate the difference between formal and informal balance. With formal balance both size and weight must be equal. With informal balance the weights must remain equal, but the sizes may change. For example, a few small paper clips may balance a large styrofoam ball.

Using Art Criticism

Have students imagine that the couple illustrated in Figure 10.8 has decided to seek the advice of a marriage counselor or minister. Ask three volunteers to role-play a first session between the couple and the professional. In preparing for their activity, the trio of students should make a list of probable quirks, worries, and problems based on Wood's acutely psychological portrait. To enhance the drama, supply a few props that appear in Wood's painting, such as a cameo pin, an apron, wire-rimmed glasses, and a dark jacket.

254

FIGURE 10.7 This entrance to the Federal Reserve Building in Washington, D.C., is very important looking. The symmetrical arrangement of vertical and horizontal shapes gives the building a secure, stable look.

Cram, Goodhue, and Ferguson. Federal Reserve Building. 1935. Washington, D.C. Façade. Photography by Sandak, Inc., Stamford, Connecticut.

FIGURE 10.8 This painting has become a symbol of what people mean when they talk about, "the good old days." It represents a Midwestern farmer and his daughter. The models were the artist's sister and his dentist. By using formal balance, Wood gives the work a stiff, serious mood, but by switching to approximate symmetry rather than pure symmetry, he adds that nostalgic, "folksy" look.

Grant Wood. *American Gothic*. 1930. Oil on beaverboard. 76 × 63.3 cm (29⅞ × 24⅞"). Collection, Friends of American Art Collection. © 1987 The Art Institute of Chicago, Chicago, Illinois. 1930.

MEETING SPECIAL NEEDS

Learning Disabled The Interdisciplinary activity above demonstrates that the types of formal balance are concrete arrangements of elements and can be easily defined and understood. However, informal balance is elusive, vague, and difficult to comprehend, since it must be felt and cannot be measured. This means that for students who have learning disabilities, experimenting with an assortment of objects of various densities on the balance scales will make the concept easier to grasp. When they understand how objects that are different in size can have the same real weight, the concept of different visual weights seems less foreign.

FIGURE 10.9   Student work. A symmetrical still life.

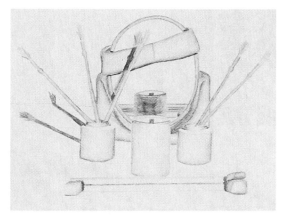

FIGURE 10.10   Student work. A still life arranged with approximate symmetry.

FIGURE 10.11   Radial balance.

3. Computer Option. Do a simple landscape drawing on the left half of the screen. Use the Select tool and the Copy, Paste, and Flip options to duplicate the drawing on the right half of the screen. This will create a symmetrical landscape. If your software does not have these options, you can simply draw a mirror image of the landscape you drew on the left half of the screen. Save the drawing. Use the Select tool to slightly rearrange the placement by moving certain objects in the landscape. Save the second drawing. Compare the two drawings. Which do you prefer? Why?

Radial Balance. Radial balance occurs *when the forces or elements of a design come out (radiate) from a central point.* The axis in a radial design is the center point. In almost all cases the elements are spaced evenly around the axis to form circular patterns (Figure 10.11).

Radial balance is really a complicated variation of symmetry. While symmetry means only two matching units, designs with radial balance may involve four or more matching units. (Figure 10.12). The design seen in a kaleidoscope is a good

FIGURE 10.12   Notice how the radial design of this tray starts with four matching units at the center. As the design moves outward, the repetitions become more complicated and increase to eight around the rim of the tray.

Southeastern Song dynasty. *Carved Lacquer Circular Tray.* 1127–1279. Black, red, and yellow lacquer on wood. 5.2 × 34.9 cm (2⅛ × 13¾"). Arthur M. Sackler Gallery, Smithsonian Institution, Washington, D.C. Arthur M Sackler Collection.

CULTURAL PERSPECTIVES

Have students recall their experiences with kites. How did it feel to balance the kite in the air? Tell them that there are conflicting legends about the origin of the kite. Most historians agree that kites existed in China by the third century B.C. The Chinese considered kites to be vital in warfare. They were used to measure the distance from one army to the other, to carry ropes across impassable rivers, or even to frighten the enemy with the illusion of falling stars. During the fifteenth century, kites were introduced into Europe. They remained just a source of amusement until the eighteenth and nineteenth centuries. At that point the kite was used in science and technology, leading to model gliders.

LOOKING CLOSELY

Have students study Figure 10.13 then answer the questions in the caption. Encourage students to see that every scene has a phrase stitched on. Across the bottom it reads: "from the mountains . . . to the prairies . . . to the ocean." The scene in the upper left corner has a yellow Bulloch County school bus pulling in front of a modern Statesboro High School. The scene in the upper right corner contains the old-fashioned Bulloch County Courthouse. These are names from Garrison's home town. Interpretations of the design will vary. Encourage students to explain their responses.

Creating Radial Balance

1. Applying Your Skills. Automobile and travel magazines might have different wheel designs that display radial balance. Flower and seed catalogs would also be valuable resources.

2. Further Challenge. This activity requires perception drawing. You might arrange a still life using objects that have radial balance, such as clocks, wheels, baskets, round toys, round pillows, some kitchen utensils, pumpkins, and cantaloupes. If you want to use smaller objects, place some of the following on each table: an apple cut horizontally; half of an orange, lemon, or grapefruit; green pepper cut crosswise; cut cucumber; onion; or individual flowers such as daisies.

LOOKING CLOSELY

FIGURE 10.13 Garrison designed this quilt for the 100th anniversary of the Statue of Liberty. She used the traditional radial design of the Star of Bethlehem pattern to represent the light of liberty but surrounded it with scenes that celebrate liberty throughout our country. What parts of American culture do you see represented? What shapes has the artist pieced together to create the radial design of the eight-pointed star? How did the artist use radial balance to gradually change the colors? What does this quilt tell you about the artist's attitude toward her country?

Elizabeth Garrison. *Long May Our Land Be Bright*. 1986. Quilt. Private collection.

example of radial balance. The continually changing shapes at the end of the tube radiate from a central axis. Elizabeth Garrison used the traditional radial design of the Star of Bethlehem quilting pattern to represent the light of liberty. She designed this quilt to celebrate the anniversary of the Statue of Liberty (Figure 10.13).

Radial balance occurs frequently in nature. Most flower petals are arranged around a central axis and radiate outward. Many plants follow radial patterns of growth. For instance, if you cut an apple in half horizontally, you will see a radial star design. Cut an orange the same way and notice the radial pattern of segments.

You can find many examples of radial balance in architecture. Domes are designed on the principle of radial balance. Manufactured items such as gears, wheels, tires, dials, and clocks are also radial in structure. Radial designs are used by many potters to decorate the surfaces of their work because they adapt well to the rounded forms of pottery (Figure 10.14).

 Creating Radial Balance

1. Applying Your Skills. Collect magazine and newspaper photographs of at least six objects that have radial balance. Mount them for display.

2. Further Challenge. Make a series of drawings of five natural or manufactured objects that have a radial structure. Emphasize the radial quality of each object.

3. Computer Option. Use the Shape tool and the Copy and Paste options to produce a design consisting of five squares. One square should be in the center of the screen. The other four should be placed over, under, and on either side of the center square to form the shape of a plus sign (+). Use the Shape tool to draw another symmetrical shape. Copy and Paste this shape on the edge of the four outside squares that are farthest away from the center square. Continue adding shapes to create radial balance. You may add to the center square, but you must maintain radial balance

COOPERATIVE LEARNING

Have students work in groups to design a quilt that reflects the work of Elizabeth Garrison. Group members should begin by selecting a story, theme, or message that they want to depict in their quilt. Have available books, craft magazines, or catalogs from department stores that show examples of quilt patterns. Then, using large squares of paper, have them work together to plan, sketch in, and paint all the parts of the design. Let group members display their completed quilts and answer any questions other students may have about the story, theme, or message.

within the square. Save your work. Try a more complex radial design. Use the Flip and Rotate options if your computer software has them.

Informal Balance

Informal balance gives the viewer the same comfortable feeling as does formal balance, but in a much more subtle way. **Informal balance** involves *a balance of unlike objects.* This is possible because two unlike objects can have equal *visual weight* (Figure 10.15).

FIGURE 10.14   Torivio is a Native American potter who has developed her own style for decorating her pots. She repeats the designs in radial patterns, and she plans the design carefully. The motif starts out small at the top rim and then expands to the widest part of the vessel.

Dorothy Torivio. *Vase.* c. 1984. Clay. Height about 20 cm (8″). Heard Museum Collection, Phoenix, Arizona.

FIGURE 10.15   The complex shapes of the wagon and the child are informally balanced by the potted plant and the foliage in this casual scene. Informal balance gives this composition the look of a snapshot.

Thomas Eakins. *Baby at Play.* 1876. Oil on canvas. 81.9 × 122.8 cm (32¼ × 48⅜″). National Gallery of Art, Washington, D.C. John Hay Whitney Collection.

CURRICULUM CONNECTION

Social Studies   Graphic communication began with simple materials and hand-drawn designs and images, probably similar to the design in Figure 10.14, above. Many cave paintings may have been records and teaching aids for young hunters (see Figure 3.3, page 43). Petroglyphs, etched into rock, represent records and messages. Native American groups have traditions of storytelling by symbolic drawings in soft earth; sand painting is a graphic ritual for others. Have students work in groups to learn more about one of these forms of graphic communication.

GUIDED PRACTICE
(continued)

**Understanding
Art History**

Remind students that Edward Hopper was strongly influenced by Robert Henri and the Armory Show of 1913, which he took part in. Encourage students to research more about this artist and this important event, then share their findings with the class.

Promoting Discussion

Have students carefully study Hopper's painting in Figure 10.16. Then ask them to suggest words that describe the mood and the scene of the painting. Using their knowledge of the elements and principles of art, they should explain how the painting evokes their responses.

Art Is Everywhere

To foster students' awareness of balance in everyday life, suggest this: Look at city maps to see if streets are in a balanced arrangement. Washington D.C. and Paris are built with radial symmetry, with the Capitol and the Arc de Triomphe as their respective centers. Find cities that are built as a grid of balanced sections and others with streets that meander along a river or up a hill. City designs affect the way people live and move in them. Find the city centers of towns and large cities. See how the residential and business sections are balanced in relation to the center. Look at the beautiful balance in the design of cloverleaf entrances and exit ramps to expressways.

FIGURE 10.16 The many small shapes in the lower right corner of this painting balance the large shape of the stage with its closed curtain.

Edward Hopper. *First Row Orchestra.* 1951. Oil on canvas. 79.3 × 102 cm (31¼ × 40⅛"). Hirshhorn Museum and Sculpture Garden, Smithsonian Institution, Washington, D.C. Gift of Joseph H. Hirshhorn Foundation, 1966.

Informal, or *asymmetrical,* balance creates a very casual effect. It seems less planned than formal balance; however, it is not. What appears to be an accidental arrangement of elements can be quite complicated. Symmetry merely requires that elements be repeated in a mirror image. Informal balance goes beyond that. Artists consider all the visual weight factors and put them together correctly.

Of course, gravity does not pull on an object in a two-dimensional work of art. The viewer does, however, perceive the objects in the work as if gravity were in effect. Many factors influence the visual weight, or the attraction, that elements in a work of art have for the viewer's eyes.

Size and Contour. A large shape or form appears to be heavier than a small shape. Several small shapes or forms can balance one large shape (Figure 10.16).

An object with a complicated contour is more interesting and appears to be heavier than one with a simple contour. A small, complex object can balance a large, simple object (Figure 10.17).

Color. A high-intensity color has more visual weight than a low-intensity color. The viewer's eyes are drawn to the area of bright color. What does this mean in terms of balance? It means that a small area of bright color is able to balance a larger area of a dull, more neutral color as seen in the stained-glass window shown in Figure 10.18.

TEACHER TALK

Providing Resources One way of adding immediacy to the art experience for students is to arrange for them to meet and speak with local artists and craftspeople. To find out who lives and works in your area, begin by getting in touch with local art gallery dealers and curators in the education departments of local museums. It is also helpful to read reviews of art shows in your area. Even though a given artist may not live in your city, he or she will very likely be in town for the opening of the show and might be willing to visit your class. Finally, art supply stores are another source of information on local artists.

FIGURE 10.17 In this wedding portrait of Frida Kahlo and Diego Rivera, Frida depicts herself in the ribbons, jewels, and native Mexican dress she often wore. Her small body, enveloped in all the ruffles and folds, balances Diego's solid, heavy form.

Frida (Frieda) Kahlo. *Frida and Diego Rivera*. 1931. Oil on canvas. 100 × 78.7 cm (39⅜ × 31″). San Francisco Museum of Modern Art, San Francisco, California. Albert M. Bender Collection. Gift of Albert M. Bender.

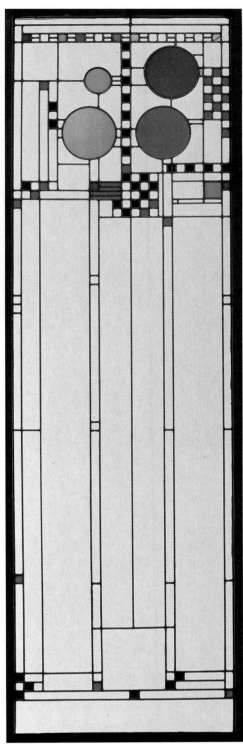

FIGURE 10.18 In the stained-glass window to the right, the bright colors of the geometric shapes balance the large area of clear glass.

Designed by Frank Lloyd Wright. American stained-glass window, one of a triptych. Twentieth century. Glass, lead, wood. 219 × 71 × 5 cm (86¼ × 28 × 2″). The Metropolitan Museum of Art, New York, New York. Purchase. Edward C. Moore, Jr., gift and Edgar J. Kaufmann Charitable Foundation gift, 1967.

MORE ABOUT . . . FRIDA KAHLO

The life and work of Mexican artist Frida Kahlo (1907–1954) was filled with pain. Born in Mexico City, Kahlo had hoped to pursue a career in medicine. A serious traffic accident during her teenage years fractured her spine and crushed her pelvis. Kahlo survived, but later endured thirty-five operations and spent much of her life in pain. While convalescing, Kahlo taught herself to paint. She showed her work to the famous Mexican muralist Diego Rivera, whom she eventually married. It was a difficult union and became one of the three main themes that Kahlo painted. Physical pain and frustration over her inability to bear a child were the other two subjects that obsessed Kahlo.

GUIDED PRACTICE
(continued)

Understanding Art History

Tell students that Jean-Honoré Fragonard was a court painter in France during the years prior to the French Revolution. Like his contemporary Antoine Watteau, Fragonard's paintings were intended to be displayed in the palaces and elegant homes of the French upper class. His themes reflected the carefree, idle lives of the aristocracy, which would soon be altered by the revolution.

Interdisciplinary: Language Arts

Ask volunteers to research examples of poetry written in the eighteenth century. Then have them select a poem that is similar in tone to Fragonard's painting. Ask the volunteers to lead a class discussion where they read the poem aloud, then discuss what both the painting and the poem suggest about the Rococo era.

Sparking Creativity

Want students to think creatively about balance and position? Suggest this: Make a mobile to experience actual balance. Open the twisted end of a wire clothes hanger. Use the hook as the top and reshape the wire into an interesting movement. Then use fine wire to attach cut shapes or found objects along the wire, trying to keep the design in balance as it hangs. Think about actual balance (so it hangs well) and visual balance (large and small shapes and colors repeated or used as accents).

FIGURE 10.19 In this Rococo painting, Fragonard balances all the cool, low-intensity colors with the warm, bright red on the dress in the foreground.

Jean-Honoré Fragonard. *A Game of Hot Cockles.* 1767–73. Oil on canvas. 115.5 × 91.4 cm (45½ × 36″). National Gallery of Art, Washington, D.C. Samuel H. Kress Collection.

Warm colors carry more visual weight than cool colors. Red appears heavier than blue, and orange appears heavier than green (Figure 10.19).

Value. The stronger the contrast in value between an object and the background, the more visual weight the object has (Figure 10.20). Black against white has more weight than gray against white. Dark values are heavier than light values. A dark red seems heavier than a light red.

Texture. As you know, a rough texture has an uneven pattern of light highlights and dark, irregular shadows. For this reason a rough surface attracts the viewer's eye more easily than a smooth, even surface. This means that a small, rough-textured area can balance a large, smooth surface. In a poster or advertisement, a block of printed words has the quality of rough texture because of the irregular pattern of light and dark. Poster designers must keep this in mind when balancing words and other visual elements.

Position. Children playing on a seesaw quickly discover that two friends of unequal weight can balance the seesaw by adjusting their positions. The heavier child moves toward the center; the lighter child slides toward the end. The board is then in balance (Figure 10.21, page 262).

In visual art, a large object close to the dominant area of the work can be balanced by a smaller object placed far from the dominant area (Figure 10.22, page 262). A large, positive shape and a small, negative space can be balanced against a small, positive shape and a large, negative space.

COOPERATIVE LEARNING

Explain to students that while viewing artworks such as *A Game of Hot Cockles* in Figure 10.19, they are given clues to the lifestyles of the subjects through their clothing. From those clues, students can research further into the historical, social, and economic status of the persons wearing them. By working in collaborative groups, students can divide the areas of research, share their findings when finished, and create artworks or reports that are more comprehensive than if done individually. Encourage students who work together in this manner to present their information to the class in the form of a creative presentation.

L O O K I N G C L O S E L Y

FIGURE 10.20 The face and head scarf of the Virgin are no lighter in value than the infant on his blanket or the shepherd's white skirt. Her face stands out so much more because it is placed against the dark value of the cave's interior, while the infant and the shepherd are placed against the midvalue tan of the ground.

Giorgione. *The Adoration of the Shepherds.* c. 1505–10. Oil on wood. 91 × 111 cm (35¾ × 43½"). National Gallery of Art, Washington, D.C. Samuel H. Kress Collection.

LOOKING CLOSELY

Have students study Figure 10.20 and consider how the artist uses color. Point out to students that although this event took place in the town of Bethlehem, the scenery depicted by Giorgione looks like European farmland, and the buildings are reminiscent of those built during the sixteenth century.

Using Informal Balance

1. Applying Your Skills.
This activity is perceptive and involves the concepts of visual weight.

2. Further Challenge.
This activity, like the previous one, requires perception, but it also calls for drawing skills. Before students try these activities, be sure that they review the factors that influence visual weight and discuss Figures 10.15 through 10.20 with you.

3. Computer Option.
As an alternative activity, have students follow these directions: Experiment with the elements used to create informal balance: size and contour, intensity of color, contrasting value, texture, and position, and relationship of positive and negative space. Then create an example of each type of informal balance by using your choice of Drawing and Shape tools, colors, and textures. Each example can be an entirely different design, or begin with elements of size and contour, to create a series of variations emphasizing the other elements listed above.

Using Informal Balance

1. Applying Your Skills.   Find five magazine illustrations, designs, or drawings that illustrate informal balance. Mount each example. Label the works, indicating how the visual weight is arranged in the illustration. Explain how the balance is achieved.

2. Further Challenge.   Create small designs using cut paper and/or fabric shapes to illustrate five weight arrangements that create informal balance (Figure 10.23, page 263). In each design keep all of the elements as alike as possible. Vary only the weight factors. For example, to illustrate differences in size, a large red circle could be balanced by several small red circles.

CURRICULUM CONNECTION

Geography Tell students that Giorgio da Castelfranco (Giorgione) was one of the first Venetian masters. Have students locate the city of Venice on a large map of Italy. Point out where the city lies in relation to Rome and Florence. Ask: How difficult would it have been for Venetian artists to journey to these cultural centers for inspiration and instruction? Would topographical features have made this trip an easy or difficult one? If a map of Venice is available, have students note the city's layout and physical makeup, such as numerous small coastal islands connected by narrow waterways. Ask how this arrangement may have facilitated trade with other cultures.

GUIDED PRACTICE
(continued)

LOOKING CLOSELY

Have students study Figure 10.22 then answer the questions in the caption. Remind them to notice that the shape of the negative space looks similar to the water except it is upside down. It is the visual balance of the positive. How does it help to balance the positive shape of the wave? The two boats with the most detail are on the right side; the boat that shows the least is on the left with the wave.

The men sit low so as not to tip the boat. Their position brings their weight closer to the base to maintain balance, to make the boat more stable. The small curved shapes are decorative, and they seem to diminish the seriousness of the situation.

Understanding Art History

To help students further appreciate the life and times of Katsushika Hokusai, whose work is shown in Figure 10.22, assign *Artist's Profile 19* in the TCR.

INDEPENDENT PRACTICE

Enrichment

Have students look through art history books that include folk art from different countries. They can also look through quilting books and magazines found in craft shops and book stores. Find examples of fabric art and compare the methods and themes with the work by Garrison in Figure 10.13 on page 256.

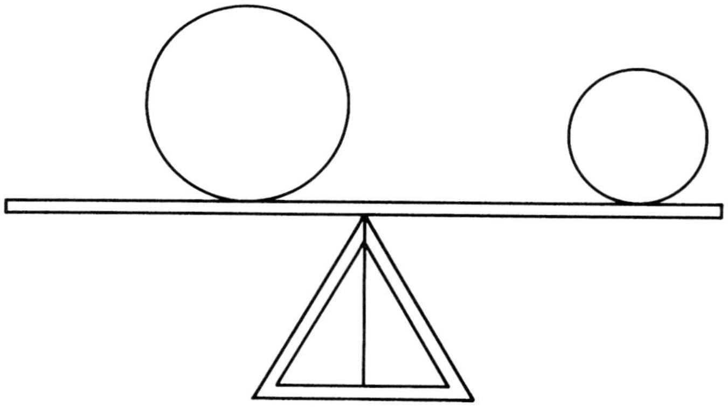

FIGURE 10.21 Does the seesaw look balanced?

LOOKING CLOSELY

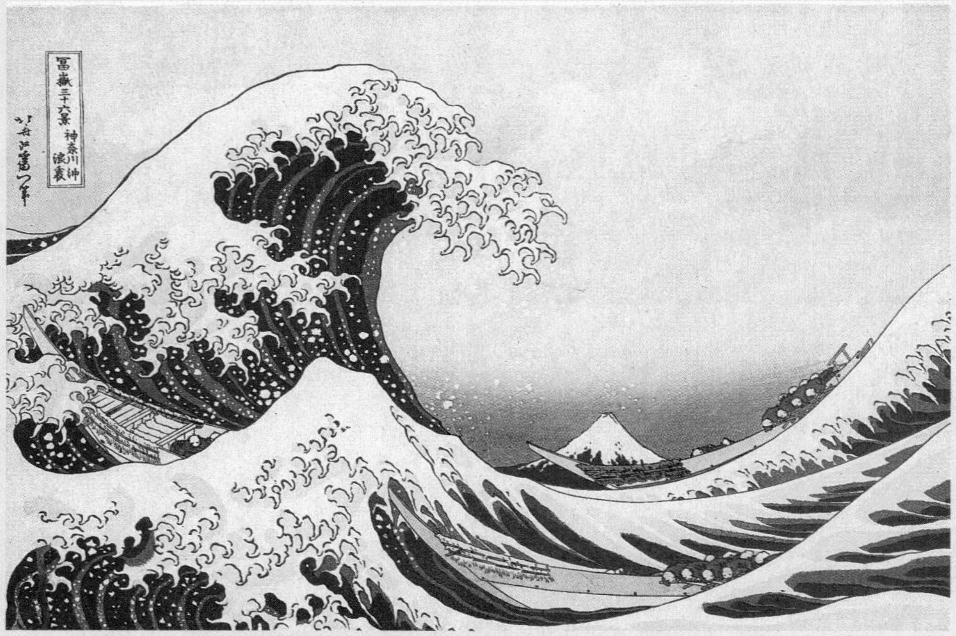

FIGURE 10.22 Notice the large wave on the left. It is balanced informally by the small triangular shape of Mount Fuji in the distance. Notice the shape of the negative space of the yellow sky. How does it help to balance the positive shape of the wave? How do the three fishing boats affect the balance of the work? Why do the men sit so low in the boats? What does their position have to do with balance? How do the many small curved shapes in the white foam of the large wave affect the mood of the work?

Katsushika Hokusai. *The Great Wave off Kanagawa* (from the series The Thirty-Six Views of Fuji). c. 1823–29. Woodblock print. 25.7 × 38 cm (10⅛ × 14 15/16"). The Metropolitan Museum of Art, New York, New York. Bequest of Mrs. H. O. Havemeyer, 1929. The H. O. Havemeyer Collection

MORE ABOUT . . . KATSUSHIKA HOKUSAI

Hokusai was born Kamamura Tokitaro to a poor family in Edo, the capital of Japan, in 1760. Because he was a younger son, he was put up for adoption and was taken in by an important artisan family. For several years he was a mirror-maker's apprentice and learned how to engrave the backs of mirrors. Applying his carving skills to wood blocks, he became a successful artist. Among the many woodblock artists, he was the only one who could cut his own blocks. Most just drew designs and gave them to carvers and printers. At the age of forty-six he became Katsushika Hokusai. He was working on some of his best work when he died at the age of eighty-nine.

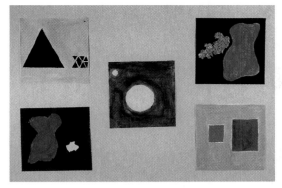

FIGURE 10.23   Student work. Informal balance.

3. Computer Option.   Use the drawing tools of your choice to create a design using informal balance. Save your work. Use the Fill Bucket tool to experiment with changes in color, value, and texture. Save experiments that you consider successful. Draw another design that illustrates informal balance. Save your work and then experiment with the new design. Once again, save experiments you consider successful. Look through the files you saved. Choose the two that you think most successfully illustrate informal balance and print them.

FIGURE 10.24   In this work the formal balance takes away from the violent impact of these "terrorists." How do lines and colors affect the feeling expressed by this work?

Bob Clements. *Evening Up the Score.* 1986. Painted wood. 274.3 × 152.4 × 15.2 cm (108 × 60 × 6″). Private collection.

THE EXPRESSIVE QUALITIES OF BALANCE

The type of balance used by an artist to organize a design has a strong impact on the feeling expressed by that design. Following are some general explanations of how artists use balance to express emotion.

Formal balance is a calm arrangement (Figure 10.24). It has been used to present a person in a dignified portrait (Figure 10.25, page 264). Formal balance has also been used in some religious paintings. Paintings used as altarpieces in churches were designed to fit in with the formal balance of the church altar. Some modern works, such as Josef Albers's *Homage to the Square: Glow* (Figure 10.26 on page 265), are symmetrical. This use of symmetry reduces complexity and allows viewers to concentrate completely on the element of color.

Government buildings, hospitals, and office buildings are designed using formal balance. One purpose of this type of balance is to imply that the people working in these buildings are stable and dignified. In colonial times, homes were built with formal balance to make them appear dignified and calm. This style is still popular today because people want their homes to look like a place where

GUIDED PRACTICE
(continued)

Exploring Aesthetics

Scatter cut shapes and found objects at random on a white cloth sheet or large piece of white paper on the floor or on a table. Ask students to describe the effect, identify the type of balance illustrated, and try to pick out a center of interest. If they find one, ask them to explain why it attracts their attention. Select a student to move the pieces around to develop a formal balance. Ask another student to change the arrangement to develop a feeling of rhythm in the composition. Have various students work with the materials to create a visual sense of movement and of the other principles. Discuss with the students the changes that take place in the developing composition.

Using Art Criticism

Have students choose an artwork from this chapter and write a brief description of the elements they find in the composition. You might have them begin with Frida Kahlo's painting in Figure 10.25. Then have them analyze, interpret, and judge the artwork. Finally, ask them to describe how the principle of balance influenced their evaluations and judgments. You might also have them study artworks from other chapters and describe how balance is used.

Understanding Art History

To help students further appreciate the life and times of Frida Kahlo, whose work is shown in Figure 10.25, assign *Artist's Profile 40* in the TCR.

FIGURE 10.25 Kahlo has organized this self-portrait using formal balance to make herself look proud and imposing.

Frida Kahlo. *Self Portrait Dedicated to Leon Trotsky.* 1937. Oil on masonite. 76.2 × 61 cm (30 × 24″). National Museum of Women in the Arts, Washington, D.C. Gift of the Honorable Clare Boothe Luce.

they can go to escape the hustle and bustle of daily life (Figure 10.27).

With approximate symmetry, artists express the same sense of calm stability, but they avoid the rigid formality of pure symmetry (Figure 10.28, page 266).

Radial design is decorative. It appears in architecture, jewelry, pottery, weaving, and textile design. It is not often used by painters in its pure form. You can, however, find loose arrangements of radiating lines in many paintings (Figure 10.29, page 266). Artists use this technique to focus attention on an important part of the painting.

Informal balance has a more natural look. When you look around your natural environment, you seldom find objects arranged with formal balance. To keep the natural quality of the real world in their works, artists use informal balance in arranging landscapes or groups of people (Figure 10.30, page 267).

Architects are using informal balance in many modern structures (see the David Wright house Figure 3.30 on page 62). Single-family suburban homes have become the symbol of casual living. These houses are designed with informal balance.

CULTURAL PERSPECTIVES

Point out that masks are perfect for demonstrating the expressive qualities of bilateral symmetry. An excellent example would be a Kwakiutl transformation mask, constructed so that the face of the outer mask could be opened to reveal another spirit inside. Some of these masks had movable parts so that during special ceremonies, if the mask was a bird, a beak would open and close. These stylized masks exaggerate the outstanding characters of each creature portrayed. Have students research and write a short report on masks and include the context in which the mask is used, the material used to make the mask, how the mask shows symmetry, and background information about the culture.

FIGURE 10.26 Albers had a strong influence on the development of American Hard-edge and Op art. He reduced line, shape, space, and texture to minimal importance and concentrated on color relationships. He created optical effects by changing the colors in the squares.

Josef Albers. *Homage to the Square: Glow.* 1966. Acrylic on fiberboard. 121.7 × 121.7 cm (48 × 48"). Hirshhorn Museum and Sculpture Garden, Smithsonian Institution, Washington, D.C. Gift of Joseph H. Hirshhorn, 1972.

FIGURE 10.27 Notice the architect's symmetrical arrangement of shapes on the front of this house. Imagine a vertical axis through the center. Do you see how the balance has been achieved?

John Vassall (Longfellow) House. 1759. Piazzas added later. Cambridge, Massachusetts. Façade. Photography by Sandak, Inc., Stamford, Connecticut.

MORE ABOUT . . . OP ART

Op art is concerned with the psychological processes of vision. Developed in the United States after 1960, this nonobjective art movement had parallels in several European countries including Germany and Italy. Op artists sought to create an impression of movement on the picture surface by means of optical illusion. In traditional paintings, the aim was to draw the viewer into the work. In contrast, Op art seems to vibrate and reach out to the viewer. Victor Vasarely is generally regarded as the founder of this movement. He used dazzling colors and precise geometric shapes to create surfaces that appear to move. They seem to project forward in places and to recede in others.

GUIDED PRACTICE
(continued)

Developing Studio Skills

Georgia O'Keeffe is famous for her paintings of parched bones and flowers. She forced viewers to take a new and different look at everyday objects. Have students experiment with O'Keeffe's style by choosing an object that is ordinary. Examine the lines, shapes, and details of the object. Have them use pencils to make sketches of the object so that it fills the paper. Instruct them to pay particular attention to the elements of line, space, texture, and shape. Also, remind them to consider how they will arrange the shape to create a pleasing balance.

Interdisciplinary: Language Arts

Essayist Joan Didion admired Georgia O'Keeffe for her refusal to compromise her values. In an essay titled "Georgia O'Keeffe," Didion celebrates O'Keeffe's fierce opposition to traditions and stereotypes. Encourage students to read the essay, then write their own evaluation of Georgia O'Keeffe's contribution to American art.

Understanding Art History

To help students further appreciate the life and times of Georgia O'Keeffe, assign *Artist's Profile 36* in the TCR.

Exploring Aesthetics

Direct students to look at Maurice Utrillo's painting in Figure 10.29. Have them work in pairs or small groups to discuss how Utrillo uses the elements of art and the principles of design. Ask: What mood or feeling do you have when looking at Figure 10.29. How do the elements and principles achieve that mood?

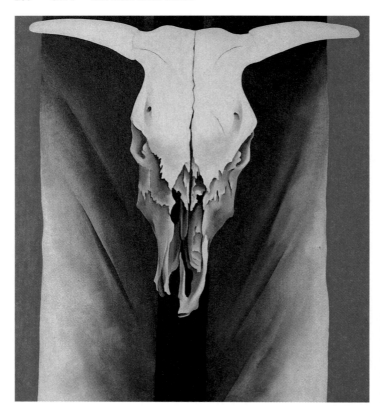

FIGURE 10.28 How has O'Keeffe arranged the shapes in this painting to create approximate, not absolute, symmetry? Would you like the painting more if it were perfectly symmetrical? Why or why not?

Georgia O'Keeffe. *Cow's Skull: Red, White, and Blue.* 1931. Oil on canvas. 101.3 × 91.1 cm (39⅞ × 35⅞"). The Metropolitan Museum of Art, New York, New York. The Alfred Stieglitz Collection, 1952.

FIGURE 10.29 The edges of the building and sidewalks, as well as the implied lines in the rows of windows and trees, radiate loosely from the vanishing point in this painting.

Maurice Utrillo. *Street at Corte, Corsica.* 1913. Oil on canvas. 60.8 × 80.7 cm (24 × 31¾"). National Gallery of Art, Washington, D.C. Ailsa Mellon Bruce Collection.

AT THE MUSEUM

Museum of Fine Arts, Houston (Houston, Texas) The Allan Chasanoff Photographic Collection: Tradition and the Unpredictable is composed of 1000 photographs on videodisk accessible through two computers in the exhibit. What makes these photographs interesting is that they are straight photographs—the image is not manipulated in the camera or in the darkroom—in which the images are confusing. For example, a photograph that looks like three balls is really a close-up of someone's back! The interactive computer program shows the photograph and asks challenging questions so the viewers have to think and form their own opinions about the photographs.

FIGURE 10.30   Notice how the large, dead tree on the left is balanced by the mass of trees in the distance on the right. Church is famous for large-scale paintings of exotic scenes such as icebergs and tropical jungles. This small painting was inspired by a sunrise he saw during the first weeks of the Civil War. It is a patriotic expression of his personal feelings about the war. He sold the rights of this image to a printmaker, and it was circulated throughout the North as a mass-produced color print.

Frederic Edwin Church. *Our Banner in the Sky*. 1861. Oil on paper mounted on cardboard. 19 × 28.9 cm (7½ × 11⅜"). Terra Museum of American Art, Chicago, Illinois. Terra Foundation for the Arts, Daniel J. Terra Collection, 1992.

 Identifying Balance

1. Applying Your Skills.   Look through the other chapters in this book to find examples of both formal and informal balance. Be sure to include symmetry, approximate symmetry, and radial balance. List the name of the work and describe how the type of balance used affects the feelings expressed.

2. Further Challenge.   Look around your neighborhood for buildings that have been constructed using formal or informal balance. Make a rough sketch of one building and describe the feeling it gives you. If you live in the city and all the buildings are too tall, look at the entrances to the buildings and sketch one of them. The entrance includes the door and all the decorative shapes around the doorway.

3. Computer Option.   Use the tools of your choice to create a complex design illustrating one of the following: formal balance, informal balance, symmetry, approximate symmetry, radial balance. Save your work and print it if possible. If your printer only prints in black and white, use colored pencils to add color. Evaluate your design. Does it meet the criteria for the kind of balance you chose to illustrate?

 GUIDED PRACTICE
(continued)

ACTIVITY   Identifying Balance

1. Applying Your Skills. Examples of formal balance using bilateral symmetry are Figures 7.20 on page 166, 7.39 on page 182, 8.29 on page 210, and 12.16 on page 326. Examples showing approximate symmetry are Figures 2.10 on page 37, 6.48 on page 151 and 11.23 on page 294. Examples of radial balance are Figures 7.21 on page 167, and 8.23 on page 203. Examples of informal balance are found in nearly all other artworks not listed above.

2. Further Challenge. If students are not able to complete this activity at home, bring in architectural magazines and let them sketch from photographs.

INDEPENDENT PRACTICE

Study Guide
   Distribute and have students complete *Study Guide 10* in the Reteaching booklet.

Enrichment
• Assign *Enrichment Activity 19* and *20* in the TCR.
• Have students select one of their artworks created before they read this chapter and write an evaluation of their use of balance.

Studio Lessons
   To expand students' familiarity with the concept of balance, these Studio Lessons are available in the TCR:
• Formal and Informal Group Portraits
• Fabric Medallion in Radial Balance
• Round Plaster Relief in Radial Balance

FOCUS

OBJECTIVE

Design and create a formal portrait of a person from history or current events.

MOTIVATOR

Talk to teachers in the areas of social studies, literature, science, and math to find out what famous people are being studied during the school year. Ask students to share what they have learned about those people. Then ask about movie, television, or music stars. Students should enjoy sharing information about these figures.

TEACH

GUIDED PRACTICE

Developing Studio Skills

If your students feel they are unable to make sketches that resemble the person, you might permit them to make photocopies of the person's face from a book, magazine, or a newspaper. The photocopy can be enlarged or reduced on the machine until it fits the proportions of the figure in the portrait.

Exploring Aesthetics

Review how various color schemes can create a central emotion or mood in a painting. For example, red can symbolize rage and anger. Blue can give a feeling of calmness or sadness. Bright colors such as yellow and orange can create a sense of excitement. A complementary color scheme creates contrast which can symbolize conflict. Analogous colors create harmony.

FIGURE 10.31 Artist unknown. *Winxiang, Prince Yi.* Qing dynasty. 1644–1911. Ink and color on silk. 186.7 × 121.9 (73½ × 48″). Arthur M. Sackler Gallery, Smithsonian Institution, Washington, D.C. Gift of Richard G. Pritzlaff.

Supplies

- Sketchbook and pencil
- Large sheet of white paper
- Yellow chalk
- Black fine-line marker
- Acrylic paints and brushes

This portrait of a Chinese prince is very different from Chinese landscape painting that one usually sees. The pose is dictated by tradition (Figure 10.31).

Notice the details in this formal portrait and think about how you can use them.

Design and create a formal portrait of a person from history or from current events. Arrange the person in a symmetrical pose in the

TECHNIQUE TIPS

Some students are intimidated by the idea of creating a portrait. The following is a list of a few helpful ideas worth reviewing:

1. The human face is three nose lengths.
2. The eyes are one eye-width apart. A third eye would fit perfectly between the two.
3. The eyes are aligned with the top of the ears.
4. The tip of the nose is aligned with the ear lobe.
5. The distance from the tip of the nose to the end of an outstretched finger extended at arm's length is 36 inches (91 cm).
6. The length of an individual's forearm from the inside fold of the wrist to the inside fold of the elbow is the length of the individual's foot.

FIGURE 10.31A Student work.

center of the composition. The figure should fill the page. Use approximate symmetry to place objects that symbolize important events in that person's life on and around the figure. Choose a color scheme that expresses a specific mood.

FOCUSING

Choose a person you have studied in history or in current events that you admire. Research information about this person. If this person is from past history, you will find information in encyclopedias or in biographies. If your subject is involved in current events, look through newspapers and the *Readers' Guide to Periodicals* for magazines that will provide information about your subject. Make visual and verbal notes about your subject in your sketchbook.

CREATING

Make rough sketches for your composition. Remember that the figure must be organized in a symmetrical pose and that it must fill most of the paper. Make some accurate sketches of details needed for the portrait such as clothing of the historical period, furniture, symbols that will surround or cover the figure, and an appropriate background setting. Choose your best design and sketch it lightly with yellow chalk on the large white paper.

Choose a color scheme that expresses the appropriate mood. Paint your composition. Use large brushes to fill in the largest shapes. Use small brushes to paint the symbols and clothing details. If necessary, use a fine-line black marker to define some of your details and labels.

Write a paragraph about your subject. Mount or mat your portrait for display. Integrate the written paragraph into your display.

CRITIQUING

Describe Name the subject of your portrait. What symbols did you select to represent the events in that person's life? How did you do visual and verbal research? Where did you look and what kind of information did you find? How did you prepare your work for display? Did you include a paragraph about the subject? How did you incorporate it into the display?

Analyze What kinds of balance did you use in your composition? Explain. Describe the color scheme you selected for this work and explain why you chose it.

Interpret What does your painting express about the subject of your portrait? Did the kinds of balance and the color scheme affect the mood? Give this work a poetic title.

Judge Which aesthetic theories would you use to judge this work? If you were to do this over, what would you do to improve it?

INDEPENDENT PRACTICE

Extension

By making several photocopies of a full-length photograph of the person, and by reducing and enlarging various parts of the person's body on the machine, students could create a collage by reassembling the differently sized parts of the figure on their paper.

ASSESS

CRITIQUING

Have students apply the steps of art criticism to their own artwork using the "Critiquing" questions on this page.

CLOSE

Have each student read his or her paragraph while displaying the portrait.

MEETING SPECIAL NEEDS

Building Self-Esteem Students with some types of disabilities may be unable to sketch or copy from a reproduction. One alternative for students with severe disabilities is to photocopy artworks which the student might then paint or color with markers, following the directions in the Studio Lesson above. Even more exciting is to transfer the design onto hooked rug mesh. The enlarged reproduction can be placed behind the mesh and the outlines of shapes drawn onto it. Then students can hook the design according to the chosen color scheme. The repetitive movements found in hooking a rug can be very satisfying.

269

FOCUS

OBJECTIVE

Design and create a paint-ing in the Impressionist style.

MOTIVATOR

If possible, have students practice some initial paintings outside, taking turns posing and painting. Encourage students to notice how the sunlight changes the surface of objects within just a one-hour period. This lesson would be most effective if taught during the early morning or late in the afternoon when the sun is at an angle, and changes in light and shadows are more noticeable.

TEACH

GUIDED PRACTICE

Developing Studio Skills

If possible, students should make the snapshot as well as the painting. If the students themselves do not have access to a camera, obtain a school camera and a roll of film for the project. Recording the order in which they shoot, allow each student to take one unposed snapshot of other students in the class. Another option is to bring in old snapshots made for the school yearbook and allow each student to select one.

FIGURE 10.32   Mary Cassatt. *Five O'Clock Tea*. 1879. Oil on canvas. 65 × 93 cm (25½ × 36½"). Courtesy of Museum of Fine Arts, Boston, Massachusetts. M. Theresa B. Hopkins Fund.

Supplies
- Sketchbook and pencil
- Snapshots you have taken
- Large sheet of white paper
- Acrylic paints and an assortment of brushes

Many late-nineteenth-century American artists painted in the Impressionist style, but Mary Cassatt was the only one who actually joined the radical French artists to show her artwork in their independent exhibitions in Paris. She followed their practice of capturing a moment of everyday life as it would look in a snapshot—one single moment in time. Like snapshots, her compositions were asymmetrical and closely cropped (Figure 10.32).

The Japanese print, which had arrived in Paris in the late 1800s, was one source of inspiration for the Impressionists' asymmetrical compositions. The Japanese printmakers were not afraid to cut off part of a figure. European artists, who had never done this, began to use this technique.

The new art of photography also influenced the compositions of the Impressionists. The camera presented them with candid, or unposed, views of people. Snapshots showed familiar subjects from new and unusual points of view. Look at Cassatt's painting. Observe how she used balance, cropped figures, and color.

270

MORE ABOUT . . . PHOTOGRAPHY

Tell students that by 1855, photography was included in the Paris World's Fair exhibition. The Royal Academy of France accepted photographs into their salon in 1859. Artists led by Jean-Auguste-Dominique Ingres formed a League of Artists Against Photography, but despite their protests, the French government officially declared photography to be art in 1862. Early photographers took the camera where the easel could not go. Paul Nada went up in a hot air balloon in the 1840s and photographed Paris from above. The ordinary person was now able to see all parts of the world through photographs.

Plan and create a painting in the Impressionist style using asymmetrical balance, a close-cropped composition, loose brushstrokes that look like dabs and dashes, and the colors of the Impressionists. This painting must be based on an unposed snapshot you have taken of your friends or family. It must include two or more people.

FOCUSING

Collect snapshots you have taken. Select one that you think will make an interesting painting. Remember that it must show asymmetrical balance, two or more people must be visible, and part of each figure must be cropped off, as are the two young women in *Five O'Clock Tea.*

CREATING

Make a large, rough sketch in your sketchbook based on the snapshot. Work on your first sketch to improve the composition as needed. Do not worry about whether the faces in the sketch and the painting look like the real people in the snapshot.

Practice using the colors of the Impressionists in your sketchbook. Use only spectral colors and white. Blues and violets replace grays, browns, and blacks even in the shadows. Apply the colors using short dabs and dashes of color. Make grays by placing complements side by side. Use white side by side with your colors and add white to some of your colors to create light values.

Using a brush and a very light value of yellow, sketch the final composition loosely onto the large sheet of white paper. Use what you have learned during practice in your sketchbook to paint your composition. Create an expressive title for your work.

Mount or mat your work for display.

FIGURE 10.32A Student work.

C R I T I Q U I N G

Describe   What is the subject matter of your work? How many people have you used? What other objects are important in the composition?

Analyze   Did you use asymmetry? Which kind of informal balance did you use? Did you keep the effect of a snapshot by cropping off parts of the figures? Did you use Impressionists' colors? How many ways did you employ white?

Interpret   Describe the difference between the look of the snapshot and the look of your finished painting. How did style affect the look of your work? Give your work a title that expresses the mood of your work.

Judge   Which aesthetic theories would you use to judge this work? If you were to do this over, what, if anything, would you do differently?

COOPERATIVE LEARNING

Tell students that an art critic of the 1800s wrote the following description of Impressionism:

The Impressionists take a canvas, some paint and brushes . . . [They] throw some tones [colors] onto the canvas and then sign it. This is the way in which the lost souls of Ville-Evard [a mental hospital] pick up pebbles from the roadway and believe they have found diamonds.

Working in pairs, have students restate this idea in their own words. Have them explain what they believe led the critic to react in this way. After having studied about Impressionist painters, do they agree or disagree with the statement?

Linoleum Print Using Radial Balance

FIGURE 10.33 Beau Dick. *Sacred Circles*. 1991. Serigraph 98/155. 50 × 50 cm (19¾″ × 19¾″). Private collection.

FOCUS

OBJECTIVE

Create a relief print that features symbols of family heritage.

MOTIVATOR

Display and have students examine prints of Rembrandt, Dürer, and other printmakers. Students would benefit by learning about other printmaking processes such as intaglio, lithography, serigraphy, and the process they are about to experience, relief printing. Students should be given the opportunity to experiment with these techniques as well as more simplified techniques that will be described in the Enrichment activity of this lesson.

TEACH

GUIDED PRACTICE

Exploring Aesthetics

Some students are disturbed when they see the lines in the negative areas. It is important that they understand that this is a special quality unique to linoleum and woodcuts.

Understanding Art History

Ask students to research the cultural traditions of the Native Americans of the Northwest coast, including information on the various arts and crafts of that area. Sources of information might include *National Geographic, Smithsonian,* encyclopedias, and books on Native Americans.

272

Supplies

- Sketchbook and pencil
- Ruler, compass, and scissors
- Tracing paper and carbon paper
- Linoleum and dark marker
- Linoleum cutting tools
- Bench hook or C clamp
- Water-base printing ink
- Brayer and inking plate
- Printmaking paper

Beau Dick was born in 1955 in the isolated village of Kingcome in British Columbia, Canada. He is a Northwest Coast Native American of the Southern Kwakiutl tribe.

The making of serigraphs (limited-edition silk-screen prints) is a new art form for the Northwest Coast artists. These artists started making serigraphs around 1970. *Sacred Circles* (Figure 10.33) was originally designed for a drum. Dick's daughter, who is a teacher in Queen Charlotte, British Columbia, asked him to design something for her students for Rediscovery Week. The Rediscovery program in Canada was begun to teach young Native Americans to rediscover their heritage as a source of self-esteem.

Beau Dick believes that the children are the future, that they are the ones to keep the traditions alive and strong. This design shows a group of young people holding hands and sitting in a circle. He depicts them holding hands to show unity and friendship. The dark round shapes in the center are stones, inside of which a bonfire is to be built. He believes the children are the ones who will rekindle the fires and the traditions of the tribes.

MEETING SPECIAL NEEDS

Learning Disabilities For students with mental retardation, the abstract quality of this lesson may pose difficulties. Having several suitable cultural symbols displayed on a poster to use as models can help them acquire concrete ideas. These might include symbols such as the peace sign, a heart, a cross, a Star of David, the recycling symbol, a stop sign, the Olympic symbol, and an American flag, as well as symbols of students' personal interests, perhaps in sports, art, or music.

Select symbols from your cultural heritage to create one or more motifs for a relief print. Produce an edition of five relief prints. Sign, date, and number your prints using proper printmaking procedures.

FOCUSING

Brainstorm with your classmates about well-known symbols for different cultures. Then discuss your cultural heritage with members of your immediate family. Choose symbols that represent your cultural identity. Select the ones you prefer and make some rough sketches for arranging them into a radial design.

CREATING

Trace the shape of your piece of linoleum onto a page in your sketchbook. Using the ruler, connect the opposite corners of the rectangle to find the center of the shape. Place the point of the compass on that center and draw the largest circle possible within that shape. Select your best design and draw it in the circle.

Trace your finished design onto the tracing paper. Use a piece of carbon paper to transfer the design from the tracing paper to the piece of linoleum.

Use a dark marker to color the lines and shapes on the areas of linoleum that will not be cut away.

Use a bench hook to hold your linoleum safely in place. You have left the linoleum in the shape of a rectangle so that it can be held in place by the bench hook. Do not cut it into a circle until all your linoleum cuts are finished. Use the narrow V-gouge to outline the shapes. To prevent injury during cutting, always move the cutting tool in an outward motion away from your body. Then use wider U-gouges to cut away the negative areas. The pattern of your cuts will show in the final print. Plan the direction of the cuts as carefully as you plan the positive shapes in your design. Finally, use the V-gouges to cut the fine lines on the positive shapes.

FIGURE 10.33A   Student work.

Squeeze out an inch (2.5 cm) of ink onto the inking plate. Roll the brayer in both directions until it is loaded with ink. Ink the linoleum.

Select your paper to make an edition of five prints. When they are dry, sign each one in pencil at the bottom of the print. Write the title on the left, the number in the center, and your name and date on the right. The number of your print is a fraction. The denominator represents the total number of the edition, and the numerator is the number of the print. Your first print should be numbered 1/5.

CRITIQUING

Describe   List and describe the symbols you used to create the motifs for your personal radial design.

Analyze   Did you use radial balance to organize the motifs? Did you use size to indicate the dominant motif? Did you use radial lines to help organize the motifs?

Interpret   What is the expressive quality of your personal print? Does it represent your family heritage?

Judge   Which aesthetic theories would you use to judge this work? If you were going to do this one more time, what, if anything, would you change?

273

GUIDED PRACTICE
(continued)

Developing Studio Skills

When researching their family heritage, students may wish to tape record family stories told by relatives. They may also be interested in writing the family history in biographical form. They could use a print as the cover for their report.

INDEPENDENT PRACTICE

Enrichment

Involve the students in various printmaking activities. The range of involvement could extend from simple vegetable prints to the more complicated processes of intaglio and lithography. To challenge the relief printers, allow them to use the subtractive method of making multicolored prints. It is recommended that the teacher and students refer to a printmaking manual for instructions for these more complicated processes.

ASSESS

CRITIQUING

Have students apply the steps of art criticism to their own artwork using the "Critiquing" questions on this page. In addition, ask the following: How did you choose a motif for the print? What new information was found about your family heritage? How was this information translated into a visual image? Do the prints adequately reflect your feelings about your heritage?

CLOSE

Ask students to write personal reflections about their designs and their cultural heritage.

TECHNIQUE TIPS

To help students enjoy this lesson, consider the following:
- Linoleum can be ordered in rolls or various sized pieces and mounted on wood blocks.
- Linoleum cutting tools can be purchased through art supply catalogs.
- The use of a bench hook is a safe method for holding the linoleum in place.
- Linoleum becomes softer if it is heated. A heating pad or the classroom heater are adequate sources of heat.
- Remind students that their prints will be mirror images of their carvings. Therefore, all letters and images will be reversed.

FOCUS

OBJECTIVE

Design and create a clay coil or pinch-pot using radial design.

MOTIVATOR

Ask students to bring to school any pieces of Native American pottery that they may have at home and share how they acquired the pieces.

TEACH

GUIDED PRACTICE

Understanding Art History

Maria Martinez was asked by archaeologists to study the ancient black-on-black pottery designs. After finding some old pieces of pottery in the area where she lived, they asked her to recreate this method of finishing pottery. Ask students to research the contemporary pottery of the Southwestern United States, including the influences and backgrounds of the potters. They should try to answer the following question: What types of motif are found on the surface of the pots?

Developing Studio Skills

To polish the clay pots, students should wait for the clay to become leather hard, then rub the surface of the pot with the back of a metal spoon or a polished stone. As they rub, students will notice a shiny appearance on the surface of the clay. This smooth surface will remain through all firings.

FIGURE 10.34   Maria and Julian Martinez. Black-on-black storage jar. 1942. Clay shaped by Maria and design painted by Julian. 47.6 x 56 cm (18¾ x 22"). Signature: Maria and Julian. Courtesy of the Museum of New Mexico, Sante Fe, New Mexico. School of American Research Collection.

Supplies
- Sketchbook, pencil, and ruler
- Clay
- Metal scraper or damp sponge
- Plastic bag (large enough to store work in progress)
- Clay tools
- Slip of a contrasting color
- Brushes

Maria Montoya Martinez, a Native American artist from the San Ildefonso Pueblo in New Mexico, learned to make pottery when she was a little girl by watching and helping her aunt and other women from the community. She met her husband, Julian, while they were attending St. Catherine's Indian School in Santa Fe, New Mexico. In addition to their community, ceremonial, and home responsibilities, Julian and Maria worked together to make pottery. She formed and polished the pottery, and he painted the surface designs.

As early as 1915, Maria's pottery stood out above all the others that were made in the area. One early critic wrote that Maria did the best polishing because she was the swiftest polisher. From the moment she picked up the pot to apply the slip, she did not put it down until the polishing was completed. In 1919 Maria and Julian began to experiment with the matte-black-on-shiny-black decorative process. This process became very popular, and by 1925 all of the San Ildefonso potters were making black-on-black ware.

After Julian died in 1943, Maria worked with Santana, her daughter-in-law, and later with her son, Popovi Da. Many experts felt that the Maria/Popovi Da period expressed the highest level of Maria's aesthetic achievement.

MEETING SPECIAL NEEDS

Physically Disabled   No matter what disabilities may befall us in our lives, no one can take away our creativity. Millions of persons bring satisfaction into their lives and into the lives of others by doing handicrafts. Beethoven composed his greatest symphonies when deaf. Milton was blind. Mary Cassatt's vision failed. Vincent van Gogh created his great paintings while dealing with neurological and emotional disability. Henri Matisse made his huge collages while in a wheelchair. Chuck Close uses an orthotic device when he paints. Disability doesn't matter; willpower and ability do.

Near the end of her life, Maria told her great-granddaughter that other people owned her pots, but she saved her greatest achievement—the ability to create—for her family. Look at Maria and Julian's pot in Figure 10.34 and begin to think of ideas for your clay pot decorated with radial designs.

Using clay, build a coil or pinch pot, smooth the outside surface, and decorate it with a design that is organized using radial balance. The radial balance will be visible when viewed from above or below. When the pot has dried, fire it.

FOCUSING

Make some rough sketches in your sketchbook to plan the form of your pot. Plan the form so that you can see the radial design from the top or bottom.

CREATING

Build your pot using the pinch pot or the coil technique. See Technique Tips 17 and 18 on page 355 in the Handbook. When you have finished forming the pot, smooth the outside by scraping it with a metal scraper and/or rubbing with a damp sponge. Be sure to store your pot in the airtight plastic bag until you have finished forming it. Then you can cover it loosely until it becomes leather-hard. Do not let it dry too fast or it will crack.

Study your pot. Make drawings of it in your sketchbook showing different points of view. Using your pencil and ruler, plan a design for your pot that uses radial balance. You may use representational symbols, abstract shapes and lines, or a combination of both to create your design.

Decide which method you will use to apply the radial design to your pot. Decorate your pot. When your pot is bone dry, fire it in the kiln. Working with a team, plan a display of your pots. Consider the color of the fired clays so that you can select contrasting colors for the display.

FIGURE 10.34A Student work.

CRITIQUING

Describe Describe the form you selected for your pot. Explain why you chose that form. Explain which technique you used to create your pot. Did you have problems with the clay cracking? What technique did you use to apply the design to your pot? How did you arrange the display of your pot?

Analyze Did you create a smooth surface on which to apply the design? Did you use radial balance to create the decorative design? Did the design fit the form of the pot?

Interpret Compare your pot to the others in the class. Did you all use the same techniques? How did that affect the look of the different pieces? Are the surface designs alike or are they different? Can you explain why?

Judge Which aesthetic theory would you use to judge this piece? If you were to do this one more time, what, if anything, would you do differently?

MORE ABOUT . . . CLAY POTTERY

It was through trade with Mexico that the Pueblo Indians of the Southwest first learned to make pottery. Sometimes pots made by the coil method are smoothed so it is not possible to tell that they were constructed with coils. Other times the ropes of clay are only partially flattened so they show on the outside. Whatever form of final decoration, the coils themselves must contain just the right balance of clay and water. If they are too dry, they will crack when they are bent. If there is too much water in the clay, the ropes will not be firm enough to withstand the weight of those above, and the pot will not hold its shape.

INTRODUCTION

Flower Day by Rivera was selected to illustrate how formal balance can turn an everyday incident into a noble and spiritual event. Bernini's angry *David*, who stands in an active, informally balanced pose, was selected for contrast to the calm, formally balanced Rivera work.

CRITIQUING THE WORK

1. Describe There are three adults and one child in the foreground, and three people in the background. In the foreground there are two women sitting on their barefooted legs, facing the large figure in the center. The figure in the center is a man. He stands, leaning forward toward the woman. His arms are bent at right angles and his fingers are locked together. His features look compressed because his head is leaning forward. He carries a large basket of lilies on his back. The figures in the background also seem to be holding flowers in their hands. There is a round form between the women on the ground that looks like rings of flowers. There are also flowers below the leaves in front of the man.

2. Analyze Rivera has used formal balance to arrange this composition to look very stiff and regal. He used approximate symmetry. The woman on the left has a shawl over her back that holds a child. Even in the background there is one head on the left and two on the right.

FIGURE 10.35 Diego Rivera. *Flower Day*. 1925. Oil on canvas. 147.4 × 120.6 cm (58 × 47½"). Los Angeles County Museum of Art, Los Angeles, California.

CRITIQUING THE WORK

1. Describe Read the credit line for the facts about *Flower Day* (Figure 10.35). Then describe the people in this work. What do they look like? What are they doing? What is the central figure carrying?

2. Analyze What kinds of line movement do you see? Does the painting look flat or does it have the illusion of three dimensions? How does the artist use space? Do the forms of the people look active or static? What kind of a color scheme has Rivera used? What kind of texture do you see in this work? Is rhythm important in this work? Explain. Why is balance an important principle in this painting?

3. Interpret Based on the visual clues you have collected and your personal experiences, write a brief paragraph explaining the meaning of this work. What do you think the artist is trying to tell us? Give the work a new title that sums up your interpretation.

Other Works By . . . Diego Rivera
Detroit Industry
Liberation of the Peon
Agrarian Leader

Other Works By . . . Bernini
Angel with the Superscription

Apollo and Daphne
Cathedral Petri
Fountain of the Four Rivers
The Ecstasy of St. Theresa
The Rape of Proserpine
The Blessed Lodovica Albertoni

FIGURE 10.36 Gianlorenzo Bernini. *David.* 1623. Marble. Life-size. Galleria Borghese, Rome, Italy.

4. Judge Do you think this is a successful work? Use one or more of the three aesthetic theories explained in Chapter 2 to defend your opinion.

COMPARING THE WORKS

Look at *Flower Day* (Figure 10.35) and *David* by Gianlorenzo Bernini (Figure 10.36). Rivera's work is a painting that looks sculptural, and Bernini's work is a freestanding, three-dimensional sculpture. Compare the central figure in *Flower Day* to the figure David. We know David represents the hero of the Old Testament story about David and Goliath. Does Rivera identify the man in his painting? Who do you think he is? List the similarities and differences between the two men. Notice their facial expressions, the movement of their bodies, the way they are dressed, and their muscles. How does balance affect the look of the two works?

277

GUIDED PRACTICE
(continued)

3. Interpret Students' paragraphs will vary. The smooth surfaces and the static forms might be interpreted as looking like statues.

4. Judge Answers will vary.

COMPARING THE WORKS

We only know that Rivera's central figure is an ordinary man. He is probably taking the flowers to sell at a festival. Because we know Rivera painted Mexican subjects, this man is probably a Mexican farmer.

Similarities: They are both men.

Differences: Rivera's work is a painting and Bernini's is a free-standing sculpture. The flower man is very still and calm looking; David is active and he looks angry. The flower man is wearing a simple shirt and pants; David is undressed except for a cloth. The man in Figure 10.35 looks smooth and simplified while David has muscles bulging all over his body that indicate intense action. Rivera uses formal balance for his figure to create a very calm, dignified noble peasant, while David is standing using informal balance. David twists his torso, and his neck twists so that his head is turned in the opposite direction of his torso. All of his weight is on his right leg. His left arm is going to swing and hurl the rock at Goliath.

EXTENSION

- Have students read more about Diego Rivera in the "Meet the Artist" feature on the following page.
- Assign *Artist's Profile 10* in the TCR.

MORE ABOUT . . . GIANLORENZO BERNINI

Gianlorenzo Bernini (1598–1680) was more than just a great Baroque sculptor. He also had a reputation as an extraordinary architect, a reputation so widespread that Louis XIV asked him to come to Paris and work out the plans for an enlargement of the Louvre Palace. Among Bernini's architectural achievements in Rome, where he spent most of his career, were the famous colonnaded piazza (square) in front of St. Peter's Basilica and the huge and impressive bronze baldachino (canopy) above the altar inside the church. Bernini was also responsible for San Andrea al Quirinale and the Scala Regia at the Vatican.

DIEGO RIVERA

Mexican, 1886–1957

Diego Rivera. *Self-Portrait.* 1941. Oil on Canvas. 61 × 43 cm (24 × 17"). Smith College Museum of Art, Northampton, Massachusetts.

In 1886 Diego Rivera was born in the small town of Guanajuato in central Mexico. Both his parents were teachers. His father also edited the local paper, *El Democratico,* a liberal newspaper concerned with the troubles and hardships of the workers. Rivera's concern for the workers, the poor, and the illiterate influenced all of his art.

As a young man, Rivera received a government grant to study art in Spain, and he traveled to France to study with Picasso. He also studied the fifteenth-century Italian murals of Raphael and Michelangelo and learned about fresco painting, later using those skills to paint his famous political murals.

When he returned to Mexico, he decided to paint only Mexican subjects. During the 1920s he received important commissions for monumental frescoes from the Mexican government. He used the simplified forms of pre-Columbian art in his work.

In 1929 he married the young artist Frida Kahlo. Her painting *Frida and Diego* (Figure 10.17, page 259) is their wedding portrait. Rivera painted many small paintings as well as murals, but he saw his murals as a way to teach people who could not read. Many of his murals have political themes. He combined the techniques of European art with the history of Mexico to create a new and individual way to portray his ideas about the people and the culture of his native land.

MORE PORTFOLIO IDEAS

Rivera painted the members of the working class, showing them with dignity. Think of an occupation that requires physical labor. Create a collage that depicts a person who performs such a service and does it well.

Rivera's painting depicts someone who is going to sell flowers at a festival in Mexico. Pick an exciting event where you have lots of fun, such as a ball game, a concert, or a festival. Create a painting of someone who has to work while everyone else is having fun. Try to express the worker's feelings about being left out of the fun.

278

DEVELOPING A PORTFOLIO

Personal Style Encourage students to observe the evolution of individual pieces of art as a way of identifying their developing style. Remind them that creative people take risks and see failure as an indication of where the creative process needs modification. For example, if they are not happy with a sketch, instead of discarding it, have them make notes about their displeasure with the design or make corrections without erasing the old. Their increased awareness of the process of artistic creation will help them recognize their choices about style. During private conferences, encourage students to articulate progress in the style of their work.

CHAPTER 10 REVIEW

Building Vocabulary

On a separate sheet of paper, write the term that best matches each definition given below.

1. The principle of design concerned with equalizing visual forces, or elements, in a work of art.
2. A dividing line that works like the point of balance in the balance scale.
3. When equal, or very similar, elements are placed on opposite sides of a central axis.
4. A special type of formal balance in which two halves of a symmetrically balanced composition are identical, mirror images of each other.
5. When the forces or elements of a design come out (radiate) from a central point.
6. A balance of unlike objects.

Reviewing Art Facts

Answer the following questions using complete sentences.

1. Why is balance important to a work of art?
2. What are the visual forces, or weights, in art?
3. What is the difference between bilateral and approximate symmetry?
4. What factors in a work of art influence the visual weight of the art elements?
5. Which carry more weight, warm or cool colors?
6. How can value affect visual weight?
7. What does a formally balanced building express?

Thinking Critically About Art

1. **Extend.** Find a mural that is located in or near your community. Research the artist, the subject, and the inspiration for the mural. Photograph the mural to share with your classmates.
2. **Research.** The Leaning Tower of Pisa (Figure 10.2, page 252) is in serious trouble. Search the *Readers' Guide to Periodicals* for recent articles about the tower and encyclopedias for background information.

What caused the tower to lean? When did it begin leaning? What has been done in the past to correct the lean? What would happen if the problem is not corrected? What has been done in recent years? Has the problem been solved? If so, how?

3. **Synthesize.** Grant Wood was an American Regionalist who created paintings about middle America such as *American Gothic* (Figure 10.8, page 254). Diego Rivera was a Mexican Muralist who created paintings about Mexican working people such as *Flower Day* (Figure 10.35, page 276). Find other works by each of the artists. Compare their styles. List the similarities and differences. Then write a paragraph explaining how each artist visually represents his own country.
4. **Analyze.** Edward Hopper, who painted *First Row Orchestra* (Figure 10.16, page 258), was not considered a member of the Regionalist school of painting. Find a book about him at the library, and look at his paintings. In what way does his subject matter and themes differ from those of the Regionalists? Explain your findings to the class using visual examples to illustrate your conclusions.

Making Art Connections

1. **Science.** Discuss balance with your science teacher to learn about the structure of life forms. Which life forms are symmetrical? Which have radial balance? Discover if any living things grow using informal balance.
2. **Math.** Discuss symmetry with your math teacher and report to the class about symmetry in mathematics.
3. **Social Studies.** Read about the "Balance of Power" and how it has affected the history of the world. What was it like in 1500, in 1914, in 1939? What is the balance of power today? Write a brief report explaining your findings.

279

Proportion

INTRODUCE

CHAPTER OVERVIEW

In Chapter 11, students learn about the relationship between mathematics and visual art, evident from the Golden Mean. They understand how scale can affect the expressive qualities of a work of art and how different cultures have different ideas about ideal proportions.

CHAPTER SUPPLIES

Refer to the "Art Supplies Grid" in the Teacher's Manual. In addition, have on hand the following special items: measuring tapes and mirrors.

FINE ART RESOURCES
Transparencies
- Claes Oldenburg. *Clothespin*
- New Guinea. *Gable Mask*
- Iroquois. *False Face Mask*
- Duane Hanson. *Football Player*

Fine Art Prints
- Beau Dick. *Bookwus Mask*
- Thomas Eakins. *Baby at Play*

FIGURE 11.1 The gigantic dancing figures seem to float across the mound of grass as they balance on three points. They visually defy the facts that they are 35 feet (10.6 m) tall and weigh 1200 pounds (544 kg).

Miriam Schapiro. *Anna and David.* 1987. Painted stainless steel and aluminum. 10.6 × 9.4 × .228 m (35′ × 31′ × 9″). Steinbaum-Krauss Gallery, New York, New York.

RESOURCES FOR CHAPTER 11

Application Activities 21, 22
Artist's Profiles 11, 14, 38, 42, 44
Cooperative Learning Activities 21, 22
Cultural Diversity in Art
Enrichment Activities 21, 22

Reteaching Activities
   Study Guide 11
   Concept Map 11
Studio Lessons 19, 20, 21
Chapter 11 Test

Proportion

" I wish my nose weren't so big!"
"This desk is too small for me!"
"You put too much salt in the stew!"

All of these complaints are about problems with proportion. **Proportion** is *the principle of art concerned with the size relationship of one part to another.*

The size of an object by itself has no meaning (Figure 11.1). We can't tell how big or small an object is unless we can compare it with something else (Figure 11.2, page 282). If you are more than 6 feet (1.8 m) tall, you must approach a doorway with caution. When you are shopping for clothes, you look for the sizes designed to fit the proportions of your body. When you are cooking, you must be sure that the proportions in your recipes are correct.

In this chapter you will learn about how artists use the elements of art to create different kinds of proportion in their works. You will begin to understand why proportion is important in both two-dimensional and three-dimensional art, and you will learn how to use proportion in your own works of art.

Objectives

After completing this chapter, you will be able to:

- Explain and recognize the Golden Mean.
- Understand how we perceive proportion and scale.
- Measure and draw human faces and bodies with correct proportions.
- Understand how artists use proportion and distortion to create meaning.

Words to Know

distortion
exaggeration
foreshortening
Golden Mean
hierarchical proportion
proportion
scale

FIRST IMPRESSIONS

Look at *Anna and David* by Miriam Schapiro. Do the figures have the proportions of average people? Read the credit information to discover the height of this sculpture. Notice the windows in the building behind the figures. That gives you an indication of the scale of the figures. How do you think this sculpture affects the mood of the people who pass it every day? How do the elements of line and color affect this mood? Why is negative space an important factor in this work?

(pages 282–287)
• The Golden Mean
• Scale

GUIDED PRACTICE

Promoting Discussion

Although most students are too self-conscious to discuss their own body proportions, probably everyone in class wishes that some of his or her proportions were different. Since this subject may be sensitive for a class discussion, encourage students to talk about the popularity of cosmetic (plastic) surgery. Have students discuss bodybuilding, weight training, and cosmetic (plastic) surgery as techniques people use to change their body proportions. How do "ideal" body proportions change among generations and cultures?

Understanding Art History

To help students further appreciate the life and times of Miriam Schapiro, whose work is shown in Figure 11.1 on page 280, assign *Artist's Profile 42* in the TCR.

Critical Thinking

Borrow a desk, table, and chair from a kindergarten classroom and the same objects from a third-grade room. Have students measure the desks, tables, and chairs and compare the differences in size and proportion between the furniture from the lower grades, then between the third-grade items and students' own classroom furniture. Ask them to speculate how designers know what measurements are appropriate for each grade level.

FIGURE 11.2 Look carefully at what seem to be cliffs. There is nothing in this picture to tell you that these are merely small piles of sand. Without anything to compare them with, you cannot tell how tall they are.

THE GOLDEN MEAN

You have just read about the importance of proportion to the function of products. Proportion is also important in creating the beauty of art objects (Figure 11.3).

Through the ages, people have sought an ideal of harmony and beauty. They have looked for a ratio (a mathematical comparison of sizes) that would produce an ideal form for figures and structures.

The ancient Greek philosopher Pythagoras found that he could apply mathematical equations to both geometric shapes and musical tones. If this is so, he thought, there must also be a way to explain other things—even the universe—in mathematical terms.

Euclid, a Greek mathematician, discovered what he considered a perfect ratio, or relationship of one part to another. He called this ratio the Golden Section, or **Golden Mean,** *a line divided into two parts so that the smaller line has the same proportion, or ratio, to the larger line as the larger line has to the whole line* (Figure 11.4). With this ratio, the ancient Greeks felt they had found the ideal proportion. It was used to control the relationship of parts in their sculpture, architecture, and even in their pottery. In math, this ratio is written 1 to 1.6. It is also written 1:1.6.

The Golden Rectangle (Figure 11.5) had sides that matched this ratio. The longer sides were a little more than half again as long as the shorter sides. This ratio was thought to be the most pleasing to the eye.

One of the many fascinating facts about the Golden Mean is its relationship to the human figure. If you divide the average adult male body horizontally at the navel, the two body measurements

---

CURRICULUM CONNECTION

Humanities Music in ancient Greece was a combination of poetry, dance, drama, and tonal art. Most Greek festivals honored gods, and music was thought to be a kind of charm connecting humans with the gods. As in all other arts, mathematics and proportion were central to Greek music. Pythagoras, a famous Greek mathematician, formulated the ratios that gave us the octave, a precursor to the scale that we use today. Our science of acoustics is based on the theories of Pythagoras and other mathematicians over the centuries. Mathematical discoveries such as periodic functions are basic to today's electronic music and voice-activated computers.

L O O K I N G
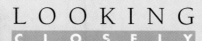

FIGURE 11.3 This heiress from the fifteenth century has some odd proportions. The red silk belt emphasizes her thin, high waist. If you use a ruler to measure, you will notice that her waist is not much wider than her head. Her lips are very full. This is supposed to symbolize a sensuous person. Notice the high forehead, which is thought to be a symbol of an intellectual person. Are these conflicting symbols? Do you think she looked like this or did the painter exaggerate her proportions to make her look more interesting?

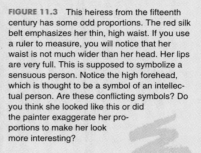

Rogier van der Weyden. *Portrait of a Lady.* c. 1460. Oil on wood. 34 × 25.5 cm (13⅜ × 10⅛″). National Gallery of Art, Washington, D.C. Andrew W. Mellon Collection.

L O O K I N G

Have students study Figure 11.3. Help them to see that the high forehead and sensuous lips are not necessarily conflicting symbols. This may have been a portrait sent to a prospective husband. A prospective husband would want a sensuous woman as well as an intelligent woman to run his household. The painter probably exaggerated her proportions.

Exploring Aesthetics

Have students take a survey to learn if people really prefer the Golden Rectangle over other rectangles. They could make up a chart showing five rectangles, one of which would have the proportions of the Golden Rectangle. This chart could be drawn on a sheet of notebook paper and the rectangles numbered. Each student would show the chart of shapes to different people and ask each person which shape he or she prefers. Encourage students to compile and discuss their findings.

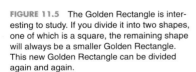

FIGURE 11.4 The ratio of the Golden Mean is 1 to 1.6.

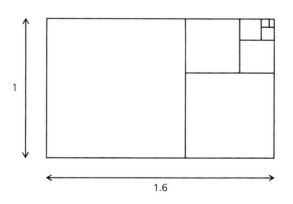

FIGURE 11.5 The Golden Rectangle is interesting to study. If you divide it into two shapes, one of which is a square, the remaining shape will always be a smaller Golden Rectangle. This new Golden Rectangle can be divided again and again.

Critical Thinking

Encourage students to become aware of how often proportion is present in their environment. For example, give this assignment to students: Notice the rectangles in your home. List and describe five that use proportions close to those of the Golden Rectangle. Instruct students to sketch the rectangles in their sketchbooks and identify the function of the object or space. Ask students to discuss the examples they observed.

AT THE MUSEUM

The National Gallery of Art (Washington, D.C.) Videodisk technology represents an exciting new direction in the study of art history. Students can access over 2500 masterpieces of American art using videodisks at the National Gallery of Art. In addition to conveying images in new, inviting, and instructional ways, the videodisks contain details of and information about each piece of art. This special project of art reproduction using computers makes American art more readily available to the public than ever before. The videodisks are available to the public for viewing at home, school, or at the museum and to teachers through a free loan program for use in the classrooms.

GUIDED PRACTICE
(continued)

Exploring Aesthetics

After students have had time to discuss the proportions of the Golden Mean in Figure 11.6, instruct them to study Claude Monet's painting in Figure 3.22, page 56. Ask them to measure the square from the right. Have them notice how the left line of the square matches a strong vertical line in the composition. Challenge them to find other examples of the Golden Mean in the text.

Promoting Discussion

Find a photograph of the pyramids that has people in it so that the students can comprehend the immensity of the pyramids. Then ask students if they have heard of someone creating a work of art on the head of a pin, or at least in miniature. Drawing on the two examples that represent extremes of proportion, encourage a discussion of how artists approach such projects.

Developing Perceptual Skills

Another important topic involving scale is the misrepresentation of scale in advertisements, such as those for jewelry. If possible, bring in jewelry shown in advertisements and let students see how small the objects really are. Warn them to read carefully to see if objects are photographed life-size or are made to appear larger.

Students also need to be conscious of scale during grocery shopping. Labels should always be studied for weights and sizes. If students help with grocery shopping, ask them to look at sizes of boxes and the weights of the contents to see if they can find examples of deceptive packaging.

284

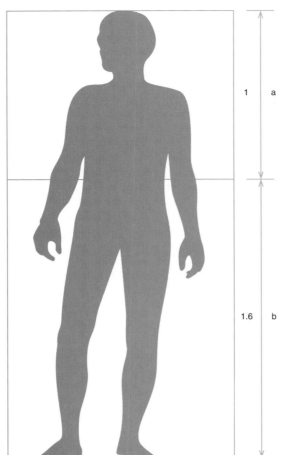

FIGURE 11.6 The relationship of the Golden Mean to the human body.

that result (head to navel = a, navel to toes = b) have a ratio of 1 to 1.6 (Figure 11.6).

The secret of the Golden Mean was forgotten with the fall of Ancient Greece. The ratio was rediscovered, however, during the Renaissance, and a book was written about it. This time the ratio was called the Divine Proportion, and it was thought to have magical qualities.

Since that time, some artists have chosen to use the Golden Mean as the basis for their compositions. Others, unaware of the mathematical ratio, used the Golden Mean just because that arrangement of parts looked good. Most artists now reject the idea that only this one rule can fit the "correct" proportions for all works of art. The ratio, however, is found in visual art so often that it is hard to ignore its importance (Figure 11.7).

Many people looked at the human body as a source for perfect proportions. As you know, artists during the Golden Age of Greece believed that the human body was the true expression of order. Statues created during that time were not realistic portraits of real people. The artists of the period showed the ideal form rather than the real form (Figure 11.8).

FIGURE 11.7 Can you find the proportions of the Golden Mean in this work?

Reginald Marsh. *Why Not Use the "L"?* 1930. Egg tempera on canvas. 91.4 × 121.9 cm (36 × 48"). Collection of Whitney Museum of American Art, New York, New York.

MORE ABOUT . . . GREEK AESTHETICS

The Greek artist was also a mathematician and philosopher. From the earliest times, in Greek sculpture, pottery, and architecture, proportion was central to the design; the philosophical concept of the human being as the highest form of creation led artists to devise the classical—or perfectly proportioned—human figure.

Logic and order were central to Greek thinking and art. The Greeks devised the Golden Rectangle—the perfect mathematical proportion—and applied it to architecture as well as sculpture. Rather than copying from a model to carve human figure sculptures, they proportioned features mathematically.

In the first century B.C., Vitruvius, a Roman writer, set down ratios for human proportion. These were later used by Leonardo da Vinci and other artists. The modern-day architect Le Corbusier applied human dimensions to architecture and city planning (Figure 11.9).

Scale

Scale is much like proportion, but there is a difference. Proportion refers to the relationship of one part to another. **Scale**, on the other hand, *refers to size as measured against a standard reference,* such as the human body. A 7-foot (2.1-m) basketball player may not look big next to other basketball players. The player will look big, however, when

FIGURE 11.8   This sculpture is idealized. The facial features and all the proportions are so perfect that you would not recognize the model even if she stood next to the work.

Greece (from Alexandria?). *Dancing Lady.* c. 50 B.C. Peloponnesian marble. 85.4 cm (33⅝") high with base; 78.7 cm (30⅞") high without base. The Cleveland Museum of Art, Cleveland, Ohio. John L. Severance Fund.

FIGURE 11.9   The sculptural form of this building is based on human dimensions.

Le Corbusier. *Chapelle Notre-Dame-du-Haut.* Ronchamp, France. 1955.

GUIDED PRACTICE
(continued)

Interdisciplinary: Math

Challenge students to look for other interesting proportional ratios in paintings and three-dimensional works and share their findings with the class.

Critical Thinking

One proportional problem that every student can relate to is the proportion of ingredients used in cooking. Ask what would happen to a chocolate cake if the cook added one teaspoon of sugar instead of one cup. What would happen to a pot of homemade vegetable soup if the cook added one cup of salt instead of one teaspoon?

Sparking Creativity

Want students to think creatively about architectural proportion? Suggest this: Proportion in architecture is achieved by organizing the many structural elements in ways that relate well to each other. For fun, design a building that is out of proportion and see how it looks. Cut paper to make the shape of columns, pediments, domes, doors, windows, and so on. Combine them to make your building. Try an over-sized dome on short columns, or windows that are too tall, too wide, or too small. When you finish, make another design that is in good proportion. Have an exhibit and talk with classmates about what is, and is not, good proportion.

TEACHER TALK

Classroom Management   The instructional strategy that is probably most familiar to art teachers is demonstration. This method of instruction is especially effective when applied to classroom activities. When preparing for a demonstration, always practice beforehand using the same materials students will be expected to use. Include continuous commentary with the demonstration, explaining in detail what you are doing and why you are doing it this way. Students receive information by way of the eyes and ears, increasing the likelihood that information will be understood and assimilated.

**Understanding
Art History**

Tell students that Claes Oldenburg created other works that are much larger in scale than normal, including a clothespin sculpture that stands ten stories high, and a soft-sculpture hamburger taller than a person. Ask the students why they think Oldenburg takes ordinary objects and makes them larger than life.

**INDEPENDENT
PRACTICE**

Extension

Some students might wish to study the proportions of other everyday objects, such as stairs, doors, and hand tools. Have students think of a unique item that is encountered frequently but often overlooked.

Art Is Everywhere

To foster students' awareness of proportion and scale in everyday life, suggest this: If you have a camera or a video recorder, take a walk to record examples of good and bad proportion in buildings. Feel the scale of the interior of a home and the interior of a public building or an amphitheater. Find churches that are designed as intimate communal space and others that seem to soar. Look for the space around buildings and see if it is in proportion to the building. Many large buildings have plazas proportioned both for movement of people and for flow of oxygen.

you see him in scale—that is, compared with a crowd of people of average height.

In art there are two kinds of scale to consider. One is the scale of the work itself. The other is the scale of objects or elements within the design.

The pyramids of Egypt are of such large scale that ordinary people are overwhelmed by their size. These pyramids were designed to be large to express the eternal strength of Egypt.

Wall paintings inside a pyramid depict the body of the pharaoh in very large scale. His servants, however, are very small in scale to emphasize their low status (Figure 3.4, page 44). When *figures are arranged in a work of art so scale indicates importance,* the artist is using **hierarchical proportion.** This arrangement disregards the actual size of figures and objects in order to indicate rank in a society. Use of scale to emphasize rank appears in the art of many cultures.

Actual works of art are usually much larger or much smaller than they appear to be when you look at photographs of them. You may have seen photos with a human hand or a human figure added for the purpose of showing the size of the objects in relation to human scale. Without some sort of measure, no illustration in any book can convey the effect of the scale of a work of art.

Some works that seem monumental in quality are really quite small in size. This is why the dimensions are always listed in the credits of the work. Try to visualize the size of a work in relation to your size. Imagine how it would look if it were in the room with you.

The picture of Claes Oldenburg's *Shoestring Potatoes Spilling from a Bag* (Figure 11.10) is not very impressive until you realize that the sculpture is 9 feet (2.7 m) tall. If you could stand beside it, the potatoes would be as tall or taller than you are, and the bag would tower an additional 3 feet (.9 m) above you. The scale of this work compared with a real bag of french fries is enormous. It is also big compared with a human being.

Variations in scale within a work can change the work's total impact. For example, interior designers are concerned with the scale of the furniture that is to be placed in a room. The designer considers the scale of the space into which the furniture will be placed. The needs of the people who will use the space must also be considered. An

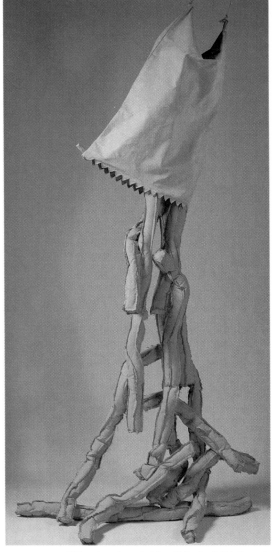

FIGURE 11.10 This soft sculpture is 9 feet (2.7 m) tall. This type of exaggerated scale is one method Pop artists used to make viewers see ordinary objects in a new way.

Claes Oldenburg. *Shoestring Potatoes Spilling from a Bag.* 1966. Acrylic, canvas, kapok, and glue. 274.3 × 116.8 × 106.7 cm (108 × 46 × 42"). Walker Art Center, Minneapolis, Minnesota. Gift of the T. B. Walker Foundation, 1966.

oversized, overstuffed sofa would crowd a small room with a low ceiling. However, the same sofa would fit comfortably in a large hotel lobby with a four-story ceiling. The large scale of the lobby would make the size of the sofa look right.

MORE ABOUT . . . CLAES OLDENBURG

American sculptor Claes Oldenburg (1929–) was born in Stockholm, Sweden. Oldenburg emigrated to the United States, studied art at Yale University and the Chicago Art Institute, and moved to New York in 1956. There he became acquainted with artists working in environmental and theatrical projects and events. In the 1960s, Oldenburg was associated with the Pop art movement. His most distinctive contribution has been monumental sculptures of a variety of everyday objects. *Spoonbridge and Cherry* is an enormous aluminum teaspoon with a handle that curves to form a bridge and a bowl that is bent upward. On the tip of the bowl is a large red cherry with an upright stem.

Experimenting with Scale

Experimenting with Scale

1. Applying Your Skills. Create a small collage scene using magazine cutouts of people, furniture, and hand-held objects such as books, combs, pencils, hair dryers, and dishes. Arrange the cutouts on a small sheet of paper using realistic, accurate scale. All the things in the scene are in scale with the people, and all the people are in correct proportion to each other (Figure 11.11). You may have to employ perspective techniques and arrange things in depth to use all of your cutouts. Draw a background environment for the scene using water-base markers, colored pencils, or crayons.

2. Further Challenge. Create a collage using the same kinds of cutouts but use unrealistic scale. The objects and furniture will not be in scale with the people (Figure 11.12). A mysterious or humorous effect is

FIGURE 11.12   Student work. Unrealistic scale.

FIGURE 11.11   Student work. Realistic scale.

created through the change in normal scale relationships. Create a background using water-base markers, colored pencils, or crayons.

3. Computer Option. Draw a figure with proportion based on average body proportions: 7½ heads high. The Line and Select tools and the Copy and Paste options can be used to quickly make the 7½-head grid that will guide your drawing. When the figure is completed, Copy and Paste the figure and then use the Resize option to change height and width of the figure. Repeat this three or four times. Have some figures that are tall and thin, others that are tall and fat, short and thin, and so on. Measure the head size of each figure you have resized. Even though the figures look very different based on height and width, the proportion related to head size will still be the same.

Experimenting with Scale

1. Applying Your Skills.
This activity can be achieved successfully by all students. Figure 11.11 will help them understand what to do. Before starting this activity, review perspective techniques in Chapter 6 on pages 136 to 138. Students will need to use these techniques to make the objects seem to fit together.

2. Further Challenge.
All students should be able to complete this exercise successfully. Figure 11.12 serves as a reference. Even though the objects will not be in scale with the people, students will still need to use perspective to make the final scene look like the unrelated objects belong together.

3. Computer Option.
If available, use video digitizing equipment to capture the portraits of students in your classroom or use different figures from other sources such as a videodisc or CD-Rom. Import the images into a drawing program. Alter the images by changing colors or using special effects such as Water Color, Oil Pastel, Smudging, and so on. Experiment using the Selection tools and Copy and Paste commands. Explore exchanging heads, bodies, or features. Use drawing tools to blend cut-and-pasted areas. With practice, it becomes difficult to tell where alterations have occurred. Challenge students to explore what they, or their friends, would look like with a famous body, head, or the eyes of a cat. Tell students that sensationalist tabloids use this technique to attract consumers' attention and sell papers.

MORE ABOUT . . . COLLAGE

Collage was first used by early Cubists and Dadaists. The Cubists were concerned with the essence of an object and painted a subject from various perspectives to express the idea of that object. In later phases of Cubism, a decorative and ornamental sensibility is evident. During this period, Picasso introduced elements other than paint onto the canvas. The Dadaists saw collage as an expression of their own theories of art. They intended to outrage and shock the art world, often with non-paint media in the context of a painting. Marcel Duchamp was the most famous of the Dadaists. He eventually abandoned oil painting altogether to make art out of found objects.

(pages 288–293)
• Drawing Human
  Proportions

GUIDED PRACTICE

Promoting Discussion

Find out whether any students have considered a modeling career. What do they know about the size of today's fashion models? Bring in a high-fashion magazine, such as *Vogue*, and a catalog from a retail department store. Point out the different proportions emphasized in the fashion photos.

Critical Thinking

Discuss how industrial designers must consider human proportions. Look around the classroom at tables, counters, sinks, scissors, pencils, brushes, paper, and windows. Think about objects at home, in factories, and examples farther from the local environment, such as space vehicles and space stations. Each time the student mentions an object, make sure that he or she explains how proportion affects the size and shape of the final product.

Exploring Aesthetics

Use large photos of individual television or movie stars to discuss beauty in facial proportions. More than likely, the conclusion will be that even idolized stars will have features that vary greatly from the ideal. This awareness will help students whose own features vary from the ideal to respect themselves.

DRAWING HUMAN PROPORTIONS

Different cultures have set different standards for human beauty. People from the Middle Ages would view us as giants (Figure 11.13). The rounded females in Rubens's Baroque paintings

FIGURE 11.13 The man who wore this armor was about 5′ 9½″ (1.7 m) tall. Would many men today fit into this armor?

English (Greenwich School). Armor of George Clifford, Third Earl of Cumberland, K. G. c. 1580–85. Steel and gold. 176.5 cm (69½″). The Metropolitan Museum of Art, New York, New York. Munsey Fund, 1932.

FIGURE 11.14 Rubens's Virgin looks much chubbier than those in most other paintings of the Virgin Mary, but hefty proportions were the favored style in the time of Rubens, so he painted Mary in that manner.

Peter Paul Rubens. *The Assumption of the Virgin.* c. 1626. Oil on wood. 125.4 × 94.2 cm (49⅜ × 37⅛″). National Gallery of Art, Washington, D.C. Samuel H. Kress Collection.

would seem overweight by today's standards (Figure 11.14). Even today there are dramatic differences between the proportions of a high-fashion model and those of the average person.

Figures

People come in a variety of sizes and shapes. Categories for clothes sizes—slim, husky, petite, tall—are just one indication of the many different shapes and sizes of people.

Although they vary in size and shape, most people do not vary with regard to proportion. The 7-foot (2.1-m) basketball player and the 5-foot (1.5-m) dancer might have the same proportions. The tall basketball player's arms, legs, and torso

---

CURRICULUM CONNECTION

Science Until the present, the relationship between human proportions and architectural forms has been studied purely for aesthetic reasons. Today there is a discipline of science called *ergonomics* that is concerned with the relationship between people and the environment. It started during World War II with the design of efficient aircraft cockpits, and it is now concerned with all areas of interface between a user and a designed interior environment. This applies to comfort and safety in the everyday environment. Kitchen counters, classroom desks, auditorium seats, shelves in stores, automobiles, and many other objects are designed for comfort and maximum efficiency.

have the same ratio to each other as the arms, legs, and torso of the dancer. Body proportions cannot be defined only in ratios of one body part to another.

The unit usually used to define the proportions of an individual figure is the length of the head from the chin to the top of the skull. The average adult is seven and one-half heads tall (Figure 11.15); a young child is five or six heads tall; and an infant is only three heads long (Figure 11.16). Many amateur paintings of children look strange because the artist has drawn the head too small in proportion to the rest of the body. When this happens, the child looks like a miniature adult.

There is one instance in which an artist may purposely distort proportion to make a drawing look more realistic. If a model is pointing at you, the arm from the fingertips to the shoulder will look shorter than it actually is. The artist will use a technique to visually shorten the arm. **Foreshortening** is *to shorten an object to make it look as if it extends backward into space* (Figure 11.17, page 290).

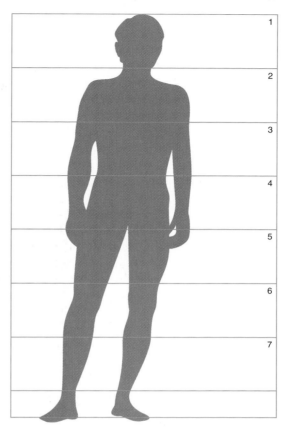

FIGURE 11.15   Average body proportions.

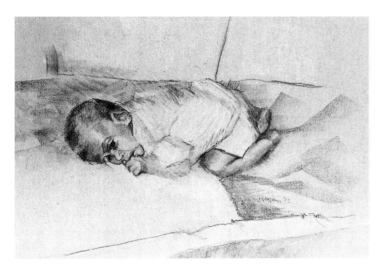

FIGURE 11.16   Notice the ratio of head to body in this sketch of an infant. Does the ratio differ from the usual adult ratio?

GUIDED PRACTICE
(continued)

**Understanding
Art History**

After students have studied Figure 11.14, ask them to point out features of Rubens's art that identify him as a Baroque artist. (See Chapter 3, page 54.)

**Developing
Perceptual Skills**

Have students observe the proportions in Figure 11.15 and then measure the proportions of the infant in Figure 11.16. An example of an infant who has the proportions of a little adult can be seen in the *Madonna and Child on Curved Throne* shown in Figure 3.14 on page 50.

ACTIVITY   **Human
Proportions**

1. Applying Your Skills.
Depending on the disposition of your students, you might team the students up in groups of two or three to record measurements. Of course you will probably want to team girls with girls and boys with boys to avoid embarrassing moments. You might assign this activity as homework, or you might ask for a few volunteers to do the measuring for the entire class. The important point is for students to understand that proportions are not just numbers created out of thin air—they are accurate.

MORE ABOUT . . . PETER PAUL RUBENS

Rubens's mother sacrificed everything so that her son could study in southern Italy. There Rubens was introduced to the Duke of Mantua, who hired him as a court painter. Among Rubens's assigned tasks was to travel widely and make copies of many paintings as well as of artworks already owned by the duke. Rubens undertook his labors very systematically and kept a complete set of finished drawings of the works he had seen. In 1608 Rubens received a letter saying that his mother was dying. He hurried back to Antwerp but was too late. Out of love and gratitude for his mother's assistance, Rubens placed one of his finest paintings on her tomb.

2. Further Challenge.
This activity might be done best in class with volunteer models. It is wise to give the model a prop or some kind of costume to make both students and model feel at ease. Before students start to draw, reassure them that they are beginners, not professional artists. They should try to capture the position and proportions of the model but not worry about facial features.

3. Computer Option.
As an alternative activity, have students follow these directions: Use a live model and the drawing tools of your choice to make several body sketches. Have the model change positions so you can try foreshortening of the arms or legs. Save and title. Then, use the Grids and Rulers option and a Selection tool to select the head on one of your drawings. Move the head down the body counting how many "heads" tall the figure is. Select the one that best represents ideal proportions. Erase the other figures or copy the ideal figure to a new page. Experiment with the Scale Selection or Resizing tool. Create some figures that are tall and thin or short and fat, but maintain the average 7½-heads proportion.

**Understanding
Art History**

Vitruvius (see bottom column on this page) wrote about how the Greeks used human proportions as the basis for architectural construction: the inch came from one joint of a finger, the palm of the hand and the foot were measures, and the cubit was the length of the forearm from the tip of the middle finger to the elbow.

FIGURE 11.17   Siqueiros used foreshortening in this painting to dramatically exaggerate his reach to grab everything he can. His hand becomes a burst of superhuman energy.

David Alfaro Siqueiros. *Self-Portrait (El Coronelazo)*. 1945. Pyroxylin on Masonite. 91 × 121 cm (35⅞ × 47¾"). Museo de Arte Moderno, Mexico City, Mexico.

ACTIVITY   **Human Proportions**

1. Applying Your Skills.   Measure your head from the top of your skull to the bottom of your chin. Because the top of your head is round, hold something flat, such as a piece of cardboard, across the top of your head to obtain an accurate measurement.

Use the length of your head as a unit against which to measure the rest of your body. In this way you can figure the relationship, or ratio, of all parts of your body to your head. You may need a friend to help you obtain accurate measurements. Determine the number of head lengths that each of the following represents: total height, chin to waist, waist to hip, knee to ankle, ankle to bottom of bare heel, underarm to elbow, elbow to wrist, wrist to tip of finger, and shoulder to tip of finger. Record the ratios and create a diagram or chart to show your findings. Compare your findings with those of your classmates. Find averages for the class, because the ratios will not be exactly alike.

2. Further Challenge.   Make a series of figure drawings using a live model. Use the sighting technique to help you see proportions. (See Technique Tip 5 on page 350 in the Handbook.) Remember, as your model's poses change, the proportions will look different. Measure what you see, not what you think you should see.

If your model is sitting facing you, the length from hip to knee may be foreshortened. This means that the amount of leg you see from hip to knee will depend upon your point of view (Figure 11.17).

3. Computer Option.   Use video digitizing software and a video camera or a scanner to capture a variety of photographs of students and objects. Use the Select tool and the Copy and Paste options to assemble a computer collage using unrealistic scale. Use the tools of your choice to manipulate the images. Images can be captured from many other sources such as videodisc. If you do not have these capabilities, use the drawing tools of your choice to create your own. Create a surrealistic scene.

Heads and Faces

As you read this section, look in a mirror or at a friend to check the examples discussed.

MORE ABOUT . . . VITRUVIUS

Vitruvius, a Roman who lived in the first century B.C., noted that the height of a person from the soles of the feet to the top of the head equals the width of the outstretched arms from finger tip to finger tip. He also recorded that if a person lies flat and extends the arms above the head, the navel becomes the center of the body's total length.

According to Vitruvian proportions, if the navel is used as a center, both the tips of the fingers and the toes will touch the circumference of a circle drawn around the person. Leonardo da Vinci's famous drawing of the human male within a circle and a square is based on the Vitruvian norm.

The front of the head is approximately oval. No one has a head that is perfectly oval—some people have narrow chins, and some have square jaws.

Because a face is approximately symmetrical, it has a central vertical axis when viewed from the front (Figure 11.18). If the face turns away from you, the axis curves over the surface of the head.

You can divide the head into four sections along the central axis. This is done by drawing three horizontal lines that divide the axis into four equal parts, as shown in Figure 11.18.

The top fourth of the head is usually full of hair. The hair may start above the top horizontal line, or it may fall below it if the person wears bangs.

The eyes usually appear on the central horizontal line. They are at the center of a person's head. Notice the width of the space between the eyes. How does it relate to the width of one eye? The bottom of the nose rests on the lowest horizontal line, and the mouth is closer to the nose than to the chin. Use the sighting technique to determine

other relationships, such as nose width, mouth width, and ear placement.

When you view a head in complete profile, or from the side, all of the vertical proportions remain the same as in the front view. However, both shape and contour change. Try to discover the new ratios (Figure 11.19). Notice the relationship between the distance from the chin to the hairline and the distance from the front of the forehead to the back of the head. Can you find a ratio to help you locate the ear in profile? Study the contour of the front of the face. Which part protrudes the most? Notice the jawline from the chin to the ear and the relationship of the neck to the head. In Figure 11.20 on page 292, Isabel Bishop has lined up the heads of the two young women so you can see how the front view and the profile proportions of their faces relate.

Notice that the facial proportions of infants are slightly different, as shown in the painting by Dürer (Figure 11.21 on page 293).

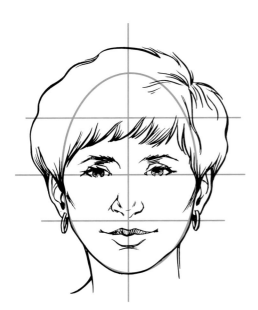

FIGURE 11.18 Facial proportions.

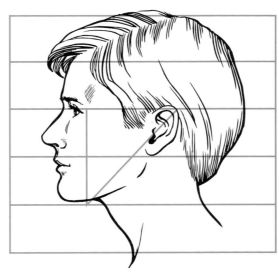

FIGURE 11.19 Profile proportions.

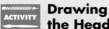 **Drawing
the Head**

1. Applying Your Skills.
Help students understand
where the central axis can be
found on a three-quarter view
by showing an example.
Parents magazine would be a
good one in which to find the
faces of children and infants.

2. Further Challenge.
This activity requires perception drawing. Emphasize
again that it is not necessary
to obtain a true likeness at
this point; draw to understand correct proportions. If
you can convince students
that accurate representation
is not important, they will be
less likely to "freeze up."

3. Computer Option.
As an alternative activity,
have students follow these
directions: Collect pictures of
faces representing three age
groups: babies or small children, adult, and elderly.
Gather front, side, and three-
quarter views. Notice the
changes in facial proportions
as babies grow and people
age. You will be making portraits representing each of
the above age categories on
three new pages. Using the
drawing tools of your choice,
draw a frontal view of a human face. Include the neck
and shoulders. The Grids
and Rulers option, if available, will help locate the
central axis and other divi-
sions. Allow enough space to
draw the side or three-quarter
view of the same face next to
the frontal view. (Use the
Page Setup menu to increase
the width and change the
page orientation, if necessary.) Make sure you have
used the correct facial proportions for each category.
Save and title your work.
Compare the results. Which
age was easier to draw?

FIGURE 11.20 The artist has placed these
heads one behind the other to give a clear idea
of the relationship between front and profile
views. What feeling has Bishop produced with
this organization? What does it tell you about
the girls?

Isabel Bishop. *Two Girls.* 1935. Oil and tempera on composition board. 50.8 × 61 cm (20 × 24″). The Metropolitan Museum of Art, New York, New York. Arthur Hoppock
Hearn Fund, 1936.

 Drawing the Head

1. Applying Your Skills. Look through magazines
for large photographs of heads. Look for adults, children, and babies. Remember that a head is not flat,
and when it is turned, the central axis moves and
curves around the shape of the head. You can always
find the axis because it goes through the center of the
nose, lips, and between the eyes. Draw the central axis
and the three horizontal dividing lines on each face
you have selected. Do you find any proportional differences among the faces of adults, children, and
infants?

MORE ABOUT . . . ISABEL BISHOP

American painter and printmaker Isabel Bishop
(1902–), has dedicated her career to capturing the
various activities of the residents of lower Manhattan. Her artistic style is evident in her use of multiple figures, high contrast of light and shadow, and
increased energy and movement. In 1925, Bishop
began to etch; she started with nude studies but
was soon depicting small vignettes of everyday life.
In 1926, she moved into her first studio on 14th St.
at Union Square in New York City, and for more
than 50 years, the Square provided her with a rich
environment of human activity to draw from.

FIGURE 11.21 As with body proportions, the facial proportions of infants are different from those of adults. The skull is large. The infant's features seem to be squeezed together in the lower half of his face.

Albrecht Dürer. *Virgin and Child with Saint Anne.* 1519. Tempera and oil on canvas, transferred from wood. 60 × 49.9 cm (23⅝ × 19⅝″). The Metropolitan Museum of Art, New York, New York. Bequest of Benjamin Altman, 1913.

2. Further Challenge. Use a mirror to study the proportions of your head. Draw a self-portrait with charcoal or pencil. Use sighting to help find accurate size and shape relationships.

3. Computer Option. Gather some pictures of the faces of babies, young children, and adults. Notice that facial proportions change with age. Use the drawing tools of your choice to draw a human face using average facial proportions. Save your work. Use the Selection tool and the Copy and Paste options to duplicate the first face you drew. To experiment with the size of facial features, use the Selection tool to select the features of the face but not the outline of the head itself. Use the Resize option to create the correct feature size for a young child. Save your work. Reduce the size even more to create the correct feature size for

an infant. The features need to be small and in the lower third of its face. Save your work. If possible, save all three faces on the same screen. Compare the three faces you have created.

How ARTISTS USE PROPORTION AND DISTORTION

Many artists use correct proportions in their work. They want every viewer to recognize the person, place, or thing being shown. These artists use correct proportion to create illusions of reality.

TEACH

(pages 293–299)
• How Artists Use Proportion and Distortion

GUIDED PRACTICE

Developing Perceptual Skills
Ask students why they think Bishop did not include background detail in *Two Girls.* What is the focal point of the painting? How does Bishop keep the viewer's attention focused there? How does Bishop convey the close relationship between the two women in the painting?

Cooperative Learning
Have students work in pairs or small groups to write the contents of the letter that the woman holds in *Two Girls.* Coach them to include information that would explain the facial expressions of the women in the painting. Have the groups read their letters to the class or incorporate the letter into a skit that they perform for the class.

Developing Studio Skills
Make a series of figure drawings using a live model. Remind students to use the sighting technique to help see proportions. Also remind them that as their model's poses change, the proportions will look different. They should keep in mind that they will measure what they see, not what they think they should see. If the model is sitting facing students, the length from hip to knee may be foreshortened. Refer back to Figure 11.17 on page 290 to reinforce the concept of foreshortening, if necessary.

GUIDED PRACTICE
(continued)

Understanding Art History

Albrecht Dürer was the first artist to complete a true self-portrait, and he was only thirteen years old at the time! As he matured as an artist, his work reflected his personal struggle with the religious controversy between the Catholic Church and Martin Luther. Eventually, he sided with Luther and became a strong advocate for change.

Using Art Criticism

After students have had a chance to study John Singleton Copley's painting in Figure 11.22, ask these questions: What do you see in this painting? What lines, shapes, spaces, colors, and textures can you identify? What has Copley said about the legendary man who rode a horse through the small town shown in Grant Wood's painting in Figure 5.3 on page 91? Do you like this painting? Why or why not?

Understanding Art History

Inform students that George Catlin was a completely self-taught artist whose first career was that of a lawyer. His life-long interest in Native American culture led him to visit various tribes and to record his impressions on canvas. He arranged an art exhibition from 1837 to 1845 and was received more enthusiastically in Europe than in the United States. Today, most of his work is in the Smithsonian Institution in Washington, D.C.

FIGURE 11.22   In this painting, Copley not only tells us what Paul Revere looked like, but he also tells us the man's profession. Revere was a silversmith, and the artist shows Revere holding a finished piece of work. The tools on the table were those used by Revere to engrave designs on the surface of his finished forms.

John Singleton Copley. *Paul Revere.* c. 1768–70. Oil on canvas. 88.9 × 72.3 cm (35 × 28½″). Museum of Fine Arts, Boston, Massachusetts. Gift of Joseph W., William B., and Edward H. R. Revere.

FIGURE 11.23   As a young man, Catlin visited forty-eight Indian tribes, and he lived with Indians in both North and South America. His paintings are an accurate record of Indian life.

George Catlin. *See-non-ty-a, an Iowa Medicine Man.* c. 1845. Oil on canvas. 71.1 × 58.1 cm (28 × 22⅞″). National Gallery of Art, Washington, D.C. Paul Mellon Collection.

This ability to show objects as though they were real seems magical to many viewers.

Most Americans have favored works of art that are accurate, realistic views of life. Early American artists were hired to paint portraits—not so much to create art as to record accurate information about real people (Figure 11.22). George Catlin recorded the life of the Native American (Figure 11.23).

Some artists use exaggeration and distortion rather than real proportion to convey their ideas and feelings. **Exaggeration** and **distortion** are *deviations from expected, normal proportions.* They are powerful means of expression. Artists can lengthen, enlarge, bend, warp, twist, or deform parts or all of the human body. By making these changes, they can show moods and feelings that are easily understood by viewers (Figure 11.24).

In the past, movie stars of the silent screen had to exaggerate facial expressions and body language

━━━━━━━━━━━━ **CURRICULUM CONNECTION** ━━━━━━━━━━━━

Radio, TV, and Film   By the turn of this century, motion pictures had become a popular attraction in amusement arcades, music halls, and vaudeville theaters. However, until the advent of the "talkies" in the 1920s, movies were silent and had to rely on the skill of actors to convey a story. Actors used exaggerated facial features and gestures to replace what their dialogue would otherwise relate. While the silent movies played, often a piano or organ player would provide live accompaniment to the action on the screen. This musician had the added responsibility of creating mood, tempo, and tone with music.

FIGURE 11.24 The intensity of feeling in this painting is almost unbearable. The twisted, tortured hands and feet of Christ are visual symbols of the entire Crucifixion. Grünewald has used just enough distortion to express the suffering without losing the reality of the moment.

Matthias Grünewald. *The Small Crucifixion.* c. 1511–20. Oil on wood. 61.6 × 46 cm (24¼ × 18⅛"). National Gallery of Art, Washington, D.C. Samuel H. Kress Collection.

to convey meaning without words. If you have ever seen an old silent movie, you have probably laughed at the exaggerated eyelid movements used to express meaning. Similarly, mimes move with graceful control that comes from years of training. Even though exaggerated or distorted, a mime's movements can convey a sense of truth (Figure 11.25 on page 296).

It takes study and skill to use exaggeration and distortion effectively. Artists who do so have first practiced the use of accurate proportion.

Edvard Munch (**ed**-vard moonk) and Pablo Picasso are two artists who used exaggeration and distortion in their work. Munch exaggerates the unity of the couple in love by eliminating all negative space between the figures (Figure 11.26 on page 296). Picasso's poor, undernourished couple in *The Frugal Repast* is not depressing because the long hands and arms of the lovers weave the withered bodies into an expression of tender togetherness (Figure 11.27 on page 297). Look for other ways in which the artist used distorted proportions.

MEETING SPECIAL NEEDS

Physically Disabled Persons with disabilities may relate to this work with special intensity upon learning that Grünewald's *The Small Crucifixion* was painted for the chapel of a lepers' hospital. It enabled those with the physical deformities resulting from leprosy to empathize with the story of Christ's suffering. In his life, Christ made special efforts to help persons with disabilities. Modern attitudes are that persons with disabilities have the same rights as persons without disabilities. A central issue today is inclusion, rather than segregation and exclusion, of persons with disabilities.

GUIDED PRACTICE
(continued)

Understanding Art History

Caricature is another powerfully expressive technique. Artists have used it since the days of ancient Egypt and Babylon, and it is still a powerful political weapon. Editorial cartoonists can sway public opinion. If you have students who are interested in this field, suggest that they research Honoré Daumier or Thomas Nast. Both of these artists were successful with the technique of caricature. Nast, an illustrator, was able to turn people against the infamous Tammany Hall political machine in New York City. His work appeared in newspapers and magazines.

Exploring Aesthetics

Ask students to explain how the medium used in Figure 11.26 affects the feeling of the work. Does the title help a viewer to interpret the image? Why or why not?

Critical Thinking

Both Figures 11.27 and 11.28 on page 298 depict a man and a woman. However, Chagall and Picasso have created quite different tones to their respective works that cause the reader to react in equally different ways. Tell students that writers accomplish the same distinction through language. To illustrate this point, ask students to begin two letters from either the men or the women in the two artworks. Each letter should express the person's feeling toward the other person in the same painting at the exact moment of the painting. Ask volunteers to read their two letters. Then compare the variations of tone in the letters.

FIGURE 11.25 A mime.

Chagall uses distortion to present a happier theme in his painting *Birthday* (Figure 11.28, page 298). The subjects of this work are the artist himself and Bella, his fiancée. The birthday is the artist's. Instead of simply showing himself leaning over to kiss Bella, Chagall used distortion. In the painting he appears to leap backward, stretch his neck like a swan, curve it around, and give Bella a kiss as he floats by. Do you think Chagall might have been thinking, "I'm so happy, I'm floating on air," when he created this work?

Artists can create feelings of great stability and calm by placing a small head on a large body. A monumental, or large and imposing, quality results. This is due mainly to placing a small head on a large, stable base. The monumental quality of Gaston Lachaise's *Walking Woman* (Figure 11.29, page 298) is created through exaggerated proportions and spacing rather than through large scale.

FIGURE 11.26 Munch has melted the two figures into one. He exaggerates the roundness of the embrace by drawing the arms as smooth curves without any elbows.

Edvard Munch. *The Kiss.* 1897–1902. Woodcut, printed in black. 46.6 × 47.4 cm (18⅜ × 18⅝"). The Museum of Modern Art, New York, New York. Gift of Abby Aldrich Rockefeller.

MEETING SPECIAL NEEDS

Physically Disabled Both Figures 11.26 and 11.27 are valuable discussion tools for teachers. Students with disabilities may be interested in knowing that Edvard Munch created some of the world's most emotional paintings, despite having tuberculosis for much of his life. Possibly, his frail health gave him even more reason and urgency to create.

Picasso's *The Frugal Repast* shows two very thin and hungry figures. Some teenage women try to emulate the bodily proportions of fashion models and become anorexic, not eating sufficiently enough to nourish their bodies. They forget that the strong bones grown in the teen years will ward off bone degeneration in later years.

LOOKING
CLOSELY

FIGURE 11.27 Notice how Picasso used distortion and exaggeration to create the atmosphere of poverty and starvation. Look at the man's face. See how the shadows under his cheekbone and around his eye are exaggerated. Notice how the tendons in his neck protrude. You can see the bones sticking out of his shoulder and elbow. Observe the elongated arms, fingers, and torsos of both figures. Why is there an empty bowl on the table? Why is there liquid in only one glass? Notice that the filled glass, the piece of bread, and the lump of food are on the woman's side of the table. Why?

Pablo Picasso. *The Frugal Repast.* 1904 (printed 1913). Etching. 46.3 × 37.6 cm (18¼ × 14¹³⁄₁₆″). The Museum of Modern Art. New York, New York. Gift of Abby Aldrich Rockefeller.

GUIDED PRACTICE
(continued)

LOOKING
CLOSELY

Have students study Figure 11.27 and answer the questions in the caption. Help students see that artists who use distortion do so for specific purposes, not because they cannot draw accurately. Allow students plenty of time to respond using their personal interpretations.

Understanding Art History

Figure 11.27 is from what is now called Picasso's "Blue Period." During this time he lived in poverty in Paris, and he was not yet famous. He later tried many different innovative styles. The most emotional work he created, *Guernica*, was painted for the Spanish exhibit at the 1937 World's Fair. Guernica was a town in Spain chosen by the Germans to test the ability of their air force to destroy towns and cities. The test was successful. The painting is a timeless expression of anguish and pain.

ACTIVITY ## Distorting Proportions

1. Applying Your Skills.
To keep this activity fun, tell students they may not use features from one photo to create the realistic proportions. The distorted face will be more fun if the students look for hats, glasses, earrings, and other accessories, as well as eyes, nose, mouth, and hair, from different faces.

2. Further Challenge.
The easiest caricatures and photos to find would be those of people in current events.

Another use of exaggeration can be seen in the features of a mask. Masks have been used in all societies, from early primitive tribes to our modern computer age (Figure 11.30, page 299). A mask allows a person to hide his or her real self and become someone, or something, else.

Masks are used in many cultures as part of religious ceremonies and rituals. In many cases the features of the mask are exaggerated for expressive purposes. There are different procedures for making and using masks. Each culture has specific traditions that are followed. Sometimes the mask appears to the person in a dream. Sometimes the mask is part of a cultural tradition. In most cases the mask is intended to aid efforts to communicate with the spirit world.

Cartoons are another way in which exaggeration can be used. Editorial cartoonists use this technique to make caricatures of famous people. The caricatures emphasize unusual facial features. Similarly, characters in comic strips are often made by using proportions that are larger than life. The most distorted comic-strip characters are often the funniest ones.

SAFETY TIP

Always supervise students carefully. Adequate supervision of students is required for both safety and liability reasons. Safety rules should be posted and explained at the start of each term and repeated regularly, especially during classroom activities and studio lessons. These rules should be rigidly enforced. At no time should students be allowed to work in the classroom without direct supervision. Teachers should also make it a rule that students not bring to class and use their own art materials unless otherwise instructed. It is possible that these art materials could contain unknown hazards.

GUIDED PRACTICE

(continued)

3. Computer Option.

As an alternative activity, have students follow these directions: Use the Brush Symmetry tool to create a symmetrical portrait. Select vertical symmetry and a brush thickness of your choice. Experiment with colors, patterns, and brush thickness to draw a fanciful human or animal mask design. Work with as large a design as possible. Save and title the mask. Now, experiment with distortion by using the Selection tool and Scale Selection or Resizing tool to change the proportion of the whole head or individual features by shrinking or exaggerating. Other manipulation tools such as Rotate, Flip, Turn, Distort, Slant, and Simple Perspective can be used. When you have achieved the desired effect, use the Save As command and retitle the work.

Exploring Aesthetics

Have students compare Chagall's painting in Figure 11.28 to Thomas Hart Benton's *I Got a Girl on Sourwood Mountain* (Figure 5.23 on page 98). Encourage them to describe the similarities and the differences.

Understanding Art History

Marc Chagall was influenced by the works of such artists as van Gogh, Gauguin, and Matisse while he studied in St. Petersburg, Russia. From there he went to Paris, France, where he was further influenced by the artistic innovations of the Cubists as well as the theories of Sigmund Freud. His own style is marked by brightly colored fantasies which draw little distinction between dreams and actual objects.

FIGURE 11.28 Chagall's painting shows a childlike belief in love's power to conquer all. He created distorted fantasies full of bright colors that looked like joyful dreams.

Marc Chagall. *Birthday.* 1915. Oil on cardboard. 80.6 × 99.7 cm (31¾ × 39¼"). Collection, The Museum of Modern Art, New York, New York. Acquired through the Lillie P. Bliss bequest.

 Distorting Proportions

1. Applying Your Skills. Cut two ovals about 9 inches (23 cm) long from any color of construction paper. Using parts cut from magazines, create one face using accurate proportions. On the second oval, create a distorted face (Figure 11.31).

2. Further Challenge. Find caricatures (cartoons in which certain features are exaggerated) of one well-known person done by two different artists. The editorial page of a newspaper is a good source. Find a photograph of the same person. Compare the three pictures by describing similarities and differences.

FIGURE 11.29 This sculpture is only 19¼ inches (48.8 cm) high and yet it has a monumental quality, because Lachaise has made the head small.

Gaston Lachaise. *Walking Woman.* 1922. Bronze. 48.8 × 26.9 × 18.9 cm (19¼ × 10⅝ × 7½"). Hirshhorn Museum and Sculpture Garden, Smithsonian Institution, Washington, D.C. Gift of Joseph H. Hirshhorn, 1966.

AT THE MUSEUM

Cleveland Museum of Art (Cleveland, Ohio) Every June the Cleveland Museum of Art holds a festive parade. The entries are based on an artwork in the museum's collection. The process of selection begins in April when the general public comes up with an idea for an art project which is related to an exhibit. Artists are hired to help the public create the entry. This parade emphasizes the museum's collection in an interactive and creative way; the museum's exhibits are basically re-created to be in the parade. To involve the community, the museum draws participants from local churches, nursing homes, and over forty cultural, educational, and medical institutions in the area.

FIGURE 11.30 Some masks were worn and some were held, but most were created for ceremonial purposes.

(left) Kwakiutl. *Wolf Mask*. Northwest Coast. 1900. Wood, copper eyes and upper teeth, haliotis shell, and paint. Height: 43 cm (17"). Milwaukee Public Museum, Milwaukee, Wisconsin.

(middle) *Mask*. New Ireland. c. 1920. Wood, paint, fiber, seashells. Height: 38 cm (15"). Milwaukee Public Museum, Milwaukee, Wisconsin.

(right) Bella Coola. *Cockle Hunter Mask*. Northwest Coast. c. 1900. Wood, horsehair, paint. Height: 33 cm (13"). Milwaukee Public Museum, Milwaukee, Wisconsin.

3. Computer Option. Use the drawing tools of your choice to draw a human face using average facial proportions. Use the Select tool and the Copy and Paste options to make four or five copies of the head and face on the same screen. Use the Select tool to experiment with the whole head and with individual facial features. Resize, Distort, Rotate, and Bend are some options that may prove useful to you. If your software does not have these options, draw the changes with drawing tools of your choice. Save your work. Compare the faces you have distorted and changed. How does the distortion affect the way you would use each face in a piece of artwork?

FIGURE 11.31 Student work. Accurate and distorted proportions.

FOCUS

OBJECTIVE

Create a clay Storyteller sculpture involving one adult interacting with many children.

MOTIVATOR

Bring several children's books to class. Ask students to read the stories aloud in class. Then discuss the human characteristics exhibited by each animal. Discuss why certain animals were given specific human characteristics or personalities. Encourage students to read the stories to younger siblings or neighborhood children so that they might get an inspiration for their clay figure.

TEACH

GUIDED PRACTICE

Understanding Art History

Around 5000 years ago the ancient Pueblos, called the Anasazi by the Navajo and archaeologists (the Pueblos do not like this name), began to spread throughout the Southwest. This migration was a result of overpopulation and a lengthy drought. Nearly 3000 years ago, the ancient Pueblos began a slow transition from hunters to agriculturalists. They began growing corn, squash, and other vegetables. They lived in multistoried dwellings called pueblos and created baskets and pottery. To avoid raiders, the Pueblos built homes atop high cliffs.

FIGURE 11.32 Annette Romero of the Cochiti Pueblo. *Storyteller Doll.* 1993. Clay and earth pigments. 20 × 10 × 17.7 cm (8 × 4 × 7″). Private collection.

Supplies

- Sketchbook and pencil
- Clay
- Clay modeling tools
- Slip and brush
- Plastic bag
- Tray or board
- Acrylic paints and assorted brushes
- Fine-line black markers

When Helen Cordero of the Cochiti Pueblo shaped the first Storyteller doll in 1964, she brought the Singing Mother, one of the oldest forms of Native American self-portraiture, into the twentieth century. In doing so, she reinvented a dying Cochiti tradition of figurative pottery.

Helen Cordero began making clay people in the late 1950s. Eventually little people came to life in her hands (Figure 11.32).

The first time Helen exhibited her work at a Santo Domingo feast day, a folk art collector named Girard bought all her little people. He asked her to make an even larger seated figure with children, and Helen thought about her grandfather, who had been a very good storyteller.

It is impossible to determine how many Storytellers Helen Cordero has shaped since 1964. It is also impossible to measure the influence of her invention, which began a revival of figurative pottery in both her own and other New Mexico pueblos. All sorts of variations have appeared. Mary E. Toya from the Jemez Pueblo made a female Storyteller in 1984 with 115 children, ten miniature pots,

MEETING SPECIAL NEEDS

Physically Disabled For some students with disabilities, it may be more appropriate to do a collage variation of the Storyteller figure. If possible, allow these students to use a glue stick to paste tiny magazine pictures of figures onto a large cut-out magazine figure. Using this method, students learn about how changes in scale can create dramatic visual effects. You could use examples of each media (clay and paper collage) to discuss the way media influences aesthetic appeal.

three baskets, two dogs, two balls, a drum and two dolls (one of which is a miniature Storyteller, less than an inch tall, with six babies). Create a clay Storyteller sculpture involving one adult interacting with many children, using proper clay construction techniques. After firing, add color.

Brainstorm with your friends to think up variations for the Storyteller project. You may depict a male or female person or an animal as the adult. The children must match the adult; for example, if you chose a bear as the adult, the children must be bear cubs. Use exaggerated scale to illustrate how an adult can enthrall children with storytelling.

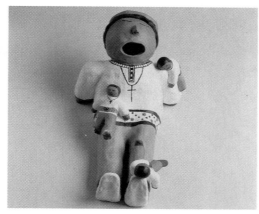

FIGURE 11.32A Student work.

CREATING

When you have selected the subject of your sculpture, make several sketches of the adult. Draw different views of your adult. Then make some rough sketches to help you think through how you will arrange the children on the adult.

Review clay construction procedures by reading Technique Tip 15 on page 354 in the Handbook. Decide which process you will use to build the adult figure. Remember that it needs to be hollow, and it needs an opening to allow the air to get inside. The storyteller's mouth would be appropriate. Decide which process will you use to create the smaller figures. Make notes about your construction plans in your sketchbook.

Collect your construction materials. Build the adult first, adding all three-dimensional details. Keep the adult stored tightly in the plastic bag while you construct the children. When you have attached all the children using scoring and slip, cover the sculpture loosely and let it dry. Check it every day to be sure that the little people are not drying too fast. They might shrink faster than the adult and crack off. When the sculpture is bone dry, fire it in the kiln.

After firing, paint the sculpture with acrylic paints. Use small brushes or fine-line markers to add linear details. You do not have to cover all the clay. Use the color of the clay as one of the predominant colors in your sculpture.

Write the story that your storyteller is narrating. Record it on tape. Arrange the Storyteller sculpture in a display. Use a tape player to tell the story to your viewers.

CRITIQUING

Describe Explain the subject of your Storyteller sculpture. How many children did you make? Which clay construction processes did you use?

Analyze How much did you exaggerate scale in your sculpture? Did you use accurate or distorted proportions? How did you incorporate the color of the fired clay into the color scheme?

Interpret What is the theme of your story? Does it match the mood of the sculpture?

Judge Which aesthetic theories would you use to judge this work? If you were to do it one more time, what, if anything, would you change?

301

MORE ABOUT . . . HELEN CORDERO

Helen Cordero was 45 years old when she began doing beadwork with her husband's cousin, Juanita Arquero, to make a little extra money. At first, most of the profits were used to buy more materials. Grandma Juana suggested that they go back to pottery. "You don't have to buy anything; Mother Earth gives it all to you." Juanita, who had learned to make pottery as a child, renewed her interest in this medium. Helen spent six months as Juanita's apprentice, learning the ancient art. However, Helen's bowls and jars never looked quite right; they kept coming out crooked. The day Juanita suggested that Helen try making figures was the day Helen's success began.

Using Distortion for Expressive Effect

OBJECTIVE

Change the mood and meaning of a two-dimensional artwork in this book by altering the proportions.

MOTIVATOR

Lead students in a critique of Botero's *The Pinzon Family*. Ask them to describe their people and objects in the painting and describe the most obvious physical characteristics of the people. Next, ask them to identify details that are not so obvious. After students have discussed the elements and principles of design used by Botero, ask them to suggest what Botero may be trying to say by distorting the physical characteristics of this family.

GUIDED PRACTICE

Understanding Art History

Discuss how distortion has been used by other artists for expressive effect. For example, Alberto Giacometti created elongated figures to evoke a feeling of loneliness, isolation, and despair from the viewer. Picasso used distortion in his earlier works for a similar effect (see Figures 1.19 on page 21 and 11.27 on page 297). El Greco painted elongated images of people to depict certain emotions. English sculptor Henry Moore demonstrated the beauty of the natural form by carving large, curved, figurative sculptures.

STUDIO LESSON: USING DISTORTION FOR EXPRESSIVE EFFECT

FIGURE 11.33 Fernando Botero. *The Pinzon Family*. 1965. Oil on canvas. 173 × 173 cm (68 × 68″). Museum of Art, Rhode Island School of Design, Providence, Rhode Island. Nancy Sayles Day Collection of Modern Latin-American Art. © Fernando Botero/VAGA, New York. 1994.

Supplies

- Selected reproduction for study
- Sketchbook and pencil
- Large sheet of white paper
- Yellow chalk and soft eraser
- Painting medium of your choice

Fernando Botero is a native of Colombia. He is one of the most popular artists in the world. After you have seen a Botero you will always recognize a Botero work. When asked about the plump proportions of the subjects in his work, he declares that he doesn't paint fat people. He gives everything in his world equal weightiness, a serious roundness he calls plasticity.

Botero has always worked in this distorted representational style. He says that if he were an abstract painter he would put a line or a spot where he needed it, but because he is a figurative painter he needs something real in order to add a particular color or form. Notice how he has used the dog's chew stick, the ball, and the lavender rod as abstract elements in this painting.

The great generals, ministers of war, dictators, and wealthy landowners in Botero's paintings look like toys. Botero has taken

302

Building Self-Esteem Students who are overweight will probably love Botero's paintings. Nevertheless, discuss this type of distortion with caution. One strategy is to also show other figures in art depicting people who are overweight. For example, Buddha's girth is an artistic convention used to exemplify spiritual qualities of abundance and fulfillment. Remind students that during Rubens's time, rounder, more fuller figures were considered desirable.

away the dignity of the rich and powerful and turned them into harmless playthings by giving them facial proportions that make them resemble infants.

In Botero's portrait of the Pinzon family, he has reduced a formal family portrait to a picture of toylike people by distorting facial and body proportions (Figure 11.33).

Choose a reproduction of a two-dimensional work in this book and change the mood and meaning by altering the proportions. All the people, animals, and objects in the work must be distorted in the same way. Choose a new color scheme to match the new mood and paint your distorted interpretation of the work.

Choose a reproduction of a realistic, two-dimensional work of art in *ArtTalk* that includes at least one person. (Do not select a student work.)

FOCUSING

Study it to see how you can alter the mood and meaning of the work by distorting its proportions. For example, what would be the effect if Picasso's couple in *The Frugal Repast* (Figure 11.27, page 297) were as plump as Botero's people?

CREATING

Make a small sketch in your sketchbook of the reproduction you have chosen. Then make a second sketch distorting the original proportions. All figures in the work should be distorted in the same style. Animals and objects may be distorted, if appropriate, to match the figures. Try a few more sketches, experimenting with different amounts and methods of distortion.

Select your best sketch. Draw it freely on the large sheet of white paper using the yellow chalk. Choose a new color scheme that will strengthen the expressive quality of your new composition. Paint your work using a paint medium of your choice.

Mount or mat your work for display.

FIGURE 11.33A

C R I T I Q U I N G

Describe Identify the reproduction you selected for this assignment. List the people, animals, and/or objects that you changed using distortion. Explain how you prepared the work for display.

Analyze Explain how and why you altered the proportions in your interpretation of the original work. Describe the color scheme and explain how it is different from the original and why you chose it.

Interpret Explain how changing proportions and color transformed the expressive effect of the work. Give your work a title that expresses the new mood of the work or one that expresses the transformation of the work through distortion.

Judge Which aesthetic theories would you use to judge this work? If you were to do this work again, what would you change?

GUIDED PRACTICE
(continued)

Developing Studio Skills
To help students be successful with this activity, suggest the following:
- Review color schemes with students. Discuss how color affects a person's mood. Also discuss how color can symbolize certain emotions. For example, red might represent anger or rage. Darker colors such as blue or blue-violet can create a more solemn feeling in a painting. Contrasting colors create excitement and movement.
- Also, review classroom procedures for painting. All brushes should be washed, messes should be cleaned up, supplies put away, and no excess paint should be left out to dry.

INDEPENDENT PRACTICE

Keeping a Portfolio
Remind students that the preliminary sketches and the final artwork for this Studio Lesson are likely considerations for their portfolios.

ASSESS

CRITIQUING
Have students apply the steps of art criticism to their own artwork using the "Critiquing" questions on this page.

CLOSE

Discuss these questions with your students: Would they hang this painting in their home? Why or why not? Do students think that the family was flattered by the way Botero portrayed them? Why or why not?

CURRICULUM CONNECTION

Language Arts Poetry expresses emotional, aesthetic, and self-fulfilling needs. Have students choose one poem by an American and one by a poet of another culture. Have them analyze the emotions expressed in the poems' words and symbols. "Lost" by Carl Sandburg is a good example.

Have students express themselves by writing a short poem. Encourage them to use any of the following poet's tools: imagery, simile, metaphor, personification, onomatopoeia, alliteration, rhyme, symbols, rhythm, or free verse.

OBJECTIVE

Working in groups, students will design and create a high-relief papier-mâché mask using distortion and exaggeration.

MOTIVATOR

Show slides, reproductions, and if available, actual masks. Discuss the similarities and differences in masks from various cultures. Notice how some masks are symmetrical and others are not. Discuss possible reasons why masks were made or worn. (Death masks were worn to give immortality; hunting masks were worn during rituals to give power.)

GUIDED PRACTICE

Understanding Art History

Ask students to research other cultures known for their masks. Students should study the various nations of Africa, Native American tribes, cultures of Central and South America, and the people of Asia. Three common purposes for masks are adornment, concealment, and ritual.

Developing Studio Skills

Suggest that various media might be applied to the surface of the mask including copper, wire, aluminum foil, metallic and neon paint, window screen nails and screws, sequins, glitter, costume jewelry, and small mirrors.

304

STUDIO LESSON: PAPIER-MÂCHÉ MASK

FIGURE 11.34 Henry Hunt, Southern Kwakiutl. *K'umugwe' (Komokwa) Mask.* 1970. Wood, copper, paint. 31.6 × 28.7 × 20.7 cm (12⅜ × 11⅓ × 8″). Royal British Columbia Museum, Victoria, British Columbia, Canada. #13215.

Supplies

- Sketchbook and pencil
- Newspaper and paper towels
- Nontoxic papier-mâché paste
- Acrylic paints and a variety of brushes
- Scissors and white glue
- Found material for decorations such as yarn and foil

The mask shown in Figure 11.34 represents the chief of the undersea world, K'umugwe' (Komokwa). The copper teeth, eyes, and eyebrows on this mask are indications of great wealth. This creature, whose dance is part of the Red Cedar Bark dance series, is a monster who causes trouble in the waters. He can stop rivers, create great waves on bodies of water, and swallow or overturn canoes. This mask was designed to be viewed on the head of a costumed figure dancing around a flickering firelight. The movements used in the dance of the K'umugwe' imitate those of a sea mammal in water, including surfacing to breathe. Notice how the wood has been carved into high relief. This is done so that the viewer will see changing shadows alternating with bright light.

Just as the K'umugwe' was used to explain things that happened in the water, you will create a myth that explains something about modern technology. Each member of the team will be an actor in the

CURRICULUM CONNECTION

History Papier-mâché originated in the Orient where it was first used to create theatrical masks and suits of lightweight armor. In the seventeenth century, exquisite snuff boxes and elegant picture frames were made from this material. The English, in the eighteenth century, perfected a process that put papier-mâché to a very practical use. Paper was boiled with chalk and glue, pressed or poured into molds, baked, and left to dry completely. The final product was a light, but strong, material that was used for ceiling molding.

A British printer invented a process that used heat to seal together several sheets of pasted paper. This material became known as papier-mâché.

drama. Each will design and create a high-relief papier-mâché mask using distortion and exaggeration to make the mask expressive. Choose a color scheme that matches the character of the mask. Paint and decorate the mask.

FOCUSING

Brainstorm with your classmates to list mysteries of modern technology. Make a list of possible themes that could be explained in a storytelling dance drama.

Divide into work teams for a planning conference. Keep notes from the conference.

Select a specific theme or topic. Choose music. Name and define the character of each participant. Write the story. Decide how you will communicate with the audience. Will you all speak lines, will a narrator tell the story, or will you act it out in pantomime? List the props and setting you will need. Plan body movements to match the music.

CREATING

Draw several ideas for your mask. Plan the side view as well as the front view. Use exaggeration and distortion to create the mood you wish your character to express.

Meet with the team to make final decisions about the masks. At this time decide on colors and the extra materials you will need for decorations. Decide if you need costumes.

Draw the final plan for your mask in your sketchbook. List the colors and special decorations you plan to add. Collect the extra materials such as yarn, costume jewelry, and fabrics.

Construct your mask. See the different directions for papier-mâché construction in Technique Tip 19 on page 355 in the Handbook. Use high relief. Make some ridges rise 2 inches (5 cm) from the surface of the mask. Plan how you will hold the mask on your head. You must be able to see through it when you are wearing it. The holes for your eyes do not have to be the eyes of the mask.

FIGURE 11.34A Student work.

When the papier-mâché is dry, paint your mask with acrylic paints. Glue on the additional decorations.

Rehearse with your group using all the props you will need for the performance, including special lighting. Perform your dance drama for the class.

CRITIQUING

Describe Explain the theme and story of your dance drama. Describe the music you used and explain why you chose it. List and explain all the characters in your drama. Describe your mask.

Analyze Did you use high relief? Explain the shadows and highlights that resulted. Explain your color scheme. Which parts of the mask did you exaggerate and distort? Did the body movements match the character of the mask and the music?

Interpret What was the message of your production? Did the audience understand the message?

Judge Which aesthetic theories would you use to judge the entire production? Are they different from the theories you would use to judge the mask? Why?

305

CULTURAL PERSPECTIVES

Worthy examples of exaggerated, distorted proportions can be found in sub-Saharan African masks and sculpture. Show your students examples of African masks and tell them how powerfully expressive these masks are. Have students describe how moods and feelings are more readily shown through elongated faces, or how grace and movement can be seen through extremely curving or spiraling forms. Tell your students that European artists at the turn of the century were greatly attracted and influenced by stylized African masks and sculptures.

Soft Sculpture

STUDIO LESSON: SOFT SCULPTURE

FIGURE 11.35 Faith Ringgold.
Mrs. Jones and Family. 1973. Mixed media.
Mrs. Jones: 152 × 30 × 41 cm (60 × 12 × 16″).
Andrew: 122 × 30 × 30 cm (48 × 12 × 12″).
Barbara: 58 × 16 × 28 cm (23 × 6½ × 11″).
Faye: 63 × 14 × 30 cm (25 × 5½ × 12″).
Faith Ringgold, Inc.

FOCUS

OBJECTIVE

Design and construct a soft sculpture symbolizing a person from history, art history, literature, or current events.

MOTIVATOR

The text says that Faith Ringgold blended her African heritage, her Europeanized education, and her African-American culture to create her art. Discuss the blending of various cultures and how it influences who we are. Ask students to think about and discuss how their backgrounds and heritage have influenced their lives.

TEACH

GUIDED PRACTICE

Understanding Art History

Tell students that Faith Ringgold is a link between the women in her family. She connects the craftswomen and storytellers of the past with her daughters, Michelle and Barbara, and the grandchildren who follow in her creative footsteps. Michelle writes fiction and teaches African-American literature, women's studies, and creative writing at the University of Oklahoma. Barbara, a mother of three, is a third grade teacher in Harlem, working toward a doctorate degree focusing on linguistic characteristics of African-American women who were raised in Harlem.

Supplies

- Sketchbook and pencil
- Paper for patterns
- Scissors and pins
- Sewing and embroidery threads
- Variety of sewing needles
- Assorted fabrics
- Stuffing material such as fiberfill
- Yarns and other trims
- Sewing machine (optional)

Faith Ringgold is an African-American artist. She is a painter, soft sculptor, and performance artist. *Mrs. Jones and Family* (Figure 11.35) represents Ringgold's family. Mrs. Jones is her mother, and Andrew is her father.

Ringgold started as a traditional painter. Her education, like that of any other art student in the 1950s, was in the European tradition. In the late 1960s, during a period when she was incorporating African designs and motifs into her painted canvases, Ringgold began to experiment first with masks and later with soft sculpture. These media enabled her to work in the center of her family. The interaction of the people in her family nourished her spirit. Notice in the sculpture *Mrs. Jones and Family* that all the dolls have their mouths open. They are all talking at once!

Look closely at the figures in Ringgold's work to see how she used media, distortion, and exaggeration to create her sculpture. Think about the techniques you can use to create yours.

306

Design and construct a soft sculpture symbolizing a person from history, art history, literature, or current events. Ringgold made the faces large according to African traditions. She made all the mouths open to indicate that her family was very talkative. Use distortion and exaggeration to emphasize the most important attributes of the person you have chosen. Select colors and fabrics to fit the personality of your sculpture and add details using stitchery and/or appliqué.

FOCUSING

Brainstorm with classmates about subjects to consider for your soft sculpture. Select the person you will symbolize. Do some research about this person. Make visual and written notes in your sketchbook. What is your person famous for? What kind of clothing is appropriate? Which features will you exaggerate? For example, if you are doing a track star, you may make the feet oversized; if you are representing a rock star, you may wish to exaggerate the mouth.

CREATING

Draw a plan for constructing your sculpture in your sketchbook. Draw your sculpture from the front, back, and sides. On a sheet of paper, make a pattern for cutting the body fabric. Cut out fabric and pin the pieces, right sides together. Sew the body together on the inside, leaving a small opening. Then turn it inside out and stuff it. You may shape a three-dimensional face, or you may use stitches and appliqué as Ringgold did. Use yarn or other material to make hair. Make clothes to fit your sculpture, or use doll clothes. Add details with stitchery. See Technique Tip 22 on pages 357–58 of the Handbook.

Arrange your soft sculpture for display. You may add props and a setting if desired. Write a few paragraphs about your sculpture and include the writing in your display.

FIGURE 11.35A   Student work.

CRITIQUING

Describe   Name the subject of your soft sculpture and explain why you selected that person. Describe the procedures you followed to construct this sculpture. List the attributes of your subject that you chose to emphasize and explain why.

Analyze   Explain how, where, and why you used distortion and exaggeration. Which colors did you select for your sculpture?

Interpret   What kind of a mood does your sculpture express? Give it a title that symbolizes the character of your subject. Do not use the subject's name.

Judge   Which aesthetic theories would you use to judge this work? If you were to do it over, what would you change?

307

MORE ABOUT . . . FAITH RINGGOLD

When asked about her different media, Faith explained that they all grew out of each other. They overlap, and she moves through the media backward and forward. Before 1970 she just painted on canvas in oils. The first dolls she created were for a lecture. At that time, she painted gourds for heads. Later, coconuts took the place of gourds. Next she made soft, realistic faces using foam rubber features that represented famous people, such as her *Martin Luther King* life-size portrait mask. The soft masks evolved into soft sculptures. Faith believes that the soft sculptures were really the people coming out of her paintings, and then as the quilts evolved, the dolls went back into the quilts.

ART CRITICISM IN ACTION

INTRODUCTION

Isabel Bishop's painting was selected to illustrate normal human proportions, as well as the contrast between the proportions of an adult and a child. Michelangelo's *Pietà* was selected to compare with Bishop's artwork because of his different treatment of a similar subject matter.

CRITIQUING THE WORK

1. **Describe** The use of tempera and oil together is unusual in contemporary art. Bishop put down a layer of tempera, and then painted glazes of oil over the tempera after the tempera was dry. This painting shows a seated woman holding a child. The woman is wearing a dress; the child appears to be wearing a dress also.

2. **Analyze** Bishop uses lines to outline the shapes of the people. Darker lines accent the woman's hair, the features on both faces, and the pleats on the woman's right sleeve. There are curved lines which define the human forms. Light horizontal lines seem to float through the whole work.

   With a minimum of shading Bishop has created the illusion of three dimensions. She also used overlapping.

   The scale of the painting is quite small. The bench is barely visible, and the figures seem to be in scale to the bench. The child is only about five and one-half heads tall, while the woman seems to be an average seven and one-half heads tall.

FIGURE 11.36 Isabel Bishop. *Waiting.* 1938. Oil and tempera on gesso panel. 73.6 × 56.5 cm (29 × 22¼"). Collection of The Newark Museum, Newark, New Jersey. Purchase, 1944. Arthur F. Egner Memorial Fund.

CRITIQUING THE WORK

1. **Describe** Read the credit line for Figure 11.36. What is unusual about the media? Describe the subject matter of the work. Can you tell what the people are wearing?

2. **Analyze** Where do you see lines? What kind of lines are they? Has the artist created the illusion of three dimensions? What kind of shapes do you see? What shape do the two overlapping figures form? What is unusual about the artist's treatment of space and depth? What is the scale of the artwork itself? Can you tell the scale of the figures in relation to other objects? Using each head to measure, are the proportions of the child the same as those of the woman?

RESOURCES BEYOND THE CLASSROOM

Other Works By . . . Isabel Bishop
Two Girls
Men and Girls Walking
Bootblack

Other Works By . . . Michelangelo
The Creation of Adam

Moses
Sistine Chapel Ceiling
David
Battle of Cascina
The Last Judgement
Studies for the Libyan Sibyl
The Conversion of St. Paul

3. **Interpret** Based upon the clues you have collected and your own ideas, write a brief paragraph explaining the meaning of the work. Then give the work a new title that sums up your interpretation.

4. **Judge** Do you think this is a successful work of art? Use one or more of the three aesthetic theories explained in Chapter 2 to defend your opinion.

COMPARING THE WORKS

Look at *Waiting* (Figure 11.36) and look at the *Pietà* by Michelangelo (Figure 11.37). In what ways are these two works similar and in what ways do they differ? Notice the subject matter. Pay attention to the way the two artists use proportion in the works and the moods expressed by the works.

FIGURE 11.37 Michelangelo. *Pietà*. c. 1500. St. Peter's Basilica, Rome, Italy.

FYI Michelangelo thought of himself as a sculptor. He thought that the creation of people from hard marble was, in some small way, related to divine creation. He loved to "liberate" human forms from cold stone. In spite of that, one of his most important achievements was a painting: the ceiling of the Sistine Chapel.

3. **Interpret** Interpretations should consider the unusual treatment of space and light. The comfortable relationship between the figures show us that they are related, probably mother and child.

4. **Judge** Answers will vary.

COMPARING THE WORKS

In both works the subject matter is the same: a mother holding her child on her lap. In Figure 11.36 a mother waits for someone or something. The sleeping child and the belongings at their side suggest they have been waiting a long time. The woman is calmly neutral. She does not hold the child with her hands; her left leg keeps the child from falling. The Michelangelo sculpture represents Mary holding the dead Jesus because of the title, *Pietà*. Mary's head is lowered, while the woman in Bishop's work holds her head upright. The proportions in the Bishop work are all normal. Michelangelo has distorted the figure of Mary so that the work would look right. Her head is in the same proportion as her son, but the rest of her body has been enlarged so that it can hold the adult body of her son comfortably.

In both works, the mother and child form the shape of a triangle. The moods in both works seem resigned—one for waiting and the other for death.

EXTENSION

- Have students read more about Isabel Bishop in the "Meet the Artist" feature on the following page.
- Assign *Artist's Profile 11* in the TCR.

MORE ABOUT . . . MICHELANGELO

The works of Michelangelo have been classified as Platonic, a reflection of his own concern with ideal forms. With sculpture, he attempted to capture the ideal form of his subjects. He viewed sculpting as a discovery process; instead of shaping stone into a form, he removed excess stone to reveal an existing essence that represented both truth and beauty. This same quest is seen in his architectural endeavors where aesthetic principles were combined with functional necessities.

CHECKING COMPREHENSION

- On a separate sheet of paper have students complete "Building Vocabulary" and "Reviewing Art Facts" on page 311.
- Assign *Application 21* and 22 in the TCR to evaluate students' comprehension.

ANSWERS TO BUILDING VOCABULARY

1. proportion
2. Golden Mean
3. hierarchical proportion
4. foreshortening
5. scale
6. distortion or exaggeration

ANSWERS TO REVIEWING ART FACTS

1. 1 to 1.6 (or 1:1.6).
2. Proportion is the relationship of one part to another; scale refers to size as measured against a standard reference.
3. Golden Rectangle.
4. The scale of the work itself and the scale of objects or elements within the design.
5. Length of the head from the chin to the top of the skull.

$\mathcal{M}$EET THE ARTIST

ISABEL BISHOP
American, 1902–88

Isabel Bishop. *Self-Portrait.* 1927. Oil on canvas. 36 × 33 cm (14⅛ × 13″). Wichita Art Museum, Wichita, Kansas. Gift of the Friends of the Wichita Art Museum, Inc.

In 1920, with financial support from an inheritance, Isabel Bishop enrolled at the Art Students' League in New York City. She had a small studio apartment on Union Square in Manhattan. After marrying and moving to Riverdale, she made the daily trip to Grand Central Station by train and then transferred to the subway, which took her to the studio. During the trips she sketched.

The subjects of her paintings were the working women she saw in the trains and from her studio window. Her concern was composition, and the subjects were a means to attack the abstract problem of time and space. She tried to express the possibility of momentary change. To her, the young women did not belong to a specific class.

The procedures she followed were unusual. First she sketched from life. From her sketchbook ideas, she selected some to become etchings. From those she selected the compositions of her paintings. She then treated a panel with eight coats of gesso, front and back. She painted a ground of loose, uneven, horizontal, gray stripes to create an undersurface that gave her paintings a sense of vibration. Then she painted on the surface with tempera. Finally, she added glazes of oil paint. The stripes always showed through. She applied the highlights with thick opaque paint and kept the shadows thin and transparent. She half concealed the people in thin shifting shadows and sparkles of light.

Her paintings took months and sometimes years to complete. There was never any point at which she felt a work was complete.

MORE PORTFOLIO IDEAS

Using tempera paint, cover a sheet of white paper with uneven, gray, horizontal stripes. Allow some white paper to show between the stripes. Make a crayon drawing based on one of the drawings in your sketchbook. Color it lightly with crayon so that the underpainting shows through.

Using acrylics, prepare a sheet of white paper with gray stripes as above. Using a brush and thinned acrylics, make a drawing over the stripes, based on a drawing in your sketchbook. Paint it using thin glazes of acrylic in the shadows. Accent the highlights using thick opaque light colors in the manner of Isabel Bishop.

310

DEVELOPING A PORTFOLIO

Assessment To help students form opinions and develop awareness of critical standards, remind them that assessment is a process of thoughtful, informed engagement of a viewer with a piece of art. Questions designed to generate critical thinking about the relative values of artwork will help them make better judgments about the work they intend to include in a portfolio. Examples are: How does the artwork demonstrate successful use of the elements of art? How are principles of art used to organize the elements? How is media used to enhance the subject of the piece? Does the artwork suggest an innovative use of form, media, or technique?

CHAPTER 11 REVIEW

Building Vocabulary

On a separate sheet of paper, write the term that best matches each definition given below.

1. The principle of art concerned with the size relationship of one part to another.
2. A line divided into two parts so that the smaller line has the same proportion, or ratio, to the larger line as the larger line has to the whole line.
3. When figures are arranged in a work of art so scale indicates importance.
4. To shorten an object to make it look as if it extends backward into space.
5. Refers to size as measured against a standard reference.
6. Deviations from the expected, normal proportions.

Reviewing Art Facts

Answer the following questions using complete sentences.

1. What is the Golden Mean ratio?
2. Explain the difference between scale and proportion.
3. What was the name for the geometric form that had sides matching the ratio of the Golden Mean?
4. What are the two kinds of scale in art?
5. What unit is usually used to define the proportions of any individual figure?

Thinking Critically About Art

1. **Extend.** Do some library research to determine how hierarchical proportions have been used in the art of different cultures. Photocopy examples to show and report your findings to the class.
2. **Analyze.** Schapiro's sculpture *Anna and David* (Figure 11.1, page 280) was based on a painting she created in 1986 called *Pas de Deux.* Find a color reproduction of the painting. Compare the sculpture to the original painting. List the similarities and differences. Explain the changes that were made to transform the work from one medium to another.
3. **Analyze.** Study the illustration of the Golden Rectangle in Figure 11.5, page 283. Look through this book to find works of art that have been organized using those proportions. Choose at least one to diagram.
4. **Apply.** Apply the four steps of art history to Albrecht Dürer's *Virgin and Child with Saint Anne* (Figure 11.21, page 293). Describe when and where it was painted. Analyze the unique features of the work. Interpret how Dürer was influenced by other artists and the world in which he lived. Finally, make a conclusion about the importance of this work.
5. **Synthesize.** Research the life and work of George Catlin. What kind of paintings did he make? What was his purpose? How did he go about accomplishing his goals? Write a report about Catlin and explain his position in the history of America as well as his place in the history of American art. Which was more important, history or art history? Why?

Making Art Connections

1. **Music.** Read about the Pythagorean theories of music. Ask your music teacher for help if necessary. Use charts, diagrams, and/or pictures to report your findings to the class.
2. **Math.** Do more in-depth research about the Golden Mean. Find out what Fibonacci's number sequence has to do with the Golden Mean. Consult your math teacher for help if necessary.
3. **Health.** The man who wore the suit of armor shown in Figure 11.13, page 288, was only 5 feet 9½ inches (176.5 cm) tall. The average man is taller than that today. What do you think nutrition has to do with the change in size?

EVALUATE

- Have students complete the *Chapter 11 Test* in the TCR.
- Alternative Assessment teaching strategies are provided below or in the Testing Program and Alternative Assessment booklet.

RETEACHING

- Have students complete *Concept Map 11* in the Reteaching booklet.
- Look through the illustrations in the other chapters of *ArtTalk* to find and list reproductions of paintings and sculptures that fit the following categories: 1) works showing realistic, accurate use of proportion; 2) works in which human proportions are exaggerated or distorted to create special effects.

Have each student select one work from each of the categories above. Ask them to write a brief statement to explain how the artist has used proportion or scale to enhance the meaning of the work.

EXTENSION

Ask students to imagine that they are interior designers. Have them list all of the measurements they would have to consider to properly design one of the following:

- a walk-in closet in which all of their clothing and linens must be stored
- the cooking space in a kitchen
- a lunch counter in a short-order restaurant.

CLOSE

Allow each student to choose a reproduction in this chapter and describe how proportion is evident in the work.

ALTERNATIVE ASSESSMENT

Instruct students to create two self-portraits in a medium of their choice. In the first work they will use accurate proportions; in the second, they will use exaggeration and distortion. Have them begin by making preliminary sketches in their sketchbooks, then proceed with the first artwork. Before they begin the second, direct them to think about the emotional effect they want the exaggerated portrait to have on viewers. Again, they should first use their sketchbooks for preliminary drawings. When the artworks are completed, have students write a critique of them, explaining how the altered proportions affect the expressive quality of the second portrait.

Variety, Emphasis, Harmony, and Unity

CHAPTER OVERVIEW

In Chapter 12, students learn that unity is the ultimate principle of design and that when all of the elements and principles work properly, the result is a unified work of art. Artists achieve the expressive qualities of unity through harmony, simplicity, proximity, repetition, and continuation.

CHAPTER SUPPLIES

For a list of the materials you will need for the Activities in this chapter, refer to the "Art Supplies Grid" in the Teacher's Manual.

FINE ART RESOURCES
Transparencies
- Vincent van Gogh. *The Night Cafe*
- Anna Mary Robertson Moses. *Calhoun*
- Kay Sage. *Danger, Construction Ahead*
- Sam Gilliam. *Ain't More Than Music*

Fine Art Prints
- Pavel Tchelitchew. *Hide-and-Seek (Cache-cache)*
- Marguerite Forach. *The Circus*

FIGURE 12.1 Jacquette makes sketches and takes photos from airplanes or tall buildings to use as references. She captures the contrast between the natural and the manufactured environment.

Yvonne Jacquette. *Town of Skowhegan, Maine V.* 1988. Oil on canvas. 198.6 × 163 cm (78⅛ × 64⅜"). Courtesy Brooke Alexander Gallery, New York, New York.

312

RESOURCES FOR CHAPTER 12

Application Activities 23, 24	Reteaching Activities
Artist's Profiles 12, 18, 32	Study Guide 12
Cooperative Learning Activities 23, 24	Concept Map 12
Cultural Diversity in Art	Studio Lessons 22, 23
Enrichment Activities 23, 24	Chapter 12 Test

Variety, Emphasis, Harmony, and Unity

Y ou have already learned about the principles of rhythm, balance, and proportion. In this chapter you will learn about three additional principles: *variety, emphasis,* and *harmony.* Even more important, you will learn about the principle of *unity.* It is only when all the elements and all the principles work together that you achieve a unified work of art.

Emphasis is a principle that enhances variety, because it creates a feeling of dominance and subordination. The dominant area is usually a focal point that attracts the attention of the viewer before the subordinate areas. Harmony enhances unity because it uses similarities and relatedness to tie elements together.

Unity and variety complement one another in the same way that positive and negative spaces complement one another. Unity and variety are like two sides of one coin. Unity controls and organizes variety, while variety adds interest to unity.

In this chapter you will see how artists have used the elements of art to create unity in their works. As you read, you will learn how to use the elements to create variety, emphasis, harmony, and unity in your own works of art.

Objectives

After completing this chapter you will be able to:

- Identify and describe variety, emphasis, harmony, and unity in your environment and in a work of art.
- Understand how artists use variety and emphasis to express their ideas and feelings.
- Understand how artists use the elements and principles of art to create unified works of art.
- Use variety, emphasis, and harmony to create your own unified works of art.

Words to Know

emphasis
focal point
harmony
unity
variety

FIRST IMPRESSIONS

Look at Figure 12.1, *Town of Skowhegan, Maine V.* How does the water affect the town in this painting? What kind of buildings do you see at the very top of the painting? Are the buildings on the right and at the bottom of the picture the same? How does the artist use the road to divide as well as unify the composition? How has she indicated the difference between the cars that are speeding on the highway and the cars that are parked? How does she unite the various conflicting factors in this painting?

313

(*pages 314–322*)
• Variety
• Emphasis

GUIDED PRACTICE

Critical Thinking

Ask students to write several paragraphs that explain how variety is present in their lives. Offer examples, such as television shows, books, academic subjects, clothes, food, and so on. Ask for volunteers to read their paragraphs aloud. Discuss the effect that lack of variety would have on their emotional well-being.

Developing Perceptual Skills

The MTV logos illustrate how one television station uses variety to keep station breaks interesting. Ask students to think of other network logos. Can they recall them vividly? Can they describe them? Do students pay attention to them if they are not interesting?

Promoting Discussion

This would be a good time to talk about logos in general. A *logo* is a symbol that represents a company or a product. Bring in examples and ask the students to identify the products, or ask each student to make a sketch of one logo seen at home and bring it to school the next day. Which logos are remembered by most students? Ask the students to guess why they are remembered. Does remembering have something to do with quality of design? With organization? When they see these logos in the environment, are they always the same, or is some variety introduced? Ask them to decide if the logos have unity.

Variety

People need variety in all areas of their lives. Imagine how boring it would be if daily routines were exactly the same every day of the week for a whole year. Imagine how visually boring the world would be if everything in it—everything—were the same color.

People put a great deal of time and effort into creating variety in their environment. They may buy new furniture or paint the walls, not because the furniture is old or the paint is peeling, but simply because they need a change. New clothes, new foods, new friends—the list of items people seek out to relieve the sameness or boredom in life is endless.

Just as people must add variety to their lives to keep it interesting, so must artists add variety to their works. **Variety** is *the principle of design concerned with difference or contrast.*

A work that is too much the same can become dull and monotonous. For example, a work composed of just one shape may be unified, but it will not hold your attention. Variety, or contrast, is achieved by adding something different to a design to provide a break in the repetition (Figure 12.2). When different elements are placed next to each other in a work of art, they are in contrast (Figure 12.3). This type of contrast, or variety, adds interest to the work of art and gives it a lively quality.

Almost every artist uses contrasting elements to balance unifying elements. Wide, bold lines complement thin, delicate lines. Straight lines contrast with curves. Free-form shapes differ from geometric shapes. Rough textures add interest to a smooth surface. The number of contrasts that can be introduced through color are limitless. The degree of contrast may range from bold to subtle. The amount of difference between the elements depends on the artist's purpose.

FIGURE 12.2 MTV has used variety to maintain interest in its logo. The shape of the logo is always the same: a heavy, solid **M** decorated with a small, thin TV, but every time you see the logo, the colors and patterns on it change. Repetition reassures the viewer that this is the same station, but variety stirs the viewer's curiosity.

Courtesy of MTV Networks.

AT THE MUSEUM

American Advertising Museum (Portland, Oregon) At the American Advertising Museum, visitors can watch TV commercials, listen to radio commercials, and admire antique radios while learning how advertising began, grew, and shaped the public's mind. Feel like you are traveling through time; they change the decade of the commercials every four days and their advertising time line tracks the history of advertising from the 1400s to the present. The American Advertising Museum also has exhibits on outdoor neon signs, print advertising, trademarks, specialty advertising, and an exhibit on how the advertising campaign is created.

FIGURE 12.3 Which elements has Pereira used to create variety in this painting? Which element do you think shows the strongest contrast?

Irene Rice Pereira. *Untitled.* 1951. Oil on board. 101.6 × 61 cm (40 × 24″). Solomon R. Guggenheim Museum, New York, New York. Gift of Jerome B. Lurie, 1981.

 Variety and Contrast

1. Applying Your Skills.   Look through the works you have produced in this course. Find one that seems dull. Study it and tell how you could add variety without destroying the unity.

2. Further Challenge.   Look through *ArtTalk* for works of art that show bold contrast of line, shape, color, value, and texture. List one work for each kind of contrast. Explain how the contrast was created.

3. Computer Option.   Draw a simple design using five or six shapes. Use the Select tool and the Copy and Paste options to make five copies of the design on the same screen. Leave one design unchanged; alter the others to show a variety of contrasts. Vary contrast in color, value, and textures by using the Fill Bucket tool. Save your work.

Emphasis

Have you ever underlined an important word or phrase several times in a letter? Have you ever raised the volume of your voice to make sure the person you were talking to understood a key point? These are just two ways that people use emphasis to focus attention on the main points in a message. In advertisements, music, news stories, your lessons at school, and your day-to-day communications, you see and hear certain ideas and feelings being emphasized over others.

Emphasis is *the principle of design that makes one part of a work dominant over the other parts.* Artists use this principle of emphasis to unify a work of art. Emphasis controls the sequence in which the parts are noticed. It also controls the amount of attention a viewer gives to each part.

There are two major types of visual emphasis. In one type, an *element of art* dominates the entire work. In the other type of emphasis, an *area* of the work is dominant over all the other areas.

Emphasizing an Element

If the artist chooses to emphasize one element, all the other elements of the work are made *subordinate*, or less important. The *dominant*, or most important element affects the viewer's perception of the total work. This element also affects the way in which all the separate items and elements in the work are perceived.

GUIDED PRACTICE
(continued)

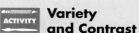 **Variety and Contrast**

1. Applying Your Skills.
This activity may seem simple, but it requires high levels of thinking. Students must describe how they would change a completed artwork by using verbal symbols (language) to describe changes in visual symbols. If there is time, have them actually revise the artwork after they have thought through the changes.

2. Further Challenge.
This activity requires perception of the bold contrast of elements in this text. Reinforce the need for each student to explain why his or her examples are accurate for the categories.

3. Computer Option.
Create a simple design unit using several geometric shapes and lines. Save and title "Basic Unit."

Now, explore ways the unit can be changed using color, line, and/or patterns to add emphasis, variety, and contrast. Select, Copy, and Paste the unit, filling a row on the page. When pasting, arrange so the background space is interesting, especially if the unit has an irregular shape. Use the Grids and Rulers option, if available, to align units. Save and title the work using the Save As command to retitle the page "Variety." Open the page with the original design unit. Make changes in color, texture, or line(s). Select, Copy, and Paste to the Clipboard. Open "Variety" page. Paste copies of the altered design unit, filling a second row on the page. Continue repeating the directions by returning to the original design unit to vary contrasts. Fill the page with rows representing these choices. Save, Print, and display.

Promoting Discussion

Key words underlined or circled in a letter, fanfares for television introductions, and gestures people make are some common types of emphasis. Ask students to identify three examples of emphasis in the school environment. What techniques are used to create the emphasis in these examples? How effective is the emphasis? What might happen if this emphasis was withdrawn?

Developing Perceptual Skills

It is important that students see the difference between the dominance of one element, as in Figure 12.4, and the dominance of an area, or focal point, as in Figures 12.5 on page 317, 12.7 on page 318, 12.8 on page 319, 12.9 on page 320, 12.10 on page 321, and 12.11 on page 322.

It is also important to point out that every work of art does not need to have one focal point. Some have several with different degrees of importance, as in Figure 12.27 on page 334, and some, as in Figures 12.4 and 12.6 on page 318, have no focal point at all.

Using Art Criticism

Have students study Bronislaw Bak's painting in Figure 12.4, which illustrates the principle of emphasis. Ask students to describe how the artist used the element of color to achieve emphasis. Which colors blend well with other colors in the work? What color schemes has he used? Which other elements besides color have been organized in the artwork?

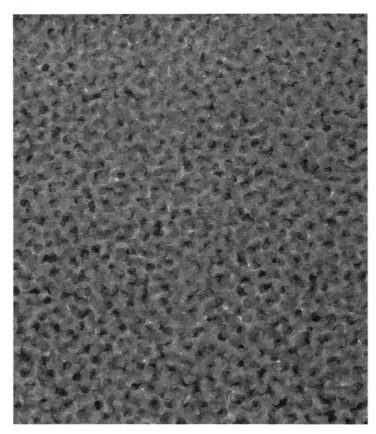

FIGURE 12.4   Redness overwhelms this painting. There is no focal point—your eyes dance from one red to another.

Bronislaw Bak. *Interpenetrations in Red.* 1980. Oil on canvas. 122 × 152.4 cm (4 × 5′). Private collection.

Sometimes the dominant element is made so strong that the whole work seems to be drenched in that element. For instance, Bronislaw Bak's *Interpenetrations in Red* (Figure 12.4) is saturated with the color red. In this painting the redness takes on a meaning all its own. It affects the viewer's perception of the painting as a whole as well as the viewer's perceptions of the separate parts.

Emphasizing an Area

Sometimes a specific area in a work of art is emphasized. This area, called the **focal point,** is *the first part of a work to attract the attention of the viewer.* The other areas are subordinate to the focal point (Figure 12.5).

It is possible for a work of art to have more than one focal point. Artists must be careful about this, however. Too many focal points cause the eye to jump around and will confuse the viewer.

Artists must decide on the degree of emphasis needed to create a focal point. This usually depends on the purpose of the work. Of course, a focal point is not necessary, and many artists don't create one in their works (Figure 12.6, page 318).

When artists do create focal points, they are usually careful not to overdo the emphasis. They make certain that the focal point is unified with the rest of the design.

Artists use several techniques to create a focal point in a work of art. Following are some examples of these techniques.

Contrast. One way to create a focal point is to place an element that contrasts with the rest of the work in that area. One large shape, for example, will stand out among small ones. One angular, geometric shape will be noticed first among rounded, free-form shapes. A bright color will dominate low-intensity colors, while a light area will dominate a dark design (Figure 12.7, page 318).

▨▨▨▨▨▨▨▨▨▨ CURRICULUM CONNECTION ▨▨▨▨▨▨▨▨▨▨

Humanities   Emphasize the comparison in the text between Bak's use of simplicity and a writer's use of simple language and syntax to strip a work of literature down to its bare essentials. Have groups of students research the power of simplicity as a statement in other movements in twentieth-century art, literature, and music. One group might concentrate on the deceptively simple sentences in works by Ernest Hemingway (e.g., *The Old Man and the Sea*), another on the minimalist compositions of contemporary composer Philip Glass, still another on the minimalist paintings of Barnett Newman. Have groups note similarities in each of these approaches to artistic expression.

FIGURE 12.5   Rembrandt uses value contrast to create a focal point in this work. Only the head and the area immediately around it are painted in light values. The background sinks into darkness.

Rembrandt van Rijn. *Self-Portrait.* 1650. Oil on canvas. 92 × 75.5 cm (36¼ × 29¾″). National Gallery of Art, Washington, D.C. Widener Collection.

TEACHER TALK

Classroom Management   When planning a display of student artwork, it is best to limit the number of words and parts to eliminate confusion. Lettering style and readability of content are important. When planning your design, limit it to these three parts: *Headline, Illustration, Information.*

Determine the best location for the display. One that is to be used as a teaching tool in the classroom should be easy to view by all students. However, you may want to think about the various locations that could be used within the school and community so that you achieve the greatest amount of visibility for the display.

GUIDED PRACTICE
(continued)

Developing Studio Skills

Have students design and create an artwork in the style of Lois Dvorak's design in Figure 12.6. Remind them that they will concentrate on a design that uses textures and shapes without a focal point. For this activity, they can use any type of paper, fabric, or materials. If possible, provide cellophane or wrapping paper that has distinct surface features. Encourage them to first make preliminary designs in their sketchbooks, then make a template for the shapes they choose. Also, remind them to play with the position of the cut-out shapes before gluing them to a piece of cardboard or heavy canvas. Encourage them to think about the decisions an artist must make when working with media and techniques like Dvorak does.

Sparking Creativity

Want students to think creatively about variety? Suggest this: Look at the many typefaces available for graphic art today. Design an alphabet of your own, working toward repetition of design elements, balance, proportion, variety, emphasis, contrast, and harmony, all working toward unity. You could cut the letters directly from printed material or draw them. Try working on a theme to unify the design, perhaps a quality like bold, graceful, nervous, rigid, happy, or a central idea such as ecology, food, fitness, architecture, and so on. Arrange the letters of the alphabet on a background that will best accent them.

FIGURE 12.6 The artist has designed this work without a focal point. In this detail you can see how one shape leads your eyes to another. Your eyes cannot find one place to rest that is more important than another.

Lois Dvorak. *The Lizards.* 1982. Handmade, hand-dyed papers and opera cloth stitched and interwoven on four layers of dowels, accented with metallic marking pen and metallic threads. 81.3 × 101.6 cm (32 × 40″). Courtesy of the artist.

FIGURE 12.7 Notice how the bright red shapes in the lower right corner catch your attention.

Horace Pippin. *Asleep.* 1943. Oil on board. 22.9 × 30.5 cm (9 × 12″). The Metropolitan Museum of Art, New York, New York. Bequest of Jane Kendall Gingrich, 1982.

An object with rough texture becomes a focal point in a design of smooth textures.

Isolation. Artists sometimes use isolation to create a focal point and thereby emphasize one part of their work. They do this by putting one object alone, apart from all the other objects (Figure 12.8). This draws the viewer's eye to the isolated object.

MORE ABOUT . . . HORACE PIPPIN

Horace Pippin (United States, 1888–1946) was a folk artist known for the strong emotions that flooded his paintings. Pippin began drawing at the age of ten. In 1917 he enlisted in the U.S. Army. He kept a war diary of sketches but lost it in the trenches when he was injured. After the war, it took nine years of exercising his stiff hand before he could paint again. At first, he painted his feelings about the war, but after a few years, he switched to painting pictures from his past. In 1942, he painted a series of paintings about the abolitionist John Brown, probably inspired by stories he had heard from his mother who had witnessed the hanging of John Brown in 1859.

LOOKING
CLOSELY

FIGURE 12.8   Neel has isolated the red chair to make it the focal point in this painting. How does the black line help? What about the color? Notice line direction. The walls, the curtains, the window, the shade, and even the windows across the street are all drawn with static lines. What kind of lines do you see around the chair? Notice how the woodwork behind the chair has been blurred. Why do you think Neel did that?

Alice Neel. *Loneliness*. 1970. Oil on canvas. 203.2 × 96.5 cm (80 × 38"). Robert Miller Gallery, New York, New York. Collection, National Gallery of Art, Washington, D.C. The estate of Alice Neel.

GUIDED PRACTICE
(continued)

LOOKING
CLOSELY

Have students study Figure 12.8 and answer the questions in the caption. Help them to see that the black line is an outline that forms a barrier between the chair and the surrounding space. Everything in the room uses vertical and horizontal lines, only the chair uses diagonals. The woodwork was blurred so that it would not detract from the isolation of the chair. The empty chair may represent someone who is not there.

Understanding Art History

Alice Neel was not recognized by the art establishment until she was in her mid-seventies. She found the strength to keep going because she believed in her work. Never doubting the quality of her own work, she knew that she was doing the right thing by remaining true to her style. Time was on her side and she lived to enjoy acclaim and financial success.

Figure 12.8 is a departure from Neel's more common subject—people. She painted only people in whom she was interested. Her brush was not for hire. Most of her subjects did not buy the finished paintings because she revealed, in harsh terms, what the world had done to them. She called her works "paintings of people" and did not like them to be called portraits. She thought that portraits had to be flattering, and Alice Neel did not want to lie. She had to paint the scars left by the psychological and emotional battles her sitters had endured.

MORE ABOUT . . . FABRICS

Fibers are the basic components of all fabrics. Natural fibers come from plants and animals like cotton, linen, wool, silk, and ramie. Manufactured fibers are formed by chemicals like acetate, acrylic, nylon, polyester, rayon, and spandex. Fibers are tiny strands that, when twisted together, make up yarns. Yarns are made into fabrics.

Fabrics have texture and color. Leather is smooth and slippery; denim is rough and rugged; corduroy is ribbed and bulky; satin is smooth; and tweed is scratchy. With all the fibers to choose from, we have the ability to create an environment filled with fabrics of beautiful colors and textures.

GUIDED PRACTICE
(continued)

Understanding Art History

Tell students of the difficulty Berthe Morisot had in achieving recognition for her art in the nineteenth century. Then have students research whether the situation for women artists has improved much during the intervening century since Morisot's time. The resource *Making Their Mark: Women Artists Move into the Mainstream, 1970–1985* contains excellent material on this subject, including statistics that compare the funding and exhibition of works by male and female artists.

 Using Emphasis

(Student Activity begins on page 322.)

1. Applying Your Skills.
This activity will help students to expand their developing awareness of advertising "propaganda." As they look for focal points, you can ask them to try to understand how the advertisers are using certain images to sell products. If some students have to use library material for this activity, have them photocopy the advertisements, then mark the points with a colored marker.

2. Further Challenge.
Allow students to choose the medium they prefer if possible. Some students may wish to use paint, some a collage of magazine pictures, others a collage using found materials. Any medium is acceptable for this activity.

If you have some students who need an extra challenge, let them make clay relief tiles to illustrate the types of focal point. If you don't have colored glazes, the tiles can be painted with acrylics after they have been bisque-fired.

FIGURE 12.9 The young woman appears to be in the center of this painting. If you measure, however, you will see that her head is to the left of the vertical axis and far above the horizontal axis. What devices has Morisot used to make the woman's face the center of interest?

Berthe Morisot. *In the Dining Room.* 1886. Oil on canvas. 61.3 × 50 cm (24⅛ × 19¾"). National Gallery of Art, Washington, D.C. Chester Dale Collection.

MEETING SPECIAL NEEDS

Mentally Disabled In thinking critically about art, students with retardation can sort art postcards into categories such as portrait, landscape, and still life. This sorting can be done in pairs to foster social growth at the same time as intellectual growth. Naturally there will be borderline cases, requiring debate which further develops understanding of the categories. Students with mental retardation may enjoy sorting the art postcards into many other concepts they are learning, for example, old times and current times, good and bad weather, males and females, young and old people.

FIGURE 12.10 In this painting all the people are staring at the preacher and the girl. The viewer becomes one of the crowd and stares too. Can you find lines in this painting that are also pointing to the two figures?

John Steuart Curry. *Baptism in Kansas.* 1928. Oil on canvas. 101.6 × 127 cm (40 × 50″). Collection of Whitney Museum of American Art, New York, New York. Gift of Gertrude Vanderbilt Whitney.

Location. *Location* is another method used to create a focal point for emphasis. A viewer's eye is normally drawn toward the center of a visual area. Thus, something near this center will probably be noticed first. Because the exact center is a dull location, most artists place the objects they wish to emphasize a bit off center. They select a location a little to the left or right of center and a little above center (Figure 12.9).

Convergence. When many elements in a work point to one item, that item becomes the focal point. This technique, called convergence, can be created with a very obvious radial arrangement of lines. It can also be achieved through a more subtle arrangement of people who are staring and pointing at the point of emphasis (Figure 12.10).

The Unusual. In a work of art, an object that is out of the ordinary can become the focal point (Figure 12.11 on page 322). In a row of soldiers standing at attention, the one standing on his head will be noticed first. The unexpected will always draw the viewer's attention.

(Figure 12.11 on page 322)

(*pages 322–333*)
• Harmony
• Unity
• Creating Visual Unity
• How Artists use Variety, Emphasis, and Harmony to Enhance Unity

GUIDED PRACTICE

Promoting Discussion

If you have students who play musical instruments, ask them to demonstrate the difference between harmony and sounds that lack harmony.

Critical Thinking

Write the following statement on the board: *The work uses variety to achieve a sense of harmony.* Divide the class into two groups and assign one group the painting in Figure 12.11, the other the painting in Figure 12.20 on page 329. Each group is to examine its own painting, paying particular attention to the elements of color, line, and shape. The group is then to discuss how the statement on the board might apply to the work.

Developing Perceptual Skills

To illustrate how space can help create harmony, gather together ten totally unrelated objects. Using tape, mark off ten rectangular shapes of equal size on the top of a table or on the floor. Be sure the shapes are large enough to contain the objects. Place one object directly in the center of each rectangle. Such an organization has more unity than if the objects were arranged haphazardly. Another way to demonstrate unity is to use the stamps that were made in Chapter 9, page 226 (Using Random Rhythm).

FIGURE 12.11   In this painting the artist has chosen a point of view that is at the eye level of the child. We see only the skirt and the hand of Ernesta's nurse.

Cecilia Beaux. *Ernesta (Child with Nurse).* 1894. Oil on canvas. 128.3 × 96.8 cm (50½ × 38⅛"). The Metropolitan Museum of Art, New York, New York. Maria DeWitt Jesup Fund, 1965.

 ACTIVITY   **Using Emphasis**

1. Applying Your Skills.   Collect a set of five magazine or newspaper advertisements that have a strong focal point. Identify the focal point in each.

2. Further Challenge.   Make a series of small designs with strong focal points using each of the following: contrast of shape, contrast of color, contrast of value, contrast of texture, isolation, location, convergence, and the unusual.

3. Computer Option.   Use the drawing tools of your choice to create a series of small designs with strong focal points, using each of the following: contrast of shape, contrast of color, contrast of value, contrast of texture, isolation, location, and convergence.

One advantage in using computers to create art is the ease with which images can be manipulated. You will be able to transform some designs to others by using the Fill Bucket tool. Others can be changed by using the Selection tool and rearranging the shapes. See if you can create all seven designs by starting with only three designs and making alterations to them. Save your work.

Harmony

Harmony is *the principle of design that creates unity by stressing the similarities of separate but related parts.*

FIGURE 12.12   Notice how often Degas repeats round shapes in this work: the hats, the ring of flowers, the round-looking bows, the young woman's head, her bodice, and her skirt. He then creates a second harmony of vertical lines. He uses thin lines in the foreground and thick ones in the background.

Edgar Degas. *The Millinery Shop.* c. 1879–84. Oil on canvas. 100 × 110.7 cm (39⅜ × 43⅜"). Art Institute of Chicago, Chicago, Illinois. Mr. and Mrs. Lewis Larned Coburn Memorial Collection, 1933.

In musical harmony, related tones are combined into blended sounds. Harmony is pleasing because the tones complement each other. In visual harmony, related art elements are combined. The result looks pleasing because the elements complement each other.

Used in certain ways, color can produce harmony in a work of art. Repetition of shapes that are related, such as rectangles with different proportions, produces harmony (Figure 12.12). A design that uses only geometric shapes appears more harmonious than a design using both geometric and

**Understanding
Art History**

Have students study Figure 12.13. Ask them to read the credit line to find out when the work was drawn. In terms of the date, the students should be able to deduce that the snake stands for the United States. Franklin's message is very clear—if the states don't unify, they will be conquered. In unity there is strength; the whole is greater than the sum of its parts.

**Developing
Perceptual Skills**

While discussing the cartoon by Ben Franklin in Figure 12.13, ask students to recall what they learned about calligraphic lines in Chapter 5. Have them point out the various widths of the letters. Encourage them to practice drawing the cartoon with a quill pen, calligraphy pens, or with tracing paper and pencil. Students may wish to make their own poster that focuses on a contemporary political issue.

Critical Thinking

Ask students to pretend they are landscape designers who are given the task to design a large part of the space around their homes or communities. (They are free to choose the area.) Ask them to make notes and sketches showing what the area looks like without any landscaping, then sketch designs that would tie the area to its surroundings. Remind them to consider the purpose of the area and how different topographic features, such as hills or rivers, might dictate some of their decisions.

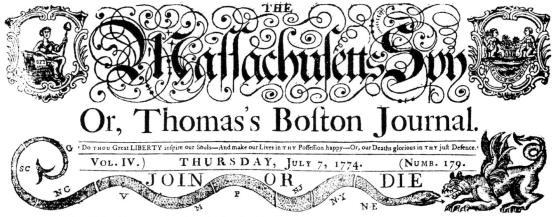

FIGURE 12.13 It is said that this cartoon was drawn by Ben Franklin. How did he use unity to convey his message? What do the parts of the snake symbolize?

Ben Franklin (attributed to). *Join or Die.* Cartoon. 1774. 5 × 7.25 cm (2 × 2⅞"). Courtesy of the Library of Congress, Washington, D.C.

free-form shapes. Even space used in a certain way can produce harmony. If all the parts in a work of art are different sizes, shapes, colors, and textures, the space between the parts can be made uniform to give the work a sense of order.

UNITY

Unity is oneness. It brings order to the world. Without it, the world would be chaotic.

Countries made up of smaller parts are political unities: the United States is such a country. Its fifty states are joined by a single federal government. As a whole unit, the United States is a world power far stronger than the combined power of the separate states (Figure 12.13).

A tree is an example of unity in nature. It is composed of roots, trunk, bark, branches, twigs, and leaves. Each part has a purpose that contributes to the living, growing tree. An electric lamp is a manufactured unit composed of a base, electric wire, sockets, bulbs, shades, and so on. All the separate

parts of the lamp work together as a unified whole to provide light. If any part does not work, the unity of the lamp is impaired.

CREATING VISUAL UNITY

In art, **unity** is *the quality of wholeness or oneness that is achieved through the effective use of the elements and principles of art.* Unity is like an invisible glue. It joins all the separate parts so they look as if they belong together.

Unity is difficult to understand at first because it is not easily defined. It is a quality that you feel as you view a work of art (Figure 12.14). As you study a work, you may think that you would not change one element or object. When this happens, you are receiving an impression that the work is a unified whole.

Unity helps you concentrate on a visual image. You cannot realize how important this is until you study a work that lacks unity. Looking at a work that lacks unity is like trying to carry on a serious

FIGURE 12.14   Rodin created this monument to honor six citizens who gave their lives in 1347 to save the city of Calais, France. Rodin showed the six men getting ready to see the king, who was laying siege to the city. Rodin spent two years modeling faces and bodies to express the men's tension and pain. Each figure would be successful as an individual statue, but Rodin has place them so that unity results. The work was designed to be placed at street level, not on a pedestal above the heads of the people.

Auguste Rodin. *The Burghers of Calais.* 1886, cast 1930s. Bronze. 2 × 2 × 1.9 m (79⅜ × 80⅞ × 77⅛"). Hirshhorn Museum and Sculpture Garden, Smithsonian Institution, Washington, D.C. Gift of Joseph H. Hirshhorn, 1966.

discussion while your little sister is practicing the violin, your brother is listening to the stereo, and your mother is running the vacuum cleaner. It would be difficult to concentrate on your conversation with all these distractions. It is the same with a work of art that lacks unity. You can't concentrate on the work as a whole, because all the parts demand separate attention.

To create unity, an artist adjusts the parts of a work so they relate to each other. A potter adjusts

GUIDED PRACTICE
(continued)

Exploring Aesthetics

Ask students to recall what they learned in Chapter 10 about balance. While studying *Snuff Containers* in Figure 12.15, ask them to identify the types of balance used. Have them also discuss the way the artists used shapes and space to create a unique design on each one. How do the designs complement the shape of the containers? What makes the designs unified?

Critical Thinking

Relate harmony to social, cultural, and political situations. How could a good sense of harmony or unity have helped the people of the former Soviet Union, the people of South Central Los Angeles, or the people and government of Haiti, to work out their differences? What tensions in families or social groups could benefit by more harmony?

Art Is Everywhere

To foster students' awareness of art in everyday life, suggest this: Find the art in your world—in lines, shapes, colors, and textures you can see, as well as lines, shapes, colors, and textures you can hear. Listen to the fine line of a flute. Feel the texture of a cello sound. Imagine the color of a saxophone playing a blues melody or a trombone belting out a march. Each musical instrument has its own qualities of sound. Listen to the sounds all around you—traffic, voices, mechanical sounds, bacon frying, and wind blowing. Composers often find inspiration for their music in these sounds.

FIGURE 12.15 The decorations on these containers were created by drilling small holes into which short lengths of wire were inserted to form the various designs. The polished surface is the result of frequent handling and an occasional application of oil.

Possibly Thonga or Shona peoples. Mozambique and Zimbabwe. *Snuff Containers.* Hard fruit shell with copper, brass, and iron wire. Largest: 6 × 7.6 cm (2⅜ × 3″). National Museum of African Art, Smithsonian Institution, Washington, D.C. Acquisition Grant from the James Smithson Society.

FIGURE 12.16 The designer of these clothes travels around the world looking for fabrics with unusual colors and textures. She then designs and creates unique patterns for her wearable art.

Florence Bayless. *Haori Coat.* 1992. Silk peau de soir, Thai silk, and silk lamé. Private collection.

CULTURAL PERSPECTIVES

Have your students collect at least two images of art from a culture other than their own from magazines or other sources that illustrate unity. Have them mount them on a small poster board or in a loose-leaf notebook. They are to include a detailed explanation on how the quality of wholeness or oneness is achieved in the two images through the effective use of the elements and principles of art.

FIGURE 12.17 Johns combines the loose brushwork of Abstract Expressionism with the commonplace objects of American Realism. His map of the United States could be pulled apart by the wild action painting, but it is unified by the harmonious, limited color scheme of a primary triad.

Jasper Johns. *Map.* 1961. Oil on canvas. 198.2 × 312.7 cm (78 × 123⅛″). Collection, Museum of Modern Art, New York, New York. Gift of Mr. and Mrs. Robert C. Scull. © Jasper Johns/VAGA, New York 1994.

GUIDED PRACTICE
(continued)

Developing Perceptual Skills

In order to help students understand the concept of unity, let them play the Unity Game. Divide the class in half by rows or tables. As you call out a category, a student from group 1 volunteers an example showing unity. A student from group 2 has to give an answer from the same category that is an example of lack of unity. For instance, if the category is "people talking," the unity example could be "agreement"—the opposite would be "disagreement or arguing." Categories suggested could include clothing (suit and tie/suit and running shorts), garden (flowers and shrubs/weeds and trash), interior decor (beige walls, brown carpet/beige walls, purple carpet). The Variety Game could be substituted using examples of variety and monotony. Close the exercise by stressing the definition of visual unity: the quality of wholeness or oneness achieved through effective use of the elements and principles of art.

Interdisciplinary: Language Arts

One of early America's outspoken literary voices was that of Henry David Thoreau who once stated that people should "Simplify. Simplify." He practiced this philosophy by living an austere, reclusive life that consisted of the barest of essentials. Ask students to consider how they would simplify their lives. Does it seem easy? How would they learn to adjust to a minimalist's lifestyle? Encourage students to read more of Thoreau's writings.

decorations on a bowl to complement the bowl's shape, size, and purpose (Figure 12.15). Clothing designers choose fabrics that complement the design and purpose of each outfit (Figure 12.16). Painters adjust the elements in a work to each other. A "busy" work with a variety of shapes and textures can be unified with a limited color scheme, for example (Figure 12.17).

Simplicity

Another way to create unity is through *simplicity.* Simplicity is not, however, easy to achieve. An artist must plan very carefully to create a good, simple design. This is done by limiting the number of variations of an element. The fewer variations the artist uses, the more unified the design will seem (Figure 12.18, page 328).

A painting in which the entire surface is covered with a single, even layer of one hue will appear strongly unified. A sculpture of a single person expresses a simple unity (Figure 12.19, page 328).

Repetition

The repetition of objects and elements can be an effective way to unify a work of art. Louise Nevelson's assemblages are a good example. As you know from reading Chapter 6, Nevelson collects objects that are not alike. This presents a problem of unity, which she solves in one or more ways. Often, she places the objects in a series of boxlike containers (Figure 12.20 on page 329). The boxes help to unify the work. She sometimes paints the entire structure the same color. Sometimes she repeats both container shape and color to unify her assemblages.

MORE ABOUT . . . ABSTRACT EXPRESSIONISM

In the 1940s, a new art movement called Abstract Expressionism took hold in America. The roots of the new movement can be traced back to the works of Kandinsky, Picasso, and especially the Surrealists. Although it gained instant recognition, it caused confusion and anger.

The movement was called Abstract Expressionism because artists applied paint freely to their huge canvases in an effort to show feelings and emotions, rather than realistic subject matter. They thought of the picture surface as if it were a flat wall and emphasized the physical action it took to paint it.

GUIDED PRACTICE
(continued)

Developing Studio Skills

Divide the class into small working groups of two or three students. Assign each group the problem of developing a composition that illustrates one of the principles of art. Include both two- and three-dimensional problems in the assignment. If the class is small, each group might be assigned several of the problems so that all of the principles are covered. Have the groups make their compositions on sheets of paper and provide them with yarn, thin sticks, found objects, and squares and circles cut from magazines.

Encourage the groups to experiment with a number of arrangements to find one that uses the space effectively and best illustrates the assigned principle. When the students have determined the best layout, they should glue the pieces into place.

Art Is Everywhere

To foster students' awareness of art in everyday life, suggest this: Cut a 1 x 1$\frac{1}{2}$ inch (2.5 x 3.8 cm) rectangle out of the center of a note card and use the card as a view finder, just as you use a camera lens. Look through the finder at your world, finding examples of all of the principles of art. Look for the rhythm of repeated rows of windows, the variety in the directions of tree branches, the contrast in light and shadow on a sunny day, or the formal and informal balance in furniture arranged in a room. Start to see your world with the eyes of an artist and you will learn to wonder.

328

FIGURE 12.18   Carr has used simplification to eliminate the details of bark, grass, and leaves. The foliage seems to be solidified into diagonally flowing living forms.

Emily Carr. *Forest, British Columbia.* c. 1931–32. Oil on canvas. 129.5 × 86.4 cm (51 × 34"). Collection of Vancouver Art Gallery, Vancouver, British Columbia, Canada. Emily Carr Trust.

FIGURE 12.19   Why was it much easier for Barlach to unify this sculpture than it was for Rodin to unify *The Burghers of Calais* (Figure 12.14)?

Ernst Barlach. *Singing Man.* 1928. Bronze. 49.5 × 55.6 × 35.9 cm (19½ × 21⅞ × 14 ⅛"). Collection, The Museum of Modern Art, New York, New York. Abby Aldrich Rockefeller Fund.

MORE ABOUT . . . EMILY CARR

Modern Canadian art can trace its origins to 1920 and a small group of landscape painters working in Toronto. These painters eventually came to be known as the Group of Seven. Their style was uniquely Canadian.

The work of the Group of Seven played an important role in the career of Emily Carr, who was to become Canada's best-known early modern artist. Like the painters in the Group of Seven, she was greatly impressed by the expressive qualities of the Fauves works and adapted their qualities to her own painting style. Emily Carr's art heralded a period of artistic activity in Canada that continues to grow in diversity and quality.

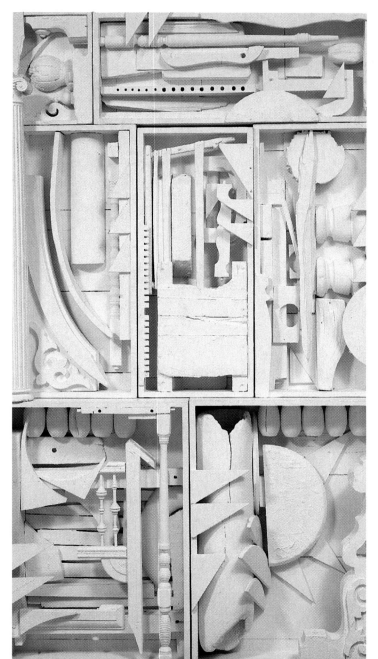

FIGURE 12.20   The use of one color and the repetition of the box shapes add to the unity of this work.

Louise Nevelson. *Dawn's Wedding Chapel I*. 1959. Wood painted white. 228 × 129 × 15 cm (90 × 51 × 6″). The Pace Gallery, New York, New York.

ART ON A SHOESTRING

As the end of a term approaches, you might be faced with a dilemma about too many odds and ends of supplies in the classroom. On the other hand, you may need supplies to finish term projects but have no budget left with which to purchase them. In either case, Louise Nevelson's assemblage provides inspiration. If you have on hand an assortment of unrelated supplies, challenge students to work in groups to create a unified assemblage. If you are low on supplies and even lower on budget, ask students each to bring ten items from home that are unneeded. Proceed with the same activity.

GUIDED PRACTICE
(continued)

Developing Perceptual Skills

Tell students that not all of Frank Lloyd Wright's designs met with the public's approval. If possible, show a reproduction of the Solomon R. Guggenheim Museum in New York City. Inform students that many people thought it looked like a giant cupcake and did not consider it an appropriate design for a museum. Ask: Why would Wright have considered it a unified design?

Understanding Art History

To help students further appreciate the life and times of Frank Lloyd Wright, assign *Artist's Profile 32* in the TCR.

Exploring Aesthetics

Have students examine Figure 12.22. Explain that commissioned portraits often represent the sitter as he or she would ideally want to be perceived. Ask students how Vigée-Lebrun presented the marquise and her children in a flattering manner. If possible, display other portraits by Vigée-Lebrun. (See Figure 8.3 on page 193.) Then have students find and study images of women in magazine advertisements. Help students see how the advertisements reflect modern perceptions of beauty and glamour, just as Vigée-Lebrun's society portraits show how women wanted to look in the late eighteenth century.

Understanding Art History

To help students further appreciate the life and times of Élisabeth Vigée-Lebrun, assign *Artist's Profile 18* in the TCR.

330

FIGURE 12.21 Wright was a genius who dared to be different. In 1936 he was asked to design a house close to this waterfall. Instead, he placed the house right over the falls. Terraces hang suspended over the running water. Even though they are made of reinforced concrete, the terraces repeat the shapes of the natural stone terraces below. The stones that make up the walls come from the building site, which ties the house more closely to its surroundings.

Frank Lloyd Wright. *Falling Water House. Bear Run, Pennsylvania.* 1936. Photography by Sandak, Inc., Stamford, Connecticut.

FIGURE 12.22 The artist has created unity by grouping the women and children close together. There is no negative space between the figures. Each one touches the next.

Élisabeth Vigée-Lebrun. *The Marquise de Peze and the Marquise de Rouget with Her Two Children.* 1787. Oil on canvas. 123.4 × 155.9 cm (48⅝ × 61⅜"). National Gallery of Art, Washington, D.C. Gift of the Bay Foundation in memory of Josephine Bay Paul and Ambassador Charles Ulrick Bay.

AT THE MUSEUM

The National Museum of Women in the Arts (Washington, D.C.)   If you live near The National Museum of Women in the Arts, you can participate in their program called "Artists + Community." Women artists, whose work is exhibited in the museum, go to women's and homeless shelters, elementary and high schools, and community centers to conduct lessons on how to create artwork. After the group watches the artist at work, they create their own art in the same genre as the artist's. Then the group critiques their own artwork, the artist's work, and each others' works. Afterwards, the museum displays the students' artworks next to the artist's work.

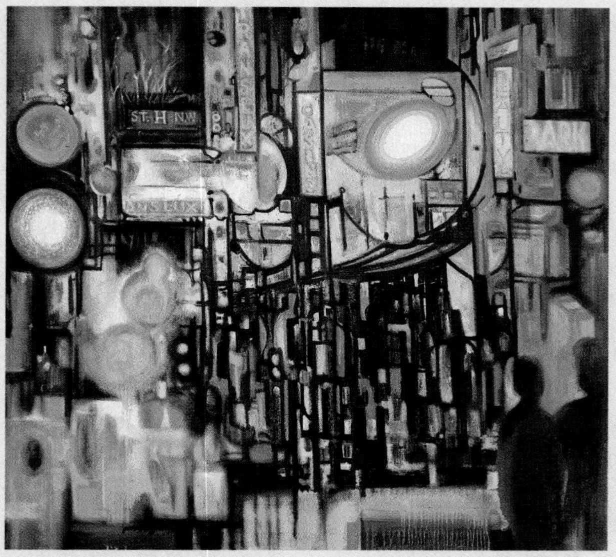

Georgia Mills Jessup. *Rainy Night, Downtown.* 1967. Oil on canvas. 112 × 122 cm (44 × 48″). National Museum of Women in the Arts, Washington, D.C.

LOOKING CLOSELY

FIGURE 12.23 Jessup has created a unified composition using many techniques. What has she simplified to unify the work? What has been repeated? Look for examples of proximity and continuity. Which area is the focal point of this work? How has the artist used variety? Notice the two people in the lower right of the work. Do you see any other hints of people in the work? What do you think the bright, round shapes represent?

Many architects are concerned with unity. Their goal is to design homes that blend with the land (Figure 12.21). They may use materials that repeat the colors and textures found in the home's environment. They may also use materials that reflect the surroundings. For instance, mirrored outside walls have been used on skyscrapers. The mirrors reflect the shapes and colors of the clouds and sky, and the buildings seem to blend with their surroundings and the atmosphere.

Proximity

Proximity, or closeness, is another way of unifying very different shapes in a work (Figures 12.22 and 12.23). This is achieved by limiting the negative space between the shapes. Clustering the shapes in this way suggests unity and coherence. The sense of unity can be made even stronger if the cluster of unlike items is surrounded by an area of negative space.

Continuation

Sometimes shapes can be arranged so that a line or edge of one shape continues as a line or edge of the next shape (Figure 12.24, page 332). This type of arrangement allows the viewer's eye to flow smoothly from one shape to the next along the continuing contour. This continuity links the different parts into a unified group.

ACTIVITY Creating Unity

1. Applying Your Skills. Using any media you wish, create small designs to illustrate the following unifying devices: simplicity, harmony of color, harmony of shape, harmony through space, proximity, and continuation.

MEETING SPECIAL NEEDS

Physically Disabled Persons with disabilities sometimes feel left out and different. They can be helped to feel a sense of psychological unity with a peer by carrying out the above activity in pairs rather than as separate individuals. Thus, in the student's mind, a connection may be realized between artistic unity and a sense of unity and agreement with another person. Just as this art exercise is about unity, likewise the pairing of students can create a sense of unity. This point is described by Herbert Read in *Education Through Art*—that a knowledge of design principles, learned through art activities, can generalize to other areas of one's life.

GUIDED PRACTICE
(continued)

LOOKING CLOSELY

Have students study Figure 12.23. Help them to see that everything in the work has been simplified. The people are silhouettes; all we can see of the lights are their round and oval shapes. The shapes of buildings and signs have been reduced so that no details show. Jessup has repeated the black lines, the round shapes, and the rectangles, as well as the shapes of the human silhouettes. Continuity is created by the black lines, both straight and curved. Proximity occurs where all the black lines seem clustered together, in almost an oval area below the center and a little to the right of center. The oval of black lines is the focal point. Variety is created by the contrast between dark and light, and the contrast between the rounded shapes, the rectangular shapes, and the variety of shapes created by the black lines.

Developing Studio Skills

Instruct students to look back at the different artworks they have created during the course. Find one work that seems to lack unity. Study it to decide which unifying devices might improve it.

ACTIVITY Creating Unity

1. Applying Your Skills. You may wish to divide the topics and have each student do one quality design rather than have each student do all six problems.

GUIDED PRACTICE
(*continued*)

2. Further Challenge.
This activity involves collage and drawing or painting. Point out the student work in Figure 12.25. Have them notice how carefully each item is cut out.

3. Computer Option.
Using the drawing tools and menus of your choice, make one example of harmony and one example of unity. Create harmony by using similar visual relationships among one of the following: shape, size, color, texture, or the arrangement in space. Save and title work.

Make a second design showing unity of the individual parts to the whole design by adjusting the elements and principles to reflect simplicity, repetition, proximity, and continuation.

Exploring Aesthetics
Have students form small groups and ask each group to create a list of ten qualities that they feel are essential for a work to be considered "art." Then have each group choose one work from the chapter that they feel is art and one they feel is not art. Each group should make a presentation and be prepared to discuss and defend their list using the information they have learned about the language of art, the elements and principles, the media, and the work of art itself.

Using Art Criticism
Have students apply the four steps of art criticism to Juan Gris's painting in Figure 12.24. Remind them that since the term is almost over, their critical analyses should reflect a thorough understanding of all the elements and principles of art.

2. Further Challenge. Suppose you have been hired to create a window display for a gift shop that sells many unrelated objects. From magazines, cut out photographs of fifteen unrelated objects that represent the merchandise to be displayed. Use as many unifying techniques as you can to create the display. Draw the window and the design for the display and glue the cutouts where the objects would be placed in the design (Figure 12.25).

FIGURE 12.24 Gris uses continuity to tie this composition together. Find out how many lines have been continued. Hold the straight edge of a ruler over a strong line direction to see how many times that line is continued throughout the painting.

Juan Gris. *Guitar and Flowers.* 1912. Oil on canvas. 112.1 × 70.2 cm (44⅛ × 27⅝″). Collection, The Museum of Modern Art, New York, New York. Bequest of Anna Erickson Levene in memory of her husband, Dr. Phoebus Aaron Theodor Levene.

3. Computer Option. Create small designs to illustrate the following unifying devices: simplicity, harmony of color, harmony of shape, harmony through space, proximity, and continuation. Take advantage of your software tools and options to make this task easier. Can you use one illustration as the basis for another? Decide which tools and options you will need to make the necessary changes. Save your work.

How Artists Use Variety, Emphasis, and Harmony to Enhance Unity

As you know, artists use variety, emphasis, and harmony to make their works more interesting and appealing. If carried to extremes, however, these principles can destroy the unity of a visual work. This means that artists must be careful to balance the contrasting qualities of variety and emphasis with harmonizing and unifying techniques to create a unified work.

Jane Wilson has successfully balanced the harmonizing and varying devices in *Solstice* (Figure 12.26). She has divided the work into two contrasting rectangles. The sky in the upper rectangle is painted with both light and dark values. The focal point of the work is the bright yellow glow of sunlight peeking through the dark clouds.

You cannot see any specific shapes in the water, shown in the lower rectangle, yet the sky is full of loose triangular shapes. These contrasting factors would pull the work apart if the artist had not used a harmonious color scheme. The entire work is composed of various values of blue, green, and yellow. She has simplified this work, showing nothing but clouds, sky, and water. She has tied the work together using repetition. The clear triangle of sky repeats the color of the water. The bright yellow of the sun is reflected along the edge of the clouds and in the water below. The active clouds are repetitions of loose triangular shapes. Without the repetitions and simple color scheme, this work might not be the unified composition that it is.

COOPERATIVE LEARNING

Consider dividing the class into two groups and assigning one group the principle of harmony and one the principle of variety. Each group is to browse through the book and write down the name and page number of ten works—other than those in Chapter 12—that exhibit the principle they have been assigned. The groups are then to trade lists and analyze the works identified in an effort to find evidence of their own principle in a work that was singled out as containing an "opposite" principle. Allow time for a discussion of the reciprocal relationship between harmony and variety.

FIGURE 12.25   Student work. A unified window display.

FIGURE 12.26   Analyze the ways in which the artist has balanced the harmonizing and varying devices in this painting.

Jane Wilson. *Solstice.* 1991. Oil on linen. 152.4 × 178 cm (60 × 70″). Fischbach Gallery, New York, New York.

Assemblage with Handmade Paper

TUDIO LESSON: ASSEMBLAGE WITH HANDMADE PAPER

STUDIO LESSON: ASSEMBLAGE WITH HANDMADE PAPER

OBJECTIVE

Create a relief assemblage that contains symbols of each student's life. Found materials that could be incorporated into the relief assemblages could include yarn, leaves, old photos, twigs, shells, sand, colored clay, feathers, costume jewelry, seeds, grasses, weeds, and dried bones.

MOTIVATOR

Bring an abandoned wasp's or hornet's nest to class. Ask students to compare its strength and texture to that of various manufactured sheets of paper. Show examples of handmade paper. If none are available, show slides or pictures from the text. If there are any papermaking artists in the area, invite one to class to demonstrate techniques.

GUIDED PRACTICE

Developing Studio Skills

Be sure that students experiment with the handmade paper before they work on their finished compositions. They need to understand how the materials behave before they use them in a finished work.

FIGURE 12.27 Lois Dvorak. *Spirit Boxes I.* 1985. Assemblage with handmade paper, construction paper, tree bark, colored pencils, pastels, and embroidery thread. 51 × 76.2 × 5.1 cm (20 × 30 × 2"). Private collection.

Supplies

- Sketchbook and pencils
- Large strong sheet of paper for background
- Your own handmade paper
- Variety of paper and fabric
- Fibers and needles
- Personal symbols
- Other found materials
- White glue
- Scissors
- Pencils, markers, and/or crayons

Spirit Boxes I is a mixed-media assemblage (Figure 12.27). The background is a sheet of paper Lois Dvorak made from cotton pulp. The swirling pattern is drawn with colored pencils and pastels. The dark tree shape is made from construction paper with pastel shading that continues the movement of the design in the background. The boxes are made from bark that was soaked and beaten into a very strong, thin paper, which was then glued and sewn together. Inside the boxes are bits of bark paper embroidered with colored threads. Notice that in some places the details in the boxes are unified with the background. Across the front of the boxes you can see very thin, transparent paper that has bits of homemade and construction paper glued in strategic places to unite the rhythmic repetition of the boxes.

Dvorak is always searching for little treasures in the environment to put in her spirit boxes, such as pieces of mica, yucca seeds, bits of bird eggshells, locust wings, hornet's nest paper, and dried-out lizards. Begin to think about how you can adapt Dvorak's techniques to your own assemblage.

Create a relief assemblage that contains symbols of your life. Each symbol should be protected in a handmade paper container just as Dvorak has protected each symbol in a spirit box. Use the principle of harmony to join the various symbols and containers into a unified composition. Use handmade papers, other papers, fabrics, fibers, and small found objects to construct the relief. Like Dvorak, add details using pencil, crayon, markers, and/or fibers.

Mentally Disabled Students with mental retardation may especially enjoy the making of paper pulp into paper. They usually enjoy the kinesthetic sensation of handling the semi-liquid pulp. Creating a piece of paper from a mass of pulp is almost a feat of magic. The moral lesson of "strength through sticking together" (the lesson taught by a Native American chief who easily broke one stick but could not break a bundle of sticks), can be applied to the fibers coming together for strength. The experience of being in a group while working on this activity may benefit persons who tend to feel outcast or isolated.

FOCUSING

Study Dvorak's assemblage, *Spirit Boxes I.* She has used several different ways to unify her work. Notice how the forms of the spirit boxes are related. Observe how the paths that weave over and under each other in the background are alike, and most of the shapes between the paths are covered with an invented texture. The boxes are placed close to each other and are held together in the branches of the tree. Can you find other ways that the artist has created unity?

Brainstorm with your classmates about objects that can be used to symbolize aspects of your life.

CREATING

Working in small groups, make handmade paper to use in this project. See the instructions for making paper in Technique Tip 21 on page 356 in the Handbook. Plan the colors you will use when making the paper, because they will be some of the colors in your final project. Collect the other materials and symbolic objects you plan to use.

Make plans for your relief assemblage in your sketchbook. List and sketch the symbolic objects you will use and explain what each represents. Design the forms of the containers. Draw each container from two or more views. List the ways that you will use harmony to unify your project.

Draw several plans for your mixed-media relief. As you draw, think about the materials you will use for construction and how you will alter them using drawing or stitching materials. Choose the best design.

Plan the procedures you need to follow to construct your work and follow your plan. Prepare your finished product for display.

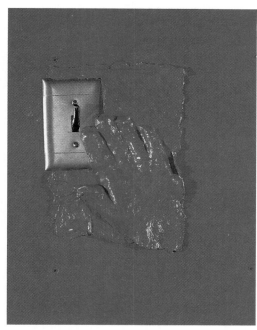

FIGURE 12.27A   Student work.

CRITIQUING

Describe   Explain the process, step by step, that you used to make paper. Describe the three-dimensional containers you made to hold the symbolic objects and explain how you constructed them.

Analyze   Which elements did you emphasize in this project? List and describe the methods you used to create harmony. Does the work have visual rhythm? Describe.

Interpret   Do the symbols you used represent only one part of your life or all of it? Are the symbols obvious or are they private and personal?

Judge   Does your work have a strong sense of unity? Which of the aesthetic theories would you use to judge this work? What, if anything, would you change to give it more unity?

335

GUIDED PRACTICE
(continued)

Developing Studio Skills
To help students be successful with this activity, consider the following suggestions:
- When students make initial sketches for their designs, provide still-life objects and photographs for ideas.
- Plastic bowls, boxes, and containers are good press molds for the assemblage.
- If there is a surface that the paper might stick to, cover it with plastic wrap before applying the paper pulp.

INDEPENDENT PRACTICE

Keeping a Portfolio
Remind students that the preliminary sketches and the final artwork for this Studio Lesson are likely considerations for their portfolios.

Extension
Allow the students to experiment with the sculptural qualities of paper pulp. A stronger mixture of glue solution may be added to the paper pulp to give it more strength for shaping. Students may want to construct wire armatures as inner supports for the sculptures.

ASSESS

CRITIQUING
Have students apply the steps of art criticism to their own artwork using the "Critiquing" questions on this page.

CLOSE

Allow time for each group to present its finished work. Ask students to explain how the work shows harmony.

CULTURAL PERSPECTIVES

Tell your students that paper was invented by the Chinese in the first century A.D. Mulberry bark, old fishing nets, or fragments of silk in water were soaked then beat to a pulp. The fibrous remains would be spread out on a framework of bamboo strips and dried. Papermaking remained a guarded secret until the eighth century. During a battle, several Chinese papermakers were taken prisoners. While in prison in Samarkand, they could not use rags or mulberry bark so they substituted local hemp and flax. In the twelfth century the craft of making paper reached Europe. By the fifteenth century, France, Germany, and the Netherlands had established paper mills.

FOCUS

OBJECTIVE

Reorganize and draw one frame from a comic strip.

MOTIVATOR

Ask students to bring in their favorite comic books or comic strips. Critique the various methods used by the artists to draw the comics. After the discussion, have students use their sketchbooks to practice some of the design methods used by comic strip artists.

TEACH

GUIDED PRACTICE

Understanding Art History

Tell students that Lichtenstein's work is considered part of the Pop art movement of the 1960s (see Chapter 3, page 63). Some Pop artists tried to show the public how the popular culture has bombarded the visual world with images of promotion and advertising beyond people's ability to ignore or resist their persuasive powers. In his paintings of Marilyn Monroe and the Campbell Soup cans, Andy Warhol demonstrates the visual repetition we face every day in the media and environment. Claes Oldenburg reproduced and enlarged common objects such as clothespins, tent stakes, and pencils on a grand scale. This method of creation makes the viewer notice the design of everyday objects.

STUDIO LESSON: ENLARGE ONE FRAME FROM A COMIC STRIP

FIGURE 12.28   Roy Lichtenstein. *Blam*. 1962. Oil on canvas. 172.7 × 203.2 cm. (68 × 80"). Yale University Art Gallery, New Haven, Connecticut. Richard Brown Baker Collection.

Supplies

- One frame cut from a comic strip
- Sketchbook, pencils, tape
- Crayons or markers
- Large sheet of white paper
- Ruler and yardstick
- Soft eraser
- Acrylic or tempera paints and brushes
- Stipple brush (optional)

When Roy Lichtenstein's paintings appeared on the scene in the early 1960s, art critics assumed that he had copied his work from the comics. Lichtenstein does not copy his subject matter. He starts with reality and then uses his excellent sense of design to reorganize the original elements into a very well-organized, strong composition (Figure 12.28). He calls what he does "quotation."

The source of his first painting was not comic strips, but bubble-gum wrappers that Lichtenstein got from his children. He continued by doing a series based on different comics. The use of strong black lines, limited color schemes, and dot patterns make his work instantly recognizable. The dots represented the benday dots used in comic strips to create light values or mixed colors.

Observe Lichtenstein's techniques and think about the comic strips you see in your daily newspaper. Consider how you can use these techniques to create your own adaptation.

Select one frame from your favorite comic strip and, in the style of Roy Lichtenstein, reorganize and redraw it. Use harmony to improve the composition of the original frame employing repetition, simplification, and continuation of line to make it a stronger, more unified

336

MORE ABOUT . . . CARTOONING

Printers in the United States usually give page sizes in inches. When printers talk about width of columns, however, they usually refer to printing measurements by using the word *picas*. There are six picas in an inch, and each inch can be broken down into tiny measurements call *points*. 12 points = 1 pica; 6 picas = 1 inch; 72 points = 1 inch.

Most newspapers reduce cartoon strips to around $6\frac{1}{2}" \times 2"$ (16.5 × 5 cm), or in printers' measurements, 34 picas long and 12 picas high. Also, point out to students that there is an average of less than thirty words per strip.

work. To keep it interesting, add variety through the use of emphasis.

FOCUSING

Study Lichtenstein's painting *Blam*. It looks like he copied a comic strip frame, but what he did was use the comic strip as the subject matter for his painting. Lichtenstein simplified the original. He omitted all the writing except *BLAM* and the numeral 3. He limited the colors to the three primaries. He repeated curved shapes such as the ovals used in the nose of the airplane and the cockpit. He has used line continuation in several places. For example, the bottom line of the wing on the right is continued in the bold, black line of the yellow explosion on the left. All the positive shapes are smooth, but the negative spaces in the background have been textured in an exaggerated imitation of the dots used to print color.

CREATING

Select one frame from your favorite comic strip, with or without color. Tape the original frame into the corner of a page in your sketchbook. With a ruler, draw a rectangle the same proportions as the original. Sketch a more unified version of the original in your rectangle. Use different methods of emphasis for variety. Make several variations of the original design. Choose the strongest, most unified composition for your final work.

Select a limited color scheme that enhances the expressive feeling of your composition. Test it in your sketchbook using crayons or markers. Plan areas of light value.

Enlarge the composition you have selected onto a large sheet of white paper using a grid. (See Technique Tip 8 on page 352 in the Handbook.) Make the final composition as large as possible.

Paint your work following the plan you made in your sketchbook. To create textured areas of light value, use stippling. Be sure to practice stippling before you use it in your final composition. Prepare your finished work for display.

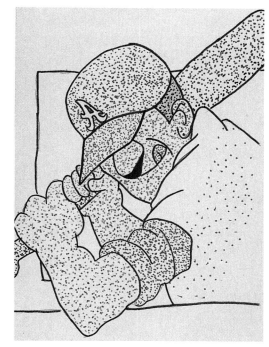

FIGURE 12.28A   Student work.

C R I T I Q U I N G

Describe   Name the comic strip you used for this project. List the objects in the frame you selected and then list the things you eliminated in your final composition.

Analyze   Explain how you used repetition, simplification, and line continuation to create harmony. Describe how you used emphasis.

Interpret   Did you change the expressive effect of the comic strip frame when you made the composition stronger and more unified? If so, how? Give this work an expressive title.

Judge   Which aesthetic theories would you use to judge this work? If you were to do this one more time, what would you change?

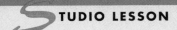
FOCUS

OBJECTIVE

Create a clay sculpture that combines two unrelated objects.

MOTIVATOR

Ask students to locate two works of art in the text that represent different specific themes. Direct them to list on paper the similarities and differences of the two pieces.

TEACH

GUIDED PRACTICE

Understanding Art History

Review the subtractive, additive, and casting processes used by sculptors. Remind students that most sculptors combine two or more of these methods. An example of the subtractive process is carving. The sculpture is created when the artist cuts away pieces of stone, clay, or wood. Michelangelo (Figure 11.37, page 309), Rodin (Figure 12.14, page 325), and Henry Moore (Figures 1.18, page 20 and 6.40, page 142) used this method. In the additive process, parts are attached to create a whole or finished sculpture. This process was utilized by David Smith (Figure 6.8, page 123) when he welded his metal sculptures. Casting involves pouring a liquid material into a mold to create a form. When the liquid dries or hardens, the mold is removed to reveal a positive shape of the mold's cavity.

FIGURE 12.29 Artist unknown. Folk art from the town of Acallan, State of Puebla, Mexico. *Fiesta Rodeo.* 1975. Ceramic with nichrome wire and acrylic paint. 55.8 × 33 × 33 cm (22 × 13 × 13″). Private collection.

Supplies
- Sketchbook and pencil
- Clay and clay tools
- Slip and brush
- Cloth-covered clay board
- Plastic bags
- Glaze or acrylic paint (optional)

Contemporary Mexican folk artists do not sign their work individually. The piece shown in Figure 12.29 comes from the town of Acallan in the State of Puebla in Mexico.

What makes this particular work so unusual is that the artist has taken two themes that are not really related and tied them together by using a balance between harmony and variety. The artist took two different themes of celebration: the secular rodeo and the religious tree of life, and carefully organized the elements of art so that the two themes merged into a unified whole. The rodeo is a worldly event. The tree of life represents the tree in the Garden of Eden from which Adam and Eve gained knowledge.

SAFETY TIPS

Before students begin this activity, review these guidelines for safety when working with clay:
- Most commercial glazes sold for school use are lead-free, but you should still read labels and check specifications before using ceramic materials or ordering supplies.
- Remind students to wash their hands thoroughly after handling clay and glazes.
- Place kilns in a separate room. If that is not possible, locate the kiln in an out-of-the-way part of the room where students are not likely to come into contact with it when it is in operation. In addition, all kilns should have local exhaust ventilation.

Notice how the artist has used contrast. The negative spaces in the rodeo fence are small rectangles, but when your eyes move up to the tree area the lines explode into active, blossoming curves.

Observe the ways in which the two themes have been related in this sculpture and think about how you will relate two themes.

Like the Mexican folk artist who combined two different themes in the sculpture, *Fiesta Rodeo*, you will create a clay sculpture that combines two unrelated objects. Create unity in your work by using a balance between variety and harmony. Use some of the following harmonizing techniques: simplification, repetition, proximity, and continuation. To help you tie the two parts together, use emphasis of an element and/or emphasis of an area.

FOCUSING

Study *Fiesta Rodeo*. Notice how the artist has unified two different themes. In your sketchbook describe how the artist has used a balance between variety and harmony to create unity. List which elements are the most important and explain why. Discuss your findings with your classmates.

Brainstorm with your classmates about different themes or objects that could be unified in a sculpture as the artist has done with *Fiesta Rodeo*. Think of your favorite school subject, your favorite after-school activity, or a hobby. Write the two ideas in your sketchbook. Make verbal and visual notes about how you could create your sculpture. Make some sketches based on your ideas. Choose your best idea. List the harmonizing techniques you want to use and which elements you will use. Then list the way you will use emphasis.

CREATING

Construct your sculpture. For proper clay construction techniques see Technique Tip 16 on page 354 in the Handbook. Between work sessions, cover your sculpture tightly with a plastic bag so the clay does not dry. When you

FIGURE 12.29A   Student work.

are finished with construction, cover your work loosely so the clay does not dry too quickly. Remember that thin clay will dry and shrink more quickly than thick clay, so cover thin areas very carefully.

When your work is bone dry, fire it in the kiln. After your sculpture is fired, you may decorate it by glazing and glaze firing the piece or painting it with acrylic paints. Prepare your work for display.

CRITIQUING

Describe   List the two different themes or objects you combined in your sculpture. Describe the clay-building techniques you used to construct your work. How did you prepare your work for display?

Analyze   Which harmonizing techniques did you use to unify your work? Describe how you used emphasis to pull the piece together visually. Does your finished product look unified?

Interpret   What is the expressive effect of your sculpture? Give your work an expressive title. Write a poem or a brief paragraph about your sculpture that expresses your feelings toward this work.

Judge   Which aesthetic theories would you use to judge this work? If you were to do this over, what would you change?

Interdisciplinary: Music

Discuss harmony as it relates to art and other areas of life. Play tapes of musical groups known for using harmony in their songs. Discuss the techniques used to harmonize the instruments and/or voices. How are these methods similar to the challenge in this Studio Lesson?

INDEPENDENT PRACTICE

Keeping a Portfolio

Remind students that the preliminary sketches and the final artwork for this Studio Lesson are likely considerations for their portfolios.

Extension

Students could play their own version of "Pictionary" in which each player, or teams of players, pulls two random nouns, written on slips of paper and placed in a hat. Students are challenged to combine the nouns into a unified drawing on the board. For example, *cup* and *tree* might look like a coffee mug with a hollow trunk as the cup and a curved branch as a handle.

ASSESS

CRITIQUING

Have students apply the steps of art criticism to their own artwork using the "Critiquing" questions on this page.

CLOSE

Ask volunteers to read their paragraphs or poems aloud and name one concept about unity that they now understand better.

TEACHER TALK

Classroom Management   Occasionally, students struggle when faced with the task of originating ideas, such as in the Studio Lesson above. In these cases, a brainstorming session can help. To help them get started try the following: Give each student two slips of paper. Have each student write the name of an object on each slip of paper. Fold the papers and put them in a container. Have one person draw two slips of paper and write the names of the objects on the board. As a class, try to develop different ideas for creating a sculpture that unifies the two objects. Now encourage them to think of two separate themes or objects that they would like to unite into a unified sculpture.

OBJECTIVE

Design and create a presentation painting of a mural for a specific site.

MOTIVATOR

If there is a mural in your city, plan a field trip to study it. Discuss its theme, the site, and the surface on which it is painted. If the artist is available, have him or her discuss what is involved in planning and painting a mural.

GUIDED PRACTICE

Understanding Art History

The earliest known murals are cave paintings where hunting scenes were painted on the walls. It is theorized that the purposes for these images included rituals and storytelling.

During the Renaissance, Giotto, Raphael, and Michelangelo painted large frescoes. Fresco is a method of painting in which water-based pigment is applied to freshly spread plaster. The plaster must be damp. As it dries, the plaster absorbs the paint. This technique is still used today by some muralists. Diego Rivera, a Mexican muralist mentioned earlier in this text (see Chapter 10, page 278), painted large frescoes. The messages in his art were often political in nature.

STUDIO LESSON: DESIGNING A MURAL

FIGURE 12.30 John Yancy. *Celebration of Arts: Vibrations of Life.* 1991. Permanent exterior mural, acrylic on panels. 2.4 × 9.7 m (8′ × 32′). Located at 1531 West 60th Street, Chicago, Illinois.

Supplies
- Sketchbook, pencil, and ruler
- Photograph of proposed site
- Enlarged photocopy of photograph
- Large sheet of white paper
- Tempera or acrylic paints
- Brushes

John Yancy received his first mural commission during his senior year in high school. He liked murals because of their scale and visibility. During his studies at The Art Institute of Chicago, he began to realize that murals inform, enlighten, and motivate people. His *Celebration of the Arts* mural depicts the programs and contributions of the Boulevard Art Center and expresses the excitement and vitality of all the visual and performing arts (Figure 12.30). The patterns on the mural portray textile designs that are seen in the masquerade ceremonies of the Yoruba people of Africa. The dancers in the mural function as dynamic, formal elements to increase movement and drama. The mural was completed with the help of a small crew of 16- to 20-year-old participants who had exhibited interest in a career in the arts.

340

Advanced Learners Artistically gifted students can make models of their mural or of a sculpture, called a *maquette* (small model), about one foot (30.5 cm) in height. This model-making experience in high school can lay the groundwork for public art competitions in later years. Many cities have a percent of their budget allocated to public art for new construction. Proposals frequently require teamwork between sculptors, landscape designers, and architects.

Yancy created the mural to let people know what was going on in the Center. Notice which elements he used to create variety and which ones he used to create harmony in the composition so that the mural became a unified whole.

Design and create a presentation painting of a mural for a specific site. Yancy used the events in the building as a theme for his mural. Choose a theme and design a mural by using subject matter that is linked to the site. Use a balance between the principles of variety, emphasis, and harmony to create a unified composition. Make your final painting to scale.

FOCUSING

Brainstorm with classmates about sites and themes for your mural designs. Decide whether you all want to work on the same theme such as the environment or the history of the community, or whether you all want to use independent themes. Then find an interesting site for your mural and choose your individual idea. Think of the subject matter you will use to express your theme.

CREATING

Photograph your site and enlarge the photograph using a photocopier. Measure the area of the photocopy on which you will place your mural. Make some rough sketches in your sketchbook. Create a unified composition by balancing the varying and unifying techniques. Because this is a plan for a large mural, you may not want to have a single focal point; you may decide to create several centers of interest. Plan your color scheme.

Select your best idea and draw it carefully with pencil on the measured area of the photocopy. Enlarge your mural plan, to scale, onto a large sheet of white paper. See Technique Tip 8 on page 352 of the Handbook for directions on using a grid to enlarge a work to scale. Paint the enlarged presentation drawing.

FIGURE 12.30A   Student work.

Arrange a display that includes the photograph, the enlarged photocopy with the drawing for the mural, the presentation painting, and a brief written statement that explains your theme, the subject matter, and why you selected them for that specific site.

CRITIQUING

Describe   Tell the theme, the subject matter, and the site you selected for your mural.

Analyze   Explain which principles of design you used to create a unified composition. Explain which color scheme you chose and why you chose it.

Interpret   What kind of a mood does your mural express? How do you think the mural would affect the site for which it was planned? Give your work an expressive title.

Judge   Which aesthetic theories would you use to judge this mural? What, if anything, would you change before you painted it on the final site?

TECHNIQUE TIP

Because this project involves public property, it might be better if you selected the sites for the murals. If the finished work can be displayed at the site, have the mural painted on plywood in the classroom and then mounted on the site when it is finished. Then you may obtain sites that are not on the school grounds, such as a shopping center or a store. It is very difficult in many school districts to get any work done after school. It is also difficult to work in a heavy traffic area or the lunchroom during the school day. If extra-curricular time is needed, it is wise to organize a weekend painting session, when everyone is fresh.

GUIDED PRACTICE
(continued)

Developing Studio Skills
If possible, have students use an opaque projector to enlarge the scale drawing onto a wall. Then a shape can be placed on the scale drawing and adjusted so that the proportions are correct.

INDEPENDENT PRACTICE

Keeping a Portfolio
Remind students that the preliminary sketches and the final artwork for this Studio Lesson are likely considerations for their portfolios.

Extension
Students may be interested in painting a fresco. Pour wet plaster into a pie tin and smooth the surface. Just as the plaster begins to harden, students should begin painting with watercolor paints. When the plaster is dry, it can be removed from the pie tin. Display the work.

ASSESS

CRITIQUING
Have students apply the steps of art criticism to their own artwork using the "Critiquing" questions on this page. In addition, ask the following: What theme was chosen for the mural? How was balance used with the principles of variety, emphasis, and harmony to create a unified design? Does the mural have a message to the viewer? What is it?

CLOSE

Ask students to speculate about what steps they would have to take if they could paint the mural at the chosen site.

INTRODUCTION

Thiebaud's painting, *Apartment Hill*, was selected because it is a symbol of human encroachment on the environment. Rembrandt's *The Mill* is a symbol of his environment.

CRITIQUING THE WORK

1. **Describe**   This work is very large. The subject is a cluster of buildings set on an impossibly steep hill, with a curved road full of cars going in both directions around the hill. The presence of people is implied in the houses, although there are no visible people in the vehicles.

2. **Analyze**   The following elements contribute to harmony: *line:* The repetition of static lines, the two major curves, and the curving hill; *shape and form:* The repetition of the two arcs and rectangles; *space:* The road, hill, and buildings are clustered together against the open negative space that surrounds them; *color:* The limited color scheme and the dominance of blue.

   The following elements introduce variety: *line:* Contrast between curved and static lines; *shape and form:* Contrast between rectangles and arcs; *color:* The use of subtle complements. Orange is seen on the right side of the hill and in different buildings on the hill; *texture:* Contrast between the rough and smooth textures.

   The principle of emphasis is seen in the dominance of blue and in the tall structures.

ART CRITICISM IN ACTION

FIGURE 12.31   Wayne Thiebaud. *Apartment Hill.* 1980. Oil on linen. 165.1 × 122 cm (65 × 48"). Nelson-Atkins Museum of Art, Kansas City, Missouri. Acquired through the generosity of the Friends of Art and Nelson Gallery Foundation.

CRITIQUING THE WORK

1. **Describe**   Read the credit line for Figure 12.31. What is the size of this work? Describe the subject matter. Do you see any people?

2. **Analyze**   Has Thiebaud created a unified composition? Which elements has he used to produce harmony? Which ones were used to introduce variety? Do you see the principle of emphasis? If you see a focal point, where is it? How did he create it?

3. **Interpret**   What message is the artist trying to express in this work? Write a brief paragraph explaining your interpretation.

342

RESOURCES BEYOND THE CLASSROOM

Other Works By . . . Wayne Thiebaud
Girl with Ice Cream Cone
Pie Counter
Seven Jellied Apples
Sunset Streets

Other Works By . . . Rembrandt
An Artist in His Studio

The Return of the Prodigal Son
The Company of Captain Frans Banning Cocq (The Night Watch)
Portrait of a Lady with an Ostrich-Feather Fan
Self-Portrait
The Stoning of St. Stephen
Anatomy Lesson of Dr. Tulp

3. **Interpret** Answers will vary. Students may see the theme as concern for the environment.
4. **Judge** Answers will vary. However, Formalism is the strongest theory for this work.

COMPARING THE WORKS

Similarities: Both works have limited color schemes, with architectural structures as the focal points. In *Apartment Hill*, trucks and cars fill the roads in both directions. In *The Mill*, we see one man rowing a sailboat and a few people are on foot. There is a hill and a road in Figure 12.31. In Figure 12.32 there is a hill upon which the windmill is perched and a road curving up the left side of the hill. In Thiebaud's scene, people are crowding out the land with their vehicles and their buildings, while Rembrandt's natural, realistic landscape has very few people.

In both works the artists have used isolation to make the architectural structures the focal point. Other principles evident are as follows: Movement through the flowing rhythm of the roads and the river; and informal balance through landscape arrangement. Even though Thiebaud has arranged the subject matter in an unrealistic manner, both works use realistic proportions and realistic scale.

Each work is a symbol of the time in which it was created.

EXTENSION

• Have students read more about Wayne Thiebaud in the "Meet the Artist" feature on the following page.
• Assign *Artist's Profile 12* in the TCR.

FIGURE 12.32 Rembrandt. *The Mill*. c. 1650. Oil on canvas. 87.6 × 105.6 cm (34½ × 41⅝″). National Gallery of Art, Washington, D.C. Widener Collection.

4. Judge Do you think this is a successful work of art? Use one or more of the three aesthetic theories explained in Chapter 2 to defend your opinion.

COMPARING THE WORKS

Look at Thiebaud's *Apartment Hill* (Figure 12.31). Now study Rembrandt's *The Mill* (Figure 12.32). Compare the two works. List the similarities and differences. Notice the color schemes, the architectural structures, transportation, and the treatment of the land masses. Notice how each artist has used isolation to create a focal point. What other principles can you find that have been used in the same way by each artist?

FYI *The Mill* is considered Rembrandt's greatest landscape painting. Many myths were told about this work. One was that it belonged to Rembrandt's father. Another was that the dark, gloomy sky was foretelling Rembrandt's financial difficulties. In truth, the sky was gloomy because the varnish had yellowed. The recent restoration of the painting has revealed the blue sky you see in this reproduction.

343

MORE ABOUT . . . REMBRANDT VAN RIJN

Rembrandt van Rijn is often referred to as the greatest Dutch painter of his era. Like his contemporaries, Rembrandt painted portraits, everyday events, historical subjects, and landscapes. However, he refused to specialize and was skilled enough to succeed in all areas. Wealthy citizens of Amsterdam were pleased with his style because he could paint the fine details of their clothing without detracting from the subject him- or herself. He was also skilled in the technique of chiaroscuro which resulted in powerful and impressive portraits.

CHECKING COMPREHENSION

- On a separate sheet of paper have students complete "Building Vocabulary" and "Reviewing Art Facts" on page 345.
- Assign *Application 23* and *24* in the TCR to evaluate students' comprehension.

ANSWERS TO BUILDING VOCABULARY

1. variety
2. emphasis
3. focal point
4. harmony
5. unity

ANSWERS TO REVIEWING ART FACTS

1. (a) The type in which an element of art dominates the entire work and (b) the type in which one area of the work is dominant over all of the other areas.
2. Dominant.
3. The degree of emphasis needed to create the focal point.
4. Contrast, isolation, location, convergence, and the unusual.
5. Simplicity, repetition, proximity, and continuation.

MEET THE ARTIST

WAYNE THIEBAUD
American, b. 1920

Wayne Thiebaud, one of California's most famous painters, has earned as many awards for excellence in teaching as he has for his painting and printmaking. He became interested in drawing in high school and later worked as a freelance cartoonist and illustrator. He continued his artwork during military service in World War II, drawing cartoons for the military base newspaper.

In 1949 he decided to become a painter. His first one-person show in New York was praised by the critics. At that time his subject matter was mass-produced consumer goods, particularly junk food, and he was considered a Pop artist. Later he became classified as an American Realist.

Since the 1970s he has concentrated on the urban landscapes of San Francisco. His primary concern is changing realistic subject matter into abstract compositions. He turns cakes into circles and figures into arrangements of spheres, triangles, and cylinders. Today Thiebaud lives and works in Sacramento and San Francisco and transforms street scenes into compositions of arcs, cubes, and networks of lines. He creates compositions that symbolize the essence of San Francisco by simplifying forms.

MORE PORTFOLIO IDEAS

Collect images that symbolize a place you know well. Organize them into a collage that expresses the essence of the place. Photocopy the collage into a black-and-white composition. Then, using a simple color scheme, paint the copy of your collage. Which looks better, the original collage or the painted photocopy?

Make some sketches of objects that symbolize your community. Then decide which abstract elements such as lines, shape, and colors symbolize your community. Create a painting simplifying details of the objects in a composition that emphasizes the abstract qualities you selected.

344

DEVELOPING A PORTFOLIO

Assessment A successful portfolio requires attention to organization. One that is carelessly put together reflects poorly on the student; therefore, encourage them to stay focused on their goals and objectives. Assessment will include an evaluation across time, materials, and artistic contents. Importantly, it will demonstrate that a student takes his or her work seriously. Remind them to give deliberate consideration to each piece of art they include, as well as to the relative merit of each piece in context with the entire portfolio. With ample assignments and opportunities to undertake projects on their own, portfolio pieces can be selected from a larger pool of works, allowing for greater variety.

CHAPTER 12 REVIEW

Building Vocabulary

On a separate sheet of paper, write the term that best matches each definition below.
1. The principle of design concerned with difference, or contrast.
2. The principle of design that makes one part of a work dominant over the other parts.
3. The first part of a work to attract the attention of the viewer.
4. The principle of design that creates unity by stressing the similarities of separate but related parts.
5. The quality of wholeness or oneness that is achieved through the effective use of the elements of art and the principles of design.

Reviewing Art Facts

Answer the following questions using complete sentences.
1. Name the two major types of visual emphasis.
2. What word is used to describe an element that is made the most important element in a comparison?
3. What must an artist consider when creating a focal point?
4. Name the five ways in which artists create a focal point.
5. Name four techniques that artists use to create unity in a work of art.

Thinking Critically About Art

1. **Analyze.** Rembrandt is known for his many self-portraits. Look through this book and list the self-portraits you find. You will have to look at the works themselves. The titles of Figures 1.1, page 4, and Figure 3.1 on page 40 do not tell you that the works are self-portraits. What do the self-portraits tell you about the different artists?

2. **Synthesize.** Artists from the past, such as Rembrandt, are easy to classify as a member of a school or movement. Contemporary artists, such as Wayne Thiebaud, move through several movements before they are finally classified. Certain artists, like Picasso, are never classified. Write a brief paper explaining why artists from the past are easy to classify, while twentieth-century artists are so difficult to classify. Select at least two artists to use as examples. Give your opinion on whether or not classifying an artist is important.

3. **Analyze.** Look through the other chapters of this book to find three examples of works in which the artist has emphasized one element, making all the others subordinate to it. List the works and explain which element has been emphasized.

Making Art Connections

1. **Music.** Do the principles of variety, emphasis, harmony, and unity play an important role in music? Bring a recording to class that illustrates each of the principles you consider important. Play it for the class and explain how the principles are used in the piece you selected.
2. **Language Arts.** Which principles of design are important in the creation of poetry? Create a poem that illustrates at least one principle discussed in this chapter. Share it with classmates.
3. **Social Studies.** Is this world moving toward a unified planet? Write a brief paper explaining your conclusions. Cite examples from ancient history, from one hundred years ago, and from the things that are happening today.
4. **Math.** Do you find examples in mathematics where unity and variety are important? Explain.

ALTERNATIVE ASSESSMENT

Suggest that students pretend they have taken an assignment to write a book titled *Everything There Is To Know About My Favorite Artist.* Challenge students to conceive a method of making a unified study of an artwork or an artist. If students prefer to work in groups, allow them to do so, but have each one submit an analysis of their methodology. Instruct them to also submit a plan of organization for the book. Remind them that they do not have to actually do the research; they are exploring the scope of a unified study. They will be expected to identify the areas of research that they would explore, such as biography, influences, artworks, social milieu, and so on.

TECHNIQUE TIPS HANDBOOK

UNIT OVERVIEW

This unit consists of a convenient reference section which offers students step-by-step procedures designed to complement and enrich the information and activities in the student text.

The first part consists of Drawing Tips that include, in addition to suggestions for drawing, guidelines for basic skills such as using a ruler, making an enlarging grid, and measuring. Painting Tips include everything from mixing paints to cleaning brushes. The Printmaking Tip focuses on stamp prints. In Sculpting Tips, students expand their familiarity with clay, paper, and papier-mâché. Other Tips is a section that includes techniques for mixed-media artworks, stitchery, making paper, and basketry. The Display Tips section recommends methods for putting the finishing touches to a completed artwork. Finally, Safety in the Art Room reminds students of safety guidelines when working with specific media, tools, and potentially hazardous materials.

Elena Bonafonte Vidotto. *Eggs.* (Detail.) 1977. Oil on panel. 25.4 × 30.5 cm (10 × 12″). National Museum of Women in the Arts, Washington, D.C. Gift of Wallace and Wilhelmina Holladay.

346

TECHNIQUE TIPS HANDBOOK

In the past, a young person who wished to become an artist had to spend time as an apprentice to a master artist. The first assignment given to the beginner was to prepare art materials for the use of the artist.

No one taught the apprentice how to appreciate art or how to use the elements of art and the principles of design. The student learned by listening and observing. If the apprentice did not learn to handle the media of art correctly, the art career was discontinued.

This unit is a reference unit. It is here to help you use the media of art. It is a collection of helpful suggestions for using a variety of tools and techniques. By referring to the information in this Handbook as you prepare your Activities and Studio Lessons, you will sharpen your skills and master the techniques needed for creating successful art projects.

347

TECHNIQUE TIPS HANDBOOK
TABLE OF CONTENTS

Drawing Tips

1	Making Contour Drawings	**349**
2	Making Gesture Drawings	**349**
3	Drawing Calligraphic Lines with a Brush	**349**
4	Using Shading Techniques	**350**
5	Using Sighting Techniques	**350**
6	Using a Viewing Frame	**351**
7	Using a Ruler	**351**
8	Making a Grid for Enlarging	**352**
9	Measuring Rectangles	**352**

Painting Tips

10	Mixing Paint to Change the Value of Color	**352**
11	Making Natural Earth Pigment Paints	**353**
12	Working with Watercolors	**353**
13	Cleaning a Paint Brush	**353**

Printmaking Tip

14	Making a Stamp Print	**354**

Sculpting Tips

15	Working with Clay	**354**
16	Joining Clay	**354**
17	Making a Pinch Pot	**355**
18	Using the Coil Technique	**355**
19	Papier-Mâché	**355**
20	Making a Paper Sculpture	**356**

Other Tips

21	Making Paper	**356**
22	Basic Embroidery Stitches	**357**
23	Weaving Techniques	**358**
24	Making a Coiled Basket	**360**
25	Making a Tissue Paper Collage	**361**

Display Tips

26	Making a Mat	**362**
27	Mounting a Two-Dimensional Work	**363**
28	Working with Glue	**363**

Safety in the Art Room — **364**

DRAWING TIPS

1. Making Contour Drawings

When you make a contour drawing, your eye and hand must move at the same time. You must look at the object, not at your drawing. You must imagine that your pencil is touching the edge of the object as your eye follows the edge. Don't let your eye get ahead of your hand. Also, do not lift your pencil from the paper. When you move from one area to the next, let your pencil leave a trail. If you do lift your pencil accidentally, look down, place your pencil where you stopped, and continue.

a. To help you coordinate your eye-hand movement, try this: First, tape your paper to the table so it will not slide around. Then, hold a second pencil in your nondrawing hand and move it around the edges of the object. With your drawing hand, record the movement.

b. If you have trouble keeping your eyes from looking at the paper, ask a friend to hold a piece of stiff paper between your eyes and your drawing hand so the drawing paper is blocked from view. You might also place your drawing paper inside a large paper bag turned sideways. A third method is to put the object on a chair and place the chair on a table. When you are standing, the object should be at your eye level. Then, place your drawing paper on the table directly under the chair. In this way you will be unable to see the paper easily.

c. When you draw without looking at the paper, your first sketches will look strange. Don't be discouraged. The major purpose of blind contour drawing is to teach you to concentrate on directions and curves. The more you practice, the more accurate your drawings will become.

d. As you develop your skills, remember that in addition to edges, contours also define ridges. Notice the wrinkles you see at the joints of fingers and at a bent wrist or bent elbow. Those wrinkles are curved lines. Draw them carefully; the lines you use to show these things will add the look of roundness to your drawing.

e. After you have made a few sketches, add pressure as you draw to vary the thickness and darkness of your lines. Some lines can be emphasized and some can be made less important through the right amount of pressure from your hand.

2. Making Gesture Drawings

Unlike contour drawings, which show an object's outline, gesture drawings show movement. They should have no outlines or details.

a. Using the side of a piece of unwrapped crayon or a pencil, make scribble lines that build up the shape of the object. Do not use single lines that create stick figures.

b. Work very quickly. When drawing people, do the head, then the neck, and then fill in the body. Pay attention to the direction in which the body leans.

c. Next, scribble in the bulk of the legs and the position of the feet.

d. Finally, add the arms.

3. Drawing Calligraphic Lines with a Brush

Mastering the technique of drawing with flowing, calligraphic lines takes practice. You will need a round watercolor brush and either watercolor paint or ink. First, practice making very thin lines.

a. Dip your brush in the ink or paint and wipe the brush slowly on the side of the ink bottle until the bristles form a point.

b. Hold the brush at the metal ferrule so the brush is vertical rather than slanted above the paper. Imagine that the brush is a pencil with a very sharp point—if you press down, you will break the point (Figure T.1).

FIGURE T.1

c. Touch the paper lightly with the tip of the brush and draw a line.

d. When you are able to control a thin line, you are ready to make calligraphic lines. Start with a thin line and gradually press the brush down to make the line thicker. Pull up again to make it thinner (Figure T.2, page 350). Practice making lines that vary in thickness.

TECHNIQUE TIPS

FIGURE T.2

5. Using Sighting Techniques
Sighting is a method that will help you determine proportions.
   a. Hold a pencil vertically at arm's length in the direction of the object you are drawing. Close one eye and focus on the object you are going to measure.
   b. Slide your thumb along the pencil until the height of the pencil above your thumb matches the height of the object (Figure T.4).
   c. Now, without moving your thumb or bending your arm,

4. Using Shading Techniques
The following techniques help create shading values.
   • **Hatching:** Use a series of fine parallel lines.
   • **Crosshatching:** Use two or more intersecting sets of parallel lines.
   • **Blending:** Use a smooth, gradual application of an increasingly dark value. Pencil lines may be blended.
   • **Stippling:** Create shading with dots.
   To be effective in forming the shaded areas, your lines and strokes must follow the form of the object. Use lines to show the surface of a flat surface. Let the lines run parallel to one edge of the surface. To show a curved surface, draw a series of parallel curved lines to give the illusion of roundness. The lines should follow the curve of the object.
   Lines or dots placed close together create dark values. Lines or dots spaced farther apart create lighter values. To show a gradual change from light to dark, begin with lines or dots far apart and bring them closer together. (Figure T.3.)

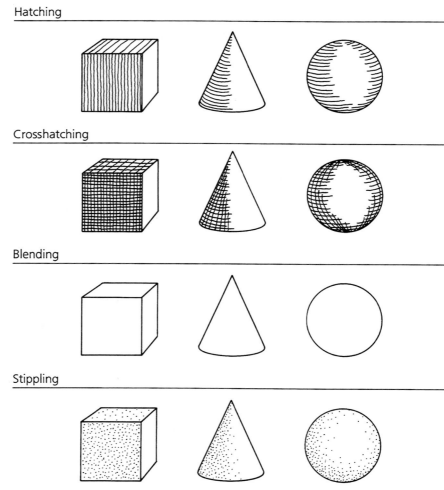

Hatching

Crosshatching

Blending

Stippling

FIGURE T.3

FIGURE T.4

subject. Imagine that the opening represents your drawing paper.

c. You can decide how much of the subject you want to include in your drawing by moving the frame up, down, or sideways.

d. You can also move the frame closer or farther away to change the focus of your drawing.

7. Using a Ruler

There are times when you need to draw a crisp, straight line.

a. Hold the ruler with one hand and the pencil with the other.

b. Place the ruler where you wish to draw a straight line.

c. Hold the ruler with your thumb and first two fingers. Be careful that your fingers do not stick out beyond the edge of the ruler.

d. Press heavily on the ruler so it will not slide while you're drawing.

e. Hold the pencil lightly against the ruler.

f. Pull the pencil quickly and lightly along the edge of the ruler. The object is to keep the ruler from moving while the pencil moves along its edge.

hold the pencil parallel to the widest part of the object. Compare the height of the object with its width. You can determine the ratio of height to width by seeing how many times the smaller measure fits into the larger measure. This method can be applied either to different parts of the same object or to two or more different objects. Use one measurement as a base measurement and see how the other measurements relate to it.

6. Using a Viewing Frame

A viewing frame helps you to zero in on an area or object you intend to draw. To make a viewing frame, do the following:

a. Cut a rectangular hole in a heavy sheet of paper (Figure T.5).

b. Hold the frame at arm's length and look through it at your

FIGURE T.5

TECHNIQUE TIPS

8. Making a Grid for Enlarging

Sometimes you must take a small drawing and enlarge it. To do this, you must first measure the size that the large, finished drawing will be. Then, using proportional ratios, reduce that size to something you can work with.

a. For example: If you want to cover a wall 5 feet high and 10 feet wide, let 1 inch equal 1 foot. Then make a scale drawing that is 5 inches high and 10 inches wide. You may work either in inches or centimeters.

b. After you have completed your small drawing, draw vertical and horizontal grid lines 1 inch apart on the drawing. Number the squares (Figure T.6).

c. On the wall, draw vertical and horizontal grid lines one foot apart.

d. Number the squares on the wall to match the squares on the paper and enlarge the

plan by filling one square at a time.

9. Measuring Rectangles

Do you find it hard to create perfectly formed rectangles? Here is a way of getting the job done:

a. Make a light pencil dot near the long edge of a sheet of paper. With a ruler, measure the exact distance between the dot and the edge. Make three more dots the same distance in from the edge. (See Figure T.7.)

b. Line a ruler up along the dots. Make a light pencil line running the length of the paper.

c. Turn the paper so that a short side is facing you. Make four pencil dots equally distant from the short edge. Connect these with a light pencil rule. Stop when you reach the first line you drew.

d. Do the same for the remaining two sides. Erase any lines that

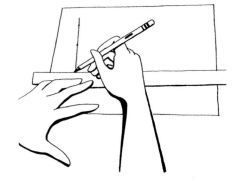

FIGURE T.7

may extend beyond the box you have made.

e. Trace over the lines with your ruler and pencil. The box you have created wil be a perfectly formed rectangle.

PAINTING TIPS

10. Mixing Paint to Change the Value of Color

You can better control the colors in your work when you mix your own paint. In mixing paints, treat opaque paints (for example, tempera) differently from transparent paints (for example, watercolors).

a. *For light values of opaque paints.* Add only a small amount of the hue to white. The color can always be made stronger by adding more of the hue.

b. *For dark values of opaque paints.* Add a small amount of black to the hue. Never add the hue to black.

c. *For light values of transparent paints.* Thin a shaded area with water. This allows more of the white paper to show through.

d. *For dark values of transparent paints.* Carefully add a small amount of black to the hue.

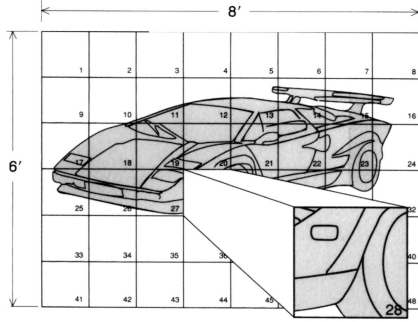

FIGURE T.6

11. Making Natural Earth Pigment Paints

Anywhere there is dirt, clay, and sand, you can find natural earth pigments.

a. Collect as many different kinds of earth colors as you can find (Figure T.8).

FIGURE T.8

b. Grind them as finely as possible. If you can, borrow a mortar and pestle from the science lab (Figure T.9). Regardless of the method you use, your finished product will still be a little gritty. It will not have the smooth texture of commercial pigment.

c. For the binder, use one part white glue to one part water. Put a few spoons of pigment into a small container and add

FIGURE T.9

some of the binder. Experiment with different proportions of pigment and binder.

d. When you have found the best proportion, apply the mixture to paper with a variety of brushes. Do not allow the brushes you use to dry before you wash them, because the glue will solidify.

e. Keep stirring your paint as you work to keep the pigment from settling. The pigment will keep indefinitely. Mix a fresh batch each time you paint, because the mixed paint is difficult to store for more than a few days.

12. Working with Watercolors

Here are some tips to control watercolor paints.

a. If you apply wet paint to damp paper, you create lines and shapes with soft edges.

b. If you apply wet paint to dry paper, you create lines and shapes with sharp, clear edges.

c. If you dip a dry brush into damp paint and then brush across dry paper, you achieve a fuzzy effect.

d. School watercolors come in semi-moist cakes. Before you use them, place a drop of water on each cake to let the paint soften. Watercolor paints are transparent. You can see the white paper through the paint. If you want a light value of a hue, dilute the paint with a large amount of water. If you want a bright hue, you must dissolve more pigment by swirling your brush around in the cake of paint until you have dissolved a great deal of paint. The paint you apply to the paper can be as bright as the paint in the cake.

13. Cleaning a Paint Brush

Rinsing a paint brush under running water will not clean it completely. Paint will remain inside the bristles and cause the brush to lose its shape. Use the following procedure to help your brushes last a long time.

a. Rinse the thick paint out of the brush under running water.

b. Do not use hot water. Gently "paint" the brush over a cake of mild soap or dip it into a mild liquid detergent (Figure T.10).

c. Gently scrub the brush in the palm of your hand to work the soap into the center of the brush. This will remove paint that you did not realize was still in the brush (Figure T.11).

d. Rinse the brush under running water while you continue to scrub your palm.

e. Repeat steps b, c, and d.

FIGURE T.10

FIGURE T.11

TECHNIQUE TIPS

FIGURE T.12

f. When your brush is thoroughly rinsed, shape it into a point with your fingers (Figure T.12).

g. Place the brush in a container with the bristles up so it will keep its shape as it dries.

PRINTMAKING TIP

14. Making a Stamp Print

A stamp print is an easy way to make repetitive designs. The following are a few suggestions for making a stamp and printing with it. You may develop some other ideas after reading these hints. Remember, printing reverses your design, so if you use letters, be certain to cut or carve them backward.

- Cut a simple design into the flat surface of a rubber eraser with a knife that has a fine, precision blade.
- Glue yarn to a bottle cap or a jar lid.
- Glue found objects to a piece of corrugated cardboard. Make a design with paperclips, washers, nuts, leaves, feathers, or anything else you can find. Whatever object you use should have a fairly flat surface. Make a handle for the block with masking tape.
- Cut shapes out of a piece of inner tube material. Glue the shapes to a piece of heavy cardboard.

There are several ways to apply ink or paint to a stamp:

- Roll water-base printing ink on the stamp with a soft brayer.
- Roll water-base printing ink on a plate and press the stamp into the ink.
- Apply tempera paint or school acrylic to the stamp with a bristle brush.

SCULPTING TIPS

15. Working with Clay

To make your work with clay go smoothly, always do the following:

a. Dip one or two fingers in water.

b. Spread the moisture from your fingers over your palms.

Never dip your hands in water. Too much moisture turns clay into mud.

16. Joining Clay

Use these methods for joining clay.

a. First, gather the materials you will need. These include clay, slip (a creamy mixture of clay and water), brush, a scoring tool (such as a fork), and clay tools.

b. Rough up or scratch the two surfaces to be joined (Figure T.13).

c. Apply slip to one of the two surfaces using a brush or your fingers (Figure T.14).

d. Gently press the two surfaces together so the slip oozes out of the joining seam (Figure T.15).

e. Using clay tools and/or your fingers, smooth away the slip that has oozed out of the seam (Figure T.16). You may wish to smooth out the seam as well,

FIGURE T.13

FIGURE T.14

FIGURE T.15

FIGURE T.16

or you may wish to leave it for decorative purposes.

17. Making a Pinch Pot

To make a pot using the pinch method, do the following:

a. Make a ball of clay by rolling it between your palms until it is round.

b. Set it on the working surface and make a hole in the top by pushing both thumbs into the clay. Stop pushing before your thumbs reach the bottom.

c. Begin to pinch the walls between your thumb and fingers, rotating the pot as you pinch.

d. Continue pinching and shaping the walls of the pot until they are an even thickness and the pot is the desired shape.

18. Using the Coil Technique

Collect all the materials you will need. These include clay, a cloth-covered board, slip and brush, scoring tool, small bowl of water, and pattern for a circular base.

a. Make a base by flattening a piece of clay to about ½ inch thick. Using the pattern as a guide, cut the base into a circle.

b. Begin a clay coil by shaping a small ball of clay into a long roll on the cloth-covered board until the roll is about ½ inch thick (Figure T.17). Your hands

FIGURE T.17

should be damp so the clay remains damp.

c. Make a circle around the edge of the clay base with the roll of clay. Cut the ends on a diagonal and join them so the seam does not show. Using scoring and slip, join this first coil to the base.

d. Make a second coil. If you want the pot to curve outward, place the second coil on the outer edge of the first coil. Place coil on the inner edge for an inward curve. Use proper joining techniques for all coils.

19. Papier-Mâché

Papier-mâché is a French term that means mashed paper. It refers to sculpting methods that use paper and liquid paste. The wet paper and paste material are molded over supporting structures such as a wad of dry paper or crumpled foil. The molded paper dries to a hard finish. The following are the three basic methods for working with papier-mâché.

Pulp Method

a. Shred newspaper, paper towels, or tissue paper into tiny pieces and soak them in water overnight. (Do not use slick magazine paper as it will not soften.)

b. Mash the paper in a strainer to remove the water or wring it out in a piece of cloth.

c. Mix the mashed paper with prepared paste or white glue until the material is the consistency of soft clay. Use the mixture to model small shapes.

d. When papier-mâché is dry, it can be sanded, and holes can be drilled through it.

Strip Method

a. Tear paper into strips.

b. Either dip the strips in a thick mixture of paste or rub paste on the strips with your fingers.

Decide which method works best for you.

c. Use wide strips to cover wide forms. Very thin strips will lie flat on a small shape.

d. If you do not want the finished work to stick to the support structure, first cover the form with plastic wrap or a layer of wet newspaper strips. If you are going to remove the papier-mâché from the support structure, you need to apply five or six layers of strips. Rub your fingers over the strips so that no rough edges are left sticking up (Figure T.18). Change directions with each layer so that you can keep track of the number. If you are going to leave the papier-mâché over the support structure, then two or three layers may be enough.

Sheet Method

a. Brush or spread paste on a sheet of newspaper or newsprint (Figure T.19). Lay a second

FIGURE T.18

FIGURE T.19

TECHNIQUE TIPS

sheet on top of the first and smooth out the layers. Add another layer of paste and another sheet of paper. Repeat this process until you have four or five layers of paper. This method is good for making drapery on a figure (Figure T.20).

b. If you let the layers dry for a day until they are leathery, they can be cut and molded any way you wish. Newspaper strips dipped in the paste can be used to seal any cracks that may occur.

Support Structures

a. Dry newspaper can be wadded up and wrapped with string or tape (Figure T.21).

b. Wire armatures can be padded with rags before the outside shell of papier-mâché is added.

c. Found materials such as boxes, tubes, and plastic bowls, can be arranged and

FIGURE T.21

taped together to form a base (Figure T.22).

d. For large figures, a wooden frame covered with chicken wire makes a good support. Push and pinch the wire into the shape you want.

FIGURE T.22

20. Making a Paper Sculpture

Another name for paper sculpture is origami. The process originated in Japan and means "folding paper." Paper sculpture begins with a flat piece of paper. The paper is then curved or bent to produce more than a flat surface. Here are some ways to experiment with paper.

- **Scoring.** Place a square sheet of heavy construction paper on a flat surface. Position the ruler on the paper so that it is close to the center and parallel to the sides. Holding the ruler in place, run the point of a knife or a pair of scissors along one of the ruler's edges. Press down firmly but take care not to cut through the paper. Gently crease the paper along the line you made. Hold your paper with the crease facing upward. You can also score curved lines, but you must do this with gradually bending curves or wide arcs. If you try to make a tight curve, such as a semicircle, the paper will not give. For a tight curve you will have to make cuts to relieve the tension.

- **Pleating.** Take a piece of paper and fold it 1 inch from the edge. Then fold the paper in the other direction. Continue folding back and forth.

- **Curling.** Hold one end of a long strip of paper with the thumb and forefinger of one hand. At a point right below where you are holding the strip, grip it lightly between the side of a pencil and the thumb of your other hand. In a quick motion, run the pencil along the strip. This will cause the strip to curl back on itself. Don't apply too much pressure, or the strip will tear. (See Figure T.20.)

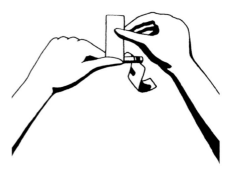

FIGURE T.20

21. Making Paper

Papermaking is a process in which fibers are broken down and reformed as a sheet. In order to make paper, collect all the materials you will need. These include a food blender, two matching stretcher frames approximately 9 x 12 inches each, rustproof window screen slightly larger than the stretchers, staple gun, duct tape, Handi Wipes towels, large pan 5 to 8 inches deep, newspapers, assorted papers, and water.

a. Make the mold by stretching the screen over the frame, stapling it at the edges, and covering the rough edges with duct tape. The second frame is the deckle, the frame that keeps the pulp in place on the mold.

b. Tear paper into 1-inch squares. Put 4 cups water and ½ cup paper scraps into the blender and blend for several minutes until the mixture is the consistency of watery cooked oatmeal.

c. Pour pulp into pan. Continue making pulp until there is about 4 inches of pulp in the pan. Additional water may be added to aid in the papermaking process.

d. Make a pad of newspapers ¼ inch thick. Unfold Handi Wipes towels and lay one on the pad; this is the blotter.

e. Align deckle on top of mold. Stir pulp to suspend paper fibers. Scoop mold and deckle under surface of water and shake to align fibers. Lift to drain excess water.

f. Remove the deckle and flip the mold and pulp onto the blotter, pulp side down against the Handi Wipes towel. Blot back of molds with a sponge to remove excess water and to compress the fibers. Remove the mold, using a rocking motion.

g. Lay another Handi Wipes towel on top of the sheet of paper and add more newspapers. Repeat the layering process.

h. Let paper dry slowly for 1–3 days. When dry, peel off the Handi Wipes.

i. To clean up, drain pulp through the mold or a sieve. Squeeze excess water from pulp and save pulp in a plastic bag for one to three days or discard it.

22. Basic Embroidery Stitches
The charts below and on the next page show the most common embroidery stitches.

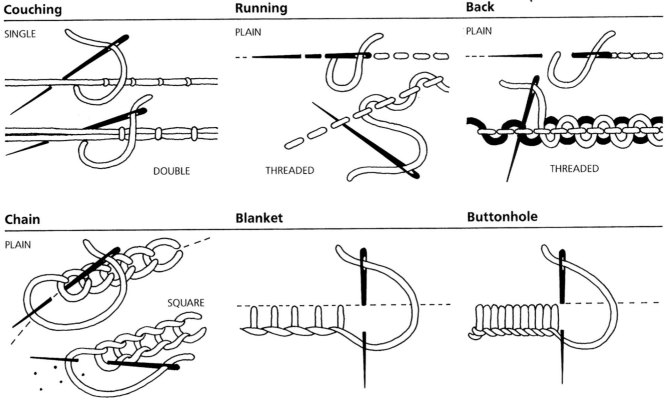

Couching	Running	Back
SINGLE	PLAIN	PLAIN
DOUBLE	THREADED	THREADED

Chain	Blanket	Buttonhole
PLAIN		
SQUARE		

FIGURE T.24

TECHNIQUE TIPS

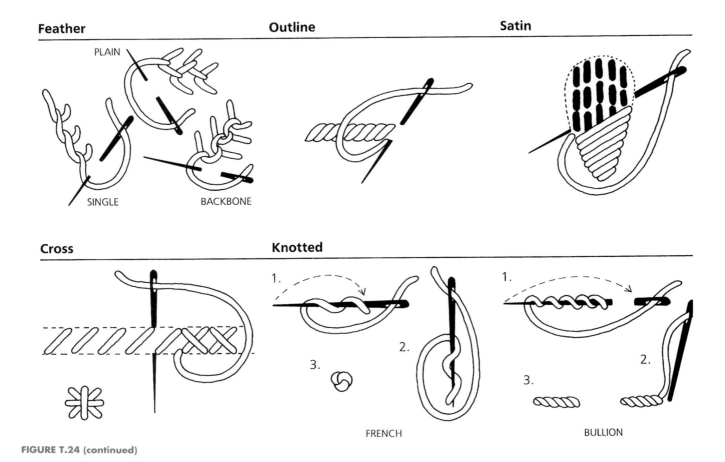

Feather

PLAIN

SINGLE   BACKBONE

Outline

Satin

Cross

Knotted

1.

2.

3.

FRENCH

1.

2.

3.

BULLION

FIGURE T.24 (continued)

23. Weaving Techniques

To make a cardboard loom, gather the materials you will need. They include cardboard, ruler, pencil, scissors, strong, thin yarn for warp, various yarns and fibers for weft, tapestry needle, comb, and dowel.

a. Measure and cut notches ¼ inch apart and ½ inch deep on opposite sides of the cardboard.

b. Tape warp thread to back of loom. Bring it to the front through the top left notch. Pull it down to the bottom of the loom and pass it through the bottom left notch to the back. Move one notch to the right and continue until you reach

the last notch. Then tape the end of the warp thread to the back. (Figure T.25)

c. Start to weave at the bottom of the loom, using a thin yarn. The weft yarns are the horizontal yarns; the easiest way to pull the weft yarn through the warp

threads is to use an over-one-under-one motion. At the end of the row, reverse directions. (Figure T.26)

d. Do not pull the weft threads too tight. Let them balloon, or curve slightly upward (Figure T.27).

FIGURE T.25

FIGURE T.26

FIGURE T.27

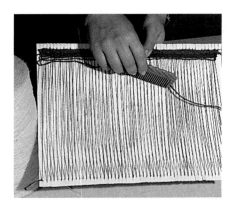

FIGURE T.28

e. After weaving several rows, pack the weft threads with a comb (Figure T.28). The tighter the weave, the stronger it will be.

f. After there is about 1 inch of tight weave, begin varying weave and materials (Figure T.29). End the process with another inch of thin, tight weave.

g. Before removing the fabric from the loom, weave in the loose ends. Cut the warp threads from the loom carefully and tie two at a time so they will not unravel.

h. Tie or sew the finished fabric to a dowel.

FIGURE T.29

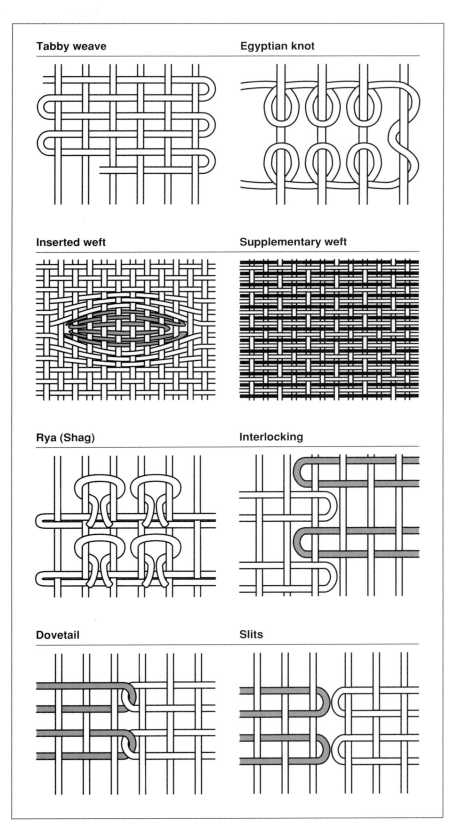

Tabby weave

Egyptian knot

Inserted weft

Supplementary weft

Rya (Shag)

Interlocking

Dovetail

Slits

TECHNIQUE TIPS

24. Making a Coiled Basket

Mastering the technique of making a coiled basket takes practice. You will need *core* material (such as heavy cord), weft wrapping materials (such as yarns and fibers), a tapestry needle, scissors, and tape.

Coiling is a stitching technique in which the continuous coils of the *core* material are stitched together with a binding material called the *weft*. The first time you try this your binding and stitches probably will not look neat. Undo the work and begin again. You want to cover the core material completely, and all your weft binding and stitches must be even and tight.

a. Trim the end of the core so it tapers. Thread the tapestry needle with a 3-foot length of weft. Using the loose weft end, begin to wind it around the core starting about 2 inches from the end. Overlap the end as you wind to anchor it. Wind the weft to about 1/2 inch from the tapered end of the core (Figure T.30).

b. Bend the core, catch the tapered end, and make a loop (Figure T.31).

c. Continue winding for about 2 inches, being sure that the tapered core is attached securely to the solid section of core material. Push the tapestry needle through the center of the loop (Figure T.32).

d. Bend the core to form a coil and bring the weft between the core and the coil. (Figure T.33) Begin winding the weft around the core from front to back. You are now ready to begin the Lazy Squaw stitch.

e. Wind the weft around the core from front to back four times. Then, bringing the weft from behind and over the core, push the needle into the center of the coil (Figure T.34). Pull tightly and hold. Continue to wrap the weft four times around the core and pull the fifth stitch into the center until you complete two coils. Hold them flat between your fingers while you work.

f. As the coiling progresses, you may wrap the weft more than four times between stitches. After the first two coils, you will no longer bring the stitch back to the center; just take it over two coils (Figure T.35). Always insert the needle from the front. This way you can see exactly where you are placing the needle. If you want to create a pattern of long stitches, this is essential.

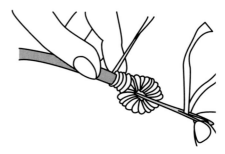

FIGURE T.32

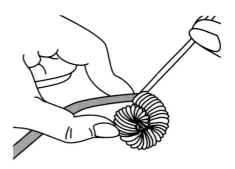

FIGURE T.33

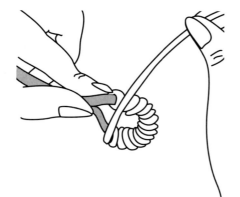

FIGURE T.30

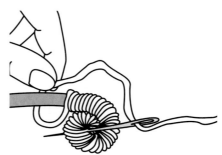

FIGURE T.34

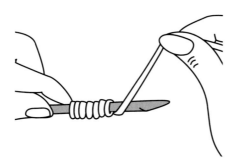

FIGURE T.31

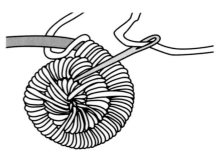

FIGURE T.35

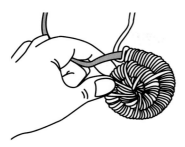

FIGURE T.36

g. Hold the coil with your left hand with the core material coming from the left, and wind the weft with your right hand so you do not tangle it with the core (Figure T.36). If you are left-handed, reverse the process. Always pull the weft very tight.

h. You will need to splice, or invisibly join, the ends of separate materials. To splice the core, taper the cut on the old and the new piece. Before working the weft, secure the spliced ends of the core by wrapping them with sewing thread or tape. Always hold the spliced area carefully until it is wrapped with the weft. Splice the weft during the wrapping, not during the stitching. Hold the tail ends of the old and the new weft together against the core as shown in Figure T.37. Wrap the new weft at least once before making a long stitch.

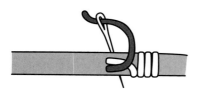

FIGURE T.37

i. When the base is the desired size, it is time to begin making the sides of the basket. If the side is to be perpendicular to the base, lay the first foundation coil directly on top of the last coil. If you want the basket to curve outward, place each new coil on the outer edge of the one below. To make an inward curve, place each coil on the inner edge of the previous coil. Use pressure from the nonstitching hand to keep the coils in place.

j. The best way to finish the basket is to taper the core and make several stitches around the last coil and the tapered coil. Then run the needle back through the wrapping stitches for about an inch and pull the weft thread through. Cut off the excess weft.

k. If you want to make a handle, simply wrap the end of the core until it is as long as you wish.

Then attach it to the other side of the top of the basket following the instructions from Step j.

25. Making a Tissue Paper Collage

For your first experience with tissue, make a free design with the tissue colors. Start with the lightest colors of tissue first and save the darkest for last. It is difficult to change the color of dark tissue by overlapping it with other colors. If one area becomes too dark, you might cut out a piece of white paper, glue it over the dark area carefully, and apply new colors over the white area.

a. Apply a coat of adhesive to the area where you wish to place the tissue.

b. Place the tissue down carefully over the wet area (Figure T.38). Don't let your fingers get wet.

c. Then add another coat of adhesive over the tissue. If your brush picks up any color from the wet tissue, rinse your brush

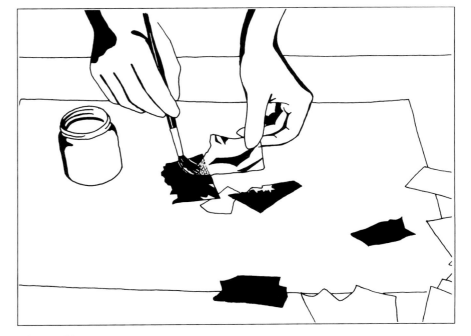

FIGURE T.38

TECHNIQUE TIPS

in water and let it dry before using it again.

d. Experiment by overlapping colors. Allow the tissue to wrinkle to create textures as you apply it. Be sure that all the loose edges of tissue are glued down.

DISPLAY TIPS

26. Making a Mat

You can add appeal to an artwork by making a mat, using the following steps.

a. Gather the materials you will need. These include a metal rule, a pencil, mat board, cardboard backing, a sheet of heavy cardboard to protect your work surface, a mat knife with a sharp blade, and wide masking tape.

b. Wash your hands. Mat board should be kept very clean.

c. Measure the height and width of the work to be matted. Decide how large a border you want for your work. (A border of approximately $2\frac{1}{2}$ inches on three sides with 3 inches on the bottom is aesthetically pleasing.) Your work will be behind the window you will cut.

d. Plan for the opening, or window, to be $\frac{1}{4}$ inch smaller on all sides than the size of your work. For example, if your work measures 9 by 12 inches, the mat window should measure $8\frac{1}{2}$ inches (9 inches minus $\frac{1}{4}$ inch times two) by $11\frac{1}{2}$ inches (12 inches minus $\frac{1}{4}$ inch times two.) Using your metal rule and pencil, lightly draw your window rectangle on the back of the board $2\frac{1}{2}$ inches from the top and left edge of the mat. (See Figure T.39). Add a $2\frac{1}{2}$-inch border to the right of the

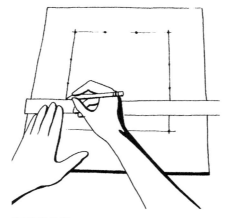

FIGURE T.39

window and a 3-inch border to the bottom, lightly drawing cutting guidelines.

Note: If you are working with metric measurements, the window should overlap your work by 0.5 cm (centimeters) on all sides. Therefore, if your work measures 24 by 30 cm, the mat window measures 23 cm (24−[2 x 0.5]) by 29 cm (30 − [2 × 0.5]).

e. Place the sheet of heavy, protective cardboard on your work surface. Place the mat board, pencil marks up, over the cardboard. Holding the metal rule firmly in place, score the first line with your knife. Always place the metal rule so that your blade is on the inside of the frame. (See Figure T.40.) In case you make an error you will cut into the window hole or the extra mat that is not used for the frame. Do not try to cut through the board with one stroke. By the third or fourth stroke, you should be able to cut through the board easily.

f. Working in the same fashion, score and cut through the board along all the window lines. Be careful not to go beyond the lines. Remove the window.

g. Cut a cardboard backing for your artwork that is slightly smaller than the overall size of your mat. Using a piece of broad masking tape, hinge the back of the mat to the backing. (See Figure T.41.) Position your artwork between the backing and the mat and attach it with tape. Anchor the frame to the cardboard with a few pieces of rolled tape.

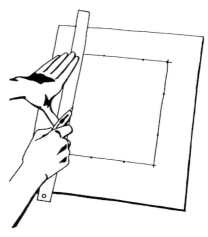

FIGURE T.40

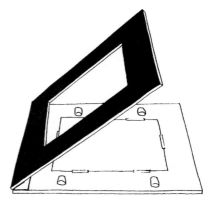

FIGURE T.41

27. Mounting a Two-Dimensional Work

Mounting pictures that you make gives them a professional look. To mount a work, do the following:

a. Gather the materials you will need. These include a yardstick, a pencil, poster board, a knife with a very sharp blade, a sheet of newspaper, and rubber cement.

b. Measure the height and width of the work to be mounted. Decide how large a border you want around the work. Plan your mount size using the work's measurements. To end up with a 3-inch border, for example, make your mount 6 inches wider and higher than your work. Record the measurements for your mount.

c. Using your yardstick and pencil, lightly draw your mount rectangle on the back of the poster board. Measure from the edges of the poster board. If you have a large paper cutter available, you may use it to cut your mount.

d. Place the sheet of heavy cardboard on your work surface. Place the poster board, pencil marks up, over the cardboard. Holding the yardstick firmly in place along one line, score the line with your knife. Do not try to cut through the board with one stroke. By the third try, you should be able to cut through the board.

e. Place the artwork on the mount. Using the yardstick, center the work. Mark each corner with a dot. (See Figure T.42)

FIGURE T.42

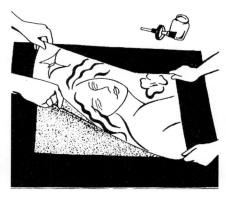

FIGURE T.43

f. Place the artwork, face down, on a sheet of newspaper. Coat the back of the work with rubber cement. (Safety Note: Always use rubber cement in a room with plenty of ventilation.) If your mount is to be permanent, skip to Step h.

g. Line up the corners of your work with the dots on the mounting board. Smooth the work into place. Skip to Step i.

h. After coating the back of your artwork, coat the poster board with rubber cement. Be careful not to add cement to the border area. Have a partner hold your artwork in the air by the two top corners. Once the two glued surfaces meet, you will not be able to change the position of the work. Grasp the lower two corners. Carefully lower the work to the mounting board. Line up the two corners with the bottom dots. Little by little, lower the work into place (Figure T.43). Press it smooth.

i. To remove any excess cement, create a small ball of dry rubber cement. Use the ball of rubber cement to pick up excess cement.

28. Working with Glue

When applying glue, always start at the center of the surface you are coating and work outward.

- When gluing papers together don't use a lot of glue, just a dot will do. Use dots in the corners and along the edges. Press the two surfaces together. Keep dots at least $\frac{1}{2}$ inch in from the edge of your paper.

- Handle a glued surface carefully with only your fingertips. Make sure your hands are clean before pressing the glued surface into place.

- Note: The glue should be as thin as possible. Thick or beaded glue will create ridges on your work.

SAFETY IN THE ART ROOM

Many artists, both students and teachers, come into daily contact with dangerous, possibly deadly materials. The unfortunate truth is that many art supplies contain high levels of chemicals, such as hexane, lead, toluene, and asbestos, and many people are unaware of the danger that these substances pose, both to art students and to teachers. In fact, the danger to art teachers, who are often exposed to toxins for several hours a day for many years, is often greater than to the students. Therefore, it is essential that all art teachers and students become aware of the potential hazards in using art materials.

Many art supplies contain materials that can cause acute illness (that is, a severe sudden illness that can be caused by a single exposure to a toxic substance and result in permanent disability or death). Long-term exposure to materials in many other art supplies can cause chronic illness (which develops gradually after repeated exposure) or cancer. Other chemicals in art supplies are sensitizers, causing allergies, particularly in children. Lead, for example, is acutely toxic and can be found in such commonly used supplies as stencil paint, oil paint, some acrylics, gessoes, ceramic glazes, copper enamels, and automotive paint in spray cans. Many highly toxic hydrocarbon-based solvents, including methyl alcohol, are used in school art programs. Other widely used art materials, such as preservatives, formaldehyde, epoxy glues, and dichromates, can contain dangerous chemicals like cadmium, nickel, silica, and pesticides.

There are three ways in which such chemicals can enter the body: absorption, inhalation, and ingestion. They can be absorbed through the skin from cuts or scrapes, resulting in burns or rashes, or into the bloodstream, moving to and damaging other parts of the body. Chemical irritants can be inhaled, causing lung problems like bronchitis and emphysema. Inhaling small particles, like the free silica in clay dust, can cause pulmonary fibrosis or asthma. Chemicals can be ingested through touching the mouth with the hands or fingers while working with supplies or unconsciously placing tools like paint brushes in or near the mouth. Since hazardous substances can easily enter the body, it is extremely important to make sure that the materials used are safe and are that they are used safely.

Labeling

Labeling can provide information on any potentially dangerous art supplies, but teachers need to be aware of what various labels mean. The label *nontoxic,* for example, does not guarantee a product's safety. According to federal regulations, toxicity means that a single exposure can be fatal to adults. The effect on young people, who are more likely to be harmed by dangerous substances, is not considered in this definition. Also, the chance of developing chronic or long-term illnesses is not addressed by the legal definition of toxicity. Repeated exposure to nontoxic materials is not always safe. Many dangerous substances, such as asbestos, can legally be defined as nontoxic. Also, some art supplies, particularly those manufactured by small or foreign companies, may be improperly labeled as nontoxic.

Not all products whose labels provide chemical components, but have no warnings or list no information at all, are safe to use. Since manufacturers are not required to disclose ingredients, products without this information or warnings are potentially hazardous.

For more complete information on the presence of hazardous substances in art supplies, teachers may request a Material Safety Data Sheet (OSHA Form 20) from the manufacturer. This sheet provides information on potential heath and fire hazards, a list of chemicals that might react dangerously with the product, and a list of all ingredients for which industrial standards exist. The manufacturer should supply this sheet on request, and a local public health official or poison control center technician can help interpret the information.

Art teachers can also take advantage of voluntary labeling standards developed by the art materials industry. The Art and Craft Materials Institute (ACMI) administers a voluntary testing and labeling program that helps to insure the safety of those who work with art materials. This system uses the labels CP, AP, and HL.

CP (Certified Product) and AP (Approved Product) labels are used mainly on products designed for younger children, while HL (Health Label) is used on products intended for older students and adults. Products labeled CP, AP, or HL (Nontoxic) are certified in a program of toxicological evaluation by a medical expert to contain no materials in sufficient quantities to be toxic or injurious to humans or to cause acute or chronic health problems. Products labeled CP, in addition, meet specific requirements of material, workmanship, working qualities, and color. HL (Cautions Required) means that the product is certified to be properly labeled in a program of toxicological evaluation by a medical expert. The Art and Craft Materials Institute makes available a list of institute-certified products. For a copy, or for more information on the institute's certification program, teachers can write to:

The Art and Craft Materials Institute
715 Boylston St.
Boston, MA 02116

Safety Rules

There are certain guidelines to be followed in selecting and using art supplies. Perhaps the most important is to know what the materials are made of and what potential hazards exist. If a material is improperly labeled, or if adequate information cannot be obtained about it, don't use it. The following rules are also helpful:

- Be sure that all materials used by younger students (ages 12 and under) have the CP or AP label and that materials used by older students and adults are marked HL.

- Don't use acids, alkalies, bleaches, or any product that will stain skin or clothing.

- Don't use aerosol cans because the spray can injure lungs.

- Use dust-producing materials (such as pastels, clays, plasters, chalks, powdered tempera, pigments, dyes, and instant papier-mâché, except the premixed cellulose type) with care in a well-ventilated area (or better yet, don't use them at all).

- Don't use solvents (including lacquers, paint thinners, turpentines, shellacs, solvent-based inks, rubber cement, and permanent markers) in the art room.

- Don't use found or donated materials unless the ingredients are known.

- Don't use old materials. Many art supplies formerly contained highly dangerous substances, such as arsenic, or raw lead compounds, or high levels of asbestos. Older solvents may contain chloroform or carbon tetrachloride.

Working conditions in the art room also affect safety. A disorderly art room leads to unsafe conditions, particularly when there are many people working close to each other. Controlling the buildup of litter and dust, insuring that tools are in good condition, and keeping workspace reasonably organized not only help prevent common accidents but also make it easier to recognize and eliminate other hazards. An orderly art room is absolutely essential to the students' and teacher's safety.

ARTISTS AND THEIR WORKS

This section contains an alphabetical list of the professional artists whose works appear in *ArtTalk*. Following each name is the nationality of the artist, birth or birth and death dates, artistic category, and the title and page reference for each work.

A

Abbot, Berenice, American, b. 1898, photographer
Façade, Alwyn Court, 129, Fig. 6.17

Albers, Josef, German, 1888–1976, painter
Homage to the Square: Glow, 265, Fig. 10.26

Albright, Ivan, American, 1897–1983, painter
The Farmer's Kitchen, 200, Fig. 8.16

Andrews, Benny, African-American, b. 1930, painter, printmaker
The Scholar, 101, Fig. 5.28

Apel, Marie, English, 1880–1970, sculptor
Grief, 141, Fig. 6.38

Arp, Jean (Hans), French, 1887–1966, painter, sculptor
Aquatique, 123, Fig. 6.9

B

Bak, Brunislaw M., American (born in Poland), 1922–1981, painter
Holocaust, 156, Fig. 7.3
Interpenetrations in Red, 316, Fig. 12.4

Bak, Hedi, American (born in Germany), b. 1924, painter
Grand Canyon #2, 194, Fig. 8.4

Balla, Giocomo, Italian, 1871–1958, painter
Dynamism of a Dog on a Leash, 236, Fig. 9.24
Street Light, 234, Fig. 9.20

Barlach, Ernst, German, 1870–1938, painter, sculptor
Singing Man, 328, Fig. 12.19

Bayless, Florence, American, b. 1922, craftsperson
Haori Coat, 326, Fig. 12.16

Bearden, Romare, African-American, 1914–1989, painter
Prevalence of Ritual: Baptism, 178, Fig. 7.37

Beaux, Cecilia, American, 1863–1942, painter
Ernesta (Child with Nurse), 322, Fig. 12.11

Benton, Thomas Hart, American, 1882–1975, painter
I Got a Girl on Sourwood Mountain, 98, Fig. 5.23
The Sources of Country Music, 61, Fig. 3.29

Bernini, Gianlorenzo, Italian, 1598–1680, sculptor
David, 277, Fig. 10.36

Bishop, Isabel, American, 1902–1988, painter
Two Girls, 292, Fig. 11.20
Waiting, 308, Fig. 11.36

Bonheur, Rosa, French, 1822–1899, painter
The Horse Fair, 224, Fig. 9.4

Botero, Fernando, Colombian, b. 1932, painter
The Pinzon Family, 302, Fig. 11.33

Botticelli, Sandro, Italian, 1445–1510, painter
The Adoration of the Magi, 135, Fig. 6.25

Brancusi, Constantin, Romanian, 1876–1957, sculptor
Torso of a Young Man, 140, Fig. 6.36

Burchfield, Charles, American, 1893–1967, painter
October Wind and Sunlight in the Woods, 223, Fig. 9.3

C

Calder, Alexander, American, 1898–1976, sculptor
Lobster Trap and Fish Tail, 237, Fig. 9.26
Varese, 108, Fig. 5.36

Carpenter, Miles Burkholder, American, 1889–1985, craftsperson, sculptor
Root Monster, 184, Fig. 7.40

Carr, Emily, Canadian, 1871–1945, painter
Above the Trees, 170, Fig. 7.27
Forest, British Columbia, 328, Fig. 12.18

Cassatt, Mary, American, 1845–1926, painter
Baby Reaching for an Apple, 24, Fig. 2.1
Five O'Clock Tea, 270, Fig. 10.32

Catlett, Elizabeth, African-American, b. 1915, printmaker, sculptor, painter
Sharecropper, 13, Fig. 1.9

Catlin, George, American, 1796–1872, painter
See-non-ty-a, an Iowa Medicine Man, 294, Fig. 11.23

Cézanne, Paul, French, 1839–1906, painter
Le Chateau Noir, 56, Fig. 3.23

Chagall, Marc, Russian, 1887–1985, painter
Birthday, 298, Fig. 11.28

Church, Frederic Edwin, American, 1826–1900, painter
Our Banner in the Sky, 267, Fig. 10.30

Clements, Bob, American, b. 1937, sculptor
Evening Up the Score, 263, Fig. 10.24

Clive, Carolyn, American, b. 1931, painter
Amplitude, 110, Fig. 5.37

Close, Chuck, American, b. 1940, painter
Janet, 246, Fig. 9.31

Copley, John Singleton, American, 1737–1815, painter
Paul Revere, 294, Fig. 11.22

Courtney-Clarke, Margaret, English, b. 1949, photojournalist
photo from *African Canvas,* 172, Fig. 7.30

Curnoe, Greg, Canadian, 1936–1992, painter
Mariposa 10 Speed, 96, Fig. 5.18
Curry, John Steuart, American, 1897–1946, painter
Baptism in Kansas, 321, Fig. 12.10

D

Dali, Salvador, Spanish, 1904–1989, painter
The Persistence of Memory, 60, Fig. 3.28
David, Jacques Louis, French, 1748–1825, painter
Death of Socrates, 115, Fig. 5.40
da Vinci, Leonardo. See Leonardo da Vinci
de Amaral, Olga, Colombian, b. 1937, fiber artist
Alquimia XIII, 203, Fig. 8.22
Degas, Edgar, French, 1834–1917, painter
Little Fourteen-Year-Old Dancer, 203, Fig. 8.21
The Millinery Shop, 323, Fig. 12.12
Dick, Beau, Canadian Native American, b. 1955, printmaker
Sacred Circles, 272, Fig. 10.33
Dillon, Leo and Diane, American, both b. 1933, graphic artists
A Wrinkle in Time cover illustration, 82, Fig. 4.13
Dodd, Lamar, American, b. 1909, painter
Night Before Launch, 19, Fig. 1.17
Dürer, Albrecht, German, 1471–1528, painter, printmaker
An Oriental Ruler Seated on His Throne, 134, Fig. 6.23
Virgin and Child with Saint Anne, 293, Fig. 11.21
Dvorak, Lois, American, 1934–1993, mixed media
The Lizards, 318, Fig. 12.6
Spirit Boxes I, 334, Fig. 12.27

E

Eakins, Thomas, American, 1844–1916, painter
Baby at Play, 257, Fig. 10.15
Baseball Players Practicing, 55, Fig. 3.21
Epstein, Sir Jacob, English (b. New York City), 1880–1959, sculptor
The Visitation, 28, Fig. 2.4
Ernst, Max, German (in America after 1941), 1891–1976, painter
The Eye of Silence, 206, Fig. 8.27
Escher, M. C., Dutch, 1898–1972, printmaker
Other World, 127, Fig. 6.13
Escobar, Marisol. See Marisol

F

Fernandes, Julio, American, b. date unknown, painter
Apollo 11, 19, Fig. 1.16
Fish, Janet I., American, b. 1939, painter
Fallen Vase, 7, Fig. 1.2
Jonathan and Lorraine, 198, Fig. 8.13

Fontana, Lavinia, Italian, 1552–1614, painter
Portrait of a Noblewoman, 125, Fig. 6.11
Fragonard, Jean-Honoré, French, 1732–1806, painter
A Game of Hot Cockles, 260, Fig. 10.19
Franklin, Ben, American, 1706–1790, statesman, philosopher
Join or Die, 324, Fig. 12.13

G

Garcia, Rupert, American, b. 1941, painter
Political Prisoner, 126, Fig. 6.12
Garrison, Elizabeth, American, b. 1914, quilter
Long May Our Land Be Bright, 256, Fig. 10.13
Gauguin, Paul, French, 1848–1903, painter
Faaturuma (The Dreamer), 154, Fig. 7.1
Ghiberti, Lorenzo, Italian, 1378–1455, sculptor
Gates of Paradise, 37, Fig. 2.10
Giorgione, Italian, 1477–1511, painter
The Adoration of the Shepherds, 261, Fig. 10.20
Giotto di Bondone, Italian, c. 1266–1337, painter
Madonna and Child, 133, Fig. 6.22
Glarner, Fritz, American (born in Switzerland), 1899–1972, painter
Relational Painting #93, 168, Fig. 7.23
Goya, Francisco, Spanish, 1746–1828, painter
The Third of May, 1808, 83, Fig. 4.14
Graves, Nancy Stevenson, b. 1940, sculptor
Rheo, 26, Fig. 2.2
Zaga, 17, Fig. 1.13
Gris, Juan, Spanish, 1887–1927, painter
Guitar and Flowers, 332, Fig. 12.24
Grünewald, Matthias, German, c. 1470/80–1528, painter
The Small Crucifixion, 295, Fig. 11.24
Gu Mei, Chinese, 17th century, painter
Orchids and Rocks, 104, Fig. 5.32

H

Hampton, James, African-American, 1909–1965, sculptor
The Throne of the Third Heaven of the Nations' Millennium General Assembly, 208, Fig. 8.28
Hanson, Duane, American, b. 1925, sculptor, painter
Traveler with Sunburn, 65, Fig. 3.33
Harrison, Wallace Kirkman, American, b. 1895, architect
United Nations Buildings, 128, Fig. 6.14
Hartley, Marsden, American, 1877–1943, painter
Blueberry Highway, Dogtown, 165, Fig. 7.18
Hassam, Childe, American, 1859–1935, painter, printmaker
Jelly Fish, 177, Fig. 7.36
Haverman, Margareta, Dutch, 1693–1750, painter
A Vase of Flowers, 31, Fig. 2.6
Hayden, Palmer, African-American, 1890–1973, painter
The Janitor Who Paints, 40, Fig. 3.1

Hepworth, Barbara, English, 1903–1975, sculptor
Figure for Landscape, 128, Fig. 6.15
Hiroshige, Andō, Japanese, 1797–1858, printmaker
Evening Rain on the Karasaki Pine, 48, Fig. 3.11
Hofmann, Hans, German (born in America), 1880–1966,
painter
Flowering Swamp, 64, Fig. 3.32
Hokusai, Katsushika, Japanese, 1760–1849, printmaker
The Great Wave off Kanagawa, 262, Fig. 10.22
Homer, Winslow, American, 1836–1910, painter
Hound and Hunter, 12, Fig. 1.8
Sketch for Hound and Hunter, 12, Fig. 1.7
Hoover, John, Native American, Aleut, b. 1919, sculptor
Loon Song, 202, Fig. 8.20
Hopper, Edward, American, 1882–1967, painter
Early Sunday Morning, 98, Fig. 5.22
First Row Orchestra, 258, Fig. 10.16
Houser, Allan, Native American, b. 1914, sculptor
Coming of Age, 233, Fig. 9.19
Hua Yen, Chinese, c. 1682–1765
Conversation in Autumn, 47, Fig. 3.10
Hunt, Henry, Canadian Native American, Kwakiutl,
1923–1985, sculptor
K'umugwe' (Komokwa) Mask, 304, Fig. 11.34
Huntington, Anna Hyatt, American, 1876–1973, sculptor
Riders to the Sea, 142, Fig. 6.39

J

Jacquette, Yvonne, American, b. 1934, painter
East River Drive, 93, Fig. 5.6
Town of Skowhegan, Maine V, 312, Fig. 12.1
Jessup, Georgia Mills, American, b. 1926, painter
Rainy Night, Downtown, 331, Fig. 12.23
Jimenez, Luis, American, b. 1940, sculptor
Vaquero, 16, Fig. 1.12
Johns, Jasper, American, b. 1930, painter
Cups 4 Picasso, 124, Fig. 6.10
Map, 327, Fig. 12.17
Johnson, Philip, American, b. 1906, architect
Johnson House, 141, Fig. 6.37
Johnson, William H., African-American, 1901–1970, painter
Jitterbugs IV, 112, Fig. 5.38

K

Kahlo, Frida, Mexican, 1907–1954, painter
Frida and Diego Rivera, 259, Fig. 10.17
Self-Portrait Dedicated to Leon Trotsky, 264, Fig. 10.25
Keyser, Louisa (Dat So La Lee), Native American,
1850–1925, weaver
Basket, 244, Fig. 9.30
Kingman, Dong, American, b. 1911, painter
Higher, Faster, and Farther, 19, Fig. 1.15
Kollwitz, Käthe, German, 1867–1945, painter, printmaker,
graphic artist
Self-Portrait, 58, Fig. 3.26

L

Lachaise, Gaston, French, 1882–1935, sculptor
Walking Woman, 298, Fig. 11.29
Lange, Dorothea, American, 1895–1965, photojournalist
Migrant Mother, 15, Fig. 1.11
Larraz, Julio, Cuban, b. 1944, painter
Papiamento, 8, Fig. 1.3
Lawrence, Jacob, African-American, b. 1917, painter
Parade, 238, Fig. 9.27
Study for the Munich Olympic Games Poster, 114,
Fig. 5.39
Le Corbusier, Swiss, 1887–1965, architect
Chapelle Notre-Dame-du-Haut, 285, Fig. 11.9
Lee, Doris, American, b. 1905, printmaker, painter
Thanksgiving, 138, Fig. 6.33
Leonardo da Vinci, Italian, 1452–1519, painter, sculptor
Ginevra de' Benci, 67, Fig. 3.36
page from his sketchbook showing movement of water,
9, Fig. 1.5
Leyster, Judith, Dutch, 1609–1660, painter
Self-Portrait, 54, Fig. 3.20
Lichtenstein, Roy, American, b. 1923, painter
Blam, 336, Fig. 12.28
Loewy, Raymond, American (born in France), b. 1893,
designer
Avanti, 74, Fig. 4.4

M

McKelvey, Lucy Leuppe, Native American, b. date
unknown, ceramicist
Whirling Rainbow Goddesses, 237, Fig. 9.25
Magritte, René, Belgian, 1898–1967, painter
The Blank Signature, 148, Fig. 6.46
Marc, Franz, German, 1880–1916, painter
The Large Blue Horses, 175, Fig. 7.34
Marisol, Venezuelan (in America since 1950), b. 1930,
sculptor
Poor Family I, 118, Fig. 6.1
Marsh, Reginald, American, 1898–1954, painter
Why Not Use the El?, 284, Fig. 11.7
Martinez, Maria and Julian, Native American, Maria:
c. 1885–1980; Julian: c. 1885–1943, ceramicists
Black-on-black storage jar, 274, Fig. 10.34
Matisse, Henri, French, 1869–1954, painter
Beasts of the Sea, 132, Fig. 6.21
Michelangelo Buonarroti, Italian, 1475–1564, sculptor,
painter
Pietà, 52, 309, Figs. 3.16, 11.37
Mitchell, Joan, American, 1926–1992, painter
Dirty Snow, 205, Fig. 8.25
Miyawaki, Ayako, Japanese, b. 1905, appliqué artist
The Red Crab, 212, Fig. 8.30
Mondrian, Piet, Dutch, 1872–1944, painter
Broadway Boogie Woogie, 176, Fig. 7.35

Monet, Claude, French, 1840–1926, painter
    Ice Floes, 161, Fig. 7.12
    Palazzo da Mula, Venice, 56, Fig. 3.22
    Poplars, 173, 174, Figs. 7.32, 7.33
Montata, Native American, b. date unknown, beadwork
    Blackfeet Man's Leggings, 121, Fig. 6.5
Moore, Henry, English, 1898–1986, sculptor
    Family Group, 20, Fig. 1.18
    Reclining Mother and Child, 142, Fig. 6.40
Morisot, Berthe, French, 1841–1895, painter
    In the Dining Room, 320, Fig. 12.9
Munch, Edvard, Norwegian, 1863–1944, painter, printmaker
    The Kiss, 296, Fig. 11.26
Murray, Elizabeth, American, b. 1940, painter
    Things to Come, 186, Fig. 7.41
Musawwir, 'Abd Allah, Islamic, 16th century, painter
    The Meeting of the Theologians, 240, Fig. 9.28
Myron, Greek, c. 480–440 B.C., sculptor
    Discobolus, 49, Fig. 3.12

N

Namingha, Dan, Native American, b. 1950, painter
    Blessing Rain Chant, 97, Fig. 5.21
Naranjo, Michael, Native American, b. 1944, sculptor
    Spirits Soaring, 150, Fig. 6.47
Neel, Alice, American, 1900–1984, painter
    Loneliness, 319, Fig. 12.8
    Marisol, 42, Fig. 3.2
Nevelson, Louise, American, 1899–1988, sculptor
    Dawn, 36, Fig. 2.9
    Dawn's Wedding Chapel, 329, Fig. 12.20
Nizami (author). Artist unknown, Persian, c. 1524–25
    Kamseh: Bahram Gur and the Chinese Princess in the Sandalwood Pavilion on Thursday, 52, Fig. 3.17

O

O'Keeffe, Georgia, American, 1887–1986, painter
    Cow's Skull, 266, Fig. 10.28
Oldenburg, Claes, American, b. 1929, painter, sculptor
    Shoestring Potatoes Spilling from a Bag, 286, Fig. 11.10
Olmstead, Frederick Law, American, 1822–1903, landscape architect
    Central Park, 77, Fig. 4.8
Orozco, José Clemente, Mexican, 1883–1949, painter
    Barricade, 62, Fig. 3.31

P

Pereira, Irene Rice, American, 1907–1971, painter
    Untitled, 315, Fig. 12.3
Perry, Lilla Cabot, American, 1848–1935, painter
    Lady with a Bowl of Violets, 66, Fig. 3.35

Picasso, Pablo, Spanish, 1881–1973, painter, sculptor
    The Frugal Repast, 297, Fig. 11.27
    Nude Woman, 59, Fig. 3.27
    The Tragedy, 21, Fig. 1.19
Pippin, Horace, African-American, 1888–1946, painter
    Asleep, 318, Fig. 12.7
Poons, Larry, American, b. 1937, painter
    Orange Crush, 158, Fig. 7.6

R

Rembrandt van Rijn, Dutch, 1606–1669, painter
    The Mill, 343, Fig. 12.32
    Self-Portrait, 317, Fig. 12.5
Renoir, Pierre Auguste, French, 1841–1919, painter
    Madame Henriot, 199, Fig. 8.15
Ringgold, Faith, African-American, b. 1930, painter, soft sculptor
    Mrs. Jones and Family, 306, Fig. 11.35
Rivera, Diego, Mexican, 1886–1957, painter
    Flower Day, 276, Fig. 10.35
Rockwell, Norman, American, 1894–1978, painter, illustrator
    Triple Self-Portrait, 70, Fig. 4.1
Rodin, Auguste, French, 1840–1917, sculptor
    The Burghers of Calais, 325, Fig. 12.14
Romero, Annette, Native American, b. 1951, ceramicist
    Storyteller Doll, 300, Fig. 11.32
Rothko, Mark, American (born in Russia), 1903–1970, painter
    Orange and Yellow, 166, Fig. 7.20
Rouault, Georges, French, 1871–1958, painter
    Christ and the Apostles, 96, Fig. 5.17
Rubens, Peter Paul, Flemish, 1577–1640, painter
    The Assumption of the Virgin, 288, Fig. 11.14
    Daniel in the Lions' Den, 215, Fig. 8.32

S

Saarinen, Eero, American, 1920–1961, architect
    Armchair, 32, Fig. 2.7
Schapiro, Miriam, American, b. 1923, painter, sculptor
    Anna and David, 280, Fig. 11.1
    Yard Sale, 201, Fig. 8.18
Shahn, Ben, American (born in Russia), 1898–1959, painter
    The Blind Botanist, 140, Fig. 6.35
Sheeler, Charles, American, 1883–1965, photographer, painter
    Catastrophe No. 2, 99, Fig. 5.24
Siqueiros, David Alfaro, Mexican, 1896–1974, painter
    Self-Portrait, 290, Fig. 11.17
Skoglund, Sandy, American, b. 1946, photographer, mixed media
    The Green House, 214, Fig. 8.31
Smith, David, American, 1906–1965, sculptor
    Cubi IX, 123, Fig. 6.8

Smith, Jaune Quick-To-See, Native American, b. 1940, painter
   Spotted Owl, 182, Fig. 7.39
Smith, Larry, American, b. 1949, painter
   North Georgia Waterfall, 144, Fig. 6.44
Spear, Laurinda, American, b. 1951, architect
   Centre for Innovative Technology, 65, Fig. 3.34
Steinlen, Théophile-Alexandre, French, 1859–1923, printmaker
   Winter: Cat on a Cushion, 27, Fig. 2.3
Steir, Pat, American, b. 1938, painter
   The Brueghel Series (A Vanitas of Style), 180, Fig. 7.38
Sullivan, Louis, American, 1856–1924, architect
   Elevator Grille, 225, Fig. 9.6
Sutej, Miroslav, Yugoslavian, b. 1936, lithographer
   Ultra AB, 14, Fig. 1.10

T

Tafoya, Juan, Native American, b. 1949, ceramicist
   Seed Pot, 203, Fig. 8.23
Tamayo, Rufino, Mexican, 1899–1991, painter
   Toast to the Sun, 169, Fig. 7.26
Thiebaud, Wayne, American, b. 1920, painter
   Apartment Hill, 342, Fig. 12.31
Tichich, Leslie Mims, American, b. 1948, craftsperson
   Body Adornment, 253, Fig. 10.6
Tintoretto, Jacopo, Italian, c. 1518–1594, painter
   Standing Youth with His Arm Raised, 102, Fig. 5.30
Torivio, Dorothy, Native American, b. 1946, ceramicist
   Vase, 257, Fig. 10.14
Town, Harold, Canadian, 1924–1990, painter
   Night Riders, 161, Fig. 7.13
Trumbull, John, American, 1756–1843, painter
   The Sortie Made by the Garrison of Gibraltar, 18, Fig. 1.14
Twiggs, Leo F., African-American, b. 1934, batik painter
   The Blue Wall, 29, Fig. 2.5
   East Wind Suite: Door, 88, Fig. 5.1

U

Utrillo, Maurice, French, 1883–1955, painter
   Street at Corte, Corsica, 266, Fig. 10.29

V

van der Weyden, Rogier, Flemish, 1399–1464, painter
   Portrait of a Lady, 283, Fig. 11.3
van Eyck, Jan, Flemish, before 1395–1441, painter
   The Annunciation, 187, Fig. 7.42

van Gogh, Vincent, Dutch, 1853–1890, painter
   Landscape at Saint-Rémy (Enclosed Field with Peasant), 200, Fig. 8.17
Vermeer, Jan, Dutch, 1632–1675, painter
   The Girl with the Red Hat, 247, Fig. 9.32
Vigée-Lebrun, Élisabeth, French, 1755–1842, painter
   The Marquise de Peze and the Marquise de Rouget with Her Two Children, 330, Fig. 12.22
   Self-Portrait, 193, Fig. 8.3

W

Warhol, Andy, American, 1928–1987, painter, printmaker
   Marilyn Monroe's Lips, 229, Fig. 9.12
White, Charles, African-American, 1918–1979, painter
   Preacher, 9, Fig. 1.4
Wilson, Jane, American, b. 1924, painter
   Solstice, 333, Fig. 12.26
Wood, Grant, American, 1892–1942, painter
   American Gothic, 254, Fig. 10.8
   Midnight Ride of Paul Revere, 91, Fig. 5.3
   Return from Bohemia, 4, Fig. 1.1
Wright, Frank Lloyd, American, 1867–1959, architect
   The David Wright House, 62, Fig. 3.30
   Falling Water House, 330, Fig. 12.21
   stained-glass window, 259, Fig. 10.18
   Taliesin West, 201, Fig. 8.19
Wyeth, Andrew, American, b. 1917, painter
   Christina's World, 33, Fig. 2.8

X

Xiong, Chaing, Laotian, b. 1953, craftsperson
   Hmong Story Cloth, 220, Fig. 9.1

Y

Yancy, John, African-American, b. 1956, muralist
   Celebration of Arts: Vibrations of Life, 340, Fig. 12.30

CHRONOLOGY OF ARTWORKS

In this section, the artworks that appear in *ArtTalk* have been arranged in chronological order. This list will enable you to see which artists were working at the same time and how the time and place in which they lived influenced their styles.

Prehistoric–1 B.C.

Artist Unknown, Altamira Caves, Spain
The Hall of the Bulls, 15,000 B.C., 43, Fig. 3.3

Artist Unknown
Statua di Donna, 2700–2600 B.C., 45, Fig. 3.5

Artist Unknown, Indian
Mohenjo-Daro, 2500 B.C., 46, Fig. 3.7

Artist Unknown, Egyptian
Methethy with His Daughter and Son, 2450 B.C., 44, Fig. 3.4

Artist Unknown, Egyptian
Figure of Hippopotamus, 1991–1786 B.C., 139, Fig. 6.34

Artist Unknown, Chinese
Ritual Wine Container, 1200 B.C., 45, Fig. 3.6

Myron, Greek, c. 480–440 B.C., sculptor
Discobolus, 450 B.C., 49, Fig. 3.12

Artist Unknown, Greco–Roman
Man of the Republic, 50 B.C., 49, Fig. 3.13

Artist Unknown, Greek
Dancing Lady, 50 B.C., 285, Fig. 11.8

Artist Unknown, Indian
Standing Vishnu, 9 B.C., 46, Fig. 3.8

A.D. 1–1399

Artist Unknown, Loma Negra, Peru
Nose Ornament, 1st–3rd centuries, 253, Fig. 10.5

Artist Unknown, Mexican, Gulf Coast
Figurine (Ball Player), 900, 53, Fig. 3.18

Artist Unknown, Coastal Huari, Tiahuanaco, Peru
Mantle, 600–1000, 225, Fig. 9.5

Artist Unknown, Southeastern Song dynasty
Carved Lacquer Circular Tray, 1127–1279, 255, Fig. 10.12

Artist Unknown, Southeast Asian
Temple at Angkor Wat, 1113–1150, 46, Fig. 3.9

Artist Unknown, Pisa, Italy
Bell Tower of the Cathedral at Pisa, 1174, 252, Fig. 10.2

Artist Unknown, French
Reims Cathedral, 1225–1299, 51, Fig. 3.15

Giotto di Bondone, Italian, c. 1266–1337, painter
Madonna and Child, 1320–30, 133, Fig. 6.22

1400–1499

van Eyck, Jan, Flemish, before 1395–1441, painter
The Annunciation, 1434–36, 187, Fig. 7.42

Ghiberti, Lorenzo, Italian, 1378–1455, sculptor
Gates of Paradise, 1425–52, 37, Fig. 2.10

van der Weyden, Rogier, Flemish, 1399–1464, painter
Portrait of a Lady, 1460, 283, Fig. 11.3

Leonardo da Vinci, Italian, 1452–1519, painter, sculptor
Ginevra de' Benci, 1474, 67, Fig. 3.36

Leonardo da Vinci, Italian, 1452–1519, painter, sculptor
page from his sketchbook c. 1475, 9, Fig. 1.5

Artist Unknown, Byzantine
Madonna and Child on Curved Throne, 1480, 50, fig. 3.14

Botticelli, Sandro, Italian, 1445–1510, painter
The Adoration of the Magi, 1481–82, 135, Fig. 6.25

Dürer, Albrecht, German, 1471–1528, painter, printmaker
An Oriental Ruler Seated on His Throne, 1495, 134,
Fig. 6.23

1500–1599

Michelangelo Buonarroti, Italian, 1475–1564, sculptor, painter
Pietà, 1500, 52, 309, Figs. 3.16, 11.37

Giorgione, Italian, 1477–1511, painter
The Adoration of the Shepherds, 1505–10, 261, Fig. 10.20

Dürer, Albrecht, German, 1471–1528, painter, printmaker
Virgin and Child with Saint Anne, 1519, 293, Fig. 11.21

Grünewald, Matthias, German, c. 1470–1528, painter
The Small Crucifixion, 1511–20, 295, Fig. 11.24

Nizami (author). Artist unknown, Persian, c. 1524–25
*Kamseh: Bahram Gur and the Chinese Princess in the
Sandalwood Pavilion on Thursday,* 1524–25, 52, Fig. 3.17

Musawwir, 'Abd Allah, Islamic, 16th century, painter
The Meeting of the Theologians, 1540–49, 240, Fig. 9.28

Tintoretto, Jacopo, Italian, c. 1518–1594, painter
Standing Youth with His Arm Raised, 102, Fig. 5.30

Fontana, Lavinia, Italian, 1552–1614, painter
Portrait of a Noblewoman, 1580, 24 125, Fig. 6.11

Artist Unknown, English
Armor of George Clifford, Third Earl of Cumberland,
1580–1585, 288, Fig. 11.13

Artist Unknown, Nigeria, Edo
Warrior Chief, Warriors and Attendants, 16th–17th centuries,
146, Fig. 6.45

1600–1699

Rubens, Peter Paul, Flemish, 1577–1640, painter
Daniel in the Lions' Den, 1615, 215, Fig. 8.32

Bernini, Gianlorenzo, Italian, 1598–1680, sculptor
David, 1623, 277, Fig. 10.36

Rubens, Peter Paul, Flemish, 1577–1640, painter
The Assumption of the Virgin, 1626, 288, Fig. 11.14

Leyster, Judith, Dutch, 1609–1660, painter
Self-Portrait, 1635, 54, Fig. 3.20

Gu Mei, Chinese, 17th century, painter
Orchids and Rocks, 1644, 104, Fig. 5.32

Rembrandt van Rijn, Dutch, 1606–1669, painter
The Mill, 1650, 343, Fig. 12.32

Rembrandt van Rijn, Dutch, 1606–1669, painter
Self-Portrait, 1650, 317, Fig. 12.5

Vermeer, Jan, Dutch, 1632–1675, painter
The Girl with the Red Hat, 1665, 247, Fig. 9.32

1700–1799

Haverman, Margareta, Dutch, 1693–1750, painter
A Vase of Flowers, 1716, 31, Fig. 2.6

Artist Unknown, Japanese
Footed Dish, 1700–1750, 229, Fig. 9.13

Hua Yen, Chinese, c. 1682–1765
Conversation in Autumn, 1762, 47, Fig. 3.10

Artist Unknown, Italian, Venice
Bedroom from the Sagredo Palace, 1725–1735, 100, Fig. 5.25

Copley, John Singleton, American, 1737–1815, painter
Paul Revere, 1768–70, 294, Fig. 11.22

Fragonard, Jean–Honoré, French, 1732–1806, painter
A Game of Hot Cockles, 1767–73, 260, Fig. 10.19

Franklin, Ben, American, 1706–1790, statesman, philosopher
Join or Die, 1774, 324, Fig. 12.13

Vigée-Lebrun, Élisabeth, French, 1755–1842, painter
Self-Portrait, 1781, 193, Fig. 8.3

David, Jacques Louis, French, 1748–1825, painter
Death of Socrates, 1787, 115, Fig. 5.40

Vigée-Lebrun, Élisabeth, French, 1755–1842, painter
The Marquise de Peze and the Marquise de Rouget with Her Two Children, 1787, 330, Fig. 12.22

Trumbull, John, American, 1756–1843, painter
The Sortie Made by the Garrison of Gibraltar, 1789, 18, Fig. 1.14

1800–1899

Goya, Francisco, Spanish, 1746–1828, painter
The Third of May, 1808, 1808, 83, Fig. 4.14

Hokusai, Katsushika, Japanese, 1760–1849, printmaker
The Great Wave off Kanagawa, 1823–29, 262, Fig. 10.22

Artist Unknown, Creek, Georgia or Alabama
Shoulder Bag, 1810–1830, 230, Fig. 9.14

Catlin, George, American, 1796–1872, painter
See-non-ty-a, an Iowa Medicine Man, 1845, 294, Fig. 11.23

Bonheur, Rosa, French, 1822–1899, painter
The Horse Fair, 1853–55, 224, Fig. 9.4

Olmstead, Frederick Law, American, 1822–1903, landscape architect
Central Park, 1858, 77, Fig. 4.8

Church, Frederic Edwin, American, 1826–1900, painter
Our Banner in the Sky, 1861, 267, Fig. 10.30

Eakins, Thomas, American, 1844–1916, painter
Baseball Players Practicing, 1875, 55, Fig. 3.21

Eakins, Thomas, American, 1844–1916, painter
Baby at Play, 1876, 257, Fig. 10.15

Renoir, Pierre Auguste, French, 1841–1919, painter
Madame Henriot, 1876, 199, Fig. 8.15

Cassatt, Mary, American, 1845–1926, painter
Five O'Clock Tea, 1879, 270, Fig. 10.32

Artist Unknown, Blackfeet, Montana
Man's Leggings, 1880, 121, Fig. 6.5

Degas, Edgar, French, 1834–1917, painter
Little Fourteen-Year-Old Dancer, 1880, 203, Fig. 8.21

Montata, Native American, b. date unknown, beadwork
Blackfeet Man's Leggings, 1880, 121, Fig. 6.5

Degas, Edgar, French, 1834–1917, painter
The Millinery Shop, 1879–84, 323, Fig. 12.12

Morisot, Berthe, French, 1841–1895, painter
In the Dining Room, 1886, 320, Fig. 12.9

Rodin, Auguste, French, 1840–1917, sculptor
The Burghers of Calais, 1886, 325, Fig. 12.14

van Gogh, Vincent, Dutch, 1853–1890, painter
Landscape at Saint-Rémy (Enclosed Field with Peasant), 1889, 200, Fig. 8.17

Artist Unknown, Chippewa, Minnesota
Man's Leggings, 1890, 121, Fig. 6.5

Artist Unknown, Northwestern Plains Indian
Feather Bonnet, 1890, 190, Fig. 8.1

Gauguin, Paul, French, 1848–1903, painter
Faaturuma (The Dreamer), 1891, 154, Fig. 7.1

Monet, Claude, French, 1840–1926, painter
Poplars, 1891, 173, 174, Figs. 7.32, 7.33

Homer, Winslow, American, 1836–1910, painter
Hound and Hunter, 1892, 12, Fig. 1.8

Homer, Winslow, American, 1836–1910, painter
Sketch for Hound and Hunter, 1892, 12, Fig. 1.7

Cassatt, Mary, American, 1845–1926, painter
Baby Reaching for an Apple, 1893, Fig. 2.1

Monet, Claude, French, 1840–1926, painter
Ice Floes, 1893, 161, Fig. 7.12

Beaux, Cecilia, American, 1863–1942, painter
Ernesta (Child with Nurse), 1894, 322, Fig. 12.11

Sullivan, Louis, American, 1856–1924, architect
Elevator Grille, 1893–94, 225, Fig. 9.6

Keyser, Louisa (Dat So La Lee), Native American, 1850–1925, weaver
Basket, 244, Fig. 9.30

1900–1949

Artist Unknown, Senufo Tribe, Ivory Coast
Equestrian Figure, 19th–20th centuries, 58, Fig. 3.25

Artist Unknown, Bella Coola, Northwest Coast
Cockle Hunter Mask, 1900, 295, Fig. 11.30

Artist Unknown, Iroquois
Corn Husk Mask, 1900, 53, Fig. 3.19

Artist Unknown, Kwakiutl
Wolf Mask, 1900, 299, Fig. 11.30

Steinlen, Théophile-Alexandre, French, 1859–1923, printmaker
Winter: Cat on a Cushion, 27, Fig. 2.3

Munch, Edvard, Norwegian, 1863–1944, painter, printmaker
The Kiss, 1897–1902, 296, Fig. 11.26

Picasso, Pablo, Spanish, 1881–1973, painter, sculptor
The Tragedy, 1903, 21, Fig. 1.19

Cézanne, Paul, French, 1839–1906, painter
Le Chateau Noir, 1900–04, 56, Fig. 3.23

Picasso, Pablo, Spanish, 1881–1973, painter, sculptor
The Frugal Repast, 1904, 297, Fig. 11.27

Artist Unknown, Bamum peoples, Cameroon
Male Figure, 1908, 57, Fig. 3.24

Monet, Claude, French, 1840–1926, painter
Palazzo da Mula, Venice, 1908, 56, Fig. 3.22

Balla, Giocomo, Italian, 1871–1958, painter
Street Light, 1909, 234, Fig. 9.20

Artist Unknown, Sundi group Kongo peoples, Congo, Zaire, and Angola
Bowl, before 1910, 226, Fig. 9.7

Perry, Lilla Cabot, American, 1848–1935, painter
Lady with a Bowl of Violets, 1910, 66, Fig. 3.35

Picasso, Pablo, Spanish, 1881–1973, painter, sculptor
Nude Woman, 1910, 59, Fig. 3.27

Marc, Franz, German, 1880–1916, painter
The Large Blue Horses, 1911, 175, Fig. 7.34

Balla, Giocomo, Italian, 1871–1958, painter
Dynamism of a Dog on a Leash, 1912, 236, Fig. 9.24

Gris, Juan, Spanish, 1887–1927, painter
Guitar and Flowers, 1912, 332, Fig. 12.24

Hassam, Childe, American, 1859–1935, painter, printmaker
Jelly Fish, 1912, 177, Fig. 7.36

Huntington, Anna Hyatt, American, 1876–1973, sculptor
Riders to the Sea, 1912, 142, Fig. 6.39

Utrillo, Maurice, French, 1883–1955, painter
Street at Corte, Corsica, 1913, 266, Fig. 10.29

Chagall, Marc, Russian, 1887–1985, painter
Birthday, 1915, 298, Fig. 11.28

Artist Unknown, New Ireland, Melanesia
Mask, 1920, 299, Fig. 11.30

Lachaise, Gaston, French, 1882–1935, sculptor
Walking Woman, 1922, 298, Fig. 11.29

Brancusi, Constantin, Romanian, 1876–1957, sculptor
Torso of a Young Man, 1924, 140, Fig. 6.36

Rivera, Diego, Mexican, 1886–1957, painter
Flower Day, 1925, 276, Fig. 10.35

Epstein, Sir Jacob, English (born in New York City), 1880–1959, sculptor
The Visitation, 1926, 28, Fig. 2.4

Kollwitz, Käthe, German, 1867–1945, painter, printmaker, graphic artist
Self-Portrait, 1926, 58, Fig. 3.26

Barlach, Ernst, German, 1870–1938, painter, sculptor
Singing Man, 1928, 328, Fig. 12.19

Curry, John Steuart, American, 1897–1946, painter
Baptism in Kansas, 1928, 321, Fig. 12.10

Hiroshige, Andō, Japanese, 1797–1858, printmaker
Evening Rain on the Karasaki Pine, 1929, 48, Fig. 3.11

Hopper, Edward, American, 1882–1967, painter
Early Sunday Morning, 1930, 98, Fig. 5.22

Marsh, Reginald, American, 1898–1954, painter
Why Not Use the El?, 1930, 284, Fig. 11.7

Wood, Grant, American, 1892–1942, painter
American Gothic, 1930, 254, Fig. 10.8

Artist Unknown, Asante people, Ghana
Wrapper, 228, Fig. 9.11

Calder, Alexander, American, 1898–1976, sculptor
Varese, 1931, 108, Fig. 5.36

Dali, Salvador, Spanish, 1904–1989, painter
The Persistence of Memory, 1931, 60, Fig. 3.28

Hartley, Marsden, American, 1877–1943, painter
Blueberry Highway, Dogtown, 1931, 165, Fig. 7.18

Kahlo, Frida, Mexican, 1907–1954, painter
Frida and Diego Rivera, 1931, 259, Fig. 10.17

O'Keeffe, Georgia, American, 1887–1986, painter
Cow's Skull, 1931, 266, Fig. 10.28

Orozco, José Clemente, Mexican, 1883–1949, painter
Barricade, 1931, 62, Fig. 3.31

Wood, Grant, American, 1892–1942, painter
Midnight Ride of Paul Revere, 1931, 91, Fig. 5.3

Carr, Emily, Canadian, 1871–1945, painter
Forest, British Columbia, 1931–32, 328, Fig. 12.18

Albright, Ivan, American, 1897–1983, painter
The Farmer's Kitchen, 1933–34, 200, Fig. 8.16

Bishop, Isabel, American, 1902–1988, painter
Two Girls, 1935, 292, Fig. 11.20

Lee, Doris, American, b. 1905, printmaker, painter
Thanksgiving, 1935, 138, Fig. 6.33

Wood, Grant, African-American, 1892–1942, painter
Return from Bohemia, 1935, 4, Fig. 1.1

Lange, Dorothea, American, 1895–1965, photojournalist
Migrant Mother, 1936, 15, Fig. 1.11

Wright, Frank Lloyd, American, 1867–1959, architect
Falling Water House, 1936, 330, Fig. 12.21

Hayden, Palmer, African-American, 1890–1973, painter
The Janitor Who Paints, 1937, 40, Fig. 3.1

Kahlo, Frida, Mexican, 1907–1954, painter
Self-Portrait Dedicated to Leon Trotsky, 1937, 264, Fig. 10.25

Abbot, Berenice, American, b. 1898, photographer
Façade, Alwyn Court, 1938, 129, Fig. 6.17

Artist Unknown, South American Indian
Featherwork Ornaments, 1938, 204, Fig. 8.24

Benton, Thomas Hart, American, 1882–1975, painter
I Got a Girl on Sourwood Mountain, 1938, 98, Fig. 5.23

Bishop, Isabel, American, 1902–1988, painter
Waiting, 1938, 308, Fig. 11.36

Rouault, Georges, French, 1871–1958, painter
Christ and the Apostles, 1937–38, 96, Fig. 5.17

Wright, Frank Lloyd, American, 1867–1959, architect
Taliesin West, 1938, 201, Fig. 8.19

Calder, Alexander, American, 1898–1976, sculptor
Lobster Trap and Fish Tail, 1939, 237, Fig. 9.26

Carr, Emily, Canadian, 1871–1945, painter
Above the Trees, 1939, 170, Fig. 7.27

Apel, Marie, English, 1880–1970, sculptor
Grief, 1940, 141, Fig. 6.38

Johnson, William H., African-American, 1901–1970, painter
Jitterbugs IV, 1939–40, 112, Fig. 5.38

Martinez, Maria and Julian, Native American, Maria: c. 1885–1980; Julian: c. 1885–1943, ceramicists
Black-on-black storage jar, 1942, 274, Fig. 10.34

Mondrian, Piet, Dutch, 1872–1944, painter
Broadway Boogie Woogie, 1942–43, 176, Fig. 7.35

Pippin, Horace, African-American, 1888–1946, painter
Asleep, 1943, 318, Fig. 12.7

Ernst, Max, German (in America after 1941), 1891–1976, painter
The Eye of Silence, 1943–44, 206, Fig. 8.27

Sheeler, Charles, American, 1883–1965, photographer and painter
Catastrophe No. 2, 1944, 99, Fig. 5.24

Siqueiros, David Alfaro, Mexican, 1896–1974, painter
Self-Portrait, 1945, 290, Fig. 11.17

Escher, M. C., Dutch, 1898–1972, printmaker
Other World, 1947, 127, Fig. 6.13

Wyeth, Andrew, American, b. 1917, painter
Christina's World, 1948, 33, Fig. 2.8

Moore, Henry, English, 1898–1986, sculptor
Family Group, 1948–49, 20, Fig. 1.18

Harrison, Wallace Kirkman, American, b. 1895, architect
United Nations Buildings, 1949, 128, Fig. 6.14

Johnson, Philip, American, b. 1906, architect
Johnson House, 1949, 141, Fig. 6.37

1950–1974

Matisse, Henri, French, 1869–1954, painter
Beasts of the Sea, 1950, 132, Fig. 6.21

Hopper, Edward, American, 1882–1967, painter
First Row Orchestra, 1951, 258, Fig. 10.16

Pereira, Irene Rice, American, 1907–1971, painter
Untitled, 1951, 315, Fig. 12.3

Wright, Frank Lloyd, American, 1867–1959, architect
The David Wright House, 1951, 62, Fig. 3.30

White, Charles, African-American, 1918–1979, painter
Preacher, 1952, 9, Fig. 1.4

Arp, Jean (Hans), French, 1887–1966, painter, sculptor
Aquatique, 1953, 123, Fig. 6.9

Artist Unknown, Mexican
Jaguar Mask, 250, Fig. 10.1

Shahn, Ben, American (born in Russia), 1898–1959, painter
The Blind Botanist, 1954, 140, Fig. 6.35

Le Corbusier, Swiss, 1887–1965, architect
Chapelle Notre-Dame-du-Haut, 1955, 285, Fig. 11.9

Rothko, Mark, American (born in Russia), 1903–1970, painter
Orange and Yellow, 1956, 166, Fig. 7.20

Tamayo, Rufino, Mexican, 1899–1991, painter
Toast to the Sun, 1956, 169, Fig. 7.26

Hofmann, Hans, German (born in America), 1880–1966, painter
Flowering Swamp, 1957, 64, Fig. 3.32

Saarinen, Eero, American, 1920–1961, architect
Armchair, 1957, 32, Fig. 2.7

Nevelson, Louise, American, 1899–1988, sculptor
Dawn's Wedding Chapel, 1959, 329, Fig. 12.20

Hepworth, Barbara, English, 1903–1975, sculptor
Figure for Landscape, 1960, 128, Fig. 6.15

Lawrence, Jacob, African-American, b. 1917, painter
Parade, 1960, 238, Fig. 9.27

Rockwell, Norman, American, 1894–1978, painter, illustrator
Triple Self-Portrait, 1960, 70, Fig. 4.1

Town, Harold, Canadian, 1924–1990, painter
Night Riders, 1960, 161, Fig. 7.13

Johns, Jasper, American, b. 1930, painter
Map, 1961, 327, Fig. 12.17

Smith, David, American, 1906–1965, sculptor
Cubi IX, 1961, 123, Fig. 6.8

Glarner, Fritz, American (born in Switzerland), 1899–1972, painter
Relational Painting #93, 1962, 168, Fig. 7.23

Lichtenstein, Roy, American, b. 1923, painter
Blam, 1962, 336, Fig. 12.28

Nevelson, Louise, American, 1899–1988, sculptor
Dawn, 1962, 36, Fig. 2.9

Warhol, Andy, American, 1928–1987, painter, printmaker
Marilyn Monroe's Lips, 1962, 229, Fig. 9.12

Burchfield, Charles, American, 1893–1967, painter
October Wind and Sunlight in the Woods, 1962–63, 223, Fig. 9.3

Loewy, Raymond, American (born in France), b. 1893, designer
Avanti, 1963, 74, Fig. 4.4

Poons, Larry, American, b. 1937, painter
Orange Crush, 1963, 158, Fig. 7.6

Bearden, Romare, African-American, 1914–1989, painter
Prevalence of Ritual: Baptism, 1964, 178, Fig. 7.37

Hampton, James, African-American, 1909–1965, sculptor
The Throne of the Third Heaven of the Nations' Millennium General Assembly, 1950–1964, 208, Fig. 8.28

Botero, Fernando, Colombian, b. 1932, painter
The Pinzon Family, 1965, 302, Fig. 11.33

Magritte, René, Belgian, 1898–1967, painter
The Blank Signature, 1965, 148, Fig. 6.46

Albers, Josef, German, 1888–1976, painter
Homage to the Square: Glow, 1966, 265, Fig. 10.26

Oldenburg, Claes, American, b. 1929, painter, sculptor
Shoestring Potatoes Spilling from a Bag, 1966, 286, Fig. 11.10

Sutej, Miroslav, Yugoslavian, b. 1936, lithographer
Ultra AB, 1966, 14, Fig. 1.10

Jessup, Georgia Mills, American, b. 1926, painter
Rainy Night, Downtown, 1967, 331, Fig. 12.23

Wright, Frank Lloyd, American, 1867–1959, architect
Stained-glass window, 1967, 259, Fig. 10.18

Carpenter, Miles Burkholder, American, 1889–1985, craftsperson, sculptor
Root Monster, 1968, 184, Fig. 7.40

Bak, Brunislaw M., American (born in Poland), 1922–1981, painter
Holocaust, 1969, 156, Fig. 7.3

Dodd, Lamar, American, b. 1909, painter
Night Before Launch, 1969, 19, Fig. 1.17

Fernandes, Julio, American, b. date unknown, painter
Apollo 11, 1969, 19, Fig. 1.16

Kingman, Dong, American, b. 1911, painter
Higher, Faster, and Farther, 1969, 19, Fig. 1.15

Twiggs, Leo F., African-American, b. 1934, batik painter
The Blue Wall, 1969, 29, Fig. 2.5

Catlett, Elizabeth, African-American, b. 1915, printmaker, sculptor, painter
Sharecropper, 1970, 13, Fig. 1.9

Hunt, Henry, Canadian Native American, Kwakiutl, 1923–1985, sculptor
K'umugwe' (Komokwa) Mask, 1970, 304, Fig. 11.34

Neel, Alice, American, 1900–1984, painter
Loneliness, 1970, 319, Fig. 12.8

Tichich, Leslie Mims, American, b. 1948, craftsperson
Body Adornment, 1970, 253, Fig. 10.6

Lawrence, Jacob, African-American, b. 1917, painter
Study for the Munich Olympic Games Poster, 1971, 114, Fig. 5.39

Artist Unknown, Ewe peoples, Volta region, Ghana
Wrapper, 1972, 242, Fig. 9.29

Johns, Jasper, American, b. 1930, painter
Cups 4 Picasso, 1972, 124, Fig. 6.10

Curnoe, Greg, Canadian, 1936–1992, painter
Mariposa 10 Speed, 1973, 96, Fig. 5.18

Ringgold, Faith, African-American, b. 1930, painter, soft sculptor
Mrs. Jones and Family, 1973, 306, Fig. 11.35

Andrews, Benny, African-American, b. 1930, painter, printmaker
The Scholar, 1974, 101, Fig. 5.28

1975–

Benton, Thomas Hart, American, 1882–1975, painter
The Sources of Country Music, 1975, 61, Fig. 3.29

Graves, Nancy Stevenson, b. 1940, sculptor
Rheo, 1975, 26, Fig. 2.2

Garcia, Rupert, American, b. 1941, painter
Political Prisoner, 1976, 126, Fig. 6.12

Jacquette, Yvonne, American, b. 1934, painter
East River Drive, 1976, 93, Fig. 5.6

Moore, Henry, English, 1898–1986, sculptor
Reclining Mother and Child, 1974–76, 142, Fig. 6.40

Houser, Allan, Native American, b. 1914, sculptor
Coming of Age, 1977, 233, Fig. 9.19

Dillon, Leo and Diane, American, both b. 1933, graphic artists
A Wrinkle in Time, 1979, 82, Fig. 4.13

Bak, Brunislaw M., American (born in Poland),
1922–1981, painter
Interpenetrations in Red, 1980, 316, Fig. 12.4

Bak, Hedi, American (born in Germany), b. 1924, painter
Grand Canyon #2, 1980, 194, Fig. 8.4

McKelvey, Lucy Leuppe, Native American, b. date unknown,
ceramicist
Whirling Rainbow Goddesses, date unknown, 237, Fig. 9.25

Mitchell, Joan, American, 1926–1992, painter
Dirty Snow, 1980, 205, Fig. 8.25

Thiebaud, Wayne, American, b. 1920, painter
Apartment Hill, 1980, 342, Fig. 12.31

Miyawaki, Ayako, Japanese, b. 1905, appliqué artist
The Red Crab, 1981, 212, Fig. 8.30

Neel, Alice, American, 1900–1984, painter
Marisol, 1981, 42, Fig. 3.2

Dvorak, Lois, American, 1934–1993, mixed media
The Lizards, 1982, 318, Fig. 12.6

Graves, Nancy Stevenson, b. 1940, sculptor
Zaga, 1983, 17, Fig. 1.13

de Amaral, Olga, Colombian, b. 1937, fiber artist
Alquimia XIII, 1984, 203, Fig. 8.22

Steir, Pat, American, b. 1938, painter
The Brueghel Series (A Vanitas of Style), 1982–84, 180,
Fig. 7.38

Torivio, Dorothy, Native American, b. 1946, ceramicist
Vase, 1984, 257, Fig. 10.14

Dvorak, Lois, American, 1934–1993, mixed media
Spirit Boxes I, 1985, 334, Fig. 12.27

Naranjo, Michael, Native American, b. 1944, sculptor
Spirits Soaring, 1985, 150, Fig. 6.47

Clements, Bob, American, b. 1937, sculptor
Evening Up the Score, 1986, 263, Fig. 10.24

Garrison, Elizabeth, American, b. 1914, quilter
Long May Our Land Be Bright, 1986, 256, Fig. 10.13

Hanson, Duane, American, b. 1925, sculptor, painter
Traveler with Sunburn, 1986, 65, Fig. 3.33

Clive, Carolyn, American, b. 1931, painter
Amplitude, 1987, 110, Fig. 5.37

Fish, Janet I., American, b. 1939, painter
Fallen Vase, 1987, 7, Fig. 1.2

Larraz, Julio, Cuban, b. 1944, painter
Papiamento, 1987, 8, Fig. 1.3

Marisol, Venezuelan (in America since 1950), b. 1930, sculptor
Poor Family I, 1987, 118, Fig. 6.1

Schapiro, Miriam, American, b. 1923, painter, sculptor
Anna and David, 1987, 280, Fig. 11.1

Xiong, Chaing, Laotian, b. 1953, craftsperson
Hmong Story Cloth, 1987, 220, Fig. 9.1

Artist Unknown, Mexican
Bird, 1988, 210, Fig. 8.29

Fish, Janet I., American, b. 1939, painter
Jonathan and Lorraine, 1988, 198, Fig. 8.13

Jacquette, Yvonne, American, b. 1934, painter
Town of Skowhegan, Maine V, 1988, 312, Fig. 12.1

Murray, Elizabeth, American, b. 1936, painter
Things to Come, 1988, 186, Fig. 7.41

Spear, Laurinda, American, b. 1951, architect
Centre for Innovative Technology, 1985–1988, 65, Fig. 3.34

Close, Chuck, American, b. 1940, painter
Janet, 1989, 246, Fig. 9.31

Twiggs, Leo F., African-American, b. 1934, batik painter
East Wind Suite: Door, 1989, 88, Fig. 5.1

Courtney–Clarke, Margaret, English, b. 1949, photojournalist
photo from *African Canvas,* 1990, 172, Fig. 7.30

Hoover, John, Native American, Aleut, b. 1919, sculptor
Loon Song, 1990, 202, Fig. 8.20

Jimenez, Luis, American, b. 1940, sculptor
Vaquero, 1990, 16, Fig. 1.12

Skoglund, Sandy, American, b. 1946, photographer,
mixed media
The Green House, 1990, 214, Fig. 8.31

Smith, Jaune Quick-To-See, Native American, b. 1940, painter
Spotted Owl, 1990, 182, Fig. 7.39

Dick, Beau, Canadian Native American, b. 1955, printmaker
Sacred Circles, 1991, 272, Fig. 10.33

Wilson, Jane, American, b. 1924, painter
Solstice, 1991, 333, Fig. 12.26

Yancy, John, African-American, b. 1956, muralist
Celebration of Arts: Vibrations of Life, 1991, 340, Fig. 12.30

Bayless, Florence, American, b. 1922, craftsperson
Haori Coat, 1992, 326, Fig. 12.16

Naminga, Dan, Native American, b. 1950, painter
Blessing Rain Chant, 1992, 97, Fig. 5.21

Tafoya, Juan, Native American, b. 1949, ceramicist
Seed Pot, 1992, 203, Fig. 8.23

Romero, Annette, Native American, b. 1951, ceramicist
Storyteller Doll, 1993, 300, Fig. 11.32

Schapiro, Miriam, American, b. 1923, painter, sculptor
Yard Sale, 1993, 201, Fig. 8.18

Smith, Larry, American, b. 1949, painter
North Georgia Waterfall, 1993, 144, Fig. 6.44

GLOSSARY

This section contains the important words and phrases used in *ArtTalk* that may be new to you. You may want to refer to this list of terms as you read the chapters, complete the exercises, and prepare to create your own works of art. You can also use the Glossary to review what you have learned in *ArtTalk*. It will help you to know that the terms used in the glossary definitions that are themselves defined elsewhere in the Glossary are in *italic*. The numbers shown in parentheses indicate the chapter in which the word is introduced.

A

Abstract art   Twentieth-century art containing shapes that simplify shapes of real objects to emphasize form instead of subject matter.

Abstract Expressionism   Painting style developed after World War II in New York City that stressed elements and principles of art as subject matter and emotion rather than planned design. Abstract Expressionism is also called *action painting* because artists applied paint freely to huge canvases (3).

Academies   Art schools that developed in western Europe after the French Revolution. They replaced the *apprentice* system.

Acrylic paint   *Pigments* mixed with an acrylic vehicle. Available in different degrees of quality: school and artists' acrylics. School acrylics are less expensive than the professional acrylics, can be washed out of brushes and clothes, and are nontoxic.

Action Painting   See *Abstract Expressionism*.

Active   Expressing movement. Diagonal and zigzag lines (5) and diagonally slanting shapes and forms (6) are active. Opposite of *static*.

Aesthetic experience   Your personal interaction with a work of art (2).

Aesthetic judgment   Values used in judging a work of art involving reasons for finding a work of art beautiful or satisfying.

Aesthetics   The philosophy or study of the nature of beauty and art (2).

Afterimage   Weak image of *complementary color* created by a viewer's brain as a reaction to prolonged looking at a color. After staring at something red, the viewer sees an afterimage of green.

Age of Faith   See *Middle Ages*.

Air brush   Atomizer operated by compressed air used for spraying on paint.

Alternating rhythm   Visual rhythm set up by repeating *motifs* but changing position or content of motifs or spaces between them (9).

Analogous colors   Colors that sit side by side on the color wheel and have a common hue (7). Violet, red-violet, and red are analogous colors. Analogous colors can be used as a *color scheme*.

Analysis   In art criticism, the step in which you discover how the work is organized (2). In art history, the step in which you determine the style of the work and how it fits into an art movement (3).

Animation   The art of moving cartoons (4). A series of drawings are photographed, and the figures seem to move when they are projected one after another.

Appliqué   An art form in which cutout fabric decorations are fastened to a larger surface to create a new design.

Apprentice   Student artist. In the *Middle Ages,* apprentices learned from master artists in *craft guilds*.

Approximate symmetry   Balance that is almost *symmetrical* (10). This type of symmetry produces the effect of stability, as formal balance does, but small differences make the arrangement more interesting.

Arbitrary color   Color chosen by an artist to express his or her feelings (7). Opposite of *optical color*.

Arch   Curved stone structure supporting weight of material over an open space. Doorways and bridges use arches.

Architect   A person who designs buildings that are well constructed, aesthetically pleasing, and functional (4).

Architecture   Art form of designing and planning construction of buildings, cities, and bridges.

Armature   Framework for supporting material used in sculpting.

Armory Show   First large exhibition of modern art in America. It was held in the 69th Regiment Armory building in New York City in 1913. The *Ashcan School* artists, who were influenced by modern European art, helped organize this exhibit.

Art   The use of skill and imagination to produce beautiful objects.

Art criticism   An organized system for studying a work of art. It has four stages: description, analysis, interpretation, and judgment (2).

Artistic style   See *style.*

Ashcan School   Group of American artists working in the early twentieth century who used city people and city scenes for subject matter (7). Originally called "The Eight," they helped organize the *Armory Show.*

Assemblage   Three-dimensional work of art consisting of many pieces assembled together.

Asymmetrical balance   Another name for *informal balance,* in which unlike objects have equal *visual weight* or eye attraction.

Atmospheric perspective   Effect of air and light on how an object is perceived by the viewer (6). The more air between the viewer and the object, the more the object seems to fade. A bright object seems closer to the viewer than a dull object.

B

Background   Part of the picture plane that seems to be farthest from the viewer.

Balance   Principle of design concerned with equalizing visual forces, or elements, in a work of art (10). If a work of art has visual balance, the viewer feels that the elements have been arranged in a satisfying way. Visual imbalance makes the viewer feel that the elements need to be rearranged. The two types of balance are *formal* (also called *symmetrical*) and *informal* (also called *asymmetrical*).

Baroque   Artistic style that emphasized movement, strong value contrast, and variety. It developed after the Reformation in the seventeenth century. Artists used movement of forms and figures toward the viewer, dramatic lighting effects, contrast between dark and light, ornamentation, and curved lines to express energy and strong emotions (3).

Bas-relief Sculpture in which areas project slightly from a flat surface. Bas-relief is also called *low relief*.

Binder A liquid that holds together the grains of pigment (7).

Blending Technique of *shading* through smooth, gradual application of dark value.

Block Piece of engraved wood or linoleum inked to make a print.

Brayer Roller with a handle used to apply ink to a surface (5).

Buttress Projecting brick or stone structure that supports an arch or *vault*. A flying buttress is connected with a wall by an arch. It reaches over the side aisle to support the roof of a *cathedral*.

Byzantine Artistic style that developed around the city of Constantinople (now Istanbul, Turkey) in the eastern Roman Empire. The style blended Roman, Greek, and Oriental art. It featured very rich colors, and figures that were flat and stiff. These works blended Greek, Roman, and Asian styles and usually had a religious theme (3).

C

Calligraphic lines Flowing lines made with brushstrokes similar to Oriental writing (5).

Calligraphy An Oriental method of beautiful handwriting (5).

Canvas Rough cloth on which an oil painting is made.

Caricature Humorous drawing that exaggerates features of a person to make fun of or criticize him or her. Caricatures are often used in editorial cartoons.

Carving Shaping wood, stone, or marble by cutting and chipping.

Cast Shaped by pouring melted material into a mold and letting it harden.

Catacombs Rock tunnels under the city of Rome that early Christians used as meeting places. Paintings on catacomb walls used secret symbols because Christianity was illegal until the fourth century.

Cathedral Main church in a district (3).

Central axis A dividing line that works like the point of balance in the balance scale. The central axis is used to measure *visual weight* in a work of art. It can be vertical (balance between sides is measured) or horizontal (balance between top and bottom is measured) (10).

Ceramics Art of making objects with clay to produce pottery and sculpture. Pottery is *fired* in a *kiln* to make it stronger.

Characters Chinese or Japanese line drawings that stand for letters, ideas, objects, or verbal sounds. They are formed by *calligraphic lines*.

Chiaroscuro The arrangement of light and shadow (6). This technique was introduced by Italian artists during the Renaissance and used widely by Baroque artists. Chiaroscuro is also called *modeling* and *shading*.

Cityscape Painting or drawing in which a city is the main feature.

Classical Referring to the art of ancient Greece and Rome. The Greeks created art based on the ideals of perfect proportion and logic instead of emotion. The Romans adapted Greek art and spread it throughout the civilized world.

Clay Stiff, sticky earth that is used in ceramics. It is wet, and it hardens after drying or heating.

Clustering Technique for creating a *focal point* by grouping several different shapes closely together (12).

Coil Long roll joined into a circle or spiral. Clay coils are used to make pottery.

Collage Two-dimensional work of art consisting of bits and pieces of textured paper and fabric pasted onto a painting (8).

Color An element of art that is derived from reflected light (7). The sensation of color is aroused in the brain by response of the eyes to different wavelengths of light. Color has three properties: *hue, value,* and *intensity*.

Color-Field Painting Twentieth-century style of painting using flat areas of color for the pure sensation of color. Artists creating color-field paintings are not trying to express emotion or use a precise design.

Color scheme Plan for organizing colors. Types of color schemes include *monochromatic, analogous, complementary, triad, split complementary, warm,* and *cool*.

Color spectrum The effect that occurs when light passes through a *prism*; the beam of white light is bent and separated into bands of color. Colors always appear in the same order, by wavelengths, from longest to shortest: red, orange, yellow, green, blue, violet. A rainbow displays the *spectrum* (7).

Color triad Three colors spaced an equal distance apart on the *color wheel* (7). The primary color triad is red, yellow, and blue; the secondary color triad is orange, green, and violet. A color triad is a type of *color scheme*.

Color wheel The *spectrum* bent into a circle (7).

Compass Instrument used for measuring and drawing arcs and circles.

Complementary colors The colors opposite each other on the *color wheel* (7). A complement of a color absorbs all the light waves the color reflects and is the strongest contrast to the color. Mixing a hue with its complementary color dulls it. Red and green are complementary colors. Complementary colors can be used as a *color scheme*.

Composition The way the principles of design are used to organize the elements (1).

Content The message the work communicates. The content can relate to the subject matter or be an idea or emotion. *Theme* is another word for content (1).

Continuation Technique for creating *unity* by arranging shapes so that the line or edge of one shape continues a line or edge of the next (12).

Contour drawing Drawing in which only *contour lines* are used to represent the subject matter (5). Artists keep their eyes on the object they are drawing and concentrate on directions and curves.

Contour lines Lines creating boundaries that separate one area from another (5). Contour lines define the edges and surface ridges of an object.

Contrast Technique for creating a *focal point* by using differences in elements (12).

Convergence Technique for creating a *focal point* by arranging elements so that many lines or shapes point to one item or area (12).

Cool colors Blue, green, and violet (7). Cool colors suggest coolness and seem to recede from a viewer. Cool colors can be used as a *color scheme*. Opposite of *warm colors*.

Craft guilds Groups of artists working in western European towns in the Middle Ages. Master artists taught *apprentices* their skills.

Crafts Art forms creating works of art that are both beautiful and useful. Crafts include weaving, fabric design, ceramics, and jewelry making.

Crayons *Pigments* held together with wax and molded into sticks.

Credit line A list of important facts about a work of art. A credit line usually includes the artist's name, the title of the work, year completed, *medium* used, size (height, width, and depth), location (gallery, museum, or collection and city), donors, and date donated (1).

Crewel   Loosely twisted yarn used in *embroidery*.

Criteria   Standards of judgment (2).

Crosshatching   The technique of using crossed lines for *shading* (5).

Cubism   Twentieth-century art movement that emphasizes structure and *design* (3). Three-dimensional objects are pictured from many different points of view at the same time.

Culture   Behaviors, customs, ideas, and skills of a group of people. Studying art objects produced by a group of people is one way to learn about a culture.

Curved lines   Lines that are always bending and change direction gradually (5).

D

Dadaists   Early twentieth-century artists using fantastic and strange objects as subject matter.

Dark Ages   See *Middle Ages.*

Decalcomania   The technique of creating random *texture* patterns by pulling apart surfaces between which blobs of paint have been squeezed (8).

Dense   Compact; having parts crowded together. Dense materials are solid and heavy. Opposite of soft.

Description   A list of all the things you see in the work (2).

Design   Plan, organization, or arrangement of elements in a work of art.

Design qualities   How well the work is organized (2). This aesthetic quality is favored by *formalism.*

De Stijl   Dutch for "the style." A painting style developed by Mondrian in Holland in the early twentieth century that uses only vertical and horizontal lines; black, white, and gray; and the three primary colors.

Diagonal lines   Lines that slant (5).

Dimension   Amount of space an object takes up in one direction (5). The three dimensions are height, width, and depth.

Distortion   Deviations from expected, normal *proportions* (11).

Divine Proportion   See *Golden Mean.*

Dome   Hemispherical *vault* or ceiling over a circular opening. A dome rises above the center part of a building.

Dominant element   Element of a work of art noticed first. Elements noticed later are called *subordinate.*

Dyes   *Pigments* that dissolve in liquid. Dye sinks into a material and stains it (7).

Dynamism   Term used by the *Futurists* to refer to the forces of movement.

Dynasty   A period of time during which a single family provided a succession of rulers (3).

E

Edition   A series of identical *prints* made from the same plate (1).

Elements of art   Basic visual symbols in the language of art. The elements of art are *line, shape, form, space, color, value,* and *texture* (1).

Embroidery   Method of decorating fabric with stitches.

Emotionalism   Theory that requires a strong communication of feelings, moods, or ideas from the work to the viewer. One of the three theories of art, the others being *formalism* and *imitationalism* (2).

Emphasis   Principle of *design* that makes one part of a work dominant over the other parts (12). The element noticed first is called *dominant;* the elements noticed later are called *subordinate.*

Engraving   Method of cutting a *design* into a material, usually metal, with a sharp tool. A *print* can be made by inking an engraved surface.

Exaggeration   Deviations from expected, normal *proportions* (11).

Expressionism   Twentieth-century art movement in which artists tried to communicate their strong emotional feelings and which stressed personal feelings rather than *composition* (3).

Expressive qualities   Those qualities that communicate ideas and moods (2).

F

Fabric   Material made from *fibers.* Cloth and felt are fabrics.

Fauves   French for "wild beasts." A group of early twentieth-century painters who used brilliant colors and bold distortions in an uncontrolled way. Their leader was Henri Matisse.

Federal Arts Project   Government program established during the Depression to create jobs for American artists.

Fiber   Thin, threadlike linear material that can be woven or spun into fabric.

Fiberfill   Lightweight, fluffy filling material made of synthetic fibers.

Figure   Human form in a work of art.

Fine art   Works of art made to be enjoyed, not used, and judged by the theories of art. Opposite of *functional art.*

Fire   To apply heat to harden pottery.

Flowing rhythm   Visual rhythm created by repeating wavy lines (9).

Focal point   The first part of a work to attract the attention of the viewer (12). Focal points are created by *contrast, location, isolation, convergence,* and use of the unusual.

Foreground   Part of the *picture plane* that appears closest to the viewer. The foreground is usually at the bottom of the picture.

Foreshortening   To shorten an object to make it look as if it extends backward into space (11). This method reproduces *proportions* a viewer actually sees, which depend on the viewer's distance from the object or person.

Form   Objects having three dimensions (6). Like a *shape,* a form has height and width, but it also has depth. Forms are either *geometric* or *free-form.*

Formal balance   Way of organizing parts of a *design* so that equal, or very similar, elements are placed on opposite sides of a *central axis* (10). Formal balance suggests stability. *Symmetry* is a type of formal balance. Opposite of *informal balance.*

Formalism   Theory that places emphasis on the *design* qualities. One of the three theories of art, the others being *emotionalism* and *imitationalism* (2).

Found materials   Natural objects (such as stones or leaves) and ordinary, manufactured objects (such as coins, keys, wire, or paper plates) found by chance that can be used to create a work of art.

Free-form shapes   Irregular and uneven shapes (6). Their outlines are curved, or angular, or both. Free-form shapes are often natural. Opposite of *geometric shapes.*

Freestanding   Work of art surrounded on all sides by space (6). A three-dimensional work of art is freestanding. Opposite of *relief* (1).

Frottage   A method of placing a freshly painted canvas right-side-up over a raised *texture* and scraping the surface of the paint (8).

Functional art   Works of art made to be used instead of only enjoyed. Objects must be judged by how well they work when used.

Futurists   Early twentieth-century Italian artists who arranged angular forms to suggest motion (9). They called the forces of movement *dynamism*.

Gallery   Place for displaying or selling works of art.

Genre painting   Paintings that have scenes from everyday life as their subject matter.

Geometric shapes   Precise shapes that can be described using mathematical formulas (6). Basic geometric shapes are the circle, the square, and the triangle. Basic geometric forms are the cylinder, the cube, and the pyramid. Opposite of *free-form shapes*.

Gestures   An expressive movement (5).

Gesture drawing   Line drawing done quickly to capture movement of the subject's body (5).

Glaze   In ceramics, a thin, glossy coating fired into pottery. In painting, a thin layer of *transparent* paint.

Golden Mean   A *line* divided into two parts so that the smaller line has the same *proportion*, or ratio, to the larger line as the larger line has to the whole line (11). Perfect ratio (relationship of parts) discovered by Euclid, a Greek Philosopher. Its mathematical expression is 1 to 1.6. It was also called the *Golden Section* and the *Golden Rectangle*. The long sides of the Golden Rectangle are a little more than half again as long as the short sides. This ratio was rediscovered in the early sixteenth century and named the *Divine Proportion*.

Gothic   Artistic style developed in western Europe between the twelfth and sixteenth centuries. Gothic *cathedrals* used pointed arches and flying *buttresses* to emphasize upward movement and featured *stained-glass* windows. *Sculpture* and painting showed humans realistically (3).

Gouache   *Pigments* ground in water and mixed with gum to form *opaque* watercolor. Gouache resembles school tempera or poster paint.

Grattage   The technique of scratching into wet paint with a variety of tools, such as forks, razors, and combs for the purpose of creating different *textures* (8).

Grid   Pattern of intersecting vertical and horizontal lines (9).

Hard-edge   In two-dimensional art, shapes with clearly defined outlines. Hard-edge shapes look dense. Opposite of *soft-edge*.

Harmony   The principle of *design* that creates *unity* by stressing similarities of separate but related parts (12).

Hatching   Technique of *shading* with a series of fine parallel *lines*.

Hierarchical proportion   When figures are arranged in a work of art so scale indicates importance (11).

Hieroglyphics   Picture writing used by ancient Egyptians.

High-key painting   Painting using many *tints* of a *color* (7). Opposite of *low-key painting*.

Highlights   Small areas of white used to show the very brightest spots (6). Highlights show the surfaces of the subject that reflect the most light. They are used to create the illusion of *form*. Opposite of *shadows*.

High relief   *Sculpture* in which areas project far out from a flat surface.

High-resolution   Producing a sharp image.

Hologram   Images in three dimensions created with a laser beam (6).

Horizon   Point at which earth and sky seem to meet.

Horizontal line   *Line* parallel to the horizon (5). Horizontal lines lie flat and are parallel to the bottom edge of the paper or canvas.

Hue   The name of a spectral *color* (7). Hue is related to the wavelength of reflected light. The primary hues are red, yellow, and blue; they are called *primary* because they cannot be made by mixing other hues together. The secondary hues, made by mixing two primary hues, are orange, violet, and green. Hue is one of the three properties of color.

Hyper-Realism   See *New Realism*.

Imitationalism   An *aesthetic* theory focusing on realistic presentation. One of the three theories of art, the others being *emotionalism* and *formalism* (2).

Implied lines   A series of points that the viewer's eyes automatically connect. Implied lines are suggested, not real (5).

Impression   Mark or imprint made by pressure.

Impressionism   Style of painting started in France in the 1860s (3). It captured everyday subjects and emphasized the momentary effects of sunlight.

Industrial designers   People who *design* the products of industry (4).

Informal balance   Way of organizing parts of a *design* so that unlike objects have equal *visual weight* or eye attraction (10). *Asymmetry* is another term for informal balance. Opposite of *formal balance*.

Intensity   The brightness or dullness of a hue. A pure *hue* is called a high-intensity *color*. A dulled hue (a color mixed with its complement) is called a low-intensity color. Intensity is one of the three properties of color (7).

Interior Designer   A person who plans the *design* and decoration of the interior spaces in homes and offices (4).

Intermediate color   A *color* made by mixing a primary color with a secondary color. Red-orange is an intermediate color.

Interpretation   The meaning or mood of the work (2).

Invented texture   A kind of *visual texture* that does not represent a real texture but creates a sensation of one by repeating *lines* and shapes in a two-dimensional pattern (8). Opposite of *simulated texture*.

Isolation   Technique for creating a *focal point* by putting one object alone to emphasize it (12).

Judgment   In art criticism, the step in which you determine the degree of artistic merit (2). In art history, the step in which you determine if the work has made an important contribution to the history of art (3).

Kiln   Furnace in which *clay* is fired in order to harden it. A kiln may be electric, gas, or wood-burning.

Kinetic sculpture   A work of art that actually moves in space (9).

L

Landscape Painting or drawing in which natural land scenery, such as mountains, trees, rivers, or lakes, is the main feature.

Landscape architect A person who *designs* playgrounds, parks, and outdoor areas around buildings and along highways (4).

Layout The way items are arranged on the page (4).

Line A mark drawn with a pointed, moving tool. Although lines can vary in appearance (they can have different lengths, widths, *textures*, directions, and degree of curve), they are considered one-dimensional and are measured by length. A line is also considered the path of a dot through space and is used by an artist to control the viewer's eye movement. There are five kinds of lines: *vertical, horizontal, diagonal, curved,* and *zigzag* (5).

Linear perspective A graphic system that creates the illusion of depth and volume on a flat surface. In one-point linear perspective, all receding lines meet at a single point. In two-point linear perspective, different sets of lines meet at different points (6).

Literal qualities The realistic qualities that appear in the subject of the work (2).

Location The technique of using placement of elements to create a *focal point* (12). Items near the center of a work of art are usually noticed first.

Logos Identifying symbols (4).

Loom Machine or frame for *weaving*.

Low-key painting Painting using many *shades* or dark *values* of a color (7). Opposite of *high-key painting*.

Low-relief See *bas-relief*.

Lucite Trademark for an acrylic plastic molded into *transparent* sheets, tubes, or rods.

M

Mannerism European sixteenth-century artistic style featuring highly emotional scenes and distorted figures.

Manufactured shapes/forms Shapes or forms made by people either by hand or by machine. Opposite of *natural shapes/forms*.

Mat To frame a picture or drawing with a cardboard border.

Matte surface Surface that reflects a soft, dull light (8). Paper has a matte surface. Opposite of *shiny surface*.

Medallion Round, medal-like decoration (10).

Media See *medium*.

Medieval Related to the *Middle Ages*.

Medium Material used to make art. Plural is *media* (1).

Mexican muralists Early twentieth-century artists whose paintings on walls and ceilings used solid *forms* and powerful *colors* to express their feelings about the Mexican Revolution. Also called *Mexican Expressionists*.

Middle Ages Period of roughly one thousand years from the destruction of the Roman Empire to the *Renaissance*. Culture centered around the Church. The Middle Ages are also called the *Dark Ages* (because few new ideas developed) and the *Age of Faith* (because religion was a powerful force.)

Middle ground Area in a picture between the *foreground* and the *background*.

Mobile Moving *sculpture* in which shapes are balanced and arranged on wire arms and suspended from the ceiling to move freely in the air currents (3).

Modeling See *chiaroscuro*.

Modular sculpture *Freestanding* sculpture that joins *modules* (9).

Module A three-dimensional *motif* (9).

Monk's cloth Heavy cloth with a basket weave, often used for curtains.

Monochrome One *color*. A monochromatic *color scheme* uses only one *hue* and the *values, tints,* and *shades* of that hue for a unifying effect (7).

Mortar and pestle Ceramic bowl and tool for grinding something into a powder.

Mosaics Pictures made with small cubes of colored marble, glass, or tile and set into cement.

Motif A unit that is repeated in visual rhythm (9). Units in a motif may or may not be an exact duplicate of the first unit.

Movement Principle of *design* that deals with creating the illusion of action or physical change in position (9).

Mural Painting on a wall or ceiling.

N

Natural shapes/forms Shapes or forms made by the forces of nature. Opposite of *manufactured shapes/forms*.

Negative spaces Empty spaces surrounding *shapes* and *forms* (6). The shape and size of negative spaces affect the interpretation of *positive spaces*. Negative spaces are also called *ground*.

Neoclassicism New classic. French artistic style developed in the nineteenth century after the *Rococo* style. It used *classical* features and was unemotional and realistic.

Neutral colors Black, white, and gray. Black reflects no wavelengths of light, white reflects all wavelengths of light, and gray reflects all wavelengths of light equally but only partially.

New Realism Twentieth-century American artistic style in which subjects are portrayed realistically (3). Also called *Hyper-Realism, Photo-Realism,* and *Super-Realism*.

Nonobjective art Art that has no recognizable subject matter.

O

Oil paint Slow-drying paint made by mixing *pigments* in oil and usually used on *canvas*.

Opaque Quality of a material that does not let any light pass through. Opposite of *transparent*.

Op Art Optical art. Twentieth-century artistic style in which artists tried to create the impression of movement on the surface of paintings with hard edges, smooth surfaces, and mathematical planning.

Optical color *Color* perceived by the viewer due to the effect of atmosphere or unusual light on the actual color (7). Opposite of *arbitrary color*.

Outline A *line* that shows or creates the outer edges of a *shape* (5).

P

Paint *Pigments* mixed with oil or water. Pigment particles in paint stick to the surface of the material on which the paint is applied.

Palette Tray for mixing *colors* of *paints*.

Papier-mâché French for "mashed paper." Modeling material made of paper and liquid paste and molded over a supporting structure called the *armature*.

Parallel lines *Lines* that move in the same direction and always stay the same distance apart.

Pastels *Pigments* held together with gum and molded into sticks.

Paste-up   Model of a printed page. It is photographed for the purpose of making a plate for the printing process.

Pattern   Two-dimensional decorative visual repetition (9). A pattern has no *movement* and may or may not have *rhythm.*

Perception   The act of looking at something carefully and thinking deeply about what is seen (1).

Perspective   A graphic system that creates the illusion of depth and volume on a two-dimensional surface (6). It was developed during the Renaissance by architect Filippo Brunelleschi. Perspective is created by overlapping, size variations, placement, detail, *color,* and *converging lines.*

Photogram   Image on blueprint paper developed by fumes from liquid ammonia.

Photography   A technique of capturing optical images on light-sensitive surfaces (1).

Photojournalists   Visual reporters (4).

Photo-Realism   See *New Realism.*

Picture plane   The surface of a painting or drawing.

Pigments   Finely ground, colored powders that form paint when mixed with a liquid. Pigments are also used to make *crayons* and *pastels* (7).

Plaster   Mixture of lime, sand, and water that hardens on drying.

Point of view   Angle from which the viewer sees an object (6). The shapes and forms a viewer sees depend on his or her point of view.

Polymer medium   Liquid used in *acrylic* painting as a thinning or finishing material.

Pop art   Artistic style used in the early 1960s in America featuring subject matter from popular culture (mass media, commercial art, comic strips, and advertising) (3).

Portrait   Image of a person, especially the face and upper body.

Positive spaces   *Shapes* or *forms* in two- and three-dimensional art (6). Empty spaces surrounding them are called *negative spaces* or *ground.*

Post-Impressionism   French painting style of the late nineteenth century that used basic structures of art to express feelings and ideas (3). The Post-Impressionism movement, which immediately followed *Impressionism,* was led by Paul Cézanne, Vincent van Gogh, and Paul Gauguin.

Prehistoric   Period before history was written down.

Principles of design   Rules that govern how artists organize the elements of art. The principles of design are *rhythm, movement, balance, proportion, variety, emphasis, harmony,* and *unity* (1).

Print   *Impression* created by an artist made on paper or fabric from a *printing plate, stone,* or *block* and repeated many times to produce identical images.

Printing plate   Surface containing the *impression* transferred to paper or fabric to make a *print* (1).

Printmaking   A process in which an artist repeatedly transfers an original image from one prepared surface to another (1).

Prism   Wedge-shaped piece of glass that bends white light and separates it into *spectral hues.*

Profile   Side view of a face.

Progressive rhythm   Visual rhythm that changes a *motif* each time it is repeated (9).

Proportion   Principle of art concerned with the size relationships of one part to another (11).

Protractor   Semicircular instrument used to measure and draw angles.

Proximity   Technique for creating *unity* by limiting *negative spaces* between *shapes* (12).

Pyramids   Tombs of Egyptian pharaohs, who were rulers worshiped as gods.

Radial balance   Type of balance in which forces or elements of a *design* come out (radiate) from a central point (10).

Random rhythm   Visual rhythm in which a *motif* is repeated in no apparent order, with no regular spaces (9).

Rasp   File with sharp, rough teeth used for cutting into a surface.

Realism   Mid-nineteenth-century artistic style in which artists turned away from the style of Romanticism to paint familiar scenes as they actually were (3).

Realists   Artists in the nineteenth century who portrayed political, social, and moral issues (3).

Real texture   Texture that can be perceived through touch. Opposite of *visual texture.*

Recede   To move back or become more distant.

Reformation   Religious revolution in western Europe in the sixteenth century. It started as a reform movement in the Catholic Church and led to the beginnings of Protestantism.

Regionalists   Artists who painted the farmlands and cities of America realistically (3).

Regular rhythm   Visual rhythm achieved through repeating identical *motifs* using the same intervals of *space* between them (9).

Relief   Type of *sculpture* in which *forms* project from a flat background. Opposite of *freestanding* (1).

Renaissance   The name given to the period of awakening at the end of the *Middle Ages* (3). French for "rebirth." Interest in *Classical* art was renewed. Important Renaissance artists are Leonardo da Vinci, Michelangelo, and Raphael.

Repetition   Technique for creating *rhythm* and *unity* in which a *motif* or single element appears again and again (12).

Reproduction   Copy of a work of art.

Rhythm   *Principle of design* that indicates movement by the repetition of elements (9). Visual rhythm is perceived through the eyes and is created by repeating *positive spaces* separated by *negative spaces.* There are five types of rhythm: *random, regular, alternating, flowing,* and *progressive.*

Rococo   Eighteenth-century artistic style that began in the luxurious homes of the French aristocracy and spread to the rest of Europe. It stressed free graceful movement, a playful use of *line,* and delicate *colors* (3).

Romanesque   Style of *architecture* and *sculpture* developed during the Middle Ages in western Europe that featured massive size; solid, heavy walls; wide use of the rounded Roman *arch;* and many sculptural decorations (3).

Romanticism   Early nineteenth-century artistic style that was a reaction against *Neoclassicism.* It featured dramatic scenes, bright *colors,* loose *compositions,* and exotic settings. It also emphasized the feelings and personality of the artist.

Rough texture   Irregular surface that reflects light unevenly (8). Opposite of *smooth texture.*

Rubbing   Technique for transferring textural quality of a surface to paper by placing paper over the surface and rubbing the top of the paper with *crayon* or pencil (8).

Safety labels   Labels identifying *art* products that are safe to use or that must be used with caution.

Scale   Size as measured against a standard reference. Scale can refer to an entire work of art or to elements within it (11).

Score   To make neat, sharp creases in paper using a cutting tool.

Sculpture   Three-dimensional work of art created out of wood, stone, metal, or clay by *carving,* welding, *casting,* or *modeling.*

Seascape   Painting or drawing in which the sea is the subject.

Shade   A dark *value* of a *hue* made by adding black to it. Opposite of *tint* (7).

Shading   See *chiaroscuro*.

Shadows   Shaded areas in a drawing or painting. Shadows show the surfaces of the subject that reflect the least light and are used to create the illusion of *form*. Opposite of *highlights*.

Shape   A two-dimensional area that is defined in some way. While a *form* has depth, a *shape* has only height and width. Shapes are either *geometric* or *free-form* (6).

Shiny surface   Surface that reflects bright light. Window glass has a shiny surface. Opposite of *matte surface*.

Sighting   Technique for determining the proportional relationship of one part of an object to another (11).

Silhouette   Outline drawing of a *shape*. Originally a silhouette was a *profile* portrait, filled in with a solid *color*.

Simplicity   Technique for creating *unity* by limiting the number of variations of an element.

Simulated texture   A kind of *visual texture* that imitates real *texture* by using a two-dimensional pattern to create the illusion of a three-dimensional surface (8). A plastic tabletop can use a pattern to simulate the texture of wood. Opposite of *invented texture*.

Sketch   Quick, rough drawing without much detail that can be used as a plan or reference for later work.

Slip   Creamy mixture of *clay* and water used to fasten pieces of clay together.

Smooth texture   Regular surface that reflects light evenly. Opposite of *rough texture* (8).

Soft-edge   In two-dimensional art, shapes with fuzzy, blurred outlines. Soft-edge shapes look soft. Opposite of *hard-edge*.

Soft sculpture   *Sculpture* made with fabric and stuffed with soft material.

Solvent   The liquid that controls the thickness or the thinness of the *paint* (7).

Space   The element of *art* that refers to the emptiness or area between, around, above, below, or within objects. *Shapes* and *forms* are defined by space around and within them (6).

Spectral colors   Red, orange, yellow, green, blue, violet.

Split complementary colors   One *hue* and the hues on each side of its complement on the *color wheel* (7). Red-orange, blue, and green are split complementary colors. Split complementary colors can be used as a *color scheme*.

Stained glass   Colored glass cut into pieces, arranged in a *design*, and joined with strips of lead.

Static   Inactive (5). Vertical and horizontal lines and horizontal *shapes* and *forms* are static. Opposite of *active*.

Still life   Painting or drawing of inanimate (nonmoving) objects.

Stippling   Technique of *shading* using dots.

Stitchery   Technique for decorating fabric by stitching *fibers* onto it.

Stone Age   Period of history during which stone tools were used.

Storyboards   A series of still drawings that show a story's progress for *animation*. Storyboards are an outline for the development of a film (4).

Style   The artist's personal way of using the elements of *art* and *principles of design* to express feelings and ideas (3).

Subject   The image viewers can easily identify in a work of art (1).

Subordinate element   Element of a work of *art* noticed after the *dominant element*.

Super-Realism   See *New Realism*.

Surrealism   Twentieth-century artistic style in which dreams, fantasy, and the subconscious served as inspiration for artists (3).

Symbol   Something that stands for, or represents, something else (1).

Symmetry   A special type of *formal balance* in which two halves of a balanced *composition* are identical, mirror images of each other (10).

Synthetic   Made by chemical processes rather than natural processes.

T

Tapestry   Fabric wall hanging that is woven, painted, or embroidered.

Tempera   Paint made by mixing *pigments* with egg yolk (egg tempera) or another liquid. School poster paint is a type of tempera.

Texture   Element of art that refers to how things feel, or look as if they might feel if touched. Texture is perceived by touch and sight. Objects can have *rough* or *smooth textures* and *matte* or *shiny surfaces* (8).

Tint   A light *value* of a *hue* made by mixing the hue with white. Opposite of *shade* (7).

Tonality   Arrangement of colors in a painting so that one *color* dominates the work of *art* (7).

Transparent   Quality of a material that allows light to pass through. Opposite of *opaque*.

Trompe l'oeil   French for "deceive the eye." Style of painting in which painters try to give the viewer the illusion of seeing a three-dimensional object, so that the viewer wonders whether he or she is seeing a picture or something real.

U

Undercut   A cut made below another so that an overhang is left.

Unity   The quality of wholeness or oneness that is achieved through the effective use of the elements and principles of art (12). Unity is created by *simplicity, repetition, proximity,* and *continuation*.

Unusual   Technique for creating a *focal point* by using the unexpected (12).

V

Value   The art element that describes the darkness or lightness of an object (5). Value depends on how much light a surface reflects. Value is also one of the three properties of *color*.

Vanishing point   Point on the horizon where receding parallel lines seem to meet (6).

Variety   *Principle of design* concerned with difference or contrast (12).

Vault   Arched roof, ceiling, or covering made of brick, stone, or concrete.

Vehicle   Liquid, like water or oil, that *pigments* are mixed with to make *paint* or *dye*.

Vertical lines   *Lines* that are straight up and down (5). Vertical lines are at right angles to the bottom edge of the paper or canvas and the horizon, and parallel to the side of the paper or canvas.

Viewing frame   A piece of paper with an area cut from the middle. By holding the frame at arm's length and looking through it at the subject, the artist can focus on the area of the subject he or she wants to draw or paint.

Visual arts   The arts that produce beautiful objects to look at.

Visual rhythm   Rhythm you receive through your eyes rather than through your ears (9).

Visual texture   Illusion of a three-dimensional surface based on the memory of how things feel. There are two types of visual texture: *invented* and *simulated*. Opposite of *real texture* (8).

Visual weight   Attraction that elements in a work of *art* have for the viewer's eyes. Visual weight is affected by size, *contour*, *intensity* of colors, warmth and coolness of colors, contrast in *value*, *texture*, and position.

Warm colors   Red, orange, and yellow (7). Warm colors suggest warmth and seem to move toward the viewer. Warm colors can be used as a *color scheme*. Opposite of *cool colors*.

Warp   In *weaving*, lengthwise threads held in place on the loom and crossed by *weft* threads.

Watercolor paint   *Transparent pigments* mixed with water.

Weaving   Art of making fabric by interlacing two sets of parallel threads, held at right angles to each other on a *loom*.

Weft   In *weaving*, crosswise threads that are carried over and under the *warp* threads.

Yarn   Fibers spun into strands for *weaving*, knitting, or embroidery.

Zigzag lines   *Lines* formed by short, sharp turns (5). Zigzag lines are a combination of diagonal lines. They can change direction suddenly.

Richter, Gisela M. A. *The Sculpture and Sculptors of the Greeks.* 4th ed., rev. New Haven, CT: Yale University Press, 1970.

Art History

Armstrong, Tom, et al. *200 Years of American Sculpture.* Boston: David R. Godine, Publishers, Inc., 1976. An informative look at the evolution of American sculpture.

Arnason, H. H. *History of Modern Art: Painting, Sculpture, Architecture, Photography.* 3d ed. NY: Harry N. Abrams, 1986.

Barnicoat, John. *Posters: A Concise History.* NY: Thames and Hudson, 1985. The importance of the poster, including its role in various artistic movements.

Beaton, Cecil Walter Hardy and Gail Buckland. *The Magic Image: The Genius of Photography.* NY: Viking-Penguin, Inc., 1990. An assortment of the work of over two hundred photographers since 1839, with biographical sketches.

Broder, Patricia J. *American Indian Painting and Sculpture.* NY: Abbeville Press, Inc., 1981. A good introduction to contemporary Indian art with excellent illustrations.

Chadwick, Whitney. *Women, Art, and Society.* The World of Art Series. London: Thames and Hudson, 1989.

Driskell, David. C. *Two Centuries of Black American Art.* NY: Los Angeles County Museum of Art and Random House, 1976.

Dwyer, Jane Powell, and Edward B. Dwyer. *Traditional Art of Africa, Oceania, and the Americas.* San Francisco, CA: Fine Arts Museum of San Francisco, 1973.

Etthighausen, Richard, and Oleg Grabar. *The Art and Architecture of Islam: 650–1250.* New Haven, CT: Yale University Press, 1992.

Feldman, Edmund B. *Thinking About Art.* Englewood Cliffs, NJ: Prentice-Hall, Inc., 1985. Combines aesthetics, art criticism, and art history. For the academically gifted student.

Frisch, T. G. *Gothic Art 1140-ca. 1450.* Toronto, Canada: University of Toronto Press, 1987.

Gardner, Helen. *Art Through the Ages.* 9th ed. NY: Harcourt Brace Jovanovich, Inc., 1991. An art history resource book for teachers.

Handlin, Oscar. *Statue of Liberty.* NY: Newsweek Book Division, 1980. A history of the conception and building of the symbolic statue.

Highwater, Jamake. *Arts of the Indian Americas: Leaves from the Sacred Tree.* NY: Harper & Row Publishers, Inc., 1983. Provides an excellent view of the arts of North, South, and Central American Indians, with information on culture and history of Native Americans.

Hillier, Bevis. *The Style of the Century: 1900–1980.* Franklin, NY: Amsterdam Books, 1990. A survey of style in art and industrial design from the turn of the century to the present with a look at the social, political, and economic situations that influenced each decade's sense of style.

Janson, H. W. *History of Art for Young People.* 4th ed. NY: Harry N. Abrams, Inc., 1992. Can be used for art history reports by academically advanced students.

Johnson, Una E. *American Prints and Printmakers: A Chronicle of Over 400 Artists and Their Prints From 1900 to the Present.* NY: Doubleday and Co., Inc., 1980. A survey of artists involved in printmaking in this century.

Lassiter, Barbara Babcock. *American Wilderness: The Hudson River School of Painting.* NY: Doubleday and Co., Inc., 1978. A history of this American realistic landscape school of painting.

Lee, Sherman. *A History of Far Eastern Art.* 4th ed. NY: Harry N. Abrams, 1982.

Lewinski, Jorge. *The Camera at War: A History of War Photography From 1848 to the Present Day.* NY: Simon and Schuster, 1980. A look at combat photographers, the problems they face, and the work they produce.

Sandler, Martin W. *The Story of American Photography: An Illustrated History for Young People.* Boston: Little, Brown and Co., 1979. A survey of American photographers and their work.

Sayer, Chloe. *The Arts and Crafts of Mexico.* San Francisco, CA: Chronicle Books, 1990. An overview of Mexican crafts with good discussion of history and culture. Richly illustrated.

Shadwell, Wendy J., et al. *American Printmaking, the First 150 Years.* Washington, D.C.: Smithsonian Institution Press, 1969. A thorough retrospective on American printmaking.

Taylor, Joshua C. *Learning to Look: A Handbook for the Visual Arts.* 2d ed. Chicago: University of Chicago Press, 1981.

Wilmerding, John. *American Masterpieces from the National Gallery of Art.* NY: Hudson Hills Press, 1980.

Artists

Adams, Ansel. *The Portfolios of Ansel Adams.* Boston: Little, Brown and Co., 1981. Adams's seven limited-edition portfolios in one volume. A definitive collection of his stunning photographic work.

Brown, Jonathan. *Diego de Velázquez, Painter and Courtier.* New Haven, CT: Yale University Press, 1986.

Bruzeau, Maurice. *Alexander Calder.* Translated by I. Mark. NY: Harry N. Abrams, Inc., 1979. A picture book of Calder's work.

Chambers, D. S. *Patrons and Artists in the Italian Renaissance.* Columbia, SC: University of South Carolina Press, 1971.

Feaver, William. *Masters of Caricature: From Hogarth and Gillray to Scarfe and Levine.* NY: Alfred E. Knopf, Inc., 1981. Brief biographical sketches of caricaturists of the last three centuries. Illustrated.

Hoving, Thomas. *Two Worlds of Andrew Wyeth: A Conversation with Andrew Wyeth.* Boston: Houghton Mifflin Co., 1978. Includes many examples of Wyeth's work as well as a long interview.

Kelder, Diane. *The French Impressionists and Their Century.* NY: Praeger, 1970.

Levin, Gail. *Edward Hopper: The Art and the Artist.* NY: W. W. Norton and Co., Inc., 1986. A representative collection of Hopper's work, combined with text on Hopper's development and characteristic themes.

Lisle, Laurie. *Portrait of an Artist: A Biography of Georgia O'Keeffe.* Albuquerque, NM: University of New Mexico, 1986. A fascinating account of O'Keeffe's life and work.

Locher, J. L., ed. *The World of M. C. Escher.* NY: Harry N. Abrams, Inc., 1988. A catalog of the precise, visually intricate and often stunning work of the Dutch mathematician and artist.

Rewald, John. *Post-Impressionism: From Van Gogh to Gauguin.* 2d ed. NY: The Museum of Modern Art, 1962.

Rockwell, Norman. *Norman Rockwell: My Adventures As An Illustrator.* NY: Harry N. Abrams, Inc., 1988. Rockwell's own fascinating account of his life and career.

Rubin, William, ed. *Pablo Picasso: A Retrospective.* NY: Museum of Modern Art, 1980. The catalog of the huge Picasso retrospective at the Museum of Modern Art.

Slatkin, Wendy. *Women Artists in History.* 2d. ed. Englewood Cliffs, NJ: Prentice-Hall, Inc., 1989. An important reference because most art-history books ignore the contribution of women artists.

Snyder, Robert R. *Buckminster Fuller: An Autobiographical Monologue/Scenario.* NY: St. Martin's Press, Inc., 1980. A thorough and personal depiction of Fuller's life and work.

Vasari, Giorgio. *Lives of the Artists.* Translated by Betty Burroughs. NY: Simon and Schuster, 1946.

The following books are from the Time-Life Library of Art, published by Time-Life Books, Alexandria, VA. They are excellent biographical sources, providing insight into the lives of the artists and their works, contemporaries, and times.

Brown, Dale. *The World of Velázquez* (1599–1660). 1969.

Coughlan, Robert. *The World of Michelangelo* (1475–1564). 1966.

Flexner, James Thomas. *The World of Winslow Homer* (1836–1910). 1966.

Hale, William Harlan. *The World of Rodin* (1840–1917). 1969.

Hirsch, Diana. *The World of Turner* (1775–1851). 1969.

Koning, Hans. *The World of Vermeer* (1632–1675). 1977.

Leonard, Jonathan Norton. *The World of Gainsborough* (1727–1788). 1969.

Prideaux, Tom. *The World of Whistler* (1834–1903). 1970.

Russell, John. *The World of Matisse* (1869–1954). 1969.

Schickel, Richard. *The World of Goya* (1746–1828). 1968.

Wallace, Robert. *The World of Leonardo* (1452–1519). 1966.

Wallace, Robert. *The World of Rembrandt* (1606–1669). 1968.

Wallace, Robert. *The World of Van Gogh* (1853–1890). 1969.

Wedgwood, C. V. *The World of Rubens* (1577–1640). 1967.

Wertenbaker, Lael. *The World of Picasso* (1881–). 1967.

Williams, Jay. *The World of Titian* (c. 1488–1576). 1968.

INDEX

A

Abbot, Berenice, *Façade, Alwyn Court,* 127, 129, Fig. 6.17
Above the Trees, 170, Fig. 7.27
Abstract Expressionism, 63, 64, Fig. 3.32
Active lines, 97
Active shapes and forms, 142, Fig. 6.39
  activities, 143
Activities
  Applying Your Skills
    architecture, 49, 50
    art criticism, 27, 28, 29–30, 32
    art history, 49, 50, 54, 55, 63, 65
    balance, 253, 256, 261, 267
    careers, 74, 78, 79, 81
    color, 159, 162, 163, 169, 173, 176
    credit line, 18
    drawing, 10
    emphasis, 322
    form, 123, 133
    line, 92, 94, 95, 99, 100, 102–103, 105
    painting, 11
    photography, 15
    point of view, 131
    printmaking, 14
    proportion, 287, 290, 292, 298
    rhythm, 223, 226, 230, 233, 235
    scale, 287
    shape, 122, 143
    space, 125, 128
    texture, 194, 197, 204
    unity, 331
    variety, 315
  Computer Options
    balance, 255, 256–257, 263, 267
    careers, 74
    color, 159, 163, 169–170, 173, 176
    drawing, 11
    emphasis, 322
    form, 123, 133
    line, 92, 94, 95, 100, 101, 103, 104, 105
    point of view, 131
    printmaking, 14
    proportion, 287, 290, 293, 299
    rhythm, 224, 226, 227, 230–231, 234, 235
    scale, 287
    shape, 122, 143
    space, 126, 128
    texture, 194, 197, 204
    unity, 332
    variety, 315
  Further Challenges
    architecture, 50
    art criticism, 27, 28, 30, 32
    art history, 49, 50, 54, 55, 63, 65
    balance, 253, 256, 261, 267
    careers, 74, 78, 79, 81
    color, 159, 162, 163, 169, 173, 176
    credit line, 18
    drawing, 11

    emphasis, 322
    form, 123, 133
    line, 92, 94, 95, 99, 101, 103, 104, 105
    painting, 11
    photography, 15
    point of view, 131
    printmaking, 14
    proportion, 287, 290, 293, 298
    rhythm, 223–224, 226–227, 230, 233, 235
    scale, 287
    shape, 122, 143
    space, 125, 128
    texture, 194, 197, 204
    unity, 332
    variety, 315
Additive process, 16
Adoration of the Magi, The, 135, Fig. 6.25
Adoration of the Shepherds, The, 260, 261, Fig. 10.20
Advertising artist, 73, Fig. 4.3
Aesthetic experience, 27
  activities, 27
Aesthetics, 25
Aesthetic theories, 30–31
  activities, 32
African art, 57–58, Figs. 3.24, 3.25
African Canvas, photo from, 172, Fig. 7.30
Afterimage, 157–158, Fig. 7.5
Age of Faith, 50
Albers, Josef, *Homage to the Square: Glow,* 263, 265, Fig. 10.26
Albright, Ivan, 197
  The Farmer's Kitchen, 197, 200, Fig. 8.16
Alquimia XIII, 203, Fig. 8.22
Alternating rhythm, 228–231, Figs. 9.13–9.16
  activities, 230–231
American Gothic, 253, 254, Fig. 10.8
Amplitude, 110, Fig. 5.37
Analogous colors, 165, 166, Figs. 7.19, 7.20
Analysis
  activities, 54, 55
  in art criticism, 27, 28, 34
  in art history, 42
  defined, 28
Ancient Greek art, 48, 49, Fig. 3.12
Ancient river valleys
  Chinese art, 44–45, Fig. 3.6
  Egyptian art, 44, Fig. 3.4
  Indian art, 45–46, Fig. 3.7
  Mesopotamian art, 44, 45, Fig. 3.5
Ancient Roman art, 48–49, Fig. 3.13
Andrews, Benny, *The Scholar,* 100, 101, Fig. 5.28
Angkor Wat temple, 46, Fig. 3.9
Animation, 78
  activities, 79
  career, 78, Fig. 4.9
Anna and David, 280–281, Fig. 11.1
Annunciation, The, 187, Fig. 7.42
Apartment Hill, 342–343, Fig. 12.31
Apel, Marie, *Grief,* 141, Fig. 6.38
Apollo 11, 19, Fig. 1.16
Applied art
  career, 81
  defined, 16
  judging, 31–32

  space in, 127–128
  texture in, 203–204, Figs. 8.22–8.24
Appliqué, 212
  Studio Lesson, 212–213
Applying Your Skills. *See* Activities
Approximate symmetry, 253, 254, Figs. 10.8, 10.10
  expressive qualities, 264, 266, Fig. 10.28
Aquatique, 123, 124, Fig. 6.9
Arbitrary color, 174–175, Figs. 7.34, 7.35
Architect, 76–77
  landscape architect, 77, Fig. 4.8
Architecture
  activities, 49–50
  career, 76–77
  Gothic, 50, 51, Fig. 3.15
  Romanesque, 49, 50
  space in, 126–127, Fig. 6.14
  texture in, 201, Fig. 8.19
  twentieth-century, 61–62, 64–65, Figs. 3.30, 3.34
Armchair, 31–32, Fig. 2.7
Armor of George Clifford, Third Earl of Cumberland, 288, Fig. 11.13
Armory Show of 1913, 60
Arp, Jean (Hans), *Aquatique,* 123, 124, Fig. 6.9
Art criticism, 25–37
  activities, 27, 28, 29–30, 32
  aesthetic theories, 30–31
  analysis step, 28, 34
  Christina's World example, 32–34, Fig. 2.8
  Dawn example, 34–35, Fig. 2.9
  defined, 25
  description step, 27–28, 32–34
  four-step system, 27
  interpretation step, 29–30, 34
  judgment step, 30–32, 34
  purpose of, 26–27
Art Criticism in Action, 20–21, 36–37, 66–67, 82–83, 114–115, 150–151, 186–187, 214–215, 308–309, 342–343
Art director for performing arts, 79, 80, Fig. 4.11
Art education, 80, 81, Fig. 4.12
Art history, 41–69
  activities, 49–50, 54, 55, 63, 65
  analysis step, 42
  description step, 42
  four-step system, 42
  interpretation step, 43
  judgment step, 43
Art therapists, 80
Asante peoples, *Wrapper,* 228, Fig. 9.11
Ashcan School, 60
Asian art
  ancient China, 44–45, Fig. 3.6
  ancient India, 45–46, Fig. 3.7
  China, 47, Fig. 3.10
  India, 46, 47, Figs. 3.8, 3.9
  Japan, 48, Fig. 3.11
Asleep, 316, 318, Fig. 12.7
Assemblage, 118, 119, Fig. 6.1
  Studio Lessons, 208–209, 334–335
Assembly, 16
Assumption of the Virgin, The, 288, Fig. 11.14
Asymmetrical balance. *See* Informal balance
Avanti, 74, Fig. 4.4

B

Baby at Play, 257, Fig. 10.15
Baby Reaching for an Apple, 24, 25, 28, Fig. 2.1
Background, 136
Background artists, 78
Bak, Bronislaw M.
  Holocaust, 156, Fig. 7.3
  Interpenetrations in Red, 316, Fig. 12.4
Bak, Hedi, *Grand Canyon #2,* 194, Fig. 8.4
Balance, 250–279
  activities, 253, 255, 256–257, 261, 263, 267
  central axis, 252, Figs. 10.3, 10.4
  defined, 252
  expressive qualities, 263–267, Figs. 10.24–10.30
  formal, 252–257, Figs. 10.5–10.14
  informal (asymmetrical), 257–263, Figs. 10.15–10.23
  overview, 251
  Studio Lessons, 268–275
  visual balance, 252, Figs. 10.3, 10.4
Balla, Giacomo
  Dynamism of a Dog on a Leash, 235, 236, Fig. 9.24
  Street Light, 234, 235, Fig. 9.20
Ballplayer figurine, 53, Fig. 3.18
Bamum peoples' art, 57, Fig. 3.24
Baptism in Kansas, 321, Fig. 12.10
Barlach, Ernst, *Singing Man,* 327, 328, Fig. 12.19
Baroque art, 54, Fig. 3.20
  activities, 54
Barricade, 62, Fig. 3.31
Baseball Players Practicing, 55, Fig. 3.21
Basket, 244–245, Fig. 9.30
Basketmaking, 360–361
Bas relief, 127, 129, Fig. 6.16
Bayless, Florence, *Haori Coat,* 326, 327, Fig. 12.16
Bearden, Romare, *Prevalence of Ritual: Baptism,* 178–179, Fig. 7.37
Beasts of the Sea, 132, Fig. 6.21
Beats in visual rhythm, 222–224, Figs. 9.2, 9.4
Beaux, Cecilia, *Ernesta (Child with Nurse),* 321–322, Fig. 12.11
Bedroom from the Sagredo Palace, 98, 100, Fig. 5.25
Bell Tower of the Cathedral at Pisa, 252, Fig. 10.3
Benton, Thomas Hart
  I Got a Girl on Sourwood Mountain, 97, 98, Fig. 5.23
  The Sources of Country Music, 61, Fig. 3.29
Bernini, Gianlorenzo, *David,* 277, Fig. 10.36
Binder, 11, 171
Bird, 210–211, Fig. 8.29
Birthday, 296, 298, Fig. 11.28
Bishop, Isabel
  Meet the Artist, 310
  Two Girls, 291, 292, Fig. 11.20
  Waiting, 308–309, Fig. 11.36
Blackfeet Man's Leggings, 53, 121, Fig. 6.5
Black-on-black storage jar, 274–275, Fig. 10.34
Blam, 336–337, Fig. 12.28

Blank Signature, The, 148–149, 206, Fig. 6.46
Blending, 350
Blessing Rain Chant, 97, Fig. 5.21
Blind Botanist, The, 139, 140, Fig. 6.35
Blueberry Highway, Dogtown, 164, 165, Fig. 7.18
Blue Wall, The, 29–30, Fig. 2.5
Body Adornment, 253, Fig. 10.6
Bonheur, Rosa, *The Horse Fair,* 54, 223, 224, Fig. 9.4
Botero, Fernando, *The Pinzon Family,* 302–303, Fig. 11.33
Boticelli, Sandro, *The Adoration of the Magi,* 135, Fig. 6.25
Bowl, 226, Fig. 9.7
Brahma, 47
Brancusi, Constantin, *Torso of a Young Man,* 139, 140, Fig. 6.36
Brayer, 11
Broadway Boogie Woogie, 176, Fig. 7.35
Brueghel Series, The (A Vanitas of Style), 180–181, Fig. 7.38
Brunelleschi, Filippo, 51
Burchfield, Charles, *October Wind and Sunlight in the Woods,* 222, 223, Fig. 9.3
Burghers of Calais, The, 324, 325, Fig. 12.14
Business and industry careers, 72–75
Byzantine art, 49, 50, Fig. 3.14

C

Calder, Alexander, 61, 108
  Lobster Trap and Fish Tail, 237, Fig. 9.26
  Varese, 108, Fig. 5.36
Calligraphic drawing, 103–104, Figs. 5.32, 5.33
  technique tips, 349
Calligraphy, 103
Careers, 71–85
  activities, 74, 78, 79, 81
  animation, 78
  architecture, 76–77
  art direction for performing arts, 79
  art education, 80
  business and industry, 72–75
  city planning, 77
  education and cultural enrichment, 80–81
  entertainment, 78–79
  environmental planning and development, 76–78
  exhibit and display design, 77–78
  fashion design, 74–75
  fine arts and crafts, 81
  graphic design, 72–73
  industrial design, 73–74
  interior design, 77
  landscape architecture, 77
  photography, 75
  special effects design, 78–79
  thinking about an art career, 81
Carpenter, Miles Burkholder, *Root Monster,* 184–185, Fig. 7.40
Carr, Emily
  Above the Trees, 170, Fig. 7.27
  Forest, British Columbia, 327, 328, Fig. 12.18

Cartoonist, 73
Cartoons
  activities, 298
  exaggeration in, 297
Carved Lacquer Circular Tray, 255, Fig. 10.12
Carving, 16
Cassatt, Mary
  Baby Reaching for an Apple, 24, 25, 28, Fig. 2.1
  Five O'Clock Tea, 270–271, Fig. 10.32
Casting, 16
Catastrophe No. 2, 98, 99, Fig. 5.24
Cathedrals, Gothic, 50, 51, Fig. 3.15
Catlett, Elizabeth, *Sharecropper,* 13, Fig. 1.9
Catlin, George, *See-non-ty-a, an Iowa Medicine Man,* 294, Fig. 11.23
Cave paintings, 43–44, Fig. 3.3
Celebration of Arts: Vibrations of Life, 340–341, Fig. 12.30
Central axis, 252, Figs. 10.3, 10.4
Central Park, 77, Fig. 4.8
Centre for Innovative Technology, 65, Fig. 3.34
Cézanne, Paul, *Le Chateau Noir,* 55, 56, Fig. 3.23
Chagall, Marc, *Birthday,* 296, 298, Fig. 11.28
Chapelle Notre-Dame-du-Haut, 285, Fig. 11.9
Chiaroscuro, 132
Children's proportions, 289, 291, 293, Figs. 11.16, 11.21
Chinese art, 47, Fig. 3.10
  ancient China, 44–45, Fig. 3.6
Chippewa Man's Leggings, 53, 121, Fig. 6.6
Christ and the Apostles, 95, 96, Fig. 5.17
Christina's World, 32–34, Fig. 2.8
Churches and cathedrals
  Gothic, 50, 51, Fig. 3.15
  Romanesque, 49, 50
Church, Frederic Edwin, *Our Banner in the Sky,* 264, 267, Fig. 10.30
City planning, 76, 77, Fig. 4.7
Clay
  Studio Lessons, 146–147, 274–275, 300–301, 338–339
  technique tips, 354–355
Clements, Bob, *Evening Up the Score,* 263, Fig. 10.24
Clive, Carolyn, 110
  Amplitude, 110, Fig. 5.37
Close, Chuck
  Janet, 246–247, Fig. 9.31
  Meet the Artist, 248
Coastal Huari, Mantle, 224, 225, Fig. 9.5
Coiled basket, 360–361
Coil technique, 355
Collage
  defined, 201
  display tips, 362–363
  Studio Lessons, 178–179, 240–241
  texture in, 201, Fig. 8.18
  tissue paper, 361–362
Color, 154–189
  activities, 159, 162, 163, 169, 176
  arbitrary, 174–175, Figs. 7.34, 7.35
  color schemes, 164–170, Figs. 7.17–7.27

Color (*continued*)
defined, 156
hue, 158–159, Figs. 7.7–7.9
illusion of depth and, 136, Fig. 6.30
in informal balance, 258–260, Figs. 10.18, 10.19
intensity, 162–163, Figs. 7.14–7.16
movement and, 176, Fig. 7.35
optical, 174, 175, Figs. 7.32, 7.33
pigments, 171–173, Figs. 7.30, 7.31
space and, 175
spectrum, 156
Studio Lessons, 178–185
surface texture and, 172–173
tonality, 176, 177, Fig. 7.36
value, 159–162, 352, Figs. 7.10–7.13
vision and, 156–158, 164, Figs. 7.2–7.6, 7.17
Color-blindness, 157
Color-field painting, 63
Color schemes, 164–170
activities, 169–170
analogous colors, 165, 166, Figs. 7.19, 7.20
color triads, 166, 168, Figs. 7.22, 7.23
complementary colors, 165–166, 167, Fig. 7.21
monochromatic colors, 164–165, Fig. 7.18
overview, 164
split complements, 168, Fig. 7.24
warm and cool colors, 168, 169, 260, Figs. 7.25, 7.26
Color spectrum, 156
Color triads, 166, 168, Figs. 7.22, 7.23
Color wheel, 159, Figs. 7.8, 7.9
Columbus, Christopher, 53
Comic strip artists, 73
Coming of Age, 231, 233, Fig. 9.19
Complementary colors
color scheme, 165–166, 167, Fig. 7.21
defined, 162, 163, Fig. 7.15
split complements, 168, Fig. 7.24
Composition, 17, 30
Computer graphics artist, 72–73, Fig. 4.2
Computer Options. *See* Activities
Constantine, 49
Content, 17–18, 30
Continuity and unity, 331, 332, Fig. 12.24
Contour drawing, 100–102, Figs. 5.26–5.29
technique tips, 349
Contour in informal balance, 258, 259, Fig. 10.17
Contour line, 100
activities, 100–101
Contrast. *See* Variety
Convergence and the focal point, 321, Fig. 12.10
Conversation in Autumn, 47, Fig. 3.10
Cool colors, 168, 169, Fig. 7.25
in informal balance, 260
Copley, John Singleton, *Paul Revere,* 294, Fig. 11.22
Cordero, Helen, 300–301
Corn-husk mask, 53, Fig. 3.19
Courtney-Clarke, Margaret, photo from *African Canvas,* 172, Fig. 7.30
Cow's Skull, 264, 266, Fig. 10.28

Crafts
career, 81
overview, 16–17
See also Applied art
Cram, Goodhue, and Ferguson, Federal Reserve Building, 253, 254, Fig. 10.7
Credit line, 18
activities, 18
Creek shoulder bag, 228, 230, Fig. 9.14
Criteria, 25
Crosshatching, 105, 350
Cubi IX, 122, 123, Fig. 6.8
Cubism, 59, Fig. 3.27
Curnoe, Greg, *Mariposa 10 Speed,* 95, 96, Fig. 5.18
Cuneiform writing, 44
Cups 4 Picasso, 124, Fig. 6.10
Curling paper, 356
Curry, John Steuart, *Baptism in Kansas,* 321, Fig. 12.10
Curved lines, 93–94, Fig. 5.10
degree of curve, 94–95, Fig. 5.16
expressive qualities, 98–99, 100, Fig. 5.25
spirals, 98–99
Cutting
mats, 362–363
safety note, 208, 273

D

Dadaists, 59, 206
Dali, Salvador, *The Persistence of Memory,* 60, 206, Fig. 3.28
Dancing Lady, 284–285, Fig. 11.8
Daniel in the Lions' Den, 215, Fig. 8.32
David, 277, Fig. 10.36
David, Jacques Louis, *Death of Socrates,* 54, 115, Fig. 5.40
David Wright House, The, 61, 62, Fig. 3.30
da Vinci. *See* Leonardo da Vinci
Dawn, 34–37, Fig. 2.9
Dawn's Wedding Chapel, 327, 329, Fig. 12.20
de Amaral, Olga, *Alquimia XIII,* 203, Fig. 8.22
Death of Socrates, 54, 115, Fig. 5.40
Decalcomania, 204, 205, Fig. 8.26
Studio Lesson, 206–207
Degas, Edgar
Little Fourteen-Year-Old Dancer, 203, Fig. 8.21
The Millinery Shop, 323, Fig. 12.12
Degree of curve, 94–95, Fig. 5.16
Density of forms, 140
Depth
activities, 138–139
depth perception, 129
illusion of, 135–139, Figs. 6.24–6.33
Description
activities, 28
in art criticism, 27–28, 32–34
in art history, 42
defined, 27
Design qualities
composition and, 30
defined, 30
Formalism and, 30

Detail and illusion of depth, 136, Fig. 6.29
Diagonal lines, 93, 94, Fig. 5.9
expressive qualities, 97, 98, 99, Figs. 5.23, 5.24
Dick, Beau, *Sacred Circles,* 272–273, Fig. 10.33
Dillon, Leo and Diane
Meet the Artist, 84
A Wrinkle in Time cover illustration, 82–83, Fig. 4.13
Dimension, 92–93
See also Perspective, Space
Direction of lines, 94–95, Fig. 5.15
Dirty Snow, 204, 205, Fig. 8.25
Discobolus, 48, 49, Fig. 3.12
Display designer, 77–78
activity, 78
Display tips, 362–363
Distortion and exaggeration, 294–299, Figs. 11.24–11.31
activities, 298–299
defined, 294
in masks, 297, 299, Fig. 11.30
Studio Lessons, 302–307
Dodd, Lamar, *Night Before Launch,* 19, Fig. 1.17
Dominant element, 315
Drawing
activities, 10–11
calligraphic drawing, 103–104, 349, Figs. 5.32, 5.33
contour drawing, 100–102, 349, Figs. 5.28, 5.29
defined, 7
display tips, 362–363
gesture drawing, 102–103, 349, Figs. 5.30, 5.31
overview, 7–10
Studio Lessons, 112–113, 144–145, 148–149, 268–269, 302–303
technique tips, 349–352
Duchamp, Marcel, 237
Dürer, Albrecht
An Oriental Ruler Seated on His Throne, 105, 132, 134, Fig. 6.23
Virgin and Child with Saint Anne, 291, 293, Fig. 11.21
Dvorak, Lois
The Lizards, 316, 318, Fig. 12.6
Spirit Boxes I, 334–335, Fig. 12.27
Dyes, 171
Dynamism, 235, 237
Dynamism of a Dog on a Leash, 235, 236, Fig. 9.24
Dynasty, 45

E

Eakins, Thomas, 55
Baby at Play, 257, Fig. 10.15
Baseball Players Practicing, 55, Fig. 3.21
Early Sunday Morning, 97, 98, Fig. 5.22
East River Drive, 92, 93, Fig. 5.6
East Wind Suite: Door, 88, 89, Fig. 5.1
Editions, 13
Editorial cartoonists, 73

Education and cultural enrichment
  careers, 80–81
Egyptian art, ancient, 44, 139, Figs. 3.4,
  6.34
Eighteenth-century art, 54
Eight, The, 60
Elements of art
  and analysis step of art criticism, 28
  color, 154–189
  defined, 6
  emphasizing an element, 315–316, Fig.
  12.4
  form, 122–124, Figs. 6.7–6.9
  Formalism and, 30
  line, 88–117
  overview, 6
  shape, 120–122, Figs. 6.2–6.6
  space, 124–129, Figs. 6.10–6.17
  subordinate and dominant, 315
  texture, 190–217
  value, 105, 159–162
  See also specific elements
Elevator Grille, 225, Fig. 9.6
Embroidery stitches, 357–358
Emotionalism
  activities, 32
  as aesthetic theory, 30–31
  defined, 30
  expressive qualities and, 30
Emphasis, 315–322, Figs. 12.4–12.11
  activities, 322
  of an area, 316–322, Figs. 12.5–12.11
  artists' use of, 332–333, Fig. 12.26
  defined, 315
  of an element, 315–316, Fig. 12.4
  focal point, 316–322, Figs. 12.5–12.11
  overview, 313
  Studio Lesson, 340–341
  See also Focal point
Enlarging drawings, 352
Entertainment careers, 78–79
Environmental planning and
  development careers, 76–78
Epstein, Sir Jacob, The Visitation, 28, Fig.
  2.4
Equestrian figure, 57, 58, Fig. 3.25
Ernesta (Child with Nurse), 321–322, Fig.
  12.11
Ernst, Max
  The Eye of Silence, 204, 206–207, Fig. 8.27
  techniques for texture, 204–206, Figs.
  8.26, 8.27
Escher, M. C., Other World, 124, 127, Fig.
  6.13
Etruscan arts, 48
Euclid, 282
Evening Rain on the Karasaki Pine, 48,
  Fig. 3.11
Evening Up the Score, 263, Fig. 10.24
Ewe peoples, Wrapper, 242–243, Fig. 9.29
Exaggeration. See Distortion and exaggeration
Exhibit and display designer, 77–78
Expressionism, 58–59, Fig. 3.26
  Abstract Expressionism, 63, 64, Fig. 3.32
Expressive qualities
  arbitrary color, 174–175, Figs. 7.34, 7.35
  of balance, 263–267, Figs. 10.24–10.30
  content and, 30
  defined, 30

of distortion and exaggeration, 294–299,
  Figs. 11.24–11.31
  Emotionalism and, 30
  of line, 97–100, Figs. 5.21–5.27
  of space, shape, and form, 139–143, Figs.
  6.34–6.43
  Studio Lessons, 182–183, 302–303
  value and, 161
Eye of Silence, The, 204, 206–207, Fig. 8.27
Eyes and color, 156–158, 164, Figs.
  7.2–7.6, 7.17

Faaturuma (The Dreamer), 154, 155, Fig.
  7.1
Façade, Alwyn Court, 127, 129, Fig. 6.17
Faces, 290–293, Figs. 11.18–11.21
  activities, 292–293
Fallen Vase, 7, Fig. 1.2
Falling Water House, 330, 331, Fig. 12.21
Family Group, 20, 21, 22, Fig. 1.18
Farmer's Kitchen, The, 197, 200, Fig. 8.17
Fashion designers, 74–75, Fig. 4.5
Fauves, 58
Feather Bonnet, 190–191, Fig. 8.1
Featherwork ornaments, 204, Fig. 8.24
Federal Reserve Building, 253, 254, Fig.
  10.7
Femmage, 201
Fernandes, Julio, Apollo 11, 19, Fig. 1.16
Figure for Landscape, 127, 128, Fig. 6.15
Figure of Hippopotamus, 139, Fig. 6.34
Figure (positive space), 124–126, Figs.
  6.10–6.12
Figurine (Ballplayer), 53, Fig. 3.18
Film graphics artist, 73
Fine arts, 16
  career, 81
First Row Orchestra, 258, Fig. 10.16
Fish, Janet
  Fallen Vase, 7, Fig. 1.2
  Jonathan and Lorraine, 197, 198, Fig. 8.13
Five O'Clock Tea, 270–271, Fig. 10.32
Flower Day, 276–277, Fig. 10.35
Flowering Swamp, 63, 64, Fig. 3.32
Flowing rhythm, 231–234, Figs.
  9.17–9.19
  activities, 233–234
Focal point
  defined, 316, 317, Fig. 12.5
  lack of, 316, 318, Fig. 12.6
  using contrast, 316, 318, Fig. 12.7
  using convergence, 321, Fig. 12.10
  using isolation, 318, 319, Fig. 12.8
  using location, 320, 321, Fig. 12.9
  using the unusual, 321–322, Fig. 12.11
  See also Emphasis
Folk art from the town of Acallan,
  338–339, Fig. 12.29
Fontana, Lavinia, Portrait of a Noblewoman,
  124, 125, Fig. 6.11
Footed Dish, 228, 229, Fig. 9.13
Foreground, 136
Foreshortening, 290, 291, Fig. 11.17
Forest, British Columbia, 327, 328, Fig.
  12.18
Form, 122–124

activities, 123, 133
  activity and stability, 142, Figs. 6.39, 6.40
  defined, 122
  density, 140
  expressive qualities, 139–143, Figs.
  6.34–6.43
  free-form forms, 122, 123, Figs. 6.7, 6.9
  geometric forms, 122, 123, 139, 140,
  Figs. 6.7, 6.8, 6.36
  illusion of, 132–135, Figs. 6.22–6.24
  natural vs. manufactured, 132
  openness, 141, Figs. 6.37, 6.38
  perception of, 129–131, Figs. 6.18–6.20
  shape vs., 122, Fig. 6.7
  Studio Lessons, 144–149
  surface of, 139–140, Figs. 6.34–6.36
Formal balance, 252–257, Figs.
  10.5–10.14
  activities, 253, 255, 256–257
  defined, 10.4
  expressive qualities, 263–266, Fig.
  10.24–10.28
  radial balance, 255–257, Figs.
  10.11–10.14
  symmetry, 253–255, Figs. 10.6–10.10
Formalism
  activities, 32
  as aesthetic theory, 30–31
  defined, 30
  literal qualities and, 30
Fragonard, Jean-Honoré, A Game of Hot
  Cockles, 260, Fig. 10.19
Frame
  making a mat, 362–363
  mounting pictures, 363
  viewing frame, 351
Franklin, Ben, Join or Die, 324, Fig. 12.13
Free-form forms, 122, 123, Figs. 6.7, 6.8
Free-form shapes, 121, Figs. 6.4, 6.6
Freestanding works, 16, 127
Frida and Diego Rivera, 258, 259, 278,
  Fig. 10.17
Frottage
  defined, 204
  Studio Lesson, 206–207
Frugal Repast, The, Picasso, Pablo, 295,
  297, Fig. 11.27
Further Challenges. See Activities
Futurism, 59, 235–237, Figs. 9.21, 9.24
FYI
  Michelangelo, 309
  Moore, Henry, 21
  Nevelson, Louise, 37
  Rembrandt van Rijn, 343
  Rubens, Peter Paul, 215

Game of Hot Cockles, A, 260, Fig. 10.19
Garcia, Rupert, Political Prisoner, 124, 126,
  Fig. 6.12
Garrison, Elizabeth, Long May Our Land Be
  Bright, 256, Fig. 10.13
Gates of Paradise, 36–37, Fig. 2.10
Gauguin, Paul, 55
  Faaturuma (The Dreamer), 154, 155, Fig.
  7.1
Geometric forms, 122, 123, Figs. 6.7, 6.8

Geometric forms (*continued*)
expressive qualities, 139, 140, Fig. 6.36
Geometric shapes, 120–121, Figs. 6.3, 6.5
drawing rectangles, 352
expressive qualities, 139, 140, Fig. 6.36
Gesture, 102
Gesture drawing, 102–103, Figs. 5.30, 5.31
technique tips, 349
Ghiberti, Lorenzo, *Gates of Paradise,* 36–37, Fig. 2.10
Ginevra de' Benci, 66–67, Fig. 3.36
Giorgione, *The Adoration of the Shepherds,* 260, 261, Fig. 10.20
Giotto, *Madonna and Child,* 132, 133, Fig. 6.22
Girl with the Red Hat, The, 247, Fig. 9.32
Glarner, Fritz, *Relational Painting #93,* 168, Fig. 7.23
Golden Mean, 282–285, Figs. 11.2, 11.4–11.9
defined, 282, 283, Fig. 11.4
human figure and, 282, 284–285, Figs. 11.6, 11.8
Golden Rectangle, 282, 293, Fig. 11.5
Gothic art, 50, 51, Fig. 3.15
Goya, Francisco, 55
The Third of May, 1808, 83, Fig. 4.14
Grand Canyon #2, 194, Fig. 8.4
Graphic design, 72–73, Figs. 4.2, 4.3
Grattage, 204
Studio Lesson, 206–207
Graves, Nancy
Rheo, 26, 28, Fig. 2.2
Zaga, 16, 17, Fig. 1.13
Great Wave off Kanagawa, The, 260, 262, Fig. 10.22
Greek art, 48, 49, Fig. 3.12
Green House, The, 214–215, 216, Fig. 8.31
Grid for enlarging drawings, 352
Grief, 141, Fig. 6.38
Gris, Juan, *Guitar and Flowers,* 331, 332, Fig. 12.24
Ground (negative space), 124–126, Figs. 6.10–6.12
Grünewald, Matthias, *The Small Crucifixion,* 294, 295, Fig. 11.24
Guitar and Flowers, 331, 332, Fig. 12.24
Gu Mei, *Orchids and Rocks,* 103, 104, Fig. 5.32

Hall of the Bulls, The, 43–44, Fig. 3.3
Hampton, James, *The Throne of the Third Heaven of the Nations' Millennium General Assembly,* 208–209, Fig. 8.28
Hanson, Duane, 63–64
Traveler with Sunburn, 63–64, 65, Fig. 3.33
Haori Coat, 326, 327, Fig. 12.16
Harmon Foundation, 40
Harmony, 322–324, Fig. 12.12
artists' use of, 332–333, Fig. 12.26
defined, 322
overview, 313
Studio Lessons, 334–341

Harrison, Wallace Kirkman, United Nations Buildings, 127, 128, Fig. 6.14
Hartley, Marsden, *Blueberry Highway, Dogtown,* 164, 165, Fig. 7.18
Hassam, Childe, *Jelly Fish,* 176, 177, Fig. 7.36
Hatching, 105, 350
Haverman, Margareta, *A Vase of Flowers,* 30–31, Fig. 2.6
Hayden, Palmer, *The Janitor Who Paints,* 40, 41, Fig. 3.1
Heads and faces, 290–293, Figs. 11.18–11.21
activities, 292–293
Hepworth, Barbara, *Figure for Landscape,* 127, 128, Fig. 6.15
Hierarchical proportion, 286, Fig. 3.4
Higher, Faster, and Farther, 19, Fig. 1.15
High-intensity color, 163
High-key paintings, 161, Fig. 7.12
Highlights, 132
High relief, 127, 129, Fig. 6.17
Studio Lesson, 146–147
Hinduism, 47
Hippopotamus, 139, Fig. 6.34
Hiroshige, Andō, *Evening Rain on the Karasaki Pine,* 48, Fig. 3.11
Hmong Story Cloth, 220–221, Fig. 9.1
Hofmann, Hans, *Flowering Swamp,* 63, 64, Fig. 3.32
Hokusai, Katsushika, *The Great Wave off Kanagawa,* 260, 262, Fig. 10.22
Holocaust, 156, Fig. 7.3
Holograms, 128
Homage to the Square: Glow, 263, 265, Fig. 10.26
Homer, Winslow, 144
Hound and Hunter, 11, 12, Fig. 1.8
Sketch for Hound and Hunter, 11, 12, Fig. 1.7
Hoover, John, *Loon Song,* 201–202, Fig. 8.20
Hopper, Edward, 144
Early Sunday Morning, 97, 98, Fig. 5.22
First Row Orchestra, 258, Fig. 10.16
Horizontal lines, 93, 94, Fig. 5.8
expressive qualities, 97, 98, Fig. 5.22
Horse Fair, The, 54, 223, 224, Fig. 9.4
Hound and Hunter, 11, 12, Fig. 1.8
Houser, Allan, *Coming of Age,* 231, 233, Fig. 9.19
Hua Yen, *Conversation in Autumn,* 47, Fig. 3.10
Hue, 158–159, Figs. 7.7–7.9
activities, 159
See also Color
Huichol Indian, *Sacrifice to the Mother of the Eagles,* 106, Fig. 5.35
Human figure
activities, 290, 292–293
children's proportions, 289, 291, 293, Figs. 11.16, 11.21
foreshortening, 290, 291, Fig. 11.17
Golden Mean and, 282, 284–285, Figs. 11.6, 11.8
heads and faces, 290–293, Figs. 11.18–11.21
proportions, 288–290, Figs. 11.13–11.17
Hunt, Henry, *K'umugwe' (Komokwa) Mask,* 304–305, Fig. 11.34

Huntington, Anna Hyatt, *Riders to the Sea,* 142, Fig. 6.39
Hyper-Realism, 63–64, 65, Fig. 3.33

Ice Floes, 161, Fig. 7.12
I Got a Girl on Sourwood Mountain, 97, 98, Fig. 5.23
Illusion
activities, 133, 138–139
of depth, 135–139, Figs. 6.25–6.33
of form, 132–135, Figs. 6.22–6.25
Illustrator, 73
Imitationalism
activities, 32
as aesthetic theory, 30–31
defined, 30
design qualities and, 30
Implied lines, 92, 93, Fig. 5.6
Impressionism, 55, 56, Fig. 3.22
optical color and, 174
Indian art, 46, 47, Figs. 3.8, 3.9
ancient India, 45–46, Fig. 3.7
Industrial designers, 73–74, Fig. 4.4
Informal balance, 257–263, Figs. 10.15–10.23
activities, 261, 263
color in, 258–260, Figs. 10.18, 10.19
defined, 257
expressive qualities, 264, 266–267, Figs. 10.29, 10.30
position in, 260, 262, Figs. 10.21, 10.22
size and contour in, 258, 259, Figs. 10.16, 10.17
texture in, 260
value in, 260, 261, Fig. 10.20
Intaglio, 13
Intensity, 162–163, Figs. 7.14–7.16
activities, 163
complementary colors and, 163, Fig. 7.15
defined, 163
scale of, 162, Fig. 7.14
Interior designer, 77
activity, 78
Intermediate hues, 158–159
Interpenetrations in Red, 316, Fig. 12.4
Interpretation
activities, 29–30
in art criticism, 27, 29–30, 34
in art history, 43
defined, 29
In the Dining Room, 320, 321, Fig. 12.9
Islamic art, 52–53, Fig. 3.17
Isolation and the focal point, 318, 319, Fig. 12.8

Jacquette, Yvonne
East River Drive, 92, 93, Fig. 5.6
Town of Skowhegan, Maine V, 312–313, Fig. 12.1
Jaguar Mask, 250–251, Fig. 10.1
Janet, 246–247, Fig. 9.31
Janitor Who Paints, The, 40, 41, Fig. 3.1
Japanese art, 48, Fig. 3.11

Jelly Fish, 176, 177, Fig. 7.36
Jessup, Georgia Mills, *Rainy Night, Downtown,* 331, Fig. 12.23
Jimenez, Luis, *Vaquero,* 16, Fig. 1.12
Jitterbugs IV, 112, Fig. 5.38
Johns, Jasper
  Cups 4 Picasso, 124, Fig. 6.10
  Map, 327, Fig. 12.17
Johnson House, 141, Fig. 6.37
Johnson, Phillip, *Johnson House,* 141, Fig. 6.37
Johnson, William H., 112
  Jitterbugs IV, 112, Fig. 5.38
John Vassall (Longfellow) House, 264, 265, Fig. 10.27
Joining clay, 354–355
Join or Die, 324, Fig. 12.13
Jonathan and Lorraine, 197, 198, Fig. 8.13
Judgment
  aesthetic theories, 30–31
  in art criticism, 27, 30–32, 34
  in art history, 43
  defined, 30
  of functional objects, 31–32
  of your own work, 32

K

Kahlo, Frida, 278
  Frida and Diego Rivera, 258, 259, 278, Fig. 10.17
  Self-Portrait Dedicated to Leon Trotsky, 263, 264, Fig. 10.25
Kamseh: Bahram Gur and the Chinese Princess in the Sandalwood Pavilion on Thursday, 52–53, Fig. 3.17
Kente cloth, 57
Keyser, Louisa (Dat So La Lee), *Basket,* 244–245, Fig. 9.30
Kinetic sculpture, 237
Kingman, Dong, *Higher, Faster, and Farther,* 19, Fig. 1.15
Kiss, The, 295, 296, Fig. 11.26
Kollwitz, Käthe, *Self-Portrait,* 58, Fig. 3.26
Kongo peoples, *Bowl,* 226, Fig. 9.7
K'umugwe' (Komokwa) Mask, 304–305, Fig. 11.34

L

Lachaise, Gaston, *Walking Woman,* 296, 298, Fig. 11.29
Lady with a Bowl of Violets, 66–67, Fig. 3.35
Landscape architect, 77, Fig. 4.8
Landscape at Saint-Rémy (Enclosed Field with Peasant), 200, 201, Fig. 8.17
Landscape studio lessons, 110–111, 148–149, 206–207
Lange, Dorothea, *Migrant Mother,* 15, Fig. 1.11
Large Blue Horses, The, 174, 175, Fig. 7.34
Larraz, Julio, *Papiamento,* 6, 8, Fig. 1.3
Lawrence, Jacob, 238–239
  Meet the Artist, 116
  Parade, 238–239, Fig. 9.27

Study for the Munich Olympic Games Poster, 114–115, Fig. 5.39
  as teacher, 81
Layout, 72
Layout artist, 78
Leaning Tower of Pisa, The, 252, Fig. 10.3
Le Chateau Noir, 55, 56, Fig. 3.23
Le Corbusier, *Chapelle Notre-Dame-du-Haut,* 285, Fig. 11.9
Lee, Doris, *Thanksgiving,* 138, Fig. 6.33
Leggings, 53, 121, Figs. 6.5, 6.6
Length of lines, 94–95, Fig. 5.12
Leonardo da Vinci, 51
  Ginevra de' Benci, 66–67, Fig. 3.36
  page from his sketchbook showing movement of water, 8, 9, Fig. 1.5
Leyster, Judith, 197
  Self-Portrait, 54, 197, Fig. 3.20
Lichtenstein, Roy, 336
  Blam, 336–337, Fig. 12.28
Line, 89–113
  activities, 92, 94, 95, 99–101, 102–104, 105
  calligraphic drawing, 103–104, 349, Figs. 5.32, 5.33
  contour drawing, 100–102, 349, Figs. 5.26–5.29
  defined, 91–92
  in the environment, 89–90, 92, Figs. 5.2, 5.4, 5.5
  expressive qualities, 97–100, Figs. 5.21–5.27
  gesture drawing, 102–103, 349, Figs. 5.30, 5.31
  implied lines, 92, 93, Fig. 5.6
  kinds of lines, 93–94, Figs. 5.7–5.11
  movement, 91, 92
  outline, 92, Figs. 5.4, 5.5
  ruler technique, 351
  static vs. active, 97
  Studio Lessons, 106–113
  value, 105, Fig. 5.34
  variations, 94–96, Figs. 5.12–5.20
Linear perspective
  defined, 51–52
  for illusion of depth, 137–138, Figs. 6.31, 6.32
Literal qualities, 30
  optical color, 174, 175, Figs. 7.32, 7.33
Lithography, 13
Little Fourteen-Year-Old Dancer, 203, Fig. 8.21
Lizards, The, 316, 318, Fig. 12.6
Lobster Trap and Fish Tail, 237, Fig. 9.26
Location
  on credit line, 18
  focal point and, 320, 321, Fig. 12.9
  for illusion of depth, 136, Fig. 6.28
  in informal balance, 260, 262, Figs. 10.21, 10.22
  point of view, 129–131, Figs. 6.18–6.20
  viewing frame, 351
Loewy, Raymond, 74
  Avanti, 74, Fig. 4.4
  Starlight Coupe (1953), 74
Logos, 73
  activities, 74
  MTV logos, 314, Fig. 12.2

Loma Negra, Nose Ornament, 252, 253, Fig. 10.5
Loneliness, 318, 319, Fig. 12.8
Long May Our Land Be Bright, 256, Fig. 10.13
Looking Closely
  Albright, Ivan, *The Farmer's Kitchen,* 200, Fig. 8.16
  Balla, Giacomo, *Street Light,* 234, Fig. 9.20
  Bonheur, Rosa, *The Horse Fair,* 224, Fig. 9.4
  Carr, Emily, *Above the Trees,* 170, Fig. 7.27
  Escher, M. C., *Other World,* 127, Fig. 6.13
  Fish, Janet, *Fallen Vase,* 7, Fig. 1.2
  Fontana, Lavinia, *Portrait of a Noblewoman,* 125, Fig. 6.11
  Garrison, Elizabeth, *Long May Our Land Be Bright,* 256, Fig. 10.13
  Giorgione, *The Adoration of the Shepherds,* 261, Fig. 10.20
  Graves, Nancy, *Rheo,* 26, Fig. 2.2
  Hassam, Childe, *Jelly Fish,* 177, Fig. 7.36
  Hokusai, Katsushika, *The Great Wave off Kanagawa,* 262, Fig. 10.22
  Hoover, John, *Loon Song,* 202, Fig. 8.20
  Jessup, Georgia Mills, *Rainy Night, Downtown,* 331, Fig. 12.23
  Neel, Alice, *Loneliness,* 319, Fig. 12.8
  Picasso, Pablo, *The Frugal Repast,* 297, Fig. 11.27
  van der Weyden, Rogier, *Portrait of a Lady,* 283, Fig. 11.3
Loom, cardboard, 358–359
Loon Song, 201–202, Fig. 8.20
Low-intensity color, 163
Low-key paintings, 161, Fig. 7.13
Low relief, 127, 129, Fig. 6.16

M

McKelvey, Lucy Leuppe, *Whirling Rainbow Goddesses,* 237, Fig. 9.25
Madame Henriot, 197, 199, Fig. 8.15
Madonna and Child, 132, 133, Fig. 6.22
Madonna and Child on Curved Throne, 49, 50, Fig. 3.14
Magritte, René, *The Blank Signature,* 148–149, 206, Fig. 6.46
Male figure, 57, Fig. 3.24
Man of the Republic, 49, Fig. 3.13
Mantle, 224, 225, Fig. 9.5
Manufactured shapes and forms, 132
Map, 327, Fig. 12.17
Marc, Franz, *The Large Blue Horses,* 174, 175, Fig. 7.34
Marilyn Monroe's Lips, 228, 229, Fig. 9.12
Mariposa 10 Speed, 95, 96, Fig. 5.18
Marisol, 42, 43, Fig. 3.2
Marisol, *Poor Family I,* 118, 119, Fig. 6.1
Marquise de Peze, The, and the Marquise de Rouget with Her Two Children, 330, 331, Fig. 12.22
Marsh, Reginald, *Why Not Use the El?,* 284, Fig. 11.7
Martinez, Julia, 274
Martinez, Maria and Julian, black-on-black storage jar, 274–275, Fig. 10.34

Martinez, Maria Montoya, 274–275
Masks
  corn-husk, 53, Fig. 3.19
  exaggeration in, 297, 299, Fig. 11.30
Matisse, Henri, 58
  Beasts of the Sea, 132, Fig. 6.21
Matte surface, 197, Figs. 8.11
Matting, 362–363
Media
  defined, 7
  overview, 6–7
  See also Medium
Medieval art
  Gothic, 50, 51, Fig. 3.15
  Romanesque, 50
Medium
  on credit line, 18
  defined, 6
  See also Media
Meeting of the Theologians, The, 240–241, Fig. 9.28
Meet the Artist
  Bishop, Isabel, 310
  Close, Chuck, 248
  Dillon, Leo and Diane, 84
  Lawrence, Jacob, 116
  Moore, Henry, 22
  Murray, Elizabeth, 188
  Naranjo, Michael, 152
  Nevelson, Louise, 38
  Perry, Lilla Cabot, 68
  Rivera, Diego, 278
  Skoglund, Sandy, 216
  Thiebaud, Wayne, 344
Mesopotamian art, 44, 45, Fig. 3.5
Methethy with His Daughter and a Son, 44, Fig. 3.4
Mexican folk art, 338–339, Fig. 12.29
Mexican Muralists, 62, Fig. 3.31
Michelangelo
  FYI, 309
  Pietà, 51, 52, 309, Figs. 3.16, 11.37
Middle Ages, 50, 51
Middle ground, 136
Midnight Ride of Paul Revere, 91, Fig. 5.3
Migrant Mother, 15, Fig. 1.11
Mill, The, 343, Fig. 12.32
Millinery Shop, The, 323, Fig. 12.12
Mimes, 295, 296, Fig. 11.25
Ming dynasty, 47
Minimalism, 64
Mitchell, Joan, Dirty Snow, 204, 205, Fig. 8.25
Mixed media studio lesson, 178–179
Miyawaki, Ayako, The Red Crab, 212–213, Fig. 8.30
Mobiles, 61, 237
Modeling
  chiaroscuro, 132
  sculpture technique, 16
Modules, 225
Mohenjo-Daro, 45, 46, Fig. 3.7
Mondrian, Piet, 59
  Broadway Boogie Woogie, 176, Fig. 7.35
Monet, Claude
  Ice Floes, 161, Fig. 7.12
  Palazzo da Mula, Venice, 55, 56, Fig. 3.22
  Poplars, 173, 174, Figs. 7.32, 7.33
Monochromatic colors, 164–165, Fig. 7.18

tonality vs., 176
Montata, Blackfeet Man's Leggings, 53, 121, Fig. 6.5
Moore, Henry
  Family Group, 20, 21, 22, Fig. 1.18
  FYI, 21
  Meet the Artist, 22
  Reclining Mother and Child, 142, Fig. 6.40
More Portfolio Ideas, 22, 38, 68, 84, 116, 152, 188, 216, 248, 278, 310, 344
Morisot, Berthe, In the Dining Room, 320, 321, Fig. 12.9
Mosaics, 49
Motifs
  activities, 226
  defined, 224
  modules, 225
  in rhythm, 224–225, Fig. 9.5
Mounting pictures, 363
Movement, 235, 236, Fig. 9.23
  color and, 176, Fig. 7.35
  defined, 235
  of lines, 91, 92
    direction, 94–95, Fig. 5.15
    gesture drawing, 102–103, Figs. 5.30, 5.31
Mrs. Jones and Family, 306–307, Fig. 11.35
MTV logos, 314, Fig. 12.2
Muhammad, 52
Munch, Edvard, The Kiss, 295, 296, Fig. 11.26
Murals
  Mexican Muralists, 62, Fig. 3.31
  Studio Lesson, 340–341
Murray, Elizabeth
  Meet the Artist, 188
  Things to Come, 186–187, Fig. 7.41
Musawwir, 'Abd Allah, The Meeting of the Theologians, 240–241, Fig. 9.28
Museums, 80
Myron, Discobolus, 48, 49, Fig. 3.12

N

Name on credit line, 18
Namingha, Dan, Blessing Rain Chant, 97, Fig. 5.21
Naranjo, Michael
  Meet the Artist, 152
  Spirits Soaring, 150–151, Fig. 6.47
NASA (National Aeronautics and Space Administration)
  artists hired by, 17–18, 19, Figs. 1.15–1.17
  Pioneer 10 plaque, 5
Native American art (pre-Columbian), 53, Figs. 3.18, 3.19
Natural shapes and forms, 132
Neel, Alice
  Loneliness, 318, 319, Fig. 12.8
  Marisol, 42, 43, Fig. 3.2
Negative space, 124–126, 127, Figs. 6.10–6.13
Neoclassicism, 54
Neutral colors, 159, 160, Fig. 7.10
Nevelson, Louise
  Dawn, 34–37, Fig. 2.9

Dawn's Wedding Chapel, 327, 329, Fig. 12.20
  FYI, 37
  Meet the Artist, 38
Night Before Launch, 19, Fig. 1.17
Night Riders, 161, Fig. 7.13
Nike of Samothrace, 151, Fig. 6.48
Nineteenth-century art
  activities, 55
  Impressionism, 55, 56, Fig. 3.22
  Neoclassicism, 54
  Post-Impressionism, 55, 56, Fig. 3.23
  Realism, 54–55, Fig. 3.21
  Romanticism, 54
Nizami, Kamseh: Bahram Gur and the Chinese Princess in the Sandalwood Pavilion on Thursday, 52–53, Fig. 3.17
Nonobjective art, 17
North Georgia Waterfall, 144–145, Fig. 6.44
Northwestern Plains Indian, Feather Bonnet, 190–191, Fig. 8.1
Nose Ornament, 252, 253, Fig. 10.5
Nude Woman, 59, Fig. 3.27

O

October Wind and Sunlight in the Woods, 222, 223, Fig. 9.3
Oil paint
  invention of, 52
  solvent, 171
O'Keeffe, Georgia, Cow's Skull, 264, 266, Fig. 10.28
Oldenburg, Claes, Shoestring Potatoes Spilling from a Bag, 286, Fig. 11.10
Olmsted, Frederick Law, Central Park, 77, Fig. 4.8
One-point perspective, 137, 138, Fig. 6.31
Op art, 63, Fig. 7.6
Openness, 141, Figs. 6.37, 6.38
Optical color, 174, 175, Figs. 7.32, 7.33
Orange and Yellow, 165, 166, Fig. 7.20
Orange Crush, 158, Fig. 7.6
Orchids and Rocks, 103, 104, Fig. 5.32
Oriental Ruler Seated on His Throne, An, 105, 132, 134, Fig. 6.23
Origami, 356
Orozco, José Clemente, Barricade, 62, Fig. 3.31
Other World, 124, 127, Fig. 6.13
Our Banner in the Sky, 264, 267, Fig. 10.30
Outline
  defined, 92, Figs. 5.4, 5.5
  expressive qualities, 139–140, Figs. 6.34–6.36
Overlapping for illusion of depth, 136, Fig. 6.26

P

Paint, 171–173
  basic ingredients, 11, 171
  cleaning a brush, 353–354
  making earth pigment paints, 353
  mixing, 352

safety note, 162
sources of pigment, 173
watercolors, 353
wet vs. dry, 171
Painting
activities, 11
display tips, 362–363
overview, 11
Studio Lessons, 106–107, 238–239, 270–271, 336–337, 340–341
technique tips, 352–354
Palazzo da Mula, Venice, 55, 56, Fig. 3.22
Paper
making paper, 356–357
origami, 356
papier-mâché, 304–305, 355–356
tissue paper collage, 361–362
Papiamento, 6, 8, Fig. 1.3
Papier-mâché
Studio Lesson, 304–305
technique tips, 355–356
Parade, 238–239, Fig. 9.27
Parthenon, the, 48
Patterns
activities, 226
defined, 225
in rhythm, 225–226, Fig. 9.6
Studio Lessons, 240–243
Paul Revere, 294, Fig. 11.22
Perception
activities, 131
defined, 8
of depth, 129
point of view, 129–131, Figs. 6.18–6.20
vision and color, 156–158, 164, Figs. 7.2–7.6, 7.17
Pereira, Irene Rice, *Untitled,* 314, 315, Fig. 12.3
Perry, Lilla Cabot
Lady with a Bowl of Violets, 66–67, Fig. 3.35
Meet the Artist, 68
Persistence of Memory, The, 60, 206, Fig. 3.28
Perspective, 138, Fig. 6.33
activities, 138–139
defined, 136
illusion of depth, 135–139, Figs. 6.25–6.33
linear, 51–52, 137–138, Figs. 6.31, 6.32
See also Linear perspective
Pharaohs, 44
Photography
activities, 15
career, 75, Fig. 4.6
defined, 14
display tips, 362–363
holograms, 128
overview, 14–15
Studio Lesson, 180–181
Photojournalist, 75, Fig. 4.6
Photo-Realism, 63–64, 65, Fig. 3.33
Picasso, Pablo
The Frugal Repast, 295, 297, Fig. 11.27
Nude Woman, 59, Fig. 3.27
The Tragedy, 21, Fig. 1.19
Picture plane, 136
Pietà, 51, 52, Fig. 3.16
Pigments
activities, 173

defined, 11, 171
dyes, 171
making earth pigments, 353
paint, 11, 171–173
sources, 173
Pinch pot, 355
Pins, safety note, 212
Pinzon Family, The, 302–303, Fig. 11.33
Pioneer 10 plaque, 5
Pippin, Horace, *Asleep,* 316, 318, Fig. 12.7
Placement. *See* Location
Pleating paper, 356
Point of view, 129–131, Figs. 6.18–6.20
activities, 131
viewing frame, 351
Political Prisoner, 124, 126, Fig. 6.12
Poons, Larry, *Orange Crush,* 158, Fig. 7.6
Poor Family I, 118, 119, Fig. 6.1
Pop art, 63, Fig. 12.28
Poplars, 173, 174, Figs. 7.32, 7.33
Portrait of a Lady, 282, 283, Fig. 11.3
Portrait of a Noblewoman, 124, 125, Fig. 6.11
Position. *See* Location
Positive space, 124–126, 127, Figs. 6.10–6.13
Post-Impressionism, 55, 56, Fig. 3.23
Powdered tempera, safety note, 162
Preacher, 9, Fig. 1.4
Pre-Columbian art, 53, Figs. 3.18, 3.19
Prehistoric art, 43–44, Fig. 3.3
Prevalence of Ritual: Baptism, 178–179, Fig. 7.37
Primary hues, 158, Fig. 7.7
Primary triad, 166, 168, Fig. 7.22
Principles of design
balance, 251–279
defined, 6
emphasis, 313, 315–322, Figs. 12.4–12.11
Formalism and, 30
harmony, 313, 322–324, Fig. 12.12
movement, 235, 236, Fig. 9.23
overview, 6
proportion, 281–311
rhythm, 221–249
unity, 313, 324–332, Figs. 12.13–12.24
variety, 313, 314–315, Figs. 12.2, 12.3
See also specific principles
Printing plate, 11
Printmaking
activities, 14
basic steps, 11
defined, 11
editions, 13
methods, 13
overview, 11, 13–14
relief designs, 127
Studio Lesson, 272–273
technique tip, 354
Progressive rhythm, 234–235, Figs. 9.20–9.22
activities, 235
Proportion, 281–311
activities, 287, 290, 292–293, 298–299
artists' use of, 293–299, Figs. 11.22–11.31
defined, 281
distortion and exaggeration, 294–299, Figs. 11.24–11.31

enlarging drawings, 352
foreshortening, 290, 291, Fig. 11.17
Golden Mean, 282–285, Figs. 11.2, 11.4–11.9
hierarchical, 286, Fig. 3.4
human proportions, 282, 284–285, 288–293, Figs. 11.6, 11.8, 11.13–11.21
scale, 285–287, Figs. 11.10–11.12
sighting techniques, 350–351
size and, 280–281, 282, Figs. 11.1, 11.2
Studio Lessons, 300–307
Proximity and unity, 330, 331, Figs. 12.22, 12.23
Publishing design, 73
Pulp method for papier-mâché, 355

R

Radial balance, 255–257, Figs. 10.11–10.14
activities, 256–257
defined, 255
expressive qualities, 264, 266, Fig. 10.29
Studio Lessons, 272–275
Rainy Night, Downtown, 331, Fig. 12.23
Random rhythm, 226–227, Figs. 9.7–9.9
activities, 226–227
defined, 226
Raphael, 51
Realism, 54–55, Fig. 3.21
Photo-Realism, 63–64, 65, Fig. 3.33
Reclining Mother and Child, 142, Fig. 6.40
Rectangles, drawing, 352
Red Crab, The, 212–213, Fig. 8.30
Regionalists, 60–61, 144, Fig. 3.29
Regular rhythm, 227–228, 229, Figs. 9.10–9.12
Reims Cathedral, 50, 51, Fig. 3.15
Relational Painting #93, 168, Fig. 7.23
Relief, 16
Relief printing, 13
Relief sculpture, 127, 129, Figs. 6.16, 6.17
Studio Lesson, 146–147
Rembrandt van Rijn, 199
FYI, 343
The Mill, 343, Fig. 12.32
Self-Portrait, 199, 316, 317, Fig. 12.5
Renaissance, 51
Renaissance art, 51–52, Fig. 3.16
activities, 54
Renoir, Pierre Auguste, 197
Madame Henriot, 197, 199, Fig. 8.15
Repetition
rhythm and, 224–226, Figs. 9.5, 9.6
unity and, 327, 330, 331, Figs. 12.20, 12.21
Reston, Virginia, 76, 77, Fig. 4.7
Return from Bohemia, 4, 5, Fig. 1.1
Reviews of chapters, 23, 39, 69, 85, 117, 153, 189, 217, 249, 279, 311, 345
Rheo, 26, 28, Fig. 2.2
Rhythm, 221–249
activities, 223–224, 226–227, 230–231, 233–234, 235
alternating, 228–231, Figs. 9.13–9.16
artists' use of, 235–237, Figs. 9.24–9.26
defined, 222
flowing, 231–234, Figs. 9.17–9.19

Rhythm (*continued*)
  overview, 221
  progressive, 234–235, Figs. 9.20–9.22
  random, 226–227, Figs. 9.7–9.9
  regular, 227–228, 229, Figs. 9.10–9.12
  repetition, 224–226, Figs. 9.5, 9.6
  Studio Lessons, 238–245
  visual rhythm, 222–224, Figs. 9.2–9.4
Riders to the Sea, 142, Fig. 6.39
Ringgold, Faith, *Mrs. Jones and Family,* 306–307, Fig. 11.35
Ritual Wine Container, 45, Fig. 3.6
Rivera, Diego
  Flower Day, 276–277, Fig. 10.35
  Meet the Artist, 278
Rockwell, Norman, *Triple Self-Portrait,* 70–71, Fig. 4.1
Rococo art, 54
Rodin, Auguste, *The Burghers of Calais,* 324, 325, Fig. 12.14
Roman art, 48–49, Fig. 3.13
Romanesque art, 49, 50
Romanticism, 54
Romero, Annette, *Storyteller Doll,* 300–301, Fig. 11.32
Root Monster, 184–185, Fig. 7.40
Rothko, Mark, 63
  Orange and Yellow, 165, 166, Fig. 7.20
Rouault, Georges, *Christ and the Apostles,* 95, 96, Fig. 5.17
Rough texture, 197, Figs. 8.9
Rubens, Peter Paul
  The Assumption of the Virgin, 288, Fig. 11.14
  Daniel in the Lions' Den, 215, Fig. 8.32
  FYI, 215
Ruler technique, 351

S

Saarinen, Eero, *Armchair,* 31–32, Fig. 2.7
Sacred Circles, 272–273, Fig. 10.33
Sacrifice to the Mother of the Eagles, 106, Fig. 5.35
Safety notes
  cutting, 208, 273
  paint, 162
  pins, 212
  wire pieces, 108
Sagredo Palace bedroom, 98, 100, Fig. 5.25
Scale, 285–287, Figs. 11.10–11.12
  activities, 287
  defined, 285
  hierarchical proportion, 286, Fig. 3.4
Schapiro, Miriam
  Anna and David, 280–281, Fig. 11.1
  Yard Sale, 201, Fig. 8.18
Scholar, The, 100, 101, Fig. 5.28
Scoring paper, 356
Screen printing, 13–14
Scroll paintings, 47, Fig. 3.10
Sculpture
  African, 57–58, Figs. 3.24, 3.25
  freestanding, 16
  overview, 16
  processes, 16

  relief, 16
  space in, 127, 128, Figs. 6.15–6.17
  Studio Lessons, 108–109, 146–147, 210–211, 306–307, 338–339
  technique tips, 354–356
  texture in, 201–203, Figs. 8.20, 8.21
  twentieth-century, 61
Secondary hues, 158, Fig. 7.7
Secondary triad, 166, 168, Fig. 7.22
Seed Pot, 203, Fig. 8.23
See-non-ty-a, an Iowa Medicine Man, 294, Fig. 11.23
Self-Portrait
  Kollwitz, 58, 59, Fig. 3.26
  Leyster, 54, 197, Fig. 3.20
  Rembrandt, 197, 316, 317, Fig. 12.5
  Siqueiros, 289, 290, Fig. 11.17
  Vigée-Lebrun, 193, Fig. 8.3
Self-Portrait Dedicated to Leon Trotsky, 263, 264, Fig. 10.25
Serigraph, 14
Seventeenth-century art, 54, Fig. 3.20
  activities, 54
Shade of color, 159, 160, Fig. 7.11
  low-key paintings, 161, Fig. 7.13
Shading, 132
  activities, 133
  chiaroscuro, 132
  highlights, 132
  illusion of form, 132–135, Figs. 6.22–6.24
  shadow as shape, 120, Fig. 6.2
  technique tips, 349–350
Shahn, Ben, *The Blind Botanist,* 139, 140, Fig. 6.35
Shang dynasty, 45
Shape, 120–122, Figs. 6.2–6.6
  activities, 122, 143
  activity and stability, 142, Figs. 6.39, 6.40
  as beats in visual rhythm, 222–224, Fig. 9.2, 9.4
  creating shapes, 132, Fig. 6.21
  defined, 120
  expressive qualities, 139–143, Figs. 6.34–6.43
  form vs., 122, Fig. 6.7
  free-form shapes, 121, Figs. 6.4, 6.6
  geometric shapes, 120–121, 139, 140, Figs. 6.3, 6.5, 6.36
  natural vs. manufactured, 132
  openness, 141, Figs. 6.37, 6.38
  outline, 139–140, Figs. 6.34–6.36
  perception of, 129–131, Figs. 6.18–6.20
  Studio Lessons, 144–149
Sharecropper, 13, Fig. 1.9
Sheeler, Charles, *Catastrophe No. 2,* 98, 99, Fig. 5.24
Sheet method for papier-mâché, 355–356
Shiny texture, 197, Figs. 8.12
Shiva, 47
Shoestring Potatoes Spilling from a Bag, 286, Fig. 11.10
Shoulder bag, 228, 230, Fig. 9.14
Sighting techniques, 350–351
Silent movies, 294–295
Simplicity and unity, 327, 328, Figs. 12.18, 12.19
Singing Man, 327, 328, Fig. 12.19

Siqueiros, David Alfaro, *Self-Portrait,* 289, 290, Fig. 11.17
Size
  on credit line, 18
  illusion of depth and, 136, Fig. 6.27
  in informal balance, 258, Fig. 10.16
  proportion and, 280–281, 282, Figs. 11.1, 11.2
  scale, 285–287, Figs. 11.10–11.12
Sketch for Hound and Hunter, 11, 12, Fig. 1.7
Sketching, usefulness of, 8, 10
Skoglund, Sandy
  The Green House, 214–215, 216, Fig. 8.31
  Meet the Artist, 216
Small Crucifixion, The, 294, 295, Fig. 11.24
Smith, David, *Cubi IX,* 122, 123, Fig. 6.8
Smith, Jaune Quick-To-See, *Spotted Owl,* 182–183, Fig. 7.39
Smith, Larry
  North Georgia Waterfall, 144–145, Fig. 6.44
  as teacher, 81
Smooth texture, 197–198, Figs. 8.10
Snuff Containers, 326, 327, Fig. 12.15
Solstice, 332–333, Fig. 12.26
Solvent, 11, 171
Sortie Made by the Garrison of Gibraltar, The, 17, 18, Fig. 1.14
Sources of Country Music, The, 61, Fig. 3.29
South American Indian featherwork ornaments, 204, Fig. 8.24
Southeastern Song dynasty, *Carved Lacquer Circular Tray,* 255, Fig. 10.12
Space, 124–129, Figs. 6.10–6.17
  activities, 125–126, 128, 138–139
  color and, 175
  defined, 124
  expressive qualities, 139–143, Figs. 6.34–6.43
  illusion of depth, 135–139, Figs. 6.25–6.33
  perception of, 129–131, Figs. 6.18–6.20
  positive and negative, 124–126, 127, Figs. 6.10–6.13
  as rests in visual rhythm, 222–223
  Studio Lessons, 144–149
  in three-dimensional art, 126–129, Figs. 6.14–6.17
Spear, Laurinda, *Centre for Innovative Technology,* 65, Fig. 3.34
Special effects artists, 78–79, Fig. 4.10
Spectrum, 156
Spiral lines, 98–99
Spirit Boxes I, 334–335, Fig. 12.27
Spirits Soaring, 150–151, Fig. 6.47
Split complements, 168, Fig. 7.24
Spotted Owl, 182–183, Fig. 7.39
Stability, 142, Fig. 6.40
Stained-glass windows
  Gothic, 50, 51, Fig. 3.15
  Wright, Frank Lloyd, 258, 259, Fig. 10.18
Standing Vishnu, 46, Fig. 3.8
Standing Youth with His Arm Raised, 102, Fig. 5.30
Starlight Coupe (1953), 74

Static lines, 97
Static shapes and forms, 142, Fig. 6.40
  activities, 143
Statua di Donna, 44, 45, Fig. 3.5
Steinlen, Théophile-Alexandre, *Winter: Cat on a Cushion,* 27, 30, Fig. 2.3
Steir, Pat, *The Brueghel Series (A Vanitas of Style),* 180–181, Fig. 7.38
Stencils, Studio Lessons, 110–111
Stippling, 350
Stitches for embroidery, 357–358
Storyboards, 78, Fig. 4.9
Storyteller Doll, 300–301, Fig. 11.32
Straight lines, 351
Street at Corte, Corsica, 264, 266, Fig. 10.29
Street Light, 234, 235, Fig. 9.20
Strip method for papier-mâché, 355
Studio Lessons
  Assemblage, 208–209
  Assemblage with Handmade Paper, 334–335
  Clay Plaque with High Relief, 146–147
  Clay Pot Decorated with Radial Designs, 274–275
  Coil Baskets, 244–245
  Contour Wire Sculpture, 108–109
  Creating a Rainbow Creature, 184–185
  Drawing an Outdoor Scene, 144–145
  Drawing Expressing Movement, 112–113
  Fantasy Landscape, 206–207
  Formal Portrait, 268–269
  Imagination Landscape, 110–111
  Informal Group Picture, 270–271
  Landscape Using Surreal Space, 148–149
  Linoleum Print Using Radial Balance, 272–273
  Painting with a Rhythmic Activity, 238–239
  Paper Sculpture Creature, 210–211
  Papier-Mâché Mask, 304–305
  Pattern Collage, A, 240–241
  Photo Collage and Mixed Media, 178–179
  Photo Enlargement, 180–181
  Soft Sculpture, 306–307
  Stitchery and Appliqué, 212–213
  Storyteller Figure, 300–301
  Using Color to Create an Expressive Statement, 182–183
  Using Distortion for Expressive Effect, 302–303
  Weaving with a Pattern, 242–243
  Yarn Painting, 106–107
Study for the Munich Olympic Games Poster, 114–115, Fig. 5.39
Style, 42
Subject
  defined, 17
  literal qualities, 30
  viewing frame, 351
Subordinate elements, 315
Subtractive process, 16
Sullivan, Louis, *Elevator Grille,* 225, Fig. 9.6
Sumerian art, 44, 45, Fig. 3.5
Sundi group, Bowl, 226, Fig. 9.7
Super-Realism, 63–64, 65, Fig. 3.33
Support structures for papier-mâché, 356
Surface of forms, 139–140, Figs. 6.34–6.36

Surrealism, 59–60, 206, Fig. 3.28
  Studio Lesson, 148–149
Sutej, Miroslav, *Ultra AB,* 14, Fig. 1.10
Symbol, 6
Symmetry, 253–255, Figs. 10.6–10.10
  activities, 253, 255
  approximate, 253, 254, Figs. 10.8, 10.10
  defined, 253
  expressive qualities, 263–264, Figs. 10.24–10.27

T

Tafoya, Juan, *Seed Pot,* 203, Fig. 8.23
Taliesin West, 201, Fig. 8.19
Tamayo, Rufino, *Toast to the Sun,* 168, 169, Fig. 7.26
Teachers, 80, 81, Fig. 4.12
Technique tips, 348–363
  display tips, 362–363
  drawing, 349–352
  other tips, 356–362
  painting, 352–354
  printmaking, 354
  sculpting, 354–356
Tempera, safety note, 162
Temple at Angkor Wat, 46, Fig. 3.9
Texture, 191–217
  activities, 194, 197, 204
  artists' use of, 197–206, Figs. 8.15–8.27
  color and, 172–173
  defined, 191
  in informal balance, 260
  of lines, 94–95, Fig. 5.14
  matte and shiny, 197, Figs. 8.11
  perception of, 192–195, Figs. 8.2–8.8
  rough and smooth, 196–197, Figs. 8.9
  Studio Lessons, 206–213
  value and, 196–199, Figs. 8.9–8.14
  visual texture, 193–194, Figs. 8.3, 8.4
Thanksgiving, 138, Fig. 6.33
Thiebaud, Wayne
  Apartment Hill, 342–343, Fig. 12.31
  Meet the Artist, 344
Things to Come, 186–187, Fig. 7.41
Third of May, 1808, The, 83, Fig. 4.14
Throne of the Third Heaven of the Nations' Millennium General Assembly, 208–209, Fig. 8.28
Tichich, Leslie Mims, *Body Adornment,* 253, Fig. 10.6
Tint, 159, 160, Fig. 7.11
  high-key paintings, 161, Fig. 7.12
Tintoretto, Jacopo, *Standing Youth with His Arm Raised,* 102, Fig. 5.30
Tissue paper collage, 361–362
Title on credit line, 18
Toast to the Sun, 168, 169, Fig. 7.26
Tonality, 176, 177, Fig. 7.36
Torivio, Dorothy, *Vase,* 256, 257, Fig. 10.14
Torso of a Young Man, 139, 140, Fig. 6.36
Town, Harold, *Night Riders,* 161, Fig. 7.13
Town of Skowhegan, Maine V, 312–313, Fig. 12.1
Tragedy, The, 21, Fig. 1.19
Traveler with Sunburn, 63–64, 65, Fig. 3.33
Triads, 166, 168, Figs. 7.22, 7.23

Triple Self-Portrait, 70–71, Fig. 4.1
Trompe-l'oeil painters, 127, 201, Fig. 6.13
Trumbull, John, *The Sortie Made by the Garrison of Gibraltar,* 17, 18, Fig. 1.14
Twentieth-century art, 58–65
  activities, 63, 65
  architecture, 64–65, Fig. 3.34
  Europe, 58–60, Figs. 3.26–3.28
  North America, 60–62, Figs. 3.29–3.31
  from the fifties to the future, 63–65, Figs. 3.32–3.34
Twiggs, Leo F.
  as Art Department head, 81
  The Blue Wall, 29–30, Fig. 2.5
  East Wind Suite: Door, 88, 89, Fig. 5.1
Two Girls, 291, 292, Fig. 11.20
Two-point perspective, 137, 138, Fig. 6.32

U

Ultra AB, 14, Fig. 1.10
United Nations Buildings, 127, 128, Fig. 6.14
Unity, 324–332, Figs. 12.13–12.24
  activities, 331–332
  creating, 324–327, 332–333, Fig. 12.14–12.17, Fig. 12.26
  defined, 324
  overview, 313
  Studio Lessons, 335–341
  through continuity, 331, 332, Fig. 12.24
  through proximity, 330, 331, Figs. 12.22, 12.23
  through repetition, 327, 330, 331, Figs. 12.20, 12.21
  through simplicity, 327, 328, Figs. 12.18, 12.19
  tonality and, 176
Untitled, Pereira, 314, 315, Fig. 12.3
Unusualness and the focal point, 321–322, Fig. 12.11
Utrillo, Maurice, *Street at Corte, Corsica,* 264, 266, Fig. 10.29

V

Value
  activities, 162
  of color, 159–162, 352
  creating with line, 105, Fig. 5.34
  defined, 105
  high-key vs. low-key, 161, Figs. 7.12, 7.13
  in informal balance, 260, 261, Fig. 10.20
  neutral colors, 159, 160, Fig. 7.10
  shades, 159, 160, Fig. 7.11
  texture and, 196–199, Figs. 8.9–8.14
  tints, 159, 160, Fig. 7.11
van der Weyden, Rogier, *Portrait of a Lady,* 282, 283, Fig. 11.3
van Eyck, Jan, 52
  The Annunciation, 187, Fig. 7.42
van Gogh, Vincent, 55
  Landscape at Saint-Rémy (Enclosed Field with Peasant), 200, 201, Fig. 8.17
Vanishing point, 137, 138, Figs. 6.31, 6.32

Vaquero, 16, Fig. 1.12
Varese, 108, Fig. 5.36
Variety, 313, 314–315, Figs. 12.2, 12.3
 activities, 315
 artists' use of, 332–333, Fig. 12.26
 defined, 314
 Studio Lessons, 334–335, 338–341
Vase, 256, 257, Fig. 10.14
Vase of Flowers, A, 30–31, Fig. 2.6
Vermeer, Jan, *The Girl with the Red Hat,*
 247, Fig. 9.32
Vertical lines, 93, 94, Fig. 5.7
 expressive qualities, 97, 99, Figs. 5.21,
 5.24
Video graphics artist, 73
Viewing frame, 351
Vigée-Lebrun, Élisabeth
 *The Marquise de Peze and the Marquise de
 Rouget with Her Two Children,* 330, 331,
 Fig. 12.22
 Self-Portrait, 193, Fig. 8.3
Virgin and Child with Saint Anne, 291,
 293, Fig. 11.21
Vishnu, 46, 47, Fig. 3.8
Vision and color, 156–158, 164, Figs.
 7.2–7.6, 7.17
Visitation, The, 28, Fig. 2.4
Visual balance, 252, Figs. 10.3, 10.4
Visual rhythm, 222–224, Figs. 9.2–9.4
 activities, 223–224
Visual texture, 193–194, Figs. 8.3, 8.4
 activities, 194

Waiting, 308–309, Fig. 11.36
Walking Woman, 296, 298, Fig. 11.29
Warhol, Andy, *Marilyn Monroe's Lips,* 228,
 229, Fig. 9.12
Warm colors, 168, 169, Figs. 7.25, 7.26
 in informal balance, 260
Warrior Chief, Warriors, and Attendants,
 146–147, Fig. 6.45
Watercolor technique tips, 353
Weaving
 African, 57
 space in, 128
 Studio Lessons, 242–245
 technique tips, 358–359
Whirling Rainbow Goddesses, 237, Fig.
 9.25
White, Charles, *Preacher,* 9, Fig. 1.4
Why Not Use the El?, 284, Fig. 11.7
Width of lines, 94–95, Fig. 5.13
Wilson, Jane, *Solstice,* 332–333, Fig. 12.26
Wine vessel, ancient Chinese, 45, Fig. 3.6
Winter: Cat on a Cushion, 27, 30, Fig. 2.3
Winxiang, Prince Yi, 268–269, Fig. 10.31
Wire, safety note, 108
Wood, Grant
 American Gothic, 253, 254, Fig. 10.8
 Midnight Ride of Paul Revere, 91, Fig. 5.3
 Return from Bohemia, 4, 5, Fig. 1.1
Wrapper, 228, 242–243, Fig. 9.11, Fig.
 9.29

Wright, Frank Lloyd, 61
 The David Wright House, 61, 62, Fig. 3.30
 Falling Water House, 330, 331, Fig. 12.21
 stained-glass window, 258, 259, Fig.
 10.18
 Taliesin West, 201, Fig. 8.19
Wrinkle in Time, A cover illustration,
 82–83, Fig. 4.13
Wyeth, Andrew, 63
 Christina's World, 32–34, Fig. 2.8

Xiong, Chaing, *Hmong Story Cloth,*
 220–221, Fig. 9.1

Yancy, John, *Celebration of Arts: Vibrations
 of Life,* 340–341, Fig. 12.30
Yard Sale, 201, Fig. 8.18
Yarn painting, 106–107

Z

Zaga, 16, 17, Fig. 1.13
Zigzag lines, 94, Fig. 5.11
 expressive qualities, 97, 98, 99, Fig. 5.24